The Handbook of Interior Architecture and Design

THE HA
OF IN
ARCHI
AND

NDBOOK
TERIOR
TECTURE
DESIGN

Edited by
Graeme Brooker and Lois Weinthal

BLOOMSBURY VISUAL ARTS
LONDON • NEW YORK • OXFORD • NEW DELHI • SYDNEY

BLOOMSBURY VISUAL ARTS
Bloomsbury Publishing Plc
50 Bedford Square, London, WC1B 3DP, UK
1385 Broadway, New York, NY 10018, USA

BLOOMSBURY, BLOOMSBURY VISUAL ARTS and the Diana logo are
trademarks of Bloomsbury Publishing Plc

First published in 2013
Published in paperback 2017
This edition published 2018
Reprinted 2020

A catalogue record for this book is available from the British Library.

A catalog record for this book is available from the Library of Congress.

ISBN: PB: 978-1-3500-8739-2
ePDF: 978-1-4725-3902-1
eBook: 978-1-4725-3904-5

Typeset by Apex CoVantage, LLC, Madison, WI, USA
Printed and bound in Great Britain

To find out more about our authors and books visit www.bloomsbury.com
and sign up for our newsletters.

CONTENTS

PART 2.2: ETHICS AND THE INDOOR ENVIRONMENT

PART 3: REPRESENTATION AND FABRICATION

PART 3.1: ATMOSPHERIC CONDITIONS OF THE INTERIOR

ILLUSTRATIONS

FIGURES

COLOR PLATES

TABLES

General Introduction

The Handbook of Interior Architecture and Design outlines an international survey of ideas and current research being undertaken within this discipline. This book presents a series of essays in a canon of dynamic and original work, representing current thoughts in a subject that has grown substantially in size and importance in the first part of the twenty-first century. The emergence of a significant body of research in this subject can be connected to two factors: the importance of interiors in relation to the enduring themes of contemporary society, and the changing perception of the subject within the hierarchy of creative disciplines. Social engagement in the form of human well-being and various forms of spatial occupation, ecologies of sustainability and the issues surrounding the environment, and the domestic realm and the relationships between public and private spaces in the city are all enduring themes that, along with the histories, theories, and pedagogies of the subject, form the central concerns of this discipline.

Historically the subject of interiors has been perceived as a marginal pursuit, mostly vocational in bias and lacking intellectual gravitas. It has often been misunderstood as a subject that appeared unscholarly and intellectually unsubstantiated. This was a view that was propagated mostly in the early twentieth century. It was a position that proliferated during the early stages of modernity when the realm of the interior was professionally integrated into the built environment and was no longer considered a distinct and unique entity. It is an opinion that has endured, quite often because of the alleged unprofessional and unregulated status of the designer in some parts of the world, and has persisted due to misogyny: an issue that, as some authors rightly point out in their chapters in this book, was due to the gender of its early protagonists.

Conversely, because of its ability to encompass and in turn reflect a variety of forms of human inhabitation, and because of its capacity to represent and engage with a full range of social, economic, and political issues, the practice of the creation of the interior can be considered to be a process that creates a space that is central to all human existence. The interior can be understood as the result of a complex weave of values, issues, and spatial formations; these can be both physical and mental structures. The interior can be perceived as an entity that is shaped by its use, its politics, its gender, and its history, and by many other real or unreal constructs. Therefore, the discipline of interior architecture and design can be considered to be substantial and expansive, primarily because of the many areas it can affect and engage with. This handbook presents texts examining these areas, produced by a range of scholars drawn from the fields of education, practice, theory, and journalism. It aims to substantiate the discipline through intellectual inquiry into the various strands of the subject and to demonstrate the relevance and importance of the interior realm not only to its users but also to contemporary social life.

Each chapter in the handbook provides a concise overview of a significant theme related to the interior. They encompass a vast and diverse range of issues in education, research, and practice. They span ideas as complex and diverse as human behavior, anthropology, cultural geography, history, taste, ageing, building reuse, the status of the designer, and technology. Because of its diversity the interior is often used as a vehicle for researchers and practitioners to gain insight into social issues such as patterns of consumption, gender, identity, and politics, much of which is done through the analysis of inhabited space. It is also a multidisciplinary practice that overlaps with architecture, fashion, furniture, exhibition design, graphics, and installation art. Multiplicity is at the heart of the identity of interior architecture and design. The chapters within this handbook offer a significant insight into the discipline at this time of its emergence. *The Handbook of Interior Architecture and Design* is a reflection of the discipline, a summary of its current activities, and a review of the field of research in order to afford interested parties a better understanding of its past, its present, and its future trajectories.

STRUCTURE

The book has been organized into three main chapters. Each contains subsections that seek to expand on the chapter headings. Whichever topic is being explored and whatever ideas, theories, and exemplars are being utilized, almost all of the chapters contain an emphasis that is about a sense of *living* and making the inhabitants' space their own—a fundamental dimension of the understanding of the interior realm.

Contexts

The first part of the handbook is entitled "Contexts." It explores the fundamental themes of the subject and provides an overview of the discipline's history, theory, practice, and education. The selection of essays in this part aims to contextualize current debates on interiors and their relationship to all spatial arts, including their overlapping discourses with other spatially related disciplines. They endeavor to present current thinking on interiors from across the world. This part aims to make clear ideas already prominent in the field of interiors and to clarify the interdisciplinary aspects of design research, theory, and practice.

The first section of this part is entitled "Reflecting on the Discipline" and is composed of a series of chapters that examine the key contextual factors on which interior architecture and design are founded. Histories, education, and the profession are the basic contexts, or filters, in which research and practice have taken place within the subject area. The narrative of the research that forms the context of interior architecture and design's identity is not singular but plural, and is made up of many voices and constructed from many perspectives. Different forces, practices, and cultures have each made an impact on the subject. This section traces the development and substantiation of these marks left on the subject through a series of key pieces on research and projects that have validated the subject in these fields. The section outlines key theories and research methodologies and examines their evolution in the history, education, and practice of the subject. The second part of "Contexts" is entitled "Interior Terrains" and explores the variety of territories particular to the subject. These range from building reuse to interior urbanism and various forms of occupation or uses pertinent to designers of the interior. These consist of domestic and office space, exhibition design, scenography, and so on. Each contributor examines the range of issues within these fields of interior space.

Occupancy

The second part of the handbook, entitled "Occupancy," addresses familiar conditions that shape interior spaces, such as room types, gender, and personalization. The intimate nature of interiors lends itself to these conditions because of the close proximity of people, objects, and space. While each of these areas is often explored by looking inward, the chapters in this part situate them within a larger network outside of the interior. The first section of this part, entitled "The Body, Behavior, and Space," explores these issues, with chapters that situate the body in physical and psychological environments as a means to better understand how we shape our interiors. Chapters focus on core topics at the immediate scale of the body, while including explorations of demographics, health and well-being, and identity. But the way in which we occupy spaces is changing as peripheral disciplines find their way into the interior. These disciplines, and their developing relationship to the interior, are the focus of the second section of this part, entitled "Ethics and the Indoor Environment." Chapters in this section focus on topics that include consumption and sustainability as well as politics, globalization, and the ethical dimension of inside space. Specifically, consumption is a topic that the field of interior architecture and design has come to inform through the mass media, and when placed in the context of sustainability and globalization, traditional observations are reevaluated.

Together, these two parts in "Occupancy" highlight the immediate forces that shape the interior through individual personalization, as well as the impact of political, economic, and social forces. Contributors in this part reveal the broader scope of topics affecting the ways in which traditional interiors are being informed.

Representation and Fabrication

The interior is a space that is fabricated from various ideas, processes, and constructs. Before it is built it is subject to many forms of simulation. Model making, drawing, and mediation are all representational tools, each one subject to technological change and development. Because the interior is a flexible realm, an ambiguous dimension that begins with what may loosely be described as the "inside," it can be subject to quick change. Potentially, this characteristic allows it be altered with ease, making the interior a suitable testing ground for emerging issues in many areas, including technology and representation. Most recently, the quickness with which technology can change is influencing the interior realm through new forms of digital fabrication and mediated simulation. The first section of this part looks to new developments taking place in the making and representation of interior space. This collection of chapters seeks to broaden the familiar scope of interiors-related issues in order to reevaluate conventional and unconventional forms of spatial production, much of which is based on the integration of emerging construction and representational ideas. The second section of this part is entitled "Atmospheric Conditions of the Interior." It focuses on what might be considered to be the surface conditions of inside space. Chapters address the effects that style and trends have on the interior, its ornament and decoration, the color and materiality of space, and the phenomenological dimension of these elements. Materials, technology, the environment, and sustainability issues constitute a larger proportion of the interior and are explored in a set of chapters that map these issues' history and evolution from the past right up to the present and beyond.

Until recently, the discipline has primarily been viewed through a limited lens of historical and vocational techniques. The collection of parts and chapters in this *Handbook* builds on interior architecture and design's multiplicity and the evolving nature of the discipline. This *Handbook* does not limit interiors to one definition; rather, it establishes a foundation, a source of references and influences that are utilized to broaden its scope and definition as it overlaps with and permeates into new areas of creative practice and research. Because of its ambiguous nature the field is rapidly expanding to include emerging paradigms, and it is becoming increasingly inclusive of tangential disciplines. To encompass the range of topics related to the interior—from those that are well established to those that are newly situated— the *Handbook* is organized into three overarching themes, so that these fold and integrate into a weave that contains the discipline's past, present, and future practices.

Finally, all of the chapters seek to ground core issues pertinent to the interior. The *Handbook* documents and records current ideas in the field and takes stock of the discipline at this critical juncture. Chapter contributors represent an international array of scholars, a range of writers who provide a global forum in a comprehensive range of texts, critical reflections, and unique insights into this exciting, dynamic emerging field of critical research and practice on the subject of the realm of the interior.

PART 1

Contexts

Introduction

Entitled "Contexts," this section outlines the main areas of the discipline where the majority of its research is and has been undertaken. Histories, education, practice, and the profession are territories that constitute the fundamental contexts that form the main areas of research within the subject of interiors. The narrative of interior architecture and design's identity is not a singular account but instead a story that is constructed out of many voices and from a diversity of perspectives. Therefore, chapters in this section are juxtaposed in order to promulgate differing points of view, contrary readings of similar sources, and the use of unorthodox and sometimes personal project material. Because of the interdisciplinary nature of this subject, a multiplicity of views, cultures, practices, and processes have each made an impact on the subject. This part of the book traces the development and substantiation of those marks with a series of essays containing exemplary research and projects that explore and hence substantiate interior architecture and design history, theory, and research.

REFLECTING ON THE DISCIPLINE

The first section of "Contexts" contains seven chapters that have been selected in order to explore history, theory, education, and the profession, all considered fundamental components of this discipline. The first two chapters explore the history of interiors. In the past, interior design history has been approached in a number of different ways: as a history of forms and styles; as social, cultural, and political history; as material culture; and as a history of the profession. In "Modern History and Interior Design" Anne Massey gives an overview of the key issues and moments in the history of the subject, examining a number of important exemplars of the design of interior space. The chapter is structured into three main periods: the Victorians, the modern, and postmodernity. In particular, Massey places an emphasis on the use of the term *modern,* examining its importance and also its relevance throughout the twentieth century. The chapter examines some of the fundamental issues surrounding the modernist project and the ways in which designers, artists, and architects such as the Independent Group critiqued modernism's obsessions with permanence and perennity, features that place modernity at odds with the temporal, a fundamental characteristic of the design of interior space. Conversely, any established history of the subject is contentious, and while one view of history may inform the subject, the development of a canon or paradigms may exclude other voices or narratives. In "Rethinking Histories, Canons, and Paradigms" John C. Turpin examines the history of the subject, utilizing the unorthodox or overlooked voices of the history of the discipline. He presents a view of the subject that is different from the accepted linear chronological timeline of history. His chapter is divided into four phases: "The Western Object," "The Object and Society," "Once Silent Voices," and "Other Voices." In the final section, entitled "A New Paradigm," the acknowledgment and encouragement of a multiplicity of voices are proposed as a vital way forward for a subject that is maturing and becoming confident of its own place in history.

As well as the development of its own historical narrative, the need for an established and relevant theory base for the subject has often been overlooked. Although this is rapidly changing, the design of interior space has been largely an untheorized critical discipline. In "Inhabited Space: Critical Theories and the Domestic Interior" Alexa Griffith Winton discusses the emergence of key theories in interior architecture, design, and decoration, formulating three separate but interdependent categories: the spatial envelope, the contents of interior space, and the interior's inhabitants. In order to outline a substantial and appropriate overview of critical theory and philosophy Winton uses domestic space as the critical exemplar pertinent to the study of interiors. She argues that while architectural theory has possibly inhibited the development of interior-specific theory, this imbalance is useful as a means to create a space to stimulate a meaningful critique of inside space. The emergence of interior-specific theory is concomitant with the development of particularized research methodologies. In "Methods of Research and Criticality" Gennaro Postiglione gives an exhaustive and critical examination of the variety of research methods and typologies in areas of research particular to the interior. Postiglione offers a framework of a multiplicity of research activities and processes that, he suggests, form a "hybrid" of doctrines and theories, many of which are borrowed from other creative and scientific disciplines. Postiglione gives a substantial overview of the subject area, both exploring areas of research and evaluating their relevance to the subject area. He argues that the multitude of approaches and types of interior research, as well as its openness to embracing methods from other fields, places it at the center of activity in the creative world.

In its broadest sense the education and profession of an interior architect/designer/decorator concern the design of space through human occupation. Issues surrounding the status and the title of the profession, and the education of its students, include matters such as pedagogy, processes, qualifications and the conferment of titles. These impact on fundamental issues of the status of the discipline and its agents in the field. Currently, the accepted worldwide standard educational qualification in this discipline is primarily based on the undertaking of an undergraduate degree in the subject. The type of degree undertaken is often wide-ranging in its remit. Courses vary from an emphasis on the commercial and technical aspects of the profession through to the exploration and testing of the territories and boundaries of the subject matter. Both types of courses are composed of a series of exploratory and innovative spatial design and theory projects. Whichever type of course is undertaken, an education in an interiors-based subject is a specialized discipline and one that has core characteristics. It differs from other practices and has its own unique processes and demands. In "Protected Title in Britain: An Educational Necessity?" Graham Stretton gives a historical overview of the role of education and the professional status of the designer in the United Kingdom. As an example of the development of courses he uses one of the first schools of interiors in the United Kingdom, De Montfort University in Leicester, as an exemplar of the changes to the status of education in this subject and to the status of title. Broadening the subject to incorporate Europe and the rest of the world, Kees Spanjers examines mechanisms for the legislation and regulation of the interior architect/designer/decorator in his chapter, "Regulations and Conventions: Interior Design Practice and Education." Spanjers examines how legislation and regulation vary across the world; interior design is a process that is subject to differing degrees of regulatory controls depending on the continent in which one practices. Spanjers examines and compares the varying degrees of government recognition of the title and practice of the designer, as well as the different regulatory mechanisms and educational systems across the world. Using a case study of an imaginary project, a restaurant, Spanjers compares how different regulatory cultures and the provisions for their understanding impact on the project's execution. Spanjers also outlines the professional and educational bodies across the globe and suggests that changing patterns in both need to be examined and understood. He argues that this would help courses and schools accommodate professionalism within their curriculums.

In the final essay of this section Drew Plunkett examines the function of professionals and their identity and prominence. He argues that their role has been substantially altered throughout the twentieth century. In "The Profession That Dare Not Speak Its Name" Plunkett argues that the emergence of the profession of the interior designer has largely been constructed in the last forty or so years, through key figures such as Terence Conran and Rodney Fitch. Plunkett challenges the domestic bias of many histories of the interior and instead suggests that the design of public space and the responsibilities that that entails form the basis of the role of the modern professional designer. Alongside this he makes a personal claim for the title of interior designer to be upheld and for education to acknowledge the skills and tools needed for this discipline to thrive and be ready for the twenty-first century.

INTERIOR TERRAINS

The chapters in this section outline the "landscape" of the design of inside space. The multiplicity of voices, ideas, methodologies, and disciplines that reside within and around the edges of the subject ensures that the delineation of its territories results in a boundary that is fluid and often ambiguous. It is the liminal qualities of what constitutes a specific territory of the discipline that make it an agile subject. Arguably, its flexibility and its unregulated character mean it is able to absorb new ideas and methods quickly into its processes and ways of working. Debatably, the sensibility of an interior architect/designer/decorator embodies the understanding and awareness of this dexterity. The eleven chapters in this section examine a range of territories, from the agents of the interior to processes of interiors, from the large scale of urbanism to the scale of the house. Chapters in this section also explore the types of programs and occupancies that the interior architect and designer will quite often be involved in the development of.

The sensibility of the interiorist is an important and yet often overlooked characteristic. In "Interiorizt" Suzie Attiwill formulates a proposition for practice that neatly sidesteps the age-old debate on the differences and similarities between the terms *interior architecture/design* and *decoration.* Instead, using the term *interiorizt* (the more dynamic *z* replacing the indifferent *s*), she proposes a manifesto addressing the "here and now," a reasoned and forceful proposal to invoke the future of agents in the field. Attiwell suggests that *interiorizt* is used to invite a practice that delights in the full potential of the subject to critically engage with space, keeping its remit as open and as heterogeneous as possible. The interiorizt requires a very particular type of sensibility, one that is an advocate and affirmation of the diversity and multiplicity of the practicing of interior space.

The awareness of territories and the ability to contest spatial norms is an important element of the role of the interior architect/design/decorator. In "Surface Demonstration, Neutral, Not So," Julieanna Preston examines contested territories in the form of active resistance as a gesture with particular regard to the mendacious qualities of the white wall. The formation of the chapter was prompted by the author's expulsion from her own office, an act that resulted in an installation of the same name as the chapter, one that provoked reflections on forms and gestures of resistance. In particular, Preston suggests that the dominant notion of *smoothness,* or the *seamlessness* of surface conditions, is analogous to contemporary culture and the design of interior spaces. This uniformity eradicates traces of labor and any mark of its maker. The act of repairing the wall, itself a process of erasing traces of occupancy, and the return of the surface to its "neutral" white-walled condition, while seemingly uncontentious, is symbolic of the hidden depths of a seemingly banal stud partition wall.

One particular aspect of the territory of the interior is the adaptation of existing buildings. This aligns the subject to what are often perceived as traditional aspects of architecture such as preservation, conservation, and restoration. This type of practice is also connected to what might be construed as more radical forms of built environment and site-specific disciplines such as installation art and the transform of existing space for new use. In "A Short History of the Room," Fred Scott argues that at the heart of this discipline is a space called the room. Throughout history the art of the separation of the exterior from the interior was exemplified by the Adam brothers and in particular their houses in central London. Sir John Soane started to erode the primacy of the enclosure of the room, and subsequently the modernist project finished the job. It did this by eradicating distinctions between inside and outside by the use of large panels of glazing along with the suppression of ornament in order to create universal abstract space. In this chapter Scott formulates a gentle plea that all questions of the interior and its space lie at the heart of the act of intervention, the amalgam of space, the existing building, and its new use. While the design of interior space is often closely connected to the reuse of existing spaces and buildings, a significant amount of its practical work takes place in the design of yet-to-be-built edifices. "New Occupancy" is an chapter that explores working with both existing spaces and "new build" projects. In a personal and poetic essay the author Lorraine Farrelly examines function in all of its forms and the processes and principles of new occupancy. She also examines post occupancy, as a means of assessing how interiors are subsequently inhabited.

As well as using and reusing buildings the programming of the interior requires innovative and experimental solutions in order to create new forms of space. New types of programs can emerge as the result of experimental projects, installations, or interventions that are often found in sites such as galleries and museums and that have the capability to innovate and experiment, often on a short-term basis, and without the need to respond to regular functional requirements. In "Program, Function, and Fabrication: Exhibiting the Domestic Interior," the authors Andy Milligan and Helen O'Connor explore a number of installations and site-specific projects in order to uncover possible exemplars and processes of reprogramming the interior. They explore how narrative, myth, occupation, and information are fabricated into a new experience in order to expose and reflect on new uses of interior space.

Large-scale interior spaces such as shopping centers or malls, and transport hubs such as airports and train stations, are often conceived as large urban conglomerations that may also include housing, offices, and retail space. In "Lives in Large Interiors" Thomas Kong analyzes their impact on the urban and civic spaces of Hong Kong and Singapore. He argues that the Western-centric critique of these types of spaces is often challenging and problematic. Instead, in the Far East the author shows how large, interconnected urban space can, through careful negotiation between occupants and governments, provide a point of entry for social exchange and civic sustenance. This confounds the dominance of Western urban models of city space and proposes a possible new type of model for the future of interior urbanism. The fabrication of these spaces that foster intimacy in urban-scale environments is key to the construction of successful and diverse city spaces. In "Swiss Cheese and Beanbags: Producing Interior Urbanism," Lee Stickells examines interior spaces in terms of their relational infrastructures, moving away from the idea of the interior as an enclosure and instead suggesting that notions of climate, ambience, disposition, and atmosphere form spaces of "flow" in which interior urbanism is encouraged to flourish. Stickells introduces recent examples of these types of urban "rooms" and posits an analysis of the types of social interaction that accompany them.

Within large city spaces the domestic realm, with its articulation of rooms, exemplifies the meaning of privacy. Yet in large high-density urban housing developments the dominant model of the single-nuclear-family private home, exemplified by the Western bourgeois domestic space of the nineteenth century, is redundant. Lilian Chee's essay, entitled "The Public Private Interior: Constructing the Modern Domestic Interior in Singapore's Public Housing," explores the domestic realm in the Far East.

In particular, it uses Housing Development Board (HBD) policies and apartments from 1960s and 1970s public housing in Singapore to analyze private space. Eighty percent of Singaporean residents are housed in HDB apartments, and it is considered to be a very successful housing strategy. The author counterpoints hard evidence such as public policy documents and publicity information with emotive descriptions drawn from film, poetry, and prose, lyrical material that has a long tradition in HDB estates. In addition, the author draws on visual material and feminist theory, as well as architectural history, to explore the private interior in public housing spaces.

Along with domestic space, work and cultural environments form a major part of the interior architect and designer's remit. An understanding of current research on these spaces is critical. The evolution of workspaces can be viewed in parallel to stylistic, programmatic, material, and environmental changes that have evolved from the turn of the century, leading to the current spaces for the digital knowledge economy. Most notably, the modernist era ushered in new forms of workspaces, exemplified in the Larkin Building by Frank Lloyd Wright and the Taylorist strategies of the modern efficient office. In "The Evolution of Workspace Design: From the Machine to the Network," Jeremy Myerson examines the legacy of modernist office design and explores contemporary currents and their impact on the twenty-first-century digital office. In addition to domestic and workspace environments, performative and installation spaces are methods of creating interiors that are a part of the territory of this discipline. Installations, performances, and events can alter the way in which a visitor uses, views, or interacts with a space. Performative space can consist of an intervention that may render ambiguous the threshold between the audience and the viewer. Installations may transform space to make it be seen in a new and revelatory way. In "Installation and Performance" David Littlefield examines how perspective, a way of viewing, or of being asked to view, a space, promotes a particular way of seeing and interacting with an interior. The subtle manipulation of the viewer, his or her place in a space, can render and describe new and also unintended spatial narratives.

The creation of exhibition environments has a growing history and a demanding future. In "Exhibition Design: Reflections" David Dernie charts the history of the subject. He interrogates ideas in exhibition design by utilizing Brian O'Doherty's *Inside the White Cube: The Ideology of the Gallery Space* and Nicholas Serota's *Experience or Interpretation: The Dilemma of Museums of Modern Art*. The chapter reflects on display aesthetics and their strategies, suggesting how they have informed insights into the visitor experience. The chapter posits ideas about experiential design and the ways in which spaces can communicate content-driven narratives, open to personal interpretation and increasingly diverse audiences.

In this section, all of the chapters reflect on the nature of the interior, examining how it touches on a multitude of aspects concerning space and its uses. These issues range from education to the profession, from urbanism to the room, from history to theory, and so on. The texts have been commissioned and then ordered to manifest the multiplicity of the discipline and signal its interdisciplinary nature, a characteristic that is a central part of its character and an element that forms an integral part of its DNA.

Reflecting on the Discipline

Modern History and Interior Design

ANNE MASSEY

From the Victorian era on, the modern dominates the history of interior design. *The modern* began as a dismissive label for contemporary interiors, then became the style of mainstream interior design, which in turn came under critical scrutiny. This chapter gives a broad overview of the key issues and moments in the history of the subject, through the mid-nineteenth century until the emergence of interior design as a distinct profession in the 1960s and modernism's subsequent demise. This overview accounts for stylistic change in relation to the context of cultural and political history, with reactions for and against the modern providing the organizing device. As Emma Ferry has argued,[1] the term *modern* had distinctly negative connotations in the nineteenth century; it wasn't until the twentieth century that the modern was regarded as a positive force for interior design. The modern was again called into question in the later twentieth century, with criticisms of its claims for permanence and functionality. Less is more became less is a bore.

THE VICTORIAN MODERN INTERIOR

The reign of Queen Victoria (1837–1901) spanned a time of seismic change in all aspects of design and material culture in Britain and much of the Western world. The forces of modernity, in the shape of industrialization and urbanization, made a massive impact on society. A prevalent consumer culture emerged, served by factory production and new patterns of distribution and consumption. A new, powerful, and sizable middle class emerged, residing in new suburban areas, served by new forms of transport. This affected interior design in myriad ways. The most obvious was the sheer proliferation of actual interiors, both public and private. Materials such as wallpaper, textiles, and carpets were now being mass-produced or imported.

New, fairly modest houses were being erected by speculative builders, expanding the limits of towns and cities. The new bourgeoisie decorated their homes with these new furnishings, mixing patterns and styles from the past, along with a wealth of home-crafted objects. Heavy curtains hung at the windows, which were also masked by thick lace curtains. The furniture was upholstered, stuffed with horsehair and often with internal springs. The walls were clad in pictures and portraits, prints, and decorative plaques. The cabinets were stuffed with ornaments, the corners of the rooms occupied by potted plants. The Victorian domestic interior can be characterized as a shelter, protection from the threats of modernity that lay beyond the threshold of the front door. Cushioned and shielded from exterior forces, the home, ideally, provided the ultimate safe haven. As Friedrich Engels noted about being on the streets in London in the 1840s:

> A town, such as London, where a man may wander for hours together without reaching the beginning of the end, without meeting the slightest hint which could lead to the inference that there is open country within reach, is a strange thing. This colossal centralization, this heaping together of two and a half millions of human beings at one point, has multiplied the power of this two and a half millions a hundredfold; has raised London to the commercial capital of the world.... The very turmoil of the streets has something repulsive about it—something against which human nature rebels. The hundreds of thousands of all classes and ranks crowding past each other—aren't they all human beings with the same qualities and powers, and with the same interest in being happy? And aren't they obliged, in the end, to seek happiness in the same way, by the same means? And still they crowd by one another as though they had nothing in common, nothing to do with one another, and their only agreement is the tacit one—that each keep to his own side of the pavement, so as not to delay the opposing streams of the crowd—while no man thinks to honor another with so much as a glance. The brutal indifference, the unfeeling isolation of each in his private interest becomes the more repellent and offensive, the more these individuals are crowded together within a limited space.[2]

This classic description of alienation on the modern city streets goes some way to explaining why the Victorians sought sanctuary within the shelter of the home. But the choices available for the furnishing and decoration of the home prompted anxieties for the middle-class householders about how best to furnish and decorate their domestic environment. The choice was vast, and this wave of new consumers needed guidance. But help was at hand. Starting with Mrs. Beeton's *Book of Household Management,* first published in 1861 in Britain, the complex set of rules about how to behave in the social circles of one's peers was spelled out in the new mass media. And aspects of home furnishing were included in this classic lifestyle manual, including how to best decorate a dining room. Taste was not a simple matter, and reflected one's place in society.

Beyond the realm of the household manager, taste in household furnishing was debated and attempts were made to regulate it, as design commentators observed that mass production had created a problem in terms of taste among the middle classes that needed serious attention. For example, Charles Eastlake's popular book *Hints on Household Taste* (1868) gave extensive advice to the householder. Based on articles the architect had written for magazines such as *The Queen* and *The Cornhill Magazine,* the book promised "to suggest some fixed principles of taste for the popular guidance of those who are not accustomed to hear such principles defined."[3]

This kind of advice was prevalent in Victorian society, with a growing middle class eager to follow respected mores and tacitly agreed patterns of behavior. Eastlake exemplifies the negative connotations of the modern here:

> Our modern furniture is essentially effeminate in form. How often do we see in fashionable drawing-rooms a type of couch which seems to be composed of nothing but cushions! It is really supported by a framework of wood or iron, but this internal structure is carefully concealed by the stuffing and material with which the whole is covered. I do not wish to be ungallant in my remarks, but I fear there is a large class of young ladies who look upon this sort of furniture as "elegant". Now, if elegance means nothing more than a milliner's idea of the beautiful, which changes every season—so that a bonnet which is pronounced "lovely" in 1877 becomes a "fright" in 1878—then no doubt this sofa, as well as a score of other articles of modern manufacture which I could mention, is elegant indeed. But, if elegance has anything in common with real beauty—beauty which can be estimated by a fixed and lasting standard—then I venture to submit that this eccentric combination of bad carpentry and bloated pillows is very *in*elegant, and, in fact, a piece of ugliness which we ought not to tolerate in our houses.[4]

For Eastlake and other Victorian design reformers, it was Art Furniture that was the recommended way forward for the home. They suggested a unified style and color palette, based on a refined Arts and Crafts style mingled with Georgian grace and restrained ornament. A well-preserved Victorian interior that drew from the inspiration of Eastlake is the home of the *Punch* cartoonist Linley Samborne in Stafford Terrace, located in the Kensington area of West London. Furnished in the 1870s, it perfectly reflects this upper-middle-class, educated Victorian taste. The hallway is decorated in dark green wallpaper, originally William Morris's *Diaper,* which can still be seen behind the many framed prints that decorate the walls. The flooring is a dark brown linoleum. So the muted colors and emphasis on art reflect the type of decoration recommended by reformers such as Eastlake.

However, despite reflecting the latest critical thoughts about design reform, the interior layout and design echoed the gender divisions prevalent in Victorian society. For example, there was a clear distinction between the dining room and drawing room. As Juliet Kinchin has argued:

> In the nineteenth century the private interior space of the middle-class home was increasingly defined as feminine territory, the antithesis of the public, external world of work peopled by men. Within the domestic arena, however, the key rooms tended to

be further grouped to either side of a male-female divide, the most explicit contrast being between the "masculine" dining room and "feminine" drawing room.[5]

The dining room is situated at the front of the house and is the first door to lead off from the hallway (Plate 1). In it there is an octagonal oak dining table, surrounded by eight matching chairs with dark green Moroccan leather upholstery. There are Windsor-style smoking chairs by one wall and two easy chairs by the window. This is where Samborne and his male friends would enjoy drinks and conversation after dinner. Adjacent to the dining room was the morning room, which was the space of Samborne's wife, Marion, with lighter furniture, including genuine eighteenth-century examples, and more upholstery and cushions, echoing Eastlake's point. The drawing room on the first floor contained a plethora of objects—framed prints and paintings on the wall, blue-and-white ceramics on the plate rail, a vast array of furniture in different styles and shapes. The notion that furniture in a domestic space should match in any way is a recent concept; this Victorian space was typical in that two easy chairs were placed together in a space that also included Regency and Louis XIV copies and originals in a seemingly random order. As Walter Benjamin observed about the nineteenth-century bourgeois French interior as part of his important *Arcades Project*:

> The private individual, who in the office has to deal with reality, needs the domestic interior to sustain him in his illusions. The necessity is all the more pressing since he has no intention of allowing his commercial considerations to impinge on social ones. In the formation of his private environment, both are kept out. From this arise the phantasmagorias of the interior—which, for the private man, represents the universe.

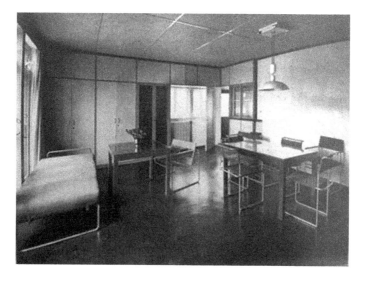

FIGURE 1   House 16, Weissenhofsiedlung, 1927. Living/sleeping area designed by Walter Gropius for the housing project, with furniture by Marcel Breuer. Courtesy of Bauhaus-Archiv, Berlin.

In the interior, he brings together the far away and the long ago. His living room is a box in the theatre of the world.[6]

A similar identification between masculinity and the dining room was made in the painting *A Bloomsbury Family* (1906–1907) by William Orpen. This depicts the Nicholson family, with the painter William Nicholson seated and shown in profile. He chose the decorations for the room, with its snuff-colored walls and decorative prints. The children sit subserviently at the dining table, while his wife stands near the threshold to the room, almost a guest in her own domestic space.[7] As Jean Baudrillard argued in 1968 in "Structures of Interior Design":

> The arrangement of furniture offers a faithful image of the familial and social structures of a period. The typical bourgeois interior is patriarchal; its foundation is the dining-room/bedroom combination. Although it is diversified with respect to function, the furniture is highly integrated, centring around the sideboard or the bed in the middle of the room. There is a tendency to accumulate, to fill and close off the space. The emphasis is on unifunctionality, immovability, imposing presence and hierarchical labelling.[8]

Advice for the householder continued to proliferate throughout the Victorian era, with the best-selling Macmillan's Art at Home series, which included Rhoda and Agnes Garrett's *Suggestions for House Decoration* (1876) and Lucy Orrinsmith's *The Drawing Room* (1877). Orrinsmith criticized the modern domestic interior in no uncertain terms:

> It must have been remarked that great artists never choose to represent an ordinary modern English house, either inside or out; the "why" is obvious. Our houses are crowded with ugly shapes disguised by meretricious ornament. The general forms are usually so bad as to require to be loaded with excrescences, which, while they blunt the critical power of the eye, leave the mind dissatisfied.[9]

THE AVANT-GARDE HOME

Apart from the criticisms of the modern home raised in contemporary advice manuals, the trend toward the artistic home among the new upper-middle-class patrons also acted as a corrective for popular taste. Architects, artists, and designers made their mark with specially designed homes with interiors that operated as a *Gesamtkunstwerk*, advertisements for their own practice and expressions of creative identity. One of the earliest examples of this type of domestic interior is the Red House, designed by Phillip Webb for William and Jane Morris in 1859. Every piece of decoration reinforces the Arts and Crafts message, from the hand-embroidered hangings to the Gothic-style wooden cabinets to the hand-knotted rugs. And the message was an anti-industrial one. The same aesthetic informs Morris's Hammersmith home and his summer retreat at Kelmscott Manor. The sparse hall of Kelmscott Manor features the simple and rustic Sussex Chair, complemented by the Morris & Co. *Strawberry Thief* chintz and oak chairs and table, decorated with eight tablemats embroidered by May Morris, William Morris's daughter, in the 1920s. Set in the Oxfordshire countryside, this rural idyll housed the Arts and Crafts philosophy in the three dimensions of the embroidered bed hangings on William Morris's bed.

The Belgian art nouveau designer Henry van der Velde emulated Morris by building a new home for himself and his new bride, complete with all furnishings, in 1895. The Villa Bloemenwerf in Uccle, a suburb of Brussels, was built in vernacular design with each room presented as a unified whole. The pale ash dining room chairs were styled in elegant, curved forms, sinuous and lightweight, but their rush seats were a rustic echo of the Sussex Chair. Made with and without arms, the chairs were subsequently produced for van der Velde's clients in more expensive materials, including padouk, mahogany, and oak with leather or cloth seats.

The same control over the entire interior was used by Victor Horta, particularly in the design of his own house in another suburb of Brussels, this time in Ixelles in 1898. The dining room presented a unified, modern interior with its walls faced with glazed white bricks, carved oak cupboards, and dining table surrounded by a set of six chairs in light oak. Horta, as the architect of his own home, designed the entire setting in which he lived. Belgian art nouveau then made an impact in France, with the architect Hector Guimard from Paris visiting Horta in 1895 and drawing on his modern influences. He returned to Paris to a complete building and interior at the Castel Beranger Apartments, Rue La Fontaine, built in 1895–1897. In the art nouveau spirit, everything was coordinated, the chairs, tables, and even doorknobs harmonizing in a fluid, asymmetrical whole. Guimard had a studio in the block, complete with an art nouveau fireplace, doorways, and wall treatments, which he advertised on a picture postcard as the "Style Guimard" in the early part of the twentieth century—another example of self-promotion on behalf of the designer.

The Scottish avant-garde architect Charles Rennie Mackintosh also designed the interior of his own home at 120 Mains Street (now preserved by the University of Glasgow) with signature high-backed chairs. In the dining room, the dark-stained oak chairs have backs that tower 53 in. (135 cm) from the floor, creating an intimate space. The walls are also dark, decorated with somber brown, rough wrapping paper. This is contrasted with the white-painted ceiling. The designer also used these characteristic high-backed chairs to great effect in the various tearooms he designed in Glasgow, for example, those located at Ingram Street in 1900 for Mrs. Cranston, a teetotaler and reformer. The furniture was all painted white, with elegant high backs; this made the perfect setting for genteel ladies to sip tea. Mackintosh was also commissioned by wealthy patrons to create unique interiors to celebrate their wealth and taste.

The best-preserved example of the Mackintosh unified interior is that of Hill House. Designed for the publishing magnate Walter Blackie and built in 1902 in Helensburgh to the west of Glasgow, it is now owned by the National Trust. The no-nonsense Scottish baronial exterior conceals a delicate and simple interior. The main bedroom is painted in white with white furniture, decorated with rose-colored glass that is echoed in the window design. The drawing room is also white, with decorations of stenciled pink roses on a blue trellis background. The space is subtly subdivided, with an area for playing the piano, seats by the stylized fireplace, and a pretty window seat. The complete interior is harmonized, with wall, floor, lighting, and furniture treatments echoing an overall unique vision for the design of the modern interior.

This approach was also taken by the Wiener Werkstätte, a group of architects, artists, and designers who were greatly influenced by Mackintosh's aesthetic and also enjoyed the patronage of wealthy clients. Founded in 1903, the group designed interiors, furniture, and even clothing as well. Its first design commission was for the Purkersdorf Sanatorium, built in 1904–1905. The architect Josef Hoffman oversaw the project, designing chairs based on the cube for the main entrancethat harmonized with the geometric patterns on the floor and wall. Such perfectly coordinated interiors were a hallmark of the Wiener Werkstätte, as they were for the American architect Frank Lloyd Wright. The architect took control of the entire open plan environment, ensuring that the inhabitants of his Prairie House sit on chairs that echo the horizontals and verticals of the interior in blond oak. So this concentration by architects on the total work of art, which comprised the modern interior, continued with the development of the modern movement itself in the 1920s.

MODERN MOVEMENT INTERIORS

The design vision of the modern movement echoed the *Gesamtkunstwerk* of the earlier Arts and Crafts and art nouveau avant-garde, but the style and materials used were far more radical, and the interiors more spartan. The modern movement abandoned wood in favor of metal, and more open, skeletal designs replaced the detailed patterns of textiles or carving in the interior. But the aim remained unchanged, to order and control the interior spaces of modernist buildings and their users. The redefinition of the modern for the interior was levered by the architects and designers themselves, who were prolific in publicizing their own work through exhibitions, publications, and the designs themselves. This is part of the reason why modern architecture dominates the historiography of the interior. As the architectural historian Beatriz Colomina has argued, modern architecture only emerged at a time when the protagonists could use the methods of the mass media to advertise their work.[10] The modern movement's place in history was also guaranteed through the published writing of erudite commentators, linked with the practitioners. The most influential publication of this type is Nikolaus Pevsner's *Pioneers of the Modern Movement: From William Morris to Walter Gropius,* first published in 1936, which established an art historical approach to the history of modern architecture. Few interiors were featured, but the book reinforced the primacy of architecture as the dominant force in the development of modern design, and the primacy of modernism itself for posterity.

However, modern design represented a minority taste throughout the 1920s and 1930s, celebrated by the architects themselves and by their acolytes; it was essentially an antibourgeois movement that attempted to overthrow the clutter of the Victorian home. Reform came in the form of radical interiors that let in more light and air and were more hygienic, plain, and stark. As Penny Sparke has argued,[11] modernism succeeded in importing an industrial aesthetic into the domestic sphere. Modern movement architects reacted against the slaughter and trauma of World War I by offering a bright new future for all. One prime example was the Weissenhofsiedlung in Stuttgart, Germany, in 1927. This was an exhibition of model mass housing organized by the Deutscher Werkbund and consisted of twenty-one model dwellings in the style of the modern movement. Mies van der Rohe was instrumental in organizing the event and invited fifteen leading modern architects to take part, including Walter Gropius, Le Corbusier, and the Dutch De Stijl architect J.J.P. Oud (Fig. 1). The interior designed by Gropius is so stark, plain, and industrial it could almost be a room in a hospital. The walls are plain, the floors shiny but covered in one color, and the furniture constructed from tubular steel. This includes the B4 and Wassily, tubular steel chairs by Mies van der Rohe's Bauhaus colleague Marcel Breuer. These puritanical chairs are set off by a tubular steel–framed daybed and ceiling pendant light, developed by Marianne Brandt at the Bauhaus. Functionality is also key, with built-in cupboards from floor to ceiling. The industrial aesthetic characterizes modernism's design for mass housing, resonating with Grete Schutte-Lihotzky's highly efficient Frankfurt Kitchen of 1926. Although it measured only 170 × 75 in. (3.5 × 1.9 m), it had a wealth of storage and work space, a foldaway ironing board, and movable lighting. Based on time and motion studies and the work of scientific management, this was the ultimate functional kitchen for the modest dwelling of the 1920s.

Modern movement architects were also capable of the grand gesture. A prime example is the German Pavilion in Barcelona, designed by Mies van der Rohe. Created for the 1929 International Barcelona Exhibition, the pavilion was constructed from luxurious materials including shimmering gold marble and reflective brass. The simple structure was virtually not an interior at all, with the space encased in huge swathes of plate glass, framed in metal. Erected to house the official opening ceremony conducted by the Spanish King Alfonso XIII and Queen Victoria Eugenie, the deserted space is dominated by the two Barcelona Chairs, specially designed by Mies van der Rohe with Lilly Reich, along with their matching footstools. Placed on a black carpet, the chairs were constructed from chromium-plated steel in a complex arrangement that was bolted together in early examples. Isolated in the space against the onyx dore marble wall, and the ornamental pool outside, the chairs are larger than life. The perfectly matched dimensions of 30 in. (75 cm) deep, 30 in. (75 cm) high, and 30 in. (75 cm) long are much more imposing than those of the average chair, some 20 in. (50 cm) wide. The chairs were also extremely heavy and could not be easily maneuvered around the space. The chair went into commercial production straight away and was redesigned by Mies van der Rohe in 1950, after Reich had died, using the new material of stainless steel with less expensive upholstery of cow leather.

Like Mies van der Rohe, the modernist architect Le Corbusier worked closely with a female collaborator, Charlotte Perriand, to produce iconic chair designs. Le Corbusier was excessively concerned with space, cleanliness, and order. His designs for private residences, such as the Villa Savoye at Poissy (1929–1931), featured a perfectly white stuccoed exterior, sweeping interior spaces, and extensive open plan arrangements around minimal fixtures and fittings. Perriand joined his practice in 1927 and developed three chairs for his design projects at the time. The B301 sling-back chair was designed to enhance conversation. The chair was constructed from tubular steel with leather straps for armrests, with the seat and back made from animal skin. One of the key designs was the Grand Confort. This consisted of a tubular steel frame that cradled leather-covered, soft cushions. The B306 chaise longue was also designed at this time. Le Corbusier and Perriand's furniture designs were included at the Salon d'Automne in 1929 in the "One-Room Flat." Le Corbusier's cousin, Pierre Jeanneret, was also credited with the designs, although it is probably the case that he mainly oversaw the business side of things. The furniture was displayed on a green glass floor that was illuminated, enhancing the luminosity of the green glass table. Around the table were placed four B302 swivel chairs in black leather and chrome. For Le Corbusier, chairs were equipment for houses, which in themselves were machines for living in. Writing in *Vers Une Architecture (Towards a New Architecture)* in 1923, he declared:

> If we eliminate from our hearts and minds all dead concepts in regard to the houses and look at the question from a critical and objective point of view, we shall arrive at the "House Machine," the mass-production house, healthy (and morally so too) and beautiful in the same way that the working tools and instruments which accompany our existence are beautiful.[12]

The architecture Le Corbusier had created was, in his mind and that of his fellow modernists, a permanent solution. The built-in furniture and unadorned surfaces indicated a commitment to everlasting good design. It also stipulated against any attempt to create a homely interior, with very little scope for the occupants to make changes and reflect any element of fashionability. As Hilde Heynen and Gulsum Baydar, and also Christopher Reed, have demonstrated, modern architecture stifled the domestic.[13] And this suppression can be linked with issues of identity, particularly around both gender and sexuality. While the impact made by modern architecture was limited during the interwar years, in the postwar years it ironically became the fashionable style for domestic and public interiors.

COLD WAR CULTURE

Modernism became mainstream partly as a result of a popular will to create a better future for society following the ravages of World War II. For example, efforts made by the newly founded British Council of Industrial Design attempted to influence popular taste and tempt homemakers to furnish their new abodes using modern design, renamed *the contemporary*. The style was celebrated at the Festival of Britain in 1951, with a swath of temporary pavilions promoting the message of a bright new future using the futuristic elements of modern architecture to entertain all. The Homes

FIGURE 2   An image used to promote the Homes and Gardens Pavilion at the Festival of Britain, 1951. Created by the British Council of Industrial Design, this is an idealized, contemporary-style living space for the ideal young couple. Taken from the *South Bank Exhibition Guide* (London: Her Majesty's Stationery Office, 1951), p. 69. Collection of Anne Massey.

and Gardens Pavilion featured modernist room sets, complete with spindly furniture, modernist fabrics, and plain-colored walls (Fig. 2). The United States also used modernism for propaganda reasons. Mass housing, shopping malls, factories, and corporate headquarters were built in the modern style across the country. Gone were the idealist notions of the prewar avant-garde, replaced by the values of a liberal consumer culture.

The development of modernism in the United States, and New York in particular, as explored by Serge Guilbaut in his excellent book *How New York Stole the Idea of Modern Art* (1983), has illuminated the appropriation of modernism on behalf of the United States and its institutions. While Guilbaut has explored this tendency in terms of fine art, it also applies to design and architecture and had begun with the opening of the Museum of Modern Art (MoMA) in the 1930s. The curatorial department for architecture and design was founded in 1932, and was the first to be created in the world. Although it did not focus on interiors, chairs were a major feature. Designer chairs were displayed in neat rows, just like the paintings. It is worth noting that currently chairs make up nearly one-quarter of MoMA's online highlights from the architecture and design collection.

The furniture displays at MoMA furthered the trend toward modern style with the *Good Design* shows of the 1950s, to which key designers such as Charles and Ray Eames contributed. MoMA also organized the *Design for Use USA* traveling exhibition at Stuttgart in 1951–1952, which was essentially part of the Marshall Plan and the spread of cold war culture. In addition, the exhibition *Fifty Years of American Art* of 1955, held in Paris and elsewhere in Europe, included contemporary American chairs.[14] Hence, in New York, modernist design was officially supported, and the designers were constructed as fine artists and enlisted to serve in the cold war, with Charles and Ray Eames at the forefront.

Charles Eames and Eero Saarinen had designed furniture for the Department of Industrial Design at MoMA's competition *Organic Design in Home Furnishings* in 1940. As part of the ensemble the pair designed a soft and sculpted upholstered side chair and a curved armchair and won first prize in both the categories of case and seat furniture. Constructed from molded plywood, the furniture was technically innovative and introduced the latest breakthrough in automobile manufacturing into the construction of the chair. The Eames continued to be showcased at MoMA, with exhibitions including *Design for Use* (1944), *New Furniture Designed by Charles Eames* (1946), and *The International Competition for Low-Cost Furniture* (1948). The Eameses characterized American cold war culture in their innovative use of high technology and new materials and helped popularize the modernist room setting.

The profession of interior design emerged during the 1960s in Britain, with the inauguration of tertiary-level courses in the subject and a postgraduate course at the Royal College of Art, led by Hugh Casson. In 1967 he commented:

> Many architects refuse to believe that such a thing as interior design exists at all. Some place it on a par with the art of the milliner or pastry cook; others seem to regard its claims for separate consideration as a personal affront.[15]

The interior design profession could be taken seriously by the architectural establishment only when the hegemony of modernism came to be challenged.

CHALLENGING MODERNISM

Qualms about the appropriateness of modernism for the design of the interior had always existed. The cartoonist Osbert Lancaster poked fun at it, traditionalists hung onto history, and the newly emerging profession of the interior decorator met the needs of the wealthy client, which by and large were not for modern interiors. Decorators such as Elsie de Wolfe worked with the wealthy elite, sourcing antiques and recreating the glamour of France in the eighteenth century.[16]

The architecture of the modern movement came under attack from a young group of architects, designers, artists, and critics at the Institute of Contemporary Arts (ICA) in London in the early 1950s. The main platform for the Independent Group's critique of modernism was its obsession with permanence. The space-time continuum was acknowledged in the work of the Independent Group in the 1950s, including the interior design work of the Smithsons, the artworks of Richard Hamilton, and the writing of Reyner Banham. The group reevaluated modernism as a style emerging at a particular moment rather than a universal, everlasting aesthetic.[17] The Independent Group also introduced elements of contemporary popular culture into its work, a surprising proportion of which concerned the interior. Richard Hamilton's collage and poster design *Just What Is It That Makes Today's Homes So Different, So Appealing?*

of 1956 (Plate 2) comprises a virtual compendium of the most up-to-date technology for the home, and the most up-to-date imagery, culled from contemporary American magazines.[18] The ephemeral was celebrated, and modernism challenged. The significance of the consumer was incorporated in the design process, and new technology acknowledged. The everyday life of the street was documented, and thresholds between outside and inside problematized. As Banham argued in his seminal article "Vehicles of Desire," published in 1955, Platonic values are outdated and lack currency:

> We eagerly consume noisy ephemeridae, here with a bang today, gone without a whimper tomorrow—movies, beach-wear, pulp magazines, this morning's headlines and tomorrow's TV programmes—yet we insist on aesthetic and moral standards hitched to permanency, durability and perennity.[19]

In the Smithsons' *House of the Future* (1956) the architects designed a domestic interior that could be thrown away or traded in when the family expanded or shrank. Created as a futuristic vision of homes in twenty-five years' time, it incorporated science-fictional flourishes, including the space-age outfits of the exhibition inhabitants (hired models).[20] This prototype, commissioned for the "*Daily Mail* Ideal Home Exhibition," was designed for a young, childless couple. The interior did not have definitively divided rooms; the inner space was fluid and arranged around a central patio, with built-in cupboards and sliding doors. Various gadgets were installed, including a self-timed shower that also dried you and incorporated a sunlamp. In the kitchen there was space for drip-drying clothes, space for home sewing, eye-level ovens, and a fridge, and one of the ovens was a microwave. There were no bed linens, as the ambient temperature was maintained for comfort. The interior surfaces were smooth, with rounded corners constructed from a wooden frame covered in a fibrous stucco. The ultimate aim was to mass-produce the living pod, cast in moldings of resin-bonded plaster. This was ultimately an exhibition design, created to illustrate a particular design approach that challenged modernism. As fellow Independent Group member John McHale commented at the time, "The attention to detailing of individual furnishing, etc., throughout reflected the designers' sensibility to varied human response, rather than the imposition of a private overall aesthetic."[21] The Independent Group was also involved in curating and designing a multitude of innovative exhibitions—the ultimate ephemeral interior. From *Parallel of Life and Art* (1953) to *Man, Machine & Motion* (1955) to *This Is Tomorrow* (1956) the group organized total environments that completely immersed the visitor but lasted for only three months.

Later critiques of modernism emanated from architects in the United States, including Robert Venturi, Denise Scott Brown, and Steven Izenour in *Learning from Las Vegas* (1972), and Italy, with the Memphis Group's (founded 1981) expansive approach to design.[22] Both were characterized by the inclusion of popular culture as a serious and powerful force to be taken into account by the designer and laid the foundations for postmodernism from the later 1970s on. Postmodernism took the ephemeral into account; it was witty and fashionable and ironic. Designs also incorporated the autonomy of the user. In a similar vein to the Smithsons' *House of the Future,* future Memphis designers contributed to the exhibition *The New Domestic Landscape* at MoMA in New York in 1972. This comprised specially commissioned microenvironments, which the user could adjust according to individual requirements.

Leading architectural theorist and designer Charles Jencks brought the term *postmodernism* into currency among designers and consumers with his book *The Language of Post-Modern Architecture* in 1977. Challenging the basic tenets of modern architecture, he designed interiors, including his own Thematic House in West London. He revived past styles in design, from Egyptian to Gothic, in the rooms, which were grouped around a central staircase. In the library, the theme was Biedermeier with specially crafted furniture in this nineteenth-century German style.

The emergence of postmodernism also prompted a more inclusive history of interior design. The subject had been dominated by modernist accounts, starting with Pevsner's, which was then amplified. Design history as a separate discipline was founded, and produced work that acted as a critique of the modernist historiography of interior design. The pioneers of modern design were superseded by the interior decorator, the DIY enthusiast, the homemaker, and the professional interior designer. A material culture perspective was also acknowledged, which took everyday experiences into account and added another dimension to design history.[23] This all culminated in the serious treatment of the interior with the launch of an academic journal, *Interiors: Design, Architecture, Culture,* by Berg in 2010, which encompasses a range of approaches to the interior from a multidisciplinary, global perspective.

The trouble is, interiors lack permanence. Much as modern architects and critics tried to freeze time in black-and-white images of the sparse interior spaces of the 1920s and 1930s, it can't be denied that any room is in a constant state of flux. Interior spaces are inhabited by a range of people, and their fixtures and fittings are renewed at an increasingly rapid pace. And so the history of the interior is in a constant state of flux, reflecting the energy and creativity of its subject.

2

Rethinking Histories, Canons, and Paradigms

JOHN C. TURPIN

INTRODUCTION

The fact that canons and paradigms exist in the telling of history is problematic; it suggests that certain ways of knowing the past have been agreed on by a group and presented to a larger public who relies heavily on what they read as "truth." Canons and paradigms, therefore, can ultimately serve "as a mechanism for the exercise of power in . . . society."[1] Combating such potentialities, noted British historiographer Keith Jenkins states that "discourses are cultural, cultivated, fabricated and thus ultimately arbitrary."[2] His suspicions regarding the objectivity of any historical narrative are anchored in a scholarly revelation that began in the middle of the twentieth century with historians like Robin George Collingwood and Edward Hallett Carr.[3] They recognize that historians shape the history they write based on their unique perspective and must therefore be read with such an understanding in mind.[4]

The concern over canons and paradigms became a topic of relevance for art/architectural history and material culture studies once these discourses moved from their early objectives of description and classification to the analysis of patterns and the determination of meanings based on content.[5] Patterns and meanings required an understanding of users, and those users were often selected from a patriarchal framework that privileged upper-class white males. *Herstory*, a neologism coined during the second-wave feminist movement, reflected the power of the then current narratives' abilities to erase women's presence—let alone contributions—from the historical narrative. This reference to gender resonates with this chapter due to the relevance of women to the experience and development of the domestic interior. Gender, however, is but one of many constructs that support the subjectivity of history and the ways in which the telling of history can be manipulated to advance the ideology or values of an individual or group. Age, class, ethnicity, and religion add to the list of possible perspectives. None represents the "truth" in its purest form; multiple perspectives are necessary to understand the complexity of any historical narrative.

The history of interiors has evolved over the last century in a manner that parallels closely not only the changing approaches toward historical inquiry, but also the development of the interior design profession. Four phases delineate this phenomenon. The first phase occurs during the nineteenth and early twentieth century, when much of the analysis focuses on the physical characteristics of objects in order to generate stylistic classifications. The articulation of period styles, particularly in the Western tradition, correlates with the prominence of the antique trade and the decorator, whose primary purpose is to recreate period rooms based on European precedents. By midcentury, historians shift from object-centered inquires to explorations between the object and the user's social patterns of daily life. The introduction of the human experience corresponds to the profession's desire to understand the relationship between the user and the object to inform design solutions. The third phase reflects the death of modernism as both a style and an epistemology. Postmodernism introduces contextual interpretation and an interest in underrepresented groups, allowing a complete reexamination of history that abandons its reliance on the myopic male perspective. The female experience with the built environment fuels a number of major publications and reflects the profession's intentional campaign to be viewed as equals in the business community. The twenty-first century (the fourth phase) is experiencing yet another evolution, in both the profession and the exploration of its history. The academy educates designers to work in interdisciplinary settings, and the history of interiors is now being examined by all manner of disciplines: art, literature, and anthropology to name just a few.

Each of these methods of inquiry has strengthened the theoretical underpinnings of the discipline and is worth exploring. The following discussion is presented as a historiography of the history of interior design, exploring each of the phases noted above. In addition, the author offers a commentary on the relationship of the profession to the historical narrative because of history's ability to shape perceptions.

PHASE I: THE WESTERN OBJECT

When it comes to paradigms, none has been more influential in the development of history than that of the Western tradition. The circumstances through which cultures have developed over the past millennia have fostered distinct ways of knowing. The Western tradition supports a linear method of thinking that defines a portion of the global population geographically because of events that occurred in and around Europe approximately four thousand years ago, particularly with the developments in Greece and Rome. The very phrase *Western tradition* implies a detachment from an Eastern tradition, in which glancing blows between the two hemispheres are treated only as opportunities for one tradition to assimilate the knowledge of another without acknowledging the true impact of the other culture. Consider the effect of gunpowder on historical events in Europe even though it was first discovered in China. This mindset devalues these other cultures.

History books concerning all of the creative arts—which include architecture, interiors, fine arts, furnishing, and decorative arts—continue to focus their efforts on Europe and the West. Those who attempt to incorporate traditions outside of the Eurocentric tradition struggle because the narrative has been written so deeply into our way of knowing. A truly global approach to history has yet to be realized. Consequently, the power of the Western paradigm must be recognized as an overarching framework that rejects well over half of the global population's contribution to and experience of the built environment.

But, to be fair, this development was not entirely intentional. As curious minds began to inquire about the past they were limited by the access they had to "history." That which was considered most ancient—and most accessible—to Europeans was Greece and Rome. The number of buildings still standing from Imperial Rome and the Golden Age of Greece offered opportunities for direct observation, as indicated by the Grand Tour taken by architects at the end of their formal education, beginning in the eighteenth century. Travel to Greece had been a dangerous journey prior to about 1750. James Stuart (an English archaeologist, architect, and artist) and Nicholas Revett (an amateur architect and artist) embarked on an expedition to Athens in 1751 to engage in serious archaeological inquiry. Their publication, *The Antiquities of Athens* (1762), was one of the first accurate surveys of ancient Greek architecture. Unintentional victims of Western social constructs, Stuart and Revett, two men who had been allowed to expand their understanding of the world through education, participated in what had already become the patriarchal domination of knowledge. Specific to this chapter, one need only consider the globally perceived pursuit of architecture as a male endeavor, while interior design is relegated to the female.

Early historical texts are similar in that they focus on the analysis of objects. This should be of little surprise. Benjamin Bloom, an educational psychologist, developed a classification of levels of intellectual behavior in the middle of the twentieth century.[6] Development begins with knowledge or simply being able to describe or identify some "thing." Stuart and Revett's careful recording of Greek architecture is a good example of this initial phase—the recording and classification of what exists. This approach defines the first phase of inquiry into the history of interiors, which was essentially a series of categorical analyses into architecture, furniture, fine art, and the decorative arts within the framework of the Western tradition that privileged European models.

The act of historical classification mirrored the scientific approach to understanding the natural world. Early scientists used working hypotheses to stimulate investigation. Empirical evidence was then gathered from the senses, particularly observation, through experimentation. The identification of similarities and patterns justified or proved the hypotheses. Consequently, the categorization of "things"—whether natural or manmade—underscored the early stages of knowing, as well as an attempt by historians to reconstruct history exactly as it happened. Chronology became an accepted method for communicating information that relied on classification and categorization in order to enhance understanding. For example, Batty Langley's *The Builder's*

Director or Bench-Mate from 1767 focused on Greek, Roman, and Gothic architectural characteristics, presented chronologically in order to emphasize the development of a particular building tradition. To assist reader comprehension, Langley's publication relied heavily on more than 500 images and was marketed accordingly. The underlying challenge, however, was the public's lack of interest in history beyond the romantic fantasies. Almost a century later, Albert Jacquemart wrote about the social perceptions of being a historian in *A History of Furniture* (1878). "Until within these last few years, those who devoted themselves to researches after old furniture, antiquities, Venetian glass, painted or lustrous potteries, were looked upon as eccentric or mad."[7] He continued to vocalize his frustrations that the public did not understand the value of archaeological research and its ability to provide a history of humankind and of civilization.

During the nineteenth century publications continued to focus on European styles presented categorically and chronologically. In the United States, a social phenomenon was responsible for the growing interest in European styles. At the end of the Civil War, a number of Americans became incredibly wealthy due to their investment in certain industries, such as the railroad and steel, that proved extremely profitable during the Reconstruction Era (1865–1877). Many of these newly rich Americans vaulted from the middle class to the upper class due to their dramatic change in financial status. The existing upper class resisted the acceptance of these individuals because they threatened the distribution of social power. In an attempt to visually validate their new status, this new "leisure class"—as coined by Thorstein Veblen—began a building campaign of magnificent homes in the European tradition.[8] The strategy was to associate themselves with the old aristocracies in Europe by constructing villas, chateaux, and castles reminiscent of those found in France, Italy, and England. Because they were not bred to have the same level of "taste" as the existing upper class, the leisure class relied on the services of architects and decorators. The decorators quickly realized that their future lay in the reproduction of period rooms to fulfill the desires of their clients. The antique trade burgeoned as the upper class consumed historical artifacts at an alarming rate. Fees based on purchases motivated the design decisions of some of the decorators. Historically inaccurate rooms dripping with fabric and stuffed with furnishings and decorative arts were often the result.

Capitalizing on the trend of period rooms, novelist Edith Wharton (1862–1937) and architect Ogden Codman Jr. (1863–1951) defined "natural good taste" for American society as anything of English, Italian, or French design from the Renaissance forward. This criterion justified a means by which decorators and clients alike could measure or criticize what became the accepted elements for successful domestic interiors. Wharton and Codman's *The Decoration of Houses* (1897) anchored the practice of interior decoration to the production of period rooms—for better or worse—and fostered the spawning of countless publications focused on historical styles for interiors and furnishings during the early part of the twentieth century. Helen Candee's (1906) *Decorative Styles and Periods in the Home* and Emily Post's (1930) *The Personality of a House: The Blue Book of Home Design and Decoration* reinforced the Western object-centered, chronological narrative in the public sector, while Frank Alvah Parsons's (1916) *Interior Decoration: Its Principles and*

Practice and Sherrill Whiton's (1937) *Elements of Interior Decoration* effectively integrated the model into the American educational system.

The "Western object" paradigmatic approach to writing history effectively served the discipline of interior design. As a profession, historical texts provided necessary information to assist decorators and designers in the reproduction of domestic period rooms commissioned by the wealthy. As a discipline, these early narratives laid the historical and theoretical foundations for future scholarly inquiry. General classification offered a knowledge base that other researchers continued to explore at a greater depth. The effectiveness of this type of narrative during the learning process remains evident as the vast majority of history texts used in programs across the world continue to include—at some level—an object-centered, chronological narrative.

PHASE II: THE OBJECT AND SOCIETY

With the growing number of historical texts documenting the various periods and styles of furniture, scholars turned their attention to the relationship between the object and the user as an indicator for understanding the built environment as an artifact of society. Inquiry extended beyond asking "What is it?" to "Why does it look this way?" Extrinsic forces such as economics, politics, and social behaviors provided provocative and informative frameworks for understanding the development of designed objects. The layering of social history onto the inquiry into objects augmented the historical narrative, and a new paradigm made its debut.

The timing of these studies parallels a growing shift in interior decoration. During the early part of the twentieth century, the concept of interior decoration started to spread beyond the exclusive boundaries of the social elite, which immediately brought into question issues of finances. The middle class could not offer the same carte blanche opportunities to the decorators and designers. In addition, the production of period rooms did not necessarily respond to modern needs and social patterns, especially for the middle-class housewife, who saw her domestic responsibilities increase as servants within the home became less feasible.[9] Researchers analyzed the design of kitchens and offered space-saving techniques to supplement new technologies to assist the housewife. The function and usage of domestic environments became much more prevalent in advice books and shelter magazines. The United States' growing fascination with hygiene also motivated a different approach to the design of interiors. As designers began to expand their clienteles to include a much larger range of socioeconomic levels, each with very different preferences and needs, historians began analyzing their subjects through a contextual lens that addressed issues of class and economics. Though historians were not ready to write about the middle of the twentieth century from a historical point of view, they did adopt a method from their current context.

By midcentury, historians like John Summerson shifted from object-centered inquires to explorations between the object and the context in which it was conceived. *Georgian London* addressed the impact of social, economic, and financial circumstances on the development of architecture during the late Stuart and Georgian period by discussing the impact of taste and wealth on British citizens and designers.[10] According to Summerson, the social construct of taste (a class derivative) imbued certain individuals with persuasive powers in the design of the built environment. Inigo Jones, one of his examples, along with his Catholic king, James I, heralded the designs of the Italians, which became the foundation for the styles to come. Both taste and wealth played major roles in the design decisions made during the seventeenth century in London. Summerson continued to frame his discussion of the built environment through topics like mercantilism and politics. The object became a manifestation of much larger social concepts, just like the production of objects during the middle of the twentieth century.

Just over a decade after the publication of *Georgian London,* John Gloag published *Georgian Grace* (1956). While the work was admittedly grounded in much of Summerson's existing work, Gloag furthered the exploration of objects as artifacts of social behaviors and patterns. He connected the concept of good living with that of food and drink and the preceding impact on the design of furnishings. Side tables, for example, were originally little more than a flat surface. However, when eating became a much more involved, social, and "gracious" event, designers added drawers and cupboards—and even spaces for chamber pots—to reflect the civility of the time. The introduction of tea had equally dramatic effects on both social behavior and the furniture that supported the new, exotic ritual. New decorative objects—like tea caddies and tea chests—populated the home. Gloag even discussed the effect of tea drinking on the design of the drawing room itself, noting a renewed interest in both japaning and chinoiserie. The exploration of tea's effect on Britain permitted a dialogue between East and West and its impact on design.

England continued to be of interest to scholars exploring the relationship of social patterns and the built environment. Mark Girouard studied the development of the English country house from the Middle Ages to the twentieth century. In the preface, he articulates the significance of social patterns.

> Even the most knowledgeable country-house enthusiasts tend to think in terms of architects, craftsmen or family history, but to know surprisingly little about *how families used the houses* which architects and craftsmen built for them...the results so greatly increased my understanding of country houses [italics added].[11]

His analysis requires that he understand the politics of each period and the ways the house reflected at least a desire for social power. Girouard tracks this theme, noting that the owners of the medieval home valued bravery and leadership, while a sixteenth-century lord privileged education and the arts. The impact on the interior of these homes was the proliferation of books and artwork. By the nineteenth century English homes mirrored the cultural emphasis on morality, thus the separation of male and female zones in the home to prevent unacceptable behavior.

Summerson, Gloag, and Girouard combined anthropological sensitivities with the formal analysis that had previously defined and essentially created the early historical narratives. Their work expanded the understanding of the built object by introducing critical contextual discussions embedded in the social and cultural systems of the object's origins. The object transcended its own existence as a simple product of the human imagination to become a manifestation of rituals, beliefs, and values unique to the individual user and designer/craftsman.

The incorporation of social patterns greatly enhanced the historical narrative of interior design. From a disciplinary viewpoint, the objects in the interior became much more valuable as cultural blueprints that helped scholars understand not only simply what was made, but also how it reflected attitudes, beliefs, and values. For people who no longer have the ability to speak to us, the interior—its compositions and components—reveals how they lived. Unlocking the anthropological messages embedded within these objects provided such research with an added level of significance. As Jacquemart predicted, the study of objects would tell us about human civilization. The relevance of the interior goes far beyond asking "what it is" to understanding "why it looks that way."

For the profession, interior design experienced significant change during the middle of the twentieth century. Interior designers began offering their services to the public through the design of hospitals, retail stores, office environments, and all other types of interior spaces. The emphasis shifted from mere aesthetics to user-centered design—the understanding that design can improve an individual's quality of life at home or work. For example, under the leadership of Florence Knoll (b. 1917), the Knoll Planning Unit brought a new approach to the design of corporate interiors. The approach was based on a systematic assessment of all end users in a corporate design project. Knoll and her team interviewed and assessed executives and clerical staff alike in regard to their daily work routines. They analyzed workflow, productivity, and daily patterns before the design work began. The result was a holistic interior space that promoted efficiency and well-being at all levels of the organization.

Although the paradigm of the Western tradition remained firm, the growing fascination of "reading" the interior environment to reveal social and cultural patterns brought a new level of rigor and respect to the nascent discipline of interior design history. The new paradigm brought validity and credibility. It mirrored the shift in the industry from an emphasis on high-end, residential designs defined by period rooms and antiques to a greater understanding of the needs of the user and the ways design can improve the quality of their life. However, the narrative still remained exclusive and did not recognize the role of women and minorities in the development of the profession. The history of interior design continued to be a history predominantly privileging the contributions of the white male architect. It would take a social revolution to create a new historical paradigm.

PHASE III: ONCE SILENT VOICES

Throughout the twentieth century minorities struggled for equality—some for the most basic human rights. Race, gender, and sexual orientation were tools used by upper-class white males to maintain control and power over every aspect of society. Laws attempted to rectify the situation, but progress did not match expectations or needs. By the 1960s, the American political landscape emerged as a flash pan for social rebellions. African Americans fought for civil liberties, women wanted control over their own bodies and the right to pursue opportunities outside the home, and a new generation wanted to be free of their parents' conservative way of living. The people demanded change.

Design experienced a similar tension as modernism's effect on the built environment was coming to an end. With the Nazi closure of the Bauhaus in the 1930s, American schools of design witnessed a flood of modernist ideologists who redefined the education of a generation of architects and designers. The emphasis on socialist reform and good design for all through standardization and mass production attempted to universalize the human experience. Although well intentioned, its failure was memorialized by the destruction of the Pruitt-Igoe housing project in 1972—just sixteen years after its completion. According to Charles Jencks, the demolition marked the day "modern architecture died."[12]

In both society and design, Americans realized that they had been trapped in a world of binary oppositions: yes/no, black/white, good/bad, male/female, public/private, modernism/historicism. Modernism and structuralism (a method used for historical research) strategically sorted American life into two broad categories: that which was valued and that which was not. The earlier work of historians like Carr, who recognized the subjectivity of history, experienced a revival of sorts in that minority groups—especially women—were ready to have their story included in the historical narrative of American culture. This would be the first serious challenge to the existing historical paradigms in many disciplines.

Though interior decoration was born from the male-dominated work of the upholsterer and cabinetmaker, women made great strides in the profession beginning with Candace Wheeler (1877–1959), Elsie de Wolfe (1865–1950), and Nancy McClelland (1877–1959) in the late nineteenth and early twentieth centuries. This first generation of "lady decorators" made significant contributions but were systematically omitted, devalued, or ignored in virtually all historical narratives leading up to the twenty-first century.[13] Between 1970 and 2005, scholars turned their attention to underrepresented groups; in the case of interior design, women were the first target.

In 1971 Linda Nochlin asks the definitive question at the most opportune moment in history, the peak of second-wave feminism: "Why have there been no great women artists?"[14] In this quote, excerpted from an article by the same name, Nochlin questions the normative quality of the current research methodologies accepted by academic establishments on historical subjects. Of specific interest is the value and validity of the white, Western male viewpoint, unconsciously accepted as the only viewpoint. From a feminist approach, Nochlin deconstructs the methods by which art historians labeled or prioritized "great" artists. She objects to the exclusion of social institutions in certain methodologies for the more illusive phenomenon of an inherent, spiritual quality of the "genius." This term is often attached to privileged names (most often male) in a monograph authored by a male. Nochlin proposes that this implies the male's ability or right to define even the most metaphysical parameters of human existence without accountability.

Dolores Hayden responds to Nochlin's question and delves into the gender politics of housing design in *The Grand Domestic Revolution* (1981).[15] The first heading in her introduction—"A Lost Feminist Tradition"—makes clear the thesis of her publication. She explores, challenges, and deconstructs the socially constructed role of the female in the domestic environment. In a male society whose individuals are measured constantly by their political or financial accomplishments, women's inability to access these opportunities and the absence of financial compensation for domestic work systematically omit them from the historical narrative. Hayden's analysis of the feminine experience during the twentieth century identifies the female as a subject with unique experiences that had been ignored by historians. For design scholars, countless questions are brought to the forefront as the female's impact on the environment had not been fully explored.

Following the work of Nochlin, Hayden, and a number of other feminist scholars, women started to receive greater attention. History was being rewritten as new narratives evolved from perspectives not previously considered. Early historical surveys, such as Isabelle Anscombe's (1984) *A Woman's Touch: Women in Design from 1860 to the Present Day*, focused on "women designers whose work contributed to the modern house and its furnishings."[16] Anscombe presents biographical information regarding the various designers and contextualizes their life and work in relation to both social history and prevailing design movements. The reading of history through the lens of the female experience—at least relative to the design fields—gained momentum slowly. Publications like Judy Attfield and Pat Kirkham's *A View from the Interior* (1988), Elizabeth Danze and Debra Coleman's *Architecture and Feminism* (1996), and Brenda Martin and Penny Sparke's *Women's Places: Architecture and Design 1860–1960* (2003) offered discrete scholarly examinations on a wide range of events and situations in which the lives of women intersected with design. A representative example includes women and the development of the modern kitchen in Germany, women and the development of the profession of interior design, and women and the development of personal identity.

Poststructuralism's interest in exploring underrepresented groups spread to other marginalized groups as well. Issues of sexuality and the built environment appeared in Beatriz Colomina's *Sexuality and Space* (1992) and Aaron Betsky's *Queer Space: Architecture and Same-Sex Desire* (1997). A sampling of essays has Colomina exploring the male gaze and the design of the interior, while Betsky examines homosexuality and the construction and interpretation of space.

All of these texts challenged at its very core the highly subjective nature of history and the white male rubric that so narrowly defined what was considered to be of value to future generations. The expansion of the historical narrative to include previously and currently marginalized groups continues to inform and strengthen our understanding of the human condition, the human experience, and its influence on the built environment and visa versa.

The social revolutions of the 1960s and 1970s had significant impacts on the development of the profession. In 1961 one of the largest professional organizations changed its name from the American Society of Interior Decorators to the American Society of Interior Designers. The majority of the membership—now women—attempted to detach their professionalism from a nomenclature that had become a liability during the twentieth century. The modern movement reinterpreted terms like *decorator* and *decoration* by constantly devaluing their worth. The white male architects retooled language to suppress the growing popularity of the field of interior design.[17] Undeterred, interior design forged ahead to validate its services by creating an accrediting body for educational programs (Foundation for Interior Design Education and Research; now the Council for Interior Design Accreditation, established 1970) and a qualifying exam (National Council for Interior Design Qualification, established 1974). Interior design had become a profession and sought state legislation for certification and licensure in the United States. Women played major roles in all of these developments in an attempt to validate their participation in and relevance to the public sphere.

PHASE IV: OTHER VOICES

The fourth phase actually occurred simultaneously with the previous phase. Scholarship resulting from second-wave feminism naturally led to cross-disciplinary explorations as researchers from women's studies, sociology, and American history began uncovering the female experience. This trend has continued but not always with the specific intent of examining underrepresented groups. Jeremy Aynsley and Charlotte Grant's *Imagined Interiors: Representing the Domestic Interior since the Renaissance* (2006) and Julia Prewitt Brown's *The Bourgeois Interior* (2008) are two such examples.

Aynsley and Grant state up front that their publication is the result of "a research programme bringing together scholars from many disciplines in an attempt to further the study of the domestic interior."[18] According to the authors, a sampling of the disciplines in which the interior has become of great interest includes archaeology, anthropology, art history, design history, architecture, material culture studies, literature, media studies, psychology, and politics. In one of the short essays, Mark Jones elucidates the impact of the temperance movement on the design of the home through a study of its literature. Amanda Girling-Budd and Harriet McKay each consider the effects of capitalism on the interior by studying advertisements and retail catalogs respectively. In her book *The Bourgeois Interior,* Julia Prewitt Brown, a professor of English, analyzes the interior as described in great works of literature to uncover prevailing bourgeois values that do not change over time. Clearly, a wide range of disciplines have come to realize the significance of the home (or interiors) and its embedded messages about the culture that created it.

The profession responded to the growing interest in cross-disciplinary exploration by reconstructing pedagogical philosophies and business structures. Schools began creating interdisciplinary experiences so that students could understand the value of collaboration—the buzzword for the first decade of the twenty-first century. They were, in part, responding to the professions' desire to hire all manner of designers and professionals from allied disciplines so that they could provide a complete package of services for the built environment. However, the academies realized the value of interdisciplinary collaboration outside of the design disciplines and sought partnerships with business and health sciences during the design process. Cutting-edge design firms, seeing the potential of this new strategy, have begun hiring staff who might come from anthropology, sociology, or psychology in order to help them better understand their clients' needs and desires and thus create a stronger end product.

The radical departure from the structuralist paradigm in the latter portion of the twentieth century with its endless voices analyzed by multiple disciplines makes clear the realization that history is neither static nor knowable in its entirety. The white male narrative's exclusivity allows it to be more easily contained within a single narrative. The fact that any book claims the title "History of the World" is misleading to say the least. All manner of disciplines now recognize the value of diverse experiences, from the homemaker to the debutante, from the laborer to the business mogul, from the aboriginal tribesman to the Prince of Wales, and every combination in between. These stories challenge historians across the globe to preface their discussions by clarifying the scope and perspective of their narrative and recognizing that at any given moment—thanks to the intellectual power of the Internet—that story might be challenged, altered, or even debunked. The Western white male paradigm is now relevant only in that it is just one version of history.

A NEW PARADIGM?

The difficulty in telling/writing any history is evident in the growing discourse of historiography during the twentieth and now twenty-first centuries. Add to that the complexity of the interior itself, and the challenge becomes daunting. To understand interiors one must study the individual objects and their participation in a larger ensemble, whether it is the arrangement on the table or the composition of the room or the layout of the home as defined by the architecture in a rural or urban setting. The objects are meaningful only once they come in contact with humans, whether it is during or after production.[19] Consequently, as in all histories, the great challenge is scope. No history text can discuss fully all the relationships and meanings embedded in interiors across time and place. A comprehensive narrative would have to address each item individually and its relationship as part of a larger whole, and then extrapolate the meaning through all users of the space, for it is certain that the male and the female, the young and the old, the gay and the straight, the African and the Asian, and so on, will all construct different meanings and relationships with the interior. Postmodern methodologies released history from its previously myopic chains by realizing that the telling of history is partially reliant on perspective and visceral experiences and is thus incomplete unless fully inclusive.

The paradigms and canons mentioned in this chapter are outgrowths of the cultures that produced them and the natural process of human learning. The male perspective that dominated Western culture for millennia valued political achievements as a reflection of social survival above all else. Narratives relied on winners and losers, whether the threat was internal or external. The consequences of this criterion alone excluded a vast majority of the population and numerous aspects of society, such as domestic life, which hindered the development of a robust history of interiors prior to the twenty-first century.

In regards to the process of learning, scholars begin by seeing and recording; they then place their observations in context and search for meaning; the level of interpretation grows ever more complex as they recognize that a person's individuality redefines the object's meaning and is therefore always in flux. One could say that according to Bloom's taxonomy, historians interested in the interior as a subject of study have moved beyond knowledge, comprehension, and analysis to synthesis and evaluation—at least until a new subject matter is uncovered. Nonetheless, the previous restrictions experienced by older methodologies and the criteria that created the paradigms and canons have now been lifted.

In the writing of history, the issue is no longer one of "truth." What matters is the objective of the historical narrative. It must have an intent, which defines its limitations and perhaps exposes the bias of the author. That which is left out is just as important as that which is left in. Introductory, educational texts will continue to rely on the paradigm of the Western object because of pedagogical conservatism and the notion that all designers should be exposed to certain facts during their education, but that does not necessarily reflect the current needs of the profession. As designers embark on global projects in areas of the world they may have never visited, they must possess the skills to research the region, its people, and its culture or new technologies required by the function of the space. With all of the scholarship produced in the areas of design and education, the future of the profession—at least for now—relies heavily on compassion, curiosity, and critical thinking.

In closing, historical narratives are subjective, incomplete, and innately exclusionary. The idea of a canon or paradigm is by its very nature problematic. This does not suggest, however, that historical narratives are not useful. History informs the self and the collective. The absence of the perfect method pressures historians "to commit to honest investigation."[20] If the methods are transparent, then so, too, are the limitations and thus the truth of the narrative.

3

Inhabited Space: Critical Theories and the Domestic Interior

ALEXA GRIFFITH WINTON

Inhabited space transcends geometric space.

—*Gaston Bachelard*[1]

While the interior and its design remain a largely untheorized area of cultural production, recent applications of critical theory from a wide range of disciplines emphasize the interior as a site of rich scholarly inquiry particularly suited to this type of discursive analysis. This chapter addresses potential means of theorizing the interior—an intrinsically interdisciplinary construct—through three separate but interdependent categories: the spatial envelope, the contents of interior space, and users or inhabitants. It is limited in scope to the domestic interior, which, as Gwendolyn Wright has argued, is the central preoccupation with twentieth-century architects, and aims to build on recent scholarship that greatly strengthens the theoretical foundations of interiors studies, including *Intimus,* edited by Mark Taylor and Julieanna Preston, and *Toward a New Interior,* edited by Lois Weinthal.[2]

The first category of analysis in this chapter is the threshold, that transitional space that divides both interior from exterior and room from room. While many critics, theoreticians, and practitioners of the interior address the threshold itself, it has not received extensive attention from scholars of the interior despite widespread acknowledgment of the significance of the distinction between inside and outside. I will also examine Walter Benjamin's use of the interior as a means of locating his cultural and social critiques.

The second section addresses the furnishings and other objects found within the interior and the deep significance they often hold both individually and collectively, including the acts of collecting and consuming, and the role of everyday objects in the interior. The cultural critiques of Jean Baudrillard and recent explorations of the significance of things beyond their conventional exchange value, as argued in Bill Brown and Frank Trentmann's work on thing theory, elucidate this category.

The final section looks at spatial theory and other means of apprehending the experience of interior space. This section contextualizes the interior as interpreted by philosophers such as Henri Lefebvre, who argues that space is an economically and cultural charged production, and Gaston Bachelard, who interprets space through the lens of phenomenology. Interior space, and especially domestic space, is the focus of much of this analysis. The role of the users or inhabitants of a space, and their subjective experience of interiority, including the roles of gender, sexuality, and other specific expressions of interior space, are also included in this section. Examples include theorist and historian Jasmine Rault's definition of "sapphic modernity" as a key constituent of modernist interior design, Henry Urbach's analysis of the social and physical implications of the closet, and George Wagner's exploration of the role of technology in the midcentury bachelor's pursuit of women as a kind of prey.

The goal of this chapter is not to articulate a fixed discursive apparatus within which to analyze the interior and its design (which may be impossible) but rather to attempt to reveal some of the many ways in which critical theory and philosophy can both respond to and potentially inform the design of interior space.

THRESHOLDS OF EXPERIENCE: TRANSITIONAL SPACES AND TRANSGRESSIVE BOUNDARIES

Danger lies in transitional states, simply because transition is neither one state nor the next, it is undefinable.

Mary Douglas[3]

The interior, in theory as in practice, is understood as binary and even dialectical. It is always defined against what it is not: the outside world, the public realm. Furthermore, as Lynne Walker has argued, these binary categories often serve to diminish the significance of specifically domestic interiors, privileging instead the facade over the inside, the public building over the private home.[4] This seemingly obvious distinction also often calls into consideration other relevant concepts including privacy and publicity, class, and gender. In this regard, the threshold or boundary between the interior and the outside and between distinct interior rooms or spaces provides a rich context for expanding theories of the interior.

The threshold dividing the domestic interior from the outside world directly engages the notion of comfort, one of the most complex and key aspects of the interior. Beginning in the eighteenth century, both architects and inhabitants placed increasing emphasis on both defining and obtaining comfort within the interior.[5] Over time, thresholds exhibited shifting levels of permeability, signifying changing degrees of comfort with intrusions into the traditionally private realm of home.

While Walter Benjamin in *The Arcades Project* describes the nineteenth-century bourgeois interior as a hard shell lined with velvet, in which complete retreat from the outside world was the ideal, by the middle of the nineteenth century the blurring of conventional boundaries between inside space and the outside world were commonplace.[6] Benjamin's reading of the encased Victorian interior is supported by a number of contemporary literary and historical examples of extreme retreat, including Marcel Proust's retreat to his dark and silent cork-lined bedroom and Joris-Karl Huysman's 1884 novel *Against Nature,* in which the protagonist Des Esseintes—an overly sensitive young man who recently inherited a large fortune—cannot tolerate the aesthetic and sensual assaults of modern Paris, withdrawing instead to his meticulously designed house, in which he exerts control over the smallest details.[7] In *The Arcades Project,* Benjamin argued that the burgeoning French middle class collapsed nearly all aspects of their experience into the interior, seeking to interiorize gardens and other public, nondomestic spaces. "The bourgeois who came into ascendency with Louis Philippe set store by the transformation of near and far into the interior. He knows but a single scene: the drawing room."[8]

For Benjamin, the interior possessed both phantasmagoric and ritualistic qualities, with the threshold occupying a central place within the potentially enchanted space of the interior:

> Threshold magic. At the entrance to the skating rink, to the pub, to the tennis court, to resort locations: *penates*. . . . This same magic prevails more covertly in the interior of the bourgeois dwelling. Chairs beside an entrance, photographs flanking a doorway, are fallen household deities, and the violence they must appease grips our hearts even today at each ringing of the doorbell.[9]

The threshold itself can be defined in many ways: by location, function, and material. Etymologically it can mean an opening or beginning as well as an obstacle, and as Catherine Murphy has demonstrated, thresholds are fundamentally and necessarily ambiguous and time-based constructs, referring to both physical and psychological states of being.[10] Some can be transgressed by the body; some are transparent or translucent and purely visual, dominated by the gaze more than by bodily spatial experience.

Theories of psychoanalysis also directly address the significance of the boundary or threshold. Sigmund Freud viewed the unconscious mind as an interior space containing, among other mental impulses, consciousness, all within a drawing room (corroborating Benjamin's definition of bourgeois life as concentrated within this space). Freud defines the boundary between mental impulses and consciousness as the threshold acting as a "watchman," policing the strict divisions between these two states.[11] Freud's own working and living environments employed thresholds to powerful effect. As Diana Fuss describes, Freud strictly segregated the two distinct areas of his professional practice, psychoanalysis and writing, kept separate by a threshold that bisected his office space.[12]

The consequences of the breakdown of this border, of the failure of the watchman to keep unwanted impulses at bay, are expressed through Rodion Romanovich Raskalnikov, the protagonist of Dostoevsky's *Crime and Punishment,* who describes his retreat to his living quarters in animal rather than human terms in explanation of his premeditated murder of the elderly pawnbroker Alyona Ivanovna: "Then I hid in my corner like a spider. You were in my kennel, you saw it....And do you know, Sonya, low ceilings and cramped rooms cramp the souls and mind! Oh, how I hated that kennel! And yet I didn't want to leave it. I purposely didn't want to!"[13] Dostoyevsky uses Raskalnikov's description of his inhuman living quarters—his kennel—and his inability to leave them after the murder to project the character's intense psychological decompensation.

The role of domestic privacy and the extent to which the interior can signify its inhabitant are recurring themes across a wide cross section of disciplines. The French writer Georges Perec, whose work was intimately engaged in everyday life, wrote of his own private interior space and the significance of the threshold in demarcating it:

> On one side, me and *my place,* the private, the domestic (a space overfilled with my possessions: my bed, my carpet, my table, my typewriter, my books, my odd copies of the *Nouvelle Revue Française*); on the other side, other people, the world, the public, politics. You can't simply let yourself slide from one into the other, can't pass from one to the other, neither in one direction nor in the other. You have to have the password, have to cross the threshold, have to show your credentials, have to communicate, just as the prisoner communicates with the world outside.[14]

In the abodes of both Perec and the fictional Raskalnikov, separated by a century, the interior projects physical manifestations of their inner selves.

MATERIAL THRESHOLDS

New building materials and construction methods began to transform not only interiors but also the way they were inhabited, beginning with the extensive use of concrete and glass by the early twentieth century. Increasing use of large expanses of glass in domestic architecture blurred the conventional distinctions between inside and outside, potentially exposing much of what had been private life to the outside world at large.

To early modernist designers such as Adolphe Behn, as well as to early twentieth-century critics and theoreticians such as Benjamin, the visually permeable qualities of glass suggested a concomitant social transparency, with the potential to abolish the conventional bourgeois preoccupation with personal discreetness and physical comfort as manifest in the domestic interior. For Benjamin, transparency "put and end to dwelling in the old sense," and to Behne it performed the necessary task of extinguishing comfort: "Glass has an extra-human, super-human quality. Therefore, the European is right when he fears that glass architecture might become uncomfortable....Away with coziness! Only where comfort ends does humanity begin!"[15] Behne expressed this view of glass in his review of Paul Scheerbart's 1914 utopian manifesto, *Glass Architecture,* in which primarily colored and translucent glass is used to create a lapidary interior space intended to improve civilization through design, starting with the domestic interior. This effect of this brittle and luminous material on the interior is highly significant, for, as Charles

Rice argues, it is impossible to leave one's trace within an interior made of glass, as neither dust nor the impressions of everyday life imprint themselves on this material.[16]

Pierre Chareau's Maison de Verre, built in Paris from 1928 to 1932, offers another example of the use of light-permeable materials in creating paradoxical boundaries and thresholds within the interior. As Sarah Wigglesworth has observed, the house itself has two identities: a private house and an obstetrician's office or surgery, and the divisions between these spaces (as well as the discrete areas within each separate space) are at points intentionally heightened and/or obscured, often through the use of movable and translucent partitions. Wigglesworth describes the provocative use of perforated metal screens dividing the bedroom from the bathroom, in which "the body at its toilette is silhouetted by the light from wall-mounted lamps, and can be seen titillatingly veiled through the porous screen."[17] Thus, this degree of penetrability allows for the preservation of the appearance of privacy, while in fact using the outline of the body to create a series of suggestive vignettes.

Poststructuralist philosophers continued to explore the effects of glass on the divisions between public and private. Jean Baudrillard, in his 1968 *System of Objects* (which devotes significant attention to the interior and its contents), posits that the presence of glass "facilitates faster communication between inside and outside, yet at the same time it sets up an invisible but material caesura which prevents such communication from becoming a real opening onto the world."[18] For Baudrillard, the primarily function of glass is to permit the world at large to visually penetrate interior spaces, a direct counterpoint to Benjamin's opaque protective shell.

Recent scholarship on glass—specifically large glass windows—in the postwar domestic environment, in which one's interior and related modes of living are intentionally exposed, highlights the intrinsic conflict in our desire to both reveal and conceal ourselves through our interiors. While Sylvia Lavin has identified how the "spatial excitement of the glazed corners in [Richard] Neutra's bedrooms recalls the erotic translucency of new products for the bed and bath and the voyeuristic pleasures of picture windows," Margaret Maile Petty extends the analysis of the increased exposure of the private realm afforded by glass, identifying the potential anxiety wrought by the "binary tension of the scopophilic and narcissistic gaze, of both desiring to view these private spaces and to see oneself within in them."[19] In both analyses, glass's materiality and its effects are directly engaged in redefining the cultural role of the interior and public access to it.

THINGS: THE STUFF OF DWELLING

In the most extreme instance, the dwelling becomes a shell. The nineteenth century, like no other century, was addicted to dwelling. It conceived the residence as a receptacle for the person, and it encased him with all his appurtenances so deeply within the dwelling's interior that one might be reminded of the inside of a compass case, where the instrument with all its accessories lies embedded in deep, usually violet folds of velvet.

Walter Benjamin[20]

Things today are shaking our fundamental understandings of subjectivity, agency, emotions, and the relations between humans and nonhumans.

Frank Trentmann[21]

The significance of the interior is found not merely in the disposition of interior spaces; the functional and symbolic objects located within it collaborate with the spatial construct of the interior and together work to define the space and its inhabitants, and scholarship from outside histories of architecture and material culture has increasingly focused on the importance of "things" as key social and cultural signifiers. As the American literary scholar Bill Brown observes, "Human subjects and material objects constitute one another."[22] This view of objects in context is expressed by Bloomsbury writer Lytton Strachey, who described his childhood home as an integrated system that literally constituted his identity: "To reconstruct, however dimly, that grim machine, would be to realize with some distinctness the essential substance of my biography."[23]

The significance of the everyday object is highlighted by recent scholarship on the larger implications of things, referred to as *thing theory*. Thing theory offers historians and theorists a means of apprehending the larger meaning of objects beyond their function or their monetary value, instead incorporating them into the analysis of whole systems of cultural practice. This has direct relevance to the critical understanding of the interior, given the number of (domestic) things incorporated into the routines of daily life. As described by historian Frank Trentmann in his argument in favor of greater scholarly attention to things as they relate to practice:

Practices thus look beyond possessions. Instead of taking either object or individual as its starting point, research on practices focuses on how users, things, tools, competence, and desires are coordinated. The life of objects, in other words, is not prior to or independent of social practices but codependent. This also means that value is not based in a product or its meanings but in how it is put to use. An object such as the chair acquires its durability because it has become tightly connected with practices, norms, and symbolic meaning.[24]

While histories of architecture long tended to focus on those objects and interiors that represent agency and power, neglecting the domestic environments of the common individual, philosophers and historians of material culture have long been interested in the study of domestic furniture as a means of apprehending value systems and modes of living. This emphasis on the critique of everyday articles of living as an essential tool in decoding wider social and cultural practices is articulated in historian Daniel Roche's *History of Everyday Things,* in which he suggests that the composition and arrangement of domestic furniture actually reflect the social structures of a given historical period. As he describes, "Furniture reveals to us a state of society through its significance, giving material form to needs and referring to the silent language of symbols."[25] This notion is taken further by Jean Baudrillard in his *System of Objects* in which he posits that the decoration and furnishing of the French postwar bourgeois home—his primary focus—is fundamentally patriarchal in nature. Rather than performing a decorative or aesthetic function, the primary objective of the arrangement of this interior, according to Baudrillard, is symbolic; the role of the furniture is to "personify human relationships, to fill the space they share between them.... They have as little autonomy in this space as the various family members enjoy in society."[26]

Baudrillard extends this notion of objects performing the identity of subjects to the act of collecting, the fruits of which are often displayed in the domestic interior. One's desired image can be located directly in one's individual possessions and the environment they create. According to Baudrillard, the collected object contributes to "the creation of a total environment, to that totalization of images of the self that is the basis of the miracle of collection. For what you really collect is always yourself."[27] In this sense, the objects themselves are no longer functional but rather symbolic in nature.

In further exploring the role of collecting within the study of the interior, we return again to Walter Benjamin. For Benjamin, the collector "is the true resident of the interior," and the interior itself is the "étui of the private individual."[28] The interior, according to Benjamin's reading, suggests a detective story in which careful observation of its contents may reveal the traces of everyday life.[29] For Benjamin, as for Baudrillard, the collector strips objects of both their exchange value and their use value, supplanting in their stead a system based on connoisseurship, in which the collector projects herself into an idealized past, as represented through the collection.

Another impetus for heightened scholarly awareness of furniture and interior objects is the increased stress on the significance of everyday life, as evidenced by the work of French scholars such as Daniel Roche, whose *History of Everyday Things* sought to expand understanding of eighteenth-century French culture through the meticulous study of estate inventories of nonaristocratic households. These inventories, mandated by the state, itemized every object in the possession of the deceased, no matter how poor; if a French citizen lived indoors, the state sealed his or her abode and recorded all his or her worldly possessions upon death. The domestic interior is both the theoretical subject matter and the raw source material for Roche, for whom articles of furniture articulate and "symbolize the course of life: the chest, the bed, the table and chairs, the kneading-trough, the clock."[30] For Roche, culture is found not in the palaces of the aristocracy but rather in the details of everyday life as reflected of everyday people, their possessions, and the ways they stored and used them.

The connection between bodies and things is an essential avenue of exploration for critical studies of the interior, and the body is itself arguably a thing, simultaneously creating and formed by its environment. Historian Lynne Walker identifies the central role of women's bodies in the Victorian home, "which both produced and was partly produced by the home and its special atmosphere of domesticity, characterized by family life, cozy intimacy, and a sense of comfort and well-being, a middle class ideal that affected all social groups."[31] In this example, the woman's body and its domestic environs are symbiotic entities, dependent on each other to define one another. This type of nuanced analysis can extend our understanding of all aspects of living in the Victorian home, and by extension the significance of the domestic interior.

SPATIAL THEORY AND THE INTERIOR

The philosophical implications of interior space, and more specifically domestic space, are highly complex. As Lynne Walker has argued, the home is the product of both tangible and intangible elements, including language, social constructs, and space, among numerous other categories.[32] Spatial theory, a methodology that is itself derived from a wide array of disciplines, including sociology, geography, and philosophy, as a field of study aims to dissect the many layers that combine—like Japanese lacquer—to shape the production and experience of space. According to spatial theory, space—whether domestic or public—is never merely a container or envelope. Instead, it is, as defined by French sociologist and philosopher Henri Lefebvre, a socially constructed concept, made by those inhabiting it, a claim reinforced by the title of his pioneering work on spatial theory, *The Production of Space,* first published in 1974.

In *The Production of Space*—informed by his Marxist views—Lefebvre defines space as a producible and reproducible commodity, directly tied to capital. He defines three main types of space: absolute space, understood as natural or spontaneous space that is created rather than produced; abstract space, formed by the dominant political and economic forces, tending toward homogeneity, fostering a stratification of classes, and produced by and in the service of hegemonic forces; and differential space, a space of resistance that is implicitly made possible within absolute space.[33]

While Lefebvre directs his argument primarily at urban and public space, aspects of spatial theory and its concomitant definition of society and its structure are relevant to study of the interior as well. The view of space and certain spatial practices as a producible commodity was shared by Baudrillard, who connects it specifically to the modern interior: "As directly experienced, the project of a technological society implies . . . a world no longer given but instead produced—mastered, manipulated, inventoried, controlled: a world in short, that has to be *constructed.*"[34]

Lefebvre's notion of differential space is also of key significance to the interior. The same hierarchies of power and strategies of resistance can be read into domestic space, particularly in its architectural forms, albeit on an intimate scale. As Victoria Rosner observes in her study of the central role of the interior and the practices of everyday life for the Bloomsbury Group, "The plan of the house deploys walls as barriers that stratify the home, defining and organizing social groups and domestic activities into a hierarchical relationship. But there is a difference between the blank spaces of the floor plan and the lived experience of the household."[35] Thus, the interior is never the sum of its architectural components, or the objects within it, but is rather produced by the people who inhabit it.

French philosopher Gaston Bachelard's *The Poetics of Space* explores the domestic dwelling from a phenomenological position, breaking it down into types of space and the experiences found in them, including corners, drawers, nests, and shells, in addition to the house in its entirety and in the context of the outside world. Bachelard locates the importance of this dwelling or house in its particulars as much as in its universalities. For him, the house "constitutes a body of images that give mankind proofs or illusions of stability."[36]

Memories, both individual and collective, conspire to give the house its central place in our collective experience, and Bachelard draws on psychoanalytical, philosophical, and literary interpretations of the mimetic faculty in his definition of the interior space, and argues for a complementary form of investigation to psychoanalysis based on an in-depth exploration of one's memories of one's home, which he called *topoanalysis*.[37] While Bachelard and Lefebvre differ in many respects, in their emphasis on the significance of the domestic interior beyond its physical properties, they are in agreement.

For Bachelard, the ability to conceal and or reveal aspects of one's self is located within typologies of storage furniture: chests, drawers, and wardrobes. These objects are containers of memory and experience, access to which is firmly controlled by their user, and signify the human need for privacy.[38] For theorist Henry Urbach, the evolution of the closet space as a replacement for these furnishings has key implications for the complex performance of concealing and revealing gay identity within the home. Urbach defines two closets: one physical and one social. The ambiguity contained within the closet is expressed in closets' minimization within the architectural plan, wherein they are merely outlined with no additional details. If the person living "in the closet" possesses two identities, so too does their closet contain one set of costumes for each persona.[39]

The interior as a type of cultural battleground, particularly in the early modernist period, is explored by Jasmine Rault, whose theory of "sapphic modernity" proposes a homocentric—if not homosexual—foundation as a common factor uniting the work of the many prominent women working in interior design in the early twentieth century. For Rault, despite the radical differences in styles and professional focus, the work of Elsie de Wolfe, Eileen Gray, Edith Wyld, Elizabeth Eyre de Lanux, and many others is linked by their use of interior design as a form of resistance directly challenging existing social norms and inextricably connected to modern life. As Rault argues, "They designed to enable the possibility of living sapphic lives, not only divorced from the confines of conventional heterosexuality but also intimately connected to the modern."[40]

The significance of the interior in projecting the exaggeratedly heterosexual identity of the postwar *Playboy* bachelor against the increasingly feminine control of the domestic realm is the subject of George Wagner's essay "Lair of the Bachelor." Wagner identifies the potentially destabilizing assumptions relating to space, place, and gender for the single workingman in the period after World War II: "If the home is the space of the woman, and if space is either masculine or feminine, what constitutes male space, and what role do women, or homosexuals, play in it?"[41] Wagner argues that the bachelor pad (as articulated by *Playboy* magazine in a series of illustrated articles in the late 1950s) defines the urban apartment of the single (straight) man as a bulkhead against the "feminization of the suburban domestic realm" and "operates as a strategy of recovery of the domestic realm by the heterosexual male."[42]

Thus, whether for the lesbian designer of the early twentieth century or the single man in midcentury, the interior, its configuration, and its contents performed essential acts of gender and sexual identity, signifying how things *could* and *should* be for the inhabitant and thereby highlighting the interior's most ambiguous or contentious aspects.

CONCLUSION

The connections between the individual and interior space are articulated through literature, philosophy, and critical theory. These links can be read into all aspects of the domestic environment, from the spatial envelope to the smallest items contained within it. It is from this position of plurality and interdisciplinarity that theories of the interior can continue to develop. While the dominance of architectural theory has arguably inhibited the development of critically informed interior studies, this imbalance can be used to stimulate meaningful critique of the interior. As both Lynne Walker and Lucinda Havenhand have argued, studies of the interior must embrace the marginality of the interior and further elucidate the implications of this marginal condition if interior design is to break away from the discipline of architecture, both in theory and in praxis.[43] Many areas of cultural criticism intersect directly with aspects of the interior, both materially and in terms of social practice. Going forward, theories of the interior will be greatly enriched by careful integration of established methodologies from philosophy, sociology, history, economics, anthropology, studies of material culture and literature, and architecture. By embracing the lack of center intrinsic to interior studies and drawing from this wide array of scholarly methods, a meaningful body of critical studies will continue to develop.

4

Methods of Research and Criticality

GENNARO POSTIGLIONE

DOMAINS AND DEFINITIONS

The aim of this chapter is to define and highlight a number of specific activities (methods and actions) that relate to the field of interiors and are used during the development of a typical research to advance disciplinary knowledge. Such emblematic activities have been demonstrated by some exemplary studies that—in different geographic and cultural contexts—represent significant references in the discipline of interior design.

> As a domain of knowledge of reality, the design of interiors is mainly expressed by the shaping of substantial essences and values implicit in the needs and utilities that demand to come to light in order to favour their recognition. The discipline of interiors is thus conceived as a form and practice of knowledge of the world.[1]

In this context, interiors can be compared to any other art practice,[2] and the works produced by the discipline of interiors can thus be related to those of the world of art and therefore be the object of multidisciplinary studies.

In order to identify and describe research methods in interiors, it is necessary to define the inquiry target and the site of the epistemological framework of the discipline. To quote works developed by Stéphane Hanrot,[3] we can say that a discipline exists whenever an epistemological framework legitimizes it, that is, whenever it is possible to identify:

- The object (as the discipline's outcome)
- A practice
- A form of knowledge
- A form of research
- A teaching

In the case of interiors (both interior architecture and interior design), five areas contribute to recognizing the discipline:

- Its objects are the works produced by the interiors discipline; along with a practice, they form the field of the survey and study of interiors.
- Its practice (as activity and process) is all that is affected by the design activity aimed at the production of works.
- Its knowledge is the aggregate of notions developed from both works and phenomena in the interiors field.
- Its teaching is the group of activities required, on the one hand, to convey knowledge of interiors and, on the other hand, to introduce interiors-related practice and research.
- Its research is the group of activities required to organize, support, assess, and develop knowledge of interiors. Its objects of study are interiors-related works, practices, and phenomena.

However, as shown by research conducted in the second half of the twentieth century on authors and historians of architecture,[4] the architectural disciplines and their theories were hardly ever based on scientific parameters but were often closer to real doctrines,[5] where knowledge of observed phenomena merged with statements about what was considered the most appropriate way of developing the project. This was due to the productive character found in such disciplines along with their historical-critical aspect. Research on the interior, therefore, can be conceived only as a hybrid of doctrines and theories, as the scientific method cannot be fully and exclusively applied to art practice. To use the tripartite distinction proposed by Christopher Frayling,[6] we can say there is research into (or about) design, research for (practical) design, and research through (or by) design.[7]

FRAMEWORKS, TYPOLOGIES, AND METHODS

Research Frameworks

This chapter refers almost exclusively to research into/about design and only marginally to research through design, while avoiding research for design, since all research activities related to actual production (e.g., surveys of requirements) belong to an operational field that is quite distinct from studies aimed at advancing knowledge and producing historical and disciplinary theoretical insights.

Research through Design

As far as research through design is concerned, it is important to note that this operational field is typical of the art practices where it is sometimes possible to identify a productive activity with a speculative and cognitive aspect. Practitioner and researcher coincide, as do the object of study and the result of design activity. This practice aims to know what doing means by doing: a survey of disciplinary foundations, mostly aimed at developing (quasi-) theories that produce theoretical advances and at the same time also legitimize practice.[8]

Practice-based theories are not about explanations and justifications (knowing why) but about establishing facts (knowing what) and instructions for action (knowing how).[9] In this field there is no operational protocol, no method; each author independently and personally defines the survey scope of his or her practice. As an example, we refer to the Scandinavian modernist master Sigurd Lewerentz's (1885–1975) late work: St. Peter's church in Klippan, in southern Sweden (1962–1966).

Here, the elderly architect dealt with what is an age-old relation in architecture, the connection between construction and decoration, where the decoration (one of the operational articulations of the interiors) is intended as a representation of architecture. For Klippan, decoration carries its own independent values in terms of materials and shapes rather than expressing the contents of construction; it neither denies nor contradicts these contents, according to the tradition from the Renaissance on, but is the bearer of material and formal autonomous values.[10] Lewerentz's incursion disrupts this tradition from the inside, as it takes construction as a paradigm and analyzes its structure and deepest expressions: Klippan's walls deconstruct in their own texture. The entire design process pervades figuration that appears as the nonorthodox representation of an orthodox and skillfully managed building knowledge. Only a closer survey may reveal the subversive and conflicting elements between what appears and what actually exists: the walls become matter through the ashlars' and mortar's texture, just as floors, windows, and door frames dematerialize and are reduced to mere openings, while the roof becomes an independent architectural figure.[11]

Research in and on Design

Research in a discipline is a "systematic inquiry directed towards the creation of knowledge"[12] and can be divided into three main typologies:[13]

- By application: that is, the nature of its possible application
- By inquiry mode: that is, the nature of the information and data to be collected and also the nature of the data analysis
- By objectives: that is, the goals and tasks the research wants to accomplish

These typologies intersect with the following operational articulations:

- Research methods: research paths to be used to pursue the research goals
- Research actions: actions and tools—linked to specific disciplines—to be used to carry out the research methods

The three main typologies and the two operational articulations are not mutually exclusive, so that a study classified as falling within one of the typologies may also, at the same time, fall into the other typologies.[14]

Research Typologies

Research by Application

The first research typology is based on the application of the results of the research and may be either basic or applied. The primary goal of basic research is the advancement of knowledge and of the theoretical understanding of the relations connecting the variables involved in a certain process. It may be exploratory, descriptive, or explanatory, although the most common is exploratory research, often instigated by the researcher's curiosity, interest, and intuition. Most studies in the field of art practices, and hence also in the interiors field, fall into the domain of basic or pure research, since they usually have little practical or operative impact.[15]

In contrast, the goal of applied research is to find practical and specific solutions. It is usually descriptive and empirical and is founded on existing basic research. In the interiors domain, applied research is mainly typical of research by design, or is used whenever cognitive advancement is developed by relying on practice and is action related.[16]

Charles Rice's work *The Emergence of the Interior* (2007)[17] can be considered as belonging to the domain of pure research, as it sets out to acquire knowledge about the underlying historical and psychoanalytical foundations of interiors. Herein the research can also be said to be "reflective" as it unfolds a reexamination of the interior, aiming to frame and demonstrate new ways of thinking about the interior, rather than new ways to design interiors. Thus, even though in the second part of the book Rice pursues the identification of spatial and image-based "trajectories," the study is not intended to either legitimate a practice or establish a theory of practice but is directed toward an understanding and explication of the discipline of interiors.

Stanley Abercrombie's *A Philosophy of Interior Design* (1990)[18] provides, by contrast, a basis for developing a theory of interior design practice and can be considered as applied research. Each chapter of the study unfolds a reference for interiors as it describes a particular aspect of the discipline, which is interpreted in an attempt to reveal its philosophical potential. Taken together, however, the chapters form a progression in which Abercrombie pursues the underlying principles signifying the quality of interior space in increasing detail.

What should, however, be considered as the most consistent and broadest study in interiors-related theoretical research is undoubtedly Gianni Ottolini's *Forma e significato in architettura* (1996), where the author sets out to explain meaning and form in architecture starting from the interior's foundational dimension.

On the other hand, references for applied research can be found in Adriano Cornoldi's *Architettura dei luoghi domestici* (1994) or John Kurtich and Garret Eakin's *Interior Architecture* (1993). Kurtich and Eakin's book presents historical and modern examples of interior architecture, explaining design principles and the links between art, architecture, and interior design. Moreover, the authors show interest in and respect for the enclosing architecture, sensitivity to human experience, the primacy of light and color, and furnishings as an extension of architecture, thus transforming their research from pure speculation into a study with consequences for practice.[19]

In *Architettura dei luoghi domestici,*[20] in contrast, Adriano Cornoldi analyzes the close and deep connections linking form and life in private spaces. The book begins with an analysis of the ideal house in the past, followed by a presentation of the most relevant models of houses in Western contemporary society and a future projection of the house and the practice of domestic design. To this end, the author relies on a typical operative research approach where historical-critical studies are not aimed simply at advancing the knowledge of works but at legitimizing a practice and building a theory.

Research by Inquiry Mode

The second way of recognizing and typifying research, called the research inquiry mode, relates to the process of finding answers to questions, which can be either qualitative or quantitative. In qualitative research, the researcher's role receives greater critical attention because the possibility that he/she can take a "neutral" position is seen as more problematic. In addition, qualitative research approaches analysis holistically and contextually, rather than being reductionist and isolationist, as in the case of quantitative approaches. Qualitative data analysis can take a wide variety of forms, as it differs from quantitative research in its focus on language, signs, and meaning.[21]

In this sense the research in Gianni Ottolini and Vera De Prizio's *La casa attrezzata* (2005)[22] is particularly relevant. In its first part, the two authors—following a quantitative approach—classify the elements integrating architecture and interior decoration in categories, each with a specific name: equipped interior boundaries, equipped exterior boundaries, inner balconies, bathroom and kitchen blocks, three-dimensional environment blocks, and multifunction structural components. The study arranges the classified elements by levels of growing integration and clarifies their contents—now using a qualitative approach—by interpreting the drawings and photos that illustrate the text or by directly referring to the specific descriptions at the end of the book, each illustrating a particular piece of equipment.

Research by Objectives

The third articulation of research defines groups of studies based on the goals and tasks the research intends to reach. Four goals can be recognized: to describe, interpret, explore, and critically read the object of study.

Descriptive Research

Descriptive research aims to rigorously and systematically describe the object of study. It explains phenomena as they exist and is used to identify and obtain information on the characteristics of a particular issue. The best approach prior to developing descriptive research is often to conduct a survey investigation and collect and systematize notions and documents, which can be either primary or secondary sources.[23]

In descriptive research, as well as in interpretative and exploratory research, the study of secondary sources is crucial not just to establish a wide frame of knowledge reference on the research object but above all to prevent the study of primary sources from proceeding without a proper background of notions and thus developing the same actions already taken by other researchers.

This category includes traditional historical studies such as Stanley Abercrombie's *A Century of Interior Design 1900–2000* (2003), Renato De Fusco's *La Storia dell'Arredamento* (1985), and Mario Praz's *An Illustrated History of Interior Decoration* (1964), which survey and describe interiors. In addition, this includes research projects with a historical-critical or interpretative character such as the above-mentioned *La casa attrezzata* (2005) as well as *Il progetto domestico* (1986) by Georges Teyssot, and others presented in following sections devoted to operational articulations of research typologies, such as *L'interno nell'interno* (2001) by Imma Forino, *La Disoluciòn de la Estancia* (2005) by José Morales, and *Re-Readings* (2005) by Graeme Brooker and Sally Stone.

Interpretative (Explanatory or Analytical) Research

Since the main goal of interpretative research is to understand and explain works or phenomena, it is often also defined as explanatory or analytical. It is a continuation of descriptive research, but here the researcher studies and explains why or how something is happening. It can often be comparative, in that it compares different aspects or even different works or phenomena by relying on research methods based on logical argumentation and case studies. When investigation is accomplished by going into depth in other fields of knowledge, or by exploiting extra- and interdisciplinary approaches, this qualifies as critical practice work,[24] where the goal is pursuing wider knowledge of the study object beyond the disciplinary field of concern.

An example can be the already mentioned work by Charles Rice (*The Emergence of the Interior*, 2007), the first part of which can be considered as critical-interpretative in its objectives, since the study of Walter Benjamin and Sigmund Freud is used as a means for reexamining and pursuing the elaboration of an understanding of the emergence of the interior. In relating the physical emergence of the interior as a bourgeois and modern manifestation of the individual with elements of psychoanalysis, the author pursues an elaborate understanding of the interior by means of logical argumentation, herein criticizing earlier conventional readings of it. On the other hand, Forino's *L'interno nell'interno* (2001) is a more traditional example of interpretative research as it is based—relying on logical argumentation and case studies—on the interpretation of a disciplinary phenomenon using disciplinary tools and methods: a particular form of envelope combining architecture and interior decoration, *the interior in the interior*.[25]

Exploratory Research

The main feature of exploratory research, compared to the other three goals, is its focus on (historical or current) works or phenomena that are still little known, or undersurveyed domains and study objects that lack a fully developed reference literature. In this perspective an emblematic work is Manolo De Giorgi's *Carlo Mollino: Interni in piano-sequenza* (2004),[26] an analysis of the Turin-born architect's work through an interpretative device derived from his work: the sequence shot, a filmmaking technique that links spaces in a sequence and in an osmotic succession, just like in Mollino's interiors, where furniture plays a relevant role. De Giorgi defines furniture as both complex morphological transfigurations and catalyzing elements.

Given the inherently exploratory character of critical practices, any research relying on them for its development may also be rightfully considered as exploratory research, as demonstrated by Giuliana Bruno's *Atlas of Emotion* (2002), a passionate reconsideration of the cognitive paradigm and of cartography as an expression of power and ideological influence. The exploration proposed in the atlas narrates the terrae incognitae of "emotional geography," a sort of sentimental writing on space that records the cultural power of emotions in history and establishes connections relating places, forms of knowledge, theories, arts, and artifacts through their emotional power. So the author guides us on a trip through art, architecture and cinema and the cultural and sensory practices that take shape and move in space and are generated by space.[27]

Operative Research

The notion of operative research[28] means attempting a critical linking of theory and practice and defines studies aimed at advancing knowledge of works and legitimizing a practice. *Operative* denotes a specific reflection on essential conditions, and defined sets of knowledge close to practice to bridge the gap between design (as a mental, subjective, embodied process) and criticism (as an abstract, objective, and distanced process).[29] Along with research by design, operative research represents a crucial relational junction between a merely cognitive activity (research) and a purely operational activity (design practice).

The reflective and analytical justification of one's own design practice (and eventually those of others) leads back to critiquing one's own (and eventually others') ideas and work, and this is usually done within a historical perspective.[30] History is used not just as a subject of study for the advancement of knowledge on (historical or current) works but as a means to build the legitimization of one's own theory. This holds true regardless of the fact that the concept of operative research—related to the use of history—has found its own theoretical formalization in architecture within Manfredo Tafuri's thought and work, most extensively in his essay "Il progetto storico,"[31] where he defines what he calls *Critica operativa* (operational criticism).

For this reason, in the study of interiors, history plays a major role not just for the development of knowledge, as in any other discipline, but also for the development of design theories and practices. During the twentieth century, this role underwent a substantial change as history went from being used instrumentally (the modern movement's historiography) to becoming a fully historical paradigm—Colin Rowe's formalist structuralism and Manfredo Tafuri's critical history[32]—based on history's disciplinary independence. Then, in the current phase, the study of history has ceased to be the only paradigm for the development of a theory, since there are no longer general and all-embracing narratives. History has been replaced by partial, fragmented, dissonant, transversal histories, the legitimacy of which is based on the coherence of their method and, most of all, on the usefulness of the results. It is an epistemological pluralism that argues for the uselessness of indisputable and universal paradigms[33] and grants architecture, as well as interiors, its own identity and disciplinary independence, while also proposing the obsolescence of the traditional dualism of theory versus practice, practical action versus theoretical action.[34]

In order to understand the operational and cognitive impact of this specific research typology, we can, for example, refer to the work and thought of authors like Alison and Peter Smithson, Sverre Fehn, and Carlo De Carli as well as many other contemporary or past masters who mainly developed their theory of practice within a critical and operational interpretation of history. Gio Ponti (1891–1979), for example, whose work was linked to the definition of domestic space and interiors, found its roots in the vernacular expressions of a spontaneous architecture. He illustrated this in his famous article "*La casa all'italiana* [The Italian-style Home]" (1928), published as an editorial in the first issue of the magazine he directed for several years, *Domus*.[35] In this article he gave a synthetic description of his research and of the foundations and inspirations of his poetic vision.[36]

But over time, particularly in the second half of the twentieth century, other so-called postcritical positions have come to develop alongside the historicist one. By making design gradually independent from history, they have pursued their own foundation in a radical autonomy of practice that is thus described as an activity linked to "the diagrammatic, the atmospheric and the cool performance."[37]

One example is Rem Koolhaas's position and the extradisciplinary nature of his critical thought and operative sources, which are focused on forms of knowledge and artifacts that are unrelated to strictly architectural fields and principles.[38] Similarly, Andrea Branzi's work can be duly considered as a lifelong speculation aimed at defining an idea of architecture that is more than the justification of itself and establishes a wider theoretical frame of reference that is offered to experts, practitioners, students, and even users. His ideas, which began in Florence with Archizoom Associati in 1966[39] and the theoretical design of *No-Stop City* (1969),[40] can also be associated with the domain of research by design. His most recent work, *Modernità debole e diffusa* (2006), as he explains, "has two goals: analyse the new elements the twenty-first century is introducing in the world of design, the passage from strong and concentrated modernity to a weaker and diluted modernity, and at the same time understand whether such passage provides an opportunity to project a future for nonfigurative architecture."[41] Such architecture would then become an urban semisphere, as it would be fundamentally conceived around, and starting from, the idea of the interior as a primary space.

Research Methods and Actions

Research Methods

Research methods emphasize different methods of data collection, referring to what kind of patterns will be used for collecting the data needed for research inquiry. These are defined when drafting the research strategy[42] or when defining what systems should be used to reach the research goals. For this reason, rather than a typology in itself these represent an operational articulation of research and are based on simulation and modeling, logical argumentation, case studies, and action.

Simulation and Modeling

Surveys, redrawing, and modeling can provide a way to read elements and collect data and information since they are broken down into a simpler form. It is interesting to note that drawing and modeling are the same tools used in the development of design practice and that the surveys making use of such methods are particularly interesting precisely for their practice-related processes. In this context the tradition of Italian historical-critical research is particularly emblematic for the systematic survey of historical and current interiors based on redrawing and modeling that has been conducted since the 1970s.[43] Mainly developed in the schools of architecture in Milan, Venice, and Naples, such research is represented by studies undertaken by Gianni Ottolini and Roberto Rizzi,[44] which are aimed at a precise and full-scale survey of paradigmatic interiors through modeling and redrawing of the most relevant environments at a detailed scale (1:50 and 1:20); by the research developed by Adriano Cornoldi[45] on adapting typological theories from architecture to apply to the interiors field, largely based on axonometric sections and perspectives as well as on the redrawing of plans and sections; and by the pioneering research developed by Filippo Alison[46] on the historical-critical and design study of furniture using both small-scale models (1:33, 1:10, and 1:3) and mock-ups, as well as 1:1 redrawing and prototyping and producing objects in a meaningful collaboration between academic research and small and medium enterprises in the world of interiors.

Logical Argumentation

Argumentation is the interdisciplinary study of how conclusions should and can be, and actually are, reached through logical reasoning. It includes debate and negotiation concerned with reaching mutually acceptable conclusions. Works based on logical argumentation are formed in part by studies based on mathematical logic and in part by studies that develop their reasoning through canons of interior logic typical of the context and age (and hence the culture) they belong to. The latter group includes research in the field of interiors where the author's rhetorical and discursive skills combined with his or her disciplinary background lead to the achievement of the intended goals in terms of knowledge advancement.[47]

In *Home, a Short History of an Idea* (1989), Witold Rybczynski argues his idea of the evolution of domestic space by means of the description and interpretation of houses from the Middle Ages until the 1980s. Living spaces are described in terms of comfort, well-being, and privacy, three essential concepts that allow the author to discuss the evolution of the home and home living and to describe a new and different history of interiors based not on style evolutions and aesthetic canons but on a precise idea of progress revolving around the growing self-awareness developed over time by people.[48]

In addition to research using forms of knowledge typical of the interiors discipline, this family of studies also includes critical practices related to extradisciplinary fields.[49] It is up to the researcher's logical-argumentative skills, combined with his or her ability to dominate the forms of knowledge that are considered most useful and appropriate to his or her goals, to define in each instance the study's operational scope and cross-disciplinary character.[50]

In *Intentions in Architecture* (1965), Christian Norberg-Schultz fashioned an impressive intellectual edifice with content that included Gestalt psychology, the mechanics of perception, information theory, modern analytic philosophy, and, in particular, linguistic analysis and the general theory of signs and symbols. The purpose was to develop an integrated theory of architectural description and architectural intention (including the intention of the user as well as that of the designer) that could be claimed as a theory of interior space.

Case Study

A case study is a research methodology commonly used in social science and is based on an in-depth investigation of a single individual, group, or event. Case studies may be descriptive, explanatory, or explorative and form a research approach situated between concrete data-collection techniques and methodological paradigms.[51]

Case study research includes the analysis of both single and multiple cases; it can include quantitative evidence and rely on multiple sources of evidence, and it can benefit from the prior development of theoretical propositions. Case studies should not be confused with qualitative research since they can be based on any mix of quantitative and qualitative evidence, according to the nature of the investigation, its objectives, and the nature of the data to be collected.[52] Three main types of information-oriented cases may be distinguished, even though these types are not exhaustive: critical cases, extreme cases, and emblematic cases.[53] They can be analyzed by taking into account either single cases or multiple cases.[54]

In the case of José Morales's study *La Disolución de la Estancia* (2005), the goal was to analyze the history and evolution of domestic space by investigating a large number of houses designed during the twentieth century by famous architects in order to define an interpretative theory of the transformation of domestic space. These case studies were chosen as representatives of evolutionary themes in interiors history, and each one is identified by a key subject.[55]

Action Research

Action research is an interactive inquiry process that balances problem-solving actions, implemented in a collaborative context, with data-driven collaborative analysis or research to understand underlying causes and enable future predictions about personal and organizational change.[56] In terms of the learning process, Stephen Kemmis and Robin McTaggart argue that action research is a way of experimenting with one's practice in order to improve and develop one's knowledge.[57] Action research represents, then, a work method that connects theory and practice in the "ideas-in-action" aggregate. Action research is mostly used in industrial design studies and in architecture, mainly by researchers in urbanism and in all other disciplines involving sociology and social science. Conversely, it is hardly present in the field of interiors.

Research Actions

With reference to the three phases of research development (collection, analysis, and interpretation), this section focuses on the real activities of data collection related to both selected research methods and the inquiry mode. This section regards *how* one should collect the data needed for the research inquiry: the research actions are defined by the research strategy and require specific tools related to the study design. While the main actions performed for data collection may be listed and shared by several research domains (such as observation, literature review, archival research, etc.), some of the tools the researcher must use belong instead to the specific field one works in.

Based on the reviewed studies, one of the most common interiors-related research tools—besides firsthand observation—is surveys, not just as a quantitative activity of measurement and transcription of the object of study but also as a focus on detail, or as a quantitative and qualitative activity that records materials, techniques, and technologies used by architects to produce their works.

A peculiar feature of historical interiors-related research is the limited access to primary sources or to the very interiors that, because of their often ephemeral nature, left no trace of their existence. Therefore, research can rely only on indirect sources. These secondary sources are mainly paintings, prints, and other similar reproductions of interiors, later replaced by photographs and most recently also by film footage. In this context, even literature becomes a valuable source.[58]

Other kinds of literary sources are the descriptions that reveal characters and lifestyles, illustrating behaviors related to the use of space and objects: these sources are mainly adopted by social-anthropological studies focusing on interiors, dwelling culture, and so on.[59] Interview-based techniques of data collection, belonging to a tradition of social studies, are not particularly developed in the interiors field, where they are used only by researchers analyzing the impact of architecture on its users' behavior. In this sense, a good example is "Post-Occupancy," a research study edited by OMA and Rem Koolhaas (2006).[60]

CONCLUSIONS

As a conclusion to this short review of interiors-related research methods, it may be interesting to note that, as for all studies related to critical research, the social approach practiced during the 1960s and 1970s, although still infrequently used, has largely been replaced by a wider cultural approach. This can be seen in the proliferation of studies, articles, and essays that over the last decade have expanded interior design's gnosiological status and transformed research on interiors from a typological and deterministic approach to a procedural and open paradigm. As a consequence, the world of interiors has expanded both as a study object and as a product of practical activity, redirecting interest toward an approach that has ceased to recognize disciplinary boundaries as operational perimeters and has instead grounded practice in a procedural context. Being ongoing and far from complete, such transformations are felt as part of the pursuit of a new identity for the interiors discipline, also greatly influencing research actions and methods.[61]

5

Protected Title in Britain: An Educational Necessity?

GRAHAM STRETTON

The protected title of interior design or interior architecture is commonplace in most of the developed world, including large parts of North America, Europe, the Pacific basin, and the Middle and Far East. The sheer act of protection requires a clear definition of the role of the interior designer or interior architect, influencing both educational syllabi and content within universities and colleges, while further dictating or controlling the operational modes of design in practice.

In the United Kingdom the status of protected title has never been achieved for this discipline. It could be argued that, without educational and professional constraints, a British educational experience in interior design produces more creative students, able to take a transdisciplinary approach to problem solving, and thus better equips them to practice design in the global economy/wider world. Conversely, it could also be argued that the absence of professional and educational control has been a major factor in interior design's lack of status in the United Kingdom.

A clear historical understanding of interior design education, its place within the British educational system, and its relationship with the interior design profession and with professional bodies and associated professional bodies is an important prerequisite for the debate on the future of interior design education. Reflective historical judgments and reviews of "design in practice" have already been chronicled in contemporary published material, yet little collation and analysis of the education of the interior designer in the United Kingdom have been undertaken.

This chapter initiates research on both historical and contemporary educational issues that contribute to the United Kingdom's lack of protected title for interior design, thus better informing the debate. It uses a framework of examples to explore and explain the present status of interior design education in Great Britain. The framework considers

- The Crace family, exploring their direct and indirect influence on education for interiors;[1]
- The influence of London society and its juxtaposition with legislation and the requirements of an emerging and growing industry;
- National key educational developments within the typical "provincial" town/city of Leicester while it engaged and embraced art and design education;[2] and
- The college's interaction with the National Design School, London, and changes brought about by Parliamentary directives.

MEDIEVAL TRAINING IN INTERIOR DECORATION AND INTERIOR DESIGN

Medieval guilds, formed to protect the livelihoods of like-minded merchants, enforced parity by initiating and conforming to minimum proficiency standards, defending the rights of guildsmen, and setting up apprenticeships. London guilds appeared first, receiving a royal charter in 1394.

The Worshipful Company of Painters—Stainers was the twenty-eighth guild formed, gaining its royal charter in 1581. These two names represent two organizations that merged around 1502. The stainers were decorators and gilders of wood, stone, and metal, and the other group is reputed to have worked on cloth.[3] It is a common mistake to assume that this guild only undertook painting and decorating. While it has incorporated these activities, it has a long association with the arts. The terms *art painter* and *art decorator* were commonly used to distinguish the works of liverymen from those of common painters.[4]

Historical records at Painter Stainers Hall were lost during World War II bombing, but it is known that this guild had formed strong relations with the royal court. The first recorded occasion of works being executed was a large "panel painting" of King Richard II in 1394 by Gilbert Prince.[5] This is the earliest surviving portrait of a British monarch and is located in Westminster Cathedral.

Indentured apprenticeships were the most common way of acquiring the skills and knowledge of one's selected trade. By the late seventeenth century this took seven years. Examples from this period include Peter Monamy,[6] who was indentured to William Clarke, a master of the Worshipful Company of Painters—Stainers; and James Thornhill (purportedly the first decorator to be knighted). Both completed their apprenticeships on the same day in March 1704. Monamy and Thornhill had successful careers as interior decorators and were commissioned to undertake decorations throughout London and in country houses. Both were born into wealth, having many relations and good connections in trade and guilds across a wide range of industries. Thornhill was commissioned to undertake the Painted Hall in Greenwich Hospital in 1715.

Typically, both Monamy and Thornhill practiced as wall-panel painters and portrait or fine art painters. However, the distinction between art painter and fine art painter was becoming established. Thornhill twice attempted to start "free" academies for drawing. The second attempt at forming an academy included attendees such as William Hogarth, who later married Thornhill's daughter. Hogarth in turn was a founder of the St. Martin's Lane Academy. In 1768 the Royal Academy was formed from many who were "artist" members of St. Martin's Lane Academy. However, this did not include Thomas Chippendale and other notable designers who were not artists or architects.

The Worshipful Company of Painters—Stainers noted that

> when the Royal Academy was founded in 1768 many artists joined that in preference to the Painters' Company, so, although we retained our links with the fine arts and regularly elect the Presidents of the Royal Academy as Honorary Liverymen, we had to find other ways to develop.[7]

Both Sir Joshua Reynolds and Charles Catton were founding members of the Royal Academy and in 1784 were liverymen/masters of the Worshipful Company of Painters—Stainers. In *TheHistory of the Royal Academy of Arts,* William Sanby wrote:

> One means of employment for painters for nearly a century after the Restoration was the internal decoration of the royal palaces and the mansions of the nobility by an adaptation of the plafond[8] painting which was so popular in France under Louis XIV. We have mentioned Verrio and Laguerre, and even Rubens, as so employed; and the chief occupation of Sir James Thornhill was the painting of walls and ceilings, for which he was paid by measurement, at so much per yard. Thus for the designs in the great hall of Greenwich Hospital he received £3 per yard. Copyists were employed on an inferior scale, to fill up panels with landscapes and subjects from the old masters at forty or fifty shillings each, and this tended to depreciate the demand for works of a higher character. Many artists, and these men of ability, often found employment in painting coach-panels with groups of allegorical figures, flowers, & c. Among them were included Hogarth, Catton, and Cipriani.[9]

It must be remembered that much of the work was undertaken with the help of assistants. During the seventeenth and eighteenth centuries, through trade and land acquisitions, larger statements of position and wealth were being sought and implemented. The older system of having one or two apprentices no longer worked. New ways of working and production were needed. There were not enough skilled practitioners who could provide the skills and knowledge required. Artisans needed to be trained and made aware of the historical context within which they worked.

> The widening divide between fine and decorative arts resulted in the formation of The Royal Academy in 1768, although the Painter Stainers Company was far larger. In fact the Company's first Book of Apprentices lists over 4,000 names between 1666 and 1796. At over thirty on average per year the demand for high quality Painter Stainers was very high.[10]

The formation of the Royal Academy, which promoted exhibitions and prizes, the profits from which funded training in art, sculpture, and architecture, represented the growing divide between the arts/architecture and artisan practitioners. Acrimonious debate and dialogue during this period precluded one overall direction for the development of the decorative arts. This divide was either directly or inadvertently supported by royal patronage, as in the case of the Royal Academy, which was formed in 1768 despite the royal family's patronage of the already existing Society of Artists (founded in 1761), which included artisans.

ROYAL PATRONAGE

During the Georgian period, royalty led the way in fashion and decoration. Contextually, it was probably the Crace family that had the most famous long-term design relationship with the British monarchy. All the Craces were apprenticed via the Worshipful Company of Painters and became masters of the company at various times, from Edward Crace (ca. 1750) to John Dibblee Crace, who was the inaugural president of the Incorporated Institute of British Decorators (IIBD) from its inception in 1899 until his death in 1919.[11]

Edward Crace; his son, John C. Crace; and his grandson, Fredrick Crace, were best known for design works undertaken for His Royal Highness the Prince of Wales, notably Windsor Castle, Buckingham Palace, and the Royal Pavilion in Brighton. Establishments wishing to be closely associated with royal fashion and taste employed the same designers:

> Splendid improvements have been made recently in the Assembly Rooms of The Old Ship, at Brighton under the most competent management and skill of Mess. Crace & Sons whose talents as artists have been so incomparably displayed in the magnificent designs and execution of the interior decorations of the Pavilion.[12]

While they had royal patronage, no Crace belonged to the Royal Academy, even though Fredrick Crace was keeper to the king's pictures (George III). It is also interesting to note that John Gregory Crace was called on by the Royal Academy to paint over William Kent's ceiling in the Royal Academy although he was not an academician.[13]

Several architects trained at, or associated with, the Royal Academy became dissatisfied with the standard of education there and formed the precursor to the Royal Institute of British Architects (RIBA), motivated by the rise of the professional training in Italy, France, and Germany. It took several years for the profession of architecture to develop in the United Kingdom: "Public bodies that were often the patrons of new buildings tended to regard the architect as merely one of the tradesmen involved in the construction process, and looked to secure designs in the cheapest way."[14] Despite this view, architecture received royal patronage with the granting of a royal charter in 1837. It was not until 1904 that an Architectural Educational Board was formed to recognize architectural schools, although examination systems were in place prior to this.[15]

While the status of the architect was becoming divorced from the process of building, the artist had overshadowed the status of the art painter. Art decorator did not establish itself as a profession. Arguably, art decorators who were leaders in their field were on a par with architects in the design and application of schemes for the interior; however, the art decorator was considered a trade because the art decorators' own workforce carried out the implementation of the design.

During this period architects sometimes also trained and practiced as art painters or art decorators, both in the United Kingdom and in Europe, notably Paris. Royal Academy members also undertook art decoration work, which was traditionally worked directly on the panel but later shifted toward being worked on canvas panels that were then applied within the interior.

Throughout this period architects and "commercial" decorators had working relationships that were symbiotic but could lead to public discourse and controversy, often played out through letters to *The Times* and articles in the press about who had originated which design. Architects had already laid claim to being the lead designer within projects. Royal Academy art painters in turn claimed that architects did not provide the right wall spaces to allow for the creation of good art panels. With the development of "society," high-end decorators, mainly London-based companies such as Crace, Cowtan, Green, and King, all argued that this polarization of who undertakes the work of art painter and art decorator was masking a greater problem. There were not enough artisan painters being trained to undertake the growing amount of panel painting required.

Within Crace & Co. some notable working relationships with architects were formed, specifically between John Nash and Fredrick Crace,[16] Augustus Pugin and John Gregory Crace,[17] and William Burges and John Dibblee Crace. As Helen Smith points out, quoting James Green (of Green & King, decorators, Baker Street) from a *Building News* article: "Speaking broadly, there is no intermediate grade between the painter (the better class of which we call decorator) and the fully educated professional artist, who paints for the academy."[18] Similar observations support the line taken by Select Committee on the School of Design ordered by the House of Commons, which concluded in its report of July 27, 1849, that the middle ground was being filled by foreign artists. Green believed that the ability to draw a figure was a prerequisite for the artisan painter-decorator. However, John Dibblee Crace stated that a student may be able to learn the fundamentals of his art while in the environments of a school of design but would not be able to "become an able designer, without working for those who are already well acquainted with it."[19] He thought it necessary for practicing designers and artists to be associated with the developing schools of design.

EDUCATION: THE HIGH-END ART DECORATOR
DURING THE VICTORIAN PERIOD

The growth of art schools from the mid- to late Victorian period came out of Britain's desire to maintain dominance in manufactured goods. The resultant requirement to train artists and designers in the field of practical art to design and decorate manufactured objects became paramount.

The relationship in most cities between the art school and the museum/art gallery mirrored the complexities and political changes that surrounded the Victoria and Albert Museum and the South Kensington School. The formation of the National Schools of Design in 1837 is well documented by the Victoria and Albert Museum, whose summary (including a bibliography)[20] is a seminal source.

In 1849 the House of Commons Select Committee Papers on the School of Design[21] are both reflective of the past (giving a sound reflective analysis of the aims and attainments after twelve years) and predictive of the future (giving direction for colleges during the remaining Victorian period). Such was the importance of the subject that the Parliamentary Committee included Sir Robert Peel, the prime minister at the time. To summarize, it was thought that the elementary design being taught was satisfactory but that beyond this schools had not improved decorative designs for manufacturers, and all the provincial schools reported declining revenues and were in debt.[22]

When John Dibblee Crace came before the same Select Committee he described himself as a decorator and responded that he was active professionally, working on the Houses of Parliament among other commissions. He considered students from the School of Design ill-prepared to undertake design work and had employed only one ex-student, who soon understood his deficiencies and left of his own accord. He normally employed between eight and twenty artists working on decoration, a small number of whom were French or German, trained under their own educational systems. Along with other submissions he called for a two-level educational split within the School of Design such that the elementary-level students would become well versed in the ability to draw, this being considered the basis for all design work. Crace, as a decorator, also expounded the necessity for the advanced course to be more closely associated with work in practice and by inference asserted that the education of the decorator/designer required firsthand knowledge. He noted that for every twelve artists working there can be only one designer.[23]

Several key changes were proposed, including establishing a pyramid structure in which the provincial centers would be more directly under the control of the School of Design and splitting the structure of the schools between the administration and the delivery, where named paid appointees were to be held directly responsible for implementation. Regular inspections of the provincial centers were to be carried out, and the delivery in London was to be of a higher level.

The name—whether it should be School of Design or School of Art—caused much debate during the next fifty years. In 1853 Prince Albert proposed a name change to "Trade Schools," but both manufacturers and students generally rejected a focus on designing for industry in favor of more generalized art teacher training.[24] Manchester, Glasgow, Edinburgh, Nottingham, Stoke, Hanley, and most industrial towns in the north of England and Scotland had growing industries that required tradesmen and artisans with training in the decorative arts. Schools were started and supported by a combination of local benefactors and public subscription. Full records and numbers of students are included in the appendices of the 1849 Parliamentary Select Committee document. However, despite local specialist design requirements the numbers of students were low in comparison with the growth of industry.

One can take Leicester as a typical example of a growing industrial town. In the 1849 documents it is noted that Leicester, Liverpool, Bristol, and Macclesfield had made repeated applications for a school of design.[25] Although public awareness was raised and industrialists promised annual donations in excess of £90 (equivalent to about $15,000 in 2013), a school was not formed at this time.[26] In 1862 another public meeting in Leicester raised the question of initiating a school of art.[27] The Leicester Literary and Philosophical Society (founded in 1835) was the main driver in the formation of both a museum and a school of art and design. The representative of the National School of Design was Mr. Hammersley, head of the Manchester school. Having transferred to Nottingham, Hammersley was also the representative at the public meeting in Leicester in 1862.[28] The meeting was divided into two parts, one on the art requirements of Leicester and the other on the amount and type of government aid.[29] Hammersley was concerned that a school had not been started after his previous visits and suggested this was due to the principal industry, hosiery, not seeing the necessity for a school of art.[30] In Leicester the School of Art finally held its first classes in 1870. An observer looking at the prospectus noted that

> on a perusal of the prospectus we find that the arrangements include morning classes for the ladies and gentlemen, and evening classes for partisans. For the latter, there are elementary classes, advanced classes, mechanical and architectural classes, and junior art classes: and there are, besides female classes.
>
> …In future years, then, we may hope for happy results in this locality—in the refinement of the general taste, in the extension of the love of art, and in a consequent extension for testing principles to every branch of trade manufacturers to which they can be applied—to architecture, house decoration, mechanical drawings, patterns of manufactured goods, and so forth. There is, indeed, a wide field to which a good School of Art in Leicester may extend its benefits.[31]

The above format seems to have been followed by most provincial schools: there are three distinct categories of students studying at different times of day that reflect both their gender and their status. Reinforcing this plea for drawing, a letter was sent to the same newspaper approximately two months later extolling John Gregory Crace's plea that every child should be encouraged to draw, whatever trade or occupation he or she might follow.[32]

In 1870 there were 20,290 students in the United Kingdom studying in 113 schools. Leicester during this first year had 269 students, 90 more than the national average. However, it was noted that the day students (ladies and gentlemen) wanted to study landscapes. Trade and artisan students generally studied in the evening. From 116 students Leicester submitted 1,182 pieces of work to the examiners at the National School of Design. Eight students were awarded national prizes.

In 1876 the Leicester New Walk museum opened, incorporating study classrooms for the Leicester College of Art and a depository for a selection of the traveling artifacts of the National School of Design. The relationship between the museum/art gallery and the art school again followed the national trend. The growth of both museum and school meant that the facilities available were no longer large enough and were suitable only for lecture- or studio-based activities.

During the last thirty years of the century much had changed within decoration. Room panels painted by art decorators were generally declining despite a small upsurge within Arts and Crafts. When painted panels were used, they were generally restricted to wealthy high-society clients or to public and religious buildings. The growing middle and professional classes demanded new ways to proclaim their status through their domestic residences. The use of wallpapers and decorative painting techniques required new skills from those who decorated homes or supplied fixtures and fittings. House decorators and house painters became a fast-growing phenomenon. Women were growing in status and were playing a more important role in trends in, and selection of, decorations, furniture, and artifacts.[33]

Every major town and city had principal decorators who could design and show clients a scheme by means of drawings and sketches; they could meet the needs of their clients in terms of taste and style that matched the client's aspirations. In major cities the leading decorators supplied the complete design and installation service, with furniture and fittings, often also holding public exhibitions of work, including furniture and artifacts. In London, the Society of Arts advertisements include Crace & Sons, Morant, Boyd & Blandford, and Gillows & Co.

Industry required more workers holding a range of skills and knowledge in practical art. John Ruskin and others debated the validity and worth of the curriculum within art school education. Like many in the City of London, the guilds were concerned and developed alternative educational and training systems. The Worshipful Company of Painters-Stainers set up evening classes in 1873, which became a prototype for the City and Guild (C&G) qualifications that were established five years later. It also awarded prizes in support of technical education. C&G became a separate entity in 1878, replacing the guild apprenticeship system, and ran jointly with the City of London Corporation.

Within each major town or city, local high-end painters and decorators had formed local associations. In 1894 these local painting and decorating associations joined together at a convention in Manchester to form the National Association of Master Painters for England and Wales, incorporated in 1895.[34] Meanwhile, another group formed as the National House Painters Association. The Worshipful Company of Painters-Stainers was also at the forefront, awarding prizes within these bodies for students/apprentices who achieved high levels of attainment; it continues to undertake this role today.

By the end of the Victorian period architects were becoming established as a profession with developing codes of practice and methods of operating. The majority of painting and decorating companies were turning to new techniques and applications based on developments in manufactured finishes and paints. High-street stores were developing in-house design facilities, a cross between a design service and a personal shopper that particularly targeted the newfound aspirations of women, who were taking control of the design of domestic housing. High-end decorators and upholsterers were providing a complete service from inception to completion of a decorating project, often providing a scheme that suited the client's aesthetic requirements, usually a contemporary interpretation of historical decorative styles.

LATE VICTORIAN AND EDWARDIAN CHANGES IN DESIGN EDUCATION

The Worshipful Company of Painters-Stainers decided to form a new educational institute in 1899. Initially called the Institute of British Decorators it changed its name four times during the next ninety years to reflect changes in the status and perception of interior design: Institute of British Decorators; Incorporated Institute of British Decorators; Incorporated Institute of British Decorators and Interior Designers; and British Institute of Interior Design At the time of the institute's incorporation, the Worshipful Company of Painters—Stainers proposed and supported an application for the institute to receive a royal charter. Records found to date do not show why this did not progress.

In a lecture, John Gregory Crace began by discussing the training of the "art-workman." He decried learning by rote. He preferred that every child would learn to draw, as drawing was the core to understanding and should be taught in all schools, especially for those students intending to undertake trades having any association with art. It was perceived that there was still an area of education and practice above the level of a full technical certificate (FTC) and the lower three levels of C&G awards. Generally it was thought that these were young artisans who had undertaken their apprenticeships and attended technical schools who now aspired to achieve the higher levels of creative design. Drawing on the analogy of speech Crace suggested that there were three phases: learning speech by drawing anything of interest; learning to coordinate the hand and eye; and being taught the rules and attending a government-supported school of design to perfect drawing, geometry, and design. "Knowledge is the result of careful study."[35]

John Dibblee Crace, who had sold the family business to Cowtan & Cowtan,[36] turned his energies toward his own academic studies, the improvement of educational studies for decorators (designers), and the support of the Palestinian cause. Initially, application for membership was by license. The founding members and early membership were the leaders and principals of interior decorating and upholstering companies that supplied the complete design and installation service. The IIBD subsequently developed an assessment and examination system in two parts, with an intermediate and a final examination. Building on studies and examinations at C&G and FTC, only high-achieving students undertook studies to pass these exams or present work for assessment by the institute.

The period of Crace's presidency of the IIBD reflected the perceived need for educational training and the acclamation of the status of the art decorator and his or her place within the built environment. The early public and membership lectures were geared toward maintaining the high level of skills and knowledge required by the top end of this profession/trade. From contemporary newspaper reports it is evident that the relationships at the presidency level between the RIBA and IIBD were cordial and harmonious; both presidents were honored guests and guest lecturers for each other. Crace was appointed a contributing visitor/honorary member of the RIBA, and most presidents of the RIBA became honorary members of the IIBD.

By 1897 the Leicester College of Art and the Leicester College of Technology had moved into a purpose-built building that is still used today as part of De Montfort University. The college syllabus that is available included:

Part 1: Freehand drawing by class lecture on blackboard, time and memory drawing, model drawing, practical plane and solid geometry and its application to design, perspective and its application to drawing interiors, landscapes and models, light and shades from casts, elementary design, plant drawing, elementary modelling and flat tinting.

Part 2: A similar content to an advanced stage with the addition of Sciography, History of Art and Ornament as applied to industry, flat design and relief design, the study of plant and its application to design form, architectural ornament, architectural design, History of Architecture and Architectural Ornament, and plasterwork.

Compared to earlier prospectuses from the National School and other provincial institutions the makeup of the courses is similar. As can be seen from the course contents, they tended to have generic structures with little difference between disciplines, with the direction being chosen by the staff.

In 1900 Augustus Spencer, head of the Leicester School of Art, was appointed to become head of the Royal College of Art.[37] The direction and syllabus content in Leicester changed radically with the appointment of Benjamin J. Fletcher as head. Although a protégée of Spencer, Fletcher understood that changes to the curriculum were necessary, having come from and trained in the cauldron of the Industrial Revolution, Coalbrookdale. He was also aware of changes in education, having studied at and visited German and Austrian educational establishments that further confirmed his intended direction. In 1901 the syllabus was changed, reflecting an industrial design bias and approach. The design of the new building, built in several stages, reflected both the changes in art and design education and the growing independence of the municipal authorities. The curriculum and facilities that developed during this period are closer to what we would now recognize as a college of art and design.

The IIBD recognized the decline of "art painting" and "art decorating" as a requirement within interiors. The debates in the 1920s turned toward what or who the "interior decorator" was, how he or she should be trained, and what his or her relationship with architects was.[38] Two important debates took place between the IIBD and the RIBA in January 1927 and January 1929, the first on the question whether the relationship between architects and decorators was satisfactory, and the second with a view to their closer cooperation. These, with other corresponding IIBD debates, reviewed the current state of relations. Most contributors were polarized between "trade" painters and decorators, on the one hand, and architects who would not work with design decorators, on the other. Traditional IIBD members lamented the lack of skills now present among top-end art painters and art decorators, and progressive architects stated that the painted panel was no longer required as modernism was related to space, light, and volume. More enlightened contributors foresaw the requirement for a new type of decorator/designer. An unnamed lecturer from the Northern Polytechnic predicted the development of a designer as a person who would be able to manipulate and create new internal spaces. The designer would be responsible for the design of the lighting and mechanical infrastructure, the manipulation of space, and the aesthetic design across the whole building. In another debate attention was drawn to the profession of the interior architect in Germany.

This confusion and lack of direction reflected the political and economic changes happening in the Western world. By 1933 a new syllabus had grown, developed, and established areas of specialism. It also reflected the changes in public awareness of design and changes in design through the influence of modernism, *moderna* (Spanish-influenced modernism, typified in England by the use of verdant pan tile pitched roofs and Spanish-influenced matching interiors), and art deco and the retro developments of neoclassical, mock Tudor, and so on. The suite of courses offered at Leicester was listed in a prospectus titled "House Painting, Decorating and Sign Writing," stating:

> Specially promising students will have the opportunity to attend life classes in conjunction with mural painting and decoration.... Students may be prepared for the examination of City & Guilds Institute, The National Painter and Decorators Joint Education Committee, The Board of Education, and the Institute of British Decorators.[39]

The progression of levels was still evident, from tradesman through craftsman to artisan and designer, or by day pupils undertaking an arts/drawing-biased studio curriculum.

The IIBD was therefore promoting both pathways through education so that students could achieve the highest award possible. During the second half of the 1930s a student/associate pressure organization built up across the country. The "99" association called for enfranchisement for associates of the IIBD and requested that membership should be granted only via examination in light of the proposal for permission to apply for a second time for a royal charter. Because of World War II the royal charter application was never processed.

POSTWAR EDUCATION

In 1948 the Leicester College of Art incorporated seven schools. The School of Architecture and the School of Building had been created, but courses for painting, decorating, and sign writing were still part of the School of Industrial Design in 1950. By 1952 full-time courses were being developed whereby selected good students could undertake the three-year course in their selected field without sitting the intermediate certificate in arts and crafts. Candidates who wished to qualify as specialist art teachers and who had taken this route had to retrospectively complete the intermediate examination within one year of completing the Ministry of Education's National Diploma in Design.

The National Diploma in Design's interior design course consisted of studies in design and color, printed textiles, model making, upholstery or plastering, painting and decorating, pottery, woven fabric, drawing (objective and geometric), perspective, still-life painting, lettering, and history (architecture, interiors, and furniture). The National Diploma in Design's decorator course consisted of similar studies in surface treatments, graining, marbling, broken color, gilding, lining and glasswork, decoration, pattern and design, geometry and perspective, color drawing, and decorative brushwork.

This was the first time that a course had the title "interior design." Viewing the two syllabi, however, reveals emerging differences between the content of the interior design and decorator courses. It can be noted that the National Diploma in Design in interior design includes a cross-disciplinary approach that also reflects the content required by the IIBD, with a strong craft design-based understanding.

NATIONAL COUNCIL FOR DIPLOMAS IN ART AND DESIGN, 1961–1974: THREE-DIMENSIONAL DESIGN

By 1966 a change of emphasis can be seen in the delivery of the course. For interior design the Leicester School of Art prospectus notes that the National Diploma in Art and Design (Dip. AD, formerly national Diploma of Design) was delivered as a three-year generic course with specialisms during the third year. Emphasis was placed on the understanding of materials and processes, believing that interior design was part of industrial design and that a more broad-based cross-disciplinary approach was required for design students.[40] The students were expected to undertake personal studies and develop personal skills and knowledge and not base their studies on purely repetitive skills.

> The investigation of materials, aims and techniques is part of a creative process in which materials and ideas, perceptions and skills, are inter-dependent,—as the development of technical ability parallels creative growth. In the studio and workshop the student is constantly directed towards the recognition, understanding, and exploration of basic principles of visual communication; in the lecture theatre room and library, he or she widens his or her horizon of the arts and disciplines of civilisation.[41]

There then follows an extensive list of equipment and workshops available for the student. The students undertook project-based inductions using the workshops during their first year, along with design methodologies; research into requirements, planning, measurement, and ergonomics; human needs and living factors; and building construction and materials. The third element of study included the term *applied science,* being mechanics, heat, light, sound, and electricity.

The third year of study was directed toward the area of specialism. In the interior design course this consisted of two-week projects at twenty-seven hours per week covering housing, education, health, transport, commerce, industry, entertainment, government, and religion. Projects were then selected and carried through to completion.

This change of direction went hand-in-hand with changes in secondary education. Brian Aylward, A. W. Hodge, and Ken Baynes undertook an experiment with the A-level design syllabus in which most of the assessments resulted from the second year of studies through a cross-disciplinary approach to workshops and equipment.[42] This approach was accepted by the Schools Council and administered by the Oxford Delegacy of Local Examinations.[43] The Gateway Grammar School[44] adjacent to the Leicester College of Art and Design (Fletcher) building constructed one of the first purpose-built design blocks, where students were encouraged to implement this approach.[45] This syllabus firmly makes interior design part of an industrial design/three-dimensional design environment.

Conversely, in 1961 the alternative interior design course at Leicester was in the Painting and Decorating Department within the School of Building. This was a British Institute of Interior Decoration and Interior Design (BIID and ID) course. The department commenced a four-year full-time course in 1965. The origins of this refer back to the development from the trade to City and Guilds qualifications and the successful completion of an FTC. Before 1965 in Leicester the top students could apply by examination for the BIID and ID qualifications and membership. The School of Building and the School of Architecture shared the same building.

In 1961 the National Council for Diplomas in Art and Design was formed as a separate trust initiated by the Ministry of Education, with the responsibility for setting standards and approving courses. Five subcommittees were formed to administer this. Interior design was part of the Three-Dimensional Design subcommittee, which had the responsibility of forming visiting teams to approve the standard of both facilities and delivery of curriculum.

With the formation of Leicester Polytechnic in 1969 all building trade and associated courses left the campus to form Southfield's College, which later merged with Charles Keene College to form Leicester College. Courses that were not Higher Education (HE) level followed this route, while the remaining HE level courses merged with the School of Architecture and formed the School of the Built Environment. The BIID interior design course closed. The full-time students transferred to Trent Polytechnic (Nottingham). Trent had an established BIID interior design course exempt from external intermediate and final examinations.[46] The transformation of colleges into polytechnics and the formation of the Council for National Academic Awards (CNAA) finally separated training for trade from bachelor's-degree courses for art and design.

Under the CNAA there were initially five interior design courses on a national basis: three in England and two in Scotland. These were drawn from good three-year Dip. AD and four-year BIID courses, which had normally gained accreditationfrom students' taking the intermediate and final exams. Leicester Polytechnic's Dip. AD (interior design) was one of those courses (see Table 5.1).

Under the CNAA, courses in interior design became more homogenized, being restricted in cohort numbers and expectations of outcomes. Both the BIID and the

INSTITUTION NAME DURING CNAA	FIRST CNAA CONFERMENT	LATEST CONFERMENT	COURSE ORIGIN
Brighton	1975	1991	Dip AD
Buckinghamshire College of Higher Education	1978	1992	Dip AD
Chelsea School of Art and Design, The London Institute	1991	1992	Dip AD
City of Birmingham Polytechnic	1977	1992	BIID
Duncan and Jordanstone College of Art	1981	1989	BIID
Glasgow School of Art	1980	1983	BIID
Kingston Polytechnic	1975	1984	BIID
Leeds Polytechnic	1975	1992	?
Leicester Polytechnic	1975	1992	Dip AD
Northern Polytechnic/Polytechnic of North London	1983	1992	BIID
Manchester Polytechnic	1975	1992	Dip AD
Middlesex Polytechnic	1978	1992	?
Sheffield City Polytechnic	1983		?
South Glamorgan Institute of HE	1985	1992	BIID
Teesside Polytechnic	1978	1992	BIID
Trent Polytechnic	1980	1992	BIID
Ulster College: The Northern Ireland Polytechnic	1976	1986	?

HONORS DEGREE TITLE 2011/12	CURRENT INSTITUTION NAME	DEPARTMENT / SCHOOL
BA, Interior Architecture	University of Brighton	Faculty of Arts (including Architecture)
BA, Interior & Spatial Design	Chelsea School of Art and Design, University of the Arts, London	Department of Design & Communication
BA, Interior Design	BIAD, Birmingham City University	School of Fashion, Textiles, and Three Dimensional Design
BDes, Interior Environmental Design	DJCAD, University of Dundee	
BA, Interior Design	Glasgow School of Art	
BA, Interior Design	Kingston University, London	School of Architecture & Landscape Architecture
BA, Interior Architecture and Design	Leeds Metropolitan University	School of Architecture, Landscape, & Design
BA, Interior Design	De Montfort University, Leicester	School of Design, Faculty AD&H
BA, Interior Architecture and Design	London Metropolitan University	School of Architecture and Spatial Design
BA, Interior Design	Manchester Metropolitan University	Manchester School of Art
BA, Interior Architecture	Middlesex University	Art, Design, & Media
BA, Interior Design	Sheffield Hallam University	Art & Design
BA, Interior Architecture	Cardiff Metropolitan University	Note: Well respected, good course; closed due to restructuring
BA, Interior Design BA, Interior Architecture	Teesside University	Art & Design
BA, Interior Architecture and Design	Nottingham Trent University	School of Architecture, Design, & Built Environment
BDes, Interior Design (subject to approval, 2012)	University of Ulster	Art, Design, & Built Environment

Society of Industrial Artists and Designers ran associate and licentiate assessment panels and advisory boards during this time, for both students and graduates. Courses not approved by the CNAA continued to run as diploma courses in interior design. Discussions took place between BIID and the Department of Education and Science to initiate an interior technician class, similar to architectural technician courses, but this did not come to fruition. Most nondegree courses undertook Business and Technician Education Council (BTEC) qualifications.

In 1992 polytechnics and other approved higher education institutions were granted the right to award degrees under individual royal charters forming university status "post 92," with a central HE quality system council overseeing standards. This enabled the new universities to review their delivery and content of subject areas. De Montfort University reverted to a cross-disciplinary approach for interior design, in which students undertook a bachelor's in three-dimensional design (interior design). Other new universities generally carried on with the course title bachelor's in interior design.

Unless required by professional requirements or parliamentary decrees the new universities did not want outside bodies unduly influencing the content of the new degrees. Prior to 1988, there were two British professional interior design associations that supported the discipline, as discussed below.

PROFESSIONAL BODIES WITH RESPONSIBILITY FOR THE PRACTICE OF INTERIOR DESIGN PRIOR TO 1988

The BIID was incorporated in 1899 under the title of the Incorporated Institute of British Decorators. The original founders were prominent decorators imbued with the principles of the Art and Crafts movement. In parallel with the BIID's educational and professional developments the term *interior designers* was added to the institute's title in 1972, and in 1975 it was finally registered as the British Institute of Interior Design. It is administered by its elected officers and council, drawn from six district committees: Scottish, Irish (all of Ireland), Australian, and, representing England, Northern, Midlands, and Southern. The institute also had an active overseas section with members in most areas of the world.

The memorandum and articles of the association have been amended at various times since they were first created after 1899, but by 1980 the council decided that complete revision of the memorandum and articles was required to bring the institute up to date. The review was completed in 1982 with this principal objective:

> To encourage the better understanding, care and improvement of interior design, being all that comprehensive range of activities which contribute to the interiors and other aspects of the built-in environment of whatever nature in design and realisation to promote the status on qualification of members of the Institute in their relationship with the community at large.[47]

The institute accepted education as one of its main aims from the beginning, as can be seen in this chapter. The craft bias was reduced, and greater attention was paid to the development in contemporary architecture and its constructional bases, with the main emphasis being placed on design. During the 1960s, thirteen full-time courses were registered.

In 1969, in order to promote the CNAA degree status, it agreed to cease holding examinations. As can be seen from Table 5.1, five BIID centers were initially approved, two in Scotland and three in England. The others in the table subsequently received validation. With a bachelor's degree with honors, qualified students would be accepted as associates to the institute providing they could also produce evidence of at least twelve months of professional practice.

From 1950 on, the development of professional documentation was a continuous process, with codes of practice that in essence allowed practitioners to operate on a professional scale of fees while allowing an alternative "turn-key" approach.

The Chartered Society of Designers had been formed in 1930 as the Society of Industrial Artists. In 1963 it added the word *Designer* to its name. The society received a royal charter in 1976 and changed to its current name in 1986. Like the BIID, it developed an equivalent memorandum and scale of fees. The Interior Panel also developed equivalent contractual documentation that mirrored the small works' agreements of the RIBA.

In 1986, when the Office of Fair Trading abolished mandatory fee scales, this had a major effect on the meaning and practice of the professional bodies that had developed from the mid-Victorian era with articles of memorandum and scales of fees that protected the profession.

Both the BIID and the Society of Industrial Artists and Designers (Interior Panel) assessed the future of interior design education in 1981. They started a liaison committee that looked at the viability of pursuing protected title for interior design following the European Court ruling in favor of French interior architects. Again, while this did not proceed, the liaison between the two bodies developed into negotiations on their merger. Now that they did not have direct influence on education, it was incumbent on them to achieve better recognition for interior design. In 1988 the BIID merged with the Chartered Society of Designers, but their lofty ideals were not fulfilled. The Chartered Society of Designers ran into financial difficulties and downsized its directorate and obligations. Although a founding member, it withdrew from the International Federation of Interior Architects and Designers and the European Council of Interior Architects. Equally, the traditionalist "art decorators" within the BIID formed a new association called the Faculty of Decoration.[48]

DRAWING CONCLUSIONS

The various attempts at formulating and protecting the title of interior design or interior architect have been subject to unfortunate timing by those who have sought this. John Gregory Crace could have promoted this when he was in favor with Prince Albert around 1845, while serving on the commission for the Great Exhibition. John Dibblee Crace could also have promoted this, as an acknowledged influential scholar at the time of the formation of the Institute of British Decorators, when the royal charter did not proceed. Had this been carried through by the act of application it would have defined the nature of the profession.

Despite the changes in design during the early 1920s the institute looked backward for design inspiration to the heyday of ornament and period styles when art decorators could demonstrate their design knowledge and skills. By the end of the decade young designers and students were looking toward new definitions for their profession. This corresponded to developments in education, where interior decoration was either moved toward schools of building or stayed within schools of art and design; in the latter, as in the example of Leicester, it was encompassed by industrial design. Had the Society of Industrial Designers achieved a royal charter during the National Diploma of Design period prior to CNAA degrees, then it would undoubtedly have had more influence on the development of the profession.

The table of CNAA degrees further demonstrates the changes in name and department mirrored in Leicester. Interior design in the United Kingdom, being between architecture, industrial design, and interior decoration and lacking the strong support of one professional organization, is subject to university and college organizational changes.

From the five honors-degree courses in the early 1970s, there are now seventy-four honors-degree courses in interior design or interior architecture in 2012.[49] Some courses are placed in schools of architecture, and others are placed in schools of design or industrial design; both schools share a common first-year curriculum. Undergraduate and postgraduate courses in interior design and interior architecture have developed since 1992. Within leading courses, staff research profiles are becoming prevalent, matching the undoubted professional expertise underpinning all UK interior courses. Decreases in funding for arts and humanities education will further affect the development, profile, and content of this body of courses.

Against this, several new professional bodies in the United Kingdom are now promoting and claiming sovereignty over the discipline, but it is hard to reconcile their narrow interpretations of a professional interior designer with a wider interpretation of interior design that clearly demonstrates the energy of both outcomes and approaches to the discipline that are shown within the majority of degree courses within the United Kingdom.

Approximately six years ago, leading interior design programs within the United Kingdom formed the organization Interior Educators, which encompasses the diverse range of interpretations of and backgrounds to the discipline. Virtually all undergraduate interior design degree courses in the United Kingdom are members of Interior Educators. This has become the forum formost of the intellectual discourse on the future of education within the discipline.

6

Regulations and Conventions: Interior Design Practice and Education

KEES SPANJERS

Shortly after I graduated, as I was starting my practice, I was working on the design of two converted apartments. I felt insecure about the egress way I had constructed and went to the local fire-inspection office for advice. A senior fire inspector kindly looked at my plans and listened to my explanation, then nodded his head, smiled at me, and said, "You know better than that; even a pregnant woman with a crying baby in her arms should be able to escape safely." I slunk off, a lesson learned.

Ever since, in my office the final question after reviewing a design is, "And where does the pregnant lady with the crying child go?" Only after that question is satisfactorily answered does the design pass to the next phase, which often includes review by a code consultant. Thanks to our commonsense question he seldom comes back with additional health and safety issues. On the contrary, many times he suggests simplifications because we have overdone it. Mostly we leave it as it is; who wants to bargain with safety?

The general practice of every interior designer deals with health, safety, and welfare issues all the time. Even decorative materials can be combustible, and when it comes to space planning and circulation, an ill-considered design can plainly be hazardous. Not all those who name themselves interior designers seem to be aware of this, however, which leads to a lot of misunderstanding about what interior design is and what it can achieve. Professional interior designers therefore seek recognition, and to achieve that many look to the government. The general idea is that legislation of the profession will bring clarity to the market and recognition of the professional interior designers' added value. But is it the government's task to regulate a profession or protect its citizens?

THE SCOPE OF WORK

It is beyond the scope of this chapter to list all the activities interior designers are engaged in. However, to define the position, a little insight into the field is necessary.

Interior design is a broad and versatile discipline that interfaces with architecture, design, and the humanities. Interior designers are working in the residential market, retail, leisure industry, bars and restaurants, offices and workplaces, set and exhibition design, hospitality, health care, education, and public buildings. More and more interior designers are specializing in a particular part of the market or engaging in only a specific field, such as color advice.

Interior designers can manage a full project independently, from initial design to delivery and often beyond that, and in doing so collaborate with multiple contributors and collaborators. More and more they are working in a multidisciplinary environment in which the boundaries between the different disciplines are dissolving. They can be employed by or work together with architects; communication, marketing, and spatial design consultants; with management consultants, LEED[1] consultants, or Internet technology specialists. The increasing complexity of society requires an expanding specialization of design and consultancy services. Many projects require the setting up of ad hoc teams of consultants who each bring their own field of expertise and responsibility. In such a multidisciplinary approach it is often difficult to see where the work of one professional ends and that of another starts.

In most cases, the work of the interior designer extends beyond the furnishing and styling of existing architectural spaces. Interior design specifies programs of use and adapts them to suit human needs and functions, in a way that serves human affections and perceptions. Interior designers design interior spaces in a comprehensive way. Spaces must meet the physical and aesthetic needs of the people using them, taking into consideration health, safety, and well-being and complying with building codes and occupancy regulations. Designers' work includes space planning, integration of mechanical and electrical needs, and interior fittings and furniture. Interior design integrates many aspects of our spatial perception. It has common ground with architecture, landscape architecture, graphic design, and product design but also with ergonomics, psychology, and anthropology.

But the main task of the interior designer is, of course, to design: to design with complete affinity for human beings and their social and organizational behavior, to design on the cutting edge of fashion and environmental quality, to design self-assuredly, with a strong vision, as active mediators between humans and their environment, between users and their everyday surroundings.

THE ROLE OF THE GOVERNMENT

Today's growing awareness of the quality of our living environment is the result of government policy as well, and is also a subject for constant concern. It is, after all, one of government's major tasks to protect its citizenship against hazards. Authorities do this in various ways: by taking repressive action in cases of disasters (like the fire brigade extinguishing fires), by enacting laws and regulations and enforcing their observance (like the police monitoring the traffic and issuing tickets when necessary), and by proactively mapping risks and qualifying to what extent such risks are acceptable (like building dikes to prevent natural disasters). A democratic government practices these tasks under the influence of a political decision-making process. The same citizens a government has to protect are also its principals and financiers.

On their side citizens have a responsibility of their own that goes beyond observing laws and regulations, and it is exactly that private responsibility, alongside collective responsibilities, that makes society complex and is a cause for many conflicts. It is in the interest of society as a whole that a free exchange of people, goods, and services can take place, and that all have equal opportunities. Therefore, governments have to see to free trade and protect intellectual property. No single group may be benefited or granted rights above others, unless the health, safety, and well-being of third parties are at stake.

To foster well-being and quality of life is an equally important task of the government. It is achieved by furthering good education, research, and development and by initiating and stimulating programs that promote cultural and historical understanding.

All this has a direct impact on the professional practice of the interior designer, who takes a position at the forefront of society and designs for the future. But besides being challenging, all those rules and regulations are also restraints that can make the design process a tough exercise. A well-prepared designer will know how to handle all restrictions, but even the most seasoned designer will sometimes encounter cases that cannot be solved even with creativity, especially when working abroad or outside of known jurisdictions.

PROFESSIONAL RECOGNITION AND LEGISLATION

By recognizing that certain groups of professionals are more influential with respect to the health, safety, and well-being of citizens, the government takes responsibility as a guiding body and also improves the social embedding of that responsibility in those particular disciplines. In some cases governments go a step further and, by means of legislation, make certain groups responsible for certain tasks, excluding others from the same. Thus, as a civilian you can trust that after an accident a well-trained and qualified doctor will be called to your bedside.

Generally, three stages of recognition and legislation of a profession can be discerned. In the first stage, the authorities recognize the existence of a profession without further restrictions by classifying it in public registers. This classification serves a role primarily in statistics and is of limited value for professionals and the public. Nonetheless, the least you may expect as a professional is that your profession is listed correctly, which is not always the case, as we shall see further on. Interior design has only recently been classified as a profession in most countries. In 1997 it was first registered in the North American Industry Classification System (NAICS)[2] as a subindustry of specialized design services, where it was described as follows:

> 541410 Interior Design Services This industry comprises establishments primarily engaged in planning, designing, and administering projects in interior spaces to meet the physical and aesthetic needs of people using them, taking into consideration building

codes, health and safety regulations, traffic patterns and floor planning, mechanical and electrical needs, and interior fittings and furniture. Interior designers and interior design consultants work in areas, such as hospitality design, health care design, institutional design, commercial and corporate design, and residential design. This industry also includes interior decorating consultants engaged exclusively in providing aesthetic services associated with interior spaces." As well the original tekst as the update are available online at the given link (use code 541410). For the purpose of this essay the original tekst is sufficient.

In 2007 this definition was adopted in the International Standard Industrial Classifications List of Economic Activities compiled by the United Nations Statistics Division,[3] where it is listed as follows:

7410 Fashion design related to textiles, wearing apparel, shoes, jewelry, furniture and other interior decoration and other fashion goods as well as other personal or household goods' and 'activities of interior decorators.

These categories exclude "architectural design," which is listed under code 71, together with engineering, landscape design, and urban planning. The 2007 revision of ISIC was adopted by many countries, which led to some conflicts regarding existing statistics codes. For example, in Germany, where the profession "interior architecture" is legally protected, it was previously listed as one of the architectural professions (code 71) but because of the ISIC revisions was potentially going to be moved to the design professions (code 74). After negotiations among the Bundes Architektenkammer, the Bund Deutscher Innenarchitekten BDIA, the Allianz Deutsche Designer, the European Council of Interior Architects, and the Statistisches Bundesamt, two listings were created for "interior architecture": "71.11.2 Buros fur Innenarchitektur" and "74.10.3 Interior Design und Raumgestaltung." Note the English term "interior design" in the second listing.[4]

A more extensive kind of recognition of the profession is title protection, where the authorities take measures to protect the use of the title interior designer or interior architect or similar nomenclature. With title protection only qualified and/or registered professionals may use the title, but the pursuit of the profession as such is not protected. Anybody can do the job, as long as they don't use the title. By preserving the name the authorities intend to bring clarity to the market, without regulating the market as such. In most countries or states where title protection exists, registered interior designers do not automatically have more extensive rights than nonregistered persons (such as applying for or signing building permits), but generally acquiring such rights is easier. For the client, working with a registered professional means certainty about the level of training and experience of the service provider.

In the most comprehensive form of recognition or legislation, the authorities can reserve the pursuit of the profession, meaning that only qualified professionals who comply with given standards of education and professional experience may provide certain services, to the exclusion of all others. This is the case for many medical professions, lawyers, auditors, and architects, and in some countries and states also for interior designers.

Such a practice act is a kind of market regulation that may lead to conflicts with others who presume they have the right skills to render that particular service. The nature of the protected services therefore has to be clearly defined to avoid legal disputes.

Title and practice acts regulate the markets in the jurisdictions where they are in force but lead to many hindrances when practicing across borders. The profession and its educational requirements, tasks, and competences often are ambiguously defined. This makes it difficult for professionals who are legally registered in their home country to operate in a host country, and it is even more problematic for professionals originating from countries where the profession is not legislated who want to work in a jurisdiction where legislation is in place. Since the authorities have a principal obligation to support an open market, all kinds of exceptions and transitional provisions are applicable. Within the European Community a Directive on the Recognition of Professional Qualifications[5] is in effect, but if one realizes that more than 800 professions are in some way regulated in some member country it's clear that this is a tough matter.

In some countries the licensing of the interior design profession is regulated not by the government but by private organizations. This is the case, for example, in France, where the professional organizations of architects and interior architects enforce a register that regulates the qualifications and educational requirements of interior architects, the Conseil Français des Architectes d'Intérieur.[6] Only those who are registered here are allowed to use the title interior architect, which finds validation in the fact that the title architect is legally protected; those using this title without being registered in the architects' register or the interior architects' register will be relentlessly summoned. A similar situation is found in the state of California (United States), where the California Council for Interior Design Certification,[7] a nongovernmental organization, regulates the use of the title "certified interior designer" to avoid legal disputes that often lead to conflicts with other professionals.

Terminology is another cause of misunderstandings. In most parts of continental Europe the common title is interior architect, and in some countries this title is regulated, while in other countries titles such as interior designer, decorator, or a local derivative are regulated. This leads to situations that hinder the pursuit of interior architecture or interior design. Because in some countries the title architect is reserved for registered architects, interior professionals there are forced to call themselves interior designers or decorators, although the scope of their work and responsibilities equals that of the architect. Whether such constraints are of a protectionist nature or are intended to benefit the health, safety, and welfare of the public will be a cause of discussion for a long time to come.

CONTIGUOUS LEGISLATION

Besides title acts and practice acts in pursuit of the profession, interior designers are faced with a multitude of rules and regulations that influence their work. Interiors are the user side of buildings. Designing interiors means transforming built spaces into ready-to-use rooms. In that respect it is important to realize that the life cycle of a building includes many users, and thus the building's interiors are subject to constantly changing views.

The buildings we construct to protect us from wind, weather, natural disasters, burglary, and the like are at the same time a source of hazards. They may collapse or burst into flames, poor indoor air quality may affect our health, and excessive energy use will ultimately cause permanent harm to our living environment. So here the civil services have the task of protecting our health, safety, and welfare. Obviously, this applies to public buildings, hospitals, schools, transportation hubs, shopping centers, hotels and restaurants, offices, and businesses, where we as users typically have no direct influence on the construction and furnishing of the building and its maintenance. But it also applies to our residential environment, especially, of course, in communal apartment buildings, but to a smaller extent also in the single private home. By means of building codes and a permit system for constructing, renovating, and maintaining buildings, and the monitoring of compliance with requirements, the government contributes to a safe and healthy environment. Although the intent of those regulations is the same in most countries and states, the elaboration of the goals in practical legislation differs enormously.

Apart from structural and fire safety there are many other aspects that affect the designers and users of buildings and interiors. Building use is determined in zoning plans, strict requirements exist for the protection of cultural heritage, additional safety measures are required in public buildings, and access and usability for handicapped persons are mandated. Generally, all specific building-related regulations are assembled in coherent legislation and permits, but in some countries a multitude of different and sometimes conflicting rules and regulations are in effect. Many of the building regulations are directly or indirectly applicable to the design of interiors, including egress requirements, fire and smoke hazard reduction, requirements to material, structural safety, air quality, energy efficiency, and durability.

However, building-related rules and regulations are not the whole story for the interior designer. Additional legislation may affect the design, especially for specific uses like health care, education, and hospitality. Most countries have regulations for hygiene and food safety; the Hazard Analysis and Critical Control Points[8] protocol is globally accepted as an instrument to control the origin and treatment of food in all stages, and the protocol also affects the planning and layout of restaurants, food stores, and other places where food is handled.

In addition, legislation on working conditions—ranging from indoor smoking bans to the ergonomic qualities of office furniture—affects the design of places where people are employed. During construction, safety and working conditions on the site are subject to regulations that may fall under the responsibility of the designer. Administrative rules affect the designer in conducting business, including rules regarding competition and contracting that affect the selection of contractors or even of the designer.

Legislation can be achievement oriented or can give a precise description of the dos and don'ts. Interpretation can cause divergent understandings and legal problems, which then can lead to even more rigid regulations. The construction industry is an important economic force, so legislation has a great impact on local economies. Inspections and enforcement can make authorities accessories to a certain extent, which in the case of disasters may lead to political consequences. For all these reasons legislation has become a many-headed monster, and controlling all aspects of it a matter for specialists.

Nonetheless, the interior designer is expected to have at least a basic knowledge and understanding of all rules and regulations that affect a design and its execution.

RESPONSIBILITY AND LIABILITY

Thus, as interior designers we are subject to extensive government interference intended to protect the health and safety of people. While delivering a project, we act as coordinators responsible for the just implementation of rules and regulations. A part of that responsibility may be delegated to third parties like special consultants or contractors, who each take their part of the required permits. But we should never forget that beyond all the responsibility covered by permits we have our own accountability to design a good and usable interior, safe and healthy for everyone who may reasonably be expected to use it. This will be the implicit demand of every client and the legitimate expectation of all users.

With responsibility comes liability. In a more and more legalized society an aggrieved party will not be satisfied with excuses like "I didn't know" or "I didn't think of it." Professionals are expected to know their responsibilities and act accordingly. Mistakes will be counted against you and may have far-reaching consequences. Nonobservance of legislation may be subject to penalty or even imprisonment, and losses will be recovered. Even more important may be the reputation damage that will result from such failures and that may damage the professional community as a whole.

The designer's degree of responsibility for mistakes, whether they were made by the designer or by others involved with the design, differs by country. Some countries have a heavy claim culture, while in other cultures problems are solved mutually with a good talk or over a stiff drink. Designers can purchase liability insurance, and clients will often demand such insurance. Most professional organizations require professional indemnity insurance as an important condition for membership. But consider that insurance may cover the damage but will not soften the blow.

A CASE STUDY

To gain insight into how all these rules and regulations work out in different countries around the world I conducted a small survey. What do we need for a design commission for the interiors of a restaurant? I presented the question in the form of the following case study to a number of practicing interior designers from all corners of the globe.

A former warehouse in a booming historic district is to be converted into a restaurant. The building itself is not listed as a historic building. The program is for an upscale restaurant with international cuisine, serving lunch and dinner, run by a renowned local chef. The existing space is 29 ft., 6 in. × 78 ft., 9 in. × 14 ft., 9 in., for a total area of approximately 2,300 sq. ft. (9 m wide × 24 m deep × 4.5 m high, or 216 sq m). The front and back facade face the street. The floors and ceiling are concrete (noncombustible). Walls are brick; there is a row of concrete columns in the middle of the room. There is an underfloor space providing access to ducts, pipes, and other services hung or laid therein and of a height sufficient for crawling. Facades may not be altered but are suitable for the purpose.

The commission to the interior designer is to completely design the conversion of the raw space into an attractive and functional restaurant, including space planning; design and decoration; incorporation of electrical, mechanical, and HVAC installations; kitchen equipment; and so on. While no structural work is expected, the interior designer will be responsible for design coordination, on-site inspection, compliance with applicable regulations, and the acquisition of the necessary permits.

All respondents agreed that this is a typical interior designer's job, but unfortunately some had to conclude just from the brief that in their country or state such a job could not be fully executed by a designer, at least not as the person with final responsibility and/or not without the help of an architect or of specialized consultants or contractors who would take responsibility for some or all of the required permits. The latter is especially the case in Great Britain and a great number of North American states, while on the European continent and in Asia all declared that the interior designer could take full responsibility for executing the job (with or without the help of consultants). It is noteworthy that in all states or countries where there is some form of legislation on the profession the designers were able to do the work.

Foreign designers or foreign-educated designers would have the same possibilities to execute the job as locals, according to the politically correct answer of all respondents. But recent research by the European Council of Interior Architects[9] shows that in many cases this is a "yes but…" When asked about hindrances when working abroad (but within the European Union) many designers reported problems. Access to the profession is difficult, especially for interior designers from a home country without legislation when working in a host country where legislation is applicable. The right to sign for permits is often obstructed by minor bureaucratic meddling; insurance policies do not fully cover the work abroad, and so on. The common workaround would, of course, be to involve a local partner, but still all this red tape is against the principle of an open market within the European Union, as promoted by the authorities.

But even in a designer's home country things are getting complicated when it comes to the necessary permits. In all countries our restaurant project would need permits before the work could be executed. Mostly, a range of different permits are required, and the applicable regulations sometimes vary from state to state or even county to county. In some countries (or states or counties) the application procedure is open for all, assuming the correct paperwork and drawings can be supplied. This is the case in such countries as Great Britain, Sweden, the Netherlands, and Australia. More often, however, some or all of the necessary permits can be acquired only by licensed professionals. Sometimes (for example, in Norway and Germany) the interior designer can acquire the authority to apply for the general building permit, if he or she has the proper education and experience, subject to limitations on the maximum size of the project. But very often we see that a building permit can be acquired only by a licensed architect, excluding the interior designer from taking responsibility for the procedures regarding health, safety, and well-being.

In all cases additional permits are needed for specific aspects of the project, which can be acquired by specialist consultants or contractors such as construction engineers; mechanical, electrical, and plumbing engineers; health and safety consultants;

food and drug consultants; fire safety consultants; and so on. Commonly, these specific permits can be acquired only under the operation of the general building permit. If the latter can be obtained only by a registered architect, then the architect takes responsibility for the whole and will want to carefully review the design.

The common workaround to obtain all necessary permits is to appoint a number of special consultants or involve contractors who are licensed to obtain the specific permit. The interior designer, the client, or the owner of the project can arrange to contract such consultants and serve as coordinator and intermediary for their services. Whatever the case, the complexity of the procedure leads to extra costs for the client and delays procurement. In general, it means a more subordinate position for the interior designer, who becomes part of a multidisciplinary team. One respondent even stated that it marginalizes the authority and professional status of the interior designer. It is noteworthy to observe that in those states or countries where legislation on the interiors profession is in effect the registered designer will mostly be entitled to manage the project in its entirety.

A more interdependent role for the interior designer has its advantages, though. Under most jurisdictions the applicant for the permit is the one who is liable, unless the contract appoints the interior designer as the overall project manager. In general, though, the interior designer would be responsible only for the design, and with a choice of consultants who have to take responsibility for critical parts there wouldn't be much left to be responsible for. But beware; cooperation between so many consultants can be difficult in itself, and the legal implications of poor cooperation can be even more painful.

Are there any other pitfalls with our nice little restaurant project? Respondents named but a few: time and budget constraints often due to slow approval procedures, additional requirements after the final inspection, unions requiring specific labor deployment, dissension between the building owner and leaseholder, complaints or even formal obstruction from neighborhood committees or individuals, cheating contractors, unyielding utility companies, and, above all, budget control and financing in general. Everything that happens on the television shows happens in the real world, all the time!

THE INTERNATIONAL DIFFERENCES

The international landscape of interior design knows mountains and valleys. In some countries, like the Netherlands, the profession is fully established. There is a legal register of interior architects that requires a master's degree in interior architecture (six years of special higher education) plus at least two years of qualified professional practical experience, as well as a compulsory continuous professional development program. The pursuit of the profession is open to everyone, however; only the title is protected, and building permits and other necessary permits can be acquired by anyone, if the proper documentation is provided.

On the other side of the spectrum there are countries where the profession does not seem to exist officially or, to say the least, is not recognized by the building authorities. But of course interior design is practiced in one way or another everywhere. A question is whether practitioners are able to go beyond styling and decoration without needing to consult a range of other professionals in order to compile a technically and legally feasible design and acquire the necessary permits. The answer is no in many countries, such as Italy, Singapore, Indonesia, and Malta, and in most U.S. states.

Interior design legislation is often seen as the lubricant that gives designers the right to practice where other legislation, such as laws that regulate architects, prohibits such. Sometimes this works, but often we see that some sort of legislation of the interior design discipline does not automatically give designers all necessary rights to acquire the required permits. The authorities with the competency to make legislation on professional recognition are not always the same as the ones that establish building legislation. But many advocates of interior design legislation who seem more interested in the higher standing the new status brings the profession also overlook the connection. In their quest to obtain the highly desired status as independent creative consultants they undervalue the practicalities that accompany full recognition of the profession.

One may wonder if this is a problem. Building construction has become a complex business, and hardly any professionals, including architects, can manage without the assistance of specialized consultants. As creative entrepreneurs interior designers will have found a way to work around practical and legal obstacles in the pursuit of their profession. Clients often are not aware of any hindrances and expect to get the best possible design for the best possible price in the least possible time. The involvement of multiple consultants may complicate such expectations, but as long as adversities are overcome they will reconcile. In one way or another it will affect the design and/or the designer if he or she is not in a position to take full responsibility for the design. It may be a cause of changes during the process, it will give others a serious interest in the design, it may affect the position of the designer, but above all in the end it will cost the client more.

A reverse side of interior design legislation can be that it excludes others from being active in the trade. This brings interesting new players to the discussion. Of course, architects have always been protective of their professional license, using the argument of the health, safety, and well-being of the public. But being exclusive also makes them indispensable, and that does not harm business. When interior designers succeed in convincing legislators of their capabilities and the public concern with professional recognition, they maneuver themselves into the same position. Many businesses will be affected if the title interior designer (or similar nomenclature) or even the "act" of designing interiors is reserved to licensed professionals only. What about those engaged in kitchen and bath design, home decoration, office furnishing, store design, and so on? It is important to draw a clear line with respect to the scope of restrictive legislation, and to do so not from the viewpoint of the required competencies of the service provider but from the notion of consumer protection.

In this regard a 2010 Florida federal court decision[10] gave an interesting view on the limitations and precision required in the creation of legislation. Florida's interior design practice act, which has been in effect since 1994, came under attack because it was said to be anticompetitive. The court upheld the practice act but found the restriction on the use of the title interior designer unconstitutional and limited the scope of the act to "professional design services provided to a client relating to *nonstructural* interior elements of a *nonresidential* building or structure" (italics by the author). The first issue, the ban on the use of the title interior designer, was already addressed by the American Society of Interior Designers,[11] whose legislative policy since 2009 no longer aims to limit, restrict, or prevent anyone from using the title interior designer and instead promotes use of the title registered, certified, or licensed interior designer for state-qualified designers.[12] The second part of the ruling, however, clearly defines (and limits) the scope of the work that is reserved to registered interior designers. While this ruling on the one hand limits the anticompetitive aspects of professional legislation, it on the other hand champions the public interest in having certain (specified) design tasks in certain (specified) building types executed by qualified design professionals, in this case registered interior designers.

THE PURSUIT OF THE PROFESSION

At this point in the chapter, we have seen how the pursuit of the profession and the legal complications vary in countries around the world. More important is what it does to the self-esteem of the designers and the interpretation of their job. Many designers are not interested in all the legal complications of their proceedings, and either leave this part of their job to specialized consultants or stay away from it all together. In practice, this means that their work is limited to the styling and decorative aspects that can be exercised without touching on legal limitations. And it is precisely that aspect of interior design that is highly popular in the media; books, magazines, and television shows are packed with extreme makeovers, (re-)decoration plans, and designer adoration. Next to women's apparel, interior design is probably the most popular subject, and not just in the magazines one reads in the dentist's or hairdresser's waiting room. There is nothing wrong with that, of course, but is such superficial design indicative of how we want the world to see design and designers? Obviously not.

As designers we may preach that our designs are unique and have an intangible added value for the welfare of people, and all that may be true, but when we come to the core of it, our work primarily deals with health and safety issues just as architects and engineers do. And as we have seen, to protect the health and safety of people permits are required for almost all substantial interior design work. When we want to take ownership of our profession, and materialize the predicted added value in real-life built environments, we have to take the role of manager and coordinator of the whole design and execution process. We must show leadership and see to it that all parties involved receive and deliver the correct information. What we see, however, is consultants and contractors who take control over their part of the job and complete the detailing according to their own insight once they have received the overall design, which may result in an interior that differs considerably from the original designer's intentions. If we, as interior designers, want to prevent that, we have to take action and claim control, including responsibility for the required permits. To do that, we need to demonstrate the skills and knowledge needed to conduct the orchestra, including a basic understanding of all the individual instrument scores the piece requires.

PROFESSIONAL ORGANIZATIONS

Around the globe individual interior designers have joined forces in professional organizations. It's the aim of these organizations to advocate for the profession by providing a unified voice to elevate its status and to educate the public about interior design. They do so by supporting education, sharing knowledge, building community, and engaging in advocacy and outreach. Usually they have set minimum standards of professional education and experience to distinguish their membership as the real professionals, to separate the sheep from the goats. The members are committed to a code of conduct to ensure professional integrity and ethics, and often professional liability insurance is required. Through these measures professional organizations aim to fulfill clients' expectations and governments' demand for professionalism and reliability, in nonregulated jurisdictions as well as in countries with a high level of certification of the profession.

Sometimes professional organizations perform tasks assigned by the authorities, such as examination, certification, or registration of interior designers (Turkey, Philippines, Malaysia, Iceland) or the evaluation of building plans (Spain). Sometimes they do so by their own authority, filling a felt gap in the legal recognition of interior designers (the Conseil Français des Architectes d'Intérieur[13] in France, the National Council for Interior Design Qualification[14] in North America). Some countries have only one association, whereas some have multiple organizations, each with its own market approach and views. Some associations are solely committed to interior design or interior architecture, whereas others are multidisciplinary interest groups. The Swedish Association of Architects[15] is an example of such an organization that serves the interests of associated architects, interior architects, landscape architects, and urban planners equally, while the Design Institute of Australia[16] and the Institute of Designers in Ireland[17] are examples of organizations that serve interior designers, industrial designers, communication designers, and the like.

On the international level national organizations join forces to promote and serve the profession. In Europe the European Council of Interior Architects[18] is a strong cooperation of sixteen national organizations that provides common standards such as admission levels and exchange programs, the European Charter of Interior Architecture Training, and the Educational Recognition program. In the Asia Pacific region, the Asia Pacific Space Designers Association[19] is a looser association of fourteen organizations, whose main activity is organizing a biannual congress. The Consejo Iberoamericano de Diseñadores de Interiores[20] is a regional organization that groups eleven Latin American organizations. In North America the situation is somewhat different, with three larger direct membership–based associations (the American Society of Interior Designers,[21] the International Interior Design Association,[22] and the Interior Designers of Canada[23]) that each consist of many regional chapters. On the global level the International Federation of Interior Architects and Designers[24] serves a membership of some thirty national organizations.

Recognition and legislation are important issues on the agendas of national, regional, and global professional organizations. In Belgium, Hong Kong, Singapore, and many other countries and states, a strong lobby for interior design legislation is in progress, with some expecting to be successful shortly. However meaningful these efforts may be, it would be sensible to look beyond recognition and focus on the profession's own ability to practice and deliver, meaning to conform to applicable rules and regulations.

EDUCATION AND TRAINING

There is one other issue in our short survey that all respondents agreed on: interior design training is about design thinking and generally leaves the practicalities of delivering a project to the first years of practice. There, they are typically learned by trial and error, often to the frustration of the designers themselves and all authorities, clients, and others involved. One need think only of the possible fatalities and the reputation damage involved to understand that this needs to be changed.

Interior design as a profession is taught in many schools throughout the world, in courses ranging from do-it-yourself short-term Internet courses to five- or six-year full-time higher education at the master's-degree level, and even PhD programs. It is obvious that this is where the lack of understanding for the profession starts. Everybody understands that an architect, engineer, lawyer, or doctor needs a proper education of at least five years; why, then, is interior design sometimes offered as a "fun course"? Why study five years if in other places you can do it in three or even two years, or even three days? To create a basic understanding of what interior design is and what it can achieve we must set up a minimum body of knowledge and required training, which must include a fundamental understanding of health, safety, and welfare issues, next to the necessary personal and artistic development of the students. We have to draw a line to delineate where the fun ends and professionalism starts. And the profession will have to draw that line by itself; don't expect providers of courses or even educational authorities to give up the fun courses as long as there is a demand for them. And there will be.

Various attempts to compile such a body of knowledge and to set minimum standards for the profession have been made. In Europe the European Council of Interior Architects has compiled the European Charter of Interior Architecture Training, which sets minimum standards of educational level and practical experience for the membership of the associated organizations. In North America the National Council for Interior Design Qualification exam has become a general requirement in those states where the profession is regulated. In general, legislation comes with educational requirements and, more and more, practical training experience and required continuous professional development programs—but, alas, not in places where no legislation is in place. Here, self-regulation is the obvious solution, and most professional organizations already follow that path. In North America the Council for Interior Design Accreditation[25] was established some forty years ago by the leading professional organizations to develop accreditation standards for interior design education. In Germany the Akkreditierungsverbund für Studiengänge der Architektur und Planung[26] has done the same since 2002.

The European Council of Interior Architects started a voluntary educational recognition program[27] in 2009. Also, educators have united themselves in organizations that aim to bring some unity to the diverse field of interior design education: the Interior Design Educators Council[28] in North America, Interior Educators[29] in the United Kingdom, the Interior Design Educators Association[30] in Australia, Interiors Forum Scotland[31] in Scotland, and Interiors Forum World[32] in Italy.

Still, it is—and should be—the responsibility of individual schools of interior architecture/design to define their course outlines. Some schools may put relative emphasis on interior design at a conceptual level, while others may concentrate on spatial and architectural design, often with attention to construction details and specifications. However, the role of the profession as a whole is to span all the skills of operation in planning and design, which means that a basic understanding of the health and safety issues must always be part of the curriculum. For many schools this means there is still a long way to go on a path that is not considered sexy but is indispensable if we want our great future thinkers to be able to practice and deliver.

CONCLUSION

The perception of interior design is proportional to the practitioner's ability to design, coordinate, and deliver a project, inclusive of obtaining the necessary permits. The interior designer who is unable to fulfill legal requirements and take full responsibility for the design ultimately sees his or her role diminished to decoration and styling. Interior design legislation does not automatically imply a license to be eligible to acquire permits. But we do see that in those jurisdictions where interior design legislation is in place it is usually easier for designers to become qualified.

Building codes and associated legislation focus on the protection of the health, safety, and welfare of the people. So does interior design. Understanding code issues and mastering the required skills and knowledge are pivotal for interior designers' recognition and ability to practice and deliver. Health, safety, and well-being issues and their technical implications and implementation should therefore be an equal part of the teaching curriculum. Authorities, clients, and above all users must be confident that a professionally designed interior is not only attractive but also usable, safe, and comfortable.

I started this article by sharing a learning moment from the early days of my own practice, which was in the 1970s. Recent research[33] has determined that a fire in an average living room some forty years ago took fifteen minutes to develop. Today, because of the use of more combustible materials in furniture and interior materials, a similar fire develops in just three minutes, leaving the inhabitants barely time to escape. Such findings keep me alert every day, as it is I who is responsible; maybe not fully for the wrong materials in the furniture I chose but at the very least for providing the possibility to exit the room in a timely and safe manner.

The entry level of the interiors profession? Knowing how to get out!

The Profession that Dare Not Speak its Name

DREW PLUNKETT

Interior design has the trappings of an established profession but not the associated status. Its practitioners, whether employers or employees, lack the confident self-regard of architects, doctors, lawyers, and members of every other professional body that scrutinizes the content and quality of its own professional training and the maintenance of its professional ethics.

In its present incarnation the profession is little more than forty years old. Arguments can be made for painters of caves and hangers of tapestries, for society decorators such as Syrie Maughan and Elsie de Wolfe, as early practitioners, but examination of those or any other antecedents will reveal very little about the profession today, which is made up of a different kind of person and operates in a different kind of way. This chapter sets out a personal perception of the professions' recent evolution and speculates about its future.

Around the beginning of the nineteenth century the artisans who fitted out the private places of the great and powerful found their client base broadening with the emergence of a substantial and prosperous middle class keen to emulate the grandeur of upper-class homes. The more entrepreneurial artisans recognized that they could attract custom if they also offered aesthetic advice, the cost of which they would subsume in profits ostensibly made on the manufacture and installation of finishes, furniture, and fittings. They provided a template for designers today who cover the cost of advice by the profits from sales in their shops and showrooms, and the office planners whose design work is funded by sales of their products. This is a legitimate way of doing business, and it provides a service but perhaps not a professional one. A professional should offer impartial advice and be paid for that alone.

The current model of practice may have a brief history, but enough time has passed to make objective appraisal possible. Economic imperatives, which determine that most interiors have a life span of little more than five years, mean that even the best are razed with a rapidity unknown in architecture. That accelerated destruction has, however, resulted in an accelerated evolution that offers substantial evidence, albeit primarily experiential and anecdotal, with which to speculate.

The speculation is United Kingdom–centric but necessarily so since the world observed, and largely absorbed, the rejection of prevalent mores and aesthetic presumptions that was acted out for it in the London of the 1960s. In a few doggedly fashionable enclaves a few individuals, like Max Glendinning and Jon Weallans, spoke the first words of a new interior design language. Like their predecessors they worked for a rarefied stratum of society, but it was now one bound not by the values of a status quo but by what was, in retrospect, an innocent iconoclasm. New interiors were likely to be public rather than private places, shops and restaurants where the new iconoclasts could display their accoutrements and accessories to a wondering and frequently outraged world.

What began in those pockets of central London spread outward and began the colonization of provincial cities and towns. A new mode of interior design practice emerged and proliferated. Terence Conran, who had established a modest studio in 1956 and had made his name first as a furniture designer and then as a retailer with his Habitat chain in the 1960s, expanded his design practice in the 1970s as a discrete business, independent of his retailing empire. Rodney Fitch established his multidisciplinary, interior design–led practice and with it began to explore the application of branding, which was to become a fundamental component in commercial interior design. Conran led on restaurant design, Fitch on retail design.

The 1960s also saw the high point of the postwar building and planning boom that reconfigured public buildings and city centers. It failed to elicit public enthusiasm for neobrutalist modernism but did generate appreciation of traditional building materials and detail and a ground swell of support for the retention rather than blanket demolition of existing buildings. It was enough for a building to be premodern to escape destruction. Architectural merit was not a prerequisite. It became necessary to accommodate fresh, financially viable functions to resuscitate what were extant but frequently redundant shells. In new buildings the interior had normally been the work of the architect responsible for the shell, and the received wisdom was that it should have direct stylistic affinity with the exterior. Designers working in period buildings were presented with the luxury of interacting with existing shells, and cross-fertilization with contemporary predilections provoked richer composite environments.

Architects themselves were not immune to nostalgia, and a few modernists began to question the movement's canons and mantras. The reappraisal was most persuasively articulated by Robert Venturi and Denise Scott Brown in the United States, and their analyses provoked a reconsideration of fundamentals by a body of significant practitioners, first in the United States and then across western Europe. Charles Jencks categorized their thinking and output as postmodern, but although they looked for inspiration to premodernist architecture, their reworkings of familiar motifs owed as much to Las Vegas and Disney. The appetite for the cartoon classicism that emerged was quickly sated.

In Italy the manifestos of the Studio Alchimia and Memphis groups also advocated embellishment of the austere modernist vocabulary, although they aspired to tap into visceral and subliminal responses to form and materials rather than stylistic nostalgia. They produced objects rather than buildings but proposed persuasive additions to the modernist palette.

Factions within the design establishment reacted, generally with anxious disapproval, to these stylistic provocations, but when the postmodern wave crashed, its excesses had been enough to recalibrate the hitherto pervasive aesthetic values.

Architects were the earliest advocates and exemplars of postmodernism, but since elaborately embellished and untested external envelopes were unlikely to cope with weather and were sure to be expensive, their first experiments were confined to the interior. Within the bland shells, labeled "sheds" in Venturi and Scott Brown's taxonomy, they had freedom to experiment with proscribed, marginalized, or neglected motifs. Their agenda and the possibilities it suggested for rewriting the visual language were appreciated and appropriated by the cohorts of interior designers who were less encumbered by theoretical procrastination and were eager to embrace new freedoms.

After Conran and Fitch and before the global impact of Philippe Starck, Britain saw the emergence of five practitioners, all working initially on a modest scale, who between them established the grammars and vocabularies of distinct interior design dialects that impacted fundamentally on the accepted language of the mainstream profession. The thinking of three of them—David Connor, Ben Kelly, and Julian Powell-Tuck—was shaped at the Royal College of Art in London under Hugh Casson, a peculiarly open-minded establishment architect who recognized that there could be, and should be, a distinctive practice of interior design and that it needed an educational model that identified and nurtured its differences. Connor brought expressionism and flamboyance. Kelly demonstrated how to deal with a diverse palette of materials, colors, and found elements. Powell-Tuck evolved elegantly restrained detailing. Eva Jiricna came to London from Czechoslovakia with training in engineering and produced retail interiors that defined the "high-tech" vocabulary. She remains its definitive exponent. John Pawson, imbued with Japanese philosophies, defined minimalism and continues to manifest its precepts with a clarity and rigour unmatched by his acolytes.

The influence of these individuals and others within their ambit built on the fission of modernism. The big bang that asserted interior design's identity and independence was recorded in *Architectural Review*'s November 1982 issue, which published the results of an interior design competition. The residential winner was an architect-designed and newly built split-level box, whose regulation whiteness was conventionally relieved by carefully deployed pieces of dark traditional furniture. The runner-up was a very small flat for a pop singer, designed by Connor. It was aggressively theatrical. All surfaces, vertical and horizontal, were faux marble, executed by a specialist painter. Monochromatic furniture was oversized and overstuffed. The judges' text suggested that they found it much the more interesting of the two and that only concern about the reaction of the architecturally orthodox, and perhaps their understandable uncertainty about how to value this deviation, prevented them from making it the winner. The few photographs published were enough to release and energize the imaginations of curious and ambitious practitioners and students.

In the upheaval and flood of new, usually small-scale projects that followed, clients were crucially important. Those who gave designers the most freedom, and required them to exploit it, came from the worlds of punk fashion and music; they wanted flamboyant and blatant innovation, not timeless elegance. They provided the impetus to drive, and the money to realize, the revitalized profession's creative ambitions. And by their selective patronage they handed aesthetic leadership to the new radicals.

As conceptual speculations were built they were disseminated through interior design trade magazines, fashion magazines, Sunday supplements, and newly created dedicated magazines, like *World of Interiors* and *Elle Decoration,* that confirmed and fed the escalating popular interest in interior design. Each month trade magazines published a few projects that became the shared topic of consideration and debate for communities of practitioners and students, who were given heroes and aspirations. Individual projects, like Kelly's Hacienda nightclub and Powell-Tuck's Metropolis recording studio, were hugely influential. Others made less dramatic impact but still offered ideas that fed the collective imagination.

The recession that struck the profession in 1989 saw the disappearance of *Designers' Journal,* probably the most ubiquitous and therefore most influential of the trade magazines, and with it went the sense of a single connected community. Information about new projects now appears on specialist websites to provide moments of shared excitement on a global rather than a national scale. Websites publish more images and fewer words, which are normally culled unedited and uncritically from designers' press releases. The only critiques are brief responses posted by random visitors to the sites. A tradition and context for interior design criticism has not had time to develop. Surviving specialist magazines are wary of causing offense and being refused access to other projects by offended designers. Popular magazines have no interest in devaluing their own content. Their journalists are not equipped to deliver analysis, and their readers do not want it. The Internet will eventually find incisive critics, and the profession will be the better for the provocation.

The 1980s saw the hectic expansion of existing practices and the proliferation of new ones. High-street fashion chains recognized that branded interior design was a crucial selling tool. Bars and restaurants needed to restyle to survive. New corporate clients tended to gravitate to the bigger, increasingly multidisciplinary design practices, and a number of these absorbed the prevalent entrepreneurial spirit too enthusiastically, relaunched themselves as public companies, and sold their shares on the stock market. Control passed to shareholders and their representatives, who did not necessarily understand, or have much patience with, the creative mechanisms they now managed. Both Conran and Fitch lost control of the companies that bore their names and moved on. Their names became the property of the new owners, who well understood their marketing value. The companies they left behind survived the recession at the end of the 1980s and the beginning of the 1990s. Many others, less well grounded, disappeared. Conran built a retailing conglomerate and started a new noneponymous design company. Fitch successfully rebranded himself as a retail strategist and in 2004 was invited to rejoin his original creation as chief executive officer.

A new, less self-indulgent profession appeared in the 1990s. Small practices felt vulnerable and worked harder and longer. Surviving larger practices, primarily designing fashion, restaurant, and bar chains, remained lean. Those who led them had learned survival strategies and tactics and understood not only competitive operating principles but also the factors that made a practice vulnerable in difficult times.

The financial profligacy of the 1980s never returned. Employment contracts were tighter and structured to make dismissal feasible in a new legislative culture that favored the employee over the employer. Practices were less altruistic, and less willing or less able than they had been in the prosperity of the 1980s to recruit graduates for their raw talent and nurture them through the first years of practice.

If postmodernism had precipitated a stylistic reorientation, the proliferation of emergent digital technologies at the end of the 1990s presented a challenge that fundamentally reshaped the profession's modus operandi. Graduates' difficulties in finding a first job were compounded as the computer began to change the operating structure of every office, eliminating the need for office drones to make precisely delineated versions of the scribbles passed to them by more senior designers. Digitally literate designers could now carry out the processes of designing and drawing more coherently and quickly and had less need for support. By the turn of the century, the first graduates who had grown up with computers and had what appeared to be an intuitive understanding of the technology that made them comfortable with all things digital were entering the profession and were better able than those only a few years older to respond to the successive waves of specialist hardware and software.

Office principals still generally belong to a time when handmade drawing was the only option and are skeptical that the computer can be an effective design tool. The level of leadership immediately below them is defensive because their dexterity at manual drawing has stamped them as creative, and, without the opportunity to immerse themselves consistently in digital drawing, they have failed to develop a digital panache to match their handmade flourishes. Adept graduates, fresh from the intensive digital drawing of their final year, have been liberated from the limitations and stylistic tics of handmade drawing.

It has become clear that to persevere romantically with hand drawing is to give the medium priority over the message. The profession's operating structures have always been prompted by changes in its essential tools. In the forty years under consideration the monochromatic imprecision of dyeline printing, which needed the sharpness of ink lines for clarity, gave way to the precision of the large-format photocopier that could cope with fuzzier pencil lines. And when photocopying was upgraded with rudimentary digital technology, colors could be reproduced and scales manipulated. Such processes were, however, no more than efficient means of copying and disseminating fragile handmade drawings. The computer makes a better and more appropriate drawing, which may be instantly transmitted anywhere in the world.

The computer will, presumably, continue to present options that will change how the profession operates and evolves. As software producers understand better what interior designers need, programs are becoming more mutually compatible and simpler to learn and use. Typing of text replaces illegible handwriting or cumbersome stencils. Mistakes are erased without damage to the virtual original. Lines are colored, and areas instantly and perfectly hatched and color washed for clarity. Designers can construct and render three-dimensional versions of their proposals more accurately and persuasively than the specialist "visualizer" whose manual skills can never match digital representation of materials, lighting, reflections, and all the other essential components that make a good interior but are the most difficult for the hand to convey.

Designers can now look at their ideas in three dimensions from the moment the first version of a plan and section is established. The machines on which they draw connect them instantly to websites with the most up-to-date information about components, materials, and relevant legislation—of which practices once held a fraction, not always up to date, in dusty box files. Designers may now connect to CNC (computer numerical control) machines that can cut, with extreme precision, the most delicate and intricate details. Auguste Choisy's suggestion in his *Histoire de l'Architecture* of 1899 that fundamental shifts in architectural style are prompted by technological innovation may be further validated by a revival of decorative detail.

The supposedly impersonal computer is giving designers the opportunity to engage more intensely with, and have more personal control over, all aspects of their creative process, but while a single designer may be able to produce all the drawings necessary for substantial projects, colleagues and collaborators have a crucial role as sounding boards, questioning presumptions made in isolation, bringing fresh imaginations to bear on unresolved problems and overwrought solutions. The ability to engage in a critical conversation is more important than willingness to draw in passive isolation.

Digital technology has also fundamentally changed clients' needs. Virtual shopping requires real retail interiors to fulfill a more complex branding role than simply providing a place for the prosaic exchange of goods for money. Bars and cafés have to compete with digital socializing and accommodate peripatetic digital workers.

In both the private and, increasingly, the public sector, outside the well-trampled areas of retail and hospitality design, clients are beginning to recognize the value that interior design can bring to their operations. Its importance as a generator of profit in the commercial sectors demonstrates, with all the objectivity of sales figures, its effectiveness as a means of engaging and persuading customers. Businesses and services that have been able to take it for granted that clients and customers would turn up because they had no options are increasingly required to compete. Dental practices, the most economically competitive of health care specialisms, have demonstrated the importance of giving patients, familiar with the environments of the high street, places that they want to be in and that suggest quality of service. Universities, dependent on vibrant student numbers for income, need socialized work environments that respond to digital learning culture. It is increasingly accepted that good environments contribute to well-being, and interior design needs to establish itself as their provider.

It is time for the profession to recognize that it must take itself seriously. Clients are prepared to do so, and designers need to treat their trust with respect. They have to confirm that what they produce is neither superficial nor ephemeral. Otherwise, the territory and the opportunities will be conceded to architects, who have no difficulty projecting gravitas when it is called for.

Recent interior projects around the world suggest that the most spectacular gestures are still most likely to be made by architects. This is not surprising since they are technically well equipped and keen to exploit the opportunity, so rarely permitted by the restrictions of exterior design, to indulge their imaginations more subjectively. Interior designers have to establish that they can also create and deliver set pieces. Their training needs to be consolidated, to teach more thoroughly the knowledge and skills that will allow them to conceptualize and build with greater ambition, to engage confidently with consultants and reassure clients. The projects they create should be of a different order from those of architects, driven by empathy for the user rather than concern for peer approval.

An ad hoc global survey of built interiors suggests that there is an aesthetic consensus, a post-postmodern international style, and this is not surprising given the economic, social, and cultural interconnectivities that unite the majority of regions and places, old and new, in which interior design practice flourishes and in which the prevailing economic model is a capitalist one. Interior designers may work across the consumerist planet, but they are essentially dealing with the same generic brief in all locations. In 2010 the Brookings Institute, in a speculation based on World Bank figures from 2005, predicted that by 2030 five billion people, nearly two-thirds of the world's population, should be classifiable as middle class, and it is safe to assume that they will demand opportunities to exercise their new spending powers in more glamorous retail and recreational environments. They will also increasingly expect better workplaces, better health facilities, and better educational institutions.

There do remain discernible territorial and national variations on the generic global aesthetic. In Britain leading practices are primarily focused on branded interiors for retail and hospitality chains. Their solutions, whatever their aesthetic merit, are obliged to be quick to install and easy to adapt to different building shells. The cost of renting or buying property, driven high by the same chains, makes independent clients wary of investing in expensive fitting-out of new premises. In most of mainland Europe small independent clients survive in greater numbers, encouraged by more modest setup costs. An abundance of good-quality existing building shells provides designers with stimulating contexts. There are fewer interesting old buildings in the malls and on the main streets of North America, where cheap, sprawling sites and low construction costs favor large projects. Small, intense interiors are found only in a few of the older, denser city centers. Interiors in Japan, after the country's brief infatuation with British and European designers in the 1980s, are back in the hands of Japanese designers, who favor a restrained palette and a taste for empty space in the unstructured confusion of their city centers. In the isolated centers of wealth that dot the planet—Singapore, Hong Kong, South Korea, the Emirates—interiors flaunt conspicuous consumption with spectacular gestures realized extravagantly and contrived to make maximum impact within bland new shells.

The BRICs (Brazil, Russia, India, and China), the new economic powerhouses, are buying enthusiastically into the prevalent global aesthetic, but this may change if the balance of influence shifts even further toward them and away from Europe and North America. Brazil, with its close links to the Iberian Peninsula, has long bought into modernism. Russia has a tradition of looking to western Europe for architectural direction. It may drift toward its indigenous architecture for inspiration, but it is more likely that such revisionism will happen in India or China, two countries that are themselves big enough and populous enough to qualify as regions with their own internal diversities. Both have distinctive architectural traditions. The modernism they have experienced to date is generally feeble, and China in particular, with its more insular tradition, may turn more readily to an indigenous aesthetic. Potentates and oligarchs are demonstrating a confident regard for their artistic heritages by buying back, in Western auction houses at spectacularly escalating prices, artifacts plundered from their cultures.

Just as it is becoming possible to find a consensus across national boundaries, continents, and cultures about the scope and conduct of interior designers' activity, those involved seem congenitally unable to agree about how to move forward as a unified profession and find a coherent, authoritative voice. Although the International Federation of Interior Architects/Designers (IFIA/D) has coherence and a clearly stated agenda concerned with educational standards and entry qualifications for professional membership, it has not yet engaged meaningfully with those countries that have no single national voice to speak for them, nor with a majority of significant practitioners in those countries that do. Nevertheless, representatives of, currently, sixty-three countries take part in what IFIA/D has described as its "global think tanks," local and international groupings that meet to consider the nature and context of present and future professional practice, which offers some hope of responsible collective deliberation.[1]

The problem of representation seems to affect the United States and the United Kingdom particularly, both of which have a plethora of potential members and a number of distinct organizations that claim to speak for their national profession but are unable to unite because of collective and individual animosities. The European council of Interior Architects functions coherently and is also devoting serious effort to formalizing qualifications for entry to the profession, recognizing the value of a specialist education consolidated by supervised experience of practice. It may be that it is easier to instigate effective transnational organizations than to find a national consensus, and it may be, given the global nature of the profession, that that is a more useful model for progress. The fundamental problem of how to identify credible national delegates for transnational collaboration remains unsolved.

Much of the obstructive rancor and confusion results from the lack of a precise definition of the interior designer's role. Owners of decorating shops are happy to perform under the label of interior designer, reluctant to be described as decorators because that also describes those who physically apply paint and paper walls. Those at the other end of the spectrum, who operate as fee-charging consultants, taking responsibility for complex construction and substantial budgets, are often wary of being classified as interior designers and frequently claim to be embarrassed to be called such, arguing that public perception then groups them with interior decorators and that their authority as technocrats is undermined.

So many anxieties seem to be about misunderstandings that the optional labels are presumed to provoke. *Interior architect* has the disadvantage of describing the discipline in relation to another field that protects its title rigorously. In 190 of the 195 countries presently computed to be in the world, no one other than those who have passed architectural examinations may use the word *architect* as a professional identity, even with a disclaimer admitting an inability to deal with "exterior design." Perversely, *interior architecture* survives in the title of a surprisingly large number of university courses, presumably as a recruiting ploy that appropriates the perceived academic respectability of architecture. Their students do not always appear to know that they cannot use the *interior architect* descriptor after graduation. The *interiorist* label is less frequently encountered and significantly more awkward to say. It has the advantage of dispensing with mention of either design or decoration but the disadvantage of perpetuating ambiguity.

It is interesting that the International Federation of Interior Architects/Designers refers only to "designers" in its publicity, and if one looks at the definition of the activity given by ICON Group International in their 2009 *Report on Interior Design Services: World Market Segmentation by City,* a wholly objective commercial market research document, it is: "This industry comprises establishments primarily engaged in planning, designing, and administering projects in interior spaces to meet the physical and aesthetic needs of people using them, taking into consideration building codes, health and safety regulations, traffic patterns and floor planning, mechanical and electrical needs, and interior fittings and furniture. Interior designers and interior design consultants work in areas, such as hospitality design, health care design, institutional design, commercial and corporate design, and residential design. This industry also includes interior decorating consultants engaged exclusively in providing aesthetic services associated with interior spaces."[2] Only the last sentence need cause any alarm.

It may be time to call a truce between designers, decorators, "architects," and architects and agree on boundaries. Why should an interior decorator not wish to declare his or her specific expertise? There is nothing to be gained from the potential embarrassment of having to admit that one lacks the knowledge necessary to fulfill a commission offered in good faith. The same self-restraint might be shown by those styling themselves interior designers, by a willingness to redirect clients to appropriate professional expertise, whether from a decorator or an architect, better suited to their needs on the assumption that referrals will be reciprocated. But such altruism might be limited. Membership of a chartered society does not necessarily confer probity.

Shades of activity that lie between the extremes will also make demarcation difficult. Designers who insert walls and levels in one project may do no more than paint walls in another, and it is as difficult to select a fabric, which will be largely subjective, as it is to detail a new mezzanine, which must be largely objective. The implications of failure in the latter may, however, be significantly more drastic and professional protection significantly more important.

There are equivalent variations of responsibility within most professions. Internal hierarchies that are clearly perceived by their members are of little consequence to a public that tends to equate their activity with that at the higher end of practice. Lawyers are assumed to be fighting for the rights of humankind rather than retention of driving licenses. Architects are assumed to be designing cathedrals rather than loft extensions. Until interior designers present a confident public face they cannot be confident of public perception.

While interior designers appear to be congenitally unsuited to acting in unison, a discipline that accounts for three-quarters of all global design practice must have a vested interest in collective action, to make clear that much of what architects are perceived to do is the territory of interior designers and that much of what interior designers are perceived to do is the territory of interior decorators.

For a profession many of whose members emerged from art schools with idealistic principles and innocent aspirations, involvement in raw commercial activity may be hard to acknowledge and may have engendered some of the low self-esteem in which members choose to hold themselves. The steady march of consumerism makes the economic world go round, and as sales returns provide objective evidence that interiors are crucial to the delivery of profit, the time has come to make sure that the place of designers within the mechanics of commerce is recognized inside and outside the profession.

The profession needs to evolve its own distinct values and to do this needs a distinct academic context and content. Otherwise, the territory it occupies, but has not yet claimed convincingly, will be conceded to architects. Interior design education needs to do a better job of giving its graduates the practical skills, the distinctive cultural hinterland, and the concomitant confidence that can match those of the architects who already hold perhaps too many strategic positions in interior design education. The profession needs to define the body of practical knowledge and essential theory crucial to it and to scrutinize how that is taught. Students should be selected for their innate creativity and then taught how to express their singular visions through the materials, techniques, and social obligations of interior design. Practical solutions to practical problems point the way in creative speculation. Appropriate theory may have more to do with economic strategies than architectural philosophies.

The profession makes demands on graduates. It wants creativity, but it wants that supported by practical knowledge. It also wants an ability and willingness to deal with administration and regulations. In the 1980s, a time of rapid expansion and few courses, practices were forced to go looking for those graduates most suited to their long-term needs, to recruit potential and nourish it within their own culture. Now they can wait for the annual influx of those with the determination to make their own opportunities, as graduates are increasingly forced to accept an "intern" culture in which they work for little or nothing to demonstrate skills that are already evident in their academic portfolio.

The problem lies with the popularity of the subject, with too many aspirants being mopped up by cash-strapped educational institutes. The inherently creative and determined survive. The majority find themselves on the lowest strata of the profession, where degree-level training is unnecessary, or in a job that has nothing to do with their study. They will be assured that "transferable skills," acquired incidentally in the course of their study, have fitted them for something lucrative, but it is questionable whether a worthwhile interior design education is an effective mechanism for developing trans-ferability. If it fulfills its obligations to the profession it requires a particular focus on particular skills. It is a vocation, but vocational training is viewed dismissively within the universities that are swallowing up art schools. The profession must demonstrate the credibility that will allow it to champion content and standards.

Postgraduation employment statistics may soon begin to suggest that the profession is a barren option for the majority who study it, applicant numbers may drop and courses may be cut, but given education's expedient decision-making processes, strong courses are as likely to be cut as weak ones. A unified profession could fight for the strong and expose the inadequate.

Courses are financially hard pressed to supply specialist teaching and tempted to di-lute curricula, to produce undergraduates unfit for the transition to professional prac-tice. To wring more money from graduates who know they need remedial instruction they concoct postgraduate courses that are even less tuned to practical training. The standard of academic achievement necessary to enroll in a postgraduate course is now lower than that needed to get a good first job. The proper postgraduate training for any interior designer remains the first few years in practice, which provide the integrated professional experience that cannot be taught in education.

There is an energy in good practices that is being squeezed from education. In Britain universities' obligation to promote research is encouraging the recruitment of teachers with little experience of, and little inclination toward, professional practice. There is no longer a meaningful role for the practitioner in the external examination process, where once a professional perception was brought to bear on the performance of both students and educators. The revised role is concerned with scrutiny of the assessment processes and needs the experience best supplied by other academics.

Financial restraints have all but eliminated the practitioner who teaches one day a week and is a role model for students and a touchstone for full-time staff. Enthusiasm for part-time teaching remains strong among practitioners who recognize an opportu-nity to hone their own skills by confronting diverse proposals of varying degrees of im-plausibility. There may be a mutually beneficial solution in the graduate intern model. Aspirant teachers might work for nothing. Some do already, and it only requires others to overcome their concern for tangible appreciation to join them. Larger practices, keen to motivate and develop staff, might send them to teach as a form of continuing profes-sional development.

A professionally regulated education is the foundation on which to build and safe-guard professional credibility. It can no longer be acceptable that anyone can unilaterally declare his or her ability to be an interior designer and begin to practice. It is unaccept-able that those deriving income from the sale of artifacts, chosen by them from the contents of their shop, can be deemed professional, because their judgment is skewed by self-interest. It is equally unacceptable that someone who has not complemented educational experience with supervised practice should be allowed to confront a profes-sional brief. Incompetence will not necessarily end in disaster, but it is likely to end in an inferior solution. A professional's obligation is to meet clients' practical needs with a solution that has an aesthetic dimension that surpasses anything they might envisage or be capable of delivering for themselves.

The first big commercial practices demonstrated how the profession might operate with efficient and effective creativity. Clients, who are often already familiar with architectural practice, want from interior designers similar management structures and procedures but a different kind of solution that comes from a different sensibility. A binding professional code of conduct, which all mature professions have, safeguards both clients and competent practitioners, who, if they conform to it, will be secure in disputes because compliance or transgression will be equally clear. A legally constituted professional body confers a status on its inaugural members that will attract others, to create a consensual voice and to consolidate identity and respect.

Conversations with practicing interior designers, all of them creatively distinguished and, to varying degrees, commercially successful, all working in what are clearly consultancy roles, reveal a reluctance on the part of most to support the idea of a regulated profession. This may be generated by affection for an outsider status that they have accepted throughout their training and their career. It may also be a fear that, as creative leaders of their profession, they will be expected to undertake the bureaucratic activities necessary to set up something as pedestrian as a regulatory body. They must be assured of their unsuitability for such a role and brought to see that it is their credibility that must be lent, to attract other members. There will be less creative but equally ambitious imaginations prepared to take on prosaic responsibilities.

It is also understandable that those who have survived and thrived in the anarchy of interior design practice have no wish to involve themselves in the equivalent of the chartered nineteenth-century institutions that shape and monitor the established professions, but it might be interesting to think about what a twenty-first-century alternative might be.

Interior Terrains

interiorizt

SUZIE ATTIWILL

A PROVOCATION

interiorizt! A new word for a twenty-first century practice! This statement, however, claims too much as *interiorizt* is quite like the Spanish word for interior designer—*interiorista*. Perhaps what is new, though, is the emphasis on *interior* not as an adjective of another practice, such as interior design, interior architecture, and interior decoration, but as interior doing, making, designing. *Interiorizt* brings *interior* to the fore as a primary activity; as a focus on practice, interiorization, techniques, and tactics. *Interiorizt* is a proposition for practicing, a way of seeing and saying, thinking and doing, attending to the question and making of interior(s) in the midst of contemporary forces that transforms ideas of inside, outside, and ways of inhabiting.

Interiorizts draw on an array of precedents and strata to test, and experiment with, the possibilities of interior making while celebrating and foregrounding interior design's concern with the designing of interiors, which includes the inside of buildings (interior architecture and interior decoration) as well as other practices of interior making such as events and installation art. In this sense, interiorizts could be seen as the next phase (or perhaps more of a bifurcation) of interior design. However, interiorizts also make a radical shift to question and attend to ideas of *interior* that underpin contemporary interior design practice, education, and research. Interiorizts address *interior* as a creative problematic *through* design.

This chapter invokes the potential of interiorizts, their connection with interior design, and the ways in which the concept of *interior* becomes a critical design proposition. Located in the middle between past and future, this text is manifesto-like to address the here and now. A series of interior designs will be sketched in as a proposed genealogy to intervene in the present moment and to invoke a current and future-becoming interiorizt.

RELATION TO INTERIOR DESIGN

Interiorizts emerge from the discipline of interior design partly because of the dynamics that surround the term *interior design* and the continual negotiations between interior decoration and interior architecture. Over the past century, interior design became defined through a process of distinction from both interior decoration and architecture. While interior design and interior decoration are now recognized as two distinct professions, there continues to be confusion about the term *interior design*. This has led to an increase in the use of *interior architecture* as a term to clarify and articulate interior design as a practice concerned with the design of spaces and not their decoration. However, the term *interior architecture* cannot be legally used in most countries in the world unless the practitioner is a qualified architect. Yet the Library of Congress—an international cataloging system—has "interior architecture" and "interior decoration" as the main subject headings used in the classification of all bibliographic material. "Interior design" is a subheading of "interior decoration." It would seem that *interior design* as a term is becoming increasingly fraught and difficult to use in a way that makes a connection to a particular practice.

Interiors is often used to overcome this issue of terminology and to bring focus to the practice as one that addresses interiors. Yet this hasn't seemed to resolve the issue of clarifying the practice. *Thinking inside the Box*—a conference convened by Interiors Forum Scotland in Glasgow in 2007—addressed interiors and in the call for papers described interiors as an "evolving and slippery discipline. Whilst the interior is everywhere, it is nevertheless ephemeral and difficult to define."[1] The problem of identity is continually raised within the discipline and frequently seen as a crisis in need of resolution. The International Federation of Interior Architects/Designers, a body representing professional organizations, initiated a series of global symposiums and workshops in 2011 under the title *Design Frontiers: The Interiors Entity* to address this identity issue.

Whether as interiors, interior design, interior architecture, or interior decoration, the word *interior* is generally understood as a given enclosed three-dimensional space and as a practice of the built environment. The word *space* is often interchangeable with *interior*. An understanding of interior—usually referred to as *the interior*—in relation to existing space, form, and structure is reiterated through the dominant narratives of interior design practice, histories, and theories. An example can be found in the introductory paragraphs to John Pile's *The History of Interior Design*, where "interiors are [defined as] an integral part of the structures that contain them—usually buildings. This means that interior design is inextricably linked to architecture and can only be studied within an architectural context."[2] The website of the International Federation of Interior Architects/Designers defines interior design/interior architecture in relation to negative space: "Firstly, that across all existing design fields—whether graphics, fashion, product design, architecture or other disciplines—interior design is the only one to have its end product grounded in the sculpting of 'negative' space rather than the production of a 'positive' object. Secondly, that at the core of interiors lies an understanding of the abstract qualities of shaping this negative space or 'void.'"[3] With the field defined in this way, the move to *interior architecture* as a term to describe this practice of interior designing seems logical. However, it is important to note that this positioning of interior as necessarily inside a preexisting thing and/or as enclosed space privileges an idea of interior as an entity or artifact where structure defines inside and outside. This reduces interior design's potential in a contemporary world where forces and technologies challenge the idea of physical structures and materiality in relation to the production of insides and outsides.

In terms of interior, what is highlighted in this repositioning is interior no longer as a given inside as implied by interior architecture and interior decoration; instead, the question of interior is posed. This could be "interior?"—a *what* kind of question that implicates a noun as an answer. It could also be posed as "?interior." Shifting the question mark to before *interior* producing a pause which opens interior in time and invites a designing. In questioning interior as ?interior, the invitation is not to provide an answer through redefining the concept of interior but to attend to it as a design, as a question in relation to practice—a *how* question that as a creative problematic needs to be addressed each time anew. It is to suspend the assumption of the middle bit—the wall, the boundary that already defines an inside—to place the question of ?interior in the world; to open it up to the exterior/outside.

The proposition and invocation of *interiorizt* is to invite a practice that affirms and highlights, draws attention to, extends, amps up, delights in interior design's potential to pose the question of interior through designing where interior becomes a process of interiorization before it becomes a space and entity. In connecting with interior design, interiorizt practice acknowledges the value of design as a creative activity and the conjunction with interior. Interior without "design" become a type, an entity, a noun as distinct from a practice, an outcome as distinct from a process. Unlike the practices of interior architecture and interior decoration, interior design has the potential to keep the question of interior open—open to an outside—as a creative, critical, contemporary proposition. For this reason, interiorizt practice is invoked as a trajectory of interior design and one that will engage and extend the discipline of interior design as a critical contemporary practice.

In the following section, a series of interior designs that address questions of interior are arranged to encourage and support a future interiorizt practice. These are not interior designs as one might encounter them in Pile's history—a collection of design as artifacts; rather, each addresses practice, interior making, different approaches, strategies, and techniques in relation to designing interior. Each is an interior design where design is understood as a drawing, a diagram, a set of instructions that set out a particular concept and way of understanding interior. While each presents a concept of interior and interior practice, this series highlights difference and variation. As a proposed genealogy they offer an opportunity to grasp the potential of posing ?interior as a design proposition.

Connections are made with each design in relation to the proposition ?interior and the concepts they create in relation to practice so that each might be useful like a box of tools or a pair of glasses:

> A theory is exactly like a box of tools....It must be useful. It must function. And not for itself. If no one uses it, beginning with the theoretician himself (who then ceases to be a theoretician), then the theory is worthless or the moment is inappropriate....It is strange that it was Proust, an author thought to be a pure intellectual, who said it so clearly: treat my book as a pair of glasses directed to the outside; if they don't suit you, find another pair; I leave it to you to find your own instrument, which is necessarily an instrument for combat. A theory does not totalize; it is an instrument for multiplication and it also multiples itself.[4]

As an interior design, each makes explicit connections with interior design as a discipline and practice. The diversity and heterogeneity in this collection celebrate the creative potential of posing ?interior and challenge any attempt to achieve one answer or solution. This variation invites and incites interiorizts to connect, invent, experiment, and manifest the potential of interior design as a practice addressing the question of ?interior *through* designing. An abundance of theoretical threads already present in interior design practice and history becomes apparent, and the potential for these to be engaged with practice, research, scholarship, and education becomes tangible.

?INTERIOR, INTERIOR DESIGNS, AND INTERIORIZATIONS

Walter Benjamin, an early twentieth-century German philosopher, offers up an interior design through his writings in which he positions "the interior" as a retreat from an exterior world of industrializing forces. For Benjamin, the collector is the "true resident" of this interior.[5] The process of collecting engages an interior/exterior dynamic where the outside is collected through a process of selection and is brought inside, into an organization and system of relations. Benjamin notes, "The true method of making things present is to represent them in our space (not to represent ourselves in their space)."[6] The dynamics between interior and exterior, inside and outside, are critical in the production of inhabitation both physically and mentally. The collector who selects things from the exterior and brings them inside engages in a process of domestication in the sense of taming, possession, and mastery. Benjamin writes of the collector's need to remove all functional references from the collected objects as part of a process of idealization to enable inhabitation:

> For the private individual, the place of dwelling is for the first time opposed to the place of work. The former constitutes itself as the interior. Its complement is the office. The private person, who in the office has to deal with reality, needs the domestic interior to sustain him in his illusions....From this arise the phantasmagorias of the interior—which for the private man represent the universe. In the interior, he brings together the far away and the long ago. His living room is a box in the theatre of the world.[7]

The interior is thus an art of genre where "the fictional framework for the individual's life is constituted in the private home" as distinct from an art of tectonics.[8]

Movement becomes a critical aspect in the production of this interior that enables both physical and mental inhabitation. The collector's motivation is described as "a struggle against dispersion"[9] where interior making involves a slowing down as a process of stabilization—sometimes to the point of stasis—to make possible this inhabitation:

> To live in these interiors was to have woven a dense fabric about oneself, to have secluded oneself in a spider's web, in whose toils world events hang loosely suspended like so many insect bodies sucked dry.[10]

The connection made between interior and movement, where movement is highlighted as implicated in interior making, is a powerful concept that reorients the way one might think about interior design—for example, ideas of inhabitation in relation to comfort through a connection with movement and slowing down become a question of stabilizing movement to produce a temporal consistency as distinct from comfort as a form of intimacy between things.

Architectural historian Charles Rice refers to Benjamin's interior design as the moment of "the emergence of the interior" in modernity. Rice positions the interior as one produced relationally and as "a conceptual apparatus." He distinguishes this from an idea of interior as defined by architectural structure.[11] In relation to the question of interior and interiorizt interests—this concept offers up different ways of thinking about interior making. Interior conceived as "apparatus" highlights modes of organization, operations, and dynamics of interior making. With reference to the writings of Benjamin, Rice observes that

> this interior is produced through an infolding....This surface does not produce a hermetic seal against the external world, but rather is activated through the inhabitant's relation to the city and its world of publicness, business and commerce, and enables a subjectivity and social identity marked "bourgeois" to be supported artefactually....The indefatigable collector understands that such a fabrication of the interior is a continual process, a set of techniques and practices that ensure the ongoing viability of a self.[12]

A different interior design is mapped out in the collaborative writings of Graeme Brooker and Sally Stone, who specifically address the discipline of interior design. This interior design also positions the concept of interior in relation to an exterior, but it is a different kind of exterior and relation from the one posed by Benjamin. Brooker and Stone write of the exterior as an existing condition within which an interior is designed. This exterior includes the building as well as other contexts both spatial and temporal, for example, history and previous patterns of occupation. "The interior is bound to its situation; it is enclosed within a building, which is, in turn, contained within its context." The interior designer responds "to the particular place that the interior inhabits."[13] Interior making becomes a process of interpretation and representation where the exterior is understood as a space of existing meaning and the past as "a package of sense."[14]

Interior design here involves the re-presentation of this existing meaning so that it can be physically and mentally inhabited, occupied, and experienced.

    This concept of exterior as an existing condition to which the interior designer responds is a familiar concept within interior design discourse. There is a sense of a structure here that is both architectural and contextual. Brooker and Stone identify a range of practices, strategies, and tactics that can be used—such as insertion, intervention, and installation. The "in-ness" of each of these actions—*in*-sertion, *in*-tervention, *in*-stallation—conjures a sense of how each happens in a context and implies a degree of stability and fixity of the exterior context so as to enable such an action to intervene, insert, or install to make an interior. From a certain angle it would seem similar to the idea of privileging the architectural context as the space within which interior design happens; however, what is active here is not an assumption that interior equates with already enclosed, three-dimensional space. Instead, it positions the practice of interior design, of interior making, in relation to exterior as an existing condition and poses ?interior within this existing order.

> The act of creating interior space is a strategy that is naturally transgressive, it is an act that interprets, conforms to, or even disobeys existing orders.[15]

An addition to this collection of interior designs is the concept of interiorist (with an *s*) presented by Michael Benedikt, a professor in architecture and urbanism, in a self-described polemic titled "Environmental Stoicism and Place Machismo." He claims there has been "a hundred year war against interiority [which] rages on" and calls for an interiorist way of attending to the world that values and places "environmental experience ahead of form-making and tectonics."[16] This statement offers a contrasting definition of interior design from those of Pile and the International Federation of Interior Architects/Designers. For Benedikt the practice of interior design is an interiorist practice, and he is critical of interior design educators and practitioners who rebrand the discipline as interior architecture, saying they have misunderstood their practice through a focus on the architectural. Along similar lines, he dismisses the definition of interior design as a practice of shaping space.

> To conceive space as "shape-able" by design is to treat it as a sculptor would. It is to transform space from something oceanic or atmospheric, from something fecund, field-like, and interiorly structured, into something with an exterior to which one could apply a tool.... Thus has an opportunity been lost to read the world as "endless interiority" and densely relational.[17]

For Benedikt, the feeling of interiority is one "of being immersed, surrounded, enclosed"; it transcends the experience of rooms and other indoor enclosures and extends to the out-of-doors.[18] In this concept of interior—this interior design—there is no exterior but an endless interiority where interior designing becomes a way of seeing and thinking that he distinguishes from an exteriorist approach and attitude. Benedikt uses the metaphors of Russian babushka dolls and an onion to describe the difference between the two

approaches. The interiorist works from the inside out, seeing and attending to surroundings as though embedded within several concave layers. Here there is a sense of proximity, of closeness, where surfaces, textures, color, touch become heightened. In contrast,
the exteriorist attends to form, the exterior of the object. Benedikt notes, however, that
this is not a question of subjectivity and objectivity as there are subjective and objective
interiorists as well as exteriorists. He aligns many qualities, practices, and people with
each attitude and approach—for example, phenomenologists and Einstein are interiorists, whereas behaviorists and Plato are exteriorists.

In relation to the provocation ?interior and interior making, Benedikt's ideas introduce an idea of interior and interiority as an endless and oceanic condition that emanates and projects from the subject who experiences and practices. He calls for interior
design to develop its own vocabulary through "articulating the interiorist world view
and all its sensitivities—sensitivities to texture, pattern, colour, style, touch, nearness,
arrangement, personality, and domesticity, to 'charged' objects (the *life* in inanimate
things), to class, and to the power of people themselves—of their clothed, warm, breathing bodies—to transform any environment by their presence."[19]

A different interior design is offered by Andrea Branzi, designer as well as interior design professor at the Politecnico di Milano. Like Benjamin, Branzi places the question of
interior in relation to the city; although Branzi's city is the twenty-first-century city with
different forces of urbanization from those of the early-twentieth-century industrial city.
Branzi challenges the concept of the built environment. The twenty-first-century city, he
claims, "is no longer just a bunch of 'architectural boxes', having transformed itself into a
territory of commodities, exchanges, information and services."[20] This city is not posed as
exterior to an interior making, as with Benjamin; instead, the city itself has become a continuous interior—an interior where there is no exterior side.[21] This continuous interior
highlights a shift from thinking about cities and urbanization in relation to architectural
form and structure to approaching them as composed of networks, relations, and movement between people, information, infrastructure, economies, agriculture, and meteorology. Space is also displaced by an idea of territory where movement is implicated in the
production of modes of inhabitation, occupation, and use.

> The city's architectural structures, once conceived for specialised functions on the basis
> of rational and sectional patterns, are now used in a disparate, improper, temporary
> fashion: it is tendentially possible to carry out "any activity anywhere". This observation
> represents a brand-new subject for the Interior Design culture and opens a new season
> of design experimentation and deeper inspection into the new frontiers of an urban real-
> ity that not only needs to be continuously "re-functionalised" in order to give hospitality
> to unexpected activities, but also witnesses a contamination of the same business, resi-
> dential and cultural activities. No more as separated environmental realities, but rather
> as active elements of an *enzymatic territory*, always changing its function and form.[22]

Juxtaposed here is another interior design—as an idea, a diagram for thinking and
practicing interior making—from a symposium called INSIDEOUT, which brought

together the practices of interior design and landscape architecture to see what could be said and thought if the middle bit between them—architecture—was taken out of the composition and questions of insides and outsides were brought to the foreground.[23] The philosopher Elizabeth Grosz presented the keynote paper, titled "Chaos, Territory, Art: Deleuze and the Framing of the Earth:" and proposed an idea of framing as a process of producing insides within an outside:

> The frame is what establishes territory out of the chaos that is the earth.... The constitution of territory is the fabrication of the space in which sensations may emerge, from which a rhythm, a tone, colouring, weight, texture may be extracted and moved elsewhere, may function for its own sake, may resonate for the sake of intensity alone.[24]

Woven through Grosz's presentation were references to the philosophy of Gilles Deleuze, including the concept of a generalized exteriority within which territories (interiors) are produced. While a frame may be a structure of enclosure, the emphasis here was on process—*framing*. The division of interior and exterior as first and foremost form and structure was shifted through a foregrounding of process and movement. Space comes after—as an outcome of framing. The concepts of interior and interiority become a question of making in an outside that is conceived as a generalized exterior that is fleeting and transitory as distinct from preexisting. Framing here is a process that separates, slows down, and arranges these dynamic forces into a temporal and spatial composition. While Grosz used the concept of framing, Deleuze writes of the constitution of an inside and interiority as a folding of the outside.[25]

An interior making through the production of a temporal consistency in relation to an outside becomes a composition of movement—"a rhythm"—that creates a space-time that enables inhabitation physically and mentally.

> The important thing is to understand life, each living individuality, not as form or as a development of form but as a complex relation between differential velocities, between deceleration and acceleration of particles.... So an animal, a thing is never separable from its relations with the world. The interior is only a selected exterior, and the exterior, a projected interior. The speed or slowness of metabolisms, perceptions, actions and reactions link together to constitute a particular individual in the world.[26]

AN INVITATION/INVOCATION

"The interior is only a selected exterior, and the exterior, a projected interior"—this statement could become an interiorizt motto. The five interior propositions presented above—Benjamin/Rice, Brooker and Stone, Benedikt, Branzi, and Grosz/Deleuze— offer up different sets of ideas, instructions, and orientations toward interior designing, each a box of tools for practicing in relation to ?interior. One encounters an array of selected exteriors and projected interiors: the collected exterior and the mimetic interior, the existing exterior and the re-presented interior, the bracketed exterior and the phenomenological interior, the impotent exterior and the continuous interior, the generalized exterior and the provisional interior. Processes of interiorization such as collecting, inserting, framing, and folding become apparent. While there could be other references and connections (and perhaps more that do not start with a *B*!), this series becomes a genealogy that intervenes in current practice and discourse to make apparent the potential in posing the question of interior as ?interior.

Projected interiors and selected exteriors proliferate, enticing interiorizts to experiment while invoking interior design as a critical, creative practice in the midst of current and contemporary forces. In contrast to concerns about slipperiness and lack of definition, this diversity becomes "differential vistas of experimentation,"[27] and the potential of interior design as a practice of interior making emerges. Fundamentals and foundations presented as unquestionable self-givens and defining elements of a discipline are not dismissed but become particular kinds of interiorizations.

Through this pair of glasses directed toward the outside in relation to the question of ?interior, contemporary concerns are amplified and highlighted as ones of interior and interior making. The potential here for the question of interior to be posed in, and engage with, contemporary forces such as urban inhabitation and subjectivity is both challenging and exciting. Interiorizts with their understanding of interior making and techniques of interiorization have a different way of seeing and responding to current forces and situations. In continually posing the question of interior as ?interior and in relation with an exterior, interiorizts bring with them an orientation that enables a critical engagement with, and transformation of, contemporary environments. The potential for ?interior to be posed, engaged, and experimented with in relation to questions of inhabitation, physically and mentally, where interior making *makes* spaces and subjects—interior spaces and interiority—through processes of interiorization invites and invokes an interiorizt practice across many scales.

If we pick up the idea of the exterior as a projected interior and the interior as a selected exterior in relation to the proposition of/provocation for interiorizt practice in the twenty-first century, what can be said and seen now? Forces such as globalization, capitalism, contemporary technologies, urban density, and war challenge existing ideas and modes of inhabitation—of place, belonging, subjectivity—and invite the production of new interiors and exteriors. For example, urbanization and inhabitation continue to be connected with questions of interior. The twenty-first century has been flagged as "the century of the city" as the number of people living in cities reaches unprecedented levels and density becomes a critical issue affecting lifestyles and modes of inhabitation.[28] Through posing ?interior, individualism and the individual become apparent as interior designs that privilege an idea of enclosed form and an idea of interior as an internalized and independent entity. The phenomena of the "intimate metropolis,"[29] where the subjectivity and individualism of contemporary society are brought to the fore, could become a focus for interiorizt practice. The psychoanalyst and social theorist Félix Guattari's call for a resingularization of subjectivity through attending to physical, social, and mental ecologies[30] invites an interiorizt practice in which interior making becomes a practice attending the invention of new modes of subjectivization and inhabitation.

Interior design as a discipline already offers up the potential for this interiorizt practice; however, there needs to be a shift from defining interior as necessarily defined by space, form, and structure so that the question of interior can be opened and posed in an outside. This then leads to questions of not only "interior?" but also "?interior" where the production of interior as a creative problematic is posed in relation to processes of interiorization. Space (whether enclosed or negative) and structure become potential outcomes of interiorizations as distinct from the predefining elements of an interiorizt practice. What if space and structure are products of twentieth-century thinking and not so useful to a twenty-first-century practice and context where contingency and change are dominant forces?

Shifts from spatial to temporal thinking in relation to design and inhabitation can be mapped in the concept of the *Gesamtkunstwerk*. This concept of a total environment connects with the question of interior as a unified and singular condition. The story of "The Poor Little Rich Man," written and published in 1900 by architect and critic Adolf Loos,[31] is a wonderful example of a total spatial environment with no relation to movement, contingency, or an outside. Here Loos tells the story of a wealthy man who engaged an architect to design his entire house in the contemporary manner as a total work of art, a *Gesamtkunstwerk*. The design was completed; the client was thrilled. On his birthday he received presents from family and friends and realized he wasn't sure where to place them, so he called the architect to come and advise him. The architect let out a scream of horror upon arrival as the man opened the front door wearing the wrong slippers for the entrance hall. The slippers were not designed for the carpet of that space and hence destroyed the whole environment. In a more recent discussion about this idea of the total environment and its presence in twenty-first-century design, a shift can be noted from a spatial emphasis to one of temporality in which the concept of the *Gesamtkunstwerk* as a total work of art continues but becomes one of "temporary totalities, nomadic encampments or natural environments composed of aggregated assemblies."[32] A distinction becomes apparent between two modes of total design in relation to different processes of making cohesive and interiorizing: one privileges space to the extent that change and exterior forces—such as birthday presents and slippers—become intrusive as they move across spatial boundaries, and another achieves a sense of unity and cohesion that is provisional and dynamic, enabling an engagement with contingency, temporality, and change.

The intention here is not to claim one over the other as the right or correct mode for interior designing in the twenty-first century; instead, it is to highlight the effects of different ideas expressed through practice and to affirm these differences and variations as an expression of a creative practice engaged with contemporary conditions. The series of interior designs presented above show how different ideas of interior implicate ways of seeing, thinking, and doing that affect and produce insides and outsides. "?interior" is a question posed in a continually changing and dynamic outside and as such invites the potential for the new. This is one reason why there is a *z* rather than an *s* in this *interiorizt* and *interiorization*. The use of *z* in words can be described as "an active *s*"; shaped like a lightning strike, a *z* brings energy and movement to a word, its reading and meaning. While interiorizt practice includes interiorists it cannot become equated with interiorism as the *z* is like a bolt out of the blue.

9

Surface Demonstrations, Neutral, Not So

JULIEANNA PRESTON

How does an interior surface participate in the politics of neutrality? In 2009 I repaired the wall surfaces of a small institutional office space as a creative form of protest against the pervasive use of neutrality as a political position and material quality without bias. This performative installation, entitled *Neutral, Not So,* tested the political agency of a generic interior surface. A script, scribbled on the wall, structured a typical nine-to-five workday as a one-act play with nine scenes that prompted a repetitive sequence of work tasks. The performance cycled through *acts of repair* (cutting, filling, sanding, wiping, and painting seventy-nine holes left in the walls by the removal of shelving), *oration* (reading aloud from texts on topics associated with neutrality), and *documentation* (archiving each scene through still and video images). Through these acts I was exploring the capacity of these walls, these interior surfaces, "to speak" (Fig. 3).

This chapter is directed by several senses of what it means to demonstrate. As *instruction,* to demonstrate imparts practical knowledge about several industrial construction products, specifically, a standard partition wall, gypsum wallboard, and white latex interior paint. Demonstration also exhibits rhetorical *expression* as a form of communicating resistance. And, finally, this chapter launches a demonstration as a *persuasive* argument relative to a political issue, specifically, the capacity of neutrality to be oppressive.

The installation, itself a demonstration in several ways, cast aspersions on two dominant notions central to interior design and contemporary culture: first, that the smoothness, seamlessness, and uniformity of industrial processes and products are motivated solely by economies that link industrial nations. With intent to overcome the aesthetic expression of craft, such economies realign notions of labor and the value of the laboring body. Every smooth, white, uniform plaster wall surface registers a desire for complete control over a material, a desire that leaves no room for blemishes or idiosyncratic traces of the maker. While labor-intensive, the mass-produced products and construction

FIGURE 3   The scene of a script on a hole-ridden wall. Copyright J. Preston 2009.

system offer no space for the laborer's creative investment. Second, there is an assumption that to be neutral is to be without color and bias, that is, to be white. As estate agents confirm, neutral-colored interiors are more attractive to buyers.[1] This assumption emphasizes the degree to which prevailing tenets of modernism serve to discipline interior environments and their occupation. Ostensibly, this chapter is about the office's two opposing white walls, which are framed by timber studs, sheathed in gypsum wallboard, and given a paint finish. Do not be fooled by the matter-of-fact manner of this description; as neither a know-how/can-do manual nor homage to material science, this chapter uses such data as a rhetorical platform to link conventional interior materials, finishes, and installation processes to the seemingly uncontentious position of neutrality.

INSTRUCTING

The scene of the performative installation was nothing more than a room measuring approximately 10 × 22 ft. (3 × 7 m) with an east-facing window. A cellular space among many in an urban environment, it is what one might call normal for a university workspace—nothing flashy, just standard issue. The performance began several days before the actual event as I shifted all my personal belongings from the office. The need to vacate the office was the result of a dispute surrounding equity in the workplace, a situation that at the time was volatile but, for the sake of this story, is only peripherally significant. Removal of all the metal bookshelves left ruptures in the walls that drew attention to the fact that they had not been safely secured to the internal structure, a frightening realization considering the weight I had just removed from them. With nothing else in the space to distract me, I mused on what made these holes offensive so as to require that they be filled up and the surface continuum resurrected. Other than reinstating the shelves in exactly the same configuration, did the holes not offer any further possibilities? Could it be that the holes revealed breaches to the wall's interior, where fumes, debris, and dead space had been banished? Did the holes insinuate a form of social neglect, abandonment, or state of impoverishment? Or did the holes impart traces of occupancy too viscerally laden, like the odor of used footwear or the stains on mattresses found at the op shop? Inherently I knew the answer had something to do with cultural codes of propriety, a sense reinforced by the fact that every time my family moved, we had to leave the house in a better state than that in which we acquired it. In academic terms, this impulse to repair the wall served to uphold what I knew to be lingering traces of a modernist ethic linked to simple forms, clean lines, and smooth surfaces. To repair and repaint was to cleanse the space and dress it in the uniform of standardized interior building products.

Interior design construction manuals provide a glimpse of what that standard uniform is (Fig. 4). A typical interior partition wall consists of timber studs or light-gauge steel units assembled as a flat, even, and rigid plane.[2] Members are located 16 or 24 in. (0.4 or 0.6 m) apart on center depending on the thickness of the drywall in order to maximize the efficiency of a standard sheet nominally measuring 4 × 8 ft. (1.2 × 2.4 m). According to New Zealand Building Standards, gypsum wallboard, also known as drywall or plasterboard, "is a sheet lining material renowned for its properties of stability, fire resistance, acoustic control and bracing. It consists of a plaster core of gypsum encased in a durable face and backing paper."[3] Sheets are fixed in a horizontal orientation directly to the skeletal frame. Screw or nail heads are sunk below the board surface to enable smooth rendering with a plaster joint compound. The wall is then "primed" with a paint designed to saturate and unify the pores of the paper coating with the spackled plaster, a process followed by several coats of finish treatment, usually white acrylic paint with a flat, satin, or low-sheen texture. A flawless wall surface is dependent on the coincidence of an industrial fabricated material, an installation process prefigured on modularity, power tools, and the attention of a "semiskilled" laborer to maintain a low degree of tolerance throughout the installation.[4] The closer these regulating standard practices are followed, the nearer the wall comes to a state of uniformity, that is, assumes an air of perfection in terms of standard contemporary construction. These practices have been promoted by the state, which regulates health and safety measures, and the manufacturer, who distributes not only the product but communication on the means by which to install and maintain it. As manufacturer advertisements attest, this is a good product! It is relatively inexpensive, lightweight, easy to install, readily available, and thermally and acoustically sound, and if that is not enough, it helps keep you safe in the event of fire! What appears as a reasonable and innocuous promotion of material "goodness" translates as a rhetorical construction of the "conception of the good," a notion usually associated with social politics and the debate on if, how, and to what degree a government should regulate independent choice and action.

> In recent years, many who call themselves liberals have maintained that the state should not favour, promote, or act on any particular conception of the good. Instead, it should simply provide a neutral and just framework within which each citizen can pursue the good as he understands it. To provide this framework, a government must sometimes interfere with liberty. It must restrict its citizens' options in order to insure security and stability, promote prosperity and efficiency, and make available various public goods. Also, if justice requires more equality than unconstrained markets can provide, the state must intervene to equalize opportunity or resources.[5]

Gypsum board's abundant presence in the marketplace extends to most home and workplace environments. Such is the reciprocal nature of supply and demand in a capitalist economy. But what does it mean to construct an interior partition that is as generic as the drafted detail that represents it? What level of choice, expression, or situated specificity does the industrial system afford? The above quote suggests that there may be some liberty at stake. If the construction of a simple and common gypsum board interior wall partition is bound up in the political economy that George Sher describes in the preceding quotation, how are the wall and the act of building the wall anything more than compliance with those forces and confirmation of gypsum's branding as a neutral product?

Acting within these insidious constraints, I felt obliged to repair the holes in order to bring this office space back into line with conditions illustrated by prominent examples of proper surface decorum. Such obligation gained prominence when weighed against the responsibilities of a person or state taking a neutral stance and those of an aggressor in the case of war:

> One of the fundamental doctrines of the modern law of neutrality is that a belligerent must refrain from committing hostile acts within the jurisdiction of a neutral power.

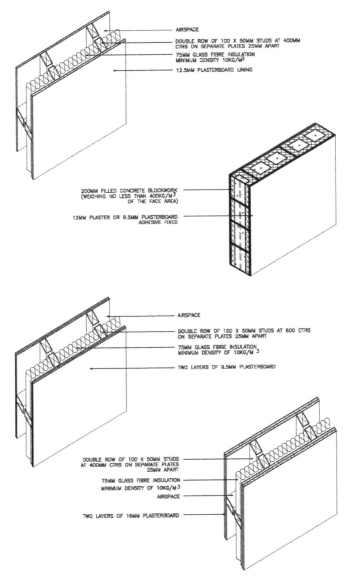

FIGURE 4   Non-load-bearing wall partition construction details. Copyright Primer 2000.

Correlatively, the neutral is under duty to prevent the commission of such acts. A bel-
ligerent's failure to respect the neutral's right makes it liable to respond in damages to
the neutral. A neutral's failure to carry out its duty makes it in turn liable to respond
in damages to the injured party.[6]

Surprisingly, my sense of duty was slightly unwarranted. While the *Residential Tenancy
Agreement*[7] outlines a legal obligation to "not damage or permit damage to the premises"
and to "leave a property clean and tidy, clear of rubbish and possessions at the end of tenancy," I found no mention in the policy or contractual agreements toward the physical

maintenance by staff of their university office spaces (Plate 3). Motivated by custom and conscience, I referred to a local building supplier for guidance on repairing these holes:

> For holes between 50 and 150 mm in diameter a plaster board patch will be required. 1. Cut away the damaged area to a neat rectangular hole. 2. Sand the area around the repair to ensure the best adhesion between the compound and the painted surface. 3. Cut a piece of plasterboard that is slightly longer (approximately 20 mm) than the hole, but small enough to fit through the hole. 4. Place a 60 mm flat head nail through the centre of the plasterboard and coat the ends with GIB Tradeset 20. 5. Insert the patch into the hole. 6. Pull toward the front using the nail. 7. Once hard (approximately 1 hr) gently push the nail back through the patch. 8. Using a broad knife, fill the hole flush to the surrounding area with GIB Tradeset 20. 9. Leave to dry for approximately 48–72 hours. This longer time is required because the plaster is very thick. 10. Apply a thin coat of GIB Plus 4 over the patched area. 11. Leave to dry and sand or wet sand the area smooth. 12. Decorate the area as required.[8]

These helpful instructions facilitated a straightforward do-it-yourself task. However, these instructions also signified an allegiance to standard industrial building material products and systems, which according to editor, typographer, writer, and critic Robin Kinross stem from the dream of "an ideology-free or ideologically neutral world made possible by advances in technology, by an abundance of material goods, by the spread of representative democracy and the eclipse of rival political systems, and by mass education."[9] Like Kinross, I am highlighting a binding relationship between material attributes and social politics such that building a simple wall is understood in a wider social context and regarded as a critical act no matter how banal the situation. What appeared to be a simple mending task proved to be vestiges of "the faith of modernism: the belief in simple forms, in reduction of elements, apparently not for reasons of style but for the most compelling reason of need—the need to save labor, time, and money, and to improve communication."[10] Such uniformity tends to infiltrate social norms through three modes of diffusion: information disseminated via mass media, sharing of best practices in an innovative environment, and imitation in an effort to blend in or gain status. The level of uniformity is factored by the number of people who have access to the information, the relevance the standard has to potential users, the degree of interpretation embedded in the standard, and the effectiveness of their implementation[11] (Fig. 5).

In their raw state, the holes spoke of the ways that this material had been manipulated to achieve its pristine and uniform state. After having been quarried, crushed, dried, and ground to a fine powder, crystalline hydrous calcium sulfate is heated to 175°C. In the process it loses most of its water content and gains its ability to fend off threatening flames.[12] A slurry of calcined gypsum, starch, water, and sizing admixtures such as rosin and alum is poured between special paper faces and passed between sets of rollers that reduce it to the desired thickness (U.S. Patent 1968). The passage from a wet formless substance to a semidry stiff plane culminates as the continuous ribbon is sheared into desired lengths and sent to cure in a high-temperature kiln. Stacked

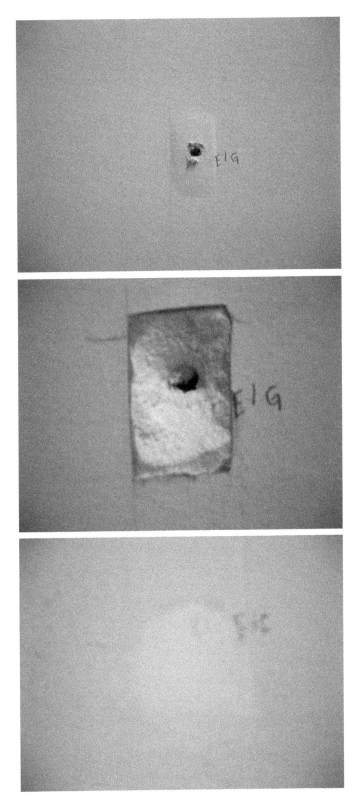

FIGURE 5   A photographic sample of hole repairs. Copyright J. Preston 2009.

and bundled on palettes according to grades of moisture susceptibility, these uniform plates prefigure a future interior. In contrast, my semi-unskilled labor highlighted plaster's propensity to elude regulation: the fine plaster dust permeated my pores, caked my nasal passages, and infiltrated every nook and cranny of the room. There was no escaping it, no containing it. Shallow reliefs of plaster (also known as "holidays") made visible in the low angle of the morning sun exposed my inexperience at wielding the trowel. Each hole revealed a unique character and a point of difference. And yet, as the performance progressed, each hole was absorbed back into the matrix of the wall in allegiance with the normative values inculcated by the dominant forces of an industrialized economy. In this way, restoring the wall's smooth, flat, and seamless surface is an act that erases difference as it upholds the status quo.

EXPRESSING

"Speak. Say everything that comes to you. Just as it comes to you, right here, now. Don't omit or exclude anything. Don't worry about contradictions or conventions. Don't organize what you say. Etc."[13]

During the performative installation, I read aloud excerpts from various texts on the subject of neutrality and allied topics addressing concepts of whiteness, standardization, uniformity, universality, and what is generic and normal. Donning a white dust coat, I stood at the far end of the room, my back to the camera and window, my face to the door and anyone that might (dare) enter. The video audibly recorded these readings and visually recorded the surface of the white coat animated by my breathing. At first my reading voice was edged by angry protest. Despite publicity generated by posters, e-mail invitations, and word of mouth, I was very much aware that I was shouting to an ungathered audience. As the day wore on, I grew increasingly weary and indifferent to whether anyone was listening at all. I took note of the words I was expressing—how my mouth shaped them, how my breath regulated their flow, how enunciation changed their meaning, and how my hand movements embellished their articulation. The surface and volume of the room echoed, absorbed, and rattled in syncopation with my voice, which was now lighter, more coy, more varied in intonation. Visitors entered, lingered, even leaned against the walls to listen. I would like to think that these orations practiced Luce Irigaray's call to use speech as enunciation machinery against a form of gendered neutrality hidden in language.[14] Using the room and its surfaces as a site to pitch a verbal protest privileged "the mother tongue," where the voice of speech is an "instrument of (re)production, as vehicle, or as object" that crosses from the inside to the outside of discourse.[15] The readings were no longer texts written for academic consumption in the detached, disinterested, and disengaged voice of proper social science research. They were no longer harnessed by objectivity's aspiration "to knowledge that bears no traces of the knower-knowledge unmarked by prejudice or skill, fantasy or judgement, wishing or striving. Objectivity is blind sight, seeing without inference, interpretation or intelligence."[16] I subverted the neutered language of these texts through the accent, amplitude, range, inflection, intensity, timbre, and volume of speech projected from my body into the room. At times this enunciation machinery extended out into the corridor and the studio space beyond the office. This transition of voice demonstrates Gui Bonsiepe's statement, gendered as it is, that "as soon as he begins to give it concrete shape, to bring it within the range of experience, the process of rhetorical infiltration begins."[17]

If rhetoric is the art of using language so as to persuade or influence others as well as the body of rules observed by a speaker or writer in order that she may express herself with eloquence, it must necessarily extend to communication via aesthetic visual and material objects. Though Kinross speaks specifically to information design, he reinforces my reasoning:

> [This is] a simple reminder that nothing is free of rhetoric, that visual manifestations emerge from particular historical circumstances, that ideological vacuums do not exist. In the context of the present rather intensely charged and volatile political atmospheres of even the "stable" Western nations, it may not be necessary to labor such truths. The rhetorical interlarding that these cultures effect in their material and visual production hardly needs decoding. That is certainly so if one thinks of the more blatant products of the Western cultures of consumption.... Therefore, we need to keep awake, applying our critical intelligences outside, as well as inside, ... questioning and resisting.[18]

It follows, then, that even a wall surface is capable of rousing a political rally to question the neutrality of commonly accepted design aesthetics. So, how might an interior surface speak? Does it do it at the bidding of a human hand, the maker, who, in the making, invests meaning into mute or dead materials? Or does this action summon expression latently residing in a product's material interior substance? Jacques Rancière assists in arguing the point:

> A "surface" is not simply a geometric composition of lines. It is a distribution of the sensible. For Plato, writing and painting were equivalent surfaces of mute signs, deprived of the breath that animates and transports living speech. Flat surfaces, in this logic, are not opposed to depth in the sense of three-dimensional surfaces. They are opposed to the "living". The mute surface of depicted signs stands in opposition to the act of "living" speech, which is guided by the speaker towards an appropriate addressee.... In opposition to the Platonic degradation of mimesis, the classical poets of representation wanted to endow the "flat surface" with speech or with a "scene" of life, with a specific depth such as the manifestation of an action, the expression of interiority, or the transmission of meaning.[19]

Engendering eloquent surfaces, manifesting a "scene" of life, I profess, is one of the mainstays of an interior design practice. The selection and specification of fabrics, paints, textures, and materials occupy the normative activities of the discipline. Orchestrating the spatial arrangement of these surfaces is a craft that draws on professional expertise. These attributes of interior design target more than competent provision of services;

these are interior design's oratory tools. For example, what could be more rhetorical than the use of color? As Kinross exclaims, "Color is perhaps like music: It can play on our senses. How, we do not quite know. But suddenly we are seduced. And is not this a rhetorical manoeuvre, in the sense of a set of rules for making information eloquent and more easily understandable, and then—more than this—for sweetening it and slipping it down our throats?"[20] Though Kinross's statement emphasizes the power of color to invoke pleasure, as a persuasive tool, it also has equal capacity to influence and punctuate social values including prejudice.

The seemingly benign use of neutral colors in interiors as a tactic to increase spaciousness and sales and "create a blank canvas" raises cause for concern. Diana Young's article "The Material Value of Colour: The Estate Agent's Tale" reveals the depths to which neutrality as a preferred aesthetic language permeates popular culture. It is here that the neutrality insinuated by shades of gray in Western science has been overturned for a fashionable hue of impersonal whiteness in Western interior environments.[21] As Young's interviews with estate agents attest, those hues signify a state of cleanliness associated with good morals and a high level of maintenance. Young writes:

> The "blank canvas" nature of walls of beige, white, magnolia or cream minimizes their material presence....In the critical discourses of modern architecture, white surface first becomes "natural" and then gradually becomes just surfaces, all references to colors ceasing. Whiteness has become a "given" of modernist history....At the point of sale or rent, colour is too personal, too emotive, and too problematic and can only mar the product, making it appear unnatural and irrational compared with the socially acceptable, genderless, given currency of neutrality as well as producing the unfortunate effect of binding the property to its vendor.[22]

This practice of using color as a rhetorical tool to erase the particularity of human presence incites a collection of critical descriptors: efficient, sobering, serious, frugal, fearful, oppressive, subduing, passive, tranquil, undemanding, "hovering on the brink of disappearance," and, most germane to my protest, "embodying a socially constructed rationality."[23] Many passionate arguments have been made around race as a dominant form of whiteness, a convenient construct of deep-seated discriminating economic and material practices that are "designed to ensure long-term survival of the culture's worldview."[24] While the use of neutral colors may prove liberating within a housing market, the perception of skin color has quite a contrary effect. Speaking to the subject of architecture and equity with a specific focus on whiteness, Craig Wilkins identifies "*whiteness* as a historical and socially produced concept that works to grant or deny different life opportunities. It is argued that *whiteness* is a form of cultural capital, similar to economic capital, and concludes that becoming aware of the advantage that *whiteness* provides is a necessary requirement to challenging it....As such, *whiteness* is often discursively hidden within concepts like neutrality or universality."[25] Whether the pigment of paint or skin, it appears that color is far from just neutral. As the preeminent tone of assumed neutrality, white and whiteness are shown to mask dirt, prejudice, imperfection, and political values operating behind and on the surface (Plate 4).

A trip to my local paint shop confirmed what is obvious to every interior designer faced with specifying colors: white is more of an idea than a reality. Every white or neutral paint sample I looked at had a hint of another color in it. Each sample I tested on the room's existing walls incited a visual phenomenal riot as it reacted with the colors in the carpet, my jersey, the facade of the building across the street, and so on.

PERSUADING

What was contentious in this performative installation?

The installation was a protest against neutrality as a common and unquestioned brand in contemporary culture. At a personal level, I was protesting a mandate made by my employer that used workplace equity policies to withdraw support for my individual development as an academic researcher. This form of neutrality upholds equal treatment for all at the expense of the pursuit of excellence for one, mediocrity in the disguise of fairness. At a professional level, this performative installation sought to expose the degree to which interiors are governed by the standard industrial materials with which they are constructed. Twenty-eight years of experience as a design practitioner and educator reinforce my opinion that the specifying of construction materials, installation processes, fixtures, and finishes does not typically engender consideration of their political inclinations nor question the ethics of the values on which they are grounded. These processes and products are so readily available and frequently upheld as exemplars of "good design" in popular and professional journals that the willpower to resist employing them is weak. This protest was about bringing this to bear, making this obvious.

Neutral, Not So was also an experiment using my laboring body and the surface of the interior to mount a public and spatial demonstration. To do this necessitated reenacting the forms of neutrality at play in the use of simple and banal building products, repairing them in line with the manufacturer's instructions and matching the color through trial and error. In one sense, my performance was not unique in that all around the world on any given day the same task is repeated by many other laborers yet without the spectacle of academic discourse orated as if it were poetry.

This creative work also draws significantly from Mark Wigley's book *White Walls, Designer Dresses,* which recharts canonical histories of modern architecture in relation to whiteness, surface, and fashion. He uncovers the spatial politics of suppression and oppression in the guise of cultural codes to what is ordinary, standard, and apparently acceptable. His cause, in part, was for architecture to recognize that it is clothing and that the default "fragile coat of white" was a dissimulation of "architectural discourse's institutionalized opposition to dissimulation."[26] Even as I revisited this book once more, looking for Wigley's definitive position on neutrality, I was struck by the tangled and multifaceted weave of the situation. He writes:

> It is not a question of the idiosyncratic and suspect desires of particular architects and historians. Rather, it is a question of the institutionalized logic that they simply reinforce and exploit. Indeed, it is the very ordinariness of such statements that marks their

force. It is the taken for granted status of these structural biases that is aligned with the white wall. They are its props. The wall can only be taken for granted when these biases are operational.[27]

Despite enduring efforts to render neutrality as fair, equitable, and unbiased, the evidence suggests neutrality may at best signal noncommitment, refusal or inability to make a choice, or it may offer a place of safe hiding. This is not the chapter that will rectify that situation by introducing a new definition or big idea, nor is the installation meant to offer a solution in terms of an aesthetic design practice. What it does do, however, is augment the existing literature with more doubt and disbelief in neutrality's own character—to be distant, uninvolved, dispassionate, without opinion, nonpositioned. It does underscore the fact that interiors are political environments and their material construction and historical interrogation are anything but neutral. Though it was written specific to the context of race and whiteness, I wish to invoke Lesley Naa Norle Lokko's question as a closing: "What are the implications—and alternatives—for both the maker and the product, if the vision [of neutrality] is no longer shared and the language no longer tolerable?"[28] I hope that I have persuaded you to at the very least add this provocation to your interior design practice as it might inform, even infect, how and what materials you specify, how your designs shape environments that might buy into paradigms that reinforce nominal, generic, standard, homogeneous space and therefore extend those qualities to the occupation of those spaces and places (Fig. 6).

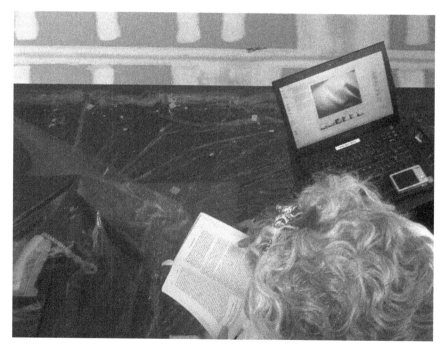

FIGURE 6   A view of the performative installation in progress. Copyright J. Preston 2009.

10

A Short History of the Room

FRED SCOTT

PART I: FORMATION

There is something in theory which hates the wall.

Colin Rowe talking at the Architectural Association in the 1970s
(paraphrasing Robert Frost)

There was once an equivalence between the art of the exterior and the art of the interior; there was also a separateness. The decline in the status of interior design since the eighteenth century parallels the decline of the room in architectural thought over the same period. The tendencies in theory were those that weakened the practice of interior design by detaching it from architectural thinking, and this was accomplished through the relegation of the idea of the room.

The room in classical buildings relies on being enclosed and connected in an orderly manner to other rooms and to the exterior, by regularly spaced doors and windows, and by a system of axes or sometimes disrupted axes. This in turn allows for a program of ornamentation to be implemented, particular to an individual room and with its own particular foci. *Ornamentation* and *order* are said to have the same etymological origin. The shape of the room is to a certain extent independent of other rooms and the exterior form of the building. This independence is mediated through the thickness of the structure, the rooms being allowed a certain freedom to slip and slide, and to acquire a variety of shapes for the walls and for the ceilings as the house is coming into being.

The equivalence between the design of the interior and the exterior is evident in the work of the Adam brothers, particularly in the designs for houses and mansions built in and around London during the latter part of the eighteenth century. With them, the practice of interior design achieved a new status.

They devised and developed a light and generally cheerful manner of decoration derived from antique sources that they had studied in Italy, a beautiful paraphrase transforming the august sobriety of the ancients into a gorgeous setting for everyday life, albeit designing houses for an exclusively elite and aristocratic clientele. The scheme of ornamentation in these houses is the spatial ordering of the rooms.

Robert is generally thought to have been the greater architectural talent. Among his other achievements, in central London his plans for the Lord Derby House and the Winfred Wynn House show his genius at adapting Renaissance axial planning into a sequence of stopped views and side-stepped axes to make a circuit, an architectural promenade within narrower frontages, so as to support the diverse social life of the houses, as well as, in the same plan, enfolding the space to allow also a graceful retreat into the more private rooms. This is how Robin Middleton describes Robert Adam's style:

> Something of this more dynamic approach to internal spaces suffuses the architecture of…Robert Adam. Adam composed his interiors as a succession of related spaces, one counterpointing the next, together making up an organic whole. His volumes, though geometrically related, were designed to be approached from oblique and unusual angles. The most celebrated example of his diagonal planning is the relationship between the second and third drawing rooms on the first floor of Derby House. London of 1773 to 1774, which he commissioned Benedetto Pastorini to record for the second volume of his Works in Architecture (1779). This view, showing the extension of space beyond the third drawing room into the Countess of Derby's dressing room, is unparalleled in contemporary architectural publications. The drama of the view, depicted in all its richness of light and shade, is new to eighteenth century conventions of domestic decorum. Other examples might be adduced, such as the arrangement of rooms on the first floor of Home House, 20 Portman Square, of 1773 to 1776, where the rooms form a circuit.[1]

Although the Adam brothers were not the first to build London terrace (or row) houses—Bedford Square was begun in 1744—nevertheless they made a significant contribution to its evolution, in particular in the contrasting of the decorated interior with the plainness of the exterior, which some have compared with how the English bourgeoisie like to consider themselves: outwardly calm and reserved, and inwardly possessed of a surprising and fanciful imagination.

Perhaps the greatest surviving works are the interventions into the two great medieval houses at Osterley and Syon House, both on the west side of London. The Etruscan room at Osterley and the use of Roman columns, dredged from the Tiber and purchased especially for the room at Syon, make direct reference to the antique inspiration for this new style of ornamentation.

Both are manifestations of the great social and political upsurge in England and in other parts of Europe. The neoclassical movement in England was adopted by sections of the ruling class as the mantle of their radicalism. To say that the English aristocracy adopted radicalism in order to avoid the fate of the French aristocrats at the hands of the Revolution is at once to simplify and disparage their motives.

It is important to understand the intense role that style played in the lives of the elite at this time, affecting all manner of things and behavior: thin dresses worn wet so that they clung in imitation of the Greek female statues of antiquity, particular stances adopted and postures of walking in supposed imitation of the golden ancient days. Political beliefs and appearances were fused in a way that we would find difficult to admit to today.

The Soane Museum at Nos. 12, 13, & 14, Lincoln's Inn Fields, London, is currently in danger of becoming all things to all architects, but it is reasonable to claim that within it can be found crucial examples of the demise of the room in architectural thought and deed.

Philip Johnson once referred to Sir John Soane as a "ceiling" architect. This is a partial and flippant remark that contains a nugget of truth. Soane's most famous ceiling, the one in the Breakfast Room in his house in Lincoln's Inn Fields, shows his mastery at using a seemingly floating canopy, connected to the sky by its lantern, to fragment and at the same time focus the space beneath it. Its geometric purity is experientially detached from the enclosing walls by the use of mirrors, internal windows, and roof lights hidden around and above its edge that flood the walls with light, making it appear sometimes as if the ceiling is afloat in the open air. This impression is reinforced by the room being sited with voids on three sides, beyond its walls: the stairwell to the south, the courtyard to the east, and the great dome over the sarcophagus on the north side.

After the tragic sequence of events that began in 1815 with the published attack on his buildings, written anonymously but quickly discovered to be by Soane's youngest son, the architect seemed to gain new resolution with regard to the completion of his museum. The loss of his wife from a broken heart and of his eldest son from tuberculosis, the permanent estrangement from the other son, and disappointments in his professional life seem to have given him a strange strength and focus, but at what a cost. The museum can have been carried forward only through an obsessive concentration; this must have been accompanied by a certain withdrawal from the public realm.

At the museum in Lincoln's Inn Field, one may compare two ideas of the arrangement of interior space in premodernist architecture. These one might call the static apprehension of space and the somatic apprehension of space. One might go on to characterize them as follows: the enfilade of the axis versus the *promenade architecturale,* the captivating set piece contrasted to the slow unfolding of spaces as one moves through them, allowing the play of clarity and obscurity, of view and denial, the sequence of incidents during the passage through the building.

The back galleries of the house, which contain the museum proper, house the collection Soane assembled during his lifetime. He had an abiding interest in funerary vases, and an enormous collection of plaster casts of details from classical buildings, hung from every available surface. The late curator Sir John Summerson once commented how different the museum looks when all the pieces are taken down for refurbishment, how it reveals the taut geometry of the underlying architectural form and Soane's continuing attachment to neoclassicism. He also said how wonderful the "handkerchief" ceiling in the Breakfast Room looked with the four bull's-eye mirrors removed, and how he thought this was evidence that Soane could never stop tinkering, even to the detriment of a particular space. Middleton has written of the museum as an episode in the history of fragmentation, leading perhaps from the baroque, the basketwork domes of Turin, to the cubists and the buildings of Louis Kahn.[2]

Paul Shepheard said that at one time, architectural decoration came off the walls and turned into possessions. The Soane Museum would seem to mark this point. One can read it as architecture shedding its decorated skin; the fragments of the classical world appear to hover like the ghost of a ruined antiquity, in front of the plain, strict, true geometry that from a particular point of view underlies the world. Here, surely, is a precursor of modernity, the impulse to distillation and clarification, the exposing of fundamentals and the wiping clean of the surface.

It is easy to picture Soane retreating into the back spaces in his later years, haunting the house at any hour. The green-coated custodians of the museum will tell you that he took to wearing a monk's habit. One imagines his spirit descending on selected subsequent curators, the two Sir John's who become indiscernible one from another as one listens to the custodians' tale. In another way Soane may be thought of as prototypically modern, as the increasingly private individual, alone in the house. And also in a way, one might think of the extensive use of mirrors as having a social as well as a spatial intention. As visitors thread their way around the building, they will intermittently catch glimpses of another, which turns out to be themselves. In this way Soane, who had grown up in an earlier age of populous houses, could give himself the affect of company without the inconvenience of the presence of others.

The Picture Gallery was one of the last rooms completed, at the rear of No. 14. It is remarkable for its ingenuity as a device for displaying a large number of pictures in a restricted space: the walls fold out to show new layers of the collection, and the strongest impact comes when the final opening breaches the integrity of the room and opens it to the void over the Monk's Parlour and beyond, past the female figure into the exterior of the Monument Court, and thus out into the indefinite.

At the same period in Revolutionary France, similar formal trends can be seen in the great building projects for the new Revolutionary Society, quintessentially in the colossal project for the *Cenotaph to Newton* by Etiénne-Louis Boullee of 1784. Here is architectural space associating itself with the discovery of the infinite, and thus aligning itself with rational scientific thought as the new atheistic basis for society. Boullee here gives clear architectural expression to the new sense of space as immeasurable. The contradiction is that the monument had to encapsulate space to do so, to render the new unifying sensibility in secret so to speak, reached along a long tunnel hidden from the established ordering of architectural space, which was of sequence and axes.

The seriousness of the undertaking, if nothing else, purges the built form of decoration. In addition, it seems that the idea of the infinite, which also contains the idea of transparency, requires a plain surface. Boullée called decoration the sterile riches of classical architecture.

Following the visionary projects of Claude-Nicolas Ledoux and Boullee, the more sober Jean-Nicolas-Louis Durand undertook a rational analysis of total architecture. Under the onslaught of his encyclopedic examination, the body of architecture withers. The corpulent form that permitted the room to have its own integrity within the plan, mediated through the thickness of the structure, becomes insupportable to the rational mind; the structure sheds its corporality. The new rationality had dissolved the ancient enclosure; the only reasonable division of infinite space is via the grid and the thin wall or screen, the back tightly corresponding with the front.[3] But France, riding on the wave of Revolution, was in advance of England in these matters throughout the first half of the nineteenth century.

The Soane Museum is perhaps the last of those houses that can be thought of as part of the public realm of the city. When Soane acquired the Sarcophagus, he gave a three-day-long party. After this, the house began to become a place of retreat and the private realm, where matters of style and taste had a different status. This shifting status is evident in the comparison of the different campaigns of two opposite designers. Both Augustus Pugin and William Morris promoted the adoption of the Gothic style, and both argued from widely different political points of view that the necessary reform of society can be achieved only through the institution of this style. Pugin was a devout Catholic convert, politically an archconservative; Morris was a socialist who became progressively more radical throughout his life.

Morris believed that through the deindustrialization of manufacture, and its replacement by craft guilds, the real and pressing horrors of the condition of the working classes could be assuaged. He believed in the beginning that a socialist utopia could be brought about based on the mutual love and practice of craftsmanship. For him also, the Gothic was an ideal, believing, as the title of the Pre-Raphaelite Brotherhood suggests, that the Renaissance had been a wrong turning in European history.

Newly married and living in the Red House, nicknamed Towers of Topsy after his wife and designed by his friend and political ally Philip Webb, Morris formulated his plan for the new society. A man of huge energies and organizing abilities, he set up a firm to make the furniture that would be imbued with these transfiguring qualities. Inevitably, a visitor one day asked if the working classes bought these products. Morris is recorded as beginning to kick hard the piece of furniture in question and saying, "No, they bloody well don't!"

Pugin in his book *Contrasts*[4] engraved views of a medieval city in 1440 where the poor lived fulsome and happy lives, under the patronage of kindly religious establishments, contrasted with the same town in 1840, composed of modern neoclassical buildings, institutions such as the Socialist Hall of Science, a city where the poor suffered a short and brutal existence, incarcerated in life and unmourned at death.

In 1875 Lord Bute commissioned Pugin's disciple William Burges to design a house in the form of a medieval dream castle, Castle Coch in the Taff Valley in South Wales. The house was raised on the existing ruins of the thirteenth-century Red Castle. Lord

Bute was thought to be the richest man in the world. His wealth came from the collieries he owned, mining the rich anthracite seams beneath the hills of the region. Life expectancy among the working classes during the height of what is called the Industrial Revolution rarely exceeded thirty years.

Burges was instructed to ensure that no coal mine would be visible from the castle. In the dining room he built into the floor at the entrance an oubliette. *Oublier* is the French verb for "to forget." This was a open-topped square hole covered by a grill, an imitation of a medieval device within which the lord's enemy, once captured, would be imprisoned and then forgotten as the household moved across the grill in and out of the dining room. Of course the client never used it for this purpose; he did, however contribute in part to Burges's beliefs in the revival of Medievalism, by the wearing of mock monks' clothing devised by the architect.

It may be a later reading of these times, but one can discern an emergent tendency in the case of Lord Bute, and in such novels as *Against Nature* by Joris-Karl Huysmans, to twin the room with solitude, with withdrawal, a place of refuge from progress at least, a shelter for the reactionary. The contrast is with the matrix of rooms that made up the Adam brothers houses, which were blatantly devised to support sociability. It is perhaps in this phase that the idea of the cell, later refined by Le Corbusier, enters the secular domain from the realms of the religious retreat and penitentiary.

So somehow, somewhere, the power of architectural style had shifted and diminished, as evidenced by the contradictory applications recalled here. Probably society had become more diffuse since Robert Adam's day, with incipient democracies indicating the emergence of a protomodern society. In the second half of the nineteenth century, taste and power were no longer the preserve of a minuscule elite. As the nineteenth century drew to a close, incipient modernism was preparing to sweep all other theories of architectural form before it, matching everywhere the spread of enfranchisement. The principal victim of this advance was to be the architectural identity and significance of the room. Its passing is marked with the loss of the ceiling as a coherent component within spatial composition.

PART II: DEMISE

The three attributes of modernism, which are transparency, commitment to a social program, and the pure surface, can be traced as they emerge following the French Revolution. They increase in intensity because of the political and tectonic advances of the nineteenth century and reach their full synthesis with the publication of Le Corbusier's *Vers une Architecture.*[5] With this they gain a moral imperative akin to inevitability. At the beginning of the "Eyes Which Do Not See" section, he proclaims:

A great epoch has begun.
There exists a new spirit.
There exists a mass of work in the new spirit, conceived in the new spirit; it is to be met with particularly in industrial production.

Architecture is stifled by custom.

The "styles" are a lie.

Style is a unity of principle animating all the work of an epoch, the result of a state of mind which has its own special character.

Our own epoch is determining, day by day, its own style.

Our eyes, unhappily, are unable yet to discern it.[6]

> Towards a New Architecture Le Corbusier, English translation by
> Frederick Etchells, London The Architectural Press. 1927 p. 82.

Le Corbusier believed that architecture had a key role in the evolution of the new age that he saw in a vision being born, from the union of anonymous mechanization and pure geometry. The book is like a poem as much as it is a reasoned argument; it is a magical attempt to copy the future. It ends with a photograph of a briar pipe, with the admonition above it: "Architecture or Revolution. Revolution can be avoided."

The modernist crusade is, of course, broad and multifaceted; the constructivists in Russia, the Bauhaus in Germany, and De Stijl in the Netherlands. All aspects of the modernist program are dependent on a surface purged of decoration. Its preparation was begun in the previous age. One sees with the visionary projects of the French Revolution, the projects by Ledoux and Boullee as previously noted, a concerted reaction against the decorated surface, reacting perhaps with clear intention against the decorative systems of ornamentation that typify rococo interiors, and thus the architecture of the ancien régime.

The impulse from the beginning is to identify the superfluous and to discard it. The excesses and the pileup of styles, the rabid eclecticism of the late nineteenth century, obviously required reform, but one might say that a reform was achieved with the emergence of the Arts and Crafts movements and art nouveau. And yet both of these were to be blown aside, marginalized by those who insisted again on a nondecorated form and surface, first Adolf Loos, and after him Le Corbusier, and after them the whole cult of modernism. The dismissal of decoration may be supposed to be the beginning of a search for fundamentals, and in the twentieth century the apostles of the fundamental are legion: Loos, Le Corbusier in the Lessons of Rome from *Vers une Architecture,* Ginsburg, Cezanne, and Mondrian. All of modernism's triumphs, the Bauhaus, De Stijl, the constuctivists, depend above all things on the plain surface.[7]

The most well-known attack written by Adolf Loos in 1908 is *Ornament and Crime.*[8] It begins thus:

> In the womb the human embryo goes through all phases of development the animal kingdom has passed through. And when a human being is born, his sense impressions are like a new born dog's. In childhood he goes through all changes corresponding to the stages in the development of humanity. At two he sees with the eyes of a Papuan, at four with those of a Germanic tribesman, at six of Socrates, at eight of Voltaire. At eight he becomes aware of violet, the colour discovered by the eighteenth century; before that, violets were blue and the purple snail was red....

The urge to decorate one's face and anything else within reach is the origin of the fine arts. It is the childish babble of painting. But all art is erotic.

A person of our times who gives way to the urge to daub the walls with erotic symbols is a criminal or degenerate. What is natural in the Papuan or the child is a sign of degeneracy in the modern adult. I made the following discovery, which I passed on to the world: *the evolution of culture is synonymous with the removal of ornamentation from objects of everyday use.*

Loos's own contribution to the dismantling of the autonomous room is the theory of *Raumplan* (spatial planning). This is a term applied later by his followers to describe the architect's attitude to the house and its plan. He himself said the following, in a footnote to the obituary for his favorite furniture maker: "This is the great revolution in architecture: the solution of the plan in space.... Just as mankind will eventually succeed in playing chess in a cube, so too other architects will, in the future, solve the plan in space." And in the last year of his life, he wrote, "I do not design plans, facades, sections, I design space. Actually there is neither a ground floor, an upper floor or a basement, there are merely interconnected spaces, vestibules, terraces.... One must connect the spaces with one another so that the transition is unnoticeable and natural, but also the most practical." This is more than an aesthetic argument; it addresses the nature of society itself.

Transparency in twentieth-century architecture is the medium for the expression of the spatial ethos of infinitude. In some ways it may be considered as an ultimate inversion of the once supposed purposes of architecture, that is, the separating of public and private realms, of the intimate from the anonymous, the solitary from the group.

One might think of transparency's emergence as the straightforward exploitation by architects of certain tectonic developments in the late nineteenth and early twentieth centuries. However, one might also think of transparency as properly appropriate only to Utopia, for a world where privacy and decorum have withered and fallen from use.

As Le Corbusier claimed, if with a typically disingenuous manner, in the modern house the exterior is the result of the interior; the relative independence of exterior and interior as manifest in classical architecture is at this point lost. The room itself is abandoned, and all that is left is the "cell," the denatured room, designated by the great man as "the biological necessity," referring, one supposes, to the purposes of sleep and reproduction, and thus just admissible within the house of the new age.

But no one can regret the loss of the room as the generator of the plan, can they? No one now would banish the modernist interpenetration of space, or the glories of transparency, to trade them for the old fixed plan, would they?

Transparency is a way to signify spatial continuum; it suggests that architectural compositions are insertions into the continuum, in recognition and support of it, appearing at least to eschew finality and enclosure. Accordingly, such insertions need to be seen as incidents within the larger schema, rather than entities and conclusions. The house now is expected to be apprehended free of enclosure, all parts seen at once. It carries with it a cubist simultaneity. Theo Van Doesburg's diagrams most clearly denote this.[9] On the tentative but wide-ranging aims of modernism, Gerrit Rietveld writes:

I prefer to see the practice of architecture as a sober self-maintenance than as a hypocritical piety.
Life as a whole is like a balance eternally looking for its centre of gravity.
From this standpoint I see architecture more as a tenuous equilibrium than as an unshakable monumentality!
Each work is only a part of the unending expressional possibilities; and an attempt toward completeness in a single work would injure the harmony.
These words are not truths but are attempts toward orientation.[10]

As Ed Hollis pointed out to me in a recent conversation, transparency is ideological. The aesthetic is consequential to this. I admit to emulating a certain North London football team in my pursuit of the subject, and here the open goal is brought to my attention, with my embarrassed thanks. The ideology has at its heart the uncertain search for the Utopia, outside of the assumed certainties of Marxism. This is the reason for persistence; it is deeper than simply a habit, our inability to lasso space in the classical manner, to enclose and compartmentalize, to treat the room as an entity with any conviction. It is that the interpenetration of spaces, the close association of interior and exterior, stands to somehow assure our equality and freedom, to signify that our fates no longer are detailed in the salons of distant authority. It is interconnectivity, and it similarly resists completion, so evading mirror symmetry in favor of asymmetry.

In practice, in the densities of cities, the problems of the everyday are obvious and manifest. Experientially it has qualities that are perhaps not often noted. The spatial continuity made possible by glass walls is available to only one of our senses. In truth the suppression of the other senses, the environmental division between inside and out, the differences in heat, sound, and humidity, is essential to our aesthetic appreciation of transparency. I seem to remember "trance" being once described as the suppression of all the senses apart from sight, and so it is that this appreciation has enchantment in it, and, because of this, traces of a dreamlike detachment from what one observes beyond the sheets of glass. In addition, with nightfall, transparent surfaces pass through a zone of disorientating ambiguity before, with darkness, the surfaces become as mirrors, establishing another different unreal infinity.

The full adoption of transparency relies on the banishment of both privacy and private property. In a less than Utopian society, it may be that transparency acquires a pathological dimension, a distinct corruption of Utopian aspirations. For instance, Robin Evans once said, referring to the Farnsworth House, that to live in a transparent house, one would need also to own the encircling landscape.[11] As it is, the cell is the consequence and the contradiction of transparency. It renders all human activities as seemingly furtive. It is intended for a specified use, for a particular function, eating, sleeping, sitting, and as such cells are the foot soldiers of functionalism.[12] The cell, the minimal enclosure, is the apparatus of the social program in architecture, of the association with the forces of reform, in particular of the house and housing. The engagement between aesthetic and social program has been an area of many difficulties in practice; indeed, the modern housing block may be the exhausted outcome of transparency and the cell struggling to find resolution.

The simple point of it all is this: the classical room had to be set aside to permit the establishment of the modernist aesthetic; universal space seeks to eradicate all sense of containment. The once separate arts of the interior and the exterior become untenable within the tenets of space as continuum, and the sense of interpenetration of exterior and interior. The idea of the room is inimical to the idea of transparency. They represent two different and opposed senses of spatiality. The art of the interior as an independent activity was relegated by developments in architectural theory in the twentieth century. What remained was interior decoration, which is not an inconsiderable practice and within which much can be achieved, but it too has been left behind by developments, to become perpetually peripheral and minor. To regain parity with the architect, the designer must redefine his or her craft as the art of intervening, of colonizing existing structures, of introducing new life into old buildings. As we must be contemporary—that is, we have the same legacy as architects—and as, in truth, the difficulty of working with the contrary natures of room and spatial continuity may occur more often in working on an existing building than in making a new one, the interior designer might therefore consider this as his or her territory, this entangled, unresolved conundrum of free space and enclosure.

The question of spatiality lies at the heart of all true works of intervention; without its consideration, the work is restricted to surface, to the not-inconsiderable realm of interior decoration. In the question of adaptation and reuse, one can readily envisage the condition where a new strategy of intervention provokes an attempted conflation of these conflicting concepts of spatiality and one can see that in the successful realization of such strategies, the art with which this amalgam or fusion of opposites is made is the key. It is the deepest difficulty, recognized and resolved in the plan through the most concentrated effort of design, ingenuity, and integrity. It is the reconciliation that finally in the end justifies the breaking of the host building at the outset. But in this initial act may be the clue to a resolution.

As I have written elsewhere, the idea of ruin is one in which the modernist and the classical might find a vehicle of coexistence in certain aspects.[13] For instance, the ruin shares with modernism a tendency to transparency, an architectonic explicitness, and a loss of decoration but it may also contain traces of the familiar arrangement of rooms, aligned in an axial manner. The idea of ruination may be a key concept in allowing a deeper integration of new and existing built form, and transparency may act as an important medium in this transposition. The essence of the ruin is incompleteness.

Here, then, is a suggestion that in the idea of the ruin, in the concept of the ruin as being addressed to the future as well as to the past, there is a potent medium for the realization of the union of contrasting spatial arrangements. This is a direction that can encourage coherence, and from which a rich complexity can arise, a depth of assimilation that might be the true measure of the work of adaptation and reuse.

11

New Occupancy

LORRAINE FARRELLY

Stripping back in its extended manifestation is the process by which the interventional designer acquires an understanding of the host building with which she or he is engaged. It is to the end of developing a structured affinity, as a preparation for the correspondence between their work and the existing. The host building needs to be understood intrinsically and in terms of its setting and to be looked at in terms of its actualities and provenance. This is an enquiry that will have both architectural and socio economic aspects.

—*F. Scott, On Altering Architecture, 2007*

The idea of reusing and reinventing existing buildings is a key consideration for contemporary designers, whether that is at the scale of a house, a skyscraper, or a whole section of a city. We need to work with what we have; the context presents the opportunities as well as the limitations for the brief. Therein lies the challenge to an interior architect and designer, architect, or urban designer: the opportunity to transform what exists, to make it relevant for our contemporary use, to think creatively about reuse of space, materials, and structures. Sometimes, and as the quote by Fred Scott cited at the start of this chapter suggests, this requires stripping something back almost to a structural frame, in order to then move forward and create new spaces for new activities to take place. This means that in a remodeled building, one that has been adapted in order to accept a new use, the new forms of occupancy will quite often draw on the vagaries of the host building. What the existing building has to offer will no doubt influence the remodeling of the space for its new use.

   This chapter explores various exemplars of new build and remodeled space in order to examine the useful or influential factors that can be utilized to create contemporary interior space and facilitate new forms of occupancy. There are important considerations when a new interior project is to be devised inside a new build project, and the significant issues for the designer when the project is but a line drawn on a page or an outline of an idea on a computer screen. It examines three case studies that have resulted in new learning spaces, interiors where new forms of occupancy are taking place that prioritize place making and inhabitation, in the processes of making space.

SPIRIT OF PLACE

Whether new build or remodeled project, the spirit or "phenomenon" of a place is an important and influential factor in its conception and subsequent development.

> What then do we mean with the word place? Obviously we mean something more than an abstract location. We mean a totality made up of concrete things having material substance, shape, texture and colour. Together these things determine an environmental character which is the essence of place.[1]

The notion of a spirit "inhabiting" a place recalls the concept of genius loci as defined as the "spirit of place." This normally refers to the scale of an urban context but can be applied to the interior of a building as well. Christian Norberg-Schulz first developed the idea of genius loci in the late 1960s when he published his seminal text in *Existence, Space and Architecture.*[2] In *Genius Loci: Towards a Phenomenology of Architecture,* published in 1979, he evolved the concept of dwelling, as considered by Martin Heidegger in "Building Dwelling Thinking," alongside genius loci and used it to define the particular processes and phenomena of making a place. Norberg-Schulz stated that "a concrete term for environment is *place.* It is common usage to say that acts and occurrences *take place.* In fact it is meaningless to imagine any happening without reference to a locality. Place is evidently an integral part of existence."[3]

He defined a *place* as a space with character and as somewhere that events occur. A place was a total phenomenon that was not easily reduced to its component parts, yet it had a character that was a result of both quantitative and qualitative definitions. He did not define *place* as an exterior or interior condition and instead suggested it was an environment where its occupant was able to "dwell" meaningfully in a particular place, in other words, an environment where occupant and space could achieve a harmonious "fit." Based on Norberg-Schulz's ideas, it would be logical to conclude that the exterior and the interior are an integral part of the genius loci of a place, inextricably linked, one inside of the other.

In many ways the relationship between inside and outside space could be described in physiological terms; by this I mean that the building could be considered to have a skeleton and a skin: a frame that forms the structure of the space and a membrane that is the outside walls that enclose it. The logical conclusion of this analogy is that the character that defines the building, its spirit that is the interior space of the building, the genius loci of a particular place, as Norberg-Schulz suggests,, then occupies the building. Therefore, whether a new build or a remodeling project, the meaningful new occupancy of a space needs to consider the *spirit* or meaningful condition of the place that is to be inhabited. As Norberg-Schulz goes on to say, "The basic act of architecture is therefore to understand the 'vocation' of the place...to belong to a place means to have an existential foothold."[4]

The outside skin has certain practical requirements to deal with the outside world, creating a shell or shelter from the climate, allowing light in, and keeping temperatures balanced. The building in its site context responds to particular issues of mass, form, materiality, and the scale of its surroundings, whether that context is the surrounding city or a landscape.

Once this scale has been determined, the interior space is defined as a particular area, and then the activities or functions of the interior can begin to occupy that space. Interior and exterior become a seamless experience; the interior spaces create their own context or frames of reference. The building's exterior has to cope with its neighbors; it has to deal with surrounding materials and forms, to define itself on a horizon, in a streetscape. It needs a sort of permanence to endure and establish itself at an urban scale.

On the other hand, the interior can be more self-referential and contained, creating a new sense of scale and identity. It has elements within it that have to have permanence, and others that are temporary and transitional, dealing with the changing expectations that the users have for the space. The functions of the spaces inform decisions regarding the location of furniture, lighting, and so on. Some are fixed elements attached to the building structure and are permanent, and others are more temporary, akin to theatrical props or scenography in the space. The latter are more easily changed as the occupants modify the interior to their own individual needs and requirements.

When the building breaks its boundaries and the interior becomes part of the outside space, that is a condition where unexpected things can happen. Where a wall opens out and the floor surface flows through from the inside to the outside, ambiguity can be created between the interior and the exterior. In this situation the polarity of the interior/exterior relationship is no longer as clearly defined. There is more informality in the way we live and work and use spaces. So the informality of function relating to these spaces requires a spatial language that is informal and temporary, allowing an easy reinterpretation and reorganization of the spaces not only in the physical dimension but also in our visualization and cerebral occupation of these spaces. We need to allow ourselves to "imagine" them as flexible, so we can think of new and unexpected activities. The space must not constrain; it needs to be suggestive of new types of uses and have a dynamic character to it, to suggest new possibilities, new types of social engagement. The space can drive new types of learning spaces; it can stimulate new interactions for thinking and communicating, as well as an experiential learning environment.

Some activities need to be located in a defined inside space for practical reasons, whereas many more activities can happen in more incidental spaces. There is much more informality in contemporary society about the way we live and work, and we need spaces that provide that flexibility—transitory spaces between inside and outside, public and private, transitory and cellular, working separately and collectively. The way we interact and communicate has these varying levels of formality, from a more structured conversation, a presentation, through to informal texting and spontaneous tweeting; our spaces and particularly our social learning spaces can reflect these possibilities.

So one could ask, where does the exterior sense of architecture end and the interior character of the spatial experience begin? If the interior and the exterior are inextricably linked, then is a meaningful inhabitation of the building reliant on seamlessness between both conditions? It is these questions that this chapter sets out to answer in the form of exploring the particular conditions of new occupancy.

UNIVERSITY OF PORTSMOUTH THIRD SPACE

University campuses provide a case study for registering how informal spaces are used and change over the course of a day, semester, and year. The integration of informal spaces provides areas of support for students to learn as they adapt to changing technologies and attitudes. An example of this is the 3rd Space, a space developed by the Project Office at the University of Portsmouth. The idea was that this space existed between the fixed lecture room and the complete informality of a student's study space at home. It needed some formality of "work" but offered group and collective learning spaces. Also, to encourage interaction over relaxation, there is a zone of "interaction" encouraging coffee and conversation. It offers a wireless environment, a space to "play" with Wii and other electronic games. The concept for "work, interaction, and play" corresponds to student modes of interaction and communication. To have an environment that is flexible in its layout and organization, and informal, results in a place that can be "owned" and occupied by students throughout the course of the day.

The site is in the students' union, a relaxation space for students. The brief for the space was that it needed to be flexible, so that space-defining elements such as furniture could be moved away to allow for other functions. Inflatable pods provide that flexibility but also offer a separation for teamwork. The space works informally, and students have appreciated the opportunity to use a space that operates as a new type of social learning space, between work and home. It has also inspired some unexpected activities, as students host fashion shows, debates, and presentations. As it has not become a formal teaching space, there is more spontaneity in terms of student use; they want to use it as a platform to engage with each other.

The way we consider the possibility of "ambiguous space" that can take on any function or character, can be inside or outside, offers more flexibility to us in the way we occupy buildings and the way we can create spaces that can evolve, as we evolve in our ways of working, communicating, and living.

Respect for the history or memory of the past of a space or building is important. As we adapt and change the architecture and spaces we use, there are aspects of the character of those spaces that are useful; they can inform a new design direction, create a starting point for a new conversation with a new "occupier." We need to be careful not to erase the past but to continue elements of it as a legacy for a new occupation of a building.

FIGURE 7   The Third Space is a new social learning environment at the University of Portsmouth. It provides a new type of "common room" for students, an informal place to work individually and collectively. Courtesy of L. Farrelly.

The idea of the palimpsest, an ancient overwritten manuscript, which was scraped back, to be written over again and again, but still had within it some trace of the past, can be a useful consideration when starting to reinvent a building. To allow subtle yet important "traces" to be clear in the new narrative brings invention to the building. There may be material references, such as an important piece of local stone or a wallpaper surface that frames some connection to the past. The connection may be more intrinsic, a structural grid or the geometry of a facade that informs a new design language.

We need to take responsibility for acting as custodians of the past, ensuring the legacy of a building, where it has value, evolves, and has relevance for the present and future. This type of reference to the past needs careful management and editing; there are many references that can be incorporated into a new design, but if there are too many, the new idea becomes overly complicated, complex, and illegible. There needs to be a careful selection, a prioritization of references. This design approach can provide a rich project that has strong visual and conceptual references to an existing building—its material, structure, and context—while also creating a new visual language, a new spatial context that builds on this past. There are many clever examples of refurbishment and redesign of old, tired buildings that have reinvigorated the existing. By pulling out some simple ideas and focusing attention on a new architectural idea, consolidating the influence of the past on the new future of the space or place, a new narrative of the building emerges. This type of creative thinking can transform our understanding of a tired space.

ARCHITECTURE PLB VETERINARY COLLEGE

An example of the reinvention of an outside courtyard to become an inside space is the Royal Veterinary College by the architects of Architecture PLB in London. This building was a series of structures mainly from the 1930s, around an open courtyard. The new scheme has turned this courtyard space into a new informal learning space. A new structure has been inserted into the space that has changed the scale of the space. The structure reads as an element of furniture, an object that is light and playful, juxtaposed with the hard brick walls that were the exterior courtyard but are now the interior edges of the atrium space. The library, museum, and dining spaces surrounding the atrium have been reconnected by this new space, creating a new social center for the campus. The

FIGURE 8 The Royal Veterinary College London courtyard was transformed by Architecture PLB when they inserted a new structure into the space underneath a glazed roof, creating new communal spaces for students. Courtesy of Timothy Soar.

FIGURE 9   The Royal Veterinary College's new structure, a soft, timber-edged space, provides a contrasting scale to the open courtyard, which has protected informal spaces to sit and relax. Courtesy of Timothy Soar.

college wanted informal spaces that contrasted with the organized spaces within the existing building. The new spaces have provided a place to sit, relax, and escape. They provide a viewing platform back into the courtyard, which has become a café beneath.

OXFORD BROOKES UNIVERSITY CAMPUS

An interesting example of the reinvention of a whole series of buildings and spaces is the new Oxford Brookes University Campus by Design Engine Architects. The design project was a campus strategy to take existing buildings and try to reinvent and rationalize a campus idea. The campus site is the reconsideration of the Gypsy Lane Campus Oxford, which comprises buildings of many physical scales and periods.

The concept is to create a new public space facing the main Headington Road, establishing a new gateway to the university and creating a new heart to the campus. The design, in effect, is trying to turn an exterior into an interior. Using fragments of existing buildings and inserting new pieces to create a new character, a new sense of place emerges. The new library and teaching building reinvents a whole city of buildings, using existing facades and creating new connection routes and internal/external space. The intention is to redefine the nature of the corridor, to the scale of the street; to use the geometries of the original 1960s building to create a new geometry that continues right

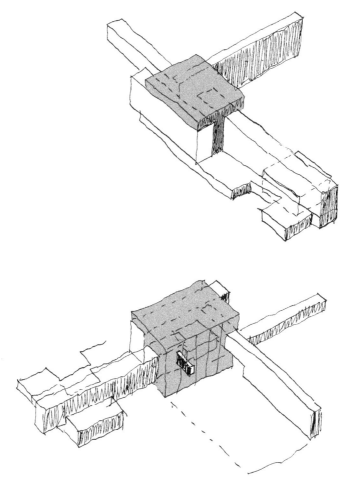

FIGURE 10 These sketches explain the concept of the Oxford Brookes University Campus by Design Engine Architects. The building concept is a series of "pegs" that fix the building on its site. Courtesy of Design Engine Architects.

through to the new applied external facade. Design Engine's architecture is character-ized by a careful interpretation of its sense of place. A subtle understanding of materials, using a carefully selected palette, is applied to shifting scales of space, form, and detail.

The concept for this site is to "fix" the buildings using three "pegs" that hold the buildings onto the site. The pegs are a series of insertions that connect back to a new forum court space and link to the existing infrastructure on the campus, physically and conceptually connecting the new to the old. This concept was delivered in the initial stages of the project and has been an enduring idea for the scheme. These pegs are both physical elements but also metaphorical connections, which is why the decision was made to use the same material inside and outside. The urban-scale idea has connected to the materiality of the large mass of the building forms and also to details of the building and its 1:1 scale.

The project is composed of a series of newly defined external and internal courts; a central anchor building and a set of peg buildings stitch the old and new parts of the campus together: a colonnade building, an extension to the Abercrombie Building, and a new pooled teaching and students' union block. The concept design is to create connections across the campus, to create a significant building that links between other buildings and spaces, some internal or external streets, and other spaces or courtyards, internally or externally. The material sensitivity reflects this ambition.

The scheme was commissioned to redefine the whole campus and identity of the university. It creates new buildings at the scale of the city, new public spaces for students and the city. The spaces within also have been developed at a range of scales; some are civic spaces interfacing between the city and the university, between the open public space and the more intimate cellular office. It is a new language of educational building: some spaces have defined uses, whereas others are less defined, allowing students to meet, learn, and connect informally.

The building works similarly. There is a hierarchy of spaces, from the individual cellular offices to common social learning spaces to open street areas. The language of the exterior, the city, has become part of the interior. The main "street" that runs through the new campus is faced now by a wall that was once an exterior facade but has been reinvented, carefully dressed in a soft oak, to become an interior wall. The old elevation has been stripped back to its structure as simple openings, and glazed panels then offer limited physical separation back to a large, covered atrium space that links the whole campus. The wall that was once heavy has become light and open, offering visual connections to the new architecture.

This newly described and reinvented set of teaching spaces relates to the open atrium that addresses the "street." The quality of natural light from the glazed roof above adds to the ambiguous sense of the space: is it an interior atrium or an open street? The new language of the building provides an interpretation that allows it to be both inside and outside at the same time. New glazed bridges link the old to the new. The new building uses its own geometry that is informed by the old building, but slightly shifted and more precise.

There are conceptual ideas that are challenged by the limitations and physical restrictions of working with the old, such as how to deal with contemporary building regulations, for example, regarding fire, access, and insulation. The idea of reusing the old is a sound principle, although the logistics and costs are more challenging than the concept. The challenge for the architect is to maintain the simplicity of the concept while solving all these practical problems without compromise.

In material terms the intention was to use materials on the inside and outside that could be visually the same but have different physical qualities, to continue this spatial ambiguity. This project offered an opportunity to design a public building that could elevate the quality of a building on the inside to the external level. In this project, the interior finishes are not of the right quality, sometimes resorting to a neutral plaster finish. The interior wall of the building has the character of the external face; the interior has assumed the character of the exterior building, and the inside is a manifestation of the outside.

The outside wall became the inside wall through a new finish or layered structure. In built terms there is a structural frame, insulation, and a clad finish, which gives an impression of a solid wall panel. In many classical buildings made from stone, the material on the inside and outside is intended to read as a solid block with carved spaces to imply a sculptural effect. The wall is neither inside or outside; rather, it is a subtle definition between both conditions. The new atrium space reinforces this sense of being outside because the materials match the color palette of the street and align with the scale of the street. The atrium is a civic space defined by urban heavy walls.

Reusing buildings, transforming facades in particular, has a dramatic effect on our perception of existing buildings. The British Museum Great Court designed by Fosters and Partners took the original design of a building by Robert Smirke, the reading room

FIGURE 11   The elevation of the "street" of the Oxford Brookes campus continues from inside to outside. The detailing is ambiguous, which could signify an inside or an outside wall. Careful detailing allows for a seamless connection. Courtesy of L. Farrelly.

of 1852 and the space around it, which was external, and transformed this "lost space" into a new interior. It reinvented the reading room, redefined it materially and physically. It was set free from the awkwardness of the spaces around it to become a beautiful sculpted stone object, with natural light from the new glazed roof highlighting stone details and openings. This is an example of the exterior becoming the interior and through that transformation becoming something extraordinary. For the Oxford Brookes University project, in a similar way, physically, the spaces in the existing Abercrombie Building are the same; however, their relationship to the new atrium has transformed and reinterpreted these spaces. The language of the new architecture can be described as a layering of new against old, of hard concrete against subtle, soft, crafted timber.

FIGURE 12 The inside elevation of the new building at Oxford Brookes University campus creates the internal "street" edge, a street that continues from inside to outside, linking the new building elements of the site. Courtesy of L. Farrelly.

Timber frames, constructed by joiners who work on cruise liners, mediate the industrial scale of the concrete and partitions. This sensitive use of materials defines the interior spaces.

The piece as a whole has been designed and conceptualized as the mediation between inside and outside, reusing and redefining existing materials with new materials and forms. The exterior has been folded into a new spatial order enclosed by an interior. Materials act as mediators for this transition. For a building such as this to be successful there needs to be a careful reading of the site, to see the possibilities of the old and the ways in which new ideas can reinvent the old, to transform it materially, functionally, formally, to become part of a new language of an architecture, and to start a new journey and legacy for the building. This concept is enduring, and the building will continue its journey and regenerate itself for another story. That narrative has yet to be written.

The idea of the informal space, the ambiguous space, is something that can exist in large-scale buildings. There are many types of spaces that have labels: office, lecture room, café. These labels suggest the activity that should take place there. The more exciting spaces are those in-between, those that have no label; they are spaces that connect the formal spaces. It is here that interesting things happen—the unexpected meeting, the chance conversation. The in-between spaces, the serendipity spaces where anything can happen, need to be factored into contemporary design.

12

Program, Function, and Fabrication: Exhibiting the Domestic Interior

ANDY MILLIGAN AND HELEN O'CONNOR

INTRODUCTION

This essay reflects on the inherent contradictions and opportunities of domestic interiors that undergo transformation from a private place (with its distinct program, functional requirements and site conditions) to a reimagined diorama within museums exposed to the public's gaze. In this transition from *lived-in place* to a *looked-at object,* the interior as museum experience undergoes a process of fabrication,[1] of building or forgery. What was conceived as a space for use takes on a new didactic role and, with this new role, new meaning. The relocated interior undergoes a rigorous curatorial reassembly of parts, which leads to the creation of an interior artifice that evokes some of the theatricality and staginess of the diorama. However, what this also offers is an opportunity to explore the interior as a hybridized museum experience seen through the lens of the emerging Internet of Things,[2] which demands alternate ways of perceiving program and function, perhaps questioning the form and existence of the museum as a physical space. In switching from a private interior to a public stage set, the interior as museum experience sheds physical, ritualistic, and metaphorical layers. Divorced from its site conditions it takes on a new purpose, is compelled to reflect the museum's narrative and adopt a new function of "exhibit" that invites public exposure and interpretation, rigorous curatorial and historical analysis, and leads to an interior that we might describe as an object/space.

Transposing an interior leads to questions first on the nature and purpose of museums; what is being exhibited? An artifact that has value and meaning in its own right? Or is it exhibited to communicate a wider narrative, to serve a wider didactic purpose? Where that didactic purpose is historical, we might accept the interior as a stage set, but where it seeks to explore the nature of interior space as a cultural phenomenon, perhaps more radical possibilities are open to us. This leads to questions about the nature of design: a discipline embedded in functionality, where spaces, services, and products exist to serve a purpose, becomes conflicted when these elements are detached from their context, represented and perceived as fine art display, and revered within the context of a gallery.

During the nineteenth century buildings were for the first time being built specifically as public museums to preserve and display the cultural treasures of empire to an increasingly discerning and curious public. Prior to this new type of civic building, collections were secreted within religious centers and later the private estates of aristocratic collectors. Running parallel to these new *mouseions,* or temples of the muses,[3] was a growing interest in both the practice of interiors and the role the interior itself held in reflecting tasteful society. Alongside this feminine development of the interior were the intellectual musings of architectural theorists and thinkers of the period, such as August Schmarsow, who shared a fascination for spatial philosophizing with Friedrich Wilhelm Joseph von Schelling (1775–1854), and the historians Alois Riegl (1858–1905), Heinrich Wölfflin (1864–1945), and Gottfried Semper (1803–1879). Von Schelling typified a particular nineteenth-century romanticized view of architecture as symbolizing a purist "sculptural art," a view that Pierre Von Meiss suggests ignored architecture's utilitarian functions. Schmarsow's own focus, however, lay in defining architecture exclusively as an abstract "spatial art" whose significance reflected a psychological expression of a particular period of history; he once remarked that "architecture is art when the design of space clearly takes precedence over the design of the object."[4]

While museum visitors were, in the recent past, afforded voyeuristic, tightly choreographed, and frequently didactic access, this nevertheless privileged the gaze and removed much of the convivial, tactile, and intimate experience an invited guest may have had in experiencing the authentic place. However, new technologies are offering up new forms of access to museums that have implications for interior and collaborative practice and research, suggesting ways in which those experiences might be personalized and made more intimate. The emerging use of QR codes, RFID (radio-frequency identification) tags, and smartphones linked to tagged museum objects has wider implications that may expand how we think of the interior, shifting its program and function beyond those normally associated with the built environment. These relatively new teleological opportunities (discussed later in the TOTem project) reflect new ways of thinking about encounter, access, and ownership. They reflect a growing democratization of the museum itself and signal a wider engagement: individuals have the potential to define what is or is not deemed culturally significant. This raises interesting questions around curatorial practice, regarding who defines which interior might be "valuable," but also exposes issues of ownership and the ways in which objects and interiors in museums should be displayed. *ReMuseum* is a participatory, mobile experiment that investigates museum processes such as collecting, displaying, valuing, and commodifying objects but exists outside the traditional dominant museum structure and reflects some of the democratic and access-related themes within the digital TOTem project.[5] Whereas the *ReMuseum* project is mobile, other approaches can occur within traditional civic museums that host and enclose interior exhibits and collections. Both the technologically enabling research of TOTem and the critical social engagement seen in *ReMuseum* could be transferred to culturally significant interiors that remain rooted to their original site and context, such as Sir John Soane's Museum. This opens up the possibility for new programmatic and functional interpretations that allow access to lost spaces (as in the case of Peter Bissenger's recreation and remodeling of Kurt Schwitter's Merzbau) and other imagined interiors.

While some interiors may be disassembled and reassembled either partially or in their entirety within larger host museums, others may be effectively fused with or conjoined into the physical fabric of a host museum. An example here is the Mackintosh House in the Hunterian Gallery at the University of Glasgow (discussed later). Others are the result of a remodeling or renovation program, such as the Geffrye Museum of the Home, with others retaining their original location and independence, such as Sir John Soane's Museum at 13 Lincoln's Inn Fields. The Geffrye Museum of the Home provides a permanent display of eleven period rooms arranged as stage sets across a historical timeline representing 400 years from the fifteenth century to the present day. Included is a restored eighteenth-century almshouse, taken back to its original condition to provide partial glimpses into the lives of London's poor. This space demands active imagination, rather than the passive, closed, and didactic *informance* that characterizes many public museum experiences. However, in the context of larger host museums, the interior exhibit seldom (if ever) achieves the type of spatial coherence or unity of Soane's museum/mausoleum.

What links these examples is the shift from *spaces of utility* to *object-spaces* for intellectual reflection. In this process interiors (and in some cases their architectural structure) become disembodied from the proximities, relationships, adjacencies, and purposes they, and their occupants, once shared—from adjoining rooms, corridors, and windows to wider exchanges with neighbors, sites, and structures. What appears to be an accurate interior exhibit is simultaneously a model, shrine, replica, archive, and hybridized object/space. Within larger museum institutions (as in Kelvingrove Art Gallery and Museum's recently renovated Charles Rennie Mackintosh exhibit and the Glasgow Style gallery in Glasgow), various interiors are set within a landscape of other museum fragments that suggests a dilution, rather than distillation, of an "authentic" interior, in which the visual takes precedence over more social and sensorial experiences. This ocular-centric tendency is described in Juhani Pallasmaa's "Hapticity and Time: Notes on Fragile Architecture," where he argues for a multisensory approach to architectural thinking that is equally applicable to the conditions placed on interior exhibits in museums:

> Every significant experience of architecture is multi-sensory; qualities of matter, space and scale are measured by the eye, ear, nose, skin, tongue, skeleton and muscle. Maurice Merleau-Ponty emphasizes this simultaneity of experience and sensory interaction as follows: My perception is [therefore] not a sum of visual, tactile, and audible

givens: I perceive in a total way with my whole being: I grasp a unique structure of the thing, a unique way of being, which speaks to all my senses.[6]

Von Meiss in "Elements of Architecture"[7] reminds us of Michel Serres's "Les Cinq Sens" (1985) and supports a need for a fuller sensual expansion of those spatial experiences that we argue are compromised when iconic interiors are reinvented in the museum. Serres reminds us of the value of sight, scent, touch, sound, taste, and our kinesthetic senses—of our physical bodies moving through space, time, and encounter. However, what we encounter in a transposed interior is the carefully choreographed narrative sequence typical of exhibition design, with didactic points along a path that lessen any serendipitous encounters and provide a one-size-fits-all experience for a wider public: "the forms buildings take may help to initiate unexpected, yet distinct, behaviours from users of the spaces; an illicit meeting in a niche, a secretive embrace within a doorway, and whilst we may design spaces it is the users who make places."[8] What this suggests is that interior exhibits shift from spaces of utility toward sites of intellectual reflection and reimagination that require the public to look beyond the obvious artifice, filter out the distraction of other people and other artifacts, and actively reimagine rituals and activity. In their preservation such interiors encourage speculative occupation, hypothesizing and collective remembering, in effect *dressing* others' rooms with our own contemporary and imaginary material, a dressing process[9] not unlike the imaginary fabrication of fictional interiors depicted in literature or heard in a radio play. This suggests that contemporary values may be projected onto culturally significant interiors from the past, which takes us further away from the authentic. Charles Rice describes similar "projections" in the views of Heidi de Mare: "that concepts such as privacy, intimacy, comfort and home were nineteenth-century sentiments that were then projected into the past and applied to seventeenth-century [Dutch] paintings, books and houses," in essence, to fabricate illusions of the past dwelling patterns of others.[10] However, Gaston Bachelard describes the positive role that imagination offers as a necessary perceptual bias that acts as a counterpoint to rationalizing, analyzing, and observing the domestic: "Space that has been seized upon by the imagination cannot remain indifferent space subject to the measures and estimates of the surveyor. It has been lived in, not in its positivity, but with all the partiality of the imagination."[11]

This contradiction between authenticity and artifice, and the actual interior as opposed to the interior's visual representations (e.g., in drawing, photography, or painting, or indeed the 1:1 diorama), is reflected in Charles Rice's essay "For a Concept of the Domestic Interior." Rice reflects on the tensions between an interior's spatial condition and its two-dimensional representations. Specifically, Rice discusses some of the contradictions in seventeenth-century Dutch genre paintings of mercantile domestic settings by Gerard Dou, Emanuel de Witte, and Jan Vermeer. Critically, Rice unearthes many of the gaps and opportunities between the physical space itself and its visual or modeled representation, casting doubt on the paintings' role as evidencing or recording the authentic interior experience.[12] Rice describes this as a curious state of "doubleness" that has some applicability to the themes within this chapter and suggests a useful conceptual structure to explore problems with the ways various disciplines study domesticity and the interior.

While interior exhibits can act as sites of collective memory and the contestation of space, these may also raise issues of authenticity and the manufacture of identity (e.g., the recreation of a Scots/Italian café in a mock streetscape in Zaha Hadid's new Glasgow Transport Riverside Museum, 2011[13]). The most obvious examples of dislocation are perhaps those interior exhibits set within the spatial envelope of a larger museum building; however, in some instances attempts have been made to retain a semblance of context. This is evident in the Mackintosh House at the Hunterian Gallery, University of Glasgow. This is a curatorial and precise "reenactment" of the home and its principal rooms—such as the original hall, dining room, studio-drawing room, and main bedroom—of Charles Rennie Mackintosh (1868–1928) and his artist wife, Margaret Macdonald Mackintosh (1864–1933). The result of a partial salvage exercise when the original tenement was demolished in 1963, the Mackintosh's House, as we now perceive it, was conceived by the architects Whitfield Partners as an integral part of the "new" Hunterian Gallery. As the museum's curator, Pamela Robertson, describes it:

> The presentation of the rooms as an exhibit was shaped by Mackintosh's aesthetic, which orchestrated interiors into a sequence of contrasting but mutually enriching spaces.... The rooms were therefore organized, (in their new location) not as a series of three-sided boxes, but located in their original interrelationship and orientation.[14]

Other areas, such as the cloakroom, kitchen, bathroom, and secondary bedrooms, have not been reconstructed at all, reminding us of the curatorial compromises (and the role subjective imagination plays in evoking missing fragments) that inevitably surface in deciding what to retain and what to reject, what is "valuable" and what is extraneous. Completed in 1981, using contemporary descriptions of the house alongside archival photographs (which we see as equally pivotal in recreating lost interiors in Schwitters's Merzbau) to direct the interior exhibit, the reconstruction contains original furniture and domestic fittings that help authenticate and direct the reworked interior and was decorated as closely as possible to the original. While the interiors presented here are unquestionably part of a gallery sequence, there are architectural anomalies: instead of entering through the front door, we emerge from the main museum directly into the hall space. The accurately reconstructed principal spaces open from the reconstructed hallway, and visitors wander around the space to experience each piece in an appropriate context, if not quite "use." Perhaps the most curious aspect of the Hunterian Gallery example is its exterior. The front door exists (as do all the windows to the principal spaces), but its location is stripped of its function and suspended several yards (meters) above street level. The exterior of the building, rendered in tooled concrete and grafted onto the body of the museum, is a strange, disembodied echo of the traditional Glasgow street elevation. The Mackintosh House represents something of a "curious hybrid, the interiors which had originally been progressive rooms created within an older building, had now become…historic interiors inserted within a modern building."[15]

SOANE: PRESENCE OF ABSENCE

However strong the attempt at curatorial authenticity, there always seems to be a sense of incompleteness and dubiety for the exhibited interior; the occupant is forever absent in the presence of active viewers. This interplay between presence and absence emerges in Sir John Soane's Museum. Operating as both a home and an essay in spatial invention, it was within his lifetime a depository for Soane's own collections and fragments; since his death it has functioned as a museum and a memorial to Soane. A domestic interior has the capacity to project the history, personality, and priorities of its creator—both consciously and unconsciously. The house is both a highly revealing and a highly controlled example, a deliberate manipulation of a message: where does it stop being a house and emerge as a museum that allows Soane to speak to future generations? To quote W. H. Auden, "I am here today but I shall be dead tomorrow and you will be active in my place, and how shall I speak to you?"[16] Soane envisaged Lincoln's Inn Fields as a house, workspace, and architectural museum and as a treasure chest of spaces containing fragments and objects collected, categorized, and assembled throughout his life. Philip Ursprung has likened Soane's collection to Walter Benjamin's *Arcades Project* as one that "resemble[s] that of a detective for whom every source, even the tiniest evidence, is potentially the key to understanding a crime."[17]

Ursprung suggests that what makes Soane's interior, and the collection of plaster casts, prints, and ephemera, so engaging is that it doesn't subscribe to an explicit, didactic, or linear narrative as is typical of exhibitions. Instead, it offers a glorious jumble of artifacts, creating surprising juxtapositions that invite chance discovery, which is difficult to program in larger civic museums. What links the collection together, however, is Soane himself: "we are confronted with the subjectivity of the curator/collector and can identify with him."[18] The history of the Soane Museum is a complex one. The house was begun as a purely domestic space, but by the time of his death Soane had reprogrammed the interior and his collections and had deliberately reinvented it as a fixed museum exhibit "for the benefit of amateurs and students,"[19] one that is even protected today in the United Kingdom by an act of Parliament. Negatively, we might see this as an uncomfortable tension and find positive value in the ongoing dialogues between the collections and successive curators.

What this also offers in relation to interior exhibits in museums is an opportunity to go beyond the lens of the curatorial archive and explore much wider ways of thinking about the interior, whether this is exhibit, habitat, or some future hybrid yet to be defined. Curiously, the way interiors are exhibited, whether in the Soane Museum or as mock interiors within a large museum, provides space to think of the interior beyond the familiar contexts of work, play, or life and suggests a territory somewhere outside the frame of reference of the built environment, evoking what Rice suggests: "as soon as 'we' forget that the interior is where 'we' live, the study of the interior will open up in new and interesting ways."[20]

LAZARUS

In addition to the dubiety or doubleness described by Rice we can consider significant interiors in museums as undergoing a form of cultural resurrection where the interior is brought back to a curated half-life. Resurrection suggests a deadening of a lived-in interior now relocated into a museum but, in effect, devoid of real life, action, and rituals. Jean Cocteau reflects some of this morbid association and considers the (Louvre) museum as a "morgue; you go there to identify your friends,"[21] supporting clichés of museums as depositories of dead objects and cultures, stuffed creatures, defunct technologies, and deadened spaces. However, new approaches are challenging this morbid cliché and again, like the TOTem project, show how the fields of product and interaction are reinventing the museum experience. In *MoLI, the Museum of Lost Interactions* research project,[22] nine predigital technologies—created between 1900 and 1979—were successfully resurrected and rebuilt as new hybrid objects. These included the Zenith Radio Hat of 1952, the world's most portable radio of its time, combined within a hat and walking cane, and the 1900 Richophone, a multiplayer-based game found in prestigious hotels and cafés in and around London, played from special Richophone booths connected through a system of telephones. While object based, these provide insights into the way interior researchers might also rethink spatial interactions, reinterpretation, and representation of interior exhibits in museums.[23] The way we think of museums is perhaps changing:

> Once considered repositories of dead, arcane, or useless artifacts, museums have, since the 1980s, become key institutions in analyses of modernity. They have been variably interpreted as expressions of elite ideologies, as sites of memory, as spaces of civic ritual, and venues for the contestation and creation of identities.[24]

NETWORKING MUSEUM OBJECTS AND EXHIBITION: TOTem

In the absence of occupants, objects within an interior museum exhibit also take on new significance. Their presence becomes heightened; occupying a privileged role in that interior, they establish points of allegorical focus as if only recently used by the absent owner. Herzog and de Meuron in exhibiting their own work have consistently played on this significance, with models and prototypes being presented as if artifacts existing in their own right (a comment that is ultimately concerned with the value of representations as embodying ideas rather than the resulting buildings), whereas Sverre Fehn describes the transformations objects often undergo when shifted from their original context and relocated into the museum as follows: "when an object [an interior] moves itself into a museum, its dialogue with the past, with the space where it was made or belonged, disappears... but time is fixed into the picture and the object is left with its aesthetic and its energy. It must survive on its own magic."[25] How the interior exhibit functions (e.g., as a didactic narrative, architectural archive, or curatorial device), and how the museum's own programmatic requirements dictate those experiences, is being transformed through technology, altering, extending, and networking our relationships with objects and spaces. This shift in focus from overtly architectural concerns toward interaction theories and ethnographic territories is evident in the TOTem project "Tales of Things and Electronic Memories."[26] This explores the phenomenon of tagging and networking objects in large civic museums that is challenging how we interact with exhibits. Conventional *exhibition interactives* play a supporting role in contemporary exhibition design (e.g., digital screens, audio guides, and other tactile devices), providing visitors with narrative bites of information at strategic points along an exhibition journey. TOTem challenges exhibition conventions by expanding how, when, and where we interact spatially, emotionally, and technologically with objects. It also suggests a democratization of this new network through smartphones. TOTem explores social memory in the emerging Internet of Things, embedding sensors and creating smart links that enable narratives between viewers and the objects they encounter, typically using a range of open-source sensors such as RFID tags, QR codes, and Arduinos. RFID tags transmit the identity and unique serial number of objects or people wirelessly. QR codes, developed initially to track auto parts, encode information in two-dimensional space and are being used in the National Museums of Scotland to tag eighty curated museum objects in *Scotland: A Changing Nation.* Concerned with the memory and value of "old" objects, TOTem explores how, in every environment, there are objects that resonate with meaning and significance but require new technologies and methods to draw these out.

With the imminent arrival of the Internet of Things,[27] new technologies will breathe life into the static interior exhibits in museums and enable richer temporal and sensorial experiences than those currently on offer. By 2020 it is estimated that the number of connected objects within the Internet of Things will exceed 50 billion. This suggests a world saturated with objects, sensors, and new forms of interconnectivity between environments, vehicles, clothing, and portable devices—each with the ability to sense, communicate, network, and produce new information. A widespread Internet of Things could transform how we live in our cities, travel, and manage our lives sustainably; how we age; and how services and entertainment adapt as our surroundings change.[28] We will be able to experience and converse with objects and environments; not only will this present opportunities for visitors to create narratives around these experiences, but networked objects in this new Internet of Things will "talk back" to visitors, and perhaps continue the conversation (tagged object to tagged device) when the museum closes. However, Russell M. Davies suggests a more convivial and important counterculture to the economic drivers currently influencing the Internet of Things and promotes a future of unrivaled creative making that connects people, not objects.[29] This also suggests scope for remaking objects, or models of objects experienced in a museum (whether an object or an interior), through three-dimensional printing, thus creating our own collections.

However, this is a research community led not by interior designers but by interdisciplinary groupings of engineers, ethnographers, computer programmers, and interaction mavericks. From an interaction and ethnographic perspective the domestic interior is used as a lab, not unlike the way scholars might study a historically significant interior within a museum. In such ethnodigital interventions "live" interiors act as hosts to objects that resemble everyday domestic items—a table to place your keys, a coffee table, a picture frame, or a tablecloth. In 2007 *The Curious Home,* an exhibition of electronic furniture that encouraged exploration and individual interpretation, used several ludic objects placed in a "live" domestic interior. These included *The Plane Tracker,* an appliance that tracks passing flight traffic and imagines views of the planes' journeys as they pass overhead; *The Local Barometer,* small devices that display text and images from local classifieds as if blown through the home; and *The Drift Table,* a table with an oculus that drifts over the landscape, giving aerial views of Britain. Unlike the Internet of Things, which is predicated on market growth, *Curious Homes* offers convivial and playful alternatives to the predictable ways in which digital technologies tend to support work, productivity, performance, consumption, and leisure. Led by Bill Gaver, the research encourages people to become active participants in digital lifestyles (and in the research project), helping individuals explore the world around them and focusing on the possibilities of playful open-ended interpretation, particularly in domestic environments. Such playful engagement could have its place in how we design future interior exhibits in museums. *Curious Homes* uses the framework of the object to veil the hidden weight-sensitive technology embedded within the domestic objects. This is not dissimilar to the house acting as a structural veil to its hidden HVAC services, or indeed the fabricated staginess of some museum interiors. While the primary aim of *Curious Homes* was to use these interactive domestic props to help map real-time behaviors and rituals, might the inclusive approach adopted here suggest exhibits as actual "live-in/be-in" interiors that invite the public to engage more directly? To play?[30]

THE DOMESTIC INTERIOR AS ART/ARTIFACT: SCHWITTERS

In transposing the interior to the gallery we change its status: it exists as a site of interpretation and reflection rather than as an everyday object of use. But examples exist of "art" that has been made as a meditation or comment on the nature of dwelling, use, and the domestic interior, and these can provide new insight on the debate. The domestic interior was the muse and the blank canvas for Kurt Schwitters's Merzbau installation. Josef Helfenstein describes the Merzbau as a work that "incorporates many branches of fine art, from architecture to assemblage, from collage to painting, transforming biographical and historical material into an abstract form."[31] Originally constructed in 1923, in Schwitters's apartment at Waldhausenstrasse 5A in Hanover, Merzbau represents an example of domestic life instigating art, a walk-in sculpture, and was recently a focus for a fabricated reworking of the lost original that has some parallels to "designed" interiors as museum experiences. Acknowledged as one of the precursors to installation art, Merzbau also underwent its own curatorial reinvention between 1981 and 1983 in a partial reconstruction by stage designer Peter Bissenger in Locarno, and later as part of the exhibition *Dada and Constructivism,* 1988–1989, at Annely Juda Fine Art, London, where a practical "travel copy" of the Merz Building was made under Bissenger's direction so that it could travel to numerous museums.[32] This example utilized wide-angle archival photography from 1933 and the recollections of Schwitters's son to analyze the original interior from very tight viewing points. Such detective work is described by Gwendolyn Webster as "the realization of what can, at best, be hinted at in the photos' limited field and monochrome two-dimensionality, the reconstruction allows us to experience first hand some sense of the very first sculpture 'in which one can go for a walk.'"[33] Developed through collage, the Merzbau can be thought of as an interior art exhibit whose original domestic setting (rather like those of Soane) evolved, mutated, and was reprogrammed over time and across various sites. It can be read as a mixed-media study and as a multidimensional museum interior. Similarly, the painstaking analysis of photography of the original influenced the recreation but also reveals some flaws in the mock-up and compromised interior reconstruction (e.g., as in the Hunterian Gallery's Mackintosh House). The Merzbau itself was perhaps never fixed and rooted but rather a nomadic entity, remaining in a perpetual state of evolution or incompleteness. After leaving Hanover in 1933, Schwitters created a second version in Oslo between 1937 and 1940, which was subsequently destroyed by fire in 1951. Ill health prevented Schwitters from completing a third version begun in England before his death in 1948.[34] Bissenger's curatorial reinvention might be seen more as another iteration of the Merzbau's existence than as a hollow reproduction/representation of it, but, however accurate it appears, it necessarily omits the architectural context that once enclosed it and therefore resembles a stage set or animated architectural walk-through.

DIORAMAS AND FABRICATIONS: WEXLER

This chapter considers how an interior may take on some of the characteristics of a curated object. It suggests that interior exhibits in museums exist as spatial simulacrums,[35] that is, an empty form devoid of spirit and a specious or fallow representation. While interiors as museum exhibits can function as valuable archives, they are also often dioramas. *Diorama* is a term applied to a tradition of museum and theatrical exhibitions, of full-scale casts, and the display of architectural fragments. Diorama acts as a convenient metaphor for the incompleteness, limitations, and isolation of some museum interiors. In "Construir/Edification," Mark Robbins describes similar limitations in exhibiting architectural exhibitions and historical building fragments in museums:

> A limitation [is] inherent in architectural exhibitions, which can rarely show the actual space or the tactile qualities of built form.... Architecture has often been made into an artifact in museological presentations, taking the form of dioramas, panoramas of city views, or interior bricolage of building parts and fragments.[36]

The term *diorama* refers to a nineteenth-century mobile theater device, a three-dimensional full-size or miniature model, or a theatrical device used in the 1800s whose invention is attributed to Louis Jacques Mandé Daguerre, who was also, curiously, a decorator.[37] He is also credited as co-inventor of the daguerreotype photographic process, and the capturing capacity of both early photography and theatrical dioramas can be seen as an illusory device that exploited depth perception. Used within a museum context, they often create a broader context or narrative, which enables interpretation of individual artifacts. In fabricating a version of the original interior, an act of curatorial editing of what should be retained and what has to be excluded results in interior exhibits that invite the gaze and that exist to be read, revered, studied, and experienced as a cultural objects: one of many cultural objects set in a sea of other curiosities. This "authentic" interior's functions are inevitably compromised and dysfunctional, and its spatiality lost in translation, existing at the boundary between curatorial accuracy, public spectacle, and diorama. Another form of artifice can be considered: that of a form of interior taxidermy not unlike the fate of other dead creatures staged within the museum to effect realness or imply a temporary absence, however static, anachronistic, or depersonalized that interior exhibit appears.

Terence Riley, in "The Architect's Room," appears to support, or at least corroborate, this dubiety of meaning between fabricated artifice and the construction of real spaces. He describes *fabrication* as a particularly slippery tectonic term that continually shifts meaning depending on the context and that "jumps between the negative sense of a falsehood and the more neutral sense of the process, or product, of making."[38] Curiously, *fabrication* in the negative sense undermines the desire for curatorial accuracy employed in recreating interior exhibits in museums. *Fabrication* also alludes to the superficial application of interior decor, where "the meaning of interior decoration corroborates the idea of the interior's deliberate fabrication, its staginess, and its distinction from architectural construction."[39] However, in "Bodybuildings: Toward a Hybrid Order of Architecture," Aaron Betsky offers an interpretation of fabrication that locates the building of space as a metaphorical or metaphysical extension of the self, suggesting that "by making a shelter, a frame, or a defined place for ourselves, we are in essence building a second, fabricated version of ourselves."[40] Within interior exhibits in museums there is no need for shelter. They provide collective spatial experiences that contradict the private access those interiors would have warranted, while aspects of the interiors' staginess seem familiar if we consider the equally staged appearance of the "show home." Such interior artifice offers no shelter; after all, these interiors have shed their own weather-tight enclosures and have become nested, like matryoshkas, in the museum. The attention to detail may include the appearance of plumbing, electric fixtures, and wiring systems on view, but these are a theatrical sham, operating as empty envelopes in rooms filled with hushed conversations.[41]

According to Debra Wilbur and Christopher Scoates, "function is the subject, not the object," of Allan Wexler's work.[42] Wexler is by training an architect but describes himself as practicing architecture as an artist rather than an architect. His work (rather like Schwitters's Merzbau above and Whiteread's *House* below) occupies the exploratory territory between architecture, art, and installation. Here he examines issues of function, the interaction between space and the body, the potential of the object/space to choreograph activity, ritual, settings, and purpose and to define narrative. Wexler's structures often appear to explore architecture and dwelling as a form of machine, one that requires operation by an absent occupant, a presence (or absence) of which the viewer is palpably aware. Indeed, as Betsky describes, they often serve to "frustrate use...[and simultaneously]...to confront us with the true nature of what it is they do."[43] A discussion of two examples of works helps illustrate this duality or doubleness. The *Crate House,* created in 1991 for the exhibition at the University of Massachusetts, Amherst (UMCA), called *Home Rooms,* was designed to address "the interdependent relationship between features of settings and features of people who use them."[44] *Crate House* was a condensation and a compression of various rituals of dwelling. The "house" is divided into four crates, for living, sleeping, cooking, and washing, with each avoiding conventional tagging as kitchen and bedroom, and each containing all the objects associated with that activity. These crates are in turn contained within a 7 sq. ft. (0.65 sq m) cube—the house. However, the individual crates must be rolled out through a door to reveal their contents and become "usable." Wexler describes these crates as resembling dioramas in a natural history museum. His work was designed to render visible the everyday, to present each functional object as an artifact. *Crate House* embodies a potential kinetic energy, dormant when contained in a gallery context but nevertheless inviting use. Conversely, *Parsons Kitchen,* designed by Wexler in 1994, builds on some of the ideas explored in the earlier *Crate House,* but here the context is materially different. Wexler was commissioned by Parsons School of Design to make a kitchen suitable for catering for exhibition openings. The kitchen itself is contained within a movable crate, which slides out from an existing recess, and unfurls to reveal the necessary utensils and workspaces, each suggesting a number of actions. In discussing the work Wexler speculated, "Which objects do I choose for optimal function? What actions do these objects imply? The objects are isolated and presented like jewels. The repetition of the forms creates pattern. Their use creates theatre."[45]

What separates these two examples is not content as much as context. *Crate House* may invite use, but its status as an art object denies this. We can argue, too, that other interior exhibits in museums, perhaps because of their heightened cultural status, may also take on the status of art object—placing previously useful interiors on the pedestal of art. *Crate House* exists purely as a "structure for reflection," not to function but instead to meditate on the relationship between a person and the space he or she occupies and, in particular, the ritual of domestic experiences. It is, as Betsky describes, a "form beyond function."[46] *Parson's Kitchen,* in its intention and in its physical context, is materially different, but that difference exists purely in the way we perceive these structures.

SPACE OBJECT: WHITEREAD

But most unforgettable of all were the walls themselves. The stubborn life of these rooms had not let itself be trampled out.

Eric L. Santer[47]

The domestic interior projects a powerful sense of its past occupation onto the eyes and imaginations of the contemporary viewer. In contrast to the culturally significant interiors mentioned previously, the artist Rachel Whiteread has described how her own childhood memories and domestic experiences (such as leaving home) were important motivations for earlier work such as *Ghost;* it was mistakenly attributed to an architectural commentary.[48] Later work, such as *House,* reflected a politicized response to the anonymity of working-class environments, what she described as a forgotten international architecture. Despite this relative anonymity, the domestic interior evokes a powerful sense of layered occupation and traces of past activity. *House* is therefore concerned with our collective experiences of the domestic interior, and while Whiteread's work is in many ways distinct from interiors within large museums, each demands some form of imagined and emotive dressing by the viewer. Such layering provides a tangible presence that remains even when ownership changes, or when the space is abandoned. While interiors as museum exhibits have been "saved," they also evoke a similar sense of abandonment, stillness, and absence. As we occupy we also invest objects with meaning and significance, akin to the reverence of art objects and religious relics, coming into partial existence through rituals, the symbolism implied in the manner of their display and use. *House* is significant in shifting focus from the exclusivity associated with the significant interiors of the famous to the anonymous domestic space, and it is also significant in that it inverts the space/object relationship, presenting the space itself as an artifact. *House* is concerned with a collective experience of the domestic, which Adrian Searle, in his critique, recognizes as the interplay between experience, memory, and association and which impacts on the emotional and spatial intelligence of viewer:

> What finally has been exposed is an empty setting, a place where people once led a life of intimacies, grew up, grew old and died. And, one might add, fucked, rowed, worried, slept, ate, shat, fought, laughed and lied. No one looks out of the windows anymore, no one puts out the milk bottles on the stoop; no one shouts—"Kevin come in your tea's ready" or returns home late from the pub and fumbles with keys in the lock.[49]

House is disturbing in that it both removes the skin of the protecting wall and forces us to look with our imaginations as well as our eyes. But the nature of its construction simultaneously denies us entry—the opportunity to mentally wander the spaces. Whiteread often describes her casts as death masks of interiors: these reflect similar morbid clichés within museums but also resonate with the fictional *OxygenHouse* (1993) by Douglas Darden and, to some extent, remind us of Soane's determination to establish his legacy through his home or mausoleum. The series of casts used by Whiteread, which began with *Ghost* and culminated in *House,*[50] reminds us of the critical role architectural casts from antiquity played in the education of architects and as focal points in exhibitions.[51] This topic is highlighted by Rachel Carley in her essay "Domestic After-lives," where she states:

> To be haunted is to bring past impressions to bear on current circumstances and rein-terpreting new phenomena in light of them. 'Ghost' bears the imagined impressions and faint glimmers of past rooms brought to bear on it by the visitation of viewers.[52]

The volume of the original space has been displaced; it no longer exists in its first itera-tion but now in the new spaces in which it is installed, and in this haunting analogy in-vites multiple insights from multiple visitors each fabricating personal fictional scenarios that reinterpret the ghost object as an intellectual springboard for spatial imaginings. Whiteread's work places us in a familiar and simultaneously strange relationship to the domestic interior—we see the space from the perspective of the enclosing wall. What we see is a full-scale three-dimensional and highly detailed tracing of space, but one that we are immediately aware is not the original but an echo/shadow of that former self.

CONCLUSIONS

This chapter reflects on the inherent contradictions and compromises in exhibiting the domestic interior. The interior is transformed from a private place, with its specific pro-grams, functional requirements, and site conditions, and recontextualized as a public spectacle within the museum. Whether displayed as fragments or near-complete interi-ors, such spaces require varying levels of fabrication to recreate the detail and character of the original. Exhibited interiors hosted in large museums can be categorized as mock stage sets, dioramas, simulacra, or mere representations. Each category offers oppor-tunities to examine program and function outside the normal constraints of the built environment. Art practice and interactive research on domestic interiors and museum objects reflect a more complex and culturally significant narrative, one that touches on issues of democracy, for example, *ReMuseum,* the changing role of the museum, widening (technological) access, and cultural ownership. New technologies seem set to transform how we access information in museum collections—in effect making us po-tential collectors of collections—but suggest scope for further interaction with exhibited interiors, and the props and objects displayed as an essential part of those interiors. This interaction suggests new modes of engaging the viewer in a dialogue that is open-ended rather than didactic. Interaction and ethnographic research, such as *Curious Homes, MoLi,* and TOTem, collectively hints at exciting changes, ways for rather static exhibited interiors to be radically transformed through these interactive surfaces and the tagging and remote accessing of these object-spaces. Where domestic spaces act as labs for eth-nographers, so too might museum interiors become "living labs" with real people enact-ing real rituals—offering a much more convivial sense of the interior exhibit as a place of being, rather than looking at and passing by deadened environments.

13

Lives in Large Interiors

THOMAS KONG

BACKGROUND

The growth of large, interconnected interior spaces housing a conglomeration of retail, commercial, office, and residential spaces has been the subject of numerous publications that have underlined the negative impact this phenomenon has on a healthy civic life. These interior environments form a large part of our everyday experience of the city and even serve as surrogate public gathering spaces. In 1989 Michael Bednar authored the book *Interior Pedestrian Places,* which gave a historical account of the growth of interior pedestrian streets in North America using significant case studies.[1] A more severe critique of the phenomenon was found in Trevor Boddy's 1992 essay, "Underground and Overhead: Building the Analogous City," which was part of a book edited by Michael Sorkin that examined the loss of public spaces in American cities.[2] The main thrust of Boddy's essay was how large interior environments, above- and below-ground pedestrian streets, had expanded and had gradually assumed the role of public spaces, becoming surrogate cities that gave a false impression of public life. Instead of sharing the diverse, inclusive civic spirit of public spaces, these privately financed, managed, and controlled interior environments were, in Boddy's view, nothing more than sanitized and hermetic spaces that promoted a culture of consumption, exclusion, and homogeneity. The essay concluded with a rallying call to find ways to resist and unfasten the analogous city's hold on "the life of the polis."[3] In an essay from the same book, Margaret Crawford chronicled the parallel development of shopping and the growth of large, all-inclusive interior environments such as the West Edmonton Mall in Calgary, designed to entertain and stimulate consumption, while simulating community and diversity.[4] The evolution of interior rooms for leisure and shopping activities can be traced to the early Parisian glass-covered arcades in the nineteenth century. Walter Benjamin, a cultural and literary critic, devoted almost thirteen years of his life to examining these precursors to modern-day shopping malls.[5] Although they do not embody the complexities and diversity of activities in a modern-day mixed-use development, these arcades nevertheless marked the transition into the consumer culture of the twentieth century. The popularity and proliferation of contemporary malls are evidence of the pervasiveness of shopping throughout all sectors of our lives; malls have, in fact, become our world. In a seminal essay titled "Bigness or the Problem of Large," Dutch architect Rem Koolhaas wrote, "Bigness no longer needs the city: it competes with the city; it represents the city; it preempts the city; or better still, it is the city. If urbanism generates potential and architecture exploits it, Bigness enlists the generosity of urbanism against the meanness of architecture."[6]

According to Koolhaas, bigness is due partly to developments in building technologies such as air-conditioning, elevators, and structural systems that enabled buildings to go wider, deeper, and higher. These big buildings eventually become autonomous objects in the landscape, containing hermetically sealed, seamless and artificial environments that have no reference and relationship to the surrounding context. They contain a multitude of uses, services, and activities and serve as surrogate public gathering spaces. Koolhaas bemoaned the lack of an understanding of the phenomenon of bigness, which would have otherwise enabled architects to engage these extra-large-scale architectural projects with greater awareness of their benefits and pitfalls.

In 2007 Kristine Miller's book *Designs on the Public: The Private Lives of New York's Public Spaces* continued the debate surrounding privately owned public spaces.[7] She discussed three case studies—the IBM Atrium, the Sony Plaza, and the Trump Tower in Manhattan—and highlighted the controversies and contestations among the building owners, the city's planning department, and civic groups over the interpretation and use of these interior spaces.

The primary concern shared by those writing on the privatization of public space is centered on the premise that public spaces embody the values of a democratic society. A public space is a space free of any restrictions, where everyone has the right of access. It is a space of civic engagement for discussion and debate on, as well as the holding of protests about, issues and concerns surrounding life in the city. The processes of privatization, as evident in these writers' arguments and the examples presented, will limit accessibility, exclude certain portions of the population who are deemed undesirable, and erode a healthy civic life.

INTERIOR URBANISM

In this chapter, I would like to recontextualize the phenomenon of large, interconnected interior environments by reexamining their presence in two Asian cities: Hong Kong, a special administrative region of the People's Republic of China, and Singapore. Both are major financial hubs in Asia and are economically successful postcolonial Asian cities intimately embedded in the global market economy. Everyday life in large, interconnected interior environments in Hong Kong and Singapore, which I term *interior urbanism*,[8] expresses an intriguing relationship between the top-down visions of the cities and the bottom-up, opportunistic use of interior and semi-interior spaces by local residents. Interior urbanism connects the city with contemporary expansive and interconnected interior spaces such as megastructures, arcades, underground pedestrian walkways, above-ground link bridges, and infrastructural spaces. It is concerned with the connectivity and expansiveness of interior spaces and their effects on our everyday lives across social, cultural, political, and geographic boundaries. As one cannot clearly separate the social environment from the spatial since the two realms are interdependent, my focus on the interior urbanism of large-scale, interconnected interior spaces provides a framework and point of entry to uncover the modes of spatial appropriation, social exchange, and continuing sustenance of these spaces. My research on Asian cities is prompted by the popular presumption that the Asian century has arrived,[9] as witnessed by the rising economic might of the region, which has shifted economic and political power as well as influence in the world's affairs away from the United States and Europe. Hong Kong and Singapore, together with neighboring cities in East, South, and Southeast Asia, are radically transforming their urban landscape with great bravado—an intense period of development last witnessed during the Industrial Revolution in Europe and the postwar era in the United States. As an architect with a long-standing practice in this region, who is intrigued by its cultural geographies, I have prepared this chapter as part of a larger investigation to come to terms with a twenty-first-century non-Western urbanism evolving from the intersection of political, economical, social, and cultural developments in Asia. This chapter is my ethnographic journey into the depths of the interior lives of the two cities, with the hope that an understanding of this phenomenon may create opportunities for an expanded role for interior design practice and education.

FILIPINO SOCIAL, RECREATIONAL, AND SHOPPING SPACE

The informal social spaces of the Filipino community—on pedestrian link bridges, in office lobbies, and on the ground floor of the HSBC bank designed by Sir Norman Foster—are unique features on Hong Kong Island every Sunday. On this rest day, Filipino migrant workers blanket the whole public plaza below the HSBC bank and other public spaces to meet friends, chat, and share a meal. The social activities often spill out to adjacent spaces in the city as they gather to send clothes, blankets, dried foodstuffs, and everyday products back to their families in the Philippines. Their presence and actions transform the financial district in Hong Kong into a mini-Philippines for a day (Fig. 13).

By creatively reappropriating used cardboard boxes as temporary floors and low walls for comfort and privacy, Filipino migrant workers convert the pedestrian link bridges into informal social spaces that snake over the city below and into adjacent office lobbies. Ever mindful of their temporary status in the city, they take great care not to dirty the spaces and at the end of the day leave no physical traces of their presence. They are fully aware that their continuing enjoyment of the unusual Sunday social space depends on maintaining a delicate harmony with the government and the owners of the buildings. The choice of Hong Kong Island as a social gathering place is also due to the

FIGURE 13   Filipina domestic workers using the pedestrian link bridges in Hong Kong as spaces for socializing. Photo by Thomas Kong.

presence of remittance agencies and shops selling Filipino food and affordable clothes, as well as churches. The informal social spaces of the Filipino community did not come about because of altruism on the part of private developers but through the concerted efforts of, and pressure from, nongovernmental organizations led by both local residents and Filipinos. In 2008 a controversy erupted over the ownership, control, and use of privately owned public spaces in Hong Kong when local residents were prevented from lingering in the outdoor space of Times Square, a mixed-use development consisting of offices and a multistory shopping mall.[10] Although the open space in question was designated as a public space to be accessible twenty-four hours a day, seven days of the week, and used for noncommercial activities like exhibitions and displays, the agreement was not adhered to by the owners, and the government failed to monitor and enforce its accessibility. The ensuing public debate provoked grassroots actions by civic groups and members of the public to challenge the owners of Times Square over the incident. Their actions ranged from loud public protest, to deliberate reclaiming of the public space by the placement of personal furniture, to the spontaneous holding of activities by social activists. The incident also prompted the government to make public a comprehensive list of privately owned public spaces in Hong Kong,[11] many of which are connecting passages, overhead link bridges between buildings, or spaces on the ground floor of commercial buildings. The negotiation and compromise between city officials and developers, who desire greater control and predictability, versus the real needs of the migrant domestic workers for spaces to socialize, is a continuous process.

AIRPORT SOCIAL, RECREATIONAL, ENTERTAINMENT, AND STUDY SPACE

The Changi Airport in Singapore has been consistently ranked among the best in the world by travelers. In 2010 it won the prestigious Skytrax World's Best Airport Award, as well as the Best Airport Leisure Amenities and Best Airport Asia.[12] However, what most foreign visitors don't know is that the airport is also a highly popular destination for students. It is not unusual to find large groups of students in Singapore studying in the coffee shops, fast-food chains, and secluded, empty spaces in the city-state's airport. For anyone unaccustomed to this ritual, it seems a rather strange habit on the part of the students to choose the airport as a place to congregate and work (Fig. 14). Given the airport's proximity to the city, connected via a safe, efficient public transport system, coupled with the availability of twenty-four-hour food outlets, it is an obvious choice for the students. The popularity of the airport as a study destination has prompted the owners of the coffee shops and food outlets to put up signs discouraging students from studying as they take up space that otherwise could be used by customers. However, with resourcefulness and ingenuity, the students continue to use the airport for purposes other than what it was intended for. Besides converting the airport into study spaces, teenagers and residents also use the huge expanse of empty spaces to socialize. On weekends, one finds families at the viewing deck of the airport or patronizing the wide array of restaurants. Groups of teenagers congregate in quiet corners to talk, while retirees find the quiet viewing decks an ideal place to spend the weekday afternoon. Couples have also used the airport as a backdrop for their all-important marriage-day photography.

FIGURE 14 Studying, among other activities, is discouraged at the Changi Airport in Singapore. Photo by Justin Zhuang.

The popularity of the space among the teenagers was co-opted by the airport management in a promotion of the Changi Airport as a shopping destination.[13] As many as 400 of them turned up in the transit lounge to perform in the manner of a flash mob to celebrate the launch of the million-dollar prize for the lucky shopper—an example in which a spontaneous and informal spatial appropriation becomes assimilated into a mainstream marketing strategy.

DANCING, SLEEPING, ROLLERBLADING, AND PROTESTING IN THE SUBWAY STATION

The large expanse of interior spaces within the network of underground passages that connect the Esplanade subway station in Singapore to the surrounding office towers, shopping malls, and the Esplanade Theatres on the Bay is designed to double up as an emergency shelter. Conceived as a civil defense shelter where residents can gather and seek protection in times of emergency, the air-conditioned spaces also serve as an alternative social as well as recreational space for urban dwellers who seek relief from the hot and humid climate. Large groups use this space to practice their social dance moves, or teenagers break-dance to music from their portable stereo sets (Fig. 15). Amid these

FIGURE 15   Teenagers use the connecting spaces of the underground subway station in Singapore to practice their dance moves. Photo by Justin Zhuang.

activities are children using the station to rollerblade, and the occasional homeless person spending the night there. When I interviewed them, the couple that brought their children to rollerblade in the subway station said the space is ideal as it is relatively empty compared to the above-ground city. It is also safe, comfortable, and free. Not unlike the Filipino migrant workers who borrowed the city for their Sunday social activities, the urban dwellers in the empty subway station are careful not to incur the disapproval of the authorities by either dirtying or damaging the property through their actions.

In 2009 a group of handicapped residents accompanied by their supporters protested inside the subway station of Hong Kong's mass transit railway against the lack of concessions for handicapped commuters.[14] The large hall in the subway station was filled with protesters who applauded and jeered as their representatives made speeches in support of their cause. For a few hours, the interior of the station took on the traditional role of an above-ground public space where residents gather to voice support for or protest for a collective cause.

LITTLE THAILAND IN SINGAPORE

The Golden Mile Complex in Singapore, either famous or infamous, depending on whether you are a politician who eschews messiness and chaos or someone who celebrates diversity and bottom-up initiatives, is an architectural landmark in the city-state.[15] Designed by Design Partnership, a local architectural firm, and completed in 1973, the Golden Mile Complex houses offices, shops, and entertainment and food outlets, as well as private apartments. The complex is a living testament to the aspirations of the megastructure movement of the 1960s. The unique stepped profile of the building acknowledges the views and the acoustic and climatic conditions of the site. More important, by consolidating a variety of programmatic requirements under one roof, the complex affords an intense and diverse interior experience, which is made more vivid by Thai migrant workers' conversion of the building into their Little Thailand. The evolution of the Golden Mile Complex into a place for Thai residents to socialize, seek entertainment, and procure Thai groceries, herbs, medicines, and other daily necessities began with the use of the complex as a departure point for the affordable long-haul bus ride to Thailand and Malaysia. Gradually, services and shops catering specifically to the Thai population started to increase and eventually took over most of the retail and commercial spaces in the complex (Fig. 16).

The activities in the Golden Mile Complex resonate with the daily temporal rhythms of the city and change from day to night.[16] After the shops close at the end of the day, the food outlets, coffee shops, and bars take on a more aggressive presence. The owners will deploy tables and chairs along the closed shop fronts, expanding their physical boundaries to cater to more customers. Although the action technically breaches the contract, it has become an accepted practice among the stall owners due to the unspoken agreement that the space will be returned to its original condition when the stall closes in the early hours of the morning. The tacit agreement is similar to how outdoor

FIGURE 16   A version of the Erawan shrine outside the Golden Mile Complex in Singapore. Photo by Thomas Kong.

spaces in Singapore are sometimes appropriated by residents for the informal collection of used cardboard boxes, newspapers, and other recycled goods. Bar hostesses, at times with their customers, linger outside the premises on the second floor of the Golden Mile Complex. Music and gyrating disco lights fill the atrium, drawing the attention of a different kind of visitor to the complex at night. The varying atmospheric conditions of this megastructure are experienced vertically across the atrium, from the highly charged lower floors to the quieter residential apartments above. Outside the complex is a small, elevated platform where a Buddhist shrine sits. It is frequented by both local and Thai residents and is very popular during religious festivals. It is not uncommon to find a visitor, a tenant, or a passenger about to embark on a trip saying a prayer at the shrine.

The plurality of lives within expansive, connected interior environments in Hong Kong and Singapore is a testament to a unique form of interior urbanism in the two cities. Some of the occupations are co-opted into the formal programmatic agendas of building owners and developers, while others are more tactical and confrontational, sustained through individual and collective tactics of contestation, negotiation, and accommodation. From my research, an ecology of conditions and factors is instrumental to the existence of diverse lives within the interior spaces. I use the word *ecology* because the conditions and factors do not act alone but are interdependent with one another in sustaining the interior activities.

DENSITY

Asian cities have some of the highest population densities in the world. With a population of over five million and limited space for building, as much as 82 percent of Singapore's population lives in high-rise public housing.[17] Hong Kong is well known for its micro and tightly compacted living quarters, which is not surprising, with 67,080 persons per square mile (25,900 persons per square kilometer).[18] In 1938 American sociologist Louis Wirth in his essay "Urbanism as a Way of Life" described the effects and consequences of a highly urbanized environment, which has high-density living and a large, heterogeneous population as its main characteristics.[19] Of interest for me is his description that living in a highly dense city forces its residents to intermingle with one another and creates a multitude of social interactions as a result. For anyone who has taken a walk down Mong Kok in Hong Kong, the experience would resonate deeply with Wirth's description. Moreover, the phenomenon of high-density living also affords greater spatial and programmatic intermixing and sharing within a compact city footprint. The spirit of sharing extends down to the everyday life of residents in Hong Kong and Singapore, where it is not uncommon for several strangers to sit around the same table and have their meals together in a restaurant. Unlike residents in the United States, who have the choice of a single-family house with a front yard and backyard for their private use, many urban dwellers in Hong Kong and Singapore utilize the city as an extension of their private living space. Families gather in the neighborhood coffee shops well into the evenings or spend their time chatting at the mall since their apartments are small. In research conducted by the Society of Community Organization, a not-for-profit organization in Hong Kong, it was found that some children in a less-well-off neighborhood in Kowloon would use fast-food outlets instead of their cramped living spaces as a place to do their homework.[20] The lack of well-designed open spaces in Hong Kong, as argued by another paper,[21] means that most residents have to resort to other spaces in the city to meet and socialize. In my own personal experience growing up in a crowded shophouse in Singapore, inhabited by an extended family of cousins, aunties, uncles, and grandparents, the houses and shops of my neighbors were my extended playground and an opportunity to be away from my family. I do not recall playing in a proper playground; I had to improvise and imagine possibilities from whatever space I found myself in. Contrary to urbanist Jane Jacob's assertion that the stability of inner-city ethnic populations creates enduring communities, sociologist Richard Sennett in his book *The Uses of Disorder* argues that instability resulting from the constant movement of people in cities means that urban dwellers need to constantly interact with newcomers.[22] Hong Kong and Singapore exemplify the kind of cities that Sennett described, as both cities attract a large percentage of expatriates and migrant workers. The persistent flow of people seeking work and other opportunities creates a dynamic and varied urban life. Being subjected to the thrown-togetherness of a densely populated environment of ceaseless flow, residents in Hong Kong and Singapore therefore have to accept, share, negotiate, and accommodate differences in their everyday life.

INTERIORS AS VESSELS

Large, interconnected interior environments in Singapore extend beyond the typical privatized and climatically controlled underground passages, above-ground link bridges, covered atria, and expanded shopping malls. A particular feature of Singapore's urban landscape is the amalgamation of public transportation and commercial, retail, residential, and recreational facilities into a synergistic urban assemblage connected by covered link ways. Contrary to the prefix *infra*'s sense of "underneath or hidden," public infrastructural buildings such as subway stations and intermodal transportation hubs are architectural statements in a city-state. A significant amount of resources and time is invested in the conceptualization, planning, and integration into the urban fabric of these types of infrastructure. They are spatially and programmatically connected to a network of buildings and open spaces, forming hubs of intensity and social interaction for urban dwellers. Getting around the city on public transportation is much more affordable than owning a car; one needs to consider not only the high initial cost of purchasing a car but the cost of maintenance and parking as well, which in land-scarce Hong Kong and Singapore can be exorbitant. Public transportation, therefore, is the main mode of traveling for many residents in both cities. The banks of escalators in the midlevel, central district of Hong Kong Island ferry residents up from the streets below to the apartments and sideways into the elevated, labyrinthine network of alleyways, eateries, and shops that offer myriad services (Fig. 17). Leslie Lu, in his article "The Asian Arcades Project: Progressive Porosity," argues that more can be done to take advantage of these urban infrastructural linkages given their effective roles as multilevel spatial and social connectors in the city.[23] If we conceive of infrastructural spaces as interior vessels that are simultaneously containers of social interactions and channels of human traffic, they do not become standalone entities in the urban landscape. The underground linking

FIGURE 17   An interior space in Hong Kong lined with shops and eateries acts as an interior connector between the subway station, adjacent street, and buildings. Photo by Thomas Kong.

passages in downtown Singapore connect retail, commercial, and cultural buildings; the existing subway system; and the above-ground public parks. Likewise, the Golden Mile Complex in Singapore, despite its conception as a megastructure in the 1970s, serves as an important departure and arrival point for the long-haul coach journeys to neighboring countries in the north.

SMALL-TRADES MENTALITY

Small, street-level trades and businesses drive cities in Asia. The vibrant street life in Hong Kong is largely due to this phenomenon. One finds food stalls intermingled with other street peddlers selling a variety of housewares, toys, and clothes along a sidewalk, next to a road, or outside the entrance of a building. Faced with the scarcity of space in the high-density urban environment, residents reclaim the narrow alleys at the back of buildings as an extension of the interior. The alleys are shielded from the sun and rain by plastic sheets stretched overhead, turning the open-air space into an interior environment housing narrow-fronted food stalls and shops that sometimes extend along the whole length of the alleyway. In other situations, stalls located opposite each other would employ the same strategy to extend their business area by transforming the existing pedestrian walkway into a partial interior (Fig. 18). This surplus, the overflowing of life within the interior out into the streets, gives Asian cities like Hong Kong a dynamic

FIGURE 18 An alleyway is transformed into an interior space for selling cooked food and dining in Hong Kong. Photo by Thomas Kong.

and lively public quality. The migration of the small-trades mentality to large-scale interiors that house a range of shops and services helps to maintain a level of messiness and diversity even when spaces are stacked vertically as opposed to spreading horizontally across the city. Besides the Golden Mile Complex, another major megastructure in Singapore is the People's Park Complex in Chinatown, which contains the same intensity and plurality of living, working, and shopping spaces within a large interior environment comprising of a podium block with high-rise residential units above. The extension of the small-trades mentality is witnessed by the number of small, privately owned shops in the People's Park Complex that mimic the vitality of the street-level shops in Chinatown.

SERVICE-CENTRIC CITIES

As a natural evolution from a deeply rooted trading mentality, both Hong Kong and Singapore have developed into highly service-centric cities, which living in a high-density urban environment supports. In Hong Kong, for example, it is not an uncommon practice for local residents to pay the neighborhood dry-cleaning shop a small fee to store their winter clothes since there is insufficient closet space in the apartments. Besides, the residents perceive this as more convenient than storing the clothes themselves. In both cities, dining out is the norm in residents' daily life. The wide range of affordable street cuisines makes dining out accessible to everyone; it also provides a hassle-free alternative to entertaining friends at home. The Urban Redevelopment Authority of Singapore in 2003 started the Civil and Community Institution scheme to integrate community facilities and services within retail and commercial spaces.[24] The extensive list of community-based uses includes services for children, disabled residents, families, the elderly, volunteer-based programs, community library, community clubs, and sports facilities managed and run by the National Sports Association and backed by the Singapore Sports Council (Fig. 19). The National Council of Social Service, which is the umbrella organization partnering with private developers to oversee the management of the scheme, will sublet the space to tenants, consisting of nongovernmental and voluntary welfare organizations. There is no rental charge except for a monthly fee for utilities and the maintenance of common areas. The assortment of services offered in Singapore's malls includes tutoring centers for primary and secondary school students, domestic help agencies, Laundromats, post offices, state-managed betting centers, remittance agencies for foreign workers, employment agencies, courier services, private nurse agencies, medical and dental clinics, pawnshops, nongovernmental organizations, and prayer rooms, to name a few.

The embedding of these services in large, interconnected interiors within a transportation network further boosts and intensifies the service-oriented attitude of residents of Hong Kong and Singapore. The plethora of affordable services caters to the varied needs of residents, from migrant workers to the middle class, and is organized along the daily flow of commuting to and from work, which makes the large, mixed-use interiors less of an exclusive and regulated space. Furthermore, the residents procuring these services

FIGURE 19 The National Volunteer and Philanthropy Center (NVPC) in Singapore is located in the Central Shopping Mall. The mall is situated directly above the Clarke Quay subway station and is part of a mixed-use development consisting of commercial, retail, and residential spaces. Photo by Justin Zhuang.

are not passive consumers. A strong social network and support activities, such as remittance centers, clinics, and tutoring centers, link consumption and socializing in the compact and densely populated city. The mall in Singapore where the Filipina domestic worker remits money back to her family is also the place for her to send parcels home, a place to socialize with her friends on Sundays in reasonably priced restaurants serving food from their homeland, to treat herself to the occasional luxury, to look for alternative employment, and to seek help if abused by her employer. In Hong Kong, shopping has also evolved to take on a unique local character that resists the pressure of cultural and spatial homogeneities. Spaces of shopping are simultaneously sites of consumption, contestation, socialization, and cultural formation for the local residents.[25] The reality on the ground, therefore, is much more layered and nuanced than envisioned by Western observers.

CLIMATE

The extension of interior spaces into the city and vice versa would not have been possible if the climate was severe. Unlike the harsh winter in North America, which demands a secure separation between indoors and outdoors, the tropical and subtropical climates of Singapore and Hong Kong, respectively, create a transitional space between the interior and the exterior that supports an open design of buildings and elevated streets. Besides facilitating cross-ventilation and visual connectivity, the porosity allows sounds and scents from the shops and food stalls to be transmitted to the street, which adds to the vitality and multisensorial qualities of the street life. On the other hand, due to the desire to escape from the humidity and heat of the tropics, large interior spaces in the city are welcome relief for the residents, who take advantage of the air-conditioned space to hold their own social and recreational activities.

SOCIOECONOMIC AND POLITICAL SETTINGS

All societies possess implicit and explicit rules regarding behaviors, expectations, and actions, which are formalized through time as laws, habits, customs, traditions, and values that become the settings for everyday life in cities. Hong Kong and Singapore are cosmopolitan Asian cities connected to the international flow of capital, trade, information, and people. Beyond the liberal economic policies that encourage free trade, Hong Kong and Singapore have through the years developed very different political systems, which have made a significant impact on, and continue to shape, the patterns of public life in both cities.

The general perception of a visitor to Singapore is of a highly organized, efficient, and orderly environment. Much of this can be attributed to the far-reaching role of the government in planning and regulating all forms of its citizens' private and public lives to ensure political stability, economic growth, religious harmony, and the maintenance of a safe living environment. Despite the charge of a draconian rule that limits freedom of expression and political dissent among the ethnically diverse population, leading to self-censorship and conformity in thinking and action, I am intrigued by the multitude of ways in which residents in Singapore are still able to reappropriate interior spaces for their own use; an infralayer of spontaneous, informal social and economic exchanges subsists quietly and comfortably alongside the more formal, official, and predictable city. The continuing, negotiated existence and tolerance are maintained as long as people abide by the tacit understanding that their spatial appropriation should not cause inconvenience or result in property damage and should not be criminal in nature or politically motivated. Therefore, social groups can hold line-dancing events in the empty subway station in the evenings, and teenagers practice break-dance routines without disturbance from the authorities. Hong Kong, on the other hand, possesses a robust civil society fully engaged in the affairs of the city; it stands ready to challenge unfair practices and policies, as well as to supplement state-provided social services. The special administrative region's fiercely independent and vocal nongovernmental organizations help ensure that the disenfranchised have a public voice. Unlike in Singapore, where the tactics of spatial appropriations are more negotiated, subtle, and less provocative, Hong Kong residents would not hesitate to mobilize social demonstrations to translate their grievances into community actions, as seen in the public protest in the subway station and over the Times Square incident.

Both cities still retain a strong social organization that extols immediate and extended family ties, coexisting with a mentality that values efficacy, speed, pragmatism, and a deep survival instinct. For Singapore, the rhetoric of vulnerability and survival is renewed every Independence Day and by the ruling party. Over time, it has become imbued into the psyche of its citizens. The few social safety nets provided by the British colonial government in Hong Kong, prior to the handover in 1997, meant that Hong Kong residents had to depend on themselves and their families to survive in a highly competitive society.[26] Eventually, this evolved to become a societal trait that created an intensely driven and family-based entrepreneurial sector in the former British colony. The notion that every situation presents an opportunity to be seized and shaped to one's practical advantage animates the formal, strategic planning decisions of the state and the informal, tactical appropriations of interior spaces by local residents. This is witnessed in Singapore with the Urban Redevelopment Authority's single-minded vision to enhance the pedestrian shopping experience by systematically linking downtown buildings via underground passages.[27] In Hong Kong, the construction of a network of partially enclosed bridges that connect commercial buildings is seen as a practical solution to separate pedestrians and vehicles in order to facilitate smoother traffic flows. On the other hand, local residents opportunistically appropriate public infrastructure and spaces of consumption for social and civic activities. Their actions reorient the generic spaces of infrastructure and consumption toward the human capacity to dwell locally over time, and the ability to improvise with creativity and resourcefulness.

CONCLUSION

The ownership, control, and use of private and public large, interconnected interiors in Hong Kong and Singapore are less clearly defined and maintained than for their Western counterparts. The porosity and ambiguity between proprietorship and the diverse uses set up permeable and shifting boundaries for transient occupations through negotiation, accommodation, and contestation. The tolerance for temporary unprogrammed and alternative uses is higher in both cities compared to the strict control and surveillance of privately owned public space in a city like New York, where such space is a common spatial typology. Even if the uses are predetermined and set within the space of consumption, the multiplicity of services catering to a large portion of the local population in Singapore and the ever-vigilant nongovernmental organizations in Hong Kong prevent these large, mixed-use interiors and privately owned public spaces from becoming restrictive and homogeneous, as feared by Western critics. Through this chapter, I hope to have presented a compelling argument that the critique of large, interconnected interior environments in the West may not strictly apply in Asia. The spatial, social, political, economic, and climatic conditions in Hong Kong and Singapore have given rise to a unique form of interior urbanism that has augmented the manifold experiences of city life, which no doubt is one important facet of an unfolding twenty-first-century urbanism in Asia.

14

Swiss Cheese and Beanbags: Producing Interior Urbanism

LEE STICKELLS

INTRODUCTION

What could it mean to discuss *interior urbanism*? The term appears contradictory: connecting the interior—and its associations of privacy, domesticity, and intimacy—with urbanity—evoking exteriority, the city, and public life. However, such oppositional taxonomies (inside/outside, private/public, community/society) are contingent and ductile. Critical to the modern city, it might be argued, is a reciprocal relationship between such dichotomies—a mutually implicating relationship between the intimate and the social.[1] The late twentieth century witnessed a proliferation of constructed environments that seem to elide these distinctions, provoking discussion of urban questions in relation to their pervasive interiority. During this period, large-scale, interconnected interior environments, housing complex mixtures of retail, commercial, recreational, and residential spaces, evolved and burgeoned. One set of examples lies in the systems of overhead and underground walkways that stitch together extensive interior spaces; in locations such as Toronto's PATH system, Hong Kong Island's central elevated walkways, and Atlanta's Peachtree Center, these linkages produce vast, and often hermetic, public interior spaces (Fig. 20). Similarly, there has been an accelerating phenomenon of enormous buildings housing complex and multilayered programs in hermetic environments—sited as autonomous objects in the urban landscape. Huge shopping centers such as the South China Mall or Dubai Mall, airport complexes such as Schiphol or Heathrow (now conceptualized as "airport cities"), and the casino developments of Las Vegas are conspicuous examples.[2] They exemplify some of the implications of an interior urbanism, particularly what Rem Koolhaas has identified as "Bigness":

> Bigness no longer needs the city: it competes with the city; it represents the city; it
> preempts the city; or better still, it is the city. If urbanism generates potential and

architecture exploits it, Bigness enlists the generosity of urbanism against the meanness of architecture.[3]

This points to an interior urbanism defined by extent—an ambiguous perceptual condition where the understanding of building versus city is made problematic through
sheer scale. Connection becomes absolute, and all is interiorized, producing an aura of
congestion.[4] Examination of the impacts of the architectural infrastructure that supports
an interior urbanism—air-conditioning, elevators, escalators, and the structural systems
that allow buildings to go wider, deeper, and higher—is valuable for engaging with the
implications of such contemporary urban environments. However, it is not the consideration foregrounded in this chapter. Rather, the focus is placed on understanding interior urbanism in terms of relational infrastructures—conceptualizing urbanity in this
case, not through scale of construction, or complexity of program, but as concerning
particular forms of social encounter.

In his discussion of the Office for Metropolitan Architecture (OMA)'s IIT building
in Chicago, Charles Rice points toward this mode of interpretation. He identifies a careful construction of interior atmospheres in the McCormick Tribune Campus Center
that intensifies moments of spatial montage. Illumination, circulation, floor levels, and
programmatic juxtaposition are used to elicit the contingent sense of relationality experienced in city streets. Rice suggests that the building's interior uses the spatial and material effects created in order to splice programmatic zones together—"producing abrupt

FIGURE 20   Hong Kong, urban interior (2011). Courtesy of Antony Westwood.

linkages and opportunistic appropriations."[5] This approach to understanding interior urbanism is a useful starting point because it shifts us away from an analytic overdetermined by ideas of the interior as enclosure and of the urban as common, open ground: a formalist paradigm of hermetic architectures and permeable cities. Instead, the focus moves toward notions of climate, ambience, and disposition.

In this chapter I take up that emphasis on the production of particular kinds of urban subjectivity and experience within architectural interiors. However, the specific trajectory will shift from attending to the production of interior "weather" atmospheres—intensities of light, color, and space—to concentrating on the production of interior atmospheres of "flow"—intensities of connection and encounter mirroring the dynamic sociability of external urban spaces. That particular sense of an interiorized urban realm is used to characterize a developing understanding of urbanity as a condition of informal encounter and conviviality being sought in architectural interiors—as diverse as offices and classrooms—to intensify spaces of learning and working. Interior urbanism is proposed here as an analytic frame to explore the contemporary linking of urban tropes with architectural interiority.

URBANITY AND SERENDIPITY

> In 1994 the mall officially replaced the civic functions of the traditional downtown. In a New Jersey Supreme Court case regarding the distribution of political leaflets in shopping malls the court declared that "shopping malls have replaced the parks and squares that were 'traditionally the home of free speech,'" siding with the protesters "who had argued that a mall constitutes a modern-day Main Street".[6]

Positive qualities of modern urbanity—the production of tolerance, civic engagement, struggles against oppression, and democratic political participation—are regularly connected with the establishment of accessible, open public spaces. A shared physical commons, where people can interact with one another and encounter difference, is often considered vital to the maintenance of a robust public sphere.[7] The phenomenon of extensive interiorization discussed in this chapter's introduction is problematic for such understandings, as it often involves the shifting of collective public activity to the inside of privately controlled building complexes. There are strong arguments that such shifts mean that the possibilities for debate and difference, vital to the public realm, are curtailed.[8] The question of the commercial shopping mall as a public space of political contestation, directly confronted in the case heard by the New Jersey Supreme Court, captures the ongoing dilemma well: if public space is an instrument of social change—a locus of forthright interaction that expands human possibilities—can the orchestrated, controlled space of the privatized interior provide the necessary legal, social, and physical openness? The uncertainty is further complicated if we recognize that public space, as a physical site of unmediated social interaction, is not necessarily commensurate with property boundaries (state-owned versus private property), nor is it a unitary space (multiple publics produce their own spaces of appearance). In addition, the broader public realm or the public sphere of political debate does not only manifest itself in material space.[9]

I am pursuing a slightly different inquiry, though: beyond arguments over the "publicness" of large, interiorized commercial spaces, why is there a frequent evocation of urbanity in the production of much less public spaces? Particularly in contemporary educational, research, and office buildings, there is a tendency to conceive relationships between form and program—between the spatial configuration and the patterns of activity and interaction it catalyzes—in terms of urban structures, activities, and atmospheres. The focus of these tactics is overwhelmingly the interior.

A clear example of this approach can be seen in the Los Angeles offices of the advertising agency TBWA\Chiat\Day, designed by Clive Wilkinson Architects in 1997 (see Plate 9). Sited in a large warehouse, where the company consolidated its offices, the project became known as "Advertising City" due to the urban character of the interior, which included a "main street," a "central park," a basketball court, billboards, and work neighborhoods. The project has been extremely influential for subsequent office design, especially in creative and media fields—a similar use of an urban interior can be seen in FAT Architects' 2002 design for the advertising agency 10's offices in Antwerp.[10] The interior resembles an elaborate, immersive theater set, featuring miniature building facades, a bridge, faux hedging, and a "town square." As FAT cofounder Sean Griffiths described it, "Using the concept of 'interior urbanism' we designed two main zones for the space connected by a bridge and a 'town square' with a basketball pitch."[11] The "urban interior" was designed for exploration and wandering through, allowing people to bump into one another. This spurring of serendipitous encounters would supposedly foster informal communication and idea sharing within the company.

In a very different context, the Ørestad Gymnasium was designed by 3XN in 2007, responding to Danish educational reforms. Its interior was similarly intended to produce a high degree of interaction and, in this case, encourage students to take active responsibility for their own learning process as well as their collective working environment (see Plate 10). A range of spaces offer students the options of learning in conventional classes, in larger assemblies, or alone, when they can flop down on beanbags with their laptops.

Although not as explicit in its appropriation of urban tropes, the interior features four boomerang-shaped "story decks" (platforms with informal seating such as beanbags) that are open toward a central core, where a broad primary staircase winds its way upward to the roof terrace. That main staircase is the core of educational and social life; it is the strongest vertical connection but also "a place to stay, watch and be seen."[12] Like the advertising agency 10's offices, Ørestad Gymnasium's internal landscape is intended to cultivate informal encounter and collaboration through a fluid set of spaces open to appropriation.

Even in working environments that are more often associated with conservative, hierarchical structures and conventional architecture—such as banking—the relational dynamics and corresponding spatial configurations of interior urbanism are being invoked. At the Macquarie Bank in Sydney, completed in 2009, Clive Wilkinson Architects (in collaboration with Woods Bagot) sought to create "a kind of vertical Greek village of the future" (Fig. 21).[13] The building's floors were divided into five neighborhoods of approximately 100 people. Within the office floors, "plazas" were designed with themes based on collaboration typologies: the "dining table," the "library," the "garden," the "tree house," the "playroom," and the "coffee house."[14] The coffee house has a particular resonance here given its long-standing importance as a site of public discussion.[15] The cup of coffee has itself come to signify a chance for people to converse beyond the constraints of purpose-governed exchanges (and to slip momentarily from assigned roles). Also consistent with the urban design approach, a "main street" on the building's first floor has communal spaces—including a café—that support larger corporate events.

FIGURE 21 Macquarie Bank in Sydney (2009), designed by Clive Wilkinson Architects in association with Woods Bago. Courtesy of Shannon McGrath.

What emerges in the production of these enclosed plazas, learning streets, and corporate main streets is an interior urbanism that functions as relational infrastructure—called on to produce casual conversation and serendipitous encounter. The urban form of the interior in such contexts is a device for enhancing productivity, creativity, and collaboration within diverse workplaces rather than for creating a collective forum for political debate and the conflictual negotiation of public life.

PERFORMING URBANITY

Underlying the production of this kind of interior urbanism is a pervasive understanding of modern urbanity as communal performance.[16] Charles Moore captured well the sense of a network of sites for scripted collectivity in his 1965 essay "You Have to Pay for the Public Life." It eloquently portrayed the seeming lack of a public realm on the West Coast of the United States: "a floating world in which a floating population can island-hop with impunity."[17] He argued that Disneyland was an important new kind of public space in this regard because

> it is engaged in replacing many of those elements of the public realm which have vanished in the featureless private floating world of southern California, whose only edge is the ocean, and whose center is otherwise undiscoverable.[18]

Critically, Moore identified Disneyland as a self-conscious attempt to create an interactive public space, where those entering agree to play-act, and agree to be watched while play-acting. Self-consciously public behavior is performed in a space with "no raw edges," where "political experience" is excluded. Moore also noted that, "curiously for a public place," an entry ticket must be bought; thus there is an agreement to pay for public life.[19]

Focusing on that requirement of admission and enclosure, the work of French semiotician Louis Marin on the structuring of utopia becomes useful for considering the production of interiority. Marin was concerned with the topology of what he termed the "utopian *figure*."[20] Although he focused on the "figure" as the textual or graphic form of utopia as a work of fiction, he also applied his thinking about utopian spatiality to Disneyland, suggesting that "these patterns and functions appear in the topography of a real space in California, and by the visitor's real use of it."[21] In his analysis of Disneyland he detailed the ways in which the original theme park was structured like a utopian island, with a series of gaps, or breaks, that produced the shift between the coordinates and systems of the outside world and those of its interior. Beginning with the abandoning of the car in the outer limit of the parking area, there followed the intermediary limit of ticket booths (including an exchange of U.S. dollars for Disney money) and the inner limit of the route made by the Santa Fe and Disneyland Railway (an embankment that physically encircled and enclosed). For Marin, the spatial patterning at Disneyland—its island-like enclosure—produced a utopic space, not simply independent of the outside (or real) world, but simultaneously open and closed. However, he saw Disneyland as a "degenerate utopia," where, as visitors entered into a fantastical projection of American values and history, the utopic representation was caught, subsumed, and changed into a myth or collective fantasy. The construction of a pseudo-public realm was critical to this process:

> This imaginary world is supposed to be what makes the operation successful. But, what draws the crowds is undoubtedly much more the social microcosm, the miniaturized and religious revelling in real America, in its delights and drawbacks. You park outside, queue up inside, and are totally abandoned at the exit. In this imaginary world the only phantasmagoria is in the inherent warmth and affection of the crowd, and in that sufficiently excessive number of gadgets used there to specifically maintain the multitudinous affect.[22]

The consequences for architecture and urbanism to follow can be clearly seen in the work of a practice such as the Jerde Partnership, an architecture and urban planning firm thoroughly associated with the concepts of "placemaking" and "experience architecture." Through placemaking (which the office describes as their key activity) the Jerde Partnership supposedly "recreates the communal pedestrian experiences upon which great cities were built, while meeting the evolving demands of rapid modernization."[23] Through the choreography of program and materiality, and the orchestration of movement and event, the Jerde Partnership claims to produce a public life of richness and diversity that responds to a broad societal "return to the communal." Chairman and founder Jon Adams Jerde asserts, "Fortunately communal experience is a designable event."[24]

The public realm—and public life—is thus evoked as a kind of shared leisure experience, whereby a themed environment coordinates sensory and symbolic cues to induce a general mood. I want to particularly draw attention to the way that urbanity becomes a coordinated, interiorized experience: the enclave becomes the basic spatial unit of the postmodern city, while material and visual cues that signal urbanity are deployed to activate an individual's internalized narratives, cuing appropriate behaviors.[25] The "experiential design," as Jerde would describe it, draws from a larger narrative framework to organize and orchestrate those impressions, but its "city life" is not necessarily commensurate with the production of a large-scale "cityscape," or the sphere of political assembly and activism. Rather, an interior urbanism emerges that is concerned with the spatial structuring of discreet atmospheres for pleasurable casual encounter; a whole taxonomy may be required for what could be described, adopting the hyperbole of Jean Baudrillard, as "spaces of circulation, ventilation and ephemeral connections."[26]

To approach and interrogate the ideas, atmospheres, and forms coalescing in the production of this particular mode of interior urbanism, three short accounts are offered here. Centered on 1992 (two years before the New Jersey Supreme Court's recognition of the mall as a public space), each indicates a conceptual strand that might be further unraveled to work through the consequences of interior urbanism, illustrating late twentieth-century anxieties over the commercially oriented interiorization of the city, the promotion of an architecture of serendipitous encounter, and the emergence of art practices fascinated with producing convivial sociability. The abrupt linkages and pre-liminary shadings of these vignettes sketch a productive area of research that directly engages with the complex, intertwined relationships between contemporary architecture, its interiors, and the multitudinous public realm.

1992(A): THE END OF URBANISM?

This book pleads for a return to a more authentic urbanity, a city based on physical proximity and free movement and a sense that the city is our best expression of a desire for collectivity. As spatiality ebbs, so does intimacy. The privatized city of bits is a lie, simulating its connections, obliterating the power of its citizens either to act alone or to act together.[27]

Taken from Michael Sorkin's introduction to *Variations on a Theme Park,* the above quote articulates the central concern of that book. Published in 1992, it exemplified an influential strand of urban discourse around that time—marking a collective anxiety about the landscape of the Western consumerist city (Fig. 22). For example, also published in the early to mid-1990s—and meditating on some of the same concerns about a decay of public life and the disappearance of public space in an aggressively privatizing world—were Mike Davis's *City of Quartz: Excavating the Future in Los Angeles* (1990), Sharon Zukin's *Landscapes of Power: From Detroit to Disney World* (1991), Richard Sennett's

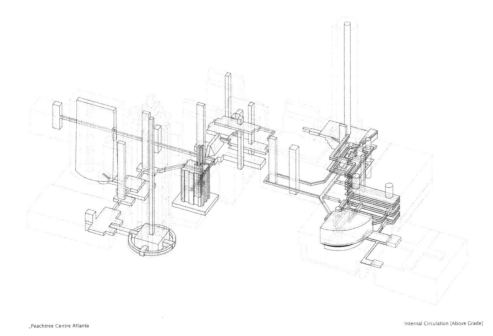

_Peachtree Centre Atlanta

Internal Circulation [Above Grade]

FIGURE 22   Peachtree Center (1970s onward), by John Portman Architects. Diagram of interior circulation above grade. Courtesy of Charles Rice and Alina McConnochie.

Flesh and Stone: The Body and the City in Western Civilization (1994), and Neil Smith's *The New Urban Frontier: Gentrification and the Revanchist City* (1996).[28]

The distinction of *Variations on a Theme Park* was its focus on the role of the built environment (especially architecture and urban design) in realizing the social and political promise of urbanity—the promiscuous mix of people and the possibilities it creates. The various essays combined to sketch a picture of an emerging (largely North American) urbanism that disrupted those possibilities, distinguished by Sorkin through three key conditions. First, there was its placelessness: a "dissipation of all stable relations to local physical and cultural geography, the loosening of ties to any specific place." Second, it was overwhelmingly focused on security, through "rising levels of manipulation and surveillance over its citizenry and with a proliferation of new modes of segregation." Third, it offered only a simulation of true urbanity, resulting in "the city as theme park."[29]

For Sorkin, that problem of the urban simulacrum was nowhere more visible than in the city's architecture. He suggested that an almost purely semiotic architecture and urban design had constructed an image of the historical city in the place of the human ecologies that actually produced and inhabited its urbanity. The "new city" was controlled, managed, and commercialized, and thus not truly urban. Instead, a phony urbanism was constructed from superficial, historicized "signs" of the public realm.

Anxiety over the "fake" and the "phony," the "simulacrum" and the "theme park" permeated the book, and it was especially directed at emerging urban interiority. In "Underground and Overhead: Building the Analogous City," Trevor Boddy worried about the "surrogate streets" of new interiorized urban pedestrian systems and their artificial rather than natural environments: "It was now possible to . . . walk from office to agency to restaurant under silkscreened banners waving in the pale wind of climate-controlled regularity."[30] M. Christine Boyer offered similar concerns about what she called "urban tableaux"—wishful projections of urban space where "the aim is theatrical: to represent certain visual images of the city, to create perspectival views shown through imaginary prosceniums in order to conjure up emotionally satisfying images of bygone times."[31]

Those anxieties reflected the connection between the concerns of the authors and a long lineage of theorizing about the impacts of urban modernity (for example, the work of Walter Benjamin, Georg Simmel, Lewis Mumford, Henri Lefebvre, and Jane Jacobs) positing critical links between the qualities of urban public space and urban engagement and citizenship. In the loss of an authentic urbanism, there is seen to be a loss of authentic urban relations—they are deemed to evaporate as their physical emplacement becomes more ephemeral. Jacobs famously linked the qualities of the street to a web of shared public trust and respect. In *The Death and Life of Great American Cities* (1961) she lamented the impacts of large-scale modernist urban regeneration on existing city neighborhoods and their fine-grained streets: "Impersonal city streets make anonymous people."[32] Similarly, in his essay in *Variations on a Theme*

Park, Boddy argued, "It may yet become apparent to all that in losing the social forum of the traditional street to the new analogous city, something important is forever departed. A zone of coexistence, of dialogue, of friction, even, is necessary to a vital urban order."[33]

1992(B): THE SOCIAL MAGIC CARPET

Also in 1992, the Dutch architectural practice OMA produced a competition entry for the design of two libraries at the Campus Universitaire de Jussieu in Paris (Fig. 23). The campus's development had been halted by the events of May 1968, and the library projects were envisaged as a way of resuscitating the modernist gridded blocks designed by Éduoard Albert. The OMA's scheme anticipated many formal and programmatic ideas that would resurface in later completed buildings (the best known of those projects is probably the Seattle Public Library, completed in 2004). The Jussieu Library project also exemplified a wider architectural interest during the 1990s in relationships between the spatial configuration of buildings (particularly the articulation of the interior) and social interactions, focused through attention to key concepts, such as "program," "event," "diagram," and "flows."[34] Documented in a postscript to *S, M, L, XL,* the scheme is described as a deradicalized reimagining of the constructivist social condenser to produce

FIGURE 23   Project for library at Campus Universitaire de Jussieu (1992), by the Office for Metropolitan Architecture (OMA). Courtesy of OMA/Hans Werlemann.

an interior urbanism: a single floor plate spirals and weaves through the building's various levels, combining the two libraries in a single formal gesture.

At Jussieu, urbanity is deliberately folded into the interior: strange, congested activity consumed by OMA's mute container. It is worth extensively quoting the project description here, to understand the spatial relations being proposed:

> We imagine its surface as pliable, a social magic carpet; we fold it to generate density, then form a "stacking" of platforms; minimal enclosure makes it a building—the culmination of the Jussieu network.
>
> These surfaces—a vertical, intensified landscape—are then "urbanized": the specific elements of the libraries are reimplanted in the new public realm like buildings in a city.... All the planes are connected by a single trajectory, a warped interior boulevard that exposes and relates all programmatic elements. The visitor becomes a Baudelairean *flâneur,* inspecting and being seduced by a world of books and information—by the urban scenario.
>
> Through their scale and variety, the effect of the inhabited planes becomes almost that of a street; this boulevard generates a system of supra-programmatic "urban" elements in the interior: plazas, parks, monumental staircases, cafés, shops.[35]

It can be seen that the emphasis here is on producing density, variety, and difference—constructing the conditions for the serendipitous encounter. The supra-programmatic ramp, as a device for throwing strangers together, is the critical spatial component: the "social magic carpet." None of the symbolic, semiotic concerns that so worried the authors in *Variations on a Theme Park*—the anxiety over authenticity—appear. Instead, the "minimal enclosure" of OMA's project is envisaged as a kind of infrastructure that encourages a "dynamic coexistence of activities" and, through their interference, generates "unprecedented events."[36]

1992(C): RELATIONAL DEVICES

In his 1992 exhibition *Untitled (Free),* the peripatetic artist Rirkrit Tiravanija cooked and served Thai curry to the (often nonplussed) visitors to the 303 Gallery in New York (Fig. 24). Visitors also came across the usually hidden elements of a gallery—packed artworks, office supplies, and the gallery director—as Tiravanija had relocated them to the public space of the gallery. *Untitled (Free)* was an early work that indicated concerns that Tiravanija continues to explore: the ways art is produced and exhibited, its economies and social processes. An important part of the show was watching the artist cook—assuming the role of performer—but a year later Tiravanija altered these dynamics.

In 1993 he contributed to the group show *Aperto 93* at the Venice Biennale. Coming upon this work, visitors now found a gas ring keeping a large pot of water on the boil. Cardboard boxes stacked up against the wall of the gallery contained packets of dehydrated Chinese soup; people were free to help themselves to the soup simply by

FIGURE 24   Rirkrit Tiravanija (b. 1961): *Untitled 1992/1995 (free/still)*. New York, Museum of Modern Art. Refrigerator, table, chairs, wood, drywall, food, and other materials; dimensions variable. Gift of Mr. and Mrs. Eli Wallach (by exchange). Acc. n.: 225.2001.© 2012. Digital image, The Museum of Modern Art, New York/Scala, Florence.

adding the water the artist had left simmering in the pot. Scattered through this scene were various pieces of camping equipment. Tiravanija—who is of Thai origin, was born in Argentina in 1961, and now divides his time between New York and Berlin—has subsequently become well known for his makeshift kitchens (gas stoves and other camping gear, boxes, crates, and sacks of provisions), which he installs in galleries, museums, and other exhibition spaces and which he either generously attends to himself or makes available to others. Significantly, in addition to the everyday provisions that ostensibly make the works, in titling and describing the materials Tiravanijia always includes the words "lots of people."[37]

The *Aperto* show has been seen as a key marker of a subsequent focus on aspects of the social by a number of contemporary artists. Tiravanija's departure point was the idea of the social sculpture pioneered by Joseph Beuys, recast to engage with the complex codings and structures of conviviality elaborated through communal eating. However, *Untitled (Free)*, his *Aperto* installation, and other similar works hover around the edges of definition. Whether they should be understood as sculpture, installation, or performance is unclear. In the free distribution of food they might, at a stretch, even be interpreted as social activism. Tiravanija himself emphasizes the social encounters his work produces: "It is not what you see that is important but what takes place between people."[38] A more productive way of thinking about the works is as relational devices, or infrastructures—containing a certain degree of randomness while provoking or managing individual and group encounters. The French curator and writer Nicolas Bourriaud has most prominently theorized such work through a "relational aesthetics": "judging artworks on the basis of the inter-human relations which they represent, produce or prompt."[39] In the collection of essays titled *Relational Aesthetics* he argues that human relations have become fully fledged artistic forms. For Bourriaud this means that "meetings, encounters, events, various types of collaboration between people, games, festivals, and places of conviviality, in a word all manner of encounter and relational invention thus represent today, aesthetic objects."[40]

   The work of artists like Tiravanija, and the discourse surrounding the notion of relational aesthetics, signals a strong contemporary interest in the exploration of spatial, aesthetic frameworks for heterogeneous forms of sociability—the production of micro-utopias. As Bourriaud puts it, "They are thus inventing models of sociality or modes of communication, drawing, more or less, immaterially on the fluxes that tie us to one another."[41] A broad range of projects—an expanded field of art and architectural practice—have emerged exploring the construction of situations that rework the possibilities for social relations, particularly the economically driven relationships that underpin the construction of urban space.[42] The relational infrastructures that produce these crucibles are often small scale, ephemeral, and bound up with the construction of intimate spaces for encounter. Tiravanija's practice, and its careful reconfiguration of gallery spaces (through the use of spatial division, furniture, cooking appliances, and objects such as books and plants), provides a good example.

CONSTRUCTING INTERIOR URBANISM

These three sketches juxtapose disparate spheres of activity and concern: ongoing academic debate around the connection between the material public realm and the public sphere of political debate, projective architectural practice exploring spatial invention, and a strand of contemporary art practice reworking the social as a medium. However, at varying scales, each also illustrates issues around the structuring of social encounters in public spaces and contributes to understanding the concept of an interior urbanism. The public space debates in *Variations on a Theme Park* highlight persistent concerns that have accompanied a growing interiority and commercial orchestration of urban space—drawing attention to ceaselessly contested understandings of the spatial and social forms that constitute the public realm. The architectural explorations of OMA—developing formal strategies for the interior staging of spontaneous encounter and serendipitous event—represent a broader interest in the spatial design of such interior urbanism. The fields of relational art and urban intervention, particularly in their configuration of relational devices or infrastructures, suggest forms of encounter that can produce relational micro-territories—seemingly, even a gas burner and some Chinese noodles can suffice. In this way, the three accounts of contemporaneous reflection on urbanity, encounter, and conviviality start to tease out the complex assemblage of concepts and desires that intersect in the production of interior urbanism.

Flowing from these circumstances there are three general, overlapping conditions that can be outlined and that structure the understanding of interior urbanism being suggested here. First, urbanity has become a privileged reference point for the structuring of contemporary architectural spaces—from the management of retail venues to the organization of offices, the fluid, complex interconnections of the urban environment form models for interior design. Second, the long-standing humanist connection of open public spaces to the development of political engagement is less certain: the dynamics of urban mingling and mixing are far from predictable, and civic practices and public culture are shaped in circuits of flow and association that are no longer reducible to the emplacement in the city square or street.[43] Last, urbanity has dispersed. Conceptually, this occurs as the experiential quality of orchestrated mingling and conviviality supplants the notion of an open public space for unmediated encounter (manifested, for example, in the ubiquitous use of "vibrancy" as a goal in urban planning and design). Physically, it emerges as the redistribution of the spatial experience of urbanity; Vito Acconci describes this contemporary condition as one where the public is redefined "as a composite of privates."[44] Urbanity is increasingly conceptualized as an experiential atmosphere, neither produced solely by the physical environment nor located solely within social relations. Rather, it occurs as a circulation of affects between people and things, produced through the conjunction of interconnected, "climate-controlled" spaces, bodies, and cultural practices. Relational devices, such as OMA's "social magic carpet," are positioned by designers as critical to affording such reciprocities.

These conditions come together prominently in certain architectural sites. For example, in the design of many recent educational, research, and office buildings, they interact with an array of aspirations and logics around innovation, mobility, creativity, flexibility, and autonomy (connected to dominant management theories, pedagogical concepts, and academic research models) to construct examples of interior urbanism.[45] Internal landscapes of congestion, encounter, and conviviality—ambient urban environments—are sought in the hopes of producing more effective and successful students, researchers, and businesses. A brief account of an approach taken in recent school design will help to distinguish this confluence.

SWISS CHEESE AND BEANBAGS

In the past decade or so, a process of "smart destruction" was undertaken in some American and Australian schools. Following the theories of educational planner and school designer Frank M. Locker—and operating like enthusiasts of Gordon Matta-Clark's "building-cuts"—school buildings were, to use Locker's term, "swiss-cheesed": openings were cut in walls to merge classrooms with corridors, create internal courtyards, install links between rooms, and increase connections between internal and external spaces.[46] Locker's contention was that in most twentieth-century schools, "design considerations were focused within the rooms, not *between* the rooms."[47]

He argued that this was a problem because new educational models require different architectural models—the isolated classroom constrains the potential for transformations in educational delivery. Locker characterized education in the twenty-first century as follows:

> Inspired by heightened concerns for effectiveness and relevancy in a changing world, the emerging education model is personalized, active, and collaborative. Students learn alone and in teams, in the classroom and in related spaces, in the school and beyond. Teachers, in their roles as guides, simultaneously coordinate various student activities, and collaborate, plan, and share time and place with other teachers. *Isolation, the mantra of twentieth century schools, is giving way to connection.*[48]

This new mantra is seen to necessitate that teachers and students have greater pedagogical and spatial variety, flexibility, and access to each other. Older schools, full of compartmentalized classrooms with four rigid walls, are described as barriers to progressive delivery. In order to "smooth out" educational space, the solution is to cut holes. Locker argued:

> Holes are more than mere openings between classrooms; they serve to facilitate a richly-developed educational delivery by reducing the physical barriers. As the classroom becomes more connected, teachers have more choices about how and where to facilitate learning.[49]

Underlying this approach is a conceptual modeling of the school in terms of an urban public space (Fig. 25). In a paper written by Prakash Nair and Annalise Gehling, Locker's colleagues at Fielding Nair International (an architecture firm that specializes in educational facilities planning), classic theories about public space design developed by Jan Gehl and Jane Jacobs were applied to learning environments, using examples of school and university campuses and exploring the emerging role of informal learning in the twenty-first century. The article "Life between Classrooms" (paraphrasing the title of Gehl's famous work *Life between Buildings*) argued that adopting the spatial components of "good public space," such as the marketplace, thoroughfare, and meeting place, would produce educational spaces that operate like the urban public realm—offering diverting activities, invitations to participation, and spontaneous interactions. The productive social and academic behaviors that would flow are, Nair and Gehling argued, "a range of highly sought-after 'soft' skills that are increasingly demanded by the business community as well as anyone with a desire for safer neighbourhoods."[50]

This example highlights the connection between the kinds of atmospheres being sought through interior urbanism and broader cultural shifts toward societies understood in terms of complex, interconnected flows:

> The world is arguably moving differently and in more dynamic, complex and trackable ways than ever before, while facing new challenges of forced mobility and uneven

FIGURE 25 Image of the café/commons at Duke School, North Carolina, United States, from Prakash Nair and Annalise Gehling, "Life between Classrooms: Applying Public Space Theory to Learning Environments." Courtesy of Fielding Nair International.

mobility, environmental limits and climate change and the movement of unpredictable risks.[51]

Social and spatial theory that is focused on the nomadic, and that emphasizes corporeal, imagined, and virtual mobility and flow over stasis and attachment, has recently
flourished.[52] Along these lines, Richard Sennett has suggested that "the modern individual is, above all else, a mobile human being."[53] The social shaping of movement and
the production of particular mobilities, through strategies and technologies to control,
restrict, and encourage mobility at all scales, are the focus of examination in a range
of disciplines from cultural geography to physiology, international law to performance
studies. Locker's concentration on producing connection over isolation in school design
exhibits an insistence on the architectural production of student mobility that invites
examination.

Connecting spatial form with the flows and activity of people, interiors can be seen as
especially important sites of control and conditioning of mobilities. They are critical in
the creation of secure spaces and boundaries, yet necessarily porous and permeable; they
are formed by bodily vectors and actions, yet also implicitly productive of them. In ply-
ing those qualities of material and social assemblage the "problem sets" being addressed
by buildings (and their designed solutions) continuously shift in their focus. It follows
that they might be interrogated for their relationship to particular logics and technologies of power that shape everyday interpersonal and institutional life. What are the implications of understanding urbanity as a privileged condition of informal encounter
and conviviality that might be produced in architectural interiors (as diverse as offices
and classrooms) and be able to intensify spaces of learning and working?

One consideration is the manner in which the interior works as an apparatus for producing particular subjectivities. The forms of mobility—flows and interactions—that
arise can be implicated in the fostering of new modes of self-governance. Interior urbanism, such as the school design of Fielding Nair, is aimed at structuring and inducing particular forms of intensified, productive social interactions (such as informal networking
and collaboration). In terms of specific architectural sites—such as classrooms, libraries,
and offices—a shift can be identified away from late nineteenth and early twentieth-
century laboratories for the application of biopolitical expertise, spaces that disciplined
corporeal energies and mobilities. By contrast, these more recent (late twentieth-century
and early twenty-first-century) architectures work to augment *self-cultivation*. They foster the self-regulation of activity through environments that—in their staging of the activity, interactions, and encounters associated with urban public space—enable flexible
working hours and studying styles and informal social interaction; they work to generate
opportunistic, independent, "creative" mobilities that structure education and work as
more autonomous and entrepreneurial. Spontaneous, "excessive" activity and interaction are enfolded within new institutional architectures. The École polytechnique fédérale de Lausanne (EPFL) Rolex Learning Centre in Lausanne (essentially a university
library), designed by Sejima and Nishizawa and Associates (known more commonly as

SANAA) and completed in 2010, typifies the aspiration to produce new spatial forms for generating and augmenting these mobilities:

> [The building] functions as a catalyst for the breeding of new relationships both within the academic realm and with society. This is a place that will be full of unintended encounters, where you might bump into an old friend, become inspired by another work group, or discover your favourite book.[54]

The building's program is spread over one single fluid space of approximately 215,000 sq. ft. (20,000 sq m) and has an interior landscape of gentle slopes and terraces that undulate around a series of internal "patios." It is described by one of its architects, Kazuyo Sejima, as an "intimate public space"; it was imagined that "this type of open space might increase the possibility for new meetings or trigger new activities."[55]

As Nair and Gehling's article directly argued, the modeling of urbanity within spaces of education is envisaged as producing young citizens attuned to twenty-first-century business models. The progressive environments described by Locker (not just the "swiss-cheesed" version but also the growing number of innovative new educational buildings) work to produce well-adjusted students who will assume responsibility for ensuring, monitoring, and acting on their own education, economic status, and health.[56]

This emphasis on spatial catalysts for producing autonomous students parallels broader pedagogical developments.[57] For instance, Majia Nadesan has traced the homologies across contemporary neoliberal economic policies in the market and the everyday discipline and character-development programs used by teachers in U.S. public schools. She points to the ways in which certain of these programs work to develop a particular kind of calculative accountability: "neo-liberal models of personhood that privilege responsible choice, within an economic calculus of value."[58] Similarly, the spatial, architectonic strategies employed in developing what Locker calls "flexible centres of personal, integrated learning"[59] might be investigated for the way they privilege students as autonomous, self-regulating agents.

Recently constructed innovative schools such as Ørestad Gymnasium in Copenhagen (discussed above) and the Australian Science and Mathematics School, designed by Woods Bagot and opened in 2003, emphasize this flexibility and autonomy both architecturally and pedagogically.[60] Their architecture is inclined toward the production of unprogrammed learning experiences and the support of individualized study plans. Spatial devices such as learning commons, studios, home bases, lounges, learning streets, and agoras are deployed to privilege students as independent, creative subjects who, as such, take responsibility for the tailoring of their own environment, education, and well-being.[61] The enfolding of urban tropes of mobility (permeability, encounter, conviviality, event) within these spaces for education is articulated through architectural models that encourage flopping down in a beanbag and chatting with colleagues—as a scaffold to instilling calculative, entrepreneurial self-care.[62]

CONCLUSION

Interior urbanism has been articulated here as the construction of particular atmospheres: spatial and material effects directed toward producing moments of intense, dynamic sociability. Critically, these architectural conditions for informal encounter are not proposed or produced for the traditional public realm of the street, plaza, or square but within the interiorized environments of schools, universities, and offices. The recurring deployment of urban tropes in the conceptualization, design, and promotion of such environments is important to consider, particularly with respect to ongoing debates about the condition of the physical public realm (and its connections to the production of public spheres of debate).[63] It may be productive to approach the notion of interior urbanism as a diagnostic instrument that offers the challenge of identifying the desires, prejudices, and assumptions at work in various projects. We might ask how such attempts to produce particular kinds of urban subjectivity and experience within interiorized environments could inform ongoing examination of the topographical contours of public spaces and the spatialization of public spheres—their scales, forms, and controls.

Further, the attempts to produce new mobilities—the movement logics of entrepreneurial, flexible, and sociable students, researchers, and workers—through the urban atmospheres of contemporary interiors also suggests a rich field of investigation. In the search for new architectural catalysts, certain practices and forms of conduct are being problematized, new concepts are put to work, and new spatialities deployed. These imply the production of subjectivities and strategies for their governance that remain ambivalent and contested. Such considerations point toward what I would argue is a vital interrogation of the ways that architecture, and its "power geometries," is employed in the affordance and conditioning of such models for learning and working. The consequences of these architectural experiments are barely understood, yet their framing of urbanity and mobility—linked with collaboration, flexibility, and sociability—is being put in the service of significant changes as innovation, creativity, and entrepreneurialism become privileged conditions across society.

15

The Public Private Interior: Constructing the Modern Domestic Interior in Singapore's Public Housing

LILIAN CHEE

PRIVACY AND INTERIORITY: INTRODUCTION

The house does not have to tell anything to the exterior; instead, all its richness must be manifest in the interior.

—Adolf Loos[1]

"Privacy" is a quality associated with both physical and psychological dimensions and is spatially bound up with the interior, in particular, the domestic interior. The development of domestic privacy as a key spatial concept, in turn, relates to the emergence of the individual subject. "Subjectivity was not simply pictured within the domestic interior; it was here that it *came into being*."[2] Unsurprisingly, the etymological progression of the word *interior* supports this relationship. Tracing the historical trajectory of what the term *interior* meant, architectural historian Charles Rice points out that as early as the eighteenth century, it not only denoted what was inside but also "designate[d] inner character and a sense of individual subjectivity."[3] Architecturally, the eighteenth-century house consisted of multipurpose spaces. These spaces gradually gave way to "specialized rooms, corridors, hallways, closets, and back-stairwells" in the nineteenth century.[4]

The cult of domesticity, and its growing demands for comfort, security, and privacy, was also fully consolidated during this time with the onslaught of consumer culture. In *The Arcades Project,* Walter Benjamin observes that nineteenth-century modernity "was addicted to dwelling."[5] Surrounded by furniture, household commodities, and a vast collection of personal bric-a-brac, the occupant cultivated a sense of self accompanied by an obsession with privacy: "to live in these interiors was to have woven a dense fabric about oneself, to have secluded oneself within a spider's web.... From this cavern, one does not like to stir."[6]

Architectural historian Gulsum Baydar Nalbantonglu argues that privacy goes beyond the oft-made opposition to "enclosure and openness."[7] Instead, the private realm has always been historically defined in relation to its corollary space, the public domain. In particular, the private domestic interior was established when the spaces of home and work were ideologically separated in terms of geographic distance during the early nineteenth century as offices, factories, workshops, and other sites of economic production were set up outside the family home.[8] Also, the progressive distinction between male and female spheres came about during this period when men went out to work as the breadwinners of the family while women remained at home to care for the children. Consequently, to maintain this hierarchy, specific gendered and familial roles in the domestic interior were circumscribed, consolidated, and performed within the specialized rooms of the household, with the husband presiding over the study and the wife in the kitchen. As paid work became more centralized, the domestic interior transformed into a haven for rest and renewal, faraway as it were from the relentless pressures of commerce and trade. The term *domesticity* is inherently more politicized than *home* because it implies a specific type of production, whether biological, material, psychological, social, or even national. Hence, the private domestic realm is a complex space bound up with one or more of these processes.

This chapter revisits the concepts of domestic interiority and privacy in a new context—by exploring their implications and modalities in the modernized island nation of twentieth-century Singapore, a country that has experienced a rapid transformation from a colonial outpost to a third-world city, and eventually to a first-world economic power, all within the short span of four decades. It discusses the construction of privacy within the domestic confines of Singapore's highly successful public housing program by its local housing agency, the Housing and Development Board (HDB), particularly during the agency's first decade, from 1960 to 1970.

The design of the HDB apartment is firmly pragmatic. It aims to provide, within affordable reach, measures of comfort, shelter, hygienic living conditions, and raised standards of living for the majority of the populace. The modular nature of the units facilitates rapid construction (Fig. 26). In fact, the early generations of HDB apartments were relatively spartan in their interior features and were homogeneous throughout in terms of their design. Only recently have there been efforts to personalize the design of these apartments. It is thus amazing to consider how diversity is managed within the interiors of such similar-looking blocks.

As the HDB apartment is unequivocally the most prevalent form of housing in Singapore, experiments and ambitions for its interiors extend beyond the state's interest. This chapter examines how privacy, interiority, and individual subjectivity were invariably shaped by three related factors—state policy, architectural utopianism, and consumer culture—in a common bid to modernize the face of public housing. Compared to the Eurocentric bourgeois historical milieu, which revolved around the individual,

FIGURE 26   Modularized and nondescript facades of the newer HDB point blocks. Courtesy of Lee Ling Wei and Najeeb Rahmat.

what does "privacy" mean in this distinct Asian context of mass housing? What are its boundaries, and how are these boundaries constructed?

The HDB is unique on two counts. First, in contrast to the common perception that privacy is primarily controlled and devised through personal agency, I suggest that the HDB interiors are instead publicly inflected situations with various public bodies having a stake in the makeup of such interiors. Second, while it is also commonly assumed that the state has an investment in public housing, the HDB apartment may be distinguished from this model in that public housing in Singapore is not a provision merely for the economically disprivileged but is home to more than three-quarters of the population. Instead, the state has always been interested precisely in the interior configuration of these apartments as a potent tool for social and familial engineering. With the aid of the apartment's interior layout, the family size and composition and class status were strategically calibrated to meet the state's policy outcomes.

Notably, the overwhelming success of the HDB program, and its enthusiastic take-up rate by almost 82 percent of Singapore's 3.9 million inhabitants, of whom 70 percent are owner-occupiers, is itself an anomaly since contemporary public housing is often marginalized as second-rate dwellings frequently beset by economic and social problems, such as class inequality, high incidence of crime, and social alienation. In contrast, the occupancy profile of the HDB is wide-ranging and includes "financially-challenged families, solid blue-collar families, and also the upper middle class and young upwardly-mobile professionals."[9]

While the public face of these blocks has been documented to the point of archival excess in photographs, drawings, reports, and discourse for social, political, historical, or economic purposes, unsurprisingly, knowledge of its interiors has fallen in the gaps of this archive.[10] There is a need to constantly read between the lines of every official document or image encountered. Despite this phenomenon, the HDB interior's rich life constantly features in contemporary Singaporean literature and film, with the domestic interior being used as a key backdrop for self-critique. These interiorized journeys pick up and describe nuances, details, experiences, and atmospheres, which are often missing from or overlooked in the public archive. As architectural theorist Giuliana Bruno iterates, they allow one to understand the interior as a "haptic space," that is, to be able to have "reciprocal contact" with how spaces are formed through a sense of movement and inhabitation.[11] This is especially important in understanding the constitution of the private domestic interior given that such spaces are normally not only physically out of bounds but also closed to another's imagination.

To this end, this chapter reads the "hard" evidence projected through official public documents against the more "emotive" descriptions of living within these interiors as narrated in film, poetry, and prose. While my aim is not to analyze these emotive narratives in any detail, the chosen excerpts are intended, as it were, to serve as intimate counterpoints for entering the space of the domestic HDB interior and to act as a counterbalance to the public documents that circumscribe but often skirt around precise descriptions of this interior space.

This unusual negotiation also places a historical, top-down perspective provided by the former evidence alongside contemporary, "lived" views from the latter. While the two voices may be asynchronous, the constancy of the HDB interior across four decades means that such contemporary perspectives allow one to inhabit these spaces as much as to criticize them. Finally, the negotiation underscores the elusive but persistent atmosphere of domestic privacy within the HDB interiors, which remains in the psyche of so many Singaporeans. As poet Cyril Wong writes, "I wake up in the place where I used to live."[12]

HIGH-RISE DOMESTICITY: THE HDB AND MODERNIZATION

> Inside four rooms with patterned floors
> and toothless furniture, framed photographs
> hang undocumented on clean white walls.
>
> —*Jane Pek*[13]

In Jane Pek's poem "Memory," she associates the HDB interior with her carefree days as a young child living in her grandparents' apartment. For Pek, the interior was clean but basic, with linoleum-covered floors and unremarkable furniture, these being reflective of her grandparents' working-class status. Seeing another elderly woman, Pek remembered what she had quickly forgotten as she grew up and moved out: "It was the HDB life—dirty, arrogant, formidable, marked by stained elevators, bamboo poles of laundry hung out of grilled windows, the buzz and blink of a thousand neon lights and television sets tuned to Channel 8 turned on at night."[14] While she shared the four rooms with her grandparents, Pek also evokes the collective extent of "HDB life" as "a thousand neon lights" emitted from surrounding households and sounds that filtered unrestricted from one unit to another. The atmosphere she remembers is not rose tinted—the elevators in her grandparents' block are stained with urine and graffiti, while the households are nondescript, with occupants from less privileged backgrounds, as the Chinese-language television channel becomes the only mode of entertainment. In comparison to the obvious cool modern touches of "grey void decks and narrow corridors" on the outside, or the "clean white walls" within the apartment, these spaces are conversely adorned by "the drift and glow of incense [which] strikes the porcelain Buddha on the red altar," or just plain "toothless furniture," and are a site where life is often frugal, with "fish porridge [as] breakfast, lunch, dinner."[15]

Pek's experience is not unique. Although the HDB apartments today cater to a wide range of occupants, the housing program was created by the Singaporean government in 1960 out of an urgent need to address a severe and mounting lack of proper, modernized housing.[16] Until then, many residents had lived in cramped, overcrowded, and insalubrious conditions, especially in the central areas, making slums, shacks, and squatter housing rampant. Health conditions in popular districts such as Chinatown were especially appalling as night-working tenants sublet their beds to others during the day, and facilities meant for a single family were serving up to fifteen families.[17] Other impending factors included a burgeoning population that increased one-and-one-half times between 1947 and 1957 (from 938,144 to 1,445,926) and threats of infectious disease, especially tuberculosis, which was endemic in the congested areas, in addition to widespread homelessness caused by frequent outbreaks of fire in the slums.[18]

Starting in 1960, 50,000 apartments were built in the first five years, and within a decade of the HDB's inception, the housing shortage was resolved. The program began with the provision of basic rental units for the poor, but a home-ownership scheme was gradually introduced in 1964. To obtain more easily the land needed for mass housing, the colonial Land Acquisition Act was amended in 1966, empowering the government to acquire any land necessary in the interest of national development at a rate of compensation determined by the state, a clause that was arguably in conflict with open-market regulations. In 2009 the World Bank held up Singapore as a model of "effective urbanization" given its success in transforming its rural slums to become "one of the cleanest and most welcoming cities in the world" in under 40 years.[19] Another strong motivation for the state to house the poor was that it was believed that eventual mass property ownership would encourage personal stakeholdership and individual commitment to raising the nation's social and economic standards.[20] Hence, a roof over one's head was implicitly tied to the country's larger ambition for economic survival.

Although the Singaporean skyline is now replete with rectilinear high-density HDB blocks, the vast majority of which were modeled in a recognizably modernist architectural language, high-rise living was adopted out of pragmatism and necessity. The first-generation residents of these apartments had originally dwelled in more communal, village-like neighborhood configurations called *kampong* (Malay for "village").[21] In such instances, social, familial, and gender norms were established around an informal and organic layout of makeshift *attap* houses, which individually, or as a whole community, could change to meet the growing demands of the households occupying the neighborhood. The concept of privacy in such cases was ambiguous since the private boundaries of one's home were fluid and easily extendable to include communal zones such as the front veranda and the wet kitchen at the rear of the house, which were both often open to the entire community as part of the *kampong*'s social network of spaces.

In this sense, the emergence of the compact and relatively sequestered HDB unit, which inevitably prioritized the nuclear family as its main occupants, echoed the architectural privatization of the bourgeois interior in its insistence on elected seclusion and newfound privacy. The first apartments in the township of Toa Payoh were small two-room rental units that had the most basic spaces for sleeping, living-dining, and washing. All other activities were to be undertaken elsewhere. For example, the elderly would gather in the shared space on the ground floor called the "void deck," children would play on the playgrounds or in the corridors, and laundry would be hung out to dry outside the unit, just within reach of the kitchen. Each apartment was accessed through a communal corridor, which usually ran the entire length of the block. The later designs catered for the ideal family size, comprising a husband, wife, and two children, as the unit size was expanded to include a second bedroom.

Yet if the bourgeois interior grew out of a singular obsession with individuated subjectivity, the concept of privacy in the HDB interior was motivated by a combination of factors and agencies desiring technological, economic, and aesthetic modernization in the trying context of 1960s Singapore. I argue that the domestic interior of the HDB apartment, in terms of its unit size and layout, its idealized furnishings, and the spatial relationship between the private unit and its shared communal spaces, all evolved in tandem with the modernizing ambitions particular to a small and tightly governed post-colonial country. During this period, the populace's and state's collective desires for modernization had divergent objectives—the former yearning for privacy and individuality, while the latter was intent of nurturing the HDB as a nucleus for procreative families. These sentiments were in no small part influenced by Singapore's physical lack of resources as well as its ethnic difference from its Southeast Asian base, a region with abundant natural resources and a large ethnic Muslim population, particularly in the neighboring countries of Malaysia and Indonesia. In contrast, Singapore's diminutive size, lack of a hinterland, and large migrant diasporic Chinese population—who have influenced a "Confucian modernity" marked by simultaneous allegiance to modernization and capitalist culture, as well as observance of tradition—set it apart from its neighbors.[22]

Before we enter a discussion into the various motivations for modernization and their impact on the HDB interior, the significance of modernization in the Singaporean context needs further reiteration. Despite strident criticism from architects like Rem Koolhaas that Singapore's modernization program—physically manifested in its pervasive HDB blocks—is ultimately a "modernity stripped of ideology," cultural theorist C.J.W.-L. Wee argues that the "Singapore modern" is in fact "an instance of the global West inside the national"; that is to say, it is not, as Koolhaas suggests, a "bad-faith copy of the West" but rather "a negotiated modernity—as an adaptation of a modernity that was and is globally circulating."[23] Highlighting that modernization in the 1960s was coterminous with the reception of the global free market and technological advancement through efficient building, upgrading, and relocation, Wee proposes that the state's solutions in its housing program, for example, are also consistent with the "utilitarian pragmatism" practiced by the People's Action Party (PAP) government since independence. In this light, the modernist HDB blocks may be read as part of "efforts at self-invention by the PAP state, drawing upon a British social-democratic model of state intervention."[24]

Wee's argument allows a different understanding of why modernization was key, particularly with regard to Singapore's sociopolitical and geographic contexts. In turn, this strategic modernization fueled the privatization of the HDB unit as different local agencies attempted to produce particular socioeconomic and political outcomes by controlling how the interior was construed as "private," that is to say, how a private domestic space within was defined in contrast to the public realm without. In each instance of self-invention, privacy was ultimately embedded into modernized ideas of domesticity, where new notions of family, social networks, and aesthetic tastes were seen as instrumental to reconfiguring class and social mobility.

PRIVACY AND DOMESTICITY: PUBLIC STRATEGIES IN THE PRIVATE INTERIOR

The body was found by one of the women along our corridor, this woman who goes to work in the morning earlier than everyone else. She always keeps her windows closed and once in a while she would bring a man back to her house. But we don't care what they do. Anyway she was always well dressed, she knew how to wear shoulder pads and stockings and sometimes when I am in the living room I see her passing in front of our house. This is when I tell my grandchildren to hurry up, put on their shoes quickly, why so dirty, just the second day of school, come, don't forget to kiss your grandmother's hand here, study hard.

—Alfian Sa'at[25]

In Alfian Sa'at's short story, the discovery of an unknown stabbing victim one morning in the common corridor is pivotal in unraveling relationships and dismantling codes of privacy. The nondescript long linear corridor of "polished cold" cement marks an uncertain threshold between public and private space ("our corridor")[26] and is used by all residents to enter their homes. As controversy sweeps over the block, the narrator reveals her prejudices about the woman, whom she is not acquainted with. The moral conduct of the latter is immediately put into question as we are told that she is likely unmarried, outwardly promiscuous, habitually secretive, and for the narrator, who views shoulder pads and stockings as indicative of a certain class, suspiciously always impeccably attired. For this armchair voyeur, the presence of this woman is as risqué as the dead man. Unable to look into the woman's locked windows, the narrator eagerly charts her comings and goings on the corridor and speculates about what goes on within her apartment, but at the same time worries about the repercussions of living in close proximity with such a person. The narrator reinforces her domestic beliefs within earshot of her mysterious neighbor by recapitulating how home is meant to anchor the family and nurture children who should in turn reciprocate by working hard and being filial to their elders.

Here, the boundaries of private versus public are amorphous within the threshold condition of the corridor, which acts like an extension of the living room (Fig. 27). More significantly, however, the codes of private space are also legislatively sustained by state policy, which determines what constitutes an idealized family unit in the HDB apartment, who is given the right to stay, and who is not. It has been noted that the public housing program constitutes one of three elements of "control, reform and reward," engineered by the state to harness a "more disciplined and uniform society."[27] In this sense, the concept of privacy in the HDB context is complicated. It aligns most closely, first, with a sense of ownership and, second, with the ideals of having personal space to operate outside the norm but doing so without upsetting the status quo. Apart from its outward provisions of material security, comfort, spiritual fulfillment, and interiority, privacy in public housing comes with its own proviso. In the home, citizens are instructed on family size, the timing of household formation and childbirth, and the language they ought to speak; they are compulsorily required to save a fifth of their income and, since 1996, to financially support their parents in old age.[28]

Enforced through housing subsidies, architectural layout, and conditions on sales and rentals, otherwise controversial policies and desired attitudes—such as ethnic integration, which ensures a fair racial distribution of occupants in each housing estate; normalized pro-family structures premised on heterosexual marriage partners intent on procreative coupling; filial piety toward parents, who form the extended family and are privately cared for; and even the influence of personal tastes and acceptable public conduct—constitute ongoing programs that are rarely contested. Housing allocation also shifted with the state's population policy. In 1973, in a bid to engineer small families, for couples that included a female work-permit holder married to a Singaporean, one of the spouses had to agree to "sterilization after the birth of the second child or

FIGURE 27   The common corridor as an extension of the living room. Courtesy of Kenneth Koh.

lose government housing subsidies and other concessions."[29] In 1993, 19.5 percent of married children lived with their parents, while 45.2 percent lived near their parents, thus "endorsing the state's constructions of the 'normal' family as the fundamental unit of society."[30] "Abnormal" households including children born out of wedlock, same-sex partners, or even two siblings living together are still discouraged by stringent sale and rental conditions and deprivation of regular housing grants.

Public exhibitions, residents' handbooks, and propaganda films were used to extend these policies. In conjunction with the HDB's first major exhibition, held at the Selegie Road/Short Street site in December 1960, a model one-room unit was constructed to educate the public on how to best furnish the apartment. The ensuing publicity photograph of this unit shows a father, a mother, and two children seated within the room, watched over by a fifth person, presumably a visitor, located significantly at the outer limits of the same space. Here, the size of the nuclear family squares with the state's population-control policy; perhaps not coincidentally, this

photograph follows on from a highly successful three-month family-planning campaign that was organized in the same year as part of the government's mass Health Education Programme.[31] While the construction of the HDB was not explicitly linked to
population-control policies, studies have suggested that the change from single-person
households and extended families to nuclear families was also accelerated by the public housing program.[32] In another instance, the state-sponsored handbook titled *New
Lives in New Homes* espouses the benefits of the nuclear-family unit, suggesting that it
will enable the family to enjoy closer ties, cultivate a greater sense of responsibility in
the husband, and relieve young couples from the frustration of dealing with the older
generation and the burden of extended relatives.[33] In *Berita Singapura: Housing Week,*
a commemorative propaganda film made in 1967 to mark the early success of the
public housing program, one scene shows a family of three—a husband, a wife, and
their teenage daughter—relaxing in a living room decked out with modern amenities
such as a television and a turntable that the daughter is busying herself with.[34] In case
we perceive this idyllic setting as unique to this family, we are then presented with another scene in which another couple looks out of their new apartment's windows to
find an exterior view of multiple identical-looking units facing them. In *Housing Week,*
the benefits of these interiors' standardization and modernization are emphasized. It
implicitly suggests that such consistency offers equal opportunity to the occupants to
make a new life for themselves. Thus, the modernized interior—here, the room "in
the sky" with the latest technological equipment, far superior to the cramped and un-
hygienic slum housing of recent memory—is also a model room and a public image
that must be maintained.

In tandem with these ideological restrictions, the early interiors may be read as also
encouraging familial groupings in their architectural layout. The toilet and shower room,
for instance, were installed as two separate spaces, accessible only through the kitchen
(Fig. 28). This meant that the two most private spaces, one for sleeping and sexuality
and the other for cleansing, were detached and connected only through two more public rooms—the living and kitchen-dining spaces (Fig. 29). Although the grouping of the
toilet and shower room was primarily for convenience of plumbing, the detachment of
the latter from the bedrooms meant that traffic between these private spaces was completely open to public scrutiny. To a certain extent, this layout privileges the legitimate
intimacy between nuclear-family members, as opposed to more transient and furtive
relationships between/with strangers or lovers. With the "neat bourgeoisie hierarchy of
privacy…disturbed," these intermediate spaces that accommodated "proper, speakable
activities" such as socializing and eating also indirectly dissuaded the traffic of publicly
unsanctioned relationships between the two private realms.[35]

As the narrator in Sa'at's short story attests through her disdain for the single promiscuous neighbor, the legislative policies and architectural layout work together to
designate the constitution of the proper private domestic realm. They describe which
desired bodies are to be housed in these apartments—those of heterosexual married
couples, preferably with children. Here, too, the concept of privacy is inherently linked
to sexuality, albeit sexuality that conforms and is procreative rather than wastefully

FIGURE 28   Shower room and toilet within the kitchen area (right side). Courtesy of San Tzer Ning Jeremy.

FIGURE 29   View from the living room toward the kitchen. Courtesy of San Tzer Ning Jeremy.

excessive. The construction of privacy through the domestic family unit requires a disciplining of the occupant's body. The interior, and also the common spaces linking all interiors, such as the corridor, is devised so that what is improper will be exposed or expunged. In this way, the HDB unit and its immediate environment mirror a system of surveillance that ultimately spatializes the "social institution of marriage" and maintains this institution through incentivized reproduction.[36] As architectural historian and theorist Mark Wigley argues, "the boundaries that define the house" need to be critiqued.[37] Similarly, in the HDB, beyond the actual physical space, it is state public ideology that delineates these boundaries and predetermines what is deemed private, insular, sacrosanct, and protected.

Yet it would be too simplistic to assume that the construction of privacy was just limited to state efforts. Other interest groups such as the local architecture community also had a hand in this modernized utopian dream. On at least two occasions, first in 1960 and then again in 1961, members of the Singapore Polytechnic Architectural Society (SPAS), consisting of architecture students, designed, constructed, and displayed interior solutions for clean, modern, and compact living.[38] Using the HDB public exhibitions as their platform, SPAS's solutions were distinctive in that they challenged the homely interiors normally projected by the state and the mass media. In an HDB exhibition held in 1961 at Macpherson Road, the society used the typical compare-and-contrast method to educate the public. Two two-room apartments were decorated in opposing styles—apartment 55 in "the usual unsanitary and haphazard manner—furnishing it with the typical beds, chairs, cupboards, etc. So realistic did it appear that for a moment it was easily mistaken for an actual dwelling." In contrast, apartment 56 used no conventional furniture, settling instead for multipurpose platforms and low-cost storage systems that presented a solution so "radical and rational" that it "discard[ed] the normal sentiments of furnishing."[39] The furnishings in apartment 56 were remarkably constructed for under SGD$300. The society promised that this "revolutionary" condition would allow eight persons to live comfortably together in a space free of clutter and excess. This unusual brief was undertaken by the SPAS to address the public's "misuse" of the two-room unit, and they purposefully overloaded the space with twice the number of occupants it was originally designed for, possibly to critique the state's idealized standards of occupation.

The proposed solution closely resembles a modernized machine for minimal living such that the conventionally separate functions of sleeping, working, eating, and entertaining could be adaptively accommodated in a limited space. Open-plan communal living in this case also meant that the idea of privacy was transformed to resemble something more akin to village or *kampong* groupings, where an extended family could comfortably reside in close proximity. The individual interior components were also conceived to be either easily constructed or found objects such as milk boxes, which could be creatively reused. This notion of self-help was meant to foster a sense of individual sufficiency, as well as the ability to create something unique for one's own home.

A cutaway axonometric drawing neatly divides the original living and bedroom spaces into nongeneric functional zones for activity and storage. Again, the hierarchies that accompany privacy are immediately dismantled as defined boundaries between private and public are erased. While this configuration apparently contradicts the state's plan for the nuclear family, it in fact reiterates the point that if a larger household is to be accommodated in the same space, then drastic measures must be taken to preserve the original public image of these interiors, whose main purpose is to propagate a healthy and hygienic environment conducive to a "stable and prosperous nation."[40] SPAS's minimal living solution has another distinction. As emphasized in the 1960 HDB *Annual Report,* where the society's model one-room unit is documented, the model interior was meant to "give a variety of ideas and suggestions on how to furnish [the] flats."[41] As such, the model HDB interior was also a conduit through which specific notions of class and taste, as reflected in the occupants' household furnishings, could be publicly cultivated and/or altered.

From 1972 to 1989, the HDB published and freely circulated to every HDB home its bimonthly magazine, *Our Home.*[42] The highlight of this magazine would invariably be a feature on an exemplary interior, almost always self-furnished by a keen do-it-yourself occupant who had an amateur interest in design. The interiors ranged from the typical white modernist ones to those that had a more exotic flair, for example, those combining Victorian (chandeliers, damask curtains, and huge armchairs) and oriental (carved wooden statues, ancient vases, antique Chinese porcelain) styles. Giving instructive taste advice on proper ornamentation, correct use of color, and avoidance of clutter, among other things, the articles are, as Jane Jacobs and Stephen Cairns argue, evidence of "micropolitics of state, subjectivity and built form."[43] Through the model homes featured in this magazine, the "Singaporean interior" was at once governed, "cultivated and contained" so that "the economic investments it entailed did not become excessive."[44] The leading local broadsheet, *The Straits Times,* similarly ran a section every weekend dedicated to home decoration. Occasionally, specific articles would be directed at HDB dwellers, suggesting budget-friendly but "tasteful" additions to the home. Toward the end of the 1960s, as increasingly larger numbers of residents also became home owners, the instructive articles veered toward advocating a more individual style in each home by the incorporation of elements from both familiar and foreign cultures. For example, in a 1967 piece that explores the range of wallpaper designs available on the market, the writer attests, "An oriental effect is given to a bedroom with Chinese interior décor...by the wallpapering of 'Linden Bower' in cherry blossom design."[45]

Yet the meshing of global and local references, and the preference for all things exotic, may be seen as a strategic move toward self-invention, and thus completely consistent with modernizing ambitions: "the alterity of Singapore's modernism lies firmly in its willingness to accommodate the very type of ornamented and phantasmagorical interior styling with which its European predecessor could not live."[46] Instead of interpreting the borrowing and assimilation of exotic Western aesthetics in the Asian context as derivative, cultural theorist Abidin Kusno similarly argues that "'Westernization'...may suggest...a destination, a process of arrival, by replication at some imagined place called 'the West'. But seen from the other [non-Western] side of the globe...[it] could also point to a departure, an exit from something one wants to leave behind, which does not necessarily imply that one would then arrive at, or replicate, a particular place called 'the West.'"[47] Thus, the construction of the private realm through phantasmagoric effects of borrowed places and times was dictated not only by popular fashion but also by the urge to reinvent the self anew (Plate 11).

CONCLUSION

Wife: In Beijing, you told me the place you live in was very special; I thought it was a villa. Actually all the Singaporeans live in similar homes: Government flats.

Husband: What's wrong with HDB flats? At least it's more sanitary than where you used to stay.

Wife: . . . the first country in the world to install urine detectors in elevators to catch people peeing.

Husband: But look, after they installed the urine detectors, they were so effective, nobody pees in the elevators anymore.

Wife: Yes, because they now pee in the corridors![48]

In the film *12 Storeys,* a China-born bride chastises her Singapore-born husband for going back on his promise of a comfortable and luxurious home. The excerpt above also intimates the fragility of privacy at the cusp of the domestic realm as surveillance technology is employed to make public, and thus control, delinquency. As a consequence, the absolute boundaries between the separate spheres of public and private are fundamentally unstable as public doctrines gradually make their way into the private domestic interior.

The modern private domestic realm is an intricate construction and, as shown, often not limited to the efforts of the individual occupant. It is instead produced "by way of a complex dialogue between the modernisms evident on drawing boards, those articulated in political rhetoric, those modelled in displays or captured in magazines, those constructed by bureaucracy, and those aspired to by residents."[49] The HDB interior is exemplary of how public values and expressions may fundamentally alter and shape the private domestic realm. More important, the constitution and construction of this private interior were seen as key to the implementation of government policies involving population control and state productivity and, more indirectly, the transformation of class status through informed notions of taste and aesthetics.

If the nineteenth-century bourgeoisie's private domestic interior could be read as an accurate summation of the individual's identity and subjectivity, then the twentieth-century Asian/Singaporean domestic interior proves to be a little more complicated. Here, the interior is produced through the subtle processes of mediation, control, negotiation, and self-invention. And, reciprocally, this interior may also obfuscate the self, which remains fragmented and enigmatic even in a person's own private domestic space.

16

The Evolution of Workspace Design: From the Machine to the Network

JEREMY MYERSON

All branches of interior design are shaped to an extent by their social, economic, and political histories. But there can be few areas of specialist practice so decisively molded by the powerful circumstances of their origins than modern office design. The type of workspace interior I want to talk about in this chapter has a history that is little more than 100 years old. This is the office as an archetype of modernism, as a by-product of the bureaucratization of industry, and as a defining phenomenon of the early twentieth century. It emerged swiftly and brutally with a design template deliberately derived from the factory floor and its attendant theories of mass production and the division of labor.

Indeed, so powerful were the social, economic, and political forces that brought the modern office into existence—and effectively reshaped the skyline of our cities—that one can argue that the more recent story of workspace interior design, certainly within the past twenty years, has been one of trying to shake off the shackles imposed by the rigid orthodoxies of modernist design. Mies van der Rohe's dictum that an office is "a machine for working in" is memorable shorthand for a movement in which functional design became the handmaiden to management efficiency in the early 1900s. That movement has been so profound that even today office interior design still struggles to depart from its pervasive legacy.

In this chapter I want to examine that legacy of modernist design allied to scientific management, describe the landmark projects and events that have served to either consolidate or undermine it, and analyze the contemporary currents—demographic, cultural, and ecological—that are starting to reposition workspace interior design toward the digital knowledge economy of the twenty-first century and away from the industrial model of economic development of the twentieth.

TWO OFFICE INTERIORS: GOOGLE AND LARKIN

At the outset it is important to acknowledge how far we have traveled in terms of design process, built outcomes, and cultural references in office interiors since the early "paper factories" that administered the emergence of mass production. So I want to start with a contemporary workspace, the Zurich office of Google, and compare its characteristics with the first great modern office scheme of the twentieth century, Frank Lloyd Wright's Larkin Building of 1904 at Buffalo, New York.

Google's Zurich office, completed in 2008, accommodates 800 staff on seven floors of a contemporary Swiss building. This interior design by architects Camenzind Evolution has been widely acknowledged as breaking new ground in office interior design for "knowledge workers."[1] There are fire poles and spiral slides to aid "fast connections" between floors, igloo-style cabins for team meetings complete with penguins sitting in a snowscape, an antique-themed library for quiet work, a games room for fun, and an "aquarium water lounge" for relaxation that allows tired staff to rest fully clothed inside a bathtub and contemplate the gentle and soothing movement of fish swimming in a series of tanks.

All of these facilities were designed in partnership with the Google workforce, tailored for their preferences and incorporated as a way to attract and retain premium staff in a competitive global knowledge economy. The interior designers adopted a codesign process with users, conducting a psychological survey and a series of one-on-one interviews and handing over some design leadership to a Google Zurich steering committee (known as Zooglers) to oversee the project.

More than a century before Google created its series of interior playgrounds for an essentially young multinational group of software engineers, programmers, and other Internet technology specialists, Frank Lloyd Wright was at work on the first truly grown-up office environment of the twentieth century. The Larkin Building at Buffalo was designed for a mail-order company—a new type of business every bit as radical and influential in its day as Internet search engine companies are now—and sited next to a railroad station to make it more efficient for workers to commute.

There were no psychological surveys, staff interviews, or steering committees in the Larkin Building—and no games rooms, fire poles, or water lounges either. Wright essentially designed the building as one large space that proclaimed the unity of the organization and the power of the business owner over the individual worker. The corporate slogan "Intelligence, Enthusiasm, Control" was emblazoned on the atrium walls. Beneath these words, mail-order clerks sat at fixed seats that pivoted from their desks and labored in total silence (conversation was banned) in serried ranks under close supervision for set hours.[2] The interior was designed to cow the worker into coglike submission to the business machine, and it worked so well that it set a template for corporate command-and-control offices grouped around atria for decades to come.

Google's Zurich office visibly embodies ideas about working in the networked knowledge economy, which explains the level of international interest it currently attracts. The scheme elevates such values as collaboration, exploration, learning, curiosity, and contemplation by creating dedicated settings to encourage them. The Larkin Building can, however, be seen as a vehicle for a different, earlier ideology of workplace interior design. Wright's project can be read as a clear demonstration of the creed of scientific management, which viewed the workplace as an integral part of a rational system of production and adopted design characteristics suited to the dominant economic model of the time. This model depended on well-run offices and factories to deliver the concept of mass production and mass marketing to a mass audience within carefully planned, centralized, and regulated hierarchies.

THE IRON FIST OF SCIENTIFIC MANAGEMENT

The concept of scientific management was pioneered by U.S. engineer Frederick Taylor (1856–1915). Taylor was a stern and puritanical figure who adapted the time-and-motion studies of the factory floor to the emerging office environment. He understood better than anyone before him how the standardization of work tools and conditions could improve productivity, and his approach spawned a whole school of twentieth-century organizational analyses and work studies.[3]

With its imposing atrium, streamlined work processes, strict protocols, clear lines of supervisory sight, and corporate sloganizing, the modern-looking Larkin Building was fast off the mark in making Taylor's ideas visible. Those ideas spread at a steady rate. In 1911, seven years after Larkin first opened its doors in Buffalo, the United States was gripped with "efficiency fever," according to historians. Taylor's ideas were held up in American business schools such as Harvard and Wharton as the means to crush trade union syndicalism and compete on more equal terms with the British Empire. His concept was also readily exportable: the American writer Judith Merkle has documented how scientific management influenced Japan, Germany (Hitler was a fan), and the rapidly industrializing USSR of Lenin (who was critical of Taylor) and Stalin (who was not).[4]

Taylor was determined to develop what he called "superior methods and machines"—to take a giant spanner to the workplace and tighten all the nuts. In the years after 1911, his well-publicized efficiency mantra was helped enormously by the gleaming new designers of the modern movement, with their own love of "efficient" and "rational" forms. Taylor's work ethic thus found a suitable work aesthetic, as the early modernists gave pride of place to the workplace as a test bed for their ideas.

It is hard to underestimate the impact on the development of office interiors that this combination of modernist design ideology and pseudoscientific analysis of management process achieved. Corporations were literally handed a blueprint to design workspaces that could truly deliver the goods in the era of the mass market. These workspaces not only worked efficiently but *looked* efficient too. By the time Wright reprised his modern office project with the visually sophisticated but even more rigidly managed Johnson Wax Building in Wisconsin (1936–1939), office interiors were even more dedicated to the needs of management efficiency above all else.

By this time the modernist pioneers such as Mies van der Rohe, Walter Gropius, and Marcel Breuer, who had emerged as leaders of the Bauhaus in 1920s Germany, were headed (via England in some cases) toward the urban business districts of the United

States, fleeing from Germany's Nazi terror in the late 1930s. The Bauhaus masters unhesitatingly marched their moral crusade about functionalist office design right into the heart of American big business.

After World War II, Le Corbusier retrospectively recognized the symbolic value of the office to the cause of the modern movement, writing in *Towards A New Architecture*, "Our modern life…has created its own objects; its own costume, its own fountain pen, its eversharp pencil, its typewriter, its telephone, its admirable office furniture."[5] Mies van der Rohe, meanwhile, was hard at work on twinning ideology with commerce. He had envisaged a towering glass office block on a triangular site as early as 1919. Once the technology was available, he realized his aims with the Seagram Building, New York, in 1958, a project regarded as representing the zenith of scientific management. This building and the nearby Union Carbide tower on Park Avenue, designed a year later by Skidmore Owings and Merrill, set the pattern for office design for the next few decades.

The irony of an architectural style conceived for worker housing amid the radical politics of 1920s Germany now being adopted by corporate North America, the very Babylon of capitalism, would not be lost on the writer and critic Tom Wolfe. In his distinctive way, Wolfe described Mies van der Rohe as putting "half of America inside German worker-housing cubes."[6] But the momentum of the new office building was irresistible. The development of steel-framed structures in architecture led to office buildings on expensive city-center sites with large, clear, lettable floor spaces unhindered by columns or obstructions. Inside buildings like Seagram and Union Carbide, office interiors became increasingly machinelike in their modular assembly of component parts.

Desks were carefully laid out in rectilinear patterns, with clerical staff inside large bull pens within the deep space; more senior executives were given, progressively, window access, perimeter offices, larger desks, more domesticated furniture (usually in wood), artworks, and private dining rooms as they moved up through the corporate hierarchy. It was this type of interior setup that was parodied brilliantly in Billy Wilder's classic 1960 film *The Apartment*—this portrayed a junior clerk (played by Jack Lemmon) ingratiating himself with senior managers in a bid to escape the office-factory floor and gain a key to the executive washroom.

The use of interior space and finishes—the territory of the interior designer—as a way to reward corporate status and entrench hierarchy was a valuable lever for a host of Taylorist followers in management. Just as modernist architects began to remodel business districts on machinelike grids, so those Taylorist followers began to treat organizations, in the management writer Charles Handy's phrase, as "giant pieces of engineering."[7] The notion of careful allocation of tasks, responsibilities, and spans of control, and in particular the emphasis on process analysis and control, fed through into the quality movement led by management experts like W. Edwards Deming and Joseph M. Juran and would eventually lead to such concepts as business process engineering, benchmarking, and downsizing.[8]

Thus it was that the efficiency mantra of Taylorism and the functionalist design dogma of the modern movement aided and abetted each other in the development of the optimum office environment. It was an alliance strictly for the bosses, and, over time, critics would increasingly point to a neglect of human factors, group psychology, changing needs, and the requirement to build elaborate networks of social relationships within organizations in order for them to be successful.

THE RISE OF KNOWLEDGE WORK

Wright's Larkin Building can point unequivocally to Taylorism (after Frederick Taylor), and by extension Fordism (after Henry Ford), as the theoretical basis for its interior organization and design. Google's Zurich office belongs to a growing body of design practice related to the rise of the knowledge worker but cannot point to an equivalent founding father of the knowledge economy for its template. The difficulty caused by the absence of a twenty-first-century equivalent of Taylor or Ford to drive forward workplace design in the knowledge era has been pointed out by the influential U.S. management expert Thomas Davenport, who dismisses most contemporary efforts to design for knowledge workers as based on "fad, fashion and faith."[9]

Davenport's view is that although companies worldwide are experimenting heavily with new office interiors, they are not learning a great deal in the process. Knowledge work departs from Taylorism in that it depends less on formula and more on the application of knowledge and learning. Instead of individuals sitting in serried ranks to follow explicit instructions within a supervised hierarchy, new working practices are emerging based on collaboration, initiative, and exploration, in which knowledge is often tacit. In this context, Google's repertoire of igloo-style meeting cabins, improvised workstations, and spiral slides belongs to a long line of gimmicks dreamed up by designers to make knowledge workers feel more creative and perform without a set script.

Knowledge work *does* have founding fathers—the term was invented in 1960, simultaneously but independently, by two American economists, Peter Drucker and Fritz Machlup. Doctors, lawyers, academics, accountants, and scientists were among the first knowledge workers they identified as a group. Drucker would later extend this definition to a new class of worker he described as "knowledge technologists": computer technicians, software designers, analysts in clinical labs, paralegals, and so on. Today the term *knowledge worker* can be routinely applied to most executive and managerial roles within business, industry, professional services, and the public sector, and a great deal of interior design expertise is aimed squarely at creating the right environment for knowledge workers. So it is surprising that we still know so little about the precise conditions in which they are most productive.

Forty years after his pioneering research on knowledge work, Drucker felt moved to comment on knowledge-worker productivity: "We are in the year 2000 roughly where we were in the year 1900 in terms of the productivity of the manual worker."[10] The productivity of the manual worker increased around fifty times during the twentieth century through process improvements of one kind or another, many of them related to environment. Can we be sure that interior design for knowledge workers will be as effective in the twenty-first century? Google's Zurich office can perhaps be seen as part of an ongoing search for solutions.

THREE WAVES OF CHANGE

Thus far I have described how the Larkin paper factory (1904) and the Google Zurich fun factory (2008) belong at opposite ends of an evolving spectrum of workspace design practice over the past 100 or so years. This spectrum has been described by leading architect and theorist Frank Duffy as comprising three great waves of change.[11] The first wave, according to Duffy, was the "Taylorist office" of the early twentieth century, a formidable engine of economic growth based around efficiency, as we have discussed; the second wave was the post-1945 emergence of the "social democratic office" in northern Europe, a light and bright postwar reaction to the darkness of fascism that elevated the role of social relations and social networks in improving productivity; and the third wave, the "networked office" that emerged after 2000, is fast reconfiguring time, place, and space in the knowledge-led economy and has companies like Google operating in its vanguard.

Google Zurich, however, embodies not only a networked element but also some essential characteristics of the social democratic model in that an enlightened employer has created a purpose-built environment in partnership with workers for mutual benefit. It is important, therefore, to explore how social democracy took hold in office design as a departure from Taylorism and what its own legacy is today.

THE SOCIAL DEMOCRATIC OFFICE

Emerging in the aftermath of World War II as northern Europe came blinking into the daylight after the darkness of fascism, the social democratic office was designed to be more communal and collegial. It was less concerned with the raw economics of efficiency than Taylorism and was often modeled on the village, neighborhood, or street. It also reflected the rising power of the white-collar unions in Germany and Scandinavia. Critically, this organizational model recognized the importance of human interactions in making work happen.

Design historian Adrian Forty has explained in his landmark book *Objects of Desire* how corporations in a postwar era of relatively full employment during the 1950s and 1960s competed with factories for staff, not by paying higher wages, but by offering more respectable and pleasant surroundings.[12] The Taylorist office wave had been led largely by developers who leased their buildings to corporate tenants; now, the social democratic wave was led by owner-occupiers who invested in purpose-built work environments for their own longer-term occupation.

The first real expression of this new wave came from the German Quickborner team, which pioneered the concept of *Bürolandschaft* (office landscaping) in the mid-1950s. The rigid, rectangular American approach to space planning gave way to more open, free-flowing lines, based on analyses of work communication, that were supposed to make for more democracy in the office. *Bürolandschaft* represented a key step forward and reworked many aspects of office design. However, as the writer Lance Knobel pointed out, open-plan landscaping of this type still allowed Big Brother to watch over workers: "Quite a few personal liberties were lost: no personal window to open or close, no light switch to control."[13]

Later, in 1973, the social democratic office took a new turn toward greater personal liberty with the Centraal Beheer insurance building at Appeldorn, the Netherlands, designed by Dutch architect Herman Hertzberger. This project created a complex, interlocking interior with an ambiguously mounting series of concrete block "work islands." Each unit housed sixteen workers, who were free to decorate the space as they wished and bring in their own pets and plants. Hertzberger's achievement was widely regarded as giving modernist office design a more human face. His solution gave staff both privacy and a sense of belonging to the communal office. Nevertheless, it was still architecture—hard concrete, fixed in time, space, and place. There was an inflexibility that a new generation of reconfigurable office systems furniture would later address.

What Hertzberger started, Norwegian architect Niels Torp completed in Sweden in the late 1980s. Torp's Scandinavian Airline Systems (SAS) building at Frosundavik just outside Stockholm perfected the model of the office as a social community, complete with park benches and tree-lined boulevards. Opened in January 1988, this building refashioned entirely the traditional concept of office life by creating a giant complex with shops, restaurants, and coffee bars lining a solar-heated internal "main street" running along the spine of the building.

The idea was for senior SAS managers to promenade up and down the "street," meeting staff informally in a social context to generate and monitor projects. Light, open, and airy under a glass roof, the SAS headquarters with its working population of 1,400 staff moved the office about as far away from Taylorism in aesthetic and organizational terms as you could get. It was a city of its own on the outskirts of a city, with a swimming pool, medical center, gym, waterside café, and conference center. It reflected the need to provide every kind of social amenity for large numbers of workers no longer based in the center of cities but transported to edge-of-town business parks.

Torp's SAS building was studied closely in the United Kingdom, and British Airways commissioned the architect to essentially repeat the project at Heathrow Airport, with the Waterside building. This was completed in 1998 at a cost of £200 million (just over $300 million). In its scale and expense, it represents the high-water mark of the social democratic office in the United Kingdom. To a considerable extent, many of Britain's better office buildings still conform to the social democratic model today. Deep space within the plan is avoided; adequate light and air are provided for all, with leafy views from narrow, fingerlike building wings de rigueur; spaces are created for spontaneous social interaction. Taking such an approach is a tacit admission that it is the informal social networks within companies that make work happen, and not the formal chains of command dictated by set bureaucracies.[14]

Interest in social theories of design led many workplace designers to reexamine historical precedents during the 1990s to discover what works best for people within tight-knit communities of 300 to 400 people. In a rebuff to the type of year-zero modernism that the Seagram building represented, medieval hilltop and bridge communities were used as metaphors for schemes. "Modern" notions of the office were beginning to break down. A project by Studios Architecture for Babcock and Brown, a private bank, on the top floor of a former coffee warehouse on the San Francisco waterfront, was typical of the period: this was designed to reflect the typology of a medieval town, with six different neighborhoods and hilltop work areas. The light and views, not an artificial grid, dictated the organization of key spatial elements—and an open space was created to allow people to gather in a way "similar to a *parvis* in front of a cathedral," according to the Studios design team.[15]

Office designers were slowly being freed from the tyranny of the grid and the adherence to adjacencies on the dreaded "org chart" that clients handed out with every brief. The span of cultural references in the workspace was being widened. Increasingly versatile office furniture systems developed by Herman Miller, Knoll, Steelcase, and the like enabled more imaginative and expansive space planning. In a further development, famous urban planning texts such as Jane Jacobs's *The Death and Life of Great American Cities* (1961) were reprinted as primers for office design.[16] Jacobs wrote about the characteristics (and characters) that made Greenwich Village such a great place to live. When architect Clive Wilkinson relocated the U.S. advertising agency TBWA\Chiat\Day to a Los Angeles warehouse building in 1998, he recreated an intelligent pastiche of the early 1960s Greenwich Village within the plan in a bid to design the perfect creative community for several hundred people.[17] A convincing stage set presented a central park, a main street, a basketball court, and "cliff dwellings"—prefabricated steel boxes stacked to accommodate workers. Vintage cars from the 1960s lined the street. The new office coincided with a revival in Chiat Day's fortunes as staff morale soared in a socially democratic workspace.

THE NETWORKED OFFICE

By the new millennium, however, the classic social democratic model was showing its limitations as companies facing unpredictable business markets began to question such bespoke, inflexible, and costly solutions to workspace needs. Frank Duffy has described how a new wave of change began to take shape in line with the emerging demands of a knowledge economy driven by digital technology. He called it the networked office. Its momentum is today being led not by developers or owner-occupiers but by service providers.

The networked office is responsive to demand and configured to add value to business processes, not simply to accommodate them. Its emphasis is on effectiveness, not just efficiency, as in the Taylorist era. It is more flexibly geared to the volatility of business change, with much shorter office leases, than the social democratic model. For the first time, virtual presence coexists with physical presence in the environment.

The networked office connects an increasingly mobile workforce with a drop-in place for know-how and resources, for coaching, mentoring, and fostering the collaborations that lead to innovation. In effect, it provides a hub for business, a place to pass through or connect to remotely, and it is the real manifestation of the organization in an increasingly virtual world. Significantly, it makes the single workplace site a node in an entire network of work. Global companies like Accenture, in adopting a networked workplace strategy, readily acknowledge this theme.

The networked office also reflects one of the fundamental shifts of the knowledge economy: the changing nature of work itself, as most people no longer do the kind of repetitive, linear, process-driven work for which the efficiency mantra of scientific management once made perfect sense. It provides greater flexibility than the social democratic model and uses new technology to make more efficient, just-in-time use of space than even Frederick Taylor could have imagined. Duffy has observed, "The new economy is characterised by a shift from value residing in tangible assets (bricks and mortar) to intangible assets such as intellectual property and knowledge."[18] New forms of accommodation such as serviced offices have simply followed suit.

This networked model has not, however, superseded the earlier waves of change in office design. Rather, it is emerging to coexist alongside them, mapping a new complexity onto the practice of workplace interiors. Every city contains examples of the Taylorist office approach, which is deeply hierarchical and resistant to change. The social democratic model continues to attract its share of paternalistic sponsors—Google among them, to judge by its campus at Mountain View, California, and its sites elsewhere. In this context, the networked office is still in the process of defining its key interior design characteristics. In some instances, on the surface at least, the networked wave is simply extending and accelerating tendencies that took shape in the heyday of the social democratic era.

A good example of this is the trend toward treating office interiors as branding statements. This narrative tendency took shape in the late 1990s as brand-owner-occupiers of socially democratic office buildings such as Reebok, Sony, Quiksilver, Toyota, Bloomberg, and others began using their workspaces as a platform to project brand values to staff, visitors, and suppliers alike. Reebok, for example, incorporated an indoor basketball court and running track into its office design; Quiksilver built a complete "beach community" with polished boardwalk and beach huts; Toyota UK adapted the forms and materials of the motor car along an internal main street at its Epsom Downs headquarters.[19]

This approach differed sharply from the Taylorist model, which paid scant regard to visualizing the different types of work being carried out in different organizations—its only interest was that the work be done efficiently. In reintroducing the storytelling element so common in the design of retail, leisure, and public spaces to the hermetically sealed modernist capsule of the office interior, there was final confirmation that the real problem-solving action in design had migrated decisively from architecture to office furnishings.

The networked era has seen some continuation of this narrative office approach. However, the "brandscapes" in networked offices today are more temporary and transient—more like stage sets—in keeping with the constant morphing of contemporary business practice. The language and techniques of stage design—of light, shadow, and pattern, as perfected for the modern era by such pioneers as Adolph Appia and Edward Gordon Craig—are today increasingly relevant for designers of office interiors.

SUSTAINABLE OFFICE INTERIORS

Where the networked office really departs from its predecessors, however, is in its attitude and commitment to sustainable design. Both the scientific management and social democratic office types unquestioningly adopted the standard industrial model of economic growth as their starting point—the former seeking to maximize efficiency at every turn, the latter seeking to ameliorate some of its less positive social effects in order to improve productivity. The worldview of both models can be summarized as believing that growth can be untrammeled and that natural and human resources can be infinitely expended to ensure the economic wheels keep turning. The legacy of both models has been wastefulness and unsustainability—all those downtown business districts lit up with office towers burning the lights all night; all those vast, expensive open-plan interiors with very low rates of occupancy; all those commuter miles just to be present in the workplace when the tasks could easily be achieved elsewhere.

Allied to more fluid and mobile ways of working, the networked office adopts a more responsible approach to the world's resources. It recognizes the limitations of the economic growth model; it provides space for when you need it, using new technology to help drive up occupancy rates; property is seen as a business tool, not simply a business cost. Indeed, the underlying strategies of using space and time more efficiently to guarantee high levels of occupancy confer on the networked office its chief green credentials.

Many workplace projects since the millennium have made a fetish of technical innovations such as attaching solar panels, brown-water systems, or wind turbines to office buildings—but an alternative view of being sustainable is simply to populate existing office space in a more intense way. The idea is that the more efficient the use of energy to heat and light that space, the less need there is to build additional space. Thus the economic development machine is slowed a little. Retrofitting and remodeling of physical space are very much on the agenda in the networked era.

A study by Pringle Brandon Consulting/UCL for the British Council for Offices (2008) predicted that organizations will seek to achieve higher density levels in their properties—a squeeze exacerbated by economic downturn.[20] Interior designers are responding with schemes that pack people in tightly, taking advantage of flat-screen computers that enables long rows of benches. In some cases, new technology is leading us back full circle to the serried ranks of Frank Lloyd Wright's Larkin workhouse. In others, Google Zurich, for example, dense and dynamic work communities are being planned to enhance creativity and productivity. It seems we are just at the start of a process in which the application of network theory, which has been around since the 1980s, will finally have an impact not just on organizational structure but on the ways organizations utilize space.

Digital pioneer Charles Armstrong, inventor of the SONAR technology system that maps and analyzes relationships at work, has described the current shift in productivity thinking as "a move from linear, straight lines to a more networked world."[21] This transition, Armstrong believes, will have an impact on office space planning that is more profound than anything seen thus far. Too many companies still cling to the org chart as a tool for designing because, says Armstrong, "it gives the illusion of something tangible and therefore manageable. But networks are essentially invisible—how do you make a map of something invisible?"[22]

THE CHALLENGE OF CHANGING DEMOGRAPHICS

In the same way that networked office space must today address a more sustainable model of development, so it must also address a more diverse workforce in terms of age and ability. Changing demographics in the shape of rapidly aging populations world-wide now represent one of the biggest challenges in workplace design. The Taylorist and social democratic models were concerned primarily with what economists call the "family formation workforce"—those from twenty to forty-five years old. The networked model brings far more people into the picture. In particular, it embraces the worldwide phenomenon of an aging workforce: in the early years of the twenty-first century there are growing numbers of older workers who will not retire from the office workplace at the normal time but will remain at work for longer, many of them on a consultancy, special-project, or part-time basis.

Several factors are driving this change. A shortfall in pension funds means many workers simply cannot afford to retire. There is a growing emphasis among managers on retaining knowledge and experience built up within the organization over several years—many older workers are also de facto knowledge workers. Age and disability dis-crimination legislation now offers more protection to older workers, and new legislation has raised the retirement age. Above all, there are the plain, unarguable demographic facts of population aging: one in two adults of working age in the European Union will be over fifty years old by 2020, for example, and nearly one-third of Japanese citizens will be over sixty-five by 2030.

With the process of aging come the multiple minor impairments that affect sensory, cognitive, and physical abilities. So office interior designers must keep an increasingly watchful eye on such matters as physical access, lighting, acoustics, air quality, ergo-nomic, assistive technology, and material finishes—all of which will have an impact on the working lives of the growing legions of older workers.

When a global research study entitled Welcoming Workplace (2008) investigated ways to improve the office environment for older workers employed in the knowledge economy, the project produced some interesting findings on what older employees really want from their workspaces.[23] The study conducted interviews and built prototype work settings in the United Kingdom, Japan, and Australia as part of a qualitative research process, engaging around eighty professionals over fifty years of age working in finan-cial services, technology, and pharmaceuticals. The results were a damning indictment of uniform open-plan environments and clean-desk policies—the dominant smart-technology solutions for knowledge workers in recent years.

The Welcoming Workplace study found that key aspects of knowledge work, such as individual concentration on complex tasks, were poorly catered for by the general design of the open-plan office. An overriding emphasis on collaboration and teamwork neglected the fact that knowledge work requires intense periods of deep, uninterrupted concentration and thinking, often undertaken alone. For older workers in particular, the need for dedicated spaces to concentrate on work is mirrored by the need for suitable spaces to contemplate—to think, relax, and physically recuperate during the working day, shielded from the daily social grind of being constantly under surveillance.

FIGURE 30   The atrium of the Larkin Building by Frank Lloyd Wright. Buffalo, New York, 1904.

Well-planned contemplation space was identified as a missing dimension in office design by the Welcoming Workplace study. Interior designers are now tasked with creating dedicated settings for each facet of knowledge work—concentration, collaboration, and contemplation. There is added impetus given that the diversity of the office population means that four generations can routinely share a single space. The universal one-size-fits-all open-plan space for all comers could be set to become a thing of the past, much like the time-and-motion exercise.

BREAKING THE BOND

Ironically, the banning of conversation and the focus on task completion in the Larkin Building at least made it a suitable place to concentrate. Google Zurich places more emphasis on collaboration and contemplation (with those fish tanks). If you want to really concentrate, you may squeeze inside one of Google's faux igloos. This is not exactly a dignified proposition for the older knowledge worker, but then Google still employs a mainly young demographic. That might change in the future as the company matures.

Indeed, as we redirect our workspace design model away from the industrial model of economic development of the last century and toward the digital knowledge economy of this one, there will be more adjustments along the way. Interior design practice will need to draw on influences as diverse as network theory, sustainable development, demographic analysis, and brand strategy to ensure that the twentieth-century bond between machinelike design and management efficiency in our workspace is well and truly broken.

17

Installation and Performance

DAVID LITTLEFIELD

The act of introducing something new to a space—something physical like an object or an installation, or temporal like a drama or a performance—can have the most profound effect. The space ought not be considered as merely a container, which may or may not have something in it; rather, the space changes state. With the introduction of the installation or the performance, the space (the interior) becomes a frame for something else, and that frame establishes a set of conditions by which the new element can be experienced, judged, and given meaning. The interior as frame, therefore, is not neutral, and it, too, can be reexperienced, rejudged, and given new meaning. An installation or performance, whether touring (and therefore designed broadly for any space) or bespoke (designed as a direct response to a particular space), can open up a series of complex relationships between interior, occupant, spectator, performer, and object.

Professor Aldert Vrij, a psychologist at the University of Portsmouth in the United Kingdom, has pioneered an innovative method to help separate genuine crime scene witnesses from those who merely pretend to have been there—or those who have only a very partial or tenuous link to the event. When asked to draw the scene in question, genuine witnesses tend to depict the space and its principal protagonists as they saw it; that is, they do not draw themselves into the picture. Liars, on the other hand, tend to include themselves in their depictions, drawing a crime scene from an imagined viewpoint in order to demonstrate their involvement in the event.[1] The veracity of spatial recall, in other words, has much to do with the way in which one depicts it. This illuminating piece of research serves to highlight a phenomenon that cannot be overestimated in spatial discourse—that space is *experienced*, rather than captured in plan/section/elevation drawings. Conventional architectural drawings encapsulate information and raw spatial data, but spaces can never be experienced in the terms described in these drawings; rather, spaces are experienced in perspective, via the widest range of sensory inputs, and always from a particular point of view. It is point of view, and the frame in particular, that is the subject of this chapter.

Spaces have meaning in relation to human action—in some cases, where spaces act as frames for a wider narrative, they have little or no meaning without the occupants as protagonists. Carlo Crivelli's 1486 painting *The Annunciation, with Saint Emidius* is a case in point. This large-format work (81.5 × 57.75 in.; 207 × 146.7 cm), hanging in London's National Gallery, depicts the moment the angel Gabriel delivers the news to Mary that she is to bear the holy child. Fortunately for the viewer, the painting is set up to enable the entire narrative to be revealed. Mary is seen kneeling in prayer within a small, but elaborately furnished, dwelling; an element of the wall (perhaps functioning as a doorway) has been peeled away to reveal Mary in this pose. Gabriel is seen, outside Mary's window, speaking with the patron saint of Ascoli, the town for which this single-perspective altarpiece was created. Most intriguingly, a bright ray of light slants diagonally from the recesses of the painting, entering Mary's little home through an arched channel in the wall, aligning perfectly to touch the Virgin's head. Perhaps this channel, which glows as the shaft of light passes through, is a preexisting feature of this very particular architecture, built expressly for the purpose shown; perhaps it appeared miraculously, making way for the laser-like ray that emanates from such a place and at such an acute angle that both door and window are inconveniently placed to allow its entrance. Without the central characters of Mary, Gabriel, and the light ray, the spaces depicted would have no meaning; Mary's dwelling would appear too small, the location of its prayerbook stand too ostentatious, the location and geometry of the arched channel too peculiar to be plausible. But, inhabited, these spaces make sense as a set in which a very specific, unique narrative can take place; we, the viewers, are given a privileged view of a particular moment. The entire architectural space is set up in order that we, as spectators, miss nothing. But in order to fit everything within the scope of the frame, the spatial characteristics depicted become odd—unbelievable, even.

Crivelli is not, of course, the only Renaissance artist to make use of this device—of creating, in effect, a two-dimensional stage set in which the viewer is placed in a position of privilege to gain the fullest understanding of the story. Antonello da Messina explores a similar principle with *Jerome in His Study* (ca. 1475; also in London's National Gallery), in which the translator of the Bible from Greek to Latin is shown at work, occupying a piece of architectural furniture set within a much larger ecclesiastical building. Usefully, an element of the building's facade is absent, or the study has been conveniently positioned in front of an opening, in order to provide the viewer with a clear view of Jerome bent over his work. The key to understanding both paintings is the acknowledgment of the viewer's relationship with the narrative via the device of the frame. The argument within this chapter develops the idea of the frame as a mediating mechanism through which internal space is perceived; the argument also explores notions of the frame as a filter that edits the view and determines what is revealed and what remains unseen, screening the ways in which space is perceived and experienced. Da Messina's *Jerome* deploys a frame that does, indeed, limit what is seen; while revealing the principal elements of the narrative, it hints at a more complex space beyond the limits of the frame. We do not see, for example, how the saint's office "furniture" continues to the left of the picture; neither can we ascertain with much certainty the plan of the church-like building he inhabits—above the study, the enveloping structure appears symmetrical, yet the building appears to recede much further to the right of Jerome than it does to the left. Indeed, on a close look, the study furniture itself is not as complete as it first appears. It is composed of separate elements that do not quite touch; elements are not aligned; there are gaps. In fact, a painting that at first sight appears symmetrical is far from it; much within the painting is out of alignment, and one half of the image merely echoes (rather than mirrors) the other. Even Jerome himself is off-center. This painting is loaded with symbolism and biographical references (the hanging cloth symbolizes washing; the peacock, immortality; and Jerome, according to legend, removed a thorn from a lion's paw, explaining the presence of the lion in the middle distance), but the composition and framing of the painting are suggestive of a subtler phenomenon—the fact that one language does not translate into another with an exact match.

French philosopher Maurice Merleau-Ponty describes the human being not as a "mind *and* a body" but as a "mind *with* a body."[2] The distinction is important, as the mind-with-body model emphasizes the mediating role of the senses, which enable the mind to form a model of the world by assembling and interpreting the stimuli presented to it via the body. Moreover, Merleau-Ponty emphasizes the very human nature of the senses and the ways in which stimuli are interpreted. The consequence, he argues, is that human beings form very partial views of the world they inhabit:

> We are rediscovering our interest in the space in which we are situated. Though we see it only from a limited perspective—our perspective—this space is nevertheless where we reside and we relate to it through our bodies. We are rediscovering in every object a certain style of being that makes it a mirror of human modes of behaviour.... This relationship is an ambiguous one, between beings who are both bodied and limited and an enigmatic world of which we catch a glimpse (indeed which we haunt incessantly) but only ever from points of view that hide as much as they reveal.[3]

"Points of view that hide as much as they reveal" reflects the nature of the frame, that limiter of perspective that arbitrates between what we see, what we do not see, and how we are able to see. The study of artificial frames—such as those provided by paintings of the Annunciation or Jerome or by more dynamic, time-based media such as films—is useful in that it emphasizes the notion that what we see or experience is always mediated, and in need of interpretation. The parameters of our senses, the physical limits of our spatial environment, the precise location in which we find ourselves, and even language itself are elements within that mediation. "The way we see things is affected by what we know or what we believe.... We never look at just one thing; we are always looking at the relation between things and ourselves. Our vision is continually active, continually moving, continually holding things in a circle around itself, constituting what is present to us as we are," writes John Berger.[4]

U.S. artist, choreographer, and filmmaker Maya Derren deployed the frames of the physical parameter and the tools of the editor to great effect in her short film *A Study in*

Choreography for Camera (1945), a collaboration with Talley Beatty.[5] In the film a dancer negotiates a series of woodland and interior spaces, but it appears that he achieves a mastery, or at least an equanimity, with the landscape only after experiencing the freedom of movement within *interior* space. The clutter, texture, and hint of claustrophobia within the early woodland scenes disappear as the dancer, through a sudden clever edit, steps into a domestic interior that provides greater room for movement—a space that is exaggerated through the presence of a mirror. The film then shifts to a large civic space, a museum interior, in which the dancer has almost unlimited room for movement (including, curiously, a pirouette of such speed that he almost achieves the condition of stillness presented by the multifaced Buddha behind him). Finally, the dancer reappears in the woodland, this time in a small clearing providing distant views, and he adopts a static posture—perhaps one of confidence or even ownership. One by one, each successive edit serves as a threshold through which the dancer passes to achieve ever greater expression. Significantly, each space is also defined by the dancer. Like the paintings described above, the relationship between space and occupant is critical; the spaces provide a frame in which the dancer can be understood (the dance itself would be meaningless without the conditions of, the mediation of, the spaces), while the spaces would be wide open to interpretation without the dancer's presence. In terms of the spaces, the performance of the dancer could be considered as a frame, a medium, through which they might be perceived and comprehended.

In this sense, the dancer is performing the role of an installation—an object or presence that serves to transform a space and the way in which it is perceived and experienced. Installations, or interventions, serve to alter the manner in which the inhabitants or visitors respond to space, shifting them away from the role of spectator and drawing them into active participation, focusing attention on the installation itself (forcing the space into the background), or recasting the space to project it, transformed, as something new. The Brazilian artist Renata Lucas, for example, has developed her work *Falha* (*Failure;* 2003) to invite the passive gallery visitor to become performer. Composed of "an articulated, portable, foldable floor that can be opened and extended onto another area—a monument that does not stand still or upright,"[6] this hinged terrain of heavy plywood sheets can be dragged into new configurations by visitors, who become interventionists within an artwork that has no definable form or physical definition, other than the condition in which visitors leave it. As a nonstatic artwork, *Falha* also embodies a certain ambiguity in that it might manifest itself as a largely flat floor surface or as a scape of abrupt peaks and troughs; through the intervention of visitors, the piece becomes more or less present. It provides a kinesthetic experience through the effort to lift a panel via its metal handle, as well as a frisson of uncertainty caused by grappling with an artwork within a gallery environment; however, some visitors might resist the temptation to alter the piece or prefer (or feel compelled by gallery etiquette) to merely look. In its flatter configuration *Falha* begins to vanish. *Falha,* therefore, is difficult to categorize in that it redefines a space through the performative whims of visitors/spectators/interventionists. It can be both space and surface, static objet d'art and a prompt for action. The way in which *Falha* defines its space depends, therefore, both on what one sees and how one chooses to become involved. Further, it is an ephemeral work. "The work is a monument that cannot sustain itself," says the artist.[7]

This sense of the ephemeral, of being more or less present, also defines the work *Above Below,* an installation by artist Caroline Broadhead in Bath Abbey (2011). Comprising a series of hundreds of parallel nylon strands, stretched as a false "ceiling" between the columns of the medieval abbey, this temporary work was an intervention of restraint and subtlety (Figs. 31 and 32). Like *Falha,* its presence depends on the viewer's position and the vagaries of time: under ambient lighting conditions and observed from below, the installation is barely perceptible, and one might pass beneath it while remaining unaware of its presence. Viewed obliquely, especially under the illumination of the Western sun, this screen glows with an intense luminosity and achieves a good deal of substance and opacity. As a horizontal screen of almost domestic height (but out of reach) the installation plays with scale and ideas of territory; the in/visible screen could be seen as gently demarcating (or alternatively blurring) the human zone within the nave from the godly vastness above. Further, and in common with *Falha,* the installation requires the observer to do more than observe—one must participate by shifting position and focus in order to allow *Above Below* to achieve a fuller expression. It is really only by moving that one can best see it, as movement creates new relationships between the viewer, the installation, and the light source.

In this sense, one could deploy philosopher Richard Wollheim's thesis to argue that *Above Below* belongs to the realm of theater and music, rather than more static art such as painting. In *Art and Its Objects* Wollheim argues that different artistic outputs (a painting, a novel, a musical score, a script) must each be considered separately as some require mediation (performance) to fulfill their intention, while others require no mediation other than a direct interpretation between the viewer and the viewed. It is an argument concerning relationships. With a painting, for example, the relationship is simple and direct; the painting

FIGURE 31 *Above Below* installation at Bath Abbey, by Caroline Broadhead. The installation is revealed at its edges, as concentrations of reflected light. Courtesy of Feilden Clegg Bradley Studios.

FIGURE 32   *Above Below,* by Caroline Broadhead (detail). Courtesy of Feilden Clegg Bradley Studios.

as an object never changes, and assessment/interpretation is one of the relationships between the artwork and the viewer. Scripts and musical scores, though still categorized as works of art, function differently; it is through their performance, and the mediation of the director/actor/musician, that the artwork can reach an audience. The raw material of the script requires interpretation; moreover, no performance can be identical with another—each will be unique. There is no universal notation that dictates exactly how every line or note should be delivered, and it is a consequence of the human condition that no one person can precisely mimic the performance of another, or even match in every way one's own performance on succeeding occasions. "A piece of music or a play cannot be performed once and for all," writes Wollheim.[8] In terms of performance, therefore, the location and timing of the authentic artwork are elusive and even illusory; while some performances may be judged to be better than others, the surest one can ever be is that they are all unique.

With installations like *Falha* and *Above Below* the occupant of the space is both viewer and interpreter—fulfilling the roles of both director and audience simultaneously. Both require a participation, an active looking, in order for the pieces to become most present and their potential for meaning, or aesthetic appreciation, to become exposed. German playwright Berthold Brecht, writing in 1948, was highly critical of conventional theater audiences, which, he believed, engaged with performances with far too passive an attitude: "True, their eyes are open, but they stare rather than see, just as they listen rather than hear. They look at the stage as if in a trance: an expression which comes from the Middle Ages, the days of witches and priests."[9] The role of *Falha* and *Above Below* is to prompt the occupant of the space to adopt a similar attitude to that of Brecht's ideal theatergoer: to become an active participant. These installations, if viewed from a position of stasis, will themselves become static.

Similar imperatives underpin a program of work at the Roman baths in Bath, England, undertaken by the author and colleagues from 2009 through 2012.[10] The project, a pilot study for the Estranged Space group, attempted to seek aesthetic value in, and re-present, a set of underground vaults beneath York Street that remain largely unknown to, and little visited by, the public (Figs. 33 and 34). The vaults, which lie

FIGURES 33 AND 34   The York Street vaults at the Roman baths, Bath. These spaces contain traces of human occupation over two millennia; it is these traces that lend the vaults their richness and authenticity. Courtesy of David Littlefield.

on the other side of the wall that defines the principal tourist and heritage zone of this protected site (awarded the UK government's heritage status of Grade 1), provide a back-of-house service function in spite of the presence of Roman artifacts and archaeology. It was this very particular (and undesigned) mix of ancient site and contemporary services, encompassed by Georgian and Victorian structures, that made the vaults an attractive proposition for exploration and interpretation. Moreover, managers at the Roman baths were actively considering ways in which these vaults could become an extension of the tourist zone, relieving pressure on the museum spaces and offering a further incentive to visit what is already one of the United Kingdom's leading visitor attractions.

The Roman baths are fed by a natural geothermal spring that was known to inhabitants in pre-Roman times, as is demonstrated by archaeological finds. The spring was contained in the Roman period, and a complex of buildings grew up around the hot waters to provide a mixture of sacred (temple) and secular (bath) spaces. The Roman drain that was built to empty the water into the nearby River Avon is still in operation. During the post-Roman era the city of Aqua Sulis declined, then reemerged during the medieval period as a market town; its Roman origins became lost and forgotten, although inhabitants continued to benefit from the hot waters. During the eighteenth century a series of building works uncovered Roman artifacts, including the bronze bust of the goddess Minerva, and by the early nineteenth century it had become clear that Bath had once been the site of a significant Roman settlement. It was not until the 1870s that excavations were undertaken by the city architect C. E. Davies, prompted by the need to investigate the cause of groundwater problems, leading to the discovery of the Great Bath that lies at the center of the Roman complex. During the following two decades land was purchased, nearby buildings demolished, and a neoclassical architectural frame erected around the site, in addition to the pump rooms that had been constructed 150 years earlier. It was during this period that the ground beneath York Street was excavated, forming the vaults that have become the site of the Estranged Space study.

Located along the southern periphery of the site, these spaces once provided a mix of baths and courtyard zones during the Roman period. In the meantime, as described above, the Georgians had built over the site, sinking basements down into what had once been the Roman ground level. An enclosed space since the 1890s, these vaults provide a zone for water pipes, gas mains, and electrical cabling and pumping systems, as well as for miscellaneous storage—including the storage of excavated material that lies, uncurated and only partially cataloged, in loose piles.

The difference between the public, curated tourist zone of the baths and the quite different zone of the York Street vaults is partly one of heritage and authenticity; located beyond the boundary of the tourist/heritage zone, the vaults represent a territory where the curatorial and conservational values of the Roman baths do not apply. Here, the Roman is not privileged over other eras. Every age takes its place matter-of-factly, and the vaults become a candid, unmediated record of human occupation, embodying something of the architectural uncanny described by Anthony Vidler as "a distancing from reality forced by reality."[11] The processes of history, society, and culture have worked themselves out on this space to create a site of spatial collision, confusion, and multiple associations. The response of visitors, including student groups, is typically one of surprise in that the condition of the space appears to be one of disrespect and neglect, especially against the background of its Roman origins and the presence of ancient artifacts. The Estranged Space project asked the question: can the vaults be re-presented, extracting or amplifying any spatial and aesthetic quality? Importantly, the project sought meaning in the entire space—the space as a cultural artifact that had evolved over the course of many centuries. Such an approach would offer a distinctive counterpoint to conventional interpretations, which create hierarchies of value, typically based on the notion that older artifacts are deserving of greater respect than newer ones. This project proceeded on the basis that every era represented within the vaults could be viewed as having equal value. The project concerned the space, rather than its constituent parts. The program became one of curating the space, shifting the way in which it might be perceived, working on both the space itself and the framework through which the space can be seen. A range of optical experiments led to the creation of a revolving light installation designed to limit the view, illuminating and revealing the space in fragments (Figs. 35 and 36).

By projecting a vertical strip of light into the space, the geology of the vaults is revealed, reducing the Roman base, Georgian walls, Victorian roof, and contemporary services into a single band, much as a geological core samples the strata and sediments of the Earth. Designed to capture the architectural section, this strip of light has the effect

FIGURE 35   Development sketch of the lighting rig used at the Roman baths, Bath. The rig went through a number of iterations before achieving the intended effect. Courtesy of David Littlefield.

of focusing the view and reducing the vaults into ephemeral concentrations of texture and color, emerging from and retreating into the darkness. Presented with only fragments of light and shade, the viewer cannot perceive the vaults as a whole; rather, one is presented with a puzzle of glimpses and abstractions, reminiscent of cubist art or the short films of László Moholy-Nagy. Socially accepted notions of good/bad, beautiful/ugly, acceptable/unacceptable become suspended as one waits for something like a complete picture to emerge. Only slowly can the viewer create a mental model of the place, but without the framework of values and aesthetic judgments one naturally brings to the act of seeing when presented with a wider, unmediated view. Presenting and framing the vaults in this manner is an act of curation, but one that requires the viewer to piece together visual clues, sensations, and impressions, as well as to negotiate the ambiguities of depth, texture, and scale (Fig. 37).

However, a complete picture of the space does not emerge—as with Crivelli's *Annunciation* or da Messina's *Jerome,* the viewer is aware that there are spaces off the picture plane that one cannot see or that never quite join, and that a sense of place is being revealed through a predetermined frame. The ray of light in Crivelli's work (as in most Annunciation images) appears improbable and from an uncertain source, although that is largely the point. Similarly, the light projection within the vaults describes unexpected paths as it strikes complex surfaces at acute angles. The installation, captured as a moving image, becomes an exercise in choreographing the relative positions of the light source, illuminated surfaces, and camera. The light projection, affixed to a surveyor's tripod, becomes a form of live drawing. As well as critiquing conventional notions of heritage and authenticity,[12] the installation investigates the use of film as a site survey tool, recording not the measurements of a space but a sense of its

FIGURE 36 The lighting rig, created with a surveyor's tripod and a bespoke lightbox and motor system. The lightbox revolves to cast a vertical strip of light. Courtesy of David Littlefield.

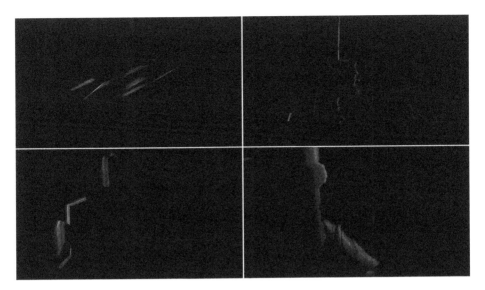

FIGURE 37 Still images from the film *Datum* (2012, Littlefield and Wilder). The revolving light installation fragments the space, revealing it as a series of abstractions. Courtesy of David Littlefield.

characteristics through the discipline of the glimpse. This act of curation and re-presentation falls somewhere between amplifying the aesthetic and spatial qualities that lie implicit within this space and creating such qualities by manipulating what one sees. It is a process of extreme spatial editing, and the revolving band of light, as it wraps across the surfaces of the vaults, reveals a set of spaces that is capable of being playful, surprising, and enchanting.[13]

This work has a close parallel with a study undertaken in Cornwall, United Kingdom, by archaeologists in the 1990s. Christopher Tilley and colleagues engaged in an archaeological study of a Stone Age settlement at Leskernick Hill, on Bodmin Moor, by using both traditional archaeological techniques and practices of creative interpretation deployed by landscape artists such as Andy Goldsworthy. In this work, which included painting, wrapping, and framing key stones on the site, the archaeologists sought to prompt an *"in situ* transformation" to re-present the past in the present.[14] Their interventions are intended as a way of engaging with the site that is more immediate and palpable than the production of professional diagrams, and more meaningful than nostalgic recreation. Indeed, they consider, in an echo of Brecht, that their temporary installations are an expression of a process of active seeing: "We are responding to the stones, not rearranging or altering them. We emphasise through this process of wrapping that seeing is not passive reception but an active process requiring participation and accumulated stocks of knowledge."[15] Further, the archaeologists came to consider that their interventions were part of a necessary process of distortion, emphasis, and even trickery, in order to convey something of the sensation of experiencing the place—a process that involved simplifying it and reducing its complexity with the aim of making a particular spatial interpretation clear.

Consciously attempting to avoid nostalgia for a vanished past or an irrational mystical relationship to culture or nature, our work does not aim at replication but *in situ* transformation, reworking a sense of place into our present-day consciousness.[16]

The work at the Roman baths attempts much the same transformation in order to celebrate the space as a living site—not as a Roman one unfortunately compromised by subsequent human activity, but as a site that gains a richness precisely because of the layering that has occurred here. These, too, are the aims of the Leskernick Hill archaeologists—to draw out the links between past and present rather than objectify the past and set it aside for our disembodied observation. Both pieces of work, therefore, seek to use art practice and notions of framing to prompt a discussion about what it means to experience a historic site in the present.

The notion of the frame is one that can be considered as a physical *artifact* (a hard edge or boundary), a matter of *attitude* or conditioning (such as an observer's willingness to participate and move beyond passivity), a *process* of determining what is seen and what is not, or even part of the human *condition* (such as the limits of language). Thus, the manner in which a designer might suggest ways for an occupant to engage with a space is just as much a frame as the very tangible structure around a painting or the finality of the film editor's cut. Design or curatorial practice becomes one of focusing meaning or affecting a relationship between the frame and the framed. As Vrij has indicated in his studies of false witnesses, the extent to which the occupant/viewer is aware of the frame of experience (whether they are inside the frame or outside it) is crucial to an understanding of space and its meaning.

A concept of such flexibility becomes a powerful and important tool in controlling the ways in which spaces are perceived, interpreted, and experienced—perhaps even *the* tool. Through a consideration of the frame, then, one might even begin to contemplate space as having little or no intrinsic value or meaning; value and meaning are implied through the mechanisms of the frame itself.

18

Exhibition Design: Reflections

DAVID DERNIE

Today exhibition design is changing like never before: museums are changing, and the combined force of the leisure, retail, and entertainment industries is setting the pace. Approaches to cultural and commercial exhibitions, once distinct, are now drawn together as display technologies cross over to create memorable visitor experiences.

Contemporary approaches to exhibition design are a far cry from the restraints of the modernist displays that dominated much of the twentieth century. It was Brian O'Doherty's *Inside the White Cube: The Ideology of the Gallery Space* (1976) that first set out how the White Cube, an icon of modernism, controlled an autonomous aesthetic of display practice, altogether removed from the character, context, or meaning of the work. Equally important to the development of our understanding of contemporary exhibition design is Nicholas Serota's text for the Walter Neurath Memorial Lecture (1996), which outlines a broader context for O'Doherty's observations, describing the historical shift in museum practice from "hanging by school" to "hanging by movement." He describes how both approaches were subject to curatorial interpretation of the works, like an art lesson, and goes on to argue that in the later twentieth century the trend is for "single artists' work seen in depth and isolation."[1]

Serota's discussion, entitled *Experience or Interpretation: The Dilemma of Museums of Modern Art,* is pivotal: he suggests that the museums of the future "will seek to promote different modes and levels of 'interpretation' by subtle juxtapositions of experience." He continues:

> In the new museum, each of us, curators and visitors alike, will have to become more willing to chart our own path, redrawing the map of modern art, rather than following a signal path laid out by the curator....Our aim is to generate a condition in which visitors can experience a sense of discovery in looking at particular paintings,

sculptures or installations in a particular room at a particular moment, rather than find themselves on the conveyor belt of history.[2]

This chapter builds on O'Doherty's seminal critique of modernist display aesthetics and develops Serota's insights into the importance of visitor experience. In part, the direction of the argument reflects contemporary practice, but it is also underpinned by an approach to exhibition, museum, and installation design that is above all participatory, that encompasses ideas of movement and *experience design* to communicate content-driven narratives. This suggests strategies for display that are less formally didactic but more relational, open to personal interpretation and diverse audiences.

The design of such participatory communication is, of course, often a subtle problem but always involves two key scales of thinking. The first is strategic: the general overall spatial structure of the show and the location of the artifacts within it, which set up dialogues between exhibits or thematic clusters. This scale is also about the design of the spaces in-between, places where visitors can stop and think, participate, and make their own sense of what is around them. The second scale of thinking concerns the detail: material, color, light, and sound. These operate like the narrator's voice, linking and interweaving references, sculpting the visible, but also alluding to what is unseen: opening doors to hidden connections. Exhibition design combines these two scales and is a kind of synthesis that structures visual and nonvisual (or indeed audible) relationships. The space of the exhibition opens up relationships between artifacts and points to a "space in-between": it concerns the interdependence of the objects, that lacuna that can engage the imagination of the visitor. In making an exhibition the designer adds an invisible substance to engage the visitor on a creative, visceral, and emotional level.[3]

An age-old device to engage people is exhibition-as-storytelling, and the idea of narrative has been central to all kinds of exhibition designs in recent times, so much so that exhibition design is regularly defined as narration. Such installations could be described as *narrative space*—settings that interweave the real, physical enclosure with the fictive, imaginary space of texts, images, or projections: *experience of narrative space oscillates between the real and the imaginary.* Narrative space concerns the poetics of contextualization, which may be explicit (direct references) but also metaphorical, where unexpected images, light and shadow, reflections, projections, or material configurations evoke distant correspondences or memories and engage the visitor more personally.

Most often, the making of narrative exhibitions involves the spaces between objects as much as the details of singular objects. In the open space between objects the visitors can inlay their own stories, recall memories and their own associations to overlay the narrative with personal value. Recently, in both cultural and commercial displays, there is a growing emphasis on creating a story line that evokes an emotional response, as a key component of the visitor experience. Clearly this is working with the psychology of advertising: colors, sounds, and contrasting rhythms of slow and fast movement that play a key role in creating a memorable, personal engagement with the object or learning experience.

This is not to suggest that a display cannot maintain a rigorous story line: the challenge is how we make that story meaningful, compelling even, to the visitor. In this respect

PLATE 1: Dining room, Linley Sambourne House, 18 Stafford Terace, Kensington, London. Courtesy of Royal Borough of Kensington and Chelsea.

PLATE 2: Richard Hamilton, *Just What Is It That Makes Today's Homes So Different, So Appealing?*, collage, 1956. DACS.

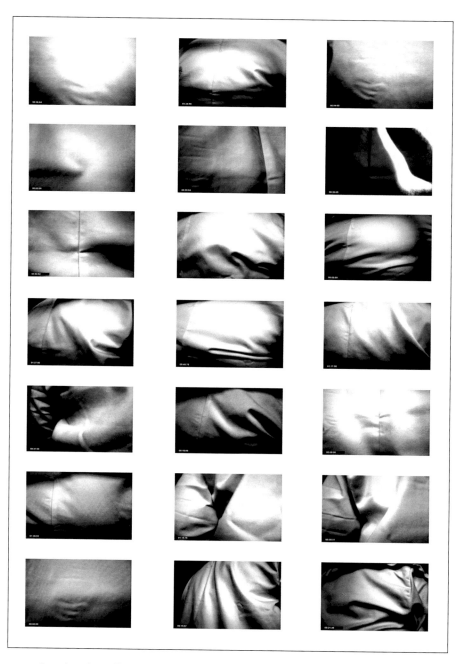

PLATE 3:   Sample video still images spoken from a white coat. Copyright J. Preston 2009.

Putty™ Y78-066-079	Spanish White™ Y88-024-082	Merino™ Y91-009-076
Pavlova™cc Y77-038-083	Half Spanish White™ Y91-020-082	Vista White™ N91-004-046
Canterbury Clay™ BR78-045-078	Double Pearl Lusta™ Y92-024-085	Black White™ N93-005-100
Colonial White™ Y89-043-083	Pearl Lusta™ Y94-018-087	Alabaster™ N96-006-099
Dutch White™ Y93-034-082	Half Pearl Lusta™ Y95-012-089	Rice Cake™ G94-010-092
Solitaire™ Y90-023-077	Quarter Pearl Lusta™ G96-012-092	Sea Fog™ N92-005-100
Bianca™ Y96-012-090	Soapstone™ N93-008-081	Wheatfield™ Y89-023-088

PLATE 4:   Anything but white, a page from *The Resene Whites & Neutrals Colour Chart*, 2009. Courtesy of Resene NZ. J. Preston.

PLATE 5: The Third Space has a series of flexible pods to provide working group pods or spaces for students. Courtesy of L. Farrelly.

PLATE 6: The central zone of the Third Space offers long shared tables to encourage collaborative learning and working. Courtesy of L. Farrelly.

PLATE 7: At the Royal Veterinary College, the placement of a raised platform in the now enclosed courtyard creates a new "sheltered" space encouraging a different scale of place and activity. Courtesy of Timothy Soar.

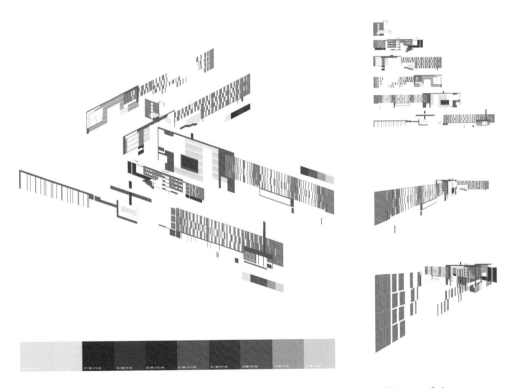

PLATE 8: The Oxford Brookes University scheme is described as a series of layers of elevations in these diagrams. These applied layers have reinvented the facades of the existing building. Courtesy of Design Engine Architects.

PLATE 9: TBWA/Chiat/Day office, 1997, designed by Clive Wilkinson Architects. Courtesy of Clive Wilkinson Architects.

PLATE 10: Independent learning in the "story deck," Ørestad Gymnasium, 2007, 3XN Architects. Courtesy of Adam Moerk.

PLATE 11: Eclectic interior furnishings contrast with the controlled HDB exterior. Photograph by Kenneth Koh.

PLATE 12: Contemplation space at Google's Zurich office, 2008. Architect: Camenzind Evolution, http://www.camenzindevolution.com. Photograph by Peter Wurmli.

PLATE 13: *Expedition Titanic*, Speicherstadt Hamburg 1997/1998. The Concentric Myth Room featured the bell that was probably rung by crew member Frederick Fleet when he saw the iceberg. Designed by Atelier Brückner with Göttz, Schulz, Haas. Photograph by Uwe Ditz.

PLATE 14: Kunsthaus Graz by Peter Cook and Colin Fournier. Photograph by David Dernie.

PLATE 15: Energy Gallery, Science Museum, London, 2004. An integrated landscape of settings for activity and learning through participation. Exhibition design by Casson Mann. Photograph by Andreas Schmidt.

PLATE 16: *Performative Space*, architectural installation designed and curated by David Dernie, at the International Biennale, Prague National Gallery, 2005. Film: Eric Parry Architects. Photograph by kind permission of David Grandorge.

PLATE 17: MoSI, Air and Space Gallery "Ascent towards the skies", David Dernie Architects with Atelierone, 2007. Collage by David Dernie.

PLATE 18: Milan Street: Theater of seduction. Photograph by David Dernie.

PLATE 19: Royal Suites at Pocono
Gardens Lodge. From Bride's
Magazine (Spring 1965).

PLATE 20: Interior view of Rolf de Maré's salon in Hildesborg home. Courtesy of Dansmuseet,
Stockholm.

PLATE 21:   Maggie's London. Photograph by Clive Parkinson.

PLATE 22:   Communal areas in Maggie's London. Photograph courtesy of Maggie's Centre.

PLATE 23: *Fortuitous Novelties* (seed pods) by Darren Browett.

PLATE 24: *Fortuitous Novelties* (seed pods) by Darren Browett.

PLATE 25: London-based Barber Osgerby's 2010 Milan furniture fair Sony project was a dim, space clad with anechoic foam to demonstrate a new chip that can transmute furnishings into audio speakers. The interior underscored the product's purity of the sound as well as the fact that retail space must provide a deep experience of its product: the new showroom must become a do-room.

PLATE 26: Leong Leong brothers Chris and Dominic set out to create retail space that offers new scenarios for living in, and interacting with, the city. For Building Fashion their $5,000, one-week installation was CNC milled as a kit of parts, slathered in a soy-based insulation foam and carved out using knives, saws, and power sanders. Photograph by Pete Deevakul.

PLATE 27: Miami's Alchemist boutique by architect Rene Gonzalez, in a parking garage by Swiss architects Herzog & de Meuron, is a glass box dressed with mirrors. It broadcasts the contents of the shop to the outside while drawing the city in. Sensors move forty-three pneumatic mirrored ceiling panels designed by the UK's Random International in sync with the movements of browsing shoppers. The shop tells us that technology does not need to be conspicuous to improve the shopping experience. Photograph by Michael Stavaridis.

PLATE 28: Miami's Alchemist boutique by architect Rene Gonzalez, in a parking garage by Swiss architects Herzog & de Meuron, is a glass box dressed with mirrors. It broadcasts the contents of the shop to the outside while drawing the city in. Sensors move forty-three pneumatic mirrored ceiling panels designed by the UK's Random International in sync with the movements of browsing shoppers. The shop tells us that technology does not need to be conspicuous to improve the shopping experience. Photograph by Michael Stavaridis.

PLATE 29: Confounding one's sense of perspective and depth, this pop-up shop for British sportswear retailer Reebok had to compete with Manhattan's visually cacophonous wholesale lighting and restaurant supply district. Borrowing from "dazzle graphics" used to camouflage WWI warships, Formavision principal Sebastien Agneessens ensured that the space made a statement with no compromises. Its boldly geometrical graphics served to generate traffic and media attention, as much as showcasing its new collections. Photograph by Jordan Kleinman.

PLATE 30: "Global vocabulary" is on "view" through a 2011 exhibition specifically designed by Zaha Hadid for a Philadelphia museum gallery. Photograph by Paul Warchol.

PLATE 31: *Form in Motion* exhibition floor plan. Permission to publish courtesy of Zaha Hadid Architects.

PLATE 32: A neutral gallery design of "streets and volumes" allows for different movement patterns and a personal realization of global possibility at the Istanbul Biennial for art. Author's photograph and copyright with permission to publish Sanaa design from ryue nishizawa.

the work of the German design studio Atelier Brückner is exemplary; their *Voyager Titanic* exhibition in Hamburg (May 1997–October 1998) combined scenography with theatrical technique to tell of how the *Titanic* sank on her maiden voyage. It focused on the dialogue between the individual visitor and the displayed object, as the source of experiencing and interpreting the event. This strategy clearly required careful attention to the display of the artifacts and, indeed, the staging of each sequential space: while there would be a clear thematic structure, the chronology of events would inevitably underscore the experience.

The design avoided the practice of establishing any heroes, so common in well-known historical accounts and in the emotional interpretations in recent films. Rather, the exhibition used five passengers as narrators without specifying whether or not they survived. The aim was not to comment on the tragedy but to let the staging of the exhibits speak for itself. The emphasis on the intimacy of experience, rather than on didactic narrative, gave the show a rich material quality and an inventive landscape of display that drew inspiration from theater and film.

The exhibition was structured around a central passageway lined in raw steel, 130 ft. (40 m) in length. Dipped in dramatic blue light, it was poignantly left empty. To either side were rooms structured around themes such as Welcome on Board, Life on Board, The Drama of the Sinking, and Rescue. Visitors constantly crossed the empty passageway before arriving at two final rooms: the Room of Silence and, like an epilogue, a room entitled Myth.

The entire length of the central hall of the exhibition—located in Hamburg's historical harbor warehouse district and contemporary with the *Titanic*—unfolded as a journey through the experience of the voyage, from the passengers boarding of the ship and life on board to the sinking of the *Titanic* and, finally, a reflection on the memory of the event. This overall chronology was overlaid by the strong individual themes in each space and was at times deliberately interrupted.

Visitors entered the passageway from an installation entitled Welcome on Board, where there was a sight line through to the final scene in the Myth room. A central "ice bell" hung silently in the distance. Its silence was matched by the cold steel walls of the passage that framed the view. The full significance of the event was powerfully communicated in the first space. Here a dialogue was constructed between a display of suitcases, lashed with ropes, and a wall of photographs of individual passengers. In its midst stood a resplendent model of the *Titanic*. Like the opening act of a drama, the impact of the whole and the anticipation of the voyage's fate were captured in an instant.

Subsequent rooms built up an image of the reality of the ship and life on board. Fragments of salvaged materials and reconstructed rooms combined with large-scale photography were used to convey a sequence of interiors that culminated in the Champagne Room (Fig. 38). This was a further theatrical experiment in that it deliberately broke the narrative structure of the other spaces: blue light and an almost imperceptible low-pitched sound combined to create an uncomfortable setting for the awkwardly housed displays. The feeling of unease provoked by this setting was reinforced by the sound of metronomes that lined the central passageway and beat ever faster, heralding the sinking of the ship.

FIGURE 38 *Expedition Titanic,* Speicherstadt Hamburg, 1997/1998. The Champagne Room with the dialectic installation of six original champagne bottles and a leather workman's boot. Designed by Atelier Brückner with Göttz, Schulz, Haas—Architekten. Photograph by Uwe Ditz.

The collision with the iceberg was itself powerfully communicated through the use of other theatrical devices, such as a sloping floor, projection of film footage of icebergs onto panels of ice, and the display of artifacts underwater. The emphasis here was on making an effective emotional connection with visitors rather than using technology to create an illusion or a realistic reconstruction. There was a deliberate emphasis on the imaginative participation of each individual: simple audiotapes recorded actors reading original accounts and quotes from surviving passengers.

The heightened tension created by the sequence of rooms was effectively countered by the first of the two final spaces: the Room of Silence. Darkened and soundproofed, it appeared to be under water—a still archipelago of cabinets, tailor made for individual yet anonymous objects intended to pay tribute to those who did not survive.

Beyond was the last room of the journey: Myth (Plate 13). This brightly lit space, framed by wavelike walls, focused on the ice bell at its center, which may have forewarned of the danger of a collision. Modern texts and quotes dealing with the ongoing interest in and never-ending metaphor of the *Titanic* disaster overlapped with messages in the form of historical newspaper reports and accounts of other shipping disasters, inviting the visitor to reflect on the broader significance of the *Titanic*'s voyage.

At no stage did the exhibition comment on, or interpret, the material in order to influence how the tragedy was read. The strength of the design was that the fragments that had survived were allowed to communicate their own message to visitors. The story of the *Titanic* was "staged," rather than simply narrated, and was portrayed through the objects themselves rather than through curatorial interpretation. Dramatic lighting, tactile and textured displays, changing temperatures, and low-tech audio environments were deftly combined to create an emotional engagement between visitors and the event.

An emphasis on this kind of narrative experience has characterized much of recent exhibition practice, as museums and galleries respond to an increasingly sophisticated and competitive leisure market. What is equally important to contemporary exhibition design is the creation of an experience that is engaging, multisensorial, and rewarding.

There is sound economic justification for such an emphasis. The idea of the *experience economy* derives from a model established by Joseph Pine and James Gilmore.[4] In today's global economy, dominated by markets of mass-produced goods and in which major Western economies are underpinned by service-sector industries, Pine and Gilmore argue that choice, and thereby economic value, is increasingly based on the quality of customers' experience. The variance of the price paid for, say, a coffee serves as a straightforward example: a coffee in a city space that provides a spectacular setting, Piazza S. Marco in Venice, for instance, can cost wildly more than the same product sold elsewhere. The differentiating factor is the physical, spatial experience. Increasingly, Pine and Gilmore argue, employees in such places become like actors and treat shoppers or visitors like guests who enter a kind of "brand theater." The shop or *destination* becomes like a stage, where a "good sensation," or emotional response to the event, is the desired result of the brand experience. This, as Pine and Gilmore explain, creates a memory in the visitor, and this is the most significant asset value—as memories of the experience are recounted and good feelings associated with the brand engagement color subsequent descriptions of the product, effectively dispersing a positive brand image. This self-generated dispersal has real economic value and rivals the investment in more traditional forms of advertising on radio or television. As a result this kind of brand experience is even privileged over direct retail exchange as exhibition or *destination design* takes on a fourth dimension—like staging an event that is scripted and interactive. We observe that major brands, from Disney to Lego, Samsung to Nike, now focus on this style of brand experience—to the extent that their flagship stores are sometimes no longer retail outlets. The value of visitors' experience during their engagement with the brand overrides the potential profits of a singular point of purchase: free souvenirs—branded trinkets that the visitor retains—will act as memory triggers well beyond the duration of the visit.

As a development of narrative practice, *experience design* such as this builds a context out of the display object or product with the aim of engaging the visitor at an emotional as well as intellectual level. In so doing it attaches a personal and enduring memory to the experience of the visit. The so-called memory economy is now recognized as a driving force behind successful brand-related design—and shortly even the more conservative museums and galleries will respond.

Essential to the creation of a memory-rich experience is the character of the physical setting, where communication is expressed as *connectivity with the individual,* clearly defined, compelling, and compressed into interactive, multisensorial environments that will transform museums and high streets alike from depositories of cultural artifacts and retail outlets into vital networks of branded experience.

A new generation of audience is emerging that differentiates less between new art and, say, new music, film, fashion, or design, and new artistic practices eschew traditional boundaries between modes of expression. The museum and brand experience needs to celebrate these new trends of interdisciplinary, creative investigation in order to keep younger audiences engaged.

At the same time, the new museum experience should not stop within the confines of the building itself; rather, it must be engaged with civic, regional, national, and international horizons. Experience design must be about establishing frameworks for change: forms, material and nonmaterial, that celebrate the shifting patterns of contemporary communication: "A museum is not just a building or even a collection, it is a place which should enrich our understanding of the world in ways that are stimulating, entertaining and enjoyable. To achieve this it needs to be part of the community, not aloof from its visitors."[5] Museums, like retail and brand events, are all *experiences of connectivity.*

With such ideas in focus, in 2006 Manchester's Museum of Science and Industry decided to pursue a comprehensive development program, integrating existing heritage buildings with new construction to shape a sustainable long-term future for the museum that was fully integrated into the Castlefield community and the broader context of the city of Manchester.

The museum-development strategy had two reciprocal dimensions. The first was the aim of setting standards for future visitor-focused displays—*as* performative spaces— that were to bring heritage to as wide an audience as possible; the second was to break down barriers to access—to create a coherent museum that is integrated with the texture and life of the modern city of Manchester.

Recalling the image, but not the meaning, of André Malraux's *museum without walls,*[6] the Museum of Science and Industry was to become a new "destination" for the city. The imposing character of the industrial buildings was to be eroded by opening up facades and tying key entrances into a series of interwoven journeys through local gardens, streets, and naturally lit exhibition halls. Strategically, the museum's story was to unfold both inside and outside of the existing warehouse buildings, creating a collage-like city-museum (Fig. 39).

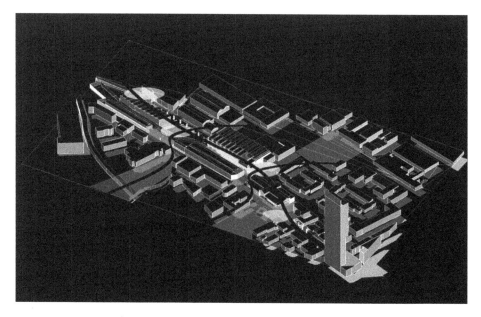

FIGURE 39   Museum of Science and Industry, Manchester in the context of the city, studied as an active city-museum. Courtesy of David Dernie.

This ambition built on a number of initiatives to engage the museum and city or surrounding community, and its story line was held by a new space—part internal, part external—that housed the Revolution Gallery (Fig. 40). In distinction to its context, the design of this low-energy space took natural form as its starting point: the object of all scientific observation. An adaptable biomimetic structure housed display spaces and was in itself an exhibition of environmental performance: like giant lilies, these lightweight forms were dynamic connectors and gatherers of people and clustered themes. Their gentle forms were to resonate with the vaulted space and textured fragments of what remained of "Cottonopolis."[7]

Here, some of the principles of Pine and Gilmore's memory economy are transferred into the experience of a theater-like space of memories. What might be called *memory design* is not primarily a question of aesthetics, or indeed technology. Memory design has a single orientation: a connection between the content of the narrative and the physical and emotional experience of the body in motion. Movement, interaction, play, and spontaneity of expression give the memory designer a distinctly new outlook compared to the static viewer of a modernist display. The conventional discourse around traditional display aesthetics is replaced with ideas and techniques drawn from theater, film, and performance, areas of visual culture that may usefully inject life into our increasingly remote institutions and at the same time generate economic benefits, as evidenced by Pine and Gilmore.

FIGURE 40   Museum of Science and Industry, Manchester. Sketch study, Revolution Gallery. David Dernie Architects with Atelierone, 2007. Courtesy of David Dernie.

In recognizing such cognate disciplines, and the inevitable overlap with the leisure industry, it is important to differentiate between entertainment, simulated environments, kitsch, and other forms of expression that communicate content with more rigor. For here the exhibition designer is not working in the realm of pure entertainment but rather creating a compelling experience that is content focused. Unlike the staging of entertainment (for its own sake), the apparatus of an exhibition installation is more like a mediating structure, heightening the drama latent in the artifacts on display, but its purpose is to tell us something about the world. Exhibitions cannot compete with the solipsistic experience of a film or the fantasy of a fairground ride; rather, their strength comes from a poetic exchange between the constructed landscape of artifacts or products and their physical and cultural context—and key to this is participation, visitors that don't just look but are imaginatively engaged with active displays.

In this sense the analogy of theater is usefully overlaid by an idea of *performativity* in exhibition design. Recently the concept of the performative in three-dimensional design has attracted international interest as a new approach to interactivity, emphasizing the dialogue between space, motion, and time. In exhibition design it tends to be identified with highly formal installations that are configured to represent movement (understood in terms of abstract data and process analysis). These complex, interactive forms are proposed as *performative statements,* structures that present something new to their context, generate a reaction, and in turn respond to movement.

The Kunsthaus in Graz, Austria, designed by Peter Cook and Colin Fournier and built as part of the European Capital of Culture celebrations in 2003, has been described as an example of performative architecture, largely, one might assume, because of its willful formal relationship to the historical context and the fact that its curvilinear form is clad in a "media facade" of programmable lighting (Plate 14). On the other hand, its rather awkwardly inclining walls and the complex forms of the building's interior make for contentious exhibition space.

Formal willfulness is in contrast to the original notion of performativity that starts within language theory. Emerging in the nineteenth century, it identified a *performative expression* as one that does not simply make a statement but in itself performs an action. It is an utterance used to express an action, as distinct to describing a condition. In the statement "I apologize," for instance, the person apologizes by saying "I apologize." The sentence is used not to describe the performance of an act but rather to perform an act— it has a performatory use; it is a performative utterance.[8]

Like performative statements in language, exhibition installations can be designed so that they are tied to actions: spatial configurations that immediately connect to a "doing." And like language, the meaning of a performative installation will be determined by its physical and cultural context.

A *performative space* is more usefully understood as one where the movement of the body is considered integral to the structuring of the environment and the landscapes of the artifacts, where movement becomes integral to communication and understanding. Visitors become quasi-performers themselves, in a sense, both spectators and part of the spectacle—they are incorporated in the creative and intellectual life that is represented.

It is a place where traditional boundaries between viewer and object or performance are eroded to create a rich and vital *memory* of a dynamic experience of the material on display.

These ideas are well illustrated by the installation *Energy Gallery "Fuelling the Future"* in the Science Museum, London, designed by Casson Mann (exhibition, museum, and interior designers) in 2004. The gallery aims to engage visitors in the crucial energy issues that face society today and in the near future. With key facts written on its walls to provide a framework for debate, this permanent installation skillfully combines perturbing information with inventive, entertaining, and interactive displays to capture the imagination and attention and to engender critical thinking by visitors of all ages (Plate 15).

The exhibition consists of a colorful landscape of eleven individual works by selected artists: the designers Casson Mann were engaged to draw these together into a coherent whole. They achieved this by first establishing a clear distinction between the two existing wings of the museum and the Energy Gallery itself. The space overlooks the east hall, through which visitors pass to enter other parts of the building, and is visible from all its levels. It reads as the culmination of a journey through the existing galleries that work around the central void.

The gallery was clearly disengaged from the existing fabric of the museum by raising its floor and lowering its ceiling. Parts of the painted ceiling were then cut into, to house lighting devices. A similar language of layered surfaces was developed for the floor and display structures. Colorful folded, veneered surfaces made from rubber-faced plywood delineate floor space and then move to become exhibition supports, projection booths, showcases, tables, and chairs. The space is almost like a stage set: colorful and luminous, the coherence of its detailing draws the diverse artworks together as a whole. At the same time it is robust and is designed to allow for change over time.

The theme of the gallery is dramatically announced to the rest of the museum by the Energy Ring, the central installation in the hall. Suspended in a three-story void, it is 14 yds. (13 m) high and comprises a LED screen, nearly 44 yds. (40 m) long, that forms a ring of moving white light. Its image heralds energy as being central to future scientific endeavor.

At a practical level, it acts as an interactive device to gain feedback from visitors. An "augmented-reality" view of the ring on four touch-screen terminals that overlook it from the exhibition area enables visitors to zap it, causing a small explosion of light to flash around it. The screens also allow visitors to change the patterns of the light and to respond to energy-themed questions. An individual's response may then be displayed on the ring for all to see.

The exhibition is immediately impressive for the way in which artists were engaged to produce installations. Partly as a consequence, the experience of the gallery is one of remarkable variety, clarity, and enjoyment. Each work engenders a different kind of interaction: movement and play become an integral part of learning. *Making Energy Useful*, for example, asks which sources of energy should be used in the future. It consists of four screens with pressure-sensitive floor areas in front of them. Symbols representing different energy sources fall down the screens, and visitors "catch" the appropriate one by moving their feet. Technologies are matched to the sources by means of a playful interaction, and at the end of an energetic game the performance of each visitor is scored. Movement, rhythm, and playfulness accompany the learning process.

Thinking about exhibitions in terms of movement, activity, and interaction challenges conventional approaches to museum and exhibition design, not as an aesthetic alternative, but in terms of new strategies for communication and learning experiences. It emphasizes the relationship between learning and play, and the architectural language of such installations eschews remnants of the old museum's hushed, whitewashed walls. This approach attracts people of all ages and social and ethnic backgrounds in an atmosphere of experiment and creative discovery.

This was the tenor of a self-build installation called *Performative Space*, set in the basement of the National Gallery in Prague at the International Biennale of 2005, which explored boundaries between architecture, the visual arts, music, and in particular theater, cinema, and the performing arts (Plate 16). It brought together international artists, photographers, filmmakers, dancers, and architects; work was deliberately selected to deflect a formal reading of contemporary architecture (so typical of the Biennale circuit). The installation was originally conceived as a movement or journey between several pavilions, between city and gallery, and between real and implied space. It was organized with a choreographic sensibility, as an interactive environment, a space for an informal dance of sorts where visitors become performers in the event they are generating.

The curatorial strategy deliberately avoided a homogeneous display of architectural objects. The resulting installation was intentionally fragmentary and formed a journey that was articulated by a sequence of textual fragments. Set against the concrete shell of the disused cinema, language, attuned to the pace and horizon of the visitor, was used to explore the relationship between the structure of the installation and the space of the imagination. The journey was like a labyrinth of discovery, a movement intended to open up an understanding between the diverse artifacts, projects, and spaces of the installation.

The idea of a "visitor's route" has always contributed to the design of exhibition layouts at some level. Here, however, movement is treated not as a circulation diagram but as a vital part of how the visitor experience is constructed: *movement animates our imaginations, and only through movement do we understand our world.*

This notion is integral to a recent proposal to restructure the Air and Space Gallery of Manchester's Museum of Science and Industry (described above). Here an experience of the wonder of flight and space travel was to be narrated using one simple performative device. A modular, lightweight ramp zigzagged its way through the nineteenth-century glazed market hall to create pockets of space for exhibit groups. As the visitor moved from the entrance, where high-level displays and distant projections conveyed the wonder of flight, the ascent took the visitor upward, to be among the planes, in the skies as it were, where planes were to be suspended at eye level. Then, as the journey progressed, the sides of the ramp were incrementally raised to obscure the world outside, until, after the visitor crossed a bridge, a ceiling was introduced, the floor surface changed from aluminum to a cushioned leather, and now, acoustically isolated, the visitor was to be surrounded by a projection of the galaxies (Plate 17).

Here the singular device of the ramp acts like an armature—a strong story line on which all the subplots can be hung: learning was to be synonymous with the excitement of a journey, both real and fictive, up into the skies through the extraordinary inventions of history and then bridging onto a darkened, silent passage, surrounded by simulated stars and dreams of the future of flight.

Today displays like this draw on the increasingly sophisticated techniques of animation and film to capture the imaginations of wider audiences at an emotional, physical, and intellectual level. And while the making of an exhibition is all about building a narrative in a specific physical context, we could refer to the space for contemporary displays as a kind of *oscillating space,* the experience of which is ever back and forth between the real and the imaginary space, the actual and the virtual existence of artifacts.

This kind of oscillating space is to be found on every commercial street, where objects for sale are creatively reimagined, reconfigured as part of the *brand experience.* Retail displays regularly use techniques borrowed from film and theater: shifting angles, montaging color, texture, and different scales of image, to draw the passerby in intimate proximity of the window's space. Here, in the multiple reflections the passerby is caught by the fascination, desire even, for the real material artifact and the projection of the brand experience that surrounds it. The commercial street has become a key space for innovation: drawing on the habitual performance of the street itself, the shopwindow has the potential to become a simulated environment, designed to create dreamlike visual experiences: *it is exhibition making as a theater of seduction,* experienced as part real, part a dreamlike escape into alternative worlds that the merchandise evokes (Plate 18).

Drawing on a critique of modernist display aesthetics, we see that exhibition design is now focused on creative narratives and the visitor experience of content. It's about creating memories, and these have economic value: good experience design that creates lasting memories will retain museum visitors and communicate the brand wider than conventional advertising.

Contemporary exhibition design eschews traditional rules of flow and circulation in favor of an understanding of body and movement as integral to the design. Movement is key to discovery and engagement: *we can say that movement is the most critical element to communication in exhibitions*—there is no experience of the display without movement. On the one hand, an exhibition may involve literal movement, play, or other themed activity, keyed to sequential displays or interactive devices. On the other hand, movement may not be literal but imaginary. Like the description of a journey to the stars (Air and Space Gallery) or to the depths of the ocean (*Voyager Titanic*) the visitor travels an imaginary journey to complete the experience. Through both real and imaginary movement, and through real and fictive space, the visitor makes the experience of the constructed narrative his or her own: it becomes a personal memory, the visitor's own story to be retold another day.

PART 2

Occupancy

Introduction

This second part, entitled "Occupancy," addresses the shaping of interior spaces, from the immediate scale of the body to larger global influences. This part consists of eleven chapters that fall under two subsections. The first subsection, "Body, Behavior, and Space," begins with chapters based in physiological and psychological perspectives to convey how influences, such as gender, behavior, and demographics, give shape and identity to the interior. Chapters provide historical and contemporary examples to better understand the evolution of the body's representation and contextualization in society. The second subsection, "Ethics and the Indoor Environment," places emphasis on larger external forces that act upon the interior but that are often out of the control of the individual. Chapters situate the interior within a larger global context to establish new paradigms informing the way we occupy interiors. Together, these topics address both tangible and imperceptible approaches to shaping interiors and reveal the complex nature of what it means to occupy.

BODY, BEHAVIOR, AND SPACE

The Vitruvian Man established a Western view of the body in architecture. It allowed for the projection of the body into geometric forms to guide the scale and proportion of architecture. In contrast, the emerging twentieth-century interior designer broke free of this image but was still tasked with negotiating the body in space. Barbara Penner's chapter, "Redesigning for the Body: Users and Bathrooms," places emphasis on the body but not in classical references—rather, from an empirical study of how the body functions in one of the most private programmed rooms, the bathroom. Penner's chapter is centered around the study of bathrooms and ergonomics by Alexander Kira in the 1960s, with research that dissolved the threshold of modesty. Penner draws out tangent issues that arose in Kira's work that included the female body as a central figure of research for the customization of bathroom fixtures and, with it, documentation that would challenge traditional practices. Designing bathrooms is a staple of interiors and often associated with luxury, as in hotels, or utility, as in airports. Manufacturers historically provided designers with a range of fixtures to select from based upon standards that rarely change. What is allowed to change is the character of these rooms but not the underlying universal fixture that Kira sought to divide and make gender specific. Penner's chapter brings visual representation to the body, while interior spaces bring visual representation to the occupant.

Post-occupancy evaluations provide a quantitative form of documenting an occupied interior, but if psychologists conducted a similar post-occupancy evaluation, the results would provide an alternative form of insight. The personalization of interiors, whether domestic or workplace, is the primary focus for psychologists Samuel D. Gosling, Robert Gifford, and Lindsay McCunn in their chapter "Environmental Perception and Interior Design." The authors apply modes of psychological evaluation established for social settings and reapply them to physical environments as a way to evaluate how occupants affect their interiors, which in turn affects the identity they project. As much as people are social creatures, the personalization of space is the physical representation of identity. The authors look at three areas for evaluations: the tangible objects made visible for others to see; atmospheric conditions of light and noise; and traces of living in the form of dust or uncleanliness. These three criteria fall in the realm of designed space, yet continue to shape the interior once the designer has left and no longer has control of the space.

In the case of accounting for ones identity through the interior, John Potvin repositions identity and personalization further in his chapter, "Guilty by Design/Guilty by Desire: Queering Bourgeois Domesticity" Potvin recognizes that while there are traditional practices surrounding the discipline of interior design, a new phenomenon has presented itself: the visualization of gay couples and their interiors as the center of focus in media. Current magazines and television shows highlight domestic interiors but also act as a base for Potvin to contrast historical characters and defining moments surrounding the domestic interior occupied by gay couples. As Gosling, Gifford, and McCunn show in their chapter, the role of objects and atmosphere are defining characteristics in establishing an identity on the interior. Potvin walks us through a selection of historical Victorian interiors pointing out effects in rooms where dark, snug, and artificially lit were characterized as more troublesome than a light, airy room. These domestic settings, coupled with gender and sexual preference were used to project judgment about one's character. In one case, Potvin looks to Oscar Wilde and the absence of a domestic interior that further characterized his identity. The intimacy of the domestic realm will always be a mainframe of media and, for better or worse, a baseline for what is acceptable in society.

The media provides a portal through which to view other peoples live. At the same time, it propagates fashion and trends, which is evident in interior design magazines and home improvement shows. Stephanie White situates her chapter, "Demographics and Identity," in the contexts of media and consumption to draw out the relationship between demographics and interior design. In order to do this, White looks to a number of underlying sources that give insight as to how products and identities are targeted at demographic groups. Two significant issues that White brings to the foreground are aspiration and assimilation as underlying currents to help explain the desire to enter into a different demographic but at the loss of traditions as some cultures seek to attain middle-class status through representations of domesticity as seen in mainstream media. White looks to representations of an emerging middle class that spans the history of pattern books to present day design magazines and television shows and their effect on shaping the interior.

Media portrayals of particular groups in society often communicate specific images of demographic groups often in their best or most pristine condition. This obfuscates other groups or demographics that may be underrepresented. The relationship between demographics and interior design is highlighted to reveal a broader connection between manufacturers, media, and interiors. Demographics are also the focus of Ong Swee Hong's chapter, "Designing for Ageing-in-Place for High-Density Living in Asia: A Comparative Analysis on Residential Design for Singapore, Japan, and Hong" to reveal a shortfall of housing for an emerging demographic in Asia. Hong tracks the growing demographic of elderly populations in Asia that are in need of new accommodations in public and private programming to meet social, cultural, physical and emotional needs. Hong points out challenges that designers face in Singapore, Japan, and Hong Kong as they design for vertical growth in high-rises versus horizontal expansion found in international precedents such as in North America and Europe. Hong emphasizes the need for reassessing living patterns and layout as a starting point for designers to be innovative with programming. The design of new high-rise buildings can respond to these future needs and places the role of flexibility and spatial configurations in the hands of the interior designer and architect at the start of the design process rather than at the end. Where smaller building footprints are a necessary part of a limited landscape, innovative programming presents itself as a solution.

Designing for ageing-in-place seeks to provide a healthy lifestyle for the elderly while balancing independence and medical care. The relationship between healthcare and interior design has been strengthened over the decades, and in the case where interiors need to accommodate patients in more severe cases, Clive Parkinson looks to the integration of experiences with art, interiors, and architecture to shape healthcare. In his chapter, "Toward Sentience," Parkinson's research calls for design to respond to the experiential rather than only the scientific, especially in cases where medicine offers no cure. In order to achieve this, the role of art, interiors, and architecture come to the foreground as a means for providing experience, placing Experience-Based Design ahead of Evidence-Based Design. In one example, Parkinson looks to the underlying goals of Maggie's Centres, centers for supporting cancer patients that originated in the United Kingdom and place emphasis on experience and emotional support as a balance to the scientific. While Evidence-Based Design offers one form of objective data, Experience-Based Design addresses the subjective, emotional side. Much like the need for balancing a healthy lifestyle and medical assistance for ageing-in-place, Parkinson shows the need for integrating the experiential in healthcare to address the emotional outcomes.

ETHICS AND THE INDOOR ENVIRONMENT

Chapters in this second subsection offer insight into larger systems and infrastructures that paints a broader picture of how we occupy interiors. Rather than shaping interiors from the inside out, these systems and infrastructures influence interiors from the out-side in. Topics such as ethics, consumption, and sustainability evolve as a reflection of a larger social context and in turn affect the practice of interior design. The last two chapters in this part position interior design within the topics of politics and globalization, which have largely been absent from the discourse of interiors. Therefore, they open up the discipline to new discussions that look outward from its traditional enclosed space, an important development as the interior has always—whether knowingly or not—engaged with social issues due to its engagement with occupation and the human in-habitation of space.

Interior designers work intimately with clients, and to guide this relationship, codes of conduct have been established with the intent to protect both client and designer. To be ethical is to uphold an ideal set of morals, and as the practice of interior design evolves, ethics and conduct must continuously be evaluated. Mary Anne Beecher, in her chapter, "The Thin Edge of the Wedge: Shifting Ethical Terrains and Interior Design in the Twenty-First Century," raises three fundamental questions about the practice of interior design as a starting point for understanding the evolution and current status of ethics in the discipline. Her questions lay a foundation upon which the evolving terrain continues to change by asking who we are as interior designers (based upon governing bodies); what we do; and how we do it. From each of these questions arise insight into the problems interior designers must resolve. Beecher looks to current interior design practices as a way to understand how an ethical framework emerges, and when analyzed from one era to the next, the shifting practice of ethics reveals the external forces that shape future conduct.

The history of interior design traditionally points to examples that focus on excess and ornament. Contemporary designers still pursue these projects, yet ethical contradic-tions now arise as interior designers are expected to be the "purveyors of beauty" which often contradicts sustainable design. Architects and interior designers are expected to be good stewards of the environment while not limiting the potential to construct in-spiring interiors, yet the two do not always complement one another in practice. Nadia Elrokhsy tackles one of the most pressing topics interior designers must undertake in her chapter, "Designing for Sustainability: A Framework for Interior Designers to Engage in Designing Experiences for Efficiency and Beyond." The traditional role of sustainable practice by interior designers includes knowledge of sustainable materials and products, which certifications and organizations make easier for practitioners to implement with product ratings and labeling. While this is a significant undertaking, Elrokhsy makes an argument for interior designers to be more strategic by considering how we use our spaces and the role of behavior as a motivator for having a greater impact on reducing energy and consumption with efficient design solutions. Specifically, the role of sharing as a form of downsizing can be applied to a range of programs, from workplace to residence. The goal is a smaller footprint that seeks to conserve energy.

An underlying current to Stephanie White's chapter in the first subsection of this part are the forces marketing and targeting have toward demographic groups that inherently affect the practice of interior design. Window-shopping is one venue for achieving these strategies, where large plate glass offers a glimpse into an otherworldly environment to captivate viewers. The storefront window is an interdisciplinary space that merges fashion, art, theater, and interior design. The combination of these fields allows for customers to embody memorable experiences, even for only a fleeting moment. Stephanie White's chapter revealed the trend toward retail and targeted audiences, and Shonquis Moreno builds upon this research and provides an overview of the traditional role of consumption in the retail environment. She does so by introducing the shift from plate glass window-shopping to online shopping and the need for distinction between the two. In her chapter, "Designing Desire," Moreno suggests that there is a need for traditional window-shopping to heighten experiences in order to create a culture, or even cult, around a product. The competition between the two forms of retail forces a restrategizing of the role of retail stores. The tactile aspect of online shopping ends with the keyboard, whereas the retail store allows for experiences that form an emotional desire. As a result, interior designers act as orchestrators of interdisciplinary approaches to the physical site of retail stores. While Moreno reveals the remaking of experiences in traditional stores, the next phase for interior designers to consider is what role, if any, they play in the experience of virtual retail.

The difference between occupying virtual and physical spaces is a practice that continues to be explored as the discipline absorbs more technology. The division between these spaces embodies complex boundaries. In drawing, poché denotes division between privacy and possession; on a map, boundaries are depicted as thin lines that represent real value—economically and politically, and how we inhabit those lines raises issues of possession and repossession. Terry Meade in his chapter, "Interior Design: A Political Discipline," makes visible the complexity of divided spaces that bring larger issues to the foreground, such as property, commerce, culture, and cyberspace networks and their effect at the global scale. These issues have changed the way we conduct day-to-day affairs, and when Meade returns to the interior, he provokes the discipline to integrate these issues into the discourse rather than limiting its scope to the safe, contained physical boundary that primarily responds to issues of style and arrangement. Meade looks through a global and political lens to see the shortfalls of the interior design discipline and its disregard of everyday complexities that lie on the exterior of an enclosed perimeter. A view through Meade's lens reveals that previous physical boundaries are dissolving and giving way to virtual boundaries, at the same time challenging traditional interior design practices.

Understanding the term *globalization* in the context of interior design is a recent theoretical endeavor. Globalization implies the migration of forms and ideas, but at the same time, it suggests the loss of regional and vernacular forms. The interior designer must now be aware of these opposing forms of practice and learn to negotiate them. Alison Snyder in her chapter, "Globalization: What Shapes a Global Interior?" looks to interior design education and practice as starting points to uncover the extent to which emphasis is placed on globalization. Snyder draws out the need to balance global and local influences in response to place, culture, and client needs. Visible results lie in the reinterpretation of traditional styles, practice, and programs. Vernacular forms give way to hybridization influenced by current technologies where new styles are generated out of vernacular traditions. Globalization positions the interior designer in new forms of practice that include being off-site or virtual with the benefit being the migration of forms at a greater speed. With this comes the collapse of traditional programmed spaces but opens up the potential for reevaluation for programmatic themes. Rather than working with programs as silos, Snyder suggests recategorizing our actions as a means for addressing global and local ways of living and working.

The chapters in this part develop the role of humans and their responses, needs, and requirements to the space in which they are situated. In all of the chapters, the interior is a central component in these explorations.

The Body, Behavior, and Space

19

Redesigning for the Body: Users and Bathrooms

BARBARA PENNER

Our needs are the needs of men. We all have the same limbs, in number, form, and size; if on this last point there are differences, an average dimension is easy to find.

Standard functions,
standard needs,
standard objects,
standard dimensions.

—Le Corbusier[1]

In this chapter, I have been asked to write about the body as a generator of interior space, a notion that summons to mind an ideal human-scale environment. But my chosen site, the modern bathroom, leads me to explore a rather different theme: the ways in which interiors can work to suppress the individual body. I argue that this was the case with the modern bathroom, which, from the 1920s onward, was a space in which specific bodily needs and the realities of everyday use were excluded, not only from design but also from representation. The bathroom was spoken about and depicted in very circumscribed ways, precisely to cleanse it of difference and to subject it to a standardized logic instead.

The extent to which these notions remain embedded in bathroom design today will be discussed in this chapter with reference to Alexander Kira's still radical 1966 work *The Bathroom*.[2] Influenced by ergonomics, *The Bathroom* and its later revised edition single-handedly sought to bring the user to the heart of design through a combination of cultural analysis, field research, and laboratory testing, culminating in a series of proposed redesigns. Even though his work is frequently hailed as a "classic of user-centered design research,"[3] Kira never managed the wholesale revolution in attitudes and standards he sought. An exploration of the book's methods will shed light on some of the difficulties of realizing user-centered human environments in practice. At the same time, it provides a tantalizing reminder of what is at stake: interior spaces that are genuinely inclusive, the holy grail of contemporary design.

SETTING STANDARDS

Although space does not permit a thorough exposition of the rise of the modernist bathroom, it is worth briefly summarizing the way in which they were treated in art and design discourse up to Kira's groundbreaking study. The starting point of this potted history will surprise few readers: Marcel Duchamp's *Fountain* (1917)—a work that was key to establishing the visual language of modernism and what might be called its cleansing drive.

There is little doubt that Duchamp was being ironic when he transformed a mass-produced urinal into a sculpture. But what is relevant here is that almost immediately an aesthetic argument in favor of the urinal's "striking, sweeping" lines was articulated by one of Duchamp's supporters.[4] And, in decades to come, it became quite normal to treat bathroom fittings as striking objects, as things of beauty. Probably the best example is modernist photographer Edward Weston's gorgeous photos of a Mexican toilet in the series "Excusado" (1925). While taking this series over a two-week period, Weston enthused, "I have been photographing our toilet, that glossy enameled receptacle of extraordinary beauty…My excitement was absolute aesthetic response to form."[5] Standardized and pristine, sanitary appliances also appealed to historians of modernism like Siegfried Giedion. In *Mechanization Takes Command* (1948), Giedion represented the naked washbasin as a triumph of progress and rationalism and chronicled, with palpable empathy, its struggle to gain its "natural form" in the face of Victorian weakness for adornment. Freed at last from "grotesque" and "feminine" ornamentation, in Giedion's eyes, the functional, manly simplicity of bathroom equipment perfectly exemplified modernist aesthetics.[6]

Modernists clearly celebrated bathroom fittings, but they did so in very particular ways, as icons of anonymous industrial processes and as embodiments of the principle form follows function. Indeed, real bodies were actively suppressed in modernist representations, which depicted bathroom fittings as objects, floating free of the context of their use. This reluctance to delve deeply into questions of setting or use is no doubt one of the reasons why, apart from stylistic changes like streamlining, bathroom equipment actually changed relatively little over the course of the twentieth century. The visionary engineer Buckminster Fuller went so far as to state that bathrooms actually demonstrated the limits of modernist architects' embrace of technological culture. Speaking with the Bauhaus in mind, he observed that the modernist enthusiasm for bathroom features almost never led to a practical concern for the design, use, or environmental problems that they represented. Modern architects, he complained, "only looked at problems of modification of the surface of end products."[7]

Insofar as modernist architects valued bathrooms as real spaces, it was on the basis that they promoted progressive social goals, such as hygiene, that would improve public health. When modernists invoked the body in this context, they were referring not to an individual sensing body, but rather to a collective social one, whose needs could be met by more efficient production and design. To best serve the needs of all, spaces needed to be standardized according to Le Corbusier with reference to average human dimensions. However, as contemporary disability activists have so effectively shown, working to average or standard human dimensions is a process that generates significant exclusions: it works around the ideal of fully functioning individuals and rejects deviations from the norm as a matter of course.[8] In the quest to raise general standards of hygiene, individual users with particular needs or challenges were thus brusquely set aside. One place, however, where they began to be given their due is in *The Bathroom*, released to a general audience in 1967 and substantially revised and reissued in 1976.

ALEXANDER KIRA'S *THE BATHROOM*

The Bathroom reports on a major study conducted at Cornell's Center for Housing and Environmental Studies between 1958 and 1965. Its aim was to establish an entirely new set of basic design criteria for bathroom facilities. In so doing, it challenged many of the conventions of modern design, particularly the neglect of individual users in all their variety and actual behavior patterns. The study's main proposition was that, in order to create effective new design criteria, both subjective factors (psychological and cultural) and objective ones (anatomical and physiological) needed to be understood, with the former acting as a set of constraints framing what was realistically possible in design at any given time or place.[9]

In order to research both functional and nonfunctional human factors, Kira divided his research activity into three parts. The first was an extensive multidisciplinary literature search; the second was a field survey of "current attitudes, practices, and problems" among one thousand middle-class households (published separately);[10] and the third was laboratory research to identify practical design issues associated with personal hygiene activities. Despite the value of the first two parts, it was the third part, the laboratory research, that has undoubtedly attracted the most attention since *The Bathroom*'s publication. Through his laboratory research, Kira suggested basic parameters for hygiene activities and developed hypotheses about how best to meet them. Most important—and this is *The Bathroom*'s most unique feature—he designed working models based on these hypotheses. This empirically based mode of working bears the hallmark of human engineering or ergonomics, which set out to assess the suitability of tools, objects, systems, or environments for human use. Kira succinctly described this creed as "fitting the activity, or the equipment, to the man, rather than vice versa," a mode of working that differed fundamentally from top-down and abstract modes of design.[11]

In order to study the man-machine interface, *The Bathroom*'s laboratory component drew specifically on task analysis. Each task or hygiene activity was described in detail, drawing on data from existing ergonomic studies or from the field survey of hygiene practices, in order to establish design considerations for different user groups—men, women, children, the aged, and the infirm. Motion picture cameras were then used to film live subjects as they performed various hygiene activities both with and without equipment ("charades") and to work out their constituent motions (Fig. 41). On the basis of these studies, Kira then calculated the optimal dimensions and configurations for equipment and—the pièce de resistance—unveiled a proposed new design to accommodate them.

Once he had gone through this exercise for each of the major hygiene activities— washing hands, face, hair, total body, and perineal region; defecation; and urination— Kira considered other related hygiene and grooming activities that take place in the bathroom (e.g., shaving and teeth brushing) and common nonhygiene activities (e.g., smoking, reading, and hand laundry). His ultimate aim was to specify design criteria for a "complete hygiene facility," including fittings, accessories, storage, and waste disposal. In these final sections, Kira most explicitly addressed practical design issues and came out in favor of a "systems approach," where prefabricated modular units could be composed to suit the owners' particular situation: family size, family life cycle, socioeconomic status, personal values, attitudes, and privacy requirements.[12]

Tellingly, he assumed each house would have one family bathroom, but, additionally, might have specialized ones, such as children's or teenage bathrooms.[13] By championing

	SMALL	MEAN	LARGE
Total height	53.4"	63.8"	74.2"
Hip (trochanter) height	26.7"	32.6"	38.5"
Trochanter to shoulder	16.6"	19.6"	22.6"
Trochanter to temple	23.7"	28.2"	32.7"
Elbow height	33.8"	40.1"	46.4"

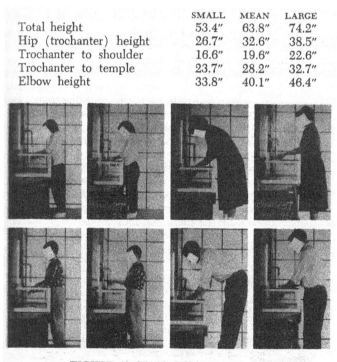

FIGURE 3. COMPARISON BETWEEN
POSTURES ASSUMED BY PERSONS OF VARYING
SIZES USING EQUIPMENT AT THE CONVENTIONAL
HEIGHT AND AT DESIRABLE HEIGHTS.

FIGURE 41 Comparison of postures assumed by persons of varying sizes using equipment at the conventional height and at desirable heights. With a chart of basic anthropometric data above. From Alexander Kira, *The Bathroom* (1967), Bantam Books, a division of Random House.

modular systems that enhanced flexibility, Kira was not, in reality, proposing a single model for bathroom design at all. Instead, he was promoting tailored units that would fit the activities of a household of users, rejecting the idea of an undifferentiated user that had long been the default modernist position and that anthropometric data and minimal space standards usually reinforced. Kira did not cite the civil rights movement of the 1960s and 1970s (including the first protests of disabled activists), but it is no stretch to see links between his project and their fight for equality and inclusion.[14] Kira believed that it was only by acknowledging and accommodating factors like sex, age, and physical ability that human environments would be improved.

A LEGITIMIZING AESTHETIC

Even Buckminster Fuller would have been impressed by the comprehensiveness of Kira's proposed redesigns throughout *The Bathroom*. But what is striking—and what remains revealing today—are the lengths to which Kira went to illustrate the bathroom user publicly. Kira was well aware that studying certain activities, namely urination, defecation, and perineal cleansing, would lead to charges of vulgarity at best and perversion at worst; indeed, a significant part of his study attempted to understand the taboos surrounding bathroom use in the first place with reference to anthropologists, sexologists, developmental psychologists, and psychoanalysts from Freud to Mary Douglas.[15] But, however he explained them, Kira knew he had a problem: the disgust and guilt associated with bathroom functions could easily prevent him from reaching the wider readership he wanted.

Hence, Kira opted for a variety of strategies to preempt such criticisms and, in particular, to contain the bathroom's "sex linkage."[16] He invented a scientific terminology to describe bathroom activities: toilets became *hygiene facilities,* and urinating or defecating became the rather sinister *elimination.*[17] When reproducing images of live models, Kira chose to only use stills of them performing innocuous activities (washing hands, getting out of bathtubs), and even then he put them in bathing suits. He also took the rather extraordinary precaution of blanking out his models' faces with little strips of paper (Fig. 41). While he may have been requested to do so by the university or by the models themselves (who Kira thanks in his introduction but never names), the gesture seems crude when measured against the sophistication and frankness of the study's methods and aims.

It is all the more remarkable, then, that a mere ten years later in his 1976 revised edition, Kira was able to dispense with the modesty shields—and the bathing suits. The marked difference between the two editions of *The Bathroom* has been attributed to the sexual revolution, something Kira hints at in his revised introduction when he states that his new images were "more natural than seemed possible a decade ago."[18] Although he does not mention them explicitly, his path was cleared by the publication of popular consciousness-raising books like Boston Women's Health Book Collective's *Our Bodies, Ourselves* in 1971 and Alex Comfort's *Joy of Sex* in 1972, which famously featured "illustrations of a hirsute couple having intercourse in a series of positions."[19]

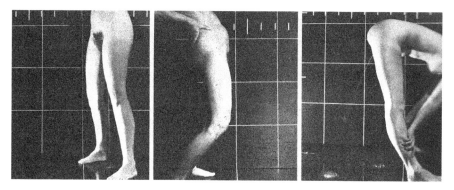

FIGURE 42   Comparative female urination postures. From Alexander Kira, *The Bathroom* (revised edition, 1976), Bantam Books, a division of Random House.

Even when seen alongside such taboo-breaking works, however, some of Kira's subjects of investigation still stand out. Consider Figure 42, Kira's comparative study of male and female urination postures. The series of three photographs running across on the top show a female model urinating in a perfectly upright position, then in a forward pelvic tilt, and, finally, in a backward pelvic tilt (Fig. 42). Kira concluded that female urinary control was improved in these positions, enabling women to project their urine stream at considerable distances (24 in. [610 mm] in the case of the backward pelvic tilt) especially if they held their labial folds apart.[20] Kira's confirmation that women were physically able to project their urine stream must have surely interested feminist psychoanalysts who, since Simone de Beauvoir, have argued that Western toilet training—which insists that women crouch to pee and not touch their genitalia as men do—is fundamental to their subordination.[21] It also subverts Freud's maxim, "anatomy is destiny," quoted by Kira in both editions of his book.

These studies no doubt struck many as gratuitous and perverse, an impression that Kira did not help when he jocularly likened the forward pelvic tilt movement to "dancing the limbo."[22] Yet their inclusion can hardly be said to be arbitrary when we recall Kira's obsession with fittings that fail to consider the realities of use due to a poor understanding of anatomy, unexamined conventions, or taboos. The failure of major plumbing manufacturers to adequately deal with female urination was one of Kira's greatest irritations: given how widely it was known that women did not sit on public facilities, he felt the continuing lack of alternatives to throne-style toilets was a classic example of how subjective factors frequently overrode objective ones in bathroom design. He was determined that his own version of a female water closet/urinal would not make the same mistake. And, indeed, it did not. Appearing later in the book, Kira's design was specifically designed to accommodate hovering.[23]

Furthermore, there is a key difference between Kira's images and those of, say, Comfort's that ultimately sets them apart. Unlike the naturalistic pencil drawings in *Joy of Sex*, Kira's photographs of human subjects plus his other images (charts, diagrams, plans, elevations, sections, and line drawings) were situated firmly within a scientific tradition that asserted their licitness. However much Kira may have spoken about pleasure, relaxation, and sex in his text, these were largely excised from his images, which visibly

FIGURE 43   Miscellaneous Phases of the Toilet: Plate 494. From Eadweard J. Muybridge, *Animal Locomotion*, 1884–86. New York, Museum of Modern Art (MOMA)/ Scala, Florence. Collotype, 18.8 × 35.1 cm. Acc.

subjected the body to rigorous scientific methods and protocols—its discipline. In their use of the gridded backdrop, for instance, Kira's urination studies distinctly recalled Eadweard Muybridge's photographic studies in *Animal Locomotion* (1887), which had put also unclothed human figures of both sexes through their paces and which also depended upon the "legitimizing aesthetic of science" for their authority (Fig. 43).[24]

While Muybridge's work may well have been a direct influence, Kira's interest in human motion and methods for capturing it had sources that were closer to home. Memomotion studies of the kind used throughout *The Bathroom* had a long lineage in American management circles. Adapted from Frederick Taylor's time-and-motion studies, they had become an integral part of human engineering research; by the 1920s, they were fundamental to efforts to improve efficiency in the home as well as the factory, thanks in large part to human engineer and psychologist Lillian Gilbreth. Gilbreth studied motion with the aim of eliminating fatigue caused by wasted movements (she called this *motion-mindedness*),[25] all with an eye to creating happier homemakers. In an interview, Gilbreth summarized her research method as follows: "First, a motion picture is made of the individual at work. The picture is taken to a laboratory and studied at leisure. Then a chart is drawn up to show every stage of the process. From this chart it can be seen whether or not some of these processes may not be cut out altogether."[26] The procedure was then repeated until the most efficient way of performing the task was found.

By the time of Kira's work, these analytic techniques were a mainstay of home engineering and management. As such, they were well-known to Kira, whose department at Cornell, the Center for Housing and Environmental Studies, enjoyed a close relationship with the College of Home Economics. Indeed, the center and college staff had previously collaborated on *The Cornell Kitchen* (1952), a research bulletin that established criteria for kitchen cabinet design and that served as the model for *The Bathroom*.[27] All the later study's main features are part of this earlier one: *The Cornell Kitchen* also sought to satisfy human and technological requirements; it deployed historical research, field surveys, and laboratory studies; and it featured an interdisciplinary research team made up of home economists, social psychologists, engineers, and architects—in this case coordinated by the Center for Housing's director, Glenn H. Beyer (who shared the responsibility for directing *The Bathroom* with Kira).[28] *The Cornell Kitchen* team went on

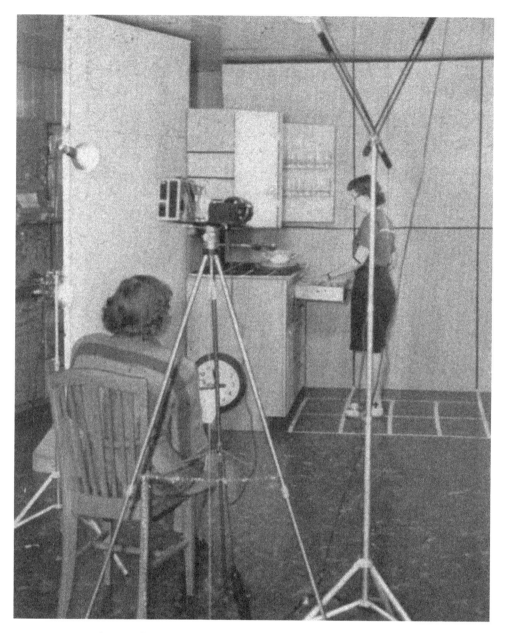

FIGURE 44   In *The Cornell Kitchen*, Cornell used "memomotion (very slow) movies to show house-wife's actions." From Gardner Soule, "New Kitchen Built to Fit Your Wife," *Popular Science* (September 1953). Bonnier Corporation. Cleared with permission via Copyright Clearance Center.

to produce five working kitchen modules—sink, mix, range, oven-and-refrigerator, and serve centers—and then studied these prototypes in use, deploying memomotion studies and energy indexes based on oxygen consumption in order to appraise factors like strain, relative effort, and floor-travel distance (Fig. 44).[29]

Through such methods, *The Cornell Kitchen* displayed the same commitment to user-centered design that would later mark *The Bathroom*. *Popular Science* summed up the philosophy as follows:

Build the cabinets to fit the woman.
Build the shelves to fit the supplies.
Build the kitchen to fit the family.[30]

The direct continuity between the two studies is most evident if we turn again to Kira's research methods and visual studies and consider them in more detail. His study of the most simple of hygiene activities, hand and face washing, was illustrated by ten studies. They were as follows:

1. Two cross-sectioned drawings. Like process charts in home engineering, these analyze "charades" of hand and face washing (i.e., without equipment), identifying the constituent motions of each activity—wetting, soaping, and reaching for controls—and the space dimensions necessary to accommodate them (Fig. 45).
2. Five memomotion stills. These show the posture of models as they use equipment—both standard and experimental—at conventional and at optimum heights (Fig. 46). The latter are determined with reference to a chart of anthropometric data of small, mean, and large body sizes.[31]
3. One drawing showing the necessary dimensions for hand and face washing equipment.
4. One comparative drawing showing conventional and necessary dimensions for lavatory equipment.
5. One rendering of Kira's experimental lavatory design responding to the criteria that emerged through the testing process.

Kira then goes on to revise his own proposed design in order to better accommodate another "significant modifier": hair washing. This willingness to continually refine designs—that is, to regard design as an ongoing dialogue with the user and to treat it as iterative—is another hallmark of home engineering.[32]

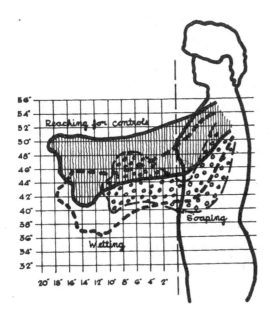

FIGURE 45 Ranges of body and arm movements while washing hands without reference to equipment. From Alexander Kira, *The Bathroom* (1967), Bantam Books, a division of Random House.

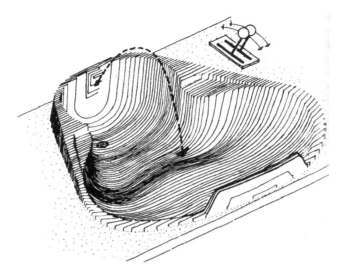

FIGURE 46   Experimental lavatory incorporating suggested criteria. From Alexander Kira, *The Bathroom* (1967), Bantam Books, a division of Random House.

Although Kira closely followed home engineers' research methods, his project necessarily departed from theirs because of the very different nature of the bathroom. When they did address the bathroom specifically, home engineers, like modernist architects, treated it as a functional space because it was part of the home's mechanical or utility core, contained the most equipment after the kitchen, and enabled necessary hygiene activities. The bathroom, however, was never fully absorbed into functionalist logic as was the kitchen, mainly because it was not a primary workspace (even if cleaning it was a significant task that fell to women).[33] As a result, even though domestic advisors from Catharine Beecher onward made efforts to educate women about hygiene and sanitary plumbing, they seemed to have comparatively few opinions about bathroom design itself.[34] The bathroom's basic form remained more or less the same as in the 1920s when the three-fixture, 5 × 7 ft. (approximately 1.5 × 2.1 m) model became standard in homes across America.[35]

Moreover, it is clear that the American public at large never really subscribed to the modernist ideal of the functional bathroom. By the time Kira began his study, the bathroom was firmly fixed in the popular mind as a sort of antikitchen, a place of privacy, pampering, and leisure—precisely the spot where an efficient homemaker might enjoy some of that precious time saved on domestic tasks. The image of a lady luxuriating in an oversized bubble bath was a stock-in-trade of advertisers; while the image's immediate source was Hollywood (picture Jayne Mansfield soaking in her famed gold-and-pink heart-shaped bath), Kira described it as Pompadour fantasy, which dangled the promise of "sensual semi-gratification" to sell products to women (Plate 19).[36] Kira was certainly was no advocate of this sybaritic version of the bathroom—quite the opposite—but his attentiveness to subjective factors meant that he did not dismiss its appeal. Rather, his tactic was to try to reshape the prevailing definition of luxury.

From the start of his research, then, Kira was well aware that encouraging bathroom reform was fraught with difficulty. The question is, who did he see as being key to reform? Home engineers wrote for a very clearly defined audience of homemakers, and their research was generally sponsored by manufacturers seeking to sell new home appliances: Christine Frederick, one of the best known, was even willing to endorse specific products. Kira was not in this position. Although *The Bathroom* was part sponsored by the American Radiator and Standard Sanitary Corporation (soon to be American Standard) and it was intimated that the corporation would produce designs along the lines Kira recommended, these were not available at the time of the study's publication.[37]

Consequently, Kira had no specific fittings to recommend, and this limited how much any single user would directly benefit from his research. Home engineers supplied basic rules, techniques, and checklists to enable homemakers to adapt their own spaces—for instance, by adjusting the placement of light switches or the heights of work surfaces. Beyond suggesting optimal heights for the installation of fittings or driving home the importance of safety bars in baths, Kira dispensed relatively little practical advice of this nature. For all his efforts to generate a greater awareness about bathroom design among the public, Kira saw his most immediate task as being to persuade the plumbing industry to adopt his criteria for bathroom equipment and to approach it as a fully integrated space. "If we are to have well designed and integrated functional facilities," he argued in the book's first edition, "the complete facility must be provided by the manufacturer."[38]

Interestingly, that same year, the architect Denise Scott Brown also made the case that manufacturers were the key to more responsive bathroom environments. After delivering a hilariously caustic critique of average powder room designs, Scott Brown tried to account for their inadequacies. She began by observing that male architects have no personal experience to fall back on in designing such spaces and no reference book to help explain women's needs (a problem that Kira hoped to remedy). But Scott Brown then mused that the real problem with the design of powder rooms is that architects were not actually involved in planning them at all; rather, they had abandoned the field to manufacturers who recommended ungenerous rule-of-thumb space allowances and supplied readymade fittings.[39] "Well, if that is the case, architects, where is your pride?" Scott Brown demanded. "Only by involving yourself deeply in the technico-industrial manufacturing processes of the twentieth century, will you be able to keep 'them' responsive to the human needs of human beings (in this case, women). Powder rooms are for people."[40]

While Kira did not cite this particular part of Scott Brown's article, he would likely have appreciated Scott Brown's rousing call to arms.[41] They were agreed in viewing "technico-industrial manufacturing processes" as the main catalyst for change, though, as we will see, Kira's view would shift with time. For now, however, the emphasis on production adds another dimension to Kira's choice of visual language. Rather than only being a legitimizing tactic to justify his overt inclusion of the user's body, his choice of visual language must also be seen as part of his strategy to speak to and to win over his main target audience: manufacturers and those as he identified as the main purchasers of sanitary fittings—architects and builders.

ARCHITECTURAL GRAPHIC STANDARDS

Given his complaints about their failures, it is significant that Kira's drawings still broadly conform to the conventions established by architectural handbooks like the American *Architectural Graphic Standards* or the European *Architects' Data*. These handbooks, sometimes referred to as "architects bibles," are reference sources that set out construction standards for designers, engineers, and builders; they specify everything from the number and type of sanitary fittings in a bathroom to the appropriate height for the toilet roll holder. Even as Kira criticized and revised the handbooks' obsolete space recommendations, he adhered to their standardized mode of depicting interiors and fittings. He also followed *Architects' Data* in showing human figures of normative dimensions, reach, and movement going about everyday activities.[42] (Bathrooms in *Architectural Graphic Standards* did not include human figures, but their dimensions referenced standard human scale.) However radical it was, Kira's work remained deeply rooted in this technocratic graphic tradition that emphasized data and dimensions, suppressing expressive techniques like shading or mimetic likeness in favor of line.

The use of graphic standards ensured that Kira's drawings would be legible and credible to his professional audience. However, there were likely some ideological reasons why he adhered to them as well. When the draftsman Charles Ramsey and specifications writer Harold Sleeper devised the American graphic standards in 1932, they reflected the larger social concerns of a community of progressive minded architects who had strong ties with Cornell, Kira's alma mater and employer. As architectural historian Paul Emmons establishes, far from being a neutral tool for architects, graphic standards were revolutionary in intent: the creation of construction standards was meant to eliminate waste, reduce costs, and improve the quality of housing for all.[43] Moreover, directly influenced by Thorstein Veblen's critique of conspicuous consumption, those behind the graphic standards consciously sought to eliminate ornament. By removing these excesses and focusing on data instead, they hoped to identify and better meet actual human needs. Architecture was to be a tool for common good.

The graphic standards' faith in data, aesthetic neutrality, and distrust of ornament fit in well with Kira's own beliefs, particularly his dislike of fashion. While he was not moralistic about it, he believed that the quest for stylish bathrooms contributed to unsuitable designs and came at the expense of comfort and safety. To his readers, particularly to those enamored of the sybaritic bathroom, he suggested, "The 'best,' and real luxury, could also be something that functions superbly instead of something ordinary fashioned from pretty and costly materials."[44] For this reason, apart from pot plants, he rarely specified materials or included ornaments in his views beyond items like perfume bottles, brushes, towels, and, in one case, a toy boat.

Yet for all his focus on producers, there is no doubting the sincerity of Kira's desire to reach a popular audience, especially in his revised edition. While the first edition of *The Bathroom* retained the overall look and feel of a scientific report, the 1976 version made obvious efforts to appeal to a mass market. It featured completely new sections on public facilities and bathrooms for the disabled and the entire text was extensively rewritten and updated. While Kira's 1967 text had already been very readable, with many popular culture references, the 1976 version was even chattier and featured a greater number of anecdotes, bits of doggerel verse, transcriptions of homosexual graffiti, and dirty jokes.[45]

However, it was the illustrations that changed most substantially—and not simply because they now included nude models. All of the report's original studies were redrawn or rephotographed, and many new images were included. Kira's redesigned

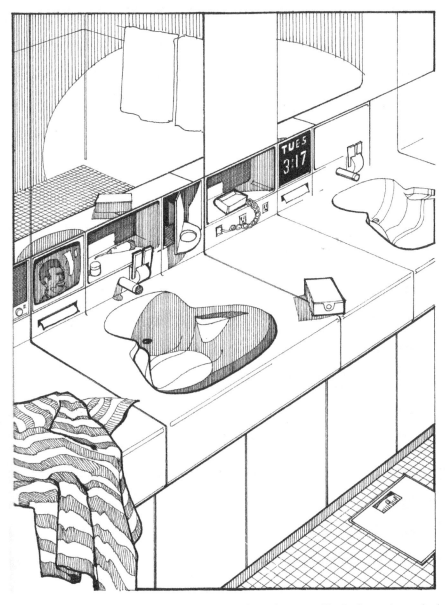

FIGURE 47 Possible approach to a lavatory. From Alexander Kira, *The Bathroom* (revised edition, 1976), Bantam Books, a division of Random House.

fittings were now shown in situ, rather than as standalone objects, and were far more artfully rendered: "Possible Approach to a Lavatory," for instance, shows two lavatories fitted into one continuous unit along with a radio, television, and digital clock—more dashboard console than counter (Fig. 47; compare to Fig. 46). And most significant of all, manufacturers' photographs of existing products were now included. This likely reflected several factors: Kira now had a greater number of ergonomic fittings to choose from (which he claimed responded to his design criteria in some way),[46] and he realized that product references were important to the consumer, whom he addressed much more directly here. In fact, since his first edition, Kira had apparently had a change of heart about the tactics needed for bathroom reform, stating, "The likelihood of fully realizing the substantive improvements described and suggested in the following pages depends very much on the consumer's level of concern and willingness to demand and pay for more rational, more convenient, and safer solutions."[47]

In other words, consumers, rather than producers, were now to be the main drivers of change. And even though Kira continued to stress the need for his redesigned fittings to work within their time-place setting and to accommodate existing social beliefs and values, this new strategy required that beliefs and values shift before many of these redesigned fittings would be in demand. But how could Kira persuade consumers that bathrooms were worth fighting for? In both editions of his book, Kira made his case largely on health and safety grounds, stressing the danger or risks associated with hygiene activities as typically practiced, from hemorrhoids to scabies to slipping in the bath. Noting the large number of injuries caused by bathtubs in his first edition, he warned sternly, "Intelligent design can only be regarded as a luxury until one stakes his life on it."[48] But he was to push the safety agenda more strongly in 1976.

More than any of the sexual revolutionaries of his era, Kira may well have owed his greatest debt to consumer advocate and activist Ralph Nader, whose rather terse endorsement appeared on the back cover of the 1976 edition of Kira's book: "An illuminating study of inadequate safety, hygiene and convenience features in bathrooms." Nader's *Unsafe at Any Speed: The Designed-In Dangers of the American Automobile* had been published in 1965, but its effects reverberated throughout the decade.[49] Many of *Unsafe at Any Speed*'s principle themes, such as manufacturers' lack of concern for safety and their preference for styling over engineering improvements, had also been voiced by Kira in 1967. But ten years later, Kira had apparently reconsidered his somewhat fuzzy earlier faith in manufacturers' willingness to reform themselves (or to be reformed by enlightened architects and builders) and now shared Nader's conviction that they would only respond to external pressure. This is likely why he relaxed his earlier prohibitions on product endorsement, photography, and gadgets. He wanted his readership to literally buy his humanistic vision of better bathrooms, achieving reform one purchase at a time.

COMPROMISE BETWEEN REALITIES

Despite these compromises and revisions, Kira's updated strategy for encouraging bathroom reform ultimately seemed no more successful than his earlier one. *The Bathroom* remains something of a curiosity. It did make a big splash in its day with extensive coverage in both the trade and mainstream media: *Time* magazine not only reported on the original publication but the revised one as well.[50] The first edition sold a hundred thousand copies in the United States alone; there were also British, German, Italian, and Japanese editions. And even though it is now out of print, the book remains a touchstone for user-centered design. Yet it has inspired few serious follow-up studies[51] and has not had a major impact on the plumbing industry, standards, and codes. While some sanitary ware manufacturers were inspired by Kira (particularly European ones like Röhm and S.C.I. Richard-Ginori) and attractive ergonomic fittings for the bathroom became widely available by the 1970s and 1980s, Kira never inspired the consumer revolution he sought.[52] Indeed, he regarded many later products such as whirlpool baths as a giant leap backward in health and safety terms.[53]

Many potential explanations for the lack of a broader take-up come to mind. But the most obvious is that the book's success always depended on its ability to articulate a convincing argument for change. While Kira's health and safety concerns were supported by some impressive numbers—275,000 people were injured each year in tubs and baths—they never had the sensational impact of Nader's who opened *Unsafe at any Speed* with the claim: "For over half a century, the automobile has brought death, injury, and the most inestimable sorrow and deprivation to millions of people."[54] And in dwelling so much on a negative argument and continually stressing the anxieties surrounding his subject, Kira failed to make the kind of simple, positive argument home engineers had so effectively used to win over their readers: redesign your kitchen and your life will be less tiring and happier—better.

Moreover, average readers—those consumers upon whom he was depending on to demand and pay for improved products—were still likely to have found some of his imagery baffling if not downright alienating. While Kira's work required the legitimizing aesthetic of science, his use of memomotion studies and his adherence to graphic standards meant that many of these remained inaccessible to the nonprofessional. One wonders, for instance, what the typical reader made of Kira's many plan views of humans seated on toilets. Unlike the typical bird's-eye perspective adopted in design handbooks, Kira's plans were done from below, in order to show both male and female genitalia, the void of the toilet hole, and the placement of necessary supports for the body (Fig. 48). Such images pushed the legitimizing aesthetic of science, the neutrality of graphic standards, and the inviolability of the body itself, to its very limits.

Kira recognized that *The Bathroom* was not always successful at containing his subject's tensions, admitting that he often found his original edition "buried among the sex novels."[55] This gap between his aims and his work's reception would probably not have surprised him; a pragmatist at heart, Kira knew that his redesigns would at best be a "compromise between realities."[56] But at times it seems as if the project's entire premise was itself fundamentally compromised. Kira found himself in the curious position of using functionalist design tools to rethink designs that he knew were not purely or even mainly functional. As he noted, "There are almost as many psychological and cultural problems to be solved in developing design criteria as there are purely physiological or

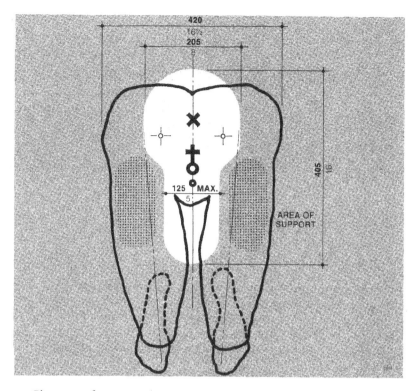

FIGURE 48 Plan view of necessary dimensions and clearances for a female pedestal water closet/ urinal. From Alexander Kira, *The Bathroom* (revised edition, 1976), Bantam Books, a division of Random House.

functional ones, and in some instances, it may almost be said that *the* problems to be solved are the psychological and cultural ones."[57]

By making the point that Kira appeared to be caught up in his subject's contradictions, this article does not seek to question the overall value of his research. Rather, it seeks to demonstrate the complexities one faces when one moves toward a more user-centered design approach that foregrounds the individual. Home engineers have long noted that a feedback loop exists between users and design—that is, a change in design according to users' preferences will change those preferences in turn.[58] But what about cases where subjective factors have so deeply shaped design parameters in the first place? Can subjective factors be reformed in advance of designs? How does one redesign a taboo?

These questions remain pertinent for interior studies. Since 1976, when Kira published the revised edition of *The Bathroom,* much has changed, academically, socially, and environmentally; probably the best example of this shift is the importance now given to providing grab bars and ergonomic fittings for the disabled, a change that Kira advocated but that is now mandated by American and English disability legislation. But with this major exception, is the average bathroom today ultimately that much better at accommodating human needs? The ever-more lush bathrooms available at the high-end of design stand in notable contrast to the uniformly desolate offerings in the public realm where mean space standards still prevail—that is, when you can find a public facility at all.[59] Any serious efforts to revamp the basics of bathroom design—for instance, attempts to introduce squat toilets or female urinals for health reasons or for convenience—remain as controversial as ever.[60]

Kira's thoughts on how bathroom reform might be achieved were always the least resolved parts of his work, but this may simply symptomatic of a larger problem identified by sociologist Harvey Molotch.[61] Molotch notes that many actors have a stake in the production and sale of even a modest bathroom interior. These actors include the organizations that set national standards, the governmental bodies that enshrine these standards in building and plumbing codes, bathroom manufacturers, architects, authors of architectural handbooks, developers, retailers, and consumers, to name only the most obvious. While Kira tended to pin his hopes for reform on one particular actor, Molotch makes clear that, for innovation to happen, "a whole lot of stars need to be aligned";[62] that is, many actors need to buy into the innovation and have enough love for it to bring it about.

While the conditions Molotch identifies are common to most interior spaces, encouraging love for bathrooms is almost uniquely difficult, as its use remains shrouded in euphemism or silence. Nobody can study the history of the modern bathroom without being acutely aware of the way that a strategic disinterest has been inscribed into modes of practice and representation. Usually unthinkingly, architects perpetuate the marginalization of users by continuing to reach for standards or design tools that fail to adequately take actual bodies and bathroom behaviors into account. Yet few are inspired to reach for new tools, possibly because bathrooms are perceived to be so overdetermined that they do not allow for much variation, let alone creativity. They also continue to be seen as trivial, tainted by their associations with mechanical services, plumbing, consumption, waste, femininity, and decoration. It is telling that, even now, the job of designing bathrooms still falls to the most junior staff in big offices—the architectural equivalent, said Kira, of "latrine duty" in the army.[63]

This embedded structural resistance to change may well be why Kira seemed to give up completely on architects in later years. In 1996, he noted with uncharacteristic bitterness that most architects still "couldn't care less" about bathrooms and attributed this indifference to the fact that "most [of them] until very recently weren't interested in interiors."[64] Perhaps he would be heartened by the new critical interest in the interior today. Researchers and practitioners in interior architecture and design have entered a phase of intense reflection, critically assessing the identity and purpose of their discipline and working out methods to suit their specific concerns. While interior architects generally share home engineers' interest in use and movement (and in sequences of movements), they are also committed to capturing spatial effects and to registering the not strictly functional potential of places. To this end, they have introduced hybrid techniques such as collage, montage, and storyboards and have pushed the conventional boundaries of architectural drawing and modelling.[65] This fresh interest in use—in all its dimensions—and related experiments in representational techniques can only be good news for the bathroom. How can the environment fit the activity? How can it fit humans in all their complexity? As Kira well knew, it is only by rigorously investigating these questions that bathrooms and the taboos surrounding them may be redesigned at last.

20

The Selection, Creation, and Perception of Interior Spaces: An Environmental Psychology Approach

SAMUEL D. GOSLING, ROBERT GIFFORD, AND LINDSAY MCCUNN

> We shape our buildings, thereafter they shape us.
>
> —*Winston Churchill (1943)*

Winston Churchill's well-known wartime remark succinctly captures the fact that the connection between people and the places in which they dwell is a two-way relationship. It is a point that is surely understood, at least implicitly, by interiors theorists, researchers, and practitioners. But what does the field of psychology have to say about the two halves of this reciprocal bond? Here we review the main theories and findings from the field of environmental psychology that can inform our understanding of the links between people and places.

PART I: HOW PEOPLE SELECT AND AFFECT INTERIOR ENVIRONMENTS

Interactionist theorists in psychology have long recognized that individuals select and create their social environments (e.g., friendships, social activities) to match and reinforce their dispositions, preferences, attitudes, and self-views.[1] David Buss used the terms "selection," "evocation," and "manipulation"[2] to delineate three broad modes of interacting with one's environment. The modes were originally developed in the context of social interactions, but they can easily be applied to physical environments to understand the ways in which humans affect interiors. People select existing spaces with interior features that they believe will allow them to express their personalities and preferences and will allow them to engage in their desired activities: an extravert may purchase a house with a large kitchen to facilitate entertaining, where the introvert prefers the property with a library. People evoke environmental features by engaging in activities that leave material traces in their wake—examples include a messy desk or a diverse collection of books on the shelves. And, perhaps of greatest relevance to interiors scholars, individuals manipulate their existing spaces, sometimes with the assistance of a professional; thus, a person may choose décor that reflects a cultural identity, use products to affect the ambient conditions, or alter the arrangement of furniture to facilitate desired activities.

The above three modes of interaction can achieve various psychological goals. But what are psychological motivations driving individuals to select, evoke, and manipulate their environments?

Psychological Motivations for Affecting Spaces

Broadly, people alter their spaces for three reasons:[3] they want to broadcast information about themselves, they want to affect how they think and feel, and they inadvertently affect their spaces in the course of their everyday behaviors.

Identity Claims

One of the ways in which people personalize their interiors is by adorning them with "identity claims"—deliberate symbolic statements about how they would like to be regarded.[4] Posters, awards, photos, trinkets, and other mementos are often displayed in the service of making such statements. One's intended audience must understand the intended message, so identity claims tend to rely on objects with shared meanings. The specific content of identity claims may vary according to the identity of the anticipated "other," with different audiences evoking different self-presentational motives—items that impress your friends may not have the same effect on your coworkers.

Thought and Feeling Regulators

Interior environments are the contexts for a wide range of activities, ranging from relaxing and reminiscing to working and playing. The effectiveness with which these activities can be accomplished may be affected by the physical and ambient qualities of the space. As we shall see in Part II of this chapter, the features of an interior environment can have an impact on the individuals who occupy those spaces. It can be hard to relax with a lot of noise around, and it is difficult to concentrate when surrounded by distractions. The environmental features conducive to one activity (e.g., socializing) are not always the same as the environments conducive to another (e.g., relaxing). Thus, many features of interior environments owe their presence to their ability to affect the feelings and thoughts of the occupant. Elements used to regulate emotions and thoughts could include photos of family, keepsakes, the color of the walls, and the music in the stereo.

Behavioral Residue

Many behaviors performed in interior environments leave some kind of discernible residue in their wake. For example, the act of tidying up one's office could result in an organized filing system. The term *behavioral residue* refers to the physical traces left in the environment by behavioral acts. Sometimes it is the lack of an act that leaves a residue. For example, the dishes in the sink are the residue of the fact that you did not clean up after eating.

There are four important features of behavioral residue. First, behavioral residue accumulates over time so it tends to reflect repeated behaviors rather than one-off acts. Second, in addition to the residue of behaviors already performed, interior environments may also contain clues to anticipated behaviors; for example, a new deck of cards and a set of poker chips suggest an occupant is planning a game of poker. Third, in addition to containing remnants of activities performed within a space, interior environments also contain residue of behaviors performed beyond the immediate surroundings. Fourth, different behaviors can result in similar environmental manifestations—a messy room could indicate sloth, or it could indicate a person who is overwhelmed with other responsibilities.

Note that three motivations—identity claims, thought and feeling regulators, and behavioral residue—are not mutually exclusive. For example, the snowboard in the corner of a room may indeed reflect exterior behaviors, but the occupant's decision to display the snowboard (rather than stow it in a closet) may also reflect a desire to make identity claims or could serve as a reminder of happy times.

Measuring the Features of Interior Environments

A small number of empirical studies have examined the specific ways in which individual differences are expressed in interior environments.[5] Before summarizing the findings to emerge from these studies, we discuss the fundamental methodological challenge faced by researchers in this domain: how to systematically record the features of spaces.

The problem of documenting space is not a simple one. Researchers must identify a method that is amenable to quantitative analyses, that permits comparisons across spaces, is sufficiently flexible to apply to a variety of spaces, and sufficiently comprehensive to capture all the relevant features that might be found in a space. Free-response descriptions of interiors are flexible, but they are hard to analyze quantitatively and are not easily compared across spaces.

Checklists of specific items are easy to quantify and facilitate comparisons across spaces but they are hard to generate and must contained hundreds or thousands of items if they are to be comprehensive; for example, Laumann and House's[6] fifty-three-item Living Room Checklist included specific-content items such as "large potted plants," "French furniture," and "sunburst clock" but could not account for the vast majority of items that one might encounter in a living room. Moreover, checklists do not capture broader configural aspects of a space.[7]

One compromise between the flexibility of free responses and the quantification potential of checklists is the use of ratings scales. For example, Kasmar's Environment Description Scale[8] used raters to document the broad global features of interior spaces in terms of ratings on sixty-six adjective pairs (e.g., appealing vs. unappealing; expensive vs. cheap). These methods are flexible, quantifiable, and facilitate comparisons across spaces, but they omit any record of specific environmental features, and they are vulnerable to the idiosyncratic interpretations of terms made by different raters. However, research has shown that such ratings typically reach high standards of reliability.[9]

To address the individual weaknesses of the itemization and rating approaches, the Personal Living Space Cue Inventory (PLSCI)[10] was designed to include both approaches. The PLSCI consists of over 700 individual items (e.g., rubber bands, fashion magazines, laundry basket) and 42 broader terms that can be rated subjectively (e.g., cheerful vs. gloomy; clean vs. dirty). The PLSCI displays adequate psychometric properties, and its viability in research settings has been demonstrated.[11]

The Expression of Psychological Attributes in Interior Environments

Most past research on manifestations of individual differences in physical environments has focused on bedrooms/dorm rooms and offices. For example, one study examined the ways in which adolescents decorated their bedrooms, focusing on the differences between the items found in boys' and girls' rooms.[12] Another study documented the features and artifacts found in living spaces and offices occupied by liberals and conservatives;[13] the study showed, for example, that conservative occupants tended to display more sports-related décor and liberals tended to have a greater variety of books in their spaces.

Lindsay T. Graham, Carson J. Sandy, and Samuel D. Gosling[14] reviewed the research documenting connections between individuals and features of physical spaces, such as bedrooms or offices. The review indicated that many different individual differences can be expressed in physical spaces. Several studies framed their analyses in terms of the widely used Big-Five model of personality.[15] The evidence suggests that all five dimensions can be manifested in living spaces, but openness and conscientiousness appear to leave the biggest imprint.[16] High-openness individuals tend to occupy spaces that are classified as "distinctive" and contain a high diversity of content items (e.g., books, magazines) and indicators of interest in various places and cultures (e.g., maps, souvenirs). The spaces occupied by conscientious occupants tend to be clean, organized, neat, and uncluttered. Openness and conscientiousness were the traits most clearly manifested in physical spaces, but others did get expressed. For example, extroverts engaged in more personalization and had offices that were classified as more inviting than offices occupied by introverts. One way the invitingness can be expressed is in terms of a relatively open chair and desk arrangement.[17]

In addition to the big five, a varied assortment of other traits have been examined, including status, need for interpersonal relationships, and locus of control. In one study, the likelihood of dropping out of college was predicted from the degree of personalization within a room;[18] specifically, individuals who personalized their rooms had lower dropout rates than did individuals who personalized them less. When the dropouts did personalize their spaces, their décor tended to be related to family and the loved ones. A similar study conducted some years later at the same university showed the opposite effect—dropouts used decoration more than nondropouts.[19] The discrepancies in findings were attributed to the small sample size and composition (only males were assessed) in the earlier William Hansen and Irwin Altman study. However, both studies found that dropouts were inclined to decorate their spaces with photos of family and friends. One interpretation of these findings is that the dorm-room décor consisted of identity claims, expressing commitment to the new college life in the nondropouts (who decorated with college-related emblems) and thought and feeling regulators designed to counter feelings of loneliness and isolation and reluctance to commit to college life in the dropouts (who decorated with reminders of home).

One study of workspaces[20] examined the connections between how a space was personalized and status. Occupants recorded the items in their workspace and gave details regarding their job, such as position and tenure within the company and how many hours per week they worked. Status in the organization was a strong predictor of the amount of personalization in an office space. But these individual difference variables were only part of the story.[21] Testifying to the complexity of the connections between occupants and their spaces, the research also revealed that other factors such as the type of workspace (e.g., a private, enclosed space vs. an open cubical) and the company's personalization policies influenced the types and amount of personalization of the workspaces.

Several studies identified substantial differences in the ways in which males and females personalized their bedrooms and office spaces. In general, women tend to decorate their spaces more than men do. In terms of specific items, compared with men, women tend to have more stuffed animals, candles, lotions, trinkets, and photos of close others such as family and friends. Men tend to have more sports equipment, CDs, stereos, and achievement-related items. These trends have been identified in several populations, including young children,[22] adolescents,[23] and college-age adults.[24]

In short, research over the past few decades has documented the ways in which individuals affect their interior spaces. But how are these spaces perceived and how do features of these spaces affect the occupants? We address these questions next.

PART II: ENVIRONMENTAL PERCEPTION AND HOW INTERIOR ENVIRONMENTS AFFECT PEOPLE

Social scientists and designers often work together to understand how individuals interact with their environments.[25] Doing so ensures that spaces in which we spend large amounts of time are functional and enjoyable. Research by environmental psychologists illuminates how particular features of indoor settings influence the attitudes and behaviors of building occupants and visitors.

This section of the chapter first introduces three important ideas about environmental perception: probabilistic functionalism, affordances, and collative properties. Then it offers examples of environmental factors that affect satisfaction, health, and performance in residential and workplace buildings. These approaches to environmental perception and research findings can be applied to spaces in the real world, where comfort and productivity are important design outcomes.

Environmental Perception

As an interior designer or as a client, how might one look at a room? The simple answer might be, in terms of possible colors, décor, and layout. However, environmental psychologists suggest three other ways that might be fruitful: probabilistic functionalism, affordances, and collative properties.

Probabilistic Functionalism

This influential approach is based on the work of Egon Brunswik,[26] who proposed that the way people perceive and interpret settings are best described by what he called the "lens model" (Fig. 49). In this model, information about a setting originally manifests itself as objective, distal cues (e.g., the actual height of a ceiling, the actual dimensions of the room), which are selectively perceived through proximal cues (e.g., that the ceiling is "low" and that the room is "boxy"), and lead to the perceiver's final evaluative conclusion, such as, "I can't work in this space." According to Brunswik, perceivers select a

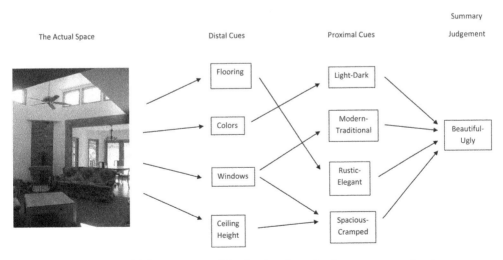

FIGURE 49   A lens model for an interior. The distal and proximal cues are examples that represent many other possibilities, and a variety of summary judgments might be considered as well. Courtesy of Robert Gifford.

subset of the many available cues in a space and reach their conclusions based on that idiosyncratic selection. Different perceivers will select and weight different cues. The successful perceiver selects the most important cues in order to function effectively in a setting. This is why Brunswik's theory is functionalist in nature.

Therefore, probabilistic functionalism conceives of environmental perception as an active attempt to extract a useful image of a place from a large number of potentially useful environmental cues, particularly in a setting that is new to a person. For example, people who visit a highly stimulating place, such as any downtown for the first time, or a large corporate workspace on the first day of a job, may not be able to sort out the important cues from those that are less important. In this situation, Brunswik predicts that people will actively seek out useful cues that the perceiver thinks will lead to a safe and successful existence in the new setting.

The probabilistic aspect of Brunswik's theory is that each cue may or may not be a perfectly valid indicator of the true nature of a setting. Rather, each cue has a particular probability of being accurate. Everyone has experienced perceptual errors and illusions in an environment. A new employee might perceive an office as good based on its large window and lovely flooring. However, over time in working in the office, the employee might pick up on other cues, such as peeling paint or a furniture arrangement that does not facilitate work performance. With experience, the perception that the office is good may shift in a negative direction. Some environmental cues are more or less accurate indicators than others.

Because of this variability in the validity or usefulness of individual cues, Brunswik integrated the idea of ecological validity into his theory. This refers to the degree of "truth" of the probabilistic relations between an objective environment and the distal cues that one selects for attention. Ecological validity represents the odds that a cue (or the cues as a group) will lead a perceiver to an effective or accurate perception of an actual space. Some cues may contribute to a highly accurate assessment of an environment, but others may not be immediately perceivable or may lead to false or undesirable impressions. For example, the widespread assumption that darker wall colors make a room look smaller has been supported empirically.[27]

Brunswik further proposes that different cues are given different weights by perceivers, in the process called "cue utilization." The perceiver's conclusion about a space is presumed to be the result of this weighting process. Overall, when cue utilization closely matches ecological validity, the perceiver's understanding of an environment will accurately reflect the objective environment. This is what often happens, but not always. Inaccurate cue utilization can occur and have serious effects. For example, if a thirsty hiker comes upon the clear water in the stream, the hiker may well decide that clear and moving water means the water is safe, but if those invisible pathogens or pollutants are present, the thirsty hiker may become ill from drinking the water.

Over time, people learn to pay attention to cues that validly represent a safe and functional path through work and life. This is what Brunswik called achievement. Although the examples given illustrate possible errors, most of our everyday perception works to keep us safe—but we had to learn. The child has to learn that the cherry color of that circular metal element on the stove is not safe. Thus, achievement varies: it is an indicator of the perceiver's accuracy in assessing the objective environment. Problems can also arise in situations with which a person is unfamiliar, especially those with environmental patterns that have a loose resemblance to those the person is used to. These problems can range from the unimportant, such as getting momentarily lost on the way to someone's office, to the fatal, such as misjudging the cues associated with a sharp curve on a highway.

Affordances

James J. Gibson[28] proposed that the environment (such as interiors) can be conceptualized as being made up of substances (e.g., steel, wood, glass) and surfaces (e.g., floors, ceilings, walls). In Gibson's framework, arrangements of substances and surfaces are called layouts, which provide affordances to perceivers. Affordances are functions of an environment that are instantly detectable by a perceiver as useful for a particular purpose. One classic affordance is that a flat horizontal expanse in front of a person affords walking. Another might be that a solid, horizontal surface situated about 18 in. (45 cm) off the ground affords sitting. This idea differs from Brunswik's in that Gibson believed that the environment provides perceivers with an immediate, direct functional assessment of some element, rather than the assessment being processed through a set of cues that are weighted and interpreted.

Gibson's approach has helped to highlight the role of the environment in human perception. One such influence has been on design education programs, which often teach that color, shape, and form are the essential elements. Gibson insisted that everyday perception does not rely on these elements and that designers should not be taught to focus so strongly on form and shape; the emphasis should be on substances and surfaces.[29] This is because, he argued, building users do not pay attention to form and shape per se, but to affordances, which are defined by substances and surfaces.

Collative Properties

Daniel Berlyne's[30] approach proposes that environments contain collative properties, which border on the distinction between cognition and perception. Collative properties are attributes of a setting that cause perceivers to compare environmental details and, generally, to stimulate interest in a setting, such as a particular interior. Some examples of a space's collative properties are novelty (i.e., perceived newness), incongruity (i.e., the sense that something is out of place or does not fit), complexity (i.e., its number of lines or shapes), and surprisingness (i.e., unexpected features).

Berlyne proposed that collative properties enhance (or do not enhance) one's aesthetic experience and desire to explore an environment through hedonic tone (i.e., the amount of beauty or pleasure experienced in a setting). Berlyne's work has motivated designers to create spaces in accordance to certain collative properties. For example, when some designers decided that modern urban forms were too simple in their lines (i.e., lacked complexity), they pioneered more curvy and articulated designs with the hypothesis that this made them more complex and thus greater in hedonic tone.[31]

This relation between complexity and preference does not apply to built environments in a linear way; rather, moderately complex settings generally elicit greater preference than either very simple or very complex settings. Berlyne's approach has helped social scientists and designers to further understand properties of settings that reliably elicit certain perceptions. Some researchers have added to the list of collative properties. One such added collative property is fittingness or how well a design suits a particular setting.[32]

The theoretical approaches of Brunswik, Gibson, and Berlyne have shaped contemporary thought concerning environmental perception and its relation to design. Next, some examples of how interiors influence behavior and well-being will be described to highlight how social science applies its theories to learn from the users and visitors of environments designed for people.

Environmental Influences at Home and Work

Every building interior could be investigated in an effort to understand how its design attributes affect individuals, and environmental psychologists have studied restaurants, prisons, schools, submarines, the international space station, polar outposts, and retails stores, among other spaces. However, this chapter will focus on two interiors in which people spend large amounts of time, residences and workplaces. Clarifying how these places promote positive behavior and wellness is important in order to avoid designs that harm these outcomes.

At Home

The physical attributes of residences obviously influence how people feel toward, and act within, them. Of course, different housing types and designs satisfy different people for different reasons, depending on their past experience, preferences, culture, stage of life, values, and so on. One goal of residential environmental psychologists is to understand which type of housing works best for whom, and why.

Housing quality clearly is one attribute that affects how people feel about their residence. Not surprisingly, individuals report greater satisfaction with their home when the physical quality of the building is greater.[33] But why is this so? One answer is that when other factors are controlled for, higher-quality residences spur greater place attachment in residents. Another is that poorer housing quality is associated with more behavior problems in children, regardless of income.[34]

Another major design element that influences residential feelings and behavior is housing form. For example, in a study of new residents in which participants were asked how they felt about their new homes, over half of those who moved into a single-family dwelling stated they were "definitely satisfied," but less than 25 percent of those who moved into an apartment said this.[35]

Although one often hears that condominiums are increasing in popularity, most people in North America still largely prefer a single-family dwelling if they can afford one. Purchasing a single-family home can symbolize wealth or achievement in adulthood. Despite being more environmentally preferable (smaller carbon footprint) and usually being less expensive, apartments and condos have been associated in some studies with poorer health and wellness, partly because of high indoor density.[36]

However, apartments and condos obviously are not always a negative influence. Siting them to take advantage of natural views, if possible, can help. Elderly residents of apartments are more satisfied if their unit overlooks a natural setting or if there is a natural setting available near the apartment building.[37] Children with visual access to nature do better in school.[38]

Besides housing quality and form, as all interior designers know or suspect, the design of a dwelling's interior also influences attitudes toward a residence. For example, individuals generally prefer higher-than-standard ceilings that are flat or have a 4:12 slope ratio and walls that meet at ninety degrees or more.[39] When shown floor-plan drawings, American university students preferred floor plans that showed the living room in the upper-right-hand corner of the drawing.[40] As one might guess, this result is not true of everyone; for example, this preference was weaker for Israeli students.[41] Much more research is necessary to form evidence-based conclusions about perceptions and preferences of room arrangements.

In contrast, colors for interiors have often been studied but not always well. Many studies have utilized small paint chips or other color samples within no particular context.[42] Results from these studies may not generalize to full-scale interiors. One recent idea suggestion is that color preferences are based on their likelihood to succeed in evolutionarily important tasks. For example, in one study women showed a stronger preference for red than men did, which was attributed to the division of labor in hunter-gatherer societies in which it was the women's job to find ripe red fruit against a background of green leaves.[43] Another approach suggests that emotions play a role: people like colors associated with things they like (e.g., blue because of water and blue skies) and dislike colors associated with things they dislike (e.g., brown for excrement).[44] Yet these studies, too, used small chips or diagrams, isolated from real environments.

In one notable exception to the usual methods, Japanese researchers showed participants slides of (full) living rooms painted in different colors. They found that preference did not particularly depend on hue but more on saturation and brightness.[45] Hue was not strongly related to preference but rather to perceived warmth. Saturation was most closely related to preference: the more saturated the wall color, the better and more comfortable the room was reported to be.

In sum, how people perceive the environmental attributes of their homes, and how those perceptions affect them, is complex. The examples above are merely that, examples of the many studies of this topic. Much more can be found in Robert Gifford's textbook on environmental psychology,[46] as well as in other sources. Physical influences are part of the larger picture, along with social aspects, culture, socioeconomic status, and individual differences, that makes research on residential satisfaction challenging and compelling.

At Work

Environmental psychologists have extensively studied work settings and often focus on the interaction between physical elements and employee productivity and well-being. An optimal design for a specific workplace can lead to higher employee satisfaction and lower absenteeism, and save organizations money. In fact, productivity can increase by 10 to 50 percent when better workplace designs are put in place.[47] This section highlights the effects of lighting and noise as examples of social science research on the physical workplace, but it certainly does not exhaust them.[48]

Lighting

Illumination consists of four main dimensions: source, fixture, amount, and arrangement. Light sources in a work setting are often a combination of natural or daylighting (e.g., sunlight) and artificial (e.g., fluorescent). Typical fixtures include ceiling and desk lamps. The amount of light is called illuminance. Lighting arrangement refers to the angle and distribution with which light strikes a work surface (e.g., uniform or nonuniform).

Unfortunately, lighting design often overlooks human preferences and needs in favor of the need for efficiency. This is the main reason why fluorescent tubes are the dominant light source in most offices and industrial workplaces. Despite their relative efficiency, employees generally do not like them. In response, many organizations have made lighting quality a priority in their decisions about office renovations. Wherever possible, giving employees the kind of light they prefer, and control over it, is a good idea.[49]

Some research shows that employee performance improves with more light.[50] Of course, optimal light levels depend on the job—someone who performs detailed work will likely require more task lighting than someone chairing a meeting in a conference room. Work surfaces are also important. Shiny surfaces can cause glare when light levels are high, especially when the light source is undiffused (e.g., a bare lightbulb). Angle also must be considered; some tasks require bright but diffused lighting (e.g., surgery), but others require sharply angled lighting to make use of shadows. For example, a textile worker searching for flaws in manufactured cloth needs angled lighting to detect them.

In general, lighting ideally should be tailored to the task and to the individual employee. This strategy would likely result in more task lighting being utilized at work, yielding an energy savings based on the reduction of energy needed to illuminate large spaces at excessive.[51]

Not surprisingly, many employees report that sunlight is desirable.[52] Although daylighting, as it is also called, in the workplace can cause complaints about glare and heat, most people prefer to be located near a window. Nevertheless, greater sunlight penetration at work is associated with higher job satisfaction,[53] and, of course, windows offer views of the outdoors, which also contribute to satisfaction and buffer the negative impacts of job-related stress.[54]

However, a balance is necessary: too much sunlight penetration is not relaxing for employees,[55] and available evidence does not show that proximity to a window increases performance,[56] even though it appears to reduce boredom.[57]

Noise

In a work setting, noise (which may be defined as "unwanted sound") might come from construction equipment, office machinery, phones, background music, communications between coworkers, or all of these sources at once! Noise is not only about the volume of sound but also its source, predictability, content, and controllability (the motorcyclist enjoys the sound made by the motorcycle, but nearby employees may not). Noise is a common complaint among employees. One study found that 99 percent of office workers thought that noise levels caused primarily by telephones and conversations significantly impaired their concentration.[58]

Noise impairs work performance, especially when the sounds occur at unpredictable intervals and are not controllable.[59] Employees who work in very noisy environments often are more aggressive, distrustful, and irritable than those working in environments with less noise.[60] Clearly, interior designers should aim to create settings in which sounds are pleasant; if noise must be part of the setting, ways should be found to give employees control over it.

Not all workplace sound is harmful or distracting. One employee might consider a certain sound to be pleasant while another may find it annoying and distracting. Preferences for and against different musical genres (or even music versus not music) are one example of how individual differences play a role. Some research finds that listening to music while working can enhance employees' satisfaction and mood state[61] and productivity.[62] However, listening to music also can sometimes harm performance and many people report that they do not enjoy listening to music while working.[63]

Designing a workplace soundscape requires consideration of all employees' characteristics if one is to create an overall plan that best encompasses noise, employee satisfaction, and productivity. As one example, noise slows reaction times and harms the memory of older individuals more than that of younger individuals.[64] As another, the performance of noise-sensitive workers naturally decreases in noisy workplaces. Some people are able to screen unwanted sounds and stimuli better than others. Extraverts are better screeners than introverts.[65] Finally, highly creative employees perform better than less-creative employees with moderate levels of noise or arousal.[66]

Noise levels in the workplace can also be important for employee health. One study showed that employees who are often exposed to unpredictable noise at work have a 60 percent greater chance of developing cardiovascular disease than other employees.[67] Even low-level noise can increase employees' stress reactions and decrease their motivation to solve problems and improve upon their work.[68] Sound and noise are part of all work settings. Therefore, designers must not overlook the potential impact of the interior's soundscape, given that the natural tendency is to focus on the visible aspects of a design.

Overall, not only do people influence and alter their interiors, those interiors also influence behavior and well-being. This begins with how they experience their interiors, and we must emphasize that different people experience the same interior differently. At home, at work, and in all the other settings in which we spend time, many aspects of the physical setting affect those who use them. These connections are very complex, but they are not random, and they are well understood in some ways and need further study in other cases.

PART III: CONCLUSION

Interior design is important because it affects the mood and behavior of those who occupy, use, or visit a space. The work summarized in this chapter underlines the strength of the multifaceted connections between individuals and the interiors in which they dwell. In the first section, we described the mechanisms by which individuals influence the interior spaces in which they live and work; we focused on the motivations driving individuals to arrange interiors in the service of communicating their values, goals, and identities to others (i.e., identity claims), to influence their cognitive and emotional states (i.e., thought and feeling regulators), and to engage in their everyday activities, which may leave material traces (i.e., behavioral residue) in their spaces. In the second section, we presented three central ideas about environmental perception (probabilistic functionalism, affordances, and collative properties). Then, drawing on decades' worth of research in the field of environmental psychology, we showed how features of spaces can have an impact on the short- and long-term behavior and psychological states of a space's occupants and those who visit it in terms of satisfaction, health, and performance. Lighting, windows, color, layout, art, furniture, plants, artifacts, and the arrangement of these elements all can influence the interactions and moods of the space's inhabitants, as well as the impressions of the occupants that are developed by visitors.

The processes discussed in this chapter are at work in all the residential, workplace, and commercial settings in which modern humans spend the vast majority of their time. Together the studies reviewed here demonstrate how a full account of interiors will require an understanding of people, how they affect interior spaces, and how they are in turn affected by spaces. As such, environmental psychology will continue to provide crucial insights into the multidisciplinary study of interiors.

21

Guilty by Design/Guilty by Desire: Queering Bourgeois Domesticity

JOHN POTVIN

To satisfy my incessant magazine craving, I often find myself either standing at news-stands browsing through magazines or simply picking up the latest issue of *Metropolitan Home, Elle Decor,* or a periodical catering to a similar demographic. In my search I tend to exclude the American edition of *Architectural Digest* given it seems slightly too out of reach and as it tends toward the lifestyles of the rich and famous, and seem-ingly not always stylish, at least according to my queer sense and bourgeois sensibility. Since 2000, I've noticed the emergence of something rather peculiar, and somewhat disruptive—that is, the significant increase in the number of articles featuring (almost exclusively) male same-sex couples' interiors and homes. These feature articles seem to appear with greater frequency over the years, ostensibly disproportionately higher than their cross-sex middle-class counterparts. Before and even after my discovery, when I would see two men portrayed in a featured home, I often started my viewing premised on the assumption that one of the two men was the proud and beaming owner of a re-designed bachelor pad, while the other was simply his equally attractive, and naturally talented, designer. However, more often than not I was wrong. So much for my—sup-posedly inherent and/or acquired—gaydar; apparently it did not work for print ma-terial. After all, in the very same magazines weren't we always forced to assume the straightness of the myriad gay designers' patrons? So disproportionate is the incursion of same-sex couples in these magazines that I have begun to question whether hetero-sexuals (and lesbians for that matter) still redesign or redecorate their homes. Could it be that as late as 2000, interior design was finally coming out of its redesigned closet and into the pages of stylish monthly magazines? Sure, it has been tacitly understood as cliché and perhaps fact that gay men (and straight women) have long served as in-terior designers, whose work has featured regularly and prominently in the very maga-zines I cite above, among others. But this was something altogether different. Here, in these glossy feature articles were same-sex couples who were not simply designers but consumers of designer services. Seemingly, overnight, sexuality had seeped through the porous boundaries of domestic space, a space traditionally represented through a silence and the taken-as-given assumption of straightness that resulted in the home appearing as if sexless. How have we gotten to this supposed time and space of inclusion? In the brief chapter that follows, I wish to explore some historical aspects which may have contributed to the phenomenon I have described above. This chapter does not, cannot, purport to provide a complete history of sexuality and gender as it intersects with interior design and the home. Rather, through a cursory survey of a few historical characters and defining moments, I wish to offer some explanations as to how we have arrived at our contemporary moment of inclusion, harmonization, and complicity. The cases as I have positioned them here affirm a comingling of sex and design. The interiors, homes, and relationships discussed also serve to expose the tensions between perversion which results in shame on the one hand and respectability, privacy, and passing below the radar on the other, a conceptualization not unlike Gayle Rubin's investigation of the cultural and institutional associations of good versus bad sex.[1]

It is a rather easy and all too facile assumption to discuss gay men's relationship to space in terms of the public domain as well as to eroticism. In fact, in *Queer Space* Aaron Betsky does a good job collapsing queer space with eroticism, lending a degree of privileged to the public sphere. Betsky defines queer space as "a useless, amoral, and sensual space that lives only in and for experience. It is a space of spectacle, consumption, dance, and obscenity. It is a misuse or deformation of a place, an appropriation of the buildings and codes of the city for perverse purposes."[2] There are a number of excellent and thoughtful studies on the intersection of homosexuality and the spaces of the public realm particularly among scholars of British cultural history.[3] And while there are also a plethora of smart books and volumes attending to the geographies of sexuality, it seems like a glaring lacuna that most scholars do not see the domestic as a landscape—or geography for that matter—that plays host to and locates sexuality.[4] The result is a sort of reification of the public/private divide by scholars who fascinate over the public domains of civility, culture, and community while through a collective silence render the home seemingly unintelligible, and, by default, feminine.[5] However, the work of one particular scholar still, almost two decades later, stands out as exemplary. In her groundbreaking volume, *Sexuality and Space,* Beatriz Colomina compels her reader to consider how architecture or more exactly space is "a system of representation" and forces us to pay heed to the idea that space is already a part of the history and realities of sexuality and the multiplicity of its performances. As I will argue throughout, space as a system of representation codes the reception and perception of interiors, defined by way of those you pass through them or stand outside peering in through the lens of social control.

In his study of the Haussmanization of Paris (1852–1870) and its processes of modernization, which gripped the City of Lights, Walter Benjamin wrote how "the bourgeois has shown a tendency to compensate for the absence of any trace of private life in the big city. He tries to do this within the four walls of his apartment."[6] The bourgeois, as a parallel development with the onslaught and affects of modernization in a constant and unnerving shock of urban development and increased chaos in Europe and North America sought refuge in the modern interior. Bourgeois ethics lead to the creation of perfect, honorable domains, domestic realms of their own devising—a perfect collective design enterprise in artificiality by an entire class in the name of individuality and subjectivity. The ethics of design and the codes of gender and sexuality were indelibly linked as a result. By the nineteenth century, the bourgeois home stood as the embodiment of the nation, its borders rendered sacred and fortified by the ever-increasing gender divide. British art and cultural critic John Ruskin wrote that the home was the

> place of Peace; the shelter, not only from all injury, but from all terror, doubt, and division. In so far as it is not this, it is not home; so far as the anxieties of the outer life penetrate into it, and the inconsistently-minded, unknown, unloved, or hostile society of the outer world is allowed by either husband or wife to cross the threshold, it ceases to be home.[7]

The fictional, though powerful, notion of the public/private divide was symbolically and architecturally defined by the threshold and maintained through the ideals of individuality, which in turn could be visualized and materialized through the objects collected, consumed, and displayed in the home. The home became a complex mapping devise for the individual, a world of his or her own divining.

QUEER DESIGN: BETWEEN AUSTERITY AND EXCESS

In 1884, Boston-born Edward Perry Warren met John Marshall while they were both students at New College, Oxford. At Oxford, Warren became obsessed with all things Hellenic and began in earnest to delve into the world of antiquities. After his university days, Warren, along with Marshall, who was to assume the role of both secretary and lover, would amass an enviable collection of rare antiquities and decorative objects for both himself and the Museum of Fine Arts in Boston. Warren and Marshall's professional and personal relationship did not initially begin with ardent passion, and Warren took great pains to woe the slightly younger man. In August 1888, he requested that Marshall broker the purchase of a set of ancient benches from Ormskirk church in Lancashire, which were to remain in the Lewes House dining room for many years. In the correspondence between the two concerning this and other deals, Marshall refrained from any reference to their future together. When he finally agreed to work as secretary, Warren assured him an annual stipend of £200 a year, excluding expenses. At the time of his consent, Marshall compelling wrote to Warren: "You were to me at first a quality, then a collection of qualities... now everything you say and do seems inseparable from you and my love to you."[8] Marshall finally succumbed in 1889 to a personal relationship with his employer.

In 1889, Warren also received the assignment of lease for Lewis House, a foreboding and large early Georgian house, a version of which had occupied the grounds since 1620. The house itself was of blue brick with a porch of cream stucco. Warren described the house as "huge, old, and not cheap. It has only three or four sunny rooms...It is the centre of Lewes and yet has a quiet garden, a paddock, greenhouse, and stables *ad lib*. Downs accessible and green woody country as well."[9] Inside, Warren furnished the house with fifteenth- to eighteenth-century furniture, Old English continental and oriental china and porcelain, over 900 ounces of silver, embroideries and brocades, and Grecian columns and statutes, the relics of times past and those of a diligent connoisseur. Among the fourteen different dinner services he owned were some produced by such venerable companies as Worcester, Minton, Capo di Monte, and Wedgewood, destined to be used in the dining room where *Adam and Eve* (1526) by Lucas Cranach hung. The forbidden apple of temptation in the picture was precisely, according to Warren, what made the picture appropriate to the room and was a rare example of the few paintings in his collection. However, Osbert Burdett and E. H. Goddard, Warren's contemporaries and first biographers, captured the atmosphere of Lewes House when they described it:

> It was to be a house of bachelors and scholars, and the "good life" was to include much fun and good fellowship, with horse to keep the men fit and good wine and food to complete their well-being. Warren differed from many scholars in not being, primarily, a man of books...scholarship to him was not an end but a means. The end was the good life as described by Aristotle and Plato, and scholarship was chiefly valuable in preserving the theory, for in the absence of the theory the "good life" itself would break down.[10]

The separated coach house became the inner sanctum, affectionately named Thebes, suggestive of its reclusive nature, devoid of the communal hubbub of the house itself, where Warren wrote studies on Greek antiquities and Uranian boy-love; it was here where Warren kept his specially commissioned version of August Rodin's famed sculpture *Le Baiser* (1904). The key to Thebes was worn around Warren's neck on a gold chain, perhaps a concession to personal adornment, practical though it was. The room's floor was of red linoleum, while the walls were half-paneled in oak, above which was painted jade-green and decorated with only one painting featuring an Elizabethan group portrait of mother and child. Two emergency bedrooms were also included in Thebes, likely occupied more by books than young men. Oak cupboards, which connected each room, were themselves repositories for additional books, ancient Greek vases, jewelry, and a tin box referred to as "the Will box."

In more public studies located in Lewes House used by Warren's various secretaries and friends, the space is consonant with his desire to enact and instill an ideal Spartan lifestyle, at whose center was the ideal youthful male as advanced by Ancient Greek civilization (Figs. 50 and 51). To this end, decorative objects were kept to a minimum, usually limited to Greek vases and bowls placed on the mantle of the fireplace while statutes of young classical male nudes rested on the desk. These spaces were perfectly suited to Warren's ideal of creating a community, a brotherhood of like-minded men. The spaces were perfect for Warren and an ideal venue to live out, in the company of numerous men (many for whom he was a benefactor), his obsession with Hellenism which culminated

FIGURES 50 AND 51   Interior view of Edward Warren Perry's Study. Courtesy of the Lewes House Archive.

in the publication of the three volume track *A Defence of Uranian Love* (1928–1930); privately published, the three volumes were produced separately, with the last two published posthumously.[11] The volumes, paeans to Uranian love, were part of a larger project seen as an embarrassment to friend and fellow pederast George Santayana, who was direct and severe in his shaming of Warren's obsessive Hellenism claiming it threatened his credibility and reputation.[12]

Warren's working room bore his emblematic Spartan design in keeping, he felt, with the ideals of self discipline, masculinity, and simplicity, the very core values of his Uranian program. Among the limited objects included on Warren's working table was a Greek marble group; a simple yet revealing reminder of his obsession. Thebes was the hallowed inner sanctum of Lewes House, removed and yet a crucial part of the space and culture of the community that gathered and thrived there. Friend, artist, and chronicler of his era, Sir William Rothenstein recounts how the house operated as

> a monkish establishment, where women were not welcomed. But Warren, who believed that scholars should live nobly, kept ample table and a well-stocked wine-cellar; in the stables were mettlesome horses, for the Downs were close at hand, and he rode daily with his friends, for the body most needs be as well exercised as the mind. Meals were served at a great oaken table dark and polished, on which stood a splendid old silver. The rooms were full of handsome antique furniture, and of Greek bronzes and marbles in place of usual ornaments... There was much mystery about the provenance of the treasures at Lewes house. This secrecy seemed to permeate the rooms and corridors, to exhaust the air of the house. The social relations, too, were often strained, and [John] Fothergill [later to become Warren's secretary after Marshall's departure] longed for a franker, for a less cloistered life.[13]

Beginning in the 1860s, men developed bachelor cultures separate and purposefully distinct from the domestic sphere, with its feminine associations and heteronormative affiliations. The choice of bachelorhood, however, was viewed as suspect, "given it suggested an abdication from patriarchy and an indifference to lineage and posterity."[14] The bachelor as a new modern type jeopardized not so much marriage per se but rather bourgeois domesticity which maintained its aesthetic and sexual order through the gendered division of labor and mythology of the separate spheres; along the public/private divide, it was in the latter wherein the bourgeois self was formed and maintained.[15] As Katherine V. Snyder posits, "Bachelors often served in cultural and literary discourse more generally as threshold figures who marked the permeable boundaries that separate domesticity, normative manhood, and high-cultural status, from what was defined as extrinsic to these realms."[16] The brotherhood Warren attempted to create, though not entirely successfully, at Lewes House was a community based on intellectually and sexually like-minded men rather than enforced through the strictures he felt were implied in the traditional family structure and hegemonic, compulsory heterosexuality. "The effect," according to Burdett and Goddard, "was to make the household seem a society apart, an isolated community. The outside world shrank to a memory."[17] The home owned by that "mad millionaire," stood foursquare as a contradiction within the gendered divide, marking the spheres as separate where a man's role was clearly defined by his public position. Clothes, accessories, and even personal articles such as towels were used by one and all without pretence to hierarchy, property, or propriety. Lewes House was a space of constant activity with a steady stream of men coming in and out, a domestic situation Warren held as ideal.

While Warren was busying himself establishing Lewes House and a homosocial community premised on Uranian love, illustrator and art critic Charles Ricketts and painter Charles Shannon began to share a home in 1887, and for over fifty years they would live and work together in numerous homes, designing them as havens for community and artistic creativity. In addition to creating art, a large part of their partnership revolved around collecting despite their meager joint income. Despite their financial health, together the couple amassed one of the most impressive and important collections of Japanese *kakemono* (wall scrolls)—popular in France and England among the aesthetes and decadents—Greek lekythoi, tanagrettes, and of course drawings and paintings by artists such as Peter Paul Rubens and the symbolist Puvis de Chavannes.

Their various homes were decorated with a Puritan rigor coupled with Art and Crafts principles. Rothenstein, who was also a friend to these two artists, commented how he was "charmed" by them and "their simple dwelling" when he was taken to The Vale by Oscar Wilde. He recalled the "primrose walls, apple-green skirting and shelves, the rooms hung with Shannon's lithographs, a fan-shaped watercolor by Whistler, and drawings by Hokusai—their first treasures, to be followed by so many others."[18] While many recall the individual objected pieces that comprised the highly respected and coveted collection of pictures, antiquities, and rare pieces (many showcased in elegant museum-like display cases in sitting rooms, in addition to being dispersed through the various rooms) that comprised the couple's collection, Rothenstein was clear to note how struck he was by the overall aesthetic affect the rooms evoked for him. Benjamin remarked on how the collector, the interior dweller, creates his world apart: the "interior is the asylum where art takes refuge…He [the collector] makes his concern the idealization of objects…The collector delights in evoking a world that is not just distant and long gone but also better."[19] The affect, however, each room conjured resulted from the sum of its parts, and Ricketts advocated that color was the key ingredient to the reception of his rooms, as it maintained "the temper of each room."[20]

The first home Ricketts and Shannon shared together beginning in 1888, (No. 4) in the The Vale, located in a cul-de-sac off the King's Road, Chelsea, was a regency house already well-known given it had previously accommodated James Abbott McNeill Whistler's long-time mistress. With Ricketts and Shannon as its new occupants, No. 4 formed a vital part of the life and activity of Bohemian London. It was in this house where the couple first developed their aesthetic and interior design program, but importantly it was also where they enlivened an important and wide-ranging circle of influential friends, which included, among others, their colleague and seemingly omnipresent dandy Oscar Wilde. While Ricketts and Shannon worked with Wilde on a number of important projects, providing exquisite illustrations and bindings suitable to his prose, their respective lifestyles couldn't have been further apart. In his less than catholic tastes, Ricketts once recalled a conversation he had with Wilde, pointedly folding their domestic programs into a thinly veiled discussion of morality. Wilde's "love of luxury," according to Ricketts, led him to "live in costly hotels and restaurants, paradises for the vulgar, and sometimes in strange company. Wilde had often smiled at the austerity of my habits…and would laughingly say 'Both you and Shannon are ascetics of art, you turn away from life and like most painters, you lack curiosity.'"[21] Wilde's luxury is too easily counterposed to Ricketts and Shannon's bourgeois, safe, and quite domestic union. For Ricketts, the sanctity of hearth and home was seemingly threatened by his friend's wild(e) ways. Ricketts, as we know, was not the only one to judge the Irish playwright by way of domestic interiors. Turning once again to Rothenstein, who, while in attendance with Wilde at Ricketts and Shannon's once commented on whether Wilde knew just "how gross, how soiled by the world he appeared, sitting in one of the white scrubbed kitchen chairs next to Ricketts and Shannon."[22]

However, nowhere is the perception of a collapse between sexual morality and the interior more painfully apparent than in the trial of the century, when Wilde and his cohort Lord Alfred Taylor were convicted of sex crimes in 1895. Taylor was charged and quickly convicted of indecency as well as with procuring for other men the services of male prostitutes, while Wilde was charged and found guilty of gross indecency. The evidence for the charges brought forward against both men was largely culled from two sources: gossip, hearsay and eyewitness testimonials; and domestic material culture. In Taylor's lodgings the police found women's clothing, a wig, and a brooch, evidence of degenerate cross-dressing. However, the majority of the reports that flooded the newspapers in the long days of the trails focused, as did the court, on the type of home Taylor kept; by the end of the nineteenth century, interior design began to operate as a composite sketch of the identity of its occupants. While no photographs or prints exist of Taylor's flat, the numerous newspaper accounts help to suggest the interior spaces he designed. In the *News of the World,* Taylor's flat was alluded to as the "snuggery at Little College-Street,"[23] whereas the *Star* characterized Taylor's rooms as "heavy draped windows, their candles burning on through the day, and the languorous atmosphere heavy with perfumes."[24] The *Evening News* also reported that the rooms Taylor rented were "draped and furnished" in a "remarkable manner" and "curious way," "perfumed and always lighted by artificial light."[25] Ed Cohen has suggested that Taylor's flat, in its perversion of normative bourgeois domesticity, mark him and Wilde as liminal figures. In so doing, "these representations constructed Taylor's and Wilde's movements in and through this space as confirmation of—if not the source for—the 'indecencies' of which they were accused."[26] Liminality, as both and at once a personal and spatial identity, subverts the signifying potential of the domestic realm to remain pure, unaffected by the vagaries and perceived evils of the outside world. In this way, then, the home is not only at risk but so too is that of the best interests and safety of the nation. Since 1885, under the Labouchère Amendment, gross indecency was no longer an issue of public safety, but deviancy was now a concern for and to be regulated within the home as well: "Any person who, *in private or public,* commits, or is a party to the commission of, or procures or attempts to procure the commission by any male person of any act of gross indecency with another male person, shall be guilty of a misdemeanour" (italics author's).[27] It light of such laws, it comes as no surprise that interior space and identity became the site of institutional and public scrutiny particularly as it concerned gender and sexuality.

In Sweden, less than a decade following Wilde's death, newspapers reported the emergence of "Wilde fever," referring to the emergence of a dandy subculture. Although it was never explicitly stated, this new type implicitly swayed with homosexuality leanings.[28] In 1911, following along in his illustrious grandmother's footsteps, the Countess Wilhelmina von Hallwyl, Rolf de Maré (1888–1964), a dandy in spirit though not in body, took to traveling the world and along the way amassed a formidable collection of Asian and African artifacts. This collection was soon to be shelved in favor of modern art, when the wealthy de Maré came into contact with fauvist and expressionist painter Nils Dardel (1888–1943), a true dandy through and through. Soon de Maré became Dardel's lover and patron, and in return the painter introduced the future impresario to some of the most important artists and cultural figures in Europe. By 1910, Dardel had moved to Paris, though he regularly returned to Stockholm for extended visits. With Dardel's shrewd artistic guidance de Maré enthusiastically and single-mindedly collected some of the most important works of modern art of his day. Although a collector at heart, this as well as his other cultural endeavors were the result of his sexual relationships. No longer his lover, Dardel soon introduced de Maré to a second and equally important figure in his life, the young ballet dancer Jean Börlin. At the time of their meeting, Börlin was a talented yet struggling dancer in the Stockholm Royal Opera. As a means to support his new lover both culturally and financially, de Maré provided Börlin with a platform for his talents when he formed the Ballets Suédois in 1920. The ballet was, importantly, an extension of de Maré's modern art collection. Numerous stages, backdrops, and costumes for the troupe were undertaken by a number of the artists whose paintings hung in de Maré's home; these included among others Giorgio de Chirico and Fernand Léger. Taking off where Sergei Diaghilev's much celebrated if at times controversial Ballets Russes had left off, de Maré installed his ballet in Paris at the Théâtre des Champs-Elysées in Avenue Montaigne, where it still stands today bracketed by the world's leading *maisons de haute couture*. The Swede was all too aware that such a modernist dance troupe would prove disastrous in his native country, especially given that a number of male and female dancers from the Royal Opera had defected, with much controversy, to join the new troupe.

Collecting provides both men and women a means through which to "participate in the feminine world of consumption in a way that simultaneously supports the masculine world of production."[29] By the end of the nineteenth century, since the onslaught of the Industrial Revolution, production and work became increasingly disassociated with the public realm of the home and became an increasing male and public domain. Parallel to this development, by the end of the nineteenth century collecting became the site of emasculation and enfeeblement according to French cultural critic Max Nordau. Collecting for Nordau not only led to effeminacy (the erosion of gender codes) but also to sterility and as a result became a national concern;[30] it was a clear act of nonproduction.

Men who collected too many objects, surrounded themselves and locked themselves within a world of often idle worship of aesthetic beauty, were seen to reside outside the domain of the heteronormative, bourgeois capital economy. The concern for collecting and design, the consumption for the home, in other words, was, as we have already seen, a national concern as it directly pertained to the codes of gender and the performances of good sexuality. In 1912, de Maré's grandmother handed over the leasehold of Hildesborg Castle in Skåne, in the south-most region of Sweden. The villa, located on the expansive grounds of Hildesborg, was converted into his home, whose redesign was completed one year later. In his 1914 painting *Reception* (Plate 20), de Dardel attempted to capture the Orientalist atmosphere and decor (both understood as feminizing and foreign influences) of the villa. In one photograph, some of the salon's exotic objects (collected on a recent trip to Asia) can be seen placed atop dark wood cabinets, while religious statuary stand prominently on delicate and sumptuously draped fabrics, which are over top of invisible tables. The room Dardel depicts is accurate in the way he has characterized a space steeped in exoticism and dripping in dark, passionate tones with its rich, brocade fire-dragon wall hanging and tiger and lion skins servicing the salon as rugs. In Dardel's picture, the space is also importantly occupied by his patron crossing the exotic room's threshold, surrounded by the young, attractive, and effete dandies who formed his all-male coterie. The spaces of the villa were likened by one contemporary to a nightclub owner's dream.[31] The painting portrayed the space and its occupants as rich, exotic, languid, and decadent. *Reception* was purchased by de Maré who significantly opted to showcase it prominently in the very space it depicted (see Figs. 52 and 53).

FIGURE 52   Interior view of Rolf de Maré's salon in Hildesborg home.

FIGURE 53   Interior view of Rolf de Maré's salon in Hildesborg home. Courtesy of Dansmuseet, Stockholm.

For the then conservative Swedish press, the spaces designed by de Maré and occupied by his community of like-minded men posed a serious threat. On September 8, 1920, the journal *Fäderneslandet (The Fatherland)* published "En celeber omyndighetshistoria" ("A Distinguished Story of Incapacity"), whose writer anonymously outed de Maré, Dardel, and Börlin. Humiliated by the scandal de Maré was causing by living a degenerate lifestyle in his villa, his grandparents were said to have paid both Börlin and Dardel to leave the estate and their grandson. While these claims were unfounded and inaccurate, nonetheless, the article submitted that the wealthy patron was living as a "ménage à trois" with Dardel and Börlin, who were "plucking the golden goose," availing themselves shamelessly of his wealth to continue their degenerate lifestyle and "perverse art," which already filled the walls of Hildesborg. The article was likely to have been penned by a disgruntled David Sprengel, a man who was denied the role of manager of the Ballets Suédois by its founder. Sprengel was at once a journalist, critic, artist, and friend of Dardel and very much considered himself a ladies' man. Sprengel cautioned de Maré that, should he continue to be open about his sexuality and private affairs (that is, make public that which must remain private, closeted even), his reputation would only be called into question and bring about scandal. Sprengel promptly offered up his own services as a normalizing and reputable force—that is, a closet in which de Maré could hide.

With increasing scandal as a result of Sprengler's scathing article as well as the all-important inauguration of the Ballets Suédois and the myriad other time consuming cultural enterprises he had initiated in 1920,[32] de Maré gradually left Sweden and settled more permanently in Paris, where he found himself a large, splendid flat in 2 Rue Saint-Simon. The formidable building is located at the corner of Boulevard Saint-Germain, the hotbed of Left Bank radical chic and even more radical sexualities in the 1920s. The spaces of the flat were ideally appointed for his bachelor-style living and his formidable collections of modern art and exotic Oriental and African objects. Picasso was a visitor and was impressed by a suite of drawings by Ernst Josephson. Isadora Duncan and Rudolph Valentino and his wife, Natasha Rambova, were also visitors to 2 Rue Saint-Simon. De Maré's home became a vital and significant meeting place for the literati of the day. The domestic sphere, the homes of immensely influential figures such as Gertrude Stein and Alice B. Toklas as well as that of Rolf de Maré, to cite only two notable examples, were sites for the collaborative exercises of modernity, modern art, and sexual identification.

Betsky has posited that the "purpose of queer space is again ultimately sex: the making of a space either for that peculiar definition of self as an engine of sexuality for the act of sex itself."[33] However, it seems to me that Betsky's claim, made 100 years after Wilde's unfortunate incarceration, only serves to reify the basic premise used against men like him, Taylor, and de Maré, further perpetuating a stereotype, albeit, perhaps true in certain cases. Betsky's definition excludes the interiors fashioned by Ricketts and Shannon and Warren and countless other male and female same-sex couples who dared to live a life of bourgeois respectability and yet outside of companionate marriage. Since 1869, when the homosexual "was called into being,"[34] the West has come through two world wars, the women's liberation movement, the struggle for racial equality, and gay liberation. At least on the surface, things have never looked better—after all, as I began with at the outset of this chapter, gay couples are everywhere in design magazines. Things must be good.

In the historically rich neighborhood of Cabbagetown in Toronto's downtown, the local community hosts the annual Cabbagetown Tour of Homes every fall. While the autumn leaves fall, dog walkers tend to their keep, and children run home gleefully after a tough day at school, the local community, with its significant, though visibly bourgeois, gay community, opens the door to eight volunteering families' homes. Each featured home boasts painstaking renovation and a preservation program that has maintained the integrity of the neighborhood's nineteenth- and early twentieth-century heritage. In the 2010 annual showing, a staggering seven out of the eight showcased homes were owned by male same-sex couples. Male same-sex couples, like those featured in the 2010 Tour of Homes, in their respectability, share with the larger community a desire to preserve the interiors of the past, while demonstrating the (social and design) progress made in the last few decades. Same-sex couples (some married others not), as Ricketts and Shannon did in their day, pass below the radar precisely because they embody bourgeois decor/um and respectability, where queerness, or too much overt indications of sexuality, is renovated and cleansed. Property and propriety now guarantee entry into the mainstream. The condo and housing boom and the legalization of same-sex marriages (in some countries), coupled with same-sex couples' desire to domesticate their relationships, purposefully turning their backs away from the stigma leveled at the community by the press, institutions, and governments in the wake of the AIDS epidemic, has led to the very phenomenon I described at the outset of this chapter. In the less than three decades since the AIDS crisis hit, gay men have come to see the interior as a way to shelter, butch-up, and gentrify their lives. The varied historical cases I have briefly outlined here and set in slight opposition to each other serve as a reminder of the ways in which sexuality and gender code domestic space and how in turn sexuality and gender affect the design and perception of these spaces. The straight, single gal, embodied perfectly and repeatedly in the hit series *Sex and the City,* and gay men, represented to varying success in series such as *Will and Grace,* remind us of the perils of single life, not of the supposed loneliness or possible merits of this unwed state but of the social pressure, stigma, and deviance these two constituencies are still burdened with when faced with the long-term prospects of single-life. Single or coupled, queer space, however you yourself wish to conceptualize it, is inscribed and marked as a space of difference, which is not limited to but must also include the varied performances, pleasures, and embodiments of sex (vanilla, Neapolitan, otherwise).

This chapter was written with my husband working across the table from me and with our dog sleeping in his plush bed beside us in our flat in a redesigned, modernized house in Old Cabbagetown, Toronto.

22

Toward Sentience

CLIVE PARKINSON

If you are given the diagnosis of cancer or dementia, the likelihood that this news is given to you in a clinical environment is high, as is that it will be given by a highly trained clinician. That you'd be concerned either for the design of the environment or the integration of the arts into this space would in all probability be an irrelevance. Given a diagnosis of any serious disease, we cling to the professionalism and speed of a responsive heath system that will act in our best interest and provide treatment that is well-considered, timely, and effective. In fact, considering design and the arts seems ridiculous in the face of illness and our own mortality. Yet there is movement that bridges the arts, health, and well-being that asserts there is a place for design and the arts alongside medicine. Moreover, there is a growing awareness among clinicians that in the face of illness and mortality, the arts offer medicine something other than scientific reductionism. Added to this, the UK think-tank *demos* conservatively estimate "that at least a fifth of NHS spending goes on end of life care and the cost of that care will rise from about £20 billion today to £25 billion in 2030...yet 40 per cent of people who die in hospital do not have medical conditions that medics can fight."[1] In the United States, the burgeoning cost of health care is potentially "the greatest threat to the country's long-term solvency, with twenty-five per cent of all Medicare spending is for the five per cent of patients who are in their final year of life, and most of that money goes for care in their last couple of months which is of little apparent benefit."[2] It seems that scrutinizing the way healthcare is delivered has never been more important.

This chapter will focus on the seemingly tenuous relationship between design, the arts, and health and argue that their potential impact on future patients is far reaching.

Much of the literature in this fast-developing field plots a neat line from the revelations of Florence Nightingale on the impact of improved sanitary conditions on Victorian public health,[3] to the not too surprising revelations of Roger Ulrich that, among other things, tells us that pleasant hospital environments reduce hospital stays.[4] We're not going to start our journey there, and although we may make passing references to eminent figures from history and contemporary research, much of this chapter will be focused on the here and now and the reality of diverse twenty-first-century life.

The idea of the patient journey is a useful place to begin because like it or not we are all consumers of health services at some point in our lives. Even for those of us in robust health, the likelihood of our final moments of life taking place inside a hospital intensive care unit (ICU) is far more probable than gently slipping away in the comfort of our own bed surrounded by those we love.

In an article for *The New Yorker,* the surgeon and writer Dr. Atul Gawande, through a first person account, painfully illustrates how modern medicine often focuses on aggressive interventions to stave off death while losing sight of the patient and of ways we can improve quality of life in people's final days. In his unflinching narrative echoing early descriptions of health services as "warehouses of the dying,"[5] he paints a picture of a health system that in its attempt to prolong life takes medicine and surgery to its furthest limits. Whist the goal of medicine and surgery is to prolong life, it runs the risk of sacrificing quality of life by pursuing every available intervention, however traumatic, for the possibility of extra time. This chapter will argue the case for more domestic-scaled care and support that enables the fullest of possible lives in the here and now.

Charles Leadbetter and Jake Garber in their report on how people die in the twenty-first-century United Kingdom, "Dying for a Change," illustrate this issue with clarity:

> Hospitals' main weaknesses…are their lack of privacy and personalisation; they are designed around professional, medical procedures and hierarchies rather than to accommodate social relationships; they deliver services for and to people but are less adept at working with them. Patients and families often complain that staff have not got the time, knowledge or skills to communicate effectively.[6]

It is my assertion that in considering all aspects of health and well-being, from the clinical setting to the communities that we live in, we must explore the extremes of the human condition to better understand how to achieve long-term cultural change in the way we design, deliver, and value public health.

Of course, any writing on healthy environments that focuses solely on clinics and hospital settings is missing the point: healthy environments are all those places that life takes place in—the streets, markets, schools, workplaces, and homes that we all inhabit. It is blindingly obvious that the environmental factors that impact on our well-being underpin everything, so a literal approach to this chapter would be to work from the crisis at Fukushima[7] outward, taking in fundamental human rights and inequalities along the way, but this is too large an area to consider here. Other more intimate factors within this spectrum might be usefully unpicked here though, ranging from patient choices to innovative partnership approaches to addressing complex health needs.

Describing how "more and more of life's inevitable processes and difficulties—birth, sexuality, aging, unhappiness, tiredness, and loneliness—are being medicalised,"[8]

Dr. Richard Smith, one-time editor of the *British Medical Journal,* argues that "medicine alone cannot address these problems and that common values and attitudes towards the management of death, while well known about in scientific circles, have yet to be acted upon because of lack of imagination."[9] While the modern version of the Hippocratic Oath[10] urges clinicians to avoid the "twin traps of over-treatment and therapeutic nihilism," it also stresses that "there is art to medicine as well as science, and that warmth, sympathy, and understanding may outweigh the surgeon's knife or the chemist's drug" and urges a focus on the human being, not the illness. Smith suggests that the arts might just be the vehicle to address these points.

Jonah Lehrer in his book *Proust was a Neuroscientist*[11] usefully expands on this theme, suggesting that creative minds might shed new light on complex scientific problems. Citing the work of, among others, Gertrude Stein and Igor Stravinsky, Lehrer uses Marcel Proust's discovery in *A la Recherche du Temps Perdu,*[12] that smell and taste produce uniquely intense memories which are dependent on moment and mood. These remembered sensations are often selective, changeable and subject to fault: "to remember is to misremember." Current scientific research shows that memories are indeed stimulated by both smell and taste, which have hard-wired connections to the hippocampus. Lehrer suggests that the artistic enquiry has preempted the scientific understanding. While there is evidence to suggest that loss of olfactory function is an indicator of dementia, smell is a neglected sense that designer James Auger suggests has a low status because of the "re-evaluation of the senses by philosophers and scientists of the eighteenth and nineteenth centuries. Smell was considered lower order, primitive, savage and bestial. Smell is the one sense where control is lost, each intake of breath sends loaded air molecules over the receptors in the nose and in turn potentially guttural, uncensored information to the brain."[13]

Auger explores our relationship with smell through his challenging "speculative design proposals" around sexual selection, health, and well-being and places it alongside the higher senses of visual and aural perception; observing that "scientists continue to study the ways that smell might have developed to warn humans of the harm of decomposing food or an approaching fire; it is up to designers to encourage people to think about what is lost when we have 'fire alarms and sell-by dates and fridges' and, for that matter, deodorants and perfume."[14]

While Lehrer doesn't manage to show that artists have consistently influenced the research direction of scientists, he does illustrate that through creative inquiry there have been dual approaches to questions of profound human interest. This parallel thirst for understanding or making sense of the world is nevertheless mired by the "mutual incomprehension"[15] between the arts and science, as writer and scientist C. P. Snow asserted in 1959, and is still an area of some difference.

Snow described this potential for the coming together of science and the arts as the third culture,[16] but much of what we describe as third culture is frequently the superficial co-opting of the other's language, symbols, and style. Often it's as obvious as a design agency co-opting imagery and words associated with the latest scientific breakthrough to inform the logo of a corporate client, or perhaps a useful sound bite from Shakespeare or Shelley is used by a scientist to make their advances more accessible to the public.

The Welcome Trust,[17] using the profits of its pharmaceutical legacy, is a major funder of innovative projects that bridge biomedical science and public understanding through the arts. From its pioneering days in the United Kingdom in the 1980s, Arts for Health[18] has influenced integrated public and participatory art alongside design intended to humanize clinical environments. Awareness of the potential of healing environments[19] has grown exponentially, as has the call for evidence of the impact of the arts on health outcomes. An early study conducted by Roger Ulrich in 1984 suggests that surgery patients with a view of nature suffered fewer complications, needed less analgesia, and were discharged sooner than those, unsurprisingly, with a view of a brick wall.[20] Studies also exist about the psychological effects of lighting, carpeting, and noise on critical-care patients, but for Ulrich, it is the view of nature or naturalistic art that, he suggests, has the biggest impact on patient outcomes.

In a number of papers however, Ulrich consistently suggests that it is only art that reflects nature that will benefit patients and that, conversely, "inappropriate art styles or image subject matter can increase stress and worsen other outcomes."[21] Similarly, he describes the "pitfalls of displaying emotionally challenging art in (the) healthcare environments... of psychiatric patients," commenting that, "patients indicated strongly negative reactions to artworks that were ambiguous, surreal, or could be interpreted in multiple ways."[22]

Isn't this a paradox? Aren't the arts supposed to be ambiguous and open to interpretation, and is this research asking the right questions? What on Earth was this abstract art that so offended, and what will the bland compromise be: a heady mix of Soylent Green[23] and *Hay Wain*?[24] Perhaps if Tracey Emin's Turner Prize–losing *My Bed*[25] were to be exhibited on a mixed-sex, multioccupancy ward, there might be room for some concern, not least on the acquired hospital infection front! But even a work as contentious as this might have a place in the atrium of a large hospital because perhaps it may just stimulate a little conversation; after all, aren't we a bit sick of those anonymous lumps of badly conceived corporate art in these cavernous glass-and-steel warehouses? At least you could curate it, change it, and move it on. Or perhaps like the inspiring education staff at the Museum of Modern Art in New York (MoMA),[26] you could work with people marginalized by illness and engage with contemporary and sometimes challenging work specifically to provoke a response. In the United Kingdom, United States, and Australia, curators and educators from galleries and museums are increasingly bringing objects to the beds of patients to experience handling the bizarre, alien, and potentially transcendent, but more of that shortly.

Typically though, hospitals get lumbered with some semipermanent prehistoric mural like the recently unveiled Michael Craig-Martin *KIDS*[27] at the Oxford Radcliffe hospital. Doubtless conceived with good intention and planned to inspire and uplift the poorly children of Oxford, in its conceit this will become a fast-ageing, five-story memento mori to the artist. Interestingly, this is one of the few arts/health stories to make it to the prime-time UK news, and an informed reader might presume the working of the celebrity artist publicity machine.

In 2003, Rosalia Staricoff published research undertaken at the Chelsea and Westminster Hospital[28] exploring the effects of "bold, challenging works of art and high quality live music and performing arts," which found that the length of stay of patients on a trauma and orthopedic ward was one day shorter when they experienced visual arts and live music, and their need for pain relief was significantly less than those in a control group; live music was very effective in reducing levels of anxiety and depression; visual arts and live music reduced levels of depression by one-third in patients undergoing chemotherapy; and staff recruitment and retention were improved.

Of course, a rational approach to integrating design into healing environments should take into account the use of natural light, noise reduction, layout and ergonomics, single-occupancy rooms, ideally with windows on a pleasant aspect and with considered way-finding. In fact, the much-lauded Evidence-Based Design (EBD) seems nothing more than a common-sense approach to design that buys into the vernacular of EBD. Some of the objective truths behind pharmacological gold standard randomized controlled trials, however, defy belief and would warrant a more rigorously forensic level of scrutiny.

Much research around EBD has time and again told us that its rigorous implementation will

- reduce staff stress and fatigue and increase effectiveness in care delivery;
- improve patient safety;
- reduce stress and improving health outcomes; and
- improve overall healthcare quality,[29]

Given the surge of interest in EBD, there are grotesquely different approaches to commissioning artists and designers in health settings. I have been involved with a number of UK NHS (National Health Service) Trusts whose approach to integrated design or inclusion of the arts amounts to a tick-box exercise; in one case, a chief executive officer demanded complete control over color schemes, way-finding, and furnishings. The resulting aesthetic, while complying with health and safety legislation, looked like an industrial-scale IKEA remainder store. If EBD is in place to reduce the likelihood of ill-formed hospital makeovers, it has to be a good thing, but if it standardizes and reduces hospitals to a corporate aesthetic, we should be skeptical.

What is apparent in much of this field of enquiry, and considering the notion of a third culture, is that the artistic element of this work is often subservient to a broader prescriptive health agenda, potentially reducing it to gloss and decoration—or as former prime minister Tony Blair described it in a Kings Fund report on Healing Environments, "the Wow Factor."[30]

One thing that's certain is that EBD and a broader understanding of the potential of integrating the arts into new healthcare buildings has spawned a range of self-styled consultants, training, accreditation, and glossy websites, all inviting you to buy into the meme that theirs is the solution to all the burgeoning health issues out there: that art and design have all the answers.

Increasingly, designers and artists are thrown a tasty challenge: redesign the hospital patient gown, encourage us all to wash our hands thoroughly, and show us how to navigate this maze of corridors and clinics. Yet research undertaken by Mary G Lankford and colleagues shows that the most influential factor on hand washing in a clinical environment wasn't the design of the facility but the behavior of senior peers in a clinical team, suggesting "that health-care worker hand-hygiene compliance is influenced significantly by the behaviour of other health-care workers."[31]

While there are examples of inspirational practice, it's critical to note that one size doesn't fit all, and where signage in a large hospital may be crucial, in a smaller setting like the Bromley by Bow Centre,[32] signage is an irrelevance: the hospitality, reception, and human interaction are the most powerful means of facilitating the patient journey and potentially affecting change—in other words, interaction and behavior are the significant factors.

I started this chapter imagining the delivery of news of a serious illness—which will in reality affect us all in some way throughout our lives. Bringing this chapter full circle leads me to two such, very real stories: that of Maggie Keswick Jenks[33] and that of a small group of people affected by dementia, who I've had the good fortune to be involved with. Jencks has been the inspiration and motivating factor behind much of my thinking for this chapter, and although I never had the good fortune of meeting her, her experience of being diagnosed with breast cancer and her personal journey perhaps best illustrate the potential of art and design as means of transformative change and the numinous potential of the built environment.

As a caveat, it is important to note here the emerging twenty-first-century secular concept of numinous, as implied by Christopher Hitchens et al.,[34] which I define as that feeling of awe, wonderment, or transcendence in the presence of natural beauty or art, or better still, the flow state we enter when we are fully engaged in creative activity. We have ample evidence of the impact of participation not only in the reduction of symptoms of ill health but, pivotally, in increased environmental mastery, personal autonomy, and civic engagement—the very factors that underpin well-being.[35]

In an article for the *Observer*, Kate Kellaway describes how Jencks, accompanied by her architect husband, Charles, recounted her experience of being given her prognosis by a consultant in an Edinburgh hospital in a way we are all too familiar with: waiting in an "awful interior" with neon lighting, and when asking the consultant, "How long have we got?" being given the reply, "Do you really want to know? Two to three months." Then, ushered into a windowless corridor because of the queue of people waiting to see the consultant, she and Charles were left to deal with these harsh facts.[36]

It was this experience, however, that set a chain of events in motion and saw Maggie and Charles exploring notions of time, space, and respect: after all, weren't these some of the most crucial needs when facing your own mortality? Maggie clearly "understood the need to feel in charge and not be a helpless passenger in a hospital production line" and devoted the remainder of her life to envisioning how this might happen.[37]

Over the last decade, the result of this experience has seen one woman's vision articulated into seven Maggie's Centres up and running and seven more in the planning with architects, including among others, Zaha Hadid, Frank Gehry, and Kisho Kurokawa.[38]

FIGURE 54   Nestling in the shadow of Charing Cross Hospital, the roof of Maggie's London, can just be seen. Photograph by Clive Parkinson.

The principles of the centers are very simple, based on what Charles Jencks describes as "the underlying notion that active involvement by patients in their own therapy can make a difference: to their attitude, to their family and friends and perhaps, even their health and outcome."[39] The design of the service and the mixture of architecture and art with the input of influential designers and architects offers the main focus, with four overarching goals:

- lowering the stress levels of patients;
- providing psychological and social support;
- helping navigate the information and treatment overload; and
- offering peace and stimulation.

Writing about her experience of treatment, Maggie describes how "at the moment most hospital environments say to the patient, in effect: 'How you feel is unimportant. You are not of value. Fit in with us, not us with you.' With very little effort and money this could be changed to something like: 'Welcome! And don't worry. We are here to re-assure you, and your treatment will be good and helpful to you."[40]

Maggie's Centres, largely funded by donations, offer exactly this support and care alongside a mix of the imaginative and the domestic, but crucially they place the

FIGURE 55   The fragrant gardens of Maggie's London. Photograph by Clive Parkinson.

individual at the center of the innovation. Visiting the award-winning Richard Rogers–designed Maggie's Centre in (see Fig. 54) London best illustrates how these environments impact the well-being of people affected by cancer and address by proxy some of the concerns highlighted by Abdul Gawande.

The center is hard to spot in the shadow of the 1970s modernist eyesore of Charing Cross Hospital in which it nestles on the permanently grid-locked Fulham Palace Road. Ironic, too, as the hospital's designer, Ralph Tubbs, was responsible for the stunning Dome of Discovery[41] at the Festival of Britain (given free reign with design, what might he have produced for Maggie's?).

Low-level and surrounded by lush foliage, the only sense that you get of this modest-sized building is the flashes of bright terracotta against the harsh backdrop of the hospital. Indeed, it's that startling Mediterranean palette that signals that you are somewhere completely different. The meandering pathway that leads you to the building is less concerned with signage (I don't think there's one in the building at all) than with coercing your curiosity. Your senses are bombarded with fragrances of lemon and rosemary, and the subtropical foliage provides shady nooks to contemplate your arrival.

This path has been taken by over sixty thousand people affected by cancer since it opened in 2008, and I wonder how typical my first impressions were. You enter the building through what feels like a domestic library, lit by the bright summer sky, and emerge straight into a large welcoming kitchen, with a giant wooden table and a fragrant

FIGURE 56   A wood-burning stove at the heart of the center. Photograph Maggie's Centre.

wood-burning stove. Didn't Frank Lloyd-Wright talk about the fire being the heart of any home? And Maggie's Centres certainly make a feature of this communal table, but this isn't a home, and its most definitely not a hospital, but the domestic is central to how this place feels, albeit on an aesthetic spectrum that many of us could only aspire to. And this is exactly what drove Maggie toward this vision—a place where people

FIGURE 57   Maggie's London. Photograph by Clive Parkinson.

facing the hurdles of serious illness would be given reassuring space, away from the harsh machinery of the clinical environment. No smell of detergent here; no clinical edge or staff separated by walls and signs. This is an open-plan space with movable walls, and as I enter, what greets me but the sound of laughter from a support group taking place. Laughter! I spend an hour or so in the center and observe people reading quietly or sitting in huddles deep in conversation. This building is modest, humane, and anything but intimidating. Importantly, it doesn't feel like a pristine space, where you can't relax, but critically (and as highlighted in the Maggie's Architectural Brief) "a calm friendly space where each individual can decide what strategy they want to adopt to support their medical treatment and their overall welfare." This might be managing stress and anxiety; it could be one of the many creative activities, or it might be getting advice with the practical, not least guidance on welfare benefits. In short, it is a place where you can engage deeply in conversation that's appropriate to you.

When I leave the center, I'm told I can take one of the fat, ripe figs growing up among the grapes that I've been eying up while we talked. A truly delicious gift alongside the warmth, exchange, and laughter.

My second story, about dementia, promises for me a more personal journey perhaps of relevance to us all, given our ageing demographic.

I was recently approached by a post-graduate student in three-dimensional design who as part of his master's, wanted to test a product he was working on. Darren

Browett[42] had been experimenting in new materials creating a range of small, hand-held objects that explored the notion of memento mori: objects loaded with memory, both literal and metaphorical.

Over the same period, I was working with occupational therapists and nursing staff on an NHS dementia assessment unit, exploring ways of engaging with the client group that went beyond reminiscence and singing old-time songs. I'd hoped to build on emerging activity taking place in Milwaukee, Wisconsin, led by Dr. Anne Davis Basting[43] and the public engagement work of MoMA: both furthering the work of the psychiatrist Professor Gene Cohen[44] and the belief that in working with people affected by dementia, we're wrong to focus on the deficits of the person and the symptoms of the disease; we should instead focus on their assets rather than getting bogged down with memory, as singling out the failing aspect of the person will ultimately frustrate and depress them, as Basting puts it in her book *Forget Memory*.[45]

Cohen took this argument further, positing that it's the symptoms of this disease that give us a potential new palette to work with, and when a person affected by dementia displays disinhibited behavior, it is in fact this disinhibition that gives rise to creative potential, often for the first time in a person's life. In short, this step-change in mind-set moves away from the signs and symptoms of a disease to a focus on the individual's assets, strengths, and satisfactions—what Cohen referred to as the "four S approach."[46]

Western culture seems over-reliant on a well-marketed pharmaceutical approach to ill-health and well-being, with an ever-increasing range of preventative medications for those at risk of disease. In the United Kingdom, people with dementia have been routinely prescribed antipsychotic medication as a method of controlling behaviors associated with the disease including wandering aimlessly, aggression, and displays of sexual promiscuity. Although the National Dementia Strategy[47] aims to address this institutional prescribing, there is an underlying concern that while these behaviors are symptomatic of the disease, they also reflect boredom, lack of liberty, frustration, and fear.

It is within this context that Browett and I tested his design to explore the possibility that his work could elicit conversation and stimulation—bearing in mind the potential of the arts to engage at a deeper emotional level rather than focusing on the intellectual. Browett was initially particularly interested in the potency of relational and shared souvenirs and memory, belonging not solely to one person but existing between people.

Building on the work of Constantin Boym,[48] investigating moments of collective memory around tragic situations, Browett produced a series of mnemonic devices which, he hypothesized, people could put their feelings into and somehow make memories more permanent: objects that could be loaded with meaning and act somehow as a catalyst to conversation and debate.

Browett took the view that "it is the personal moments that provide the measure and meaning to life, and are the events that shape us. The rights of passage of birth, childhood, love and partnership, old age and death are the emotional milestones making human experiences that are the common properties of mankind across time and culture. Objects that mark out these life events," which—he suggests, "become personal memorials and reminders of our shared humanity."[49]

Early on in his exploration, Browett investigated the complex structures of pollen and the "powerful symbolism of seeds as a metaphor to re-connect us with the natural world [representing the] beginning and end of the life of plants, and the rebirth...of seeds and fruit and the endless and ever repeating cycle."[50]

From this idea of seeds and nature, he crafted prototype designs combining new technologies and handcrafting. From his experimentation, his desire to create beautiful, high-quality, and challenging objects that were loaded with imaginative potential, he created what became known as, his "seedpods."

The pods are small articulated objects, far more robust than they look, that turn inside out on themselves. Each contains a thermoplastic seed with an embossed design of a domestic object, person, or pet. These objects, no matter how precious they may appear, demand a sense of inquiry through handling and play. I would suggest that these loaded objects offer something very different to a memento mori and possibly offer a powerful vehicle for facilitating difficult conversations akin to a secular Ars Moriendi.[51]

FIGURE 58   Maggie's London. Photograph by Clive Parkinson.

Using a participatory action research approach to his work, Browett worked with patients, family, and staff to test his design. They had a profound impact on engagement. Here's what one occupational therapist said:

> The patients were fascinated by the shape of the outer object and they shared what they thought the object was, or what it reminded them of, which encouraged thought and communication. They then worked out how to extract the centre…and were drawn to it by the bright colour…and the image etched onto the surface sparked off a whole new set of questions. The objects, stimulated speech, thought and

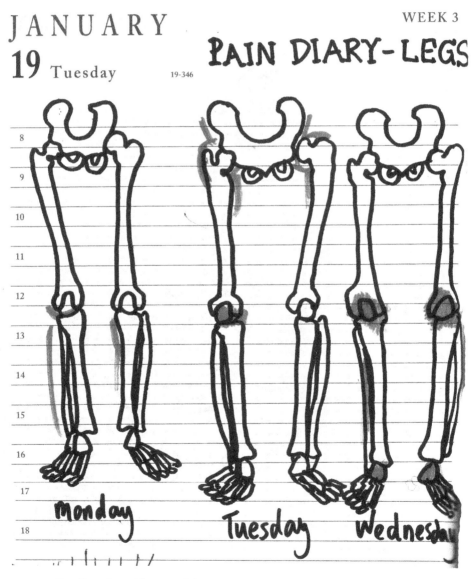

FIGURE 59   Pain Diary Legs. Photograph by Lois Blackburn (Arthur and Martha).

communication...during this session one lady who had significant word finding difficulties, was free of her symptoms.[52]

This work did impact on memory in the sense that Anne Basting illustrates, where memory is not only an act of retrieval but an act of creative storytelling using imagination based on the here and now, emphasizing that memory is relational and does not belong to one person. This small-scale research has established that through challenging design Browett's intervention has enabled

- the making of connections between personal stories and the world at large;
- exploration and exchange of ideas;
- intellectual stimulation and engagement in imaginative activity;
- participation in an activity that fostered personal growth and a wider understanding of the individual; and
- being fully absorbed in the present moment.

It is perhaps this idea of being actively absorbed in the present moment that has the most significance: the potential of regaining part of yourself. Through his practice, Browett aimed to create meaningful objects that aimed to be "cathartic in situations that are considered to be a crisis."[53] He succeeded, with many of the people involved engaging in the activity way beyond the normal few minutes, up to well over an hour—time in which the participants experienced real sentience.

FIGURE 60   Communal Kitchen. Photograph Maggie's Centre.

Globally, health services typified by the United Kingdom's fragile NHS are, in very real terms, geared toward the diagnosis and treatment of sickness and not to the promotion of health and well-being. Imagining ourselves, or our loved ones, receiving a

FIGURE 61   Marjorie Raynor. Photograph by Lois Blackburn (Arthur and Martha).

diagnosis of a serious illness is useful in beginning to understand the relevance of design and the arts in relation to the condition of being human.

I have suggested that in the face of serious health crises, the arts offer a key to making sense of our experience of being human, and contribute to humanizing the procedures and processes of treatment. Research suggests that EBD has some very real impacts on patient outcomes and, by proxy, the potential to impact on economic factors. The temptation of focusing on savings and profit for health providers leads, however, to the old trap of market forces, rather than the ethical context, being the dominant factor in healthcare delivery.

Conspicuous consumption and selfish individualism brought on by a belief in the free market and all that it offers have fed a culture of greed and materialism, which has, in part, led to the current global recession. This same consumer culture has had an insidious effect on health services, which have become target obsessed, competition driven, and rife with inequalities. Design is widely associated with beauty and aspiration and is a potent symbol of celebrity-obsessed superficiality: for whitened, straightened teeth and flawless bronzed skin. Well-being is increasingly associated with the appearance of health, and a burgeoning high-street cosmetic industry is ready to suck out your fat, pump up your lips, and take away your lines. Added to the rise in preventative health technologies, we are witnessing what the general practitioner Iona Heath describes as "a new arena of human greed, which responds to an enduring fear."[54] Our selfish individualism may also enable us to take the notion of interior design to its inevitable limits through customized DNA profiling, sex selection, and shopping list kit-formed children of the future.

We have bought into the consumer myth of our own invincibility wholesale, and our relationship with clinicians reflects this "customer is always right" retail market reality. Because I have succumbed to male-pattern baldness and the inevitable macular degeneration associated with my long years, should I treat these as disease or an inevitable consequence of ageing? Clearly I can buy eyeglasses, probably one of the most successfully designed and marketed medical devices available; I could even go the whole hog and have a hair transplant. Here then is my plea to designers, scientists, artists, and philosophers: as future patients, we must collaborate around our often divergent vision with one another to affect a paradigm shift in the way health is perceived and well-being is nurtured. There are enormous and challenging ideas to test, and the ways in which we support people toward the end of their lives should be central to this conversation.

Jonah Lehrer describes the tensions between science and art and suggests that building on C. P. Snow's third culture, in which "scientists and artists continue to describe the world in incommensurate languages"[55] that we aspire to a fourth culture in which, "art and science can be useful, and both can be true," with art acting as "a necessary counterbalance to the glories and excesses of scientific reductionism, especially as they are applied to the human experience."[56]

Writing in the *British Medical Journal,* Iona Heath provides us with some difficult food for thought around this conversation on ageing, illness, and mortality. Heath suggests that as governments strive to reduce mortality, they are ultimately fighting a losing battle, as "the mortality rate for the population will always be 100%, [and if] we continue to fight all causes of mortality, particularly in extreme old age, we have no hope of success, and we will consume an ever increasing proportion of healthcare resources for ever diminishing returns."[57]

In her paper "What Do We Want to Die From?" Heath describes the natural process of death in old age and the trap that clinicians find themselves in, as their efforts to treat one disease is met by another that takes its place. Despite all the evidence, preventative medicines like statins are prescribed to people over 70, which successfully reduce deaths from cardiovascular disease, only to increase mortality rates through cancer and dementia. She cites a U.S. study of care in people dying of advanced cancer or dementia in acute hospitals, which found that "for 24% of both groups cardiopulmonary resuscitation was attempted and that 55% of those with dementia died with feeding tubes in place."[58] Her explicit question is, "Is this what we want for ourselves or those we love—or indeed for anyone?"[59]

Succinctly, Heath comments, "Authentic health care for the old and frail has much more to do with helping to preserve their dignity, treating them with affection, and supporting their continued involvement in social activities, rather than the pursuit of ever-more elusive cures."[60] As I write this chapter, an argument is raging in the United Kingdom about assisted dying: as one of the last great taboos in society, this ethical minefield is one our fourth culture should engage in.

While patient involvement in healthcare is well-established, there is still a feeling of tokenism, lack of vision, and genuine voice. Experience-Based Design, offers something beyond Evidence-Based Design which puts patients' and users' experience at the heart of the process, echoing Kath Weston's call for theory that comes from people outside of the academic (straight) sphere, which she describes as "Street Theory," and which offers "a wellspring of explanatory devices and rhetorical strategies in their own right."[61] Experience-Based Design, as Paul Bate and Glenn Robert illustrate perfectly, pushes "to

FIGURE 62 *Fortuitous Novelties* (seed pods) by Darren Browett.

widen and intensify the search for 'better' and more effective theories and approaches to transformation, particularly those at the participative end of the spectrum."[62]

The UK Alzheimer 100 project has seen codesign put into practice and has involved "stakeholders of dementia to generate ideas and make decisions based on their experiences, rather than focusing on only improving technology and drugs."[63] My own work in the NHS builds on that of Darren Browett and has opened up the possibility of patients, caregivers, and staff influencing the design of a new dedicated dementia treatment center and giving voice to patient treatment options.

Perhaps Experience-Based Design will enable genuine engagement with civic society, in relation to health and well-being, and the broader conversations around our experience of end of life care, which while challenging, will present the most innovative of collaborations with the greatest of opportunities.

Gene Cohen reminds us, that "the optimal treatment of the patient focuses not just on clinical problems but also on the individual potential of that person. It's only when problems and potential are considered together that health is best promoted and illness best cared for. This is the ultimate art and creativity of medicine and healthcare."[64]

Through divergent thinking and convergent collaboration, the arts and sciences offer us something bigger than our transient individual egos. Designers, scientists, artists, and philosophers can facilitate something profound and nonprescribed. By engaging with wider society and addressing the deficit of imagination posited by Richard Smith,[65] this fourth culture can inform and influence a generational cultural shift around how health and well-being are understood, and ultimately how we care for each other.

Can the arts cure cancer or dementia? Of course not. But in the face of serious illness and our own mortality, do the arts have any real relevance? I suggest that the connection is profound and yet incredibly subtle. The design of Maggie's Centres and the craftsmanship of Darren Browett's seedpods are equally uplifting and life-affirming, and neither were intended as vehicles for discussions on mortality, but both offer new opportunities for deeply meaningful interaction. Our fourth culture dialogue should be less focused on superficiality and gloss and more deeply engaged with a new philosophy of how we live our lives and, explicitly, end our days. A difficult conversation perhaps but one that the arts are best placed to address, enabling a new humanist aesthetic that not only stimulates and provokes our senses but facilitates breakpoint discussion.[66]

23

Design for Ageing-in-Place for High-Density Living in Asia: A Comparative Analysis on Residential Design in Singapore, Japan, and Hong Kong

ONG SWEE HONG

INTRODUCTION

In accordance to a 2006 report presented by the Inter-Ministerial Committee on the demographics of those greater than age 65 in Singapore, it is reported that by 2030, one in five Singapore residents will be greater than 65 years old.[1] Also, with reference to a published report by the Statistics Bureau of Japan, the proportion of the aged population to total population in Japan will increase to approximately 29.2 percent by year 2020 and to 39.6 percent by 2050.[2] While in Hong Kong, according to the study by the Census and Statistic Department of Hong Kong, the projected population greater than 60 will increase to about 30.8 percent of the total population.[3] As various strategies have been adopted by each of the highlighted case-study countries to cope with the issue of rapidly ageing populations, the examination of these selected case-study countries will potentially provide insight on how high-density living environments can be modified to accommodate for the potential change in needs or suggest new directions in design to accommodate for this anticipated shift in housing type with reference to its occupants; from the sensitive remodeling of the existing residential spatial types to the design parameters required for healthy aged and potential for the adaptation of the existing optimum residential models that promotes aging-in-place to suit an Asian cultural context. Admittedly, studies in successful models that examine health and design or perhaps residential space models that promote smooth readaptation catering for aging-in-place are still on the drawing board and require rigorous understanding in a variety of factors—from understanding the design requirement of the healthy aged to culture, social, and living patterns. There suggests a potential to understand that such spatial models should be developed with relation to its occupants, with thorough understanding of the unique living space type preference of the particular culture or the living patterns of its occupants.

This idea of modifying our living environment to the needs of the aged is aligned with the concept of ageing-in-place that has been widely embraced in recent years. Studies have shown that this will result in the minimization of stress from moving the healthy aged into a nursing home and will help to maximize independence. Furthermore, with low birth rates and a rapidly ageing population, the demographic trend means that the aged will be a potentially large market sector in demand of a special housing type. In Asian society, this concept of ageing-in-place is not foreign, as the family nuclei is usually composed of three generations all housed within one living environment. Therefore, we are now faced with the question of how will the high-rise, high-density living environment adapt itself to suit the idea of ageing-in-place, while accommodating the special needs of these individuals. With reference to the case-study cities highlighted, there is a need to examine how design can promote the readaptation of our interior living environment and to anticipate for the changing needs of its occupants. Perhaps this new wave has also signaled a new search for a housing model and evolution of a new spatial model, yet, in the midst of providing for universal design, we will need to anticipate for how we also ease the transition into ageing and provide for the required infrastructure and amenities.

CHANGING DEMOGRAPHICS IN ASIA

Traditionally, Asian family structures consists of three generations of families living under the same roof, and Asian values heavily regard the aged as treasures; with emphasis on filial piety, care for elderly in Asia usually falls in the hands of their children.[4] Table 23.1 indicates that in Asia (east, southeast, central), on the average, more than 70 percent of the elderly population live with their children and grandchildren. Furthermore, it was reported that in thirty years time, Singapore will join the ranks of Japan as one of the three countries in Asia that has the highest proportion of the aged population.[5] In accordance to the Department of Statistics in Singapore, the number of residents aged 65 years and above living alone rose from 15,313 to 21,858 in 2005.[6] In 2001, according to the Hong Kong Population Census, about 14.9 percent of the overall population are aged 60 or above, and the proportion of the aged 60 and above is set to increase in Asia in years to come.

This impending "silver tsunami" might suggest new directions in design and especially in the area of spatial remodeling in existing space types, yet these might also pose some new issues in terms of care for the elderly—how the current residential models, in relation to the space and total environment, will react to this change in demographics. How can we ensure that these elderly are able to live independently, and how can

TABLE 23.1 Living Arrangement of Elderly Population (aged 60 and above)—in percentage of household, by Selected Regions and Sub-regions of the World

REGION/ SUB-REGION	LIVING ARRANGEMENT				
	ALONE (%)	COUPLE ONLY (%)	WITH CHILDREN OR GRANDCHILDREN (%)	WITH OTHER RELATIVES OR NONRELATIVES (%)	TOTAL (%)
Asia	7	16	74	4	100
East	9	20	70	1	100
Southeast	6	13	73	9	100
South-central	4	9	83	-	100
Africa	8	9	74	8	100
Europe	26	43	26	4	100
South	19	39	38	4	100
Latin America & Caribbean	9	16	62	14	100
North America	26	47	19	8	100

Source: UN 2005, Table II.5, p 36

design contribute to the aspects of healthy ageing? With the changing demographics profile in several developed or developing Asian countries, and especially coupled with traditional Asian perspectives on ageing and care for the elderly, and the social stigma of sending parents to retirement or nursing homes, there exists a potential need to integrate these residential space models and design considerations prematurely into the existing design considerations. This is particularly relevant for both Hong Kong and Singapore where faced with a shortage of land and coupled with the high-rise urban environment, there is a need to examine if the current environment can be improved or redefined to accommodate for the potential change required to deal with the impending silver tsunami.

The concepts of ageing-in-place[7] and assisted living[8] have been adopted by most countries in Asia in recent years and have been popular as living concepts for the aged in Europe and the United States. So, with the current availability of a greater choice in housing and with greater economic power, coupled with higher education levels, the retirees in Asia are aware of the choices they have regarding residential design, and the possibilities of integrating the two living concepts for the aged will be examined for the Asian contexts. It is anticipated that this generation of baby boomers will be able to give rise to more differentiated housing types for retirement living in the near future. Lifestyle and housing needs vary in the second half of life just as much or even more so than in earlier phases, depending on "social milieu, generation and age."[9]

Although we are faced with the issue of how to accommodate for our rapidly ageing population, our understanding of the existing housing typologies for retirement living and the facilities required or even the lifestyle of the medically stable elderly remain vague. Aside from understanding the basic demographic structure of rapidly ageing Asian communities, it is vital to know the different housing requirements and needs in order to design in relation to the targeted demographic. A recent *Straits Times* interview with Mr. Paul Klaassen, the founder of Sunrise Senior Living, pointed out possible new frameworks of living when faced with a rapidly ageing population. Mainly, one of the concepts behind his success in the development for housing for the aged were the ideas of flexibility and adaptation, where flexibility can be perceived as the stepped health care services the residents can have in times of need and the manner in which their existing systems can accommodate for various requirements at different stages of ageing. Therefore, it is not merely in the provision of a universal environment that reacts to the physical changes we will need for the ageing population, but the software of such residential development must adapt for the daily emotional or medical needs or the performance of daily chores for its residents. In short, there is no one-size-fits-all solution when it comes to the provision of a well-considered living environment for the aged. But, it is crucial to understand that residential design for the aged is no longer institutionalized, so the design can potentially take into consideration the need for flexibility, to be able to accommodate for individual's needs and to allow the system to be tailored to fit the different tiers of needs and requirements for ageing individuals.

Research that has shown that the living condition of the aged will directly impact their sense of well-being, hence it is important for designers to anticipate, understand, and design with relation to their needs during the planning and implementation of the design. Aside from making necessary physical provisions (in relation to universal design requirements) to facilitate ease of use of space for all, it is important for designers to understand the other aspects that will relate to good living conditions, which is designing with references to social, emotional, mental, and cultural needs of individuals, across different parts of the world. Hence, there might not be a universal solution to "universal design." For instance, it is necessary for the environment to be conducive to socializing by allowing for more community-based activities for the elderly to interact with their neighbors. Such activities facilitate the cultivation of well-being and belonging of self to the community, which can help prevent instances of neglect and to foster closer bonds between the elderly and the community. But can a certain space layout or space type facilitate social activities to occur? Questions of how design or architectural form facilitates community exchanges can be inspired through proportion studies of communal spaces to private spaces and the interface between the two mentioned space types. Can a certain manner to model space or architectural volume facilitate intracommunity exchanges? Or perhaps, will such framework be more acceptable in the East, where social living is more prized as compared to the West? This is also, perhaps, more relevant for the high-rise, high-density environment, which we will often associate with compact living spaces, and hence communal spaces will need to be strategically placed and rightfully considered in relation to their use within a vertical community.

In Hong Kong and Singapore, the two cities are facing similar issues in relation to housing and population demographic change, and it will not be possible to build beyond geographical boundaries, nor are we able to replicate the exact formats the

European and American cities are adapting for their ageing population due to our different cultural values and belief systems. So, it might be important for us to understand how we could enhance the housing provision to facilitate for better ageing-in-place with relation to the particular context of the two cities, while accommodating for future changes that might take place with this shift in demographics by understanding the potential design can have. Furthermore, it is necessary for architectural design, interior design, and space planning to consider these needs, especially in instances when the majority of the population in both cities resides in high-rise buildings that are composed of units with floor plans that are of a standard basic configuration. Therefore, design parameters necessary for any future anticipated changes due to the changing needs of occupants can be factored into design in phases of early design implementation.

UNDERSTANDING VARIOUS LIVING CONCEPTS AND DESIGN PRINCIPLES FOR THE AGED

To establish the different housing design guidelines, we will need to consider the provisions that make for healthy living conditions for the aged population; there are a few ways to start. For this chapter, we will first understand the different existing current housing typologies for the elderly and how they will react to facilitate different needs of the aged and whether these frameworks can be further expanded into a possibility of future space/environment types to be redeveloped with consideration in the context of high-rise, high-density living conditions.

Currently, nursing homes and skilled nursing facilities are residential options for elderly who depend on care providers in the fulfillment of their daily needs, and these are usually with medical facilities to accommodate for the needs of their residents. Often, elderly who are residing in the nursing home are unable to reside alone without assistance. In addition to residences with integrated medical facilities, some retirement housing providers in Europe have embraced the concept of assisted living, where there are facilities integrated in the group of retirement housing to cater for the needs of its elderly residents; they allow for individual autonomy among a communal living environment.

For the elderly who do not require as much medical attention, we have the concept of ageing-in-place, which has been gaining popularity in recent years; often the concept has to be complemented by technology to facilitate independence among the elderly, from safety at home to continuous learning. But, primarily, the concept behind ageing-in-place is not merely to minimize the stress from moving the elderly from their familiar background, but the well-being and the ability of the elderly to reside safely and healthily is a major concern. The initiative also comprises three other concepts: independent living, assisted living, and Alzheimer's care. Universal design[10] is another essential consideration for the design of such housing communities and is gaining popularity in good design for all ages and in all aspects of design. Besides these primary concepts in the provision of a healthy, accessible environment for the elderly, we have several different housing options presented in Europe, such as "Service House, Pleghem, Life Span Housing, Communal Housing, Group Home, Learn-to Housing, Congregate House, Assisted Living Housing and Home-Care-Based Nursing."[11] These varied typologies and their integrated facilities are too extensive to be covered in this chapter.

However, most of the current residential typologies for the aged are primarily designed for physically or mentally impaired residents. These might constitute a small proportion of aged populations who require extensive care in their day-to-day living, but how will design respond to the healthy aged, and are there any existing frameworks that relate to the healthy aged who might not require as much assistance but will want to reside in a health enabling condition? Also, at the same time, we will need to prevent instances of overcare[12] or undercare[13] in the provision of the residential design framework for the healthy aged.

Aside from understanding the various concepts for different elderly living arrangements, there are several design principles that must be understood from research that examine factors to consider in residential design for the aged. Victor A. Regnier had presented four theories for consideration: "Reginer and Pynoos Common Research Themes, Wilson's Assisted Living Concepts and Attributes, Cohen and Weisman's Therapeutic Goals for Dementia Facilities and Reginer and Pynoo's Environment Behaviour Principles."[14] In summary, for good residential design for the aged, we have to examine both the physical design aspects of the space and the living conditions for its residents. This can be perceived from the encouraged community living and interaction among the residents that are advocated in the mentioned theories.[15] The different needs of these individuals should to be recognized, allowing them flexibility in their ability to exercise choice and control. These points emphasize the need for the residences and the environments to aid in the inhabitants' mental stimulation, ease of orientation, and adaptation to growing needs—mental, psychological, or physical.

Designing a healthy environment for the aged is multifaceted. Housing options can respond to an understanding the physical limitation of the elderly, the mental well-being of occupants (patients suffering from dementia or Alzheimer's), physical health conditions of the occupants, or even to react to the different spectrum of ageing, and hence, with all this in mind, the variety of housing options will differ. So, it is suggested to have post-occupancy surveys or measured parameters to understand the improvements that can be made to the physical environment and to allow for design empathy toward those who might require special attention. Besides creating an accessible built environment, we will need to have structures in place that encourage interaction among the residents and facilities that support mental stimulation. This can be translated into a few strategies: to understand the possibilities of change in configuration in internal space layout or the ease of removal of internal partitioning within the typical floor plans to accommodate for flexibility in living arrangements. Hence, this might point toward further research on the materials that compose the divider panels or if these panels can be designed as a movable integrated system, where services can be integrated into the partitions; for example, these partitions can be a storage device to minimize clutter while allowing the aged flexibility to reconfigure their environment to suit their needs for space. Furthermore, the

finishes of existing homes can be considered with the possibilities of integrating amenities that might be required for safe aged living—nonslip surfaces, sensitive detailing of
the heights of door handles and switches, and careful specification of the hardware to be
selected for interior finishes. All these suggest possibilities of expanding the categories of
study on aged living into frameworks that look at the anticipation of future living conditions, while integrating one's sensitivity in understanding the aged's living needs.

EXISTING HOUSING OPTIONS FOR THE AGED
IN SINGAPORE AND HONG KONG

Provisions for housing for the aged have evolved from mere accommodations at care
homes or nursing homes. Now, the idea of aged living has been diversified to accommodate for different housing models, with the primary focus on a model that imposes
minimal physical and emotional stress on the elderly, as well as a housing model that
adapts to our varied physical needs with different stages in ageing. With the emergence of new housing models for the aged, Huber, Hugentobler, and Walthert-Galli[16]
state that most people will prefer to live in their own apartment or house. Also, with
the different needs and awareness of residences for the aged, we are seeing a new type of
housing for the aged gradually gaining popularity in Europe. These combine collective
living with different levels of care and services provided for residences which promote
independence and interaction among occupants. However, although there exist various
design guidelines and specifications recommended for universal living, the responses
and views of such design recommendations for elderly residents have yet to be studied,
nor have studies been done on such collective housing through post-occupancy surveys.

In Hong Kong, the "thrust of government's housing policy is to assist the low-income families who cannot afford private rental housing through the provision of public rental housing."[17] In order to cater to public housing requirements, the Hong Kong
government established two statutory organizations, Hong Kong Housing Authority
(HKHA)[18] and Hong Kong Housing Society (HKHS)[19] to address the needs of public housing and to provide housing assistance, as the fundamentals behind the government's housing scheme. In comparison to Singapore's public housing provision, as of
March 2010, about 30 percent of Hong Kong's population, approximately 2.06 million people, lived in public rental housing estates. As of March 2010, about 471,200
of age 60 and above, which represents about 39 percent of Hong Kong's elderly population, lived in public housing flats of HKHA and HKHS.[20] To cater to the residential
for the aged, the "HKHS is operating the pilot Senior Citizen Residence Scheme which
provides purpose-built housing with integrated health care facilities on a "lease-for-
life" basis to eligible senior citizens in the middle income group."[21] Additionally, there
are plans for two elderly housing developments in Tin Shui Wai and North Point (see
Table 23.2).

However, in Hong Kong, as the public housing residential provision is mainly determined by market forces and as the selection parameters are already in place, it will function differently as compared to Singapore, where it is greatly accessible for all. Therefore,

TABLE 23.2 Population by Type of Housing, 1996, 2001 and 2006

TYPE OF HOUSING	1996		2001		2006	
	NUMBER	% OF TOTAL	NUMBER	% OF TOTAL	NUMBER	% OF TOTAL
Public rental housing	2,391,857	38.5	2,135,624	31.9	2,129,252	31.0
Housing Authority subsidized sale flats (2)	691,895	11.1	1,080,377	16.1	1,173,115	17.1
Housing Society subsidized sale flats (3)	17,117	0.3	51,315	0.8	48,106	0.7
Private permanent housing (2)(3)	2,912,626	46.9	3,284,001	49.0	3,383,890	49.3
Temporary housing	124,617	2.0	72,035	1.1	45,504	0.7
Nondomestic housing (4)	69,254	1.1	79,142	1.2	81,413	1.2
Total	6,207,366	100.0	6,702,494	100.0	6,861,280	100.0

Source: 2006 Population By-census Office, Census and Statistic Department, The Government of Hong Kong Special Administrative Region

(1) The figures exclude persons living on board vessels.
(2) Housing Authority subsidized sale flats include flats that can be traded in the open market in the 1996 Population By-census. These flats are classified under "Private permanent housing" in the 2001 Population Census and the 2006 Population By-census.
(3) In the 1996 Population By-census, Housing Society subsidized sale flats include flats that can be traded in the open market. These flats are classified under "Private permanent housing" in the 2001 Population Census and the 2006 Population By-census.
(4) Please see "Definition of Terms" for the detailed coverage of this housing type. Since the counting rules for quarters in hospitals, penal institutions, and student dormitories adopted in the 1996 Population By-census, the 2001 Population Census, and the 2006 Population By-census are different, caution is required in making comparison. For example, students living in individual rooms in student dormitories were regarded as living in "domestic households" in the 1996 Population By census, whereas they are regarded as living in "collective households" in the 2001 Population Census and the 2006 Population By-census.

the extent of improving the existing living condition for aged living, generally lacking an impetus that might be driven by government policy, is lacking in Hong Kong. In recent years, the spectrum of housing possibilities for the second half of life increased to beyond the care homes, and in Singapore there are plans to build more retirement homes to cater for the needs of our rapidly ageing nation. Specifically, in March 2010, there was a media announcement of a site in Jalan Jurong Kechil to be released as a short-term land lease (thirty years of land lease) for development of a possible retirement housing development. While the Singapore government reacted to the projected rapidly ageing population and the possible housing options to be provided with specific relation to these people with special needs, the response from developers had been lukewarm, citing reasons of the underdeveloped property transfer law pertaining to the conversion of retirement homes for passing down to another generation and the low marginal gain for the thirty years land lease. This raises the issue whether there is a need to build new

retirement housing developments or to reexamine if the current housing can be retrofitted with facilities or be physically altered to allow for elderly to live comfortably and
independently in their existing living environment. In Singapore, changes in the infrastructure have been made in accordance to the provisions to facilitate ageing-in-place,
and a few schemes are in place to address the physical requirements to accommodate
universal design and ease of accessibility of movement. To date, about 124 housing precincts have undertaken the Lift Upgrading Programme (LUP)[22] and about 122 precincts
had completed the Main Upgrading Programme (MUP).[23]

The above illustrates the existing infrastructural changes that are proposed for Singapore and Hong Kong to accommodate for change in population demographics. Yet, these
provide the framework for understanding the potential changes that can be introduced
as a result of adapting for change in our existing physical environment and the need for
our existing residential infrastructure to respond to the changes of the requirements of
its occupants. Furthermore, these changes are necessary for Singapore and Hong Kong,
where it is more common for the residents to own the units they reside in, and hence,
these homeowners can be offered an option for their housing condition to change with
relation to their age. Yet, such modifications in the physical environment can also be
provided in the design conceptualization phase, and good planning can anticipate future
changes that might be required for the needs of the changing population demographics.

Although the concept of designing for the aged has originated and been popular in
the West, there remains a need for different interpretation of such models to succeed for
the East due to different living habits, social models, or cultural outlook. With a strong
social stigma in Asia against sending healthy aged to retirement homes or homes for
the aged or even for the healthy aged to choose to live independently, it is important to
ensure integration between these units and the existing home options available for the
healthy aged that relate to an Asian context. So, retirement villages or developments
might not be appealing for Asians as few will like to check themselves into such developments. Hence, to start the discussion, it is necessary to understand the differences in attitude toward living patterns that relate to cultural requirements of the population. First,
a culturally specific outlook regarding residential space allocation: as a result of the living
patterns and the attitude toward family life or community living, in relation to space,
shared spaces are more prized than individual living spaces in Asia. And these shared or
communal spaces can be translated to an inserted space that forms a relationship with
private areas—such as bedrooms. And, these might even point toward the need for the
conventional residential layout to be reexamined and to deconstruct the internalized
spaces, to conceive, perhaps, of a more efficient living model for single elderly in relation
to the rest of the community.

Second, there is a possibility to study the existing average family size and number of
people living within the vertical community and to allow a mix of different floor plans
for different occupants' requirements to exist within the same block. This will provide a
variety to the profile of the residents and allow a better integration of the aged into the
greater community and not to cluster all the aged population into a single block. This
also suggests a departure from the conventional housing type model in Singapore and

Hong Kong, where the arrangement of the housing units is a mix of floor plans of different sizes, but there can be a potential to examine even a mix of profiles, where the housing to be provided for healthy aged can be integrated into the new housing models that cater to the larger population. The two above points relate to potential changes and design ideas and can reshape architectural forms and the interaction between spaces and be extended into new design types or space types.

MAKING DESIGN PROVISIONS AND CONSIDERATIONS

The way to move forward for housing for the aged in Singapore and Hong Kong can be an integrative approach, where the existing housing fabric will need to cater to changes required for the population, along with enhanced care to enable living in a high-rise apartment. It is essential that during planning, policy-making, and design stages of these ageing residential projects that minimal changes are made to the existing infrastructure while simultaneously supporting the principles of ageing-in-place and community care. Yet, it must be understood that the integrative approach to ageing-in-place should not be limited to making physical improvements to our living environment, nor to make design provisions, but there must be an understanding of how to facilitate for healthy living within the highly urbanized living environment. Not concentrating on the internalized environment but the integration of the accessibilities to amenities, transportation—ensuring a barrier-free environment, ensuring independence for the elderly.

Upon understanding the various case studies and presented theories, the following considerations had been established to coincide with the various requirements to facilitate ageing-in-place.

Evaluation of the Existing System

There remains a need to understand the adequacy of the existing systems and their weaknesses to facilitate for the ability to allow for ageing-in-place. We must be able to understand the needs of the elderly in conjunction with the need for existing policies in order for design to react to and address what is lacking. Recently in Singapore, senior minister Mr. Goh Chok Tong revealed a pilot study on the elderly population residing in the Singapore Marine Parade GRC (General Constituency) to understand the needs and requirements of the elderly, as well as to facilitate government policies in response to these requirements. The study includes questions on what the elderly feel are improvements they need in their neighborhoods.

Coupled with the need to improve the living environment, home care services must be made accessible for the aged so that they do not have to relocate to a nursing home—unless necessary—and can be cared for by their relatives or family members. However, with high prices and lack of service providers in the area of home-based care, this is definitely an area to be examined in terms of government subsidy and policy changes to make this accessible to those in need. Yet with the concerns pointed out by the article "Improving

Home Care," published in the *Straits Times*,[24] the luxury of home care is often out of reach for most who require the service. Therefore, there are suggestions to examine if government subsidies can be given to those families that require the service and to facilitate the growth of this new service. Besides encouraging the elderly to live independently without the need to be relocated, the Singapore government also introduced housing incentives to children who are looking for a new home in proximity to their parents, and this rebate has proven to be effective in encouraging many three-generation families to stay in proximity, if not co-reside. This will help ease the stress on the families who will need to cater to or care for an elderly in their midst. These measures will minimize the need for the elderly to be relocated to nursing homes and the stress that might arise from this shift, in addition to reducing the strain on limited places at nursing homes.

The Singapore Building and Construction Authority (BCA) introduced the Code on Barrier-Free Accessibility in Buildings 1990 and the Code of Practice for Universal Design so that architects can translate these parameters and apply them in projects. The Hong Kong Housing Society published the "Universal Design Guidebook For Residential Development In Hong Kong" in 2005 as a guide to design and for implementation.[25] In Singapore, it is mandatory to incorporate these codes in design in recent years, and the Accessibility Fund has been set up to aid in the upgrading of existing building to be "barrier-free accessibility" compliant. In relation to the design of the physical environment, it is suggested that the local regulations or laws can allow for the aged to have various options to monetize their fixed assets to offset the costs of changing their living environment to suit their growing needs, for instance, installing additional hand-bars or anti-slip surfaces, or to widen interior openings. Yet, in Asian society, legal claims filed by parents is the last resort adopted by most.

Design and Implementation

Besides recommendation for policy and protection of legal rights for the elderly, we will need to accommodate for changes in the physical environment. For the design of homes, the interior environment must be able to accommodate for mobility, and facilities must allow for the elderly to reside independently. Emergency or call switches and similar amenities must be incorporated and be within easy reach for the occupants—repositioning of lighting switches, appropriate lighting levels at home, and the material specification of the house must allow for the elderly to move at ease. Furthermore, there must be provisions made in terms of fittings and even considerations made for the width of doorways to facilitate the movement of wheelchair-bound residents. The area of the house must allow for easy manageability in terms of cleaning, and external services must be provided to help in the regular maintenance of living conditions and house cleaning.

In addition to the maintenance of the interior environment, the exterior environment must be well-suited to allow occupants to live individually in a communal environment. Other than basing the design principles of the interior environment on barrier-free design principles, the exterior environment must also facilitate for the ease of movement to allow for the elderly to maintain contact with friends and relatives and to reinstate their confidence in their ability to navigate their environment. Furthermore, the residence should arrange activities to allow for residents to interact, as well as allowing for continual activities for mental stimulation. Yet, it is noted that we must still allow for flexibility within the communal environment, where individuals can be grouped in accordance to their needs, preferences, and services (meals, cleaning, medical, etc.).

Post-Occupancy Survey and Maintaining
a Good Living Condition

In Singapore, there are volunteer programs to make sure that the elderly are taken care of and ready to be assisted when in need. In Singapore, there exist several schemes to take care of the elderly who are residing alone; for example, the Lions Befrienders Service Association.[26] Aside from catering for potential changes in the physical environment, the Singapore government has implemented two projects, Project CHEER[27] and Project SPHERE,[28] to integrate the aged with other age groups through volunteer-initiated activities. Furthermore, the existing estate's facilities must be reevaluated and maintained on a regular basis to ensure that the occupant's needs are taken care of. Care and medical facilities should be made accessible to the elderly, especially for those who are needy of frequent care by medical personnel or home-care services. There might be a possibility to understand and reevaluate the elderly's concerns and needs prior to the estate's upgrading program, and it will be good to look into how the services for elderly (day care, medical stations, emergency stations) are planned, not only for the matured districts but all estates that anticipate changes for future needs.

CONCLUSION

The silver tsunami is not an issue restricted to the developed countries but will awash several cities in Asia in less than half-a-century's time. Therefore, measures should be in place to ease the transition into a greying society, and the challenge is particularly great in cities such as Singapore and Hong Kong, where we are constrained by our limited land area. Therefore, we will need to look into an approach that is not the same as those adopted in Europe or America but one that suits the framework of living within a high-rise urban environment and one that anticipates future directions in housing with relation to the demographic shift that is unique of the two cities. It is necessary to reevaluate the current living situation and its adaptation toward healthy living for the elderly and potential design directions that tailor toward this future direction in design. Besides altering the physical environment to facilitate for ease in mobility for the elderly, post-occupancy evaluations must be done at interim phases; policies can be reexamined to react to the impending changes that might be brought about by our rapidly ageing population and to relate to the changes in our residential environment as regards housing policies, profile of the occupants, or even to look into the conceptualization of a housing model that is flexible and unique to an Asian context.

24

Demographics and Identity

STEPHANIE WHITE

Demographic data comes from the division of a population into fine gradations of difference that can be measured, correlated, and recombined to understand trends. Spending patterns based on economic level, or spending patterns in visible minority populations, or something as particular as spending habits of 30-year-old urban versus rural women—demographic data, or statistics, when analyzed, are often the basis of policy decisions, changes in public spending, justification, for example, for a national day-care program or a regional public transport plan. It is also essential to marketing, honing advertising to specific groups at specific economic levels.

To address the targeting of demographic groups by interior designers, whether through media or consumption, we might consider some of the evidence that the designed interior (domestic and commercial) has little to do with demographics. After all, this is not how the design process is taught. Design in the modern tradition exists in an egalitarian, idealized world of functional requirements, attractive form, and innovative spatial solutions. Marketing is precisely the opposite: class, ethnicity, and income indicators are divisive; marketing and targeting depends on difference. Lifestyles are constructed and spatial propriety is central to this construction.

Design as an active process based in production and consumption sits in direct opposition to vernacular building traditions based on inherited patterns of living, which are generally static, conservative, rooted, and slow. Bernard Rudofsky's 1964 study, *Architecture Without Architects,* showed timeless, traditional, premodern forms of building that often had not changed for hundreds of years. R. W. Brunskill defined the vernacular as untutored, unprofessional building, conventional, following local expediency, never fashion. We can consider a contemporary vernacular as being buildings, furnishings, interiors, and objects immune to change or renovation, either through poverty or disinterest in trends. Of course, this is linked to a demographic group that resists change, for a wide range of reasons, making it also resistant to marketing.

"Design" on the other hand is dynamic and linked functionally to change. "Keeping up with the Joneses," that infamous dictum of mid-twentieth-century social mobility, required the purchase of new things and the throwing away of the cumbersome, traditional past. A change in social status is often signaled through the strategic deployment of potent and symbolic designed objects, spaces, and dress. The simple spatiality of class aspiration and ethnic assimilation that characterized the twentieth century has become something much more complex in the twenty-first with the advent of identity politics, underclass street culture, and the counteractive sustainability movement. However, the basic outlines are the same. Social mobility must be acknowledged, and it is acknowledged visibly through the acquisition of new things from the symbolic economy of aspiration.

Demographic data articulates certain trends, often market or manufacturer driven. Designers shape these trends and show people how to accept, to enjoy, and to strategically deploy new products.

For example, after WWII, manufacturing of tanks and armaments changed over to consumer durables, including hugely heavy steel refrigerators, stoves, and cars, enameled and plated, all to use up steel, nickel, and chromium surpluses and to keep employment high as the steel industry scaled back from wartime production. These new products were marketed relentlessly, targeting women in the home for domestic appliances and men for new cars. The size of the kitchen in the postwar house increased in size to accommodate the gargantuan new equipment. Double garages made their first appearance as the family car was no longer adequate for a family: two cars were promoted. Cities cut back on public transport that in the interwar years had consisted of streetcars and trolleys, in favor of surface and underground parking lots for the increased use of commuter automobiles: expansion into suburbia was facilitated by the availability of cars that hurtled into the city each morning on freeways.

This is a case where a geopolitical event had industrial consequences that radically changed urban, architectural, interior, and social design. Change was presented to people as something they wanted, something in which to invest their disposable income. Change must be marketed to be acceptable, and for the interior designer it means shaping the changes into something that is intensely desirable.

There is no formula for this. There are examples however.

Let us start in 1850s Britain and the United States, during the filthiest part of the Industrial Revolution, which was wreaking havoc with the environment, causing civil wars and mass migrations of peoples to cleaner spaces. It was also destroying traditional social hierarchies: money began to speak more loudly than birth. Both nations were building extensive colonial networks: the British Empire for Britain, territorial expansion throughout North and Central America for the United States—something that haunts both Europe and America still. From the middle of this stew emerged the house pattern book.

PATTERN BOOKS OF THE NINETEENTH CENTURY

Nineteenth-century pattern books, which carried through into the twentieth century in the form of house plans offered in newspapers and magazines, demonstrated, through the design and arrangements of spaces and furniture, the lineaments of upward social mobility. Pattern books were very popular in the developing United States, although the first recognized pattern book is J. C. Loudon's *Encyclopaedia of Cottage, Farm and Villa Architecture and Furniture,* London 1833. Pattern books diagram, through house plans and elevation sketches, dwellings suitable for the socially mobile in a society in flux. A. J. Downing's *The Architecture of Country Houses,* New York 1850, not only gives house plans from cottages to villas, but details brackets, window seats, and porches; it presents basic plans in a wide range of styles from Swiss to Romanesque to Georgian. It dresses basic, small houses in cloaks that reference much grander styles in the manner of J. C. Loudon, who proposes, among dozens of other situations, "A Grecian Villa, of a medium Size, for a Gentleman of Fortune."

Who would use such books? Who would need a guide to a more elaborate house than a frame farmhouse thrown up by rough carpenters or barn builders? People without traditions or with traditions that are irrelevant to their aspirations. People seek design guidance when they recognize that their traditions are not adequate to their present situation.

Whether crossing North America on the train to one's homestead or migrating from a rural hinterland to a city, there is a change of status, not always up.[1] Immigrants do suffer a setback in their economic fortunes sometimes not corrected for a couple of generations. How do they signal that their aspirations are greater than their material state? In the United States, as read in the pattern books, it was through a genteel attention to the house, to the placement of women in the house, to the aspect of the house, to the cultural references of the house, delineated by such architects as Andrew Jackson Downing and Calvert Vaux. A book is less expensive than commissioning an architect. It is a portable guide, an image, a hope that can be given to a builder anywhere. It is democratic.

It is also assimilative. A standard set of guidelines and images is given to widely differing cultural groups who have lost their pasts in the immigration process. As part of the American project, all disparate peoples were meant to become American: this is the origin of the melting pot concept. If we look at this demographically, what was the demographic that needed this early design attention? The wealthy did not need advice on how to build; they had their architects. The very poor did not build at all. The long-established had their houses built in an earlier Jeffersonian time—a generalized Georgian that represented patrician values. The niche for active design was broad: the socially, economically, and geographically mobile who, in the spirit of the frontier, were always launching into uncharted territory.

Pattern books were the medium of the nineteenth century, and in this we can include the rise of recipe books, such as Mrs. Beeton's 1861 *Book of Household Management* or Charles Eastlakes's *Hints on Household Taste,* 1868, which laid out for the first time rules of service, how to set a table, how to choose a menu. Specifically, they "encouraged working-class readers to imagine themselves in the middle-class domestic interior and assume the values of the middle class home."[2] These were primers for middle-class living because middle-class living was just being invented.

This is not just a historic phenomenon: house plans are still carried by newspapers, by DIY home stores such as Home Depot, and one can readily buy books of house plans. As so little independent house building takes place today—housing development is the domain of developers—the demographic for house plans seems more narrow, more renegade than in the nineteenth century, but perhaps it is just smaller. Off the peg house plans are for rural, unregulated areas, small towns without development pressure, and for a lower economic group that builds its own houses and needs some basic guidance. This was the prevailing condition for a country in violent social upheaval: the United States was engaged in a civil war in the 1860s; slavery was ended, sending large numbers of unassimilated African Americans to the industrialized north from the agricultural south, which consequently foundered without its labor force. The prairies in the center of the continent were opened up for settlement, and migration from Europe peaked by the end of the century: there was no status quo. The opportunity to change one's circumstances was great.

What is the lesson here for interior design of the present? Social insecurity is omnipresent. If one never changed one's social status, as happens in societies that have developed strong traditional frameworks for how to live, one would never need anything new. However, globalization of media and product has affected everyone. Inuit in Greenland watch documentaries on Australian aborigines; they also watch all the advertisements on commercial television. Our knowledge of the rest of the world is immense, breaking down the cultural autonomy of all groups, all classes, all demographic divisions.[3]

Just because we now share a lot of information doesn't mean that there are not national, regional, and civic cultural differences.[4] For example, in an oft-discussed and relatively trivial example, the bidet has never become ubiquitous in the United States. It has been available for decades, but it hasn't caught on. This isn't squeamishness; it is a different attitude to cleanliness. In a Europe or a Japan of overcrowding and limited water resources, bidets are focused, purpose-driven showers. In an America of huge spaces and near-unlimited water, full showers are used. Washing machines are vast and consume inordinate amounts of water. Hair is washed every day and then needs conditioners to overcome the results. The percentage of the house devoted to personal hygiene is large. Forests are felled for toilet paper; issues of water security will soon rival energy security—it will take an environmental collapse to change this bathroom culture.[5] Cleanliness is next to godliness: this is a precept present in American culture derived from puritan austerity of the seventeenth century. It has deep roots. In eras of prosperity or power, social anxiety is lessened, and deep roots are trusted. If the society is in turmoil, for whatever reason, and social mobility is accelerated, anxiety increases: both in those who are losing their hegemony and in those who are moving up into new territory. Signifiers become extremely important. Enter new markets for the bidet.

Are the countries in the Organization for Economic Co-Operation and Development experiencing social upheaval today? There are demographic groups in transition:

new immigrants; families displaced by unemployment, house loss, or bankruptcy; internal migration resulting from climate change, desertification, or chronic floods. Different groups largely denied access to the middle class (in the twentieth century, it was African Americans, or Chinese Canadians, Bengali British, or North African French; in the early twenty-first century, it appears to be Turkish Germans, aboriginal peoples, French *beurs*) all bear a difficult and ambiguous relationship to that middle class. If they aspire to it, and eventually occupy its structures, the cost is the loss of their own traditions. There are no longer pattern books outlining this process, but there are guidelines: the racks of interior design magazines, hours of house and garden television, miles of warehouse-style box stores selling coordinated house contents, which assume a coherent relational system to which everyone aspires.

Magazines can be seen as guidebooks to this relational system as they disseminate interior design ideas.

MAGAZINES

The development of twentieth-century printing techniques produced popular publications that gave all classes a view of life at the economic top. *Tatler & Bystander,* for example, founded in 1901 as a follower of the British aristocracy and still published, covered interior trends in the interwar period developed by Syrie Maugham, Elsie de Wolfe, and Sybil Colefax. In the United States, *Vogue* (1909) and *Vanity Fair* (1913–1936) supplied this function: examples of gracious living were disseminated not by direct exposure (the traditional method whereby one visited the houses of one's own social group) but by magazines, to be consumed by anyone. This unprecedented access to a way of life to which it was assumed most classes aspired created the figure of the interior designer as arbiter of taste. And here, taste is not associated with functionalism, or with efficiency, or with sustainability, or even attainability. It is associated with wealth.

Architectural Digest started in the United States in 1920, *Better Homes & Gardens* in 1922, *House and Garden* in 1915. These publications were, and are, read both by the people or class featured in them and by other classes who are either titillated by the sheer extravagance of living at the top or aspire to it. Again, there is a demographic here that looks for guidance and has chosen the social scale as its pathway.

Consider the careers of Billy Baldwin, Mark Hampton, David Hicks, Sister Parrish, all at their peak of influence in the 1950s and early 1960s: famous for lacking formal training but imbued with taste, which was developed in the drawing rooms of socialites, minor aristocracy, old families, and old wealth. Taste has little to do with design and much to do with discernment. In Woody Allen's 1983 film *Interiors,* a pivotal character is Eve, a New York interior designer whose control over her environment and all who occupy it is near total. This stereotype was portrayed as obsessive and illogical: fine gradations of social standing were sensed according to an indefinable set of rules. Perhaps unfairly, this points out the underbelly of the interior designer as arbiter of taste only truly understood by certain classes. This unattainable sensibility makes it all the more powerful. And yet, this sensibility was also disseminated to hundreds of thousands of people through the interiors magazines—*House & Garden*'s circulation in 1965 was over one million copies per month.[6] And there is the paradox and the attraction.

One might argue that Woody Allen's surgical dissection of New York WASP morés over a number of films signaled the end of their hegemony. The 1960s heyday of *House and Garden* guides to interior design coincided with the civil rights movement, a violent and race-driven era of America that echoes still, and with the rise of the antimaterialist counter-culture, in some ways as threatening to social order as a race riot. None of this appears in the interiors magazines of the time: it seems to have no influence at all. However, the houses and interior landscapes of old blue blood money were gradually superseded by pop culture celebrity on one hand and by the Martha Stewart phenomenon on the other.

Martha Stewart Living started in 1990. Martha Stewart made much of her Polish heritage, writing last page editorials with a fierce nostalgia for her mother's cooking. At its peak in 2002, *Martha Stewart Living*'s circulation was two million. Her success was presented as the hard-working success of all immigrants: she could cook, she canned peaches, she could paint houses, garden, and even farm, and she had unerring taste. Stewart is not from America's East Coast aristocracy; her taste has been earned. From middle-income New Jersey, she trained as a stockbroker and is known as a publishing magnate found guilty of perjury. However, she also valorized American traditions rather than borrowing from Europe; she presented collections of depression glass, McCoy pottery, Fiesta ware: products so inexpensive and so common that Stewart's selection of them appeared revolutionary and, again, democratic. Interior design in this magazine was presented as affirmative rather than aspirational.

Demographically, what accounts for this shift, from interior design as an unattainable, aristocratic ideal to a kind of affirmative cultural archive? It is perhaps connected to the rise of identity politics and a reaction to some of the processes of assimilation.

MODERNISM AND ASSIMILATION

House pattern books and interior design magazines as populist transmitters of design ideas and standards were engaged in style: the styling of a national domesticity, the style of propriety, the style of graciousness and values. Coexisting with twentieth-century populist media was the development of modernism with its initial ambitions to eschew style and decoration, to pursue design through rational, logical means. This was a role for the professional designer who worked from principles rather than personal taste. Design could be codified.

Today, the proportion of editorial to advertising in magazines is roughly 25:75, meaning that while editorial features have prestige, advertisers occupy more space. Editorial content might show grand designs of great extravagance, but advertisements carry a different message: they instruct readers in how to achieve access to a well-designed life it is assumed they desire. That achievement comes through the consumption of products. Modernity lent itself to streamlined and rationalized manufacturing processes that decreased costs and, by moving away from subjective artisanal production, removed any sense of exclusivity. The sheer democracy of modernity suited an era in the developed world where the assimilation of diverse ethnicities, religions, traditions, and circumstances was important. Nations that are internally divided squander their resources: it is politically more efficient to assimilate everyone to a model that is clearly defined, accessible, and cohesive.

The two world wars were great social levelers; society over the twentieth century became more mobile, less hierarchical: the loss of servants to munitions factories and the armed forces in WWI challenged traditional domestic relations that had relegated the kitchen and scullery to a back wing of the house. By the middle of the twentieth century, the kitchen was the center of the house.

The civil rights movement in the United States had its roots in WWII where visible minority soldiers returned home from the war and were unwilling to resume their subservient position in a segregated society. There were massive postwar movements of displaced and refugee European peoples to Britain, Canada, Australia, and the United States, and then subsequent refugee waves from Eastern Europe with the expansion of the USSR as WWII settled into the cold war.

Women in the workplace had been a necessity during both wars, releasing men to the armed forces. Forcing them back to the home in the 1950s so that veterans could be rewarded with jobs disturbed their new-found autonomy seeding second wave feminism.[7] Vaguely patrician taste was not going to bind such disparate peoples together. Instead, a clear-cut objective modernism appeared to embrace everyone.

In postwar Western economies, magazines shifted from showing how to be wealthy to how to be modern. The marketing of modern technology, materials, styles, and concepts developed a highly sophisticated use of advertisements outlining precise specifications for access to a perceived mainstream demography at the center of, generally, American culture.

Diana Rowntree in a representative 1964 modern design handbook proposes that personal taste is to be accommodated within a clean, rational, science-based analysis of space and motion. *Interior Design* is a straightforward manual of rational, clear, useful design along modernist principles reflecting a turn away from obvious class aspiration to democratic equality. Demographically speaking, who was meant to be tutored in modernist principles in the postwar era? Almost anyone who was changing from a terraced house to tower block, from an apartment to a single-family house, from Europe to North America, from the working class to the middle class.

ACCESS TO EQUALITY

It took a century and a half of enlightenment-based effort to move a great mass of society up out of the unregulated industrial environments of the nineteenth century toward better ways of living—to healthier dwellings, to more pleasure per dollar, to educating people in basic design principles, to improving quality of life. And by the mid- to late-twentieth century, interior design activity could distinguish between the sentimental and the rational, the tawdry and the authentic, the useless and the useful, between trends and innovation. The rational, the authentic, the useful, and the innovative: these are the hallmarks of modernity.

The apotheosis of the modernization of a diverse population is the IKEA phenomenon, where good design was made extremely affordable and at the same time, desirable. Added to the spare Scandinavian good looks of the IKEA product is the process: one saves money by assembling furniture oneself, thus engaging directly in the construction of a modern life. For IKEA, warehousing is reduced: in fact, product is sold from the warehouse. Products are modular and interchangeable, choices are limited—that is, just two kitchen cabinet profiles rather than comparable bespoke kitchen design firms which offer custom sizes and profiles for up to five times the price. What one sacrifices in individuality, one saves in cost. There is an understanding here that participation in IKEA's world is not about individual expression but instead indicates that one discerns that good design is not necessarily about expense. This is interior design that does not exploit social insecurity, neither does it divide the population into ethnic camps, or economic levels, or gender, or geography: it unites in a pan-modernist efficiency.

Throughout the modern era, the absence of any discussion of cultural identity is marked. Demographics appear to be irrelevant to the greater project of egalitarianism. The interior designer's and the architect's role is to reiterate the universal principles of good circulation, temperature control, adequate light, and achievable cleanliness.[8]

LATE-TWENTIETH-CENTURY ECLECTICISM

Rational, utilitarian egalitarianism began to pall in some design quarters by the last quarter of the twentieth century. Postmodern styles of late capitalism found modernist technology coexisting with rediscovered markers of status.

This corresponded with, in Britain, the erosion of the hegemony of the state as a social provider. Council housing was put up for sale; council estates and tower blocks, the Corbusian model meant to lift families out of dank and dark slum housing, were vilified and identified with violence and poverty. The privatization of social housing in Britain was synonymous with a further erosion of class consciousness, a greater feeling of personal control, and a consequent turning toward consumption,[9] although it also can be seen as a further expansion of the middle class. The United States saw the demolition of major housing projects built in the late 1950s: they too had become behavioral sinks, synonymous with African-American poverty and fractured families. By moving low-income families into home ownership, their entry into the middle class was provided.

It is one thing to achieve parity with one's ambitions; it is another thing to be content with that achievement. Hierarchization is a natural social process.[10] A completely egalitarian society is impossible, for built into social relationships is a scale of inequalities.[11] "Keeping up with the Joneses," the byword in 1950s America for social striving through consumption, is never achievable. There is always a higher position to work toward, and despite the goals of modernist equality, social standing is still represented by lifestyle.

As always, consumers are guided in their choices. By the end of the twenty-first century, in reaction to a progressive modernism, the past began to acquire a shimmering desirability with nostalgic certainty, safe hierarchies, and firm values. The Seaside, Florida phenomena, new urbanism, is the direct exemplar of a kind of pre-modern Elysium where people lived in villages with tidy wood houses and picket fences. This kind of myth-making ranges from the Prince of Wales' Poundbury to new development on the outskirts of most North American cities.

A revisitation of historic styles was also promoted by late-twentieth-century magazines. *The World of Interiors* searched the world for the visually beautiful to introduce visual complexity to a utilitarian modernism in housing and office space. Coffee table books of the 1980s and 1990s such as the almost endless series *Paris Style, New York Style, Berlin Style* presented epochs of old-world elegance in each world city as collections of objects and interiors, shadowed and romantic.[12] *Interiors, the Home since 1700,* for example, is a catalogue of the way that technology and the Industrial Revolution pushed and distorted traditions, replacing authenticity with simulacra and time-tested comfort with modern, rather than modernist innovation. Steven Parissien's anti-modernist views were typical of a *fin-de-vingtième-siècle* obsession with historical continuity ruptured by the modern movement. Parissien was just one of many writing of this era whose interior design attitudes are encapsulated in this revealing statement:

> The dilution of the Modernist ethic in the West in the 1970s laid the foundations for the cheerful eclecticism of the last two decades of the twentieth century. In many ways the design parameters of the 1980s recalled those of the 1830s: an increasingly confident and wealthy middle class, bent on conspicuous consumption and ostentatious displays of status and success; a rejection of stylistic dogma and prescription; and the assumption of a magpie-like attitude to disposing and decorating the home, a strategy which would have horrified the design purists of thirty years before.[13]

The easy acceptance of historic styles as the hallmark of success and status was in direct contradistinction to stripped-down modernist clarity where objects had no history.

However, even this broadly eclectic view of how to live with ostentation did not last long in the mainstream. The sifting of the past for decorative motifs, the historical pastiche, the architecture of Leon Krier, Robert Stern, and Venturi became identified with insincerity: the motifs referred in each case to previous eras that are no longer politically acceptable: empires, extreme class distinctions, formality. They were also associated with Reagan and Thatcherite economics, championed by some for lifting their nations out of the recession of the 1970s and listed by others as creating the foundation of economic collapse at the end of the first decade of the twenty-first century.[14]

It must be noted that while the broad strokes of design movements change, shift, and develop, they leave constituencies behind that continue their precepts. Thus, in approaching demographic divisions with a view to marketing, political affiliation is important. When Alison Clarke says that historically the construction of the household as an expressive form has been associated with the consolidation and formation of middle-class identity, it is important that the interior designer, the architect—or any sort of designer— understand the affiliative history of certain design ideologies and concepts of class.

EARLY-TWENTY-FIRST-CENTURY SEARCH FOR AUTHENTICITY

Did such late-twentieth-century changes address a changing demographic that demanded visibility, or were they the abandonment of the dream of equality in favor of a stratification that was essentially antiurban and antidemocratic, a stratification based on a new set of symbolic markers?

Increasingly, and this is perhaps a function of identity politics, the search for an authentic identity affects design. The counter-culture of the 1960s and its interest in ideas of authenticity, indigenous cultures, and exotic dress has sifted through to the mainstream. Magazines such as *Dwell, Nest, Interiors, Country Living* have their roots in such 1960s publications as the *Whole Earth Catalogue:* a search for a more authentic cultural reality than the architecture and design of either modernism, late capitalism, or historicism.

It is Pierre Bourdieu's "agents of consecration" that confer cultural legitimacy on symbolic goods—the theorizing of academics is transferred to journalists; ideas generated in salons eventually appear in movies. Middle culture defines itself in an acquisitive relationship to high culture, with a necessary time lag as the symbolic markers of high culture are manufactured for a middle class.[15] Discernment is critical here: there are privileged groups that discern value in some products and adopt them, whether they be Swedish antiques or South African township artifacts. Cool hunters and tastemakers search for cultural authenticity, whether it be one's own culture or, more likely, some distant culture.

Bourdieu also outlines the relationship between groups that dominate economically and politically (mainstream cultural production in manufacturing, retail stores, mass market magazines) and those that are independent of the economy (artists and traditional cultures). This division defines the role of the avant-garde, the artists, to initiate symbolic markers that are then mainstreamed. This is how gentrification works: artists locate certain areas, certain kinds of building fabric without discernible market value, occupy them and in so doing, change their market status. In mainstream cultural production, there is a fierce attention to economics and market, and so, Bourdieu feels, trends adopted from the avant-garde are precisely those that appear to be the most amenable to such social structures. Why, in the 1980s, were old nineteenth-century warehouses in downtown cores, abandoned because of transportation changes, access difficulties, and the decline of small manufacturing, converted to lofts first for artists, and then designers, and then young bankers—why did this happen so rapidly? The avant-garde initiated an anti-suburban symbolic marker of urban diversity, of urban *povera*—things that were anathema to a market culture but that struck a chord with enough people, a large enough demographic group, to initiate a change in attitude to downtown living, seized upon by a very conventional social structure, the real estate industry.

Whether or not interesting trends come from above or below, the process of promoting them to chosen demographics, whether middle income, working class, or the wealthy, is the same. We are not talking about content as much as we in the design field are discussing process: how changes in ways of inhabiting space are capitalized and commodified.

An early twenty-first-century interest in products outside conventional mass-market offerings and available from reconstructing economies as they enter the globalized marketplace can be read as a new avant-garde in possession of an anti-transnational authenticity. Bourdieu wrote about twentieth-century traditions and processes that generally were aspirational; in the twenty-first century, hierarchization increasingly looks inverted. However, style that comes up from the street rather than down from the salons is disseminated in a most traditional way: through popular magazines, film, music, television, and websites (Thomas, 1998). It is not so much the markers or the sources that are the most important thing in this discussion but how they are presented so as to appear desirable enough to spur consumption.

DEMOGRAPHIC DATA, THE BASIS OF TARGETED MARKETING

Demographic data per se does not indicate aspiration or goals. Demographics are statistical snapshots of life as it is being lived: the percentage of a population that plays video games, or is of Italian descent, or has children, or has teenaged children, or has 13-year-old girls. A population can be sliced into infinitely fine sections and can then, in marketing terms, be defined by the products they feel they want and therefore buy.

A survey that estimates the number of vegans in British society gives a snapshot of food consumption that would, or would not, implement vegan product sections in supermarkets. Once such sections are established, based on existing vegan presence, then they can be marketed: advertising the benefits of a vegan diet, vegan cosmetics, vegan clothing production, the vegan household, linking vegan lifestyle to larger movements such as the environmental movement. Much of this is about reading the statistics and then devising strategies that make the demographic group feel autonomous and proud to be singled out for attention. One can create a growth market for vegan products where previously vegans slipped in and out of mainstream society searching for vegan products with great difficulty.

Let us look at the example of Starbucks, a coffee store that started in Seattle for well-traveled American coffee aficionados who had tasted espresso in France, in Italy, in Turkey and on returning home could not find such coffee experience in a country where coffee had been percolated and then stewed on the stove top for a century. A fairly narrow demographic was noticed: it was that section of the postwar baby boom with enough money to travel and that, in 1971 when Starbucks began, was not yet particularly homebound or house-proud. Starbucks introduced café culture for young, upper-middle-income Americans, replacing coffee shop culture, which appealed to an older, lower-middle economic demographic. The American dream is, above all, economically aspirational: this is what Western society in general means throughout the world—more disposable income. Thus it was inevitable that Starbucks, with its moderately expensive but still accessible product, became a marker of an upwardly mobile demographic, expanding around the world. The way Starbucks designed its signage and its interiors is also telling. Starbucks first floated its *Il Giornale* style in 1986—very Italian: thin black chairs, cream tile, and in the Vancouver Starbucks, newspapers and bits of notes and pictures clipped to a datum line of picture wire stretched on all four walls at 4 ft. (1.2 m) high. This last detail was, at the time, staggeringly sophisticated: an inexpensive design touch that was clearly both ad hoc and minimal. The minimalism was bare; one could have an espresso and read the *New York Times* or *Il Giornale* without taking one's coat off. It felt European in a way that North America, outside Greenwich Village, never seemed to achieve, trying too hard and slipping into Disney versions of the Parisian café with striped awning.

The next time I was in a Starbucks in an odd (to me) location was in 2006 in Newcastle where I was startled to see the exact same Italian orange-speckled glass pendant lampshades as in all the Starbucks in Canada. It didn't look like Newcastle; it didn't look like the United States: it looked like Starbucks—no longer quite as Italian looking, more Italian-product looking. Over the years, Starbucks shifted from the vaguely uncomfortable Italian bar to something much more domestic: as the lattes got larger and puffier, so did the seating—enormous dark brown leather armchairs that forced one to lounge, to relax. We were invited to use Starbucks as a living room away from home, a social center rather than an individual caffeine and news hit. After Starbucks had expanded to almost every street corner, in every mall and every big box bookstore in fifty countries, it adopted a localization policy: rather than one design, interiors were to be regional.[16] This could have been a response to the targeting of Starbucks during antiglobalization protests: an internationally recognizable corporation, no matter what its ethical origins, is still a corporation, on the stock exchange, global in reach. Images in a *New York Times* article of 2010 showed new, local Starbucks in New York looking like versions of New York Irish bars, or indefinable arts-and-crafts whole-food interiors. In Canada, local references often resulted in the interiors of Starbucks approaching the dreary beige tiles of Tim Horton's, a coffee and doughnut outlet that occupies a wildly nationalistic role in Canadian culture. Starbucks is a case where an enterprise starts in a small, exclusive, upmarket niche that markets worldliness and, once that and all the logos are established, then goes downmarket in appearance to draw in the widest possible demographic, wherever it can be found.

Like MacDonald's, Starbucks relied on its ubiquity, its offer of variations within a limited palette, and the cachet of being an American institution.[17] Both capitalized on certain demographics and then built their product line, their outlets, and their advertising, reinforcing the identity of those belonging to, say, the Starbuck's generation. The methods of pattern books, society magazines, IKEA, and Whole Foods take as a given that whatever demographic group one is born into, one's identity is fluid and is susceptible to being shaped.

There is, in most Western-style democracies, an unwritten national project to build a middle class out of diverse and often conflicting peoples. It signifies a stable civil society. As this is happening, the shape of acceptable aspiration is quite uniform. For example, one might have been a Hungarian family emigrating to Canada in 1956 with centuries of Hungarian traditions, but once in Canada, or the United States, or Australia or

Britain, the choice of housing, furniture, and clothing was limited to what was available. From the 1930s to the 1950s, both Sears Roebuck in the United States and Eaton's in Canada sent out catalogs from which one could order a dwelling that came in a boxcar or on a flatbed truck, clothe one's family, and equip the house. Rural households had the same access to products as urban households had to retail stores. Choice was limited, neither cheap nor expensive, neither elaborate nor overly utilitarian.[18] Style was not an issue; most households had the same chesterfield and ate much the same food off the same plates. IKEA started in the immediate postwar era (1951) as a catalogue, offering ready-made lifestyle assemblages.[19] This was a time of great leveling, bringing different cultures, different classes, different geographies into equivalence through housing, interiors, food, and dress.

Once leveled, and reinforced through a great number of popular television family comedies and movies portraying middle-class, middle income nuclear families, all those who didn't fit this vision of a mainstream began to be heard from. The NAACP, the American Indian Movement, the lobby to have visible minorities appear in the media, Women's Liberation, the GLBTG movement, Canada's Multicultural Act of 1973—all these things that came to the fore in the 1970s were indications that individual identity had been suppressed for too long in favor of a social and material flattening, and that personal identity could be mobilized politically, despite identity being an ambiguous and changeable signifier.[20] When specific demographic groups struggle for public acknowledgement and visibility, it is difference, rather than grievous inequity that becomes intensely important.[21]

The beginning of the twenty-first century sees a newly complex world where identity politics are powerful enough to have challenged the hegemony of the putative middle class. There are still large population shifts of refugees, economic migrants, and displaced peoples, but there is also a transfer of wealth to what had previously been considered an underclass of ghettos and crime, added to ideological wars that indicate some problems with the assimilative melting pot concept, which, for all its goals of an egalitarian civil society, contains indigestible homegrown diversity.

We have societies divided, at war externally and internally, experiencing recession and personal economic failure. If the nineteenth and twentieth centuries provide a model, soon all these differences will be subsumed in a new project of unification. It won't be modernism—that has been tried and exhausted. At the end of the twentieth century and the beginning of the twenty-first, voracious commodification of revolutionary or countercultural trends, such as punk, was the agent of unification.[22] A new project of unification will perhaps be a focus on climate change, which is bigger than any national government, larger than any transnational corporation and is no respecter of demographic difference.

The importance of sustainability as a guiding concept, with its roots in the 1960s environmental movement, includes a nostalgia for appropriate technology, a desire for geopolitical security and for a personally acceptable way to step back from material aspirational culture.[23] Welcomed as a relatively simple alternative to the chaotic relationships of the geopolitical world, sustainability was immediately exploited in publications such as *Real Simple, Life Made Easier Every Day,* an American consumer magazine started in 2006. The environment and climate change present a clear problem with carefully approved methodologies.

How does the interior designer approach the demographics of sustainability? How will this change the shape of our interior environments? The automobile industry, after the failures from overextension in the late 2000s, markets hybrid vehicles, electric vehicle research, and very small cars to precisely the demographic that can afford a new car. In other words, the economic class with disposable income.

There are clear environmental, economic, and material goals that, for the average consumer, are not clear in discussions of carbon-trading strategies that take place at national and international levels. The bellwether in forging a new life in the era of sustainable systems will not be the person with the license plate that reads "We're spending our grandchildren's inheritance," nor will it be the climate change denier interested in maintaining the status quo—stasis is not economically productive. It will be an educated, upper-income, relatively confident class that has the wherewithal to purchase new products and has traditionally led style and taste. The complete revision of manufacturing and production of consumer durables, furnishing, and fabrics, mechanical systems and appliances all under the rubric of sustainability will be presented in a way that unites everyone in this project. Just as the advent of computers redesigned the home and the family, leading to smart houses, rearranged electrical systems, and reassigned room functions, so will sustainability mean a redesign of the home. How, for example, are those clumsy blue plastic crates to be accommodated in the well-designed kitchen?

Of course it might not be sustainability, or it might only be sustainability for a short while, but whatever the trends are, they will continue to be driven by aspiration, whether to wealth, status, taste, or to ethics. The designer, who is both a member of society and the analyst of it, must decide what change means for each demographic group. Society is uneven. There are still demographic groups without wealth that aspire to it. There are still groups without equality that want it. There are still people ill at ease with contemporary life who look to the past. There are demographic groups who want to acquire many, many things as an indication of their ability to purchase, and there are groups who revel in a new, thing-less austerity as an indication of their ultimate and enviable identity.

Ethics and the Indoor Environment

25

The Thin Edge of the Wedge: Shifting Ethical Terrains and Interior Design in the Twenty-First Century

MARY ANNE BEECHER

Despite the publication of several recent works on the topic of ethics and their relationship to the production of the built environment, the philosophical consideration of ethical practice in relationship to the practice of interior design has been generally underrepresented in contemporary scholarship.[1] This chapter explores the potential for ethical considerations to shape or clarify the interior design profession's identity, and it poses questions about the current paradigm(s) used to identify the ethical terrain on which professional interior design education and practice currently exists.

It seems that new challenges and new cultural conditions arrive with the dawn of every new century, and the latest millennial transition was no different. With the shift to the twenty-first century now more than a decade behind us, these challenges and conditions continue to reframe all kinds of design issues such as how the selection of materials that were once understood and largely agreed upon by positivist modernists should now be approached within the context of sustainable design. By looking at recent ethically charged issues identified in design literature, I hope that the questions articulated here help create challenges to what occurs at the intersection of interior design practice and ethical decision-making. Because these issues can be somewhat controversial and require nuanced considerations, it is likely that taking a refreshed look at certain ethical questions may result in a reconsideration of the place of interior design in the generation of the built environment. I will argue that by clarifying how interior design practice is ultimately understood or defined, an interior design practice that is grounded in a twenty-first-century ethical framework can be established.

Nearly every essay written on the topic of ethics and design offers up its own definition for how the concept is understood by the author. Due to the rather complex nature of ethics—in particular its association with morality—it is important to frame the extent to which a consideration of ethical issues is examined through the lens of some form of universally defined moral behavior. This can be problematic, however, when the value of pluralism and the embrace of multiple viewpoints linger as by-products of postmodernity.

For the purposes of this chapter, the consideration of ethics focuses on the actions taken by designers in response to contemporary North American cultural conditions so that ethics become rules of conduct based on principles that are agreed upon collectively by a group such as a profession—in this case, the profession of interior design.[2] By agreeing on what is generally considered fundamentally "right" and "wrong" behavior, professionals assume that certain results of practice will always occur when predictable sets of actions and guidelines are utilized. This chapter will demonstrate, however, that the clarity required for this type of agreement is rarely in place, and that is, of course, where things get a little ambiguous.

By understanding ethics as rules of behavior—agreed upon or not—it becomes important to also consider the types of motivation that encourage their use. Simply put, what conditions or circumstances are likely to cause interior designers to want to practice ethically in the first place? The answer can be posed in terms of the way that an understanding of consequences directs behavior. Ethicists typically place an understanding of consequences into two different categories: teleology and deontology. For the teleologically inclined, it is the anticipation of good consequences that motivates ethical practice. Teleological designers believe that doing what they believe to be the right thing will result in a positive outcome for themselves and for all persons involved. Such practices result in the preservation of what is good and the improvement of what isn't.

Contrastingly, designers in the deontological camp subscribe to absolutes such as a belief in the rightness of honesty. For these designers, ethical behavior is practiced out of a sense of obligation or duty with little actual concern for the outcome. The extent to which environments produced by deontological practices are improved is not necessarily the measure of their success. There are, in other words, designers who promote ethical practice because of the general good it can produce while others perform ethically because they believe that it is, simply, the right thing to do.[3]

Cultural conditions experienced in North America in the latter part of the twentieth century demonstrated that, among other things, changes in available technologies and in what one might describe as the priorities of practice, as well as shifts in the beliefs and values of the cultures served by the interior design profession, occurred at a quicker pace than ever before encountered in what historian Clive Edwards, among others, has recently argued is a two-century-long history of the profession.[4] Ethical perspectives on interior design practices once held as constants may now be understood as fluid, and the dawn of the twenty-first century may one day be seen as a critical transition period in which increasing occurrences of change in cultural attitudes were accommodated by new approaches to interior design practice.[5] As such, it may signify the beginning of a period in which some of what was once taken for granted with regard to the ethics of practice can no longer be assumed. As Judith Fosshage puts it, "To ensure that the interior design profession has a viable future, *evolving ethics* are an essential ingredient."[6]

The proposition of a shifting ethical terrain is bound to make some people nervous. After all, humans tend to take comfort in the constancy of beliefs about what is acceptable behavior and some may argue that it is easy to imagine how such repositioning might result in our heading down a slippery slope with new practices. And yet the usefulness of this cautionary rhetorical metaphor may be limited by its supposition that the direction we may head as a result of these shifts is necessarily down; that is, to a less desirable position. Instead, it is the purpose of this chapter to explore the potential of considering the use of shifting principles of ethical practice to accomplish certain positive outcomes such as having the ability to clarify the value and uniqueness of interior design's contributions to an improved built environment.

Due to constraints on the overall length of this particular discussion of ethics, I have decided to limit the considerations made here to three specific propositions, each addressing a currently contested reality of contemporary practice. Ethical considerations are frequently framed within the context of notions of identity—how the very nature of a group guides its responses to the world. Deliberations on the topic of interior design practice inevitably focus on the need to clarify the profession's identity. This is evidenced by the numerous legislative battles for interior design certification or licensure in the United States that have been waged in recent years and by activities such as the development of the International Federation of Interior Architects/Designers (IFI) "Design Frontiers: The Interiors Entity," an international policy initiative exploring, in part, the identity of interior design. One of the three propositions will, therefore, center on issues related to who we are. Because the nature of ethics also requires a consideration of actions, however, the other two propositions will focus more specifically on a consideration of what we, as a profession of designers, do and how we do it.

PROPOSITION 1

Twenty-first-century interior design practice must challenge its association with luxury in order to encourage a more altruistic premise for the work we do. If accomplished, this will ultimately support the possibility that above all else, interior design practice has an ethical responsibility to create architectural space that is responsive to and supportive of human needs.

Perhaps this first proposition seems so obvious that it should go without saying. I mean to suggest, however, that the ethical practice of interior design requires the proper accommodation of human needs and gives it priority over all of the other qualities that generate spatial designs. That is, of course, not currently the case with every designed interior produced today. But as this emphasis on the creation of environments that support the people who occupy them is often cited as a defining characteristic of interior design practice, it makes sense for this to be understood as a defining ethical principle.

Since its inception as a distinct methodological approach to creating interior environments of all kinds, interior design has been contextualized by a public perception that presumes that, as a practice, it is largely associated with excess and exclusivity rather than with humanitarian principles. At the root of this image of excess is the misperception that professional interior designers' clients are always wealthy individuals and that interior designers' work is largely residential. The profession's image as a luxury-based (and therefore extra and even expendable) practice when tough economic times demand practicality or frugality threaten the profession's ability to convey the inevitable benefits it offers participants in all types of design and building processes. This mistaken association with luxury and frivolousness also challenges the profession's capacity to communicate its role in the establishment of safe and healthy environments for the public at large.

The history of the interior design profession, as described in numerous history texts, emphasizes the long-lasting relationships that early designers often enjoyed with wealthy clients and their propensity for procuring and integrating costly materials and artistic works into designed interiors—both residential and commercial. Citing Elsie de Wolfe's work for steel magnate Henry Clay Frick or Donald Deskey and Phillip Vollmer's designs for John D. Rockefeller and Helena Rubenstein or the association of later-twentieth-century designed interiors by Andrée Putman, Philippe Starck, or Clodaugh with boutique hotels, posh corporate showrooms, and luxury penthouses, historians have celebrated the exclusive practices of individuals whose work might better be described as invocations of the so-called decorative arts than of professional interior design as it has emerged and been defined by the various professional associations in North America. Professional interior designers have long-expressed frustration at the public's presumption that their work is the selection of color schemes and textiles; code for making pretty places but not a convincing description of a serious and technical line of work. As a demonstration that this perception persists, the conservative and business-oriented *Wall Street Journal* published an article in 2011 on the fight over the deregulation of the interior design profession in Florida that invoked the image of interior designers as inhabitants of "a genial world of pastel palettes and floral motifs" and described their protest over challenges to licensing legislation in that state as "an indecorous pillow fight over who has the right to design."[7]

Threatening to outnumber such tired invocations of metaphors of frivolousness are celebrations of designed interiors with a social conscience as the emergence of specialized expertise in the design of environments such as affordable housing and long-term care facilities, for the swelling numbers of elderly persons in our aging population, dominates both education and practice today. The relevance of interior designers' understanding of human needs empowers the profession to use its knowledge base to make a difference in all types of human experiences.

The practice of interior design must therefore always produce designed spaces that acknowledge their inextricable interdependence with their human occupants. Interior space, whether public or private, has the potential to facilitate interactions—to serve not just as a backdrop for life's activities but as a factor in determining the quality of people's existence. Research has established that when the needs of people are supported and their senses are stimulated in positive ways, anxieties are lessened and wellness is enhanced.[8] Any consideration of the dimensions of this interdependence between space and people must therefore consider the role of ethics in the determination of how the profession does or should approach its work.

Despite acknowledged associations of the profession with privilege and expense, persons who are attracted to interior design are often drawn to its potential to improve environments as a means of promoting the betterment of the human condition. This acknowledges that interior design can be, at its heart, an altruistic endeavor. Time and again, I have been told by my students that they selected interior design as a career path because they want to help people. Yet even under the most supportive social circumstances, the practice of interior design is always riddled with choices that place design decisions that might best ensure the comfort, health, or safety of a building's occupants in potential conflict with design decisions that might generate a solution that better interfaces with an existing architectural context or that accommodates the available budget for a project or the values of the client. The reality of interior design practice (perhaps in contrast to the idealistic approaches taken to design within educational contexts) often places designers in positions of having to determine what ought to be done by the consideration of multiple opposing factors. This is further compounded by designers' common challenge of having to act as a conduit for someone else's perceived needs.

How can those in interior design practice overcome the conflict of having to compromise design matters that affect human satisfaction? One answer may reside in the use of Julieanna Preston and Mark Taylor's definition of "interiority"—a condition created by the "conscious and reflexive awareness of the self, identity, community and others within the social environment"—as a litmus test for whether or not a design idea is supportive of the human condition and is, therefore, ethical.[9] The notion that interiority is the result of ethical interior design practices requires the use of the body in all of its physiological and cultural complexity as the impetus for spatial solutions. Whether considering the nature of the interior of our clothing, our rooms, our buildings, or our cities (all rightfully acknowledged by Lois Weinthal as the domain of interior design), interior designers' understandings of what is possible and what is preferable in terms of human comfort, human activity, and humanity's values empowers them to position themselves as leading creators of the built environment from the inside out.[10] If the body is the vehicle through which we determine meaning in the environment, then interior designers, as the keepers of the near environment, are not just able to create supportive spaces, they are ethically obligated to do so. Because interior designers are aware of the potential of their practice to impact the lives of individuals who encounter them, there is an implicit ethical obligation to use the design and construction of interior space to advance the human condition in physical and social ways above all other factors.

PROPOSITION 2

Contemporary interior design practice requires the embrace of new strategies for designing, producing, or using solutions that do not harm organisms at the micro scale or the ecosystems they form through their production or their extended use.

The relatively recent rise of sustainable approaches to living in North America promotes a mandate for the reconsideration of many of the traditional premises of contemporary interior design practice. As most of us know, the building industry as a whole is the rightful recipient of significant blame for generating a very high percentage of the content of our landfills. Various Web-based resources put the total percentage of building-related waste in landfills at 25 to 33 percent in Canada and 25 to 40 percent in the United States.[11] Learning how to more accurately consider the potential impact of waste produced as a result of construction undertaken under their direction is, therefore, a high priority for contemporary interior design practitioners.

Understanding the other side of the equation concerning green design practices is equally critical. Designers should have a working knowledge of the origin, content, and production processes associated with the building materials, fixtures, furnishings, and equipment they specify in order to comprehend the energy embodied by their designs and the life cycle implications of those designs.

Life cycle issues also include the long-term impact of a designed interior's presence in a locale. It is this more immediate implication of the interior environment that exempli-fies its effect on living inhabitants. Designers must ask how the air quality of the envi-ronment created affects persons who occupy spaces. They must consider the quantity of energy and water consumed through occupation. It is equally important to understand the types of impacts on the environment created by the processes required to maintain an interior environment.

Whether one credits the dawn of the new environmentalism to the publication of Rachael Carson's *Silent Spring* in 1962, to the inauguration of Earth Day in the United States in 1970, or to a much more recently revealed middle-class social conscience evi-denced by a growing market for all things green, the reality is that little concern for the environmental implications of typical design practices was commonly evidenced by in-terior designers in practice prior to the early 1990s.[12]

Since the dawn of the twenty-first century, however, much has shifted with regard to the use of environmentally responsible practices. Today, the acquisition of LEED AP (Leadership in Energy and Environmental Design) credentials, for instance, has be-come one of several important benchmarks for North American interior designers who are serious about putting sustainable design principles into practice. Manufacturers of goods used by interior designers are also more forthcoming than ever with information about their production processes and the sources of the raw materials they use. Concerns about the energy expended to distribute global products have created opportunities for smaller-scale local producers to once again enjoy viable profitability, especially in parts of North America, such as the Pacific Northwest, that have already established a platform of values regarding the preservation of the environment.

This all sounds like good news with positive ethical implications, and it is. Sustain-able design practices are now often viewed by clients as desirable from both functional and economic viewpoints, especially in the sectors of educational, child care, and hospi-tality design and the design of financial institutions.[13] Still, there are important ethical considerations to be articulated in relationship to the conservation of resources and the preservation of the environment given that the premise for much interior design practice remains market-driven and is an inevitable generator of waste.

With so many favorable changes in support of environmentally responsible design practices emerging, what are some of the factors impeding the wholehearted transformation of the approach taken to interior design practice? Since its inception as a modern profession, interior design was, by its very nature, rooted in the view that change is unavoidable and even preferable. It was, therefore, a knowing participant in the consumption-based system that produced the environmental crisis in the first place. While architectural structures—those that predate WWII in particular—tend to have enjoyed preservation and successive incarnations, their interior spaces are usually treated as expendable. Spaces are repurposed. Openings are rearranged. Surfaces are stripped bare or layered with something new. Volumes are reduced or expanded.

Environmental responsibility as ethical behavior has implications within interior design practice that transcend the selection of green products and materials and the adoption of energy-efficient systems and building strategies. In Western culture, the interiors of buildings have been perceived historically as temporary environments and with few exceptions have been undervalued and treated accordingly. Seen as disposable, the material realities of discarded interiors fill our landfills just as the elimination of our interior environments erases the material culture of our existence.

Interior design may have inadvertently contributed to the undervaluing of the preservation and sustainability of designed interior space by establishing a professional framework early on that encouraged planned obsolescence. Throughout the twentieth century, modern society was hungry, and interior design was one of the many professions to have emerged with a spoon to feed its endless demand. With an early history of combining the provision of design services with the sale of goods such as furniture, interior finish materials, luminaries, and the like, interior designers established their association with consumption early on. In fact, it is the association of interior design practice with retail services that partially contributed to the denigration of the profession's reputation as a creative and truly modern design discipline in the view of new fields of professional design practice, such as industrial design, that emerged in the twentieth century.[14]

Some interior designers have justified their role in the promotion of the desire for goods by defending themselves as arbiters of taste and purveyors of beauty, although this representation, still embraced by popular culture, pits aesthetics against the values of environmental responsibility in a random and unjustifiable way. Corporate designers and those focused on the development of public space in general are far more likely to be professionals who operate outside of the world of retail. Perhaps it is no coincidence that it is smaller and more private environments such as residential spaces that are least associated with environmentally responsible practices while sustainable interior design methods are more commonly used in more institutional-scale projects that are apt to be designed by certified designers.[15]

Stereotypes about sustainable design's lack of desirable aesthetic qualities have waned as the public's taste for new products have emerged more strongly in the twenty-first century. Still, there are concerns that this round of "less is more" requires a level of compromise that is not desired by designers who fear having to abandon their principles of aesthetics in order to accommodate green ambitions. Old habits are, after all, hard to break.

An example of this frustration with the trade-offs necessitated by the sober tendencies of environmentally responsible design can be heard in Karrie Jacob's review of the 2010 National Design Triennial at the Cooper-Hewitt National Design Museum in New York City. Entitled "Too Virtuous," her article in the July/August 2010 issue of *Metropolis* criticizes the show's curators for featuring sustainable products without presenting a convincing argument for the necessity of design to a world overwhelmed by the financial challenges of the current economic crisis. Jacob claims that while work in the show represented a positive range of ways in which design has addressed the need for sustainability at a global scale, its presentation within a backdrop of minimal concrete block and cardboard elements neglected to encourage an understanding of what the many obscure products made from low-cost materials or repurposed junk actually do. "The seamless do-gooder quality of the exhibition made me claustrophobic," complained Jacob in her review. "What I saw all around me was the far end of an arc; design had gone from sexy fluff, a parade of Swarovski-studded chaises, to monastic plainness. I couldn't help thinking that the pendulum had swung too hard, too fast."[16]

Along with doubt that the spare humility of cardboard will ever really resonate with the consuming masses, Karrie Jacob also voices a skepticism that the goal to actually save the environment can actually ever be met. "Given that this world-saving project may or may not work out," she notes, "perhaps we shouldn't be so quick to dismiss that other aspect of design, the one involving pure, dumb pleasure."[17] But herein lays the rub: by drawing a line in the sand between design that attends to environmental concerns and that which appeals to an innately human appreciation of beauty, a dangerous condition of mutual exclusion is implied. And because interior design has always included aesthetic considerations as part of its practice, such a dichotomy implies that it is on the wrong side of issues that respond responsibly to the ominous environmental, political, and economic circumstances of the day.

By looking at this conundrum through an ethical lens, however, it may be possible to argue the role of interior design as that of an essential player. While interior design struggles to assert itself on a level professional playing field with the practice of architecture, it has, perhaps too often, ignored not just the value of its ability to develop strategies for adapting spaces to new uses and to help clients analyze and make shifts in their own practices to work within their own spatial conditions. By emphasizing their ability to program space in creative ways that include the efficient management of resources, the argument that design is valuable is made. But in this argument, creativity becomes less about imagining how else existing architectural space can be and more about optimizing what already exists. Because most interior spaces are temporary, they would be treated as such by being appropriately designed, complete with expiration date. Beauty must also be optimized in this scheme, and because of the value of the contribution of delight to the human condition, interior designers have an ethical obligation to provide it.

Ethics in relation to the practice of sustainable interior design should therefore be considered on the level that benefits both the organism and the ecosystem in order to reach what Craig Delancey calls "shared environmental goals."[18] When both are addressed simultaneously and successfully, the achievement of these goals enables the designer to manage both the responsible use of resources in the production of the design and the creation of spaces that support human health and well-being and the creation of a condition of interiority that mediates both body and spirit.

PROPOSITION 3

New media, new technological capabilities, and new ways of engaging a larger, more global community of designers evoke the possibility that beliefs once held constant regarding the ownership of ideas are currently and rightfully in flux.

For all intents and purposes, architecture produced prior to the modern era tended to be hand-built and specific to its local environment. Increases in industrially produced building materials and prefabrication capabilities have now all but replaced folk vernacular tendencies in North America. Many mid-twentieth-century architects, interior designers, and industrial designers attempted to establish expressions of universality in design in the form of a European-based "international style" aesthetic founded on a philosophy that promoted production using industrial means. This approach to design generated environments and objects that were thought to be suitable for use anywhere, but critics either praised the originality of the abstract simplicity that characterized much of modern design or disparaged it for its supposed inability to communicate with and appeal to the so-called masses.

Mid-twentieth-century art critics such as Clement Greenberg reinforced the idea that the quality of creative work should be equated with its originality; that is, its ability to express concepts through constructs or representations not previously known.[19] On the other hand, philosophers and critics such as Walter Benjamin and Roland Barthes raised challenging questions about the nature of originality itself as early as the 1930s. Benjamin's 1936 essay "The Work of Art in the Age of Mechanical Reproduction" explored the transformation of notions of originality in the fine arts brought on by the rise of photography as a popular means of image production. Because the photographic negative could be used to make multiple prints of the same image, photographers challenged the value of the singular or unique piece of art produced by fine artists.[20] While training to be a fine artist traditionally included the practice of copying masterworks, being able to use photography to recreate images presented artists with new interpretive opportunities that walked the line between interpretation and duplication.

Benjamin's essay on the impact of mechanical reproduction—which was not translated to English until 1969—helped establish a premise for the consideration of appropriation as a creative strategy, particularly as it was explored by photographers such as Sherrie Levine and Cindy Sherman, who both used photography in varying ways to heavily reference or literally reproduce images from previous times. By reshooting the works of Walker Evans from his own exhibition catalogue and presenting the images as her own, for instance, Levine forced her audience to question the issue of authorship in creative work. Her work, and others like it, forces the question of whether an artist owns an image just because he or she is the first one to make it or whether anyone can make claim authorship of work that is produced as a result of his or her effort.

In comparison to the debate over appropriation generated in the art world, deliberations about issues related to the authorship of design ideas and the complications caused by the appropriation of works from the past got off to a slow start. Modernists pushed for honesty in design by restricting superfluous ornament and imitative materials and encouraging the open expression of structure. Modern interior designers likewise sustained practices that valued abstract expression as a signifier of originality.

The rise of a postmodern approach to architecture and interior design in the 1980s gradually restored historical references to and imitation of—the design-based equivalent of appropriation in the visual arts—the designed environment. A desire for irony or a longing for ornament motivated the use of these elements for most designers, rather than a reckless wish to copy. Perhaps because architectural and interior design practices are ultimately businesses, the proprietary nature of interior designers' work and their often close working relationships with their clients—relationships that often included a legal obligation not to disclose names, sources, financial details, or technical construction information related to a project—reinforced that the replication of ideas rarely seemed like a good idea.

Despite the generally consistent aesthetic character of most of the designed interiors developed during various periods of the twentieth century, designers tended to operate under strict ethical codes that restricted the sharing of specific design sources or resources. Design schools drove home the message that borrowing ideas from previous projects required a level of abstraction sufficient to erase any literal reference to the original. The approach taken to the use of materials required the rejection of all things imitative and overtly decorative. As notions of creative scholarship emerged within the academic setting, design students came to view the copying of another's visual, formal, functional, or structural ideas as a form of plagiarism.

But the times, as Bob Dylan sang, they are a-changin'. Today's professional interior designer is often a specialist in the design of specific types of environments. This type of designer is sought by clients who desire specific design characteristics in a new project—often something seen as part of a previously completed project. Well-known "starchitects" and designers of all kinds produce iconic designs whose qualities are repeated in a number of settings. These works are also often interpreted by others who produce close adaptations.

In the world of furniture design, the previously held perception of a knock-off as a defiling copy of an original design has lost its edge. In tough economic times, stores dealing in knock-offs are viewed by the general public (and sometimes designers, too) as viable sources due to their remarkably lower prices. Clients often demand value over the quality once understood to be imbued only in an original design.

The extent to which these changing values are reflected in and shaped by contemporary culture remains to be seen. As already noted, the boundaries between the authentic and the artificial/imitation have been blurred to the point of indistinction on many fronts, both real and virtual. Still, shifts in attitudes toward the use of existing ideas as inspiration to be adapted as part of new work mirror the rate at which new communication models are being adopted by professional designers. Images of projects once reserved for professional audiences now appear publically on professional and social websites as well as on blogs and photo-sharing sites.

Designers are now encouraged to make use of these tools for promotion and marketing and to keep tabs on current design activities. To this end, social media expert Avi Flombaum made a keynote presentation to a group of interior design professionals at IIDEX/NEOCON Canada in Toronto, September 2010. As the cofounder of "Designer Pages," an electronic social media outlet for persons in the fields of design and architecture, Flombaum touted the promise of social media websites as modes of communication and promotion between designers and between designers and their potential clients. While Internet-based resources such as Twitter and Facebook have been harnessed by many professionals to advance their business prospects and interaction with their peers, Flombaum identified interior design as a profession that is failing to maximize the advantages such sites make available to promote and market what it has to offer.[21]

Some of the interior designers at the event expressed their reluctance to create publically accessible websites featuring images of the environments they've created or information about how key conceptual approaches to their work have been achieved. They claimed that their hesitancy has to do with the occasional legal need to protect a client's privacy or the desire to protect the intellectual property represented in an interior designer's finished project. Flombaum, however, expressed a different point of view. "To be copied," he proclaimed, "is to be famous!"[22] What was once considered unethical imitation has become, it seems, a form of flattery.

The resolution of this dilemma ("Is copying someone else's work wrong?") may be found by reframing the question in terms of how we actually define what interior design is. Saul Fisher's essay entitled ""How to Think about the Ethics of Architecture" asks whether architecture (and interior design, by extension) is a service or a product.[23] Fisher asserts that the difference between providing a service and a product is critical in terms of establishing a principle of ownership over design ideas because if interior design is a service—a premise supported by discussions already presented within the context of this chapter—then what is created is not an owned product/idea to which one can be entitled, at least by the standards established within the normal realm of American copyright law. The implication for this position is that because most designed interiors exist as part of the public environment, they are, therefore, available as inspiration, precedent, or template to all who encounter them. The built environment becomes a sort of open source space for its occupants and observers, much like the Massachusetts Institute of Technology's "OpenCourseWare" website serves as a free resource for students and educators worldwide.

According to Gerry Beegan and Paul Atkinson, technologies and their by-products have had a democratizing effect on design since the latter part of the twentieth century and the fluctuating boundaries between designers, makers, and users have all but disappeared.[24] If interior design is a verb that describes the processes we engage in as professionals instead of a noun that refers to the environments we create, then perhaps our protectionist tendencies in the name of ethics are misplaced. Would interior design be better served ultimately if it created an identity that emphasized its importance as a means to a better and more humane end?

CONCLUSION

Conceived of as a means to an end and not an end in itself, interior design is now placed in a position to emphasize that, as a profession, it is rooted in actions that result in ethically produced spaces. This chapter has attempted to demonstrate that what that has formerly meant does not necessarily hold true today. But if the consideration of interior design's place within a shifting ethical terrain can be used to secure a stronger sense of the profession's identity, then it is a worthy slope to tread.

Matters of definition between design disciplines sometimes seem murky as there are many shared perspectives on the design process and methods used to produce professional spatial designs of all kinds. Professionally oriented education lays a common ground for burgeoning architects, landscape architects, and interior designers. That is not to say that there are not fundamental differences in the manner in which different types of design problems are framed and approached by each of the disciplines, however, and these differences are hallmarks to be used to distinguish among them.

The level to which the use of research on the characteristics of occupants or users of a space acts as a point of departure from which to generate design options is a methodological difference found among the perspectives taken by different disciplines, with only a few exceptions. While it would be difficult to deny that successful architects produce designs that accommodate their client's requirements, the practice of architecture is often posed theoretically as an artistic act more driven by concept than by practical considerations and theories of environment and behavior. Interior designers' attraction to evidence-based design provides a level of credibility to their work that transcends notions of pure expressiveness.

At least in North America, how one defines interior design practice and differentiates it from the practice of other building-related professions such as architecture is generally framed by legal parameters that limit interior design practice to the addition, subtraction, or manipulation of nonstructural or non-load-bearing architectural elements. This physical limitation on interior design activity is spelled out in the wording of most legislative regulations or statutes that provide definitions of what constitutes professional interior design practice as part of either title or practice legislation. Just more than half of all Canadian provinces and American states and territories provide a restrictive legal framework that establishes who can legally use a particular title (usually "professional," "registered," "licensed," or "certified interior designer") or who can provide professional interior design services (a more contested and much less common legislative circumstance). As a result of these factors and others, interior design is all too often defined by what it does not or cannot do rather than by what it has to offer. It is my position that contemporary ethics can and should be used as a measure to determine how to frame practices in concert with values that help establish a proactive definition of what the interior design profession is.

After 200 years of attempting to clarify its public identity, Taylor and Preston's notion of interior design's purpose as a means of creating a "conscious and reflexive awareness of the self" offers a helpful, distinctive clarification. It suggests that because interior design is a methodologically unique profession, it is positioned to make a valuable contribution to the creation of a healthy and supportive built environment by privileging considerations of the body's need to be accommodated. Based on the ethically based arguments presented in this chapter, interior design, therefore, should be human-centered and unapologetically client-based. It is the profession that generates spaces that are, first and foremost, supportive of physical, intellectual, and emotional experiences at a personal or intimate scale. Interior designers should use their knowledge of the body's physical and social needs as an instrument through which to generate, mediate, and evaluate the quality of interior space.

Professional interior design practices are rooted in established theory and research and are not predicated on taste or opinion. They are best applied to the creation of public space where technical knowledge is essential to design decision-making. Professional interior designers are educated to contribute to the establishment of the public realm in a manner that sustains the health and welfare of all who encounter it. While this does not exclude professional designers from designing private space such as residences, this type of design is far less regulated and complex and is not central to our education or professional work. By focusing on the design of public space, the interior design profession positions itself to make a more significant impact on the conservation of environmental resources and the improvement of the health of the planet and of the people who occupy it.

Finally, whether designing for public or private purposes, the ways in which the design of the environment is approached must anticipate inevitable future changes, and interior spaces should be planned and built as temporary installations. As a profession, interior design should dedicate itself to the exploration of ways in which these can be places that satisfy the human need for inspiration and beauty, comfort and safety, within the context of environmental responsibility. And when new technologies or ideologies that impact the ways in which we approach the generation and sharing of design ideas emerge, interior designers must be elastic enough to adjust their approaches—both ethical and practical—in order to meet the needs of the day. Doing so ensures the relevance and distinctiveness of the interior design profession for generations to come.

26

Designing Desire

SHONQUIS MORENO

Money may make the world go round, but it is desire that makes money go round. Desire is the fulcrum of all retail consumption, and American provocateur Tobias Wong[1] knew this well. Wong put longing on display in the windows of his Wrong Store, which never really opened for business in 2007. The shop, a play on *The Wrong Gallery*, Maurizio Cattelan's temporary 2002 art installation,[2] took window shopping to the nth degree and consisted of only two elements: its vitrines and its product—covetable, purpose-made, one-off treasures by artists, designers, and architects from around the globe.[3] Wong, however, provided no means for shoppers to enter the store—passersby instead stood with their noses pressed to the glass in the time-honored tradition of kids and candy stores. With no way to handle the merchandise or to make a purchase, the wish to own the products was simultaneously inflamed and thwarted. It made the point pointedly: in retail, who is actually possessed, the product consumed or the consumer?[4]

Wrong Store represented only a brief respite: we shop everywhere now. We buy to ease our consciences at church, we pay a premium in the museum, we snap up duty-free at the airport, we dig for deals at home in our underwear, or we bargain-hunt on the curb from our mobile phones. "In the end, there will be little else for us to do but shop," Dutch architect Rem Koolhaas predicted. "Shopping is arguably the terminal form of public activity."[5]

As Koolhaas well knows, for better or for worse, interior design influences consumption, even in the most basic sense—which brands dominate the eye-level shelves and which are relegated to those we can't reach and rarely raise our gaze to? Design shapes desire shapes shopping.

It used to be that visual merchandising consisted of what the merchant had in stock—stacked, piled, ranged in a row. Think of the old general store, the five-and-dime, the farmer's market. The ancient Greeks shopped in the agora, the Romans in the

Forum, the Persians in the bazaar,[6] the Arabs in the souk, and, finally, the Americans in the mall. By now, we have seen the rise and decline of the department store, which grew up in mid-nineteenth-century England after a draper[7] began to count the weekly revenues by "department."[8] Following WWII, the two-cars-in-every-garage mentality drove suburbanites into shopping malls,[9] which were bookended by department stores, drawing business away from local shops. Convenient and immersive, they cultivated a captive audience by putting everything under one roof, supplemented with food courts that meant shoppers didn't even have to leave to eat. The significance of this addition was underscored in 1960 when IKEA founder Ingvar Kamprad discovered that customers were cutting their shopping short due to hunger and established his now famous in-store cafeterias. Megastores like IKEA or big box retailers—whose revenues, in 2003, thirty-five years after their progenitor, Thrifty Acres, opened in Grand Rapids, Michigan, finally surpassed those of the department store—have begun to compete in earnest with the department store by offering the ease of everything-under-one-roof, in-bulk warehouse retailing. In 2008, in fact, low-cost, high-volume behemoth Kmart opened a location on the same Manhattan lot where, 100 years earlier, one of the paradigms of the department store had stood—Wanamaker's—replete with an art gallery and vast street-front glazing.

Today, with the ascent of e- and m-commerce, shopping apps and group buying, we are able to research, comparison shop, and find the deepest discounts online at all hours of the day or night, which means that it is becoming increasingly difficult to get us out of our pajamas and into the store. To combat this, the physical retail space must offer something more than clearance sales and logos. What the Internet can offer is rock-bottom prices, a glut of information, convenience, and the wherewithal in this age of Facebook and Twitter to make brands into icons by creating buzz around them for good or ill. What it cannot offer is experience.

DESIGNING EXPERIENCE

The Vaudeville of Window Display

Today, many retail interiors reflect the fact that shopping has evolved from being a necessity and a chore to being a form of recreation to being entertainment. That seed was planted and flourished in the storefront.

Glass is a powerful medium. Once upon a time, windows served as the only means to engage people with their local stores and the items they needed to get by. Today, the creation of highly crafted shadowboxes, vitrines, or room-size windows synthesizes and experiments with multiple disciplines—graphic design, scenography, micro-architecture, marketing and branding, art, choreography, and performance. Even creative icons like American industrial designer Raymond Loewy, surrealist Salvador Dali, and pop art legend Andy Warhol designed windows once. Windows are cross-disciplinary, material, theatrical, temporal, and psychological and, because they are about money, political, as well. (Broken glass and, beyond it, looting are familiar components of protest and riot the world over.) For Simon Doonan, who has been the mischief-maker designing the windows of New York department store Barneys for twenty-five years, windows are vaudeville on the street. He draws gawkers by using live ducks and live students (two women, one in drag), flyswatters, toilet paper, tins of lighter fluid, and condoms. He pairs trashed mattresses with cocktail gowns to depict surreal suburban backyards and dark adult tantrums. By contrast, Tokyo industrial designers Takaaki Tani and Kazunori Matsumura of t/m, both only 28, used nothing but tall white shopping bags filled with air to mimic ghostly crowds in a series of 2010 vitrines for Tokyo department store Isetan. Especially as retail interiors become, like windows, increasingly ephemeral, convertible, and transporting, designers would do well to look through the glass for methods, related to theater, composition, and choreography, to immerse the customer in shifting, ever-new experiences.

The importance of the visual merchandiser has grown over time as several retail roles have been conflated, including planning, lighting, design, décor, and display. While retailers fear that the Internet is stealing foot traffic (and eyes on the windows) by offering more ubiquitous and immediate communication, there may be a middle ground emerging in which windows will become as interactive and participatory as they are imaginative. Augmented Reality (AR) generates a real-time view of a physical object or environment that has been interleaved with computer-generated, interactive imagery. London's Selfridges used AR in display windows in mid-2010 to allow passersby to test-drive Tissot watches by strapping a strip of black paper on their wrists and letting a mirror-like online display track their movements, replacing the two-dimensional image with three-dimensional models whose functions—compasses, diver functionality, thermometers—worked in real time. Fashion retailer H&M used an AR iPhone application[10] to enable its customers to preview and take images of its fall/winter 2010 collection virtually—from the sidewalk outside ten of its Manhattan stores. When these window shoppers selected and captured the garments in their phones, they received a 10 percent discount on future purchases.[11] Admittedly, this remains a crude application of the technology, but it will become another powerful character on the window designer's stage.

The Do-Room is the New Showroom

If the importance of the visual merchandiser has grown in recent years, it has also, according to Martin Raymond of UK trend forecaster The Future Laboratory, been supplemented by the ascent of in-store producers and experience managers. This is because the experiences of window shopping and window display have spread inside. "Stores, and the activities that consumers increasingly expect to find in them," Raymond says, "will become more like nightclubs, galleries and theatres." In rudimentary forms, this has been happening since the 1970s, but as children of the pop-up store, constant connectivity, and the three-dimensional film, youth now now expect shopping to be an entertainment and an event. And this to the degree that they walk into the experience as literally as they walk into the space. For this reason, Raymond believes that retail will have to be increasingly emotion-driven, appealing to the consumer's imagination. "This will require a new commitment to retail design that truly woos and a ramping up of service that, until now, has been found in bars, exclusive clubs, and five-star luxury hotels."[12]

But it will not just be a ramping up of entertainment that we can expect. Interiors will become the sites of immersive experiences that tap all of our senses, not just to amuse but to inform. Computer hardware giant Apple has recreated the retail store as a showroom, where it is not so important that you buy the product there (although many do) but that you fall in love and buy the product somewhere—online, on the Apple site, on other sites, in other stores. "They win every time because their product is special," says Dennis Askins, creative director of Italian fashion label Diesel. "The lesson being that if you provide quality unique product, you can use the stores to inform, educate and excite and still benefit, no matter where the product is purchased."[13]

A more extraordinary example is when London-based design studio BarberOsgerby immersed visitors to the 2010 Milan furniture fair in a dim, mineral-looking environment of pure sound and Platonic forms. They armored a warehouse with anechoic foam to demonstrate a new Sony technology, a chip that, when integrated into furnishings, transforms them into audio speakers. The space contained several vignettes of minimalist domestic luxury that served as listening zones where guests reclined, listening to the furniture sing. The interior underscored the purity of the sound that the chip, inside table lamps, credenzas, and chairs, was capable of delivering, but it also made a second, perhaps more important, point: having stalked the Web, most hunter-shoppers today know their product's specs before they set foot in the store; what they can't possibly anticipate is what kind of experience that product will engender. BarberOsgerby's interior generated individual experiences that made it clear that the new showroom must become a do-room.

"Great experiences should be front and center; the equipment is arbitrary," says Askins. "If you give people the chance to feel what it's like to drive a Ferrari at a Ferrari showroom, you'll build their passion for the brand and at least sell a t-shirt."[14]

DESIGNING PUBLIC SPACE

"Retail space is most interesting when it offers new scenarios for living in, and interacting with, the city," says New York architect Dominic Leong, who, with brother Chris, makes up Leong Leong, the studio that designed Philip Lim's L.A. flagship in 2008. For Building Fashion,[15] the brothers designed a one-week retail installation in a disused lot that both hosted events and served as a store for fashion designer Siki Im. They sprayed a converted 474 sq. ft. (44 sq m) construction trailer with a soy-based insulation foam, filling it end-to-end with a ramp, and, using knives, saws, and power sanders, carved out niches and ledges at various heights. Garments were displayed out of sight in little caves under each end of the ramp that were accessed by canted triangular apertures in the floor, leaving the bulk of the volume free for lounging guests. On a $5,000 budget, the brothers designed the space digitally, CNC-milling one of its sections as a kit of parts; they constructed it off-site and then disassembled and installed it in three days.

Removing their shoes at the door, visitors reclined, listened to music, climbed, slid, posed, and purchased. Some people seemed a little bewildered on entering the space; others didn't enter at all because they didn't want to take off their shoes. For them, it remained a spectacle. "We asked people to remove their shoes because we thought it would automatically take them out of their everyday expectations of a retail space," says Dominic. "It would be domestic, but still very public at the same time. We had no idea how people would react, but our intent was to take people out of their ordinary comfort zone by creating a space that only suggested how it should be used or experienced, but never explicitly declaring it."[16]

The store multitasked as a play space where people gathered, drank, listened to music, tried on clothes, and, because of the gloopy consistency of the foam on one's bare feet, had an experience that drew on all their senses. "I challenged them to be emotional," Im says. "This is how a store should be. There will be less and less of a physical barrier between the virtual and the real in the future, but until then we still need the tactile and sensual intervention of the store."[17] Sales were an afterthought: wholly engaging guests, whether customers or not, expanded the perception of the brand beyond the product alone. Few people left the event without knowing who their hosts had been. That said, each project also had another impact: by reinvigorating a dead space, an abandoned former real estate sales office, underneath the Manhattan High Line Park, the designers also served to form connections among the city, the brand, and the inhabitants of both.

DESIGNING EMOTION

We've seen that novelty boutiques can engage customers through the senses. They involve a scenography that, by appealing to our emotions, transcends the transaction, so that we buy into the brand with more than our money. Design can influence the consumption of not just products but of company and culture. In these environments, it is not just the inventory that is on sale; the actual purchase becomes merely a souvenir of an experience generated by the brand space. These spaces are both engaging and memorable. They appeal to the emotions. The goal? Not simply to manufacture brand loyalty but to cultivate brand affinity, a visceral, irrational connection to the company—one that converts customers into advocates, with or without short-term sales.

The Art/Commerce Hybrid

Retail designers have sown fertile ground by periodically refusing to dig trenches between art, architecture, fashion, and commerce. By resorting to extra-commercial activities, they are able to diminish our perception of the transaction and deepen our experience of the brand. Take, for instance, the Prada Transformer, an event space designed for the Italian fashion house by Rem Koolhaas' Office for Metropolitan Architecture. A vast tetrahedron that could be rotated by a construction crane into various positions to form purpose-built spaces, it opened in Seoul during the summer of 2009 and then served as a site for fashion shows, cinema, art exhibitions, and

FIGURE 63   London-based BarberOsgerby's 2010 Milan furniture fair Sony project was a dim space clad with anechoic foam to demonstrate a new chip that can transmute furnishings into audio speakers. The interior underscored the product's purity of sound as well as the fact that retail space must provide a deep experience of its product: the new showroom must be a do-room.

events—undiluted cultural experiences. Unmediated by explicit marketing, this kind of performance sends the cognoscenti right back to the Prada cash till and makes aspirants of all the rest.

The more naked hybrids of commerce and culture represent a synergistic exchange taking place among fashion, art, and architecture that has become more conspicuous in the highest end boutiques in the past decade. One no longer merely browses, tries, and buys clothes. The shopper has a bite-size experience more common to the theater or gallery: one is transported into a different world or thrust into an alien world one might not otherwise have had the opportunity (or wanted the opportunity?) to enter. One wanders through the sanitized but meticulously detailed tarpaulin-clad lean-tos of a Japanese homeless community in Tokyo's Bernhard Wilhelm store by New York–based artist Cyril Duval of Item-Idem. Or, designed by Dutch artist Germaine Kruip with fashion virtuoso Raf Simons, the New York flagship for Jil Sander is as austere but materially rich as a contemporary art gallery. It eschews the glazed frontage, asking that visitors walk blind from the cluttered Soho street into a nearly empty marble-and-mirror art installation. At the rear, Kruip created rotating vertical louvers consisting of narrow slivers of mirror that catch and release reflections of the bare interior as they turn. On the second floor, the changing rooms are cubes of mirror that the client wraps around herself like a mantle on entering and that are as sparse as Simons's clothing. It is an exquisite, hermetic fiction with a single goal: to sell "art," be it rotating shards of glass, unfolding fitting rooms, or lushly geometrical winter coats.

The promise, however, to deliver full artistic or cultural experiences has not been well- or widely kept; in general, the veneer of artistry comes to feel disingenuous in many spaces. Case in point, the message when Prada began to open its huge, high-concept and high-design epicenters in 2001 was that these stores "were created to transcend shopping and engage public space and cultural programming."[18] Indeed, the 23,000 sq. ft. (2,137 sq m) New York epicenter was built on the former site of the Guggenheim Soho—a fact lost on no one—with a hang tag of $40 million at a time when the company was hundreds of millions of dollars in debt. Since then, however, its vast zebrawood wave-cum-shoe-display-cum-amphitheater, which sacrificed a swathe of high-return, street-level retail while leaving the lower level feeling cramped, has hosted only a single (gallery-worthy) exhibition of skirts by Miuccia Prada, a brief display of skull wallpaper-plus-video projec-tions by Damien Hirst, some gorgeously graphical wall-coverings by design studio 2x4, and a handful of Tribeca Film Festival screenings. The world has waited for the exhibi-tions and performances that would redeem our acquisitive compulsions and delivery on the explicit promise that shopping would be forever altered, but there has been no signifi-cant or sustained arts programming yet.

DESIGNING THE SELF

The Boutique

It was the introduction of prêt-à-porter to the fashion industry and the free spirit of the decade that helped to create the boutique in 1960s London, with its balance of indi-viduality (the shopper's) and uniqueness (of the owner's product selection) with enter-tainment and accessibility. The accessories of retail architecture remain the same—a till, fitting rooms, display systems (racks, tables, shelves, cupboards), tightly choreographed lighting (or lack thereof), a storefront, and vitrines animated by a scenography of mer-chandise—but today more than ever, these elements must resonate with shoppers' fanta-sies and senses in a way that lasts long after they leave the shop. An unusually packaged soap or a pair of trainers becomes the token of a larger, ongoing narrative that is the brand but that is perceived as an expression of self.

In 2005, the Milan boutique of Amsterdam's favorite fashion twins Viktor & Rolf turned interior architecture on its head—literally—with dados and moldings, par-quet flooring and chandeliers, all upended. Shoppers shopped on the ceiling; garments appeared to hang upward. It was a wonderland of chic. The Alchemist boutique in Miami by architect Rene Gonzalez is no less fanciful for being entirely true-to-life. It is a poem to place, a real place. Situated in an parking garage by Swiss architects Her-zog & de Meuron, the store is a glass box dressed with mirrors that reflect either traffic threading the street below or the city's tropical skyline. This means that it broadcasts the contents of the shop to the outside while drawing the city in, making this con-stant motion the source of the space's dynamic look and feel. Sensors move forty-three pneumatic, mirrored ceiling panels (designed by the UK's Random International) in sync with browsing shoppers, stopping when they stop, moving when they move. Technology does not need to be conspicuous to improve the shopping experience. Indeed, unless it is an explicit component of the design concept, designers are increasingly burying it in the interior, rendering it invisible to—though palpable and functional for—the customer. Because tech products still lack flexibility and usually feature standard formats and looks, their presence, if conspicuous, can seem onerous, unsophisticated, and clunky; they also risk appearing quickly outdated. Instead, through the integration of a technology-driven artwork, Alchemist has been pared down to light, sky, reflections, and rotating clothing collections. This ethereal bareness is aided by a barely there display system: "The shop is meant to serve as a blank canvas where there are no rules," says co-owner Roma Cohen, who helped design the system, which consists of receiving holes ranged in a grid on the floor (like a Battleship game board) into which one pops rack poles, allowing the pattern to be altered at whim.[19] On this canvas, the fashion—the Alchemist store owners' tastes run to pieces with strong personalities: Rodarte, Chrome Hearts, Rick Owens—becomes a texture as much as the light and reflections do. The shop is a jewel box of the senses that gives visitors a fresh perspective on both what it contains and what contains it. It also happens to be one of the purest interactions one can have with Miami outside of the too-tan tans, the withered décolletés, and the leopard-print Lycra.

DESIGNING A DESTINATION

The Pop-Up Shop

In the late 1990s, looking to sell in greater volume, shops co-opted a tool used by marketers to move Halloween costumes and seasonal fireworks: simple but clever temporary retail spaces capable of generating buzz while pumping up the purchasing and creating a destination as much as an event. In 2010, Kid Robot's Manhattan pop-up, selling limited-edition art toys, consisted of a space rented between permanent tenants that was then slathered with sheets of ordinary household aluminum foil. Guerrilla marketing's most celebrated pioneer, Comme des Garçons' Rei Kawakubo, delighted shoppers with her 2004 Berlin pop-up shop, but since then everyone from Song Airlines to eBay have "popped up," including Target, which popped up floating in the middle of the Hudson River for Christmas 2003. In its customers, the pop-up—at its best, a global concept lithe enough to draw both international media and the locals—generated a sense of urgency to get there with its ever-imminent expiration date. At the same time, it leapfrogged lengthy leases and costly architecture and interiors.

Much of the time, the only way to tell the difference between a pop-up shop and a sample sale is the price tag, but the form became increasingly baroque at its peak. For four weeks in 2009, British sportswear retailer Reebok opened a pop-up sneaker shop in Manhattan's visually cacophonous wholesale lighting and restaurant supply district. Designed by local studio Formavision, the space flew in the face of the frill-free pop-up template; the space was sharpened and animated with "dazzle graphics" that tore visitors out of three dimensions and flattened them into two. This distortion of space co-opted a technique used to camouflage WWI "dazzle" warships. These brazen graphics—some suggested by the shoes, including honeycomb patterns and chevrons—both clarified and confused every surface. These patterns, developed by the British Royal Navy as military camouflage, were applied to the hulls and decking of ships for the purpose of obscuring their size, shape, and direction. The team mapped out the graphics in two dimensions and folded them into three before applying them to the walls and floors. Formavision principle Sébastien Agneessens[20] admits that, had it been a permanent store, the team would have approached it differently, using more benign colors and shapes, finer finishes and lighting. Instead, this was a temporary installation intended to serve, precisely, as an extension of both shoes and brand that would generate traffic and media attention and reposition Reebok in its industry, as much as showcase its new collections. "When we chose the location, we realized that we had to be pop and loud," Agneessens explains. "To make it work, the space had to make a statement with no compromises."[21] Confounding perspective, the furnishings became graphical devices as much as the graphics: garment racks appeared flat from the front but from an angle were revealed to be deeply crimped. The cash counter tapered into sharp points at either end, while display tables consisted of two slabs whose edges, when stacked, were slightly offset. Everywhere the blunt confronted the pointed, giving the shop an exuberant athleticism. "The pop-up store as a model is meant to privilege contemporaneity and immediacy. It should anticipate or even catalyze trends," says Rafael de Cárdenas, once a Calvin Klein designer who turned to furniture and interiors, heading up his own Manhattan studio, Architecture at Large. "The same way that content delivery has become more dynamic with YouTube and Twitter, the canonical ways of product display are giving way to new strategies valued for the simple sake of never-been-seen-beforeness. I value the flash-in-the-pan because it fingerprints and daydreams of a very specific moment in time."[22]

EDITING EXPERIENCE

The Concept Shop

Behind an unmarked London door in 1966, Biba was among the first concept shops. The press called it "a private members' club for the general public," words that could describe a balance that many retailers are still trying to achieve today. In 1980, Armand and Martine Hadida's Paris fashion shop, L'Eclaireur, was a second famed pioneer of the type: another unmarked storefront that guarded a curated selection of avant-garde designers, including Prada, Martin Margiela, and Dries van Noten and a retail approach that combined art, architecture, and fashion. The concept shop grew more widespread in the early 1990s with the success of Milan's 10 Corso Como, a gallery, café, boutique, and bookstore. The idea was to winnow the breadth of the department store into a tightly edited inventory and, at the largest scale, as in Tokyo's Opening Ceremony, turn retail departments into themed environments.

By 2010, L'Eclaireur had opened its sixth location in Paris, designed by the Belgian Studio Arne Quinze (SAQ). This outpost adds technology to the Hadida mix: embedded unevenly in the roughly accreted wood slats of the walls are 140 LCD screens fed by 32 remote signals, forming either a single large video wall or 32 separate displays—the result feels nothing like marketing. At the heart of the store, a digital artwork by local artists Naziha Mestaoui and Yacine Ait Kaci, known as Electronic Shadow, played in a darkened, secret room. The first installment of their series projected real-time, state-of-the-world statistics into a basin on the floor. The second chapter allowed visitors to change a projected image, producing a sound with each alteration, that was available for viewing (and altering) online simultaneously. "The world is changing. Retail has become a place for experience," insists Naziha Mestaoui, who suggests that on entering a shop, shoppers must not be stripped of their human complexity and reduced to being only customers. "There is a mix of influences that determines who you are and retail has to consider people not only from the perspective of branding, but in a dialog with the visitors who will spend time in the universe that the shop creates. As I said at the opening, this is not a store, this is a story. This is, as I understand it, the meaning of the name 'l'Eclaireur': it doesn't just sell objects, it sells illumination."[23]

DESIGNING LUXURY

L'Eclaireur also broadcasts exclusivity without resorting to some of the most wearying tropes of the business: the use of intimidation (as opposed to service) as a retail tool or a limited and conventional use of decadent materials—approaches that appeal all too often to the client's masochism. Lighting may be reduced to an impractical[24] darkness, severely diminished pinpoints, or the opposite, a panoptic, chandelier-like brilliance that is thought to amplify a space's exclusivity, if not its functionality. L'Eclaireur's atmosphere feels luxurious through strategic contrasts: a generous sense of space paired with hidden chambers; roughly articulated wall surfaces in combination with soft finishes. The lighting has a pragmatic chiaroscuro effect: niches of clothing are well-lit while other parts of the space are darkened to let the video pop out. When the client enters the store, she is received immediately by a salesperson, who then helps her to discover the displayed—(but actually an incomplete portion of the) collection, which serves as a tasting menu. The client is considered the host, in command of a lingering experience expected to last, whether a purchase is made or not, thirty minutes to an hour instead of the quick ten minutes that is typical. This lengthy stay is actually merited here, not because there are so many garments on display (there aren't) but because there is enough artwork to spend some time with, if you don't happen to get sucked in by the clothing. After the client indicates her tastes, the salesperson will dip into any of six cabinets of curiosities, each dedicated to a single designer, that are locked in a room that conceals the bulk of the stock behind doors that open only on command.

Now, the L'Eclaireur-type of retail space—dedicated to high-touch service, exclusivity, a forward-looking aesthetic, and the generation of an immersive and patrician sense of luxury—is not particularly innovative. Hadida's own shops did it early on, after all. But SAQ's design succeeds amply in its manufacture of a rarified atmosphere through a confection of rich ingredients—the explicit abundance of art, a highly choreographed discovery of the product, the vault of treasures secreted behind closed doors, awaiting discovery. The interior, however, privileges nothing over the client. As SAQ project lead Roel Delhoorne says, "The concept was a dressing room, not a boutique."[25]

DESIGNING CONVENIENCE

Round-the-Clock Retail

From high-brow to high-low, retailers who want to keep to regular business hours, but still wish to increase sales and lend a constant sense of both change and choice to shopping, are beginning to add vending machines to interstitial spaces: hotel lobbies, airport terminals, or cosmetic departments. Recently, these machines have become interior design elements in and of themselves.

For those who prefer self-service to high-touch customer service (read: pushy salespeople), it would be a relief to just punch a few buttons and swipe your card instead of fending off the hard sell. We share personal information with a machine instead of a human every time we use an ATM or airport self-check-in kiosk, and we're getting used to it. This growing intimacy with technology has revived a low-tech and old-school retail tool: that early twentieth-century coin-operated paradigm of Americana that served up stews, sandwiches, and sodas, saving on labor costs and staying open for business long after all the other stores had been shuttered—the automat.

In Japan during the mid-1990s, the machines were filled with flowers, tinned coffee, men's dress shirts, and porn. In the U.S. meantime, with nothing quite as compelling to save it, the vending machine faded into obscurity with the dissemination of the stale Doritos and Dr. Pepper; over the years, they became a symbol of institutionalized alienation instead of solicitous service.

Today, however, it's all about luxury vending: cosmetics brand Elizabeth Arden has opened a kiosk introducing a "virtual beauty consultant" that recommends (and vends) the appropriate product according to skin type. Fragrance manufacturer Coty allows customers to sample perfumes by exhaling a scented vapor produced at the touch of a button. In Abu Dhabi, a machine that looks more like an armored truck dispenses gold bars and coins. The U*Tique machine created by Mara Segal and RUX in 2008 vends hair and skincare products by Lancôme and Bliss, along with mink eyelashes, at a specialty boutique in Fred Segal Santa Monica. In the lobby of the Mondrian Miami hotel, the Semi-Automatic (vending) machine *is* the hotel gift shop, accepting credit cards only and offering twenty-four-hour service. Violet light illuminates the tony white shopping bags that line its glass-fronted, white shelving. The Morgans' creative director Kim Walker curated the contents, which include 24-karat-gold handcuffs, Atari Classics for PlayStation, the day-rental of a Rolls Royce Silver Shadow, $400 marabou feather vests, and paperback fiction.

The vending machine is also assuming more ordinary shifts: in 2002, UK supermarket Sainsbury's stocked a machine with 150 products, including staples like milk and bread, that became especially popular among nightshift workers. Australia's Crumpler website is designed to look and act like a machine that vends bags. And who hasn't made a last-second electronics purchase at the airport before rushing to their gate?

Technology: Finally Changing Shopping?

Once upon a time, fitting rooms were an afterthought, and, mostly, they still are. Unfortunately, when they're not an afterthought, they're overthought. Koolhaas kitted out the changing room doors of his Prada epicenter in New York with SGG Priva-Lite glass. A liquid crystal film laminated between transparent sheets of glass became opaque when the electric current was cut off with the touch of a large floor button. Shoppers' delight in this feat of magic was the doom of the doors, however: under zealous use, they broke repeatedly. In 2001, this was one example of how Prada served as a glaring example of the fact that, despite claims to the contrary, technology had not yet profoundly altered the rituals or mechanisms of shopping.

The impetus for change finally proved, instead, to be the Internet, followed swiftly by the smart phone and technologies capable of enriching reality, which have provided direct marketing with its ideal delivery method. But it's also meant that we've became so overwhelmed with input that we have turned to retail curators in gallery-like concept shops to save time and articulate our limited-edition individuality. With the rise in online shopping, with its hackable databases of personal information, its shopping histories, and its not-quite-right on-the-mark recommendations, there has been a commensurate swell in meticulously crafted shops. And these physical spaces are being created with the understanding that today the thrill of a day of shopping should be commensurate to a day of themed rides at Disneyland. By now, technology is changing both what and how we are consuming in earnest, which is, in turn, changing significant components of the retail interior. Take the new fitting-room mirror: Cisco lets shoppers use gesture control to scroll through ensembles and try them in a "mirror." This is the harbinger of the "responsive mirror," which uses multiple cameras to track motion, replaying images in high-definition video on a screen beside the (actual) mirror: the shopper can view herself in one garment at a time or view one blouse while trying on another; the earlier image will follow in any direction she turns. Soon, intelligent fitting rooms will be able to suggest pairings, alternatives, or stream any of these images to a friend's phone to elicit feedback.

As e-commerce (shopping online) evolves into m-commerce (shopping from one's mobile device), the transaction that high-end stores have already been tucking away from sight can increasingly be taken out of physical retail space altogether. Smart phone applications are turning phones into sales tools—using photo-recognition technology, for instance, to turn them into smart cosmetic compacts that allow a woman to test-drive colors on a photo of her face. With our credit card info, sizes, and preferences stored in our gadgets, we will browse nearby stores, scan the QR codes and hang tags of desired items, charge them to AT&T, and pick up our shopping bag whenever we finally walk past the store.

DESIGNING VALUES

Buy Good, Do Good

As climate concerns mount and the economy sags, retail environments and consumption have become a way to get good value while expressing one's values. Concerned with a different kind of environment in the last decade, consumers have been embracing do-gooder values and value for their money (most conveniently found on the Web). They want everything to be accessible but in a unique environment; they want good stuff, but they want it to come with good service. And today, they are looking for points of view in addition to points of sale. With the constant refrain of sustainability in the first decade of the twenty-first century, retailers are learning to anticipate how not just their products but their spaces can respond to a new set of values and a new emphasis on value. The disposable culture of the 1990s has gone out of fashion followed by an aesthetic of rustic

FIGURE 64   Leong Leong brothers Chris and Dominic set out to create retail space that offers new scenarios for living in, and interacting with, the city. For Building Fashion their $5,000, one-week installation was CNC milled as a kit of parts, slathered in a soy-based insulation foam and carved out using knives, saws, and power sanders.

chic or rough luxe and styles that favor the handmade as counterpoint to the laser-cut and the CNC-milled.

It would be too simplistic, however, to suggest that the return to values is simply a response to global crisis and economic downturn, or even a political statement. Discerning luxury in rough environments or handcrafted objects represents a turning away from the end-of-millennium excess that was glaringly reflected in the architecture of the time toward a contemplation of simpler things, a craving to discern traces of the human hand and not only the keyboard. It becomes a refreshing counterpoint to ostentation, waste, information saturation, and the unblemished nature of the products of the techno-culture. These hybrid interiors, as the zeitgeist of the era dictates, synthesize the traditional and the contemporary, familiarity and innovation, bling and asceticism. Usually these spaces are furnished and finished with objects that have (or appear to have) a history, objects salvaged or collected from a flea market or construction site, or abandoned by a previous owner. The interior bears the traces of the carpenter who assembled them. In response to CAD, Rhino, and 3D Max, in response to the pixel, designers of these spaces are trying to provide an alternative to the algorithms by recalling a time when people knew where every product they were buying had come from. Usually the surfaces are colored by the colors of the materials used to build them—grainy wood, sheer plastic sheeting, multicolored rip-ties, thick lumpy yarns—and then left unvarnished, unpainted, merely patina-ed with their own age. We mustn't mistake this approach for nostalgia, a longing to recover the past; instead, it appeals to consumers trying to carve out a place in their lives that isn't overwhelmed, in a rush, or anxious—a mental space that is neither weary nor polluted.

This is also a yearning to find our way back to each other after years of communicating through e-mails and SMSes. In Montreal, the first Atelier Lolë opened in 2010, not simply to showcase the company's sportswear and health concepts but also as a place where women who share the values of the brand can connect with one another. The design of the flagship features a so-called social wall which is embedded with ten iPads where shoppers and women around the globe can share photos taken on their phones using an app created by the brand and archived on the Lolë blog, where women can "communicate, exchange ideas and inspire one another." The brand's online greeting urges visitors to "feel motivated by the active lifestyle we live and breathe, and visit often to express your individuality and passion for life."[26] This is a more individualized opportunity for self-expression than wearing a Tommy Hilfiger logo across your chest, one that invites guests to imagine that the commercial aspect of the business has disappeared, leaving only this avuncular host of a network of likeminded people (not consumers).

Values-oriented spaces don't have to be made of hemp and recycled newspaper pulp, although designers today are even making luxe objects out of those old hippie humbugs, too. Tel Aviv's Delicatessen boutiques, designed by New York–based Guy Zucker of Z-A Studio in 2006 and 2009, are an expression of the brand's and the designer's values through retail space. In the original shop, Zucker used only linoleum and cardboard tubes to dress a 904 sq. ft. (84 sq m) storefront in a thin garment that served as the shop's display racks and window, fitting room and cash till. The entire project cost only $3,000, of which the materials represented only one-third while nonetheless proscribing the form and function of the space. The shop's second Tel Aviv incarnation featured pegboard that Zucker bought at a hardware store. On a $10,000 budget, the designer lined the two-story, 336 sq. ft. (34 sq m) shop with custom-perforated white hardboard. The grid of holes is accessorized with hooks for display but also happens to suggest a sewing pattern.

Neither space set out to be sustainable, according to Zucker; instead, he was making a comment on his own discipline by suggesting that architecture should, like fashion, use cheap materials with sophistication and make the cost of design far outstrip the cost of materials, instead of the other way around. If architects want to learn from the fashion industry, attitudes must change, Zucker insists: we can't expect every building to become a monument. "If we can invest less in 'high-end' materials," he suggests, "we might be able to give more importance to the manipulation of material and the quality of design rather than to the cost of the material; give less importance to the contractor and more importance to the designer."[27]

Designing the Digital Interior

With changes in values and a deepening hunger for imaginative escape compounded by advances in technology, graphic designers are going to have to become retail designers, too of online "interiors". Designers of every stripe will have to consider any retail space to be an interior in the shopper's mind, if not outside it. Meanwhile, consumers will always reward retailers who fabricate a good user experience, experience being the fertile word of the day. Now the shop must be a place to indulge our imaginations and aspirations, not just three-dimensional logos or warehouses. As unbreachable as Tobi Wong's Wrong Store was, so too was the corresponding online shop, an unbrowsable URL offering nothing for sale and little more than a cheeky sign reading "Closed on Mondays." Although he was urging us to greater self-awareness, he knew precisely how to keep our faces pressed up against the glass.

27

Designing for Sustainability: A Framework for Interior Designers to Design for Efficiency and Beyond

NADIA ELROKHSY

WHY? AND WHY INTERIOR DESIGN?

Interior designers need to question more broadly what role they play and become involved in the evolution of the design proposal/brief itself. This chapter suggests that the discipline of service design, along with strategic and integrative design provides a valuable format for questioning what and in what manner we consume and why to support alternatives to the "business as usual" model. The discipline of interior design can encourage a move away from the propensity for consuming more things, which advances related carbon dioxide emissions and waste, by designing "the conditions"[1] for successful interactions and experiences to live "more with less."[2] The prospects are tremendous for interior designers who take up the challenge to become stewards of our planet and support the ability to be resilient in the face of dramatic change. With a new mission and vision for our role, the interior designer can design for quality of life while influencing more sustainable ways of being.

SUSTAINABILITY—BUILDING ON A WORKING DEFINITION

Interior designers are often interested in challenging existing notions of how we live, and at the initial phase of design, question more broadly what setting to design and to support what experiences. At the heart of any definition of *sustainability* is the basic and essential question, How do we live? Investigations into green design or energy efficiency, which typically focus on materials and products, are critical, but our behaviors, habits, and rituals are essential to the study, as well. This is the space where interior design can be of great influence.

Any writing on the subject of sustainability must begin with a working definition. The topic of sustainability has been defined in many ways and through various lenses. The most commonly referenced definition is taken from the 1987 United Nations World Commission on Environment and Development report, "Our Common Future,"[3] where *sustainable development* is defined as "development that meets the needs of the present without compromising the ability of future generations to meet their own needs."[4] The difficulty is in having a global agreement on needs versus wants. Environmentalist and activist Bill McKibben[5] in his book *Deep Economy* reveals that the connection between money and happiness is much more difficult to make after one's primary needs are satisfied.[6] Nevertheless, our global economy continues to revolve around the need for ever-increasing growth and monetary wealth, which has pushed "the planet's ecological systems to the brink of failure, without making us happier."[7]

If designers are to play a part in rethinking current unsustainable lifestyles, then ecological literacy is a necessary place to begin. "Ecological footprint analysis,"[8] originally developed by scientists William Rees and Mathis Wackernagel, quantifies the amount of regenerative planetary resources required for our current consumption patterns.[9] The WWF (World Wildlife Fund For Nature) 2010 Living Planet Report states that "by 2030 humanity will need the capacity of two Earths to absorb CO_2 [carbon dioxide] waste and keep up with natural resource consumption."[10] Clearly, certain inhabitants consume and waste far and above our planet's ability to absorb the effects—challenging Earth's "carrying capacity."[11] Furthermore, coupled with ever-increasing population growth, we simply cannot extend these lifestyles across the globe to all inhabitants without consequences that challenge our ability to be resilient; a sustainable future will require a drastically different way of living.[12] In the recently published *Design Dictionary, Perspectives on Design Terminology*,[13] sustainability is defined through the lens of design. In this valuable reference, philosopher and sustainability educator Cameron Tonkinwise[14] defines *sustainability* as "a measure of the resilience of a system, the capacity of a system (and all its components) to repair itself when damaged."[15] Resilience, as introduced by famed ecologist C. S. "Buzz" Holling,[16] offers a theory and framework for relating how shocks to the system—social, environmental, and/or economic—are becoming seeds for new opportunities to design ways of bouncing back, to be "persistent, adaptable and transformable."[17] Tonkinwise expands on the definition of sustainability with the excerpt from "Our Common Future" but then quickly turns to the study of ecology as foremost to our understanding the issue—the study of biotic[18] interactions and interrelationships that help to identify the impacts of human lifestyles and processes. Physicist, systems theorist, and author of *The Hidden Connections: A Science for Sustainable Living* Fritjof Capra[19] writes that the "first step" toward sustainability "is to understand the principles of organization, common to all living systems, that ecosystems have developed to sustain the web of life."[20] Tonkinwise's definition summarizes expansive thoughts and works from experts in the sustainability arena, most especially designer Ezio Manzini.

Impacts and risks to our natural and human systems have been uncovered through a number of landmark discoveries over the centuries. Each of these discoveries evidences a network of hidden connections, connecting the environmental, social, and economic factors, exposing their interdependencies. This awareness reached our popular culture with *Silent Spring,* the seminal work of scientist Rachel Carson,[21] and more recently with the release of *An Inconvenient Truth,*[22] the documentary film of vice president Al Gore's presentation on climate change. The link between fossil fuel consumption and carbon dioxide emissions. Emphasizes benefits of designing and implementing energy efficiencies. However, as Tonkinwise points out, "If a household is convinced to buy a more efficient air-conditioner, that household will save money on its electricity bills that over time it will probably respend on extensions to the house, creating whole new spaces to be filled with furnishings and cooled/heated by air conditioners."[23] Therefore interior designers need to be asking how individuals might be motivated to live radically different lives, making associations between everyday actions and their impact.

These questions are not new to all fields of design, and, as Tonkinwise explains in his definition of sustainability, there are designers who are regularly engaged with these questions and strategies for designing. Ezio Manzini, and his colleagues, provide useful examples where designers operate as "facilitators"[24] to groups of individuals who are motivated to make changes because of a desire to improve their quality of life. Using low-impact products combined with alternative systems and services for collaborating, these "creative communities"[25] support ways of living more socially enriched lives with less materiality. International research networks, such as the Design for Social Innovation and Sustainability (DESIS), internationally coordinated by Manzini are bringing awareness, through design, by "amplifying" various local and small-scale initiatives to influence a greater impact overall.[26] What these case studies also offer is insight into how different fields of design, such as interior design, leveraging knowledge and skills related to the built environment, can design responsive and adaptable environments that serve the needs and desires of its users, with social and economic benefits supported alongside environmental benefits.

ENVIRONMENTAL DRIVERS FOR CHANGE

From Ice Ages to the Sages

Science on the "greenhouse effect"[27] and global warming, driving our heightened awareness and concern for climate change, can be mapped back to Victorian times when naturalists such as John Tyndall and scientists such as Joseph Fourier and Svante Arrhenius were driven by an interest in Earth's temperature and the question of how our planet's climate could so dramatically change that it could cause the ice ages. The scientific study of greenhouse gasses such as carbon dioxide began with an interest in understanding the past.[28] In the mid- to late 1990s, scientists studying greenhouse gasses understood that increases in recorded carbon dioxide levels, along with other human-related gas emissions—methane—would bring about increases in average global temperatures and with it climate change. Decades have passed and advancements, such as the readings from ice core samples,[29] have allowed scientists to reliably track global carbon dioxide levels, going back hundreds of thousands of years.[30]

Global warming and concerns for climate change reached international scientific consensus through the International Panel on Climate Change (IPCC). In 1988, the United Nations Environment Programme (UNEP) and the World Meteorological Organization (WMO) established this intergovernmental organization of scientists to assess the numerous, worldwide, scientific documentation of global warming and the impacts of climate change. Each IPCC update is designed to arm decision-makers with an assessment of our ability to adapt to the effects of human-related carbon uptake and to identify areas of vulnerability to climate change.[31] The 2007 IPCC Fourth Assessment Report presented more evidence than in prior IPCC reports that our planet's "unequivocal"[32] global warming is primarily caused by human behaviors and lifestyles, resulting in increases in global greenhouse gas emissions. Population growth, increasing demand for natural resources, along with advancements in technologies have allowed us to harvest and consume those natural resources at unprecedented magnitudes and are resulting in observable impacts to our environment.[33]

Designers must, therefore, question how they can assist in decoupling the relationship between growth and development in the economy, and fossil fuel energy consumption, while supporting an improved quality of life. They need to understand the significant role they and the built environment play in continuing or changing the unsustainable business-as-usual scenario of global warming and climate change. Interior designers regularly make decisions and assist others in making decisions that impact energy use, waste, and efficiencies within buildings. Additionally, interior designers influence human activities within buildings; therefore, they have the potential to influence sustainable lifestyles by designing the settings that make those patterns of behavior more attractive.

Consumption Patterns, Energy Efficiency, and the Built Environment

Many innovations in the built environment (beginning with examples in the vernacular) were developed in direct response to the climatic conditions of a place.[34] Presently, these practices have found renewed interest and advancement in the practice of environmental design (see Fig. 65).[35]

Utilizing the technologies, materials, and products available to them, interior designers have designed and can design spaces that provide comfort and delight for all the senses. Alternatively, our recent past indicates that, without efficiencies, advances in technology for building systems allowed designers to ignore climatic conditions, thereby increasing energy consumption in the operation of buildings—for example, in increased lighting, heating, and cooling loads. The 1970s energy crisis sparked an interest in design for energy efficiency and alternative sources for energy, fostering their growth and development. As the crisis abated and despite incentives for energy efficiency and alternative energy sources, the trend for using these alternatives faded, and by 2008 energy consumption for heating and electricity generation had increased, accounting for almost half of the of world's carbon dioxide emissions by sector.[36] The persistent efforts of many and growing global interest in the importance of

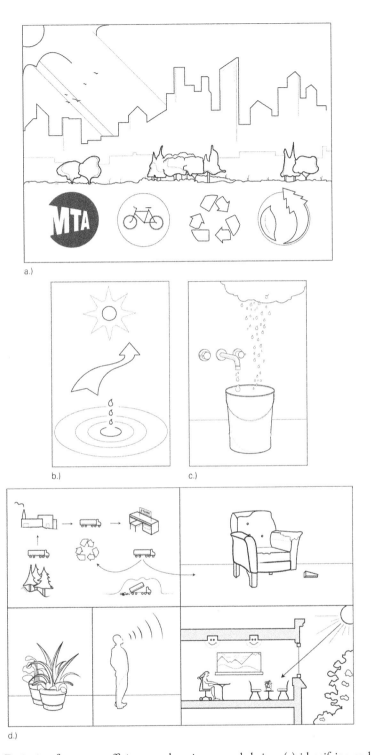

FIGURE 65 Designing for energy efficiency and environmental design: (a) identifying and leveraging the assets of the site; (b) capturing and utilizing the sun, the wind, and (c) rain fall; and (d) designing to reduce consumption and impact from raw material resourcing through use to life after use versus landfill, and designing to support health in the interiorscape. Courtesy of Nadia Elrokhsy; digitally drawn by Eli Rosenbloom.

sustainability has renewed our attention for alternatives in the design of the built environment. National and international organizations for the built environment have been established to educate people, and assess the impact of buildings on people and the environment.[37] In 1990, the UK's Building Research Establishment (BRE) organization established the nation's first process for assessing the environmental performance of a building—the Building Research Establishment Environmental Assessment Method (BREEAM).[38] A few years later, following the example of BREEAM, but with a different process, the U.S. Green Building Council (USGBC)[39] established the Leadership in Energy and Environmental Design (LEED) Green Building Rating System. There are other rating systems, but these two were firsts of their kind and continue to be most frequently referenced. Beyond energy consumption, BREEAM and LEED also address water efficiencies and indoor air quality. Air quality is of growing concern as we design more efficient and air-tight buildings. Many of the materials used emit toxic chemicals during their lifetime. Scientific research on the toxic effects of certain materials, and the intermixing of materials, is ongoing, requiring designers to stay abreast of the latest information. Various third-party product rating systems, and research from governmental and nonprofit organizations, such as the California Air Resource Board (CARB), Energy Star, GREENGUARD, Green Label, Green Seal, and Global Ecolabelling Network, to name a few, assist designers in material and product selection.[40]

Strategies for reusing and improving existing buildings is especially important for developed nations, since the existing building stock represents an already significant investment in energy—the embodied energy in its materials and products is wasted in demolition. As we work toward greater energy efficiencies in the operation of buildings, building materials and products emerge as significant in their natural resource depletion, toxicity, pollution, and waste.[41]

The systemic flows associated with materials and products are typically "cradle to grave,"[42] where a process of resourcing, manufacturing, transporting, use, and maintenance ends in waste and dumped in a landfill. Environmental impacts of this process must be accounted for and assessed in design analysis. Our economy is based on a long-standing policy of planned obsolescence, fueling a rejection of the old in favor of the new fashionable or more "convenient" thing.[43] Mountainous landfills and anthropogenic "marine debris" events—such as the "garbage patch"[44]—should challenge our notion of need and expedite alternative strategies to waste."[45] In a "cradle to cradle"[46] scenario, a material or product is recycled and made anew; however, the flows of that process must be accounted for and assessed, as well. The method used to understand and analyze these material flows and their ecological impacts over the life span of a material, product (including its component parts), and/or service is known as Life Cycle Assessment (LCA).[47] There are challenges to the success of LCA tools, which include acquiring accurate and current data about a material and/or process, the assignation of value for inputs, and the weighting, in relative importance, of one category against another. Nonetheless, LCA can be a powerful tool for interior designers and other decision-makers to uncover the process of things, identifying where environmental impacts lie in the chain of events and when common standards for comparisons can be found, to "choose the least burdensome"[48] on the environment.[49]

Efficiencies Are Not Enough

While many energy- and water-efficient strategies are hidden from human sight, others bring awareness to the daily choices we make in end-use energy consumption. Direct feedback systems through smart monitors (for example, hand-held technologies, such as mobile phones) connected to a smart grid offer users the ability to watch, in real time, their energy consumption and make necessary changes to equipment and appliances that continue to draw energy despite their not being in use. Studies indicate that energy feedback systems will motivate people to turn down or turn off to save on energy and related costs.[50]

Efficiencies alone do not have the capacity to address the environmental impacts that increased product consumption creates. Other alternative strategies become necessary, focusing on the design for "sufficiency rather than efficiency."[51] The Western practice of owning and consuming as much as we want has been masqueraded as a basic human right, and the ill effects are furthered, especially as transitional nations desire the same growth and development.[52] Questioning the importance of ownership and alternative strategies in consumption presents a challenge for interior designers to reconsider their role, as well as the tools they use, to assist in making alternative experiences to living our everyday more attractive and successful overtime.

The economic crisis of 2008, and the quick fixes that followed, uncovered another set of carefully hidden connections between consumption, growth, and economic stability. Their interdependencies have supported our patterns of consumption. Therefore it is unlikely that "a" global policy responding to climate change impacts will be implemented in the immediate future. Emerging evidence and case studies suggest that multiple solutions to sustainable living, especially collaborative innovations—from small, local-scaled collaborations to large, global-scaled collaborations—are important and provide strategies that should be, simultaneously, supported, since they are gaining momentum. Elinor Ostrom, who in 2009 was the first women to win the Nobel Prize in economics, asserts that multi-scaled approaches, utilizing local actors in a "commons" system of sharing, can result in creative and "diverse" opportunities for "experimentation and learning... maximizing the benefits at varying levels."[53]

SOCIAL DRIVERS FOR CHANGE

Creative Living Scenarios

In her book *The Grand Domestic Revolution: A History of Feminist Designs for American Homes, Neighborhoods, and Cities,* author Dolores Hayden[54] writes about the changing roles of women and the effect on the nature of home life. Factors attributed are the changing needs of families and the evolution of the "career woman," as people moved into compact, developing cities of economic opportunity. For these women of the late 1800s urban living had unique needs, including the need for social interactions, which resulted in the development of some of our first cooperative living models. In *Seven American Utopias, The Architecture of Communitarian Socialism,* Hayden[55] presents a spectrum of communal living arrangements that existed in the United States between 1790 and 1938. These examples are important references for designers, as they illustrate how the design process, the buildings, and the objects within were the perfect expression of the ideals of pioneering individuals who hoped this would support a better way of life.

Current scenarios of cohousing, including intergenerational housing schemes, exist in cities worldwide. There is an increasing need and desire for such schemes. Many enlist the help of government- and/or community-based organizations to retrofit existing buildings to accommodate these needs within a community.[56] Cohousing scenarios offer many environmental benefits, from the careful insertion of densities supporting local services to the savings in resources and energy when buildings are purpose built, or retrofitted, for shared conditions of living. Other urban insertions of cohousing encounter infrastructural roadblocks—zoning, financial, neighborhood—and their valiant and committed members put efforts into improving or changing existing conditions before they can move ahead.[57]

Creative Working Scenarios

Another trend that has gained momentum is "coworking."[58] Our continued, rapid adoption of technological advancements has allowed varying degrees of nomadic living, such as mobile working. Online collaboration, virtual offices, connecting across vast geographies that break traditional office social, temporal, and spatial boundaries mean it is quite easy to be disconnected from physical human interaction. Developed out of desire for freelancers to socialize through systematized but casual "meetups,"[59] coworking has expanded to include other self-employed, home-office workers and small-shop business people. Coworking has also opened up a possibility for "the dynamic reorganization and co-location of people, firms and activities."[60] Coworking environments are places where people, often with diverse sets of knowledge, gather to work and collaborate.[61] As the U.S. Commercial Real Estate market experiences approximately an 18 percent vacancy rate for existing office space,[62] these scenarios for social innovation may be a welcome alternative to the traditional tenant lease arrangement for office space and where interior designers could find a new design opportunity. In coworking scenarios, people self-organize based on shared needs and/or values. Additionally, brand and image identity, expertly materialized through design, including interior design, will be as important to these collaborative communities as it is to their traditional corporate counterparts—the firm.

The financially successful dot-com/information technology (IT) companies, such as Google, have eschewed traditional, hierarchical office planning for open, collaborative work-and-play space that supports creativity and extended or dynamic work hours. Exciting design concepts flourished for the companies that have the extensive space required to achieve these social benefits while addressing the real challenge of planning for sound and visual privacy.[63] Smaller firms and coworking scenarios have similar but distinct challenges in designing for sound and visual privacy. Furthermore, the social benefits that support creativity and extended or dynamic work hours for small and coworking scenarios will require a different design strategy. While environmental design demands that the interior designer consider the local services available to a site that would support efficiencies—for example, mass-transportation or bike stands and paths—interior designers could begin to investigate other existing shared or collaborative services, and design to support them, and leverage those systems to design less stuff that is individually owned and operated. Additionally, interior designers can identify prospects for new collaborations that support other social, or economic, needs, or desires, for navigating through our everyday and contribute to our well-being by designing conditions that foster more enjoyable experiences in connecting with each other.

Trending to Share

One could, undoubtedly, weave a continuous thread of examples of collective and collaborative living through the twentieth century to present day. There is a trend of people tending to opt out of ownership, connecting with various product-service systems—paying for the benefits of using a product without owning it exclusively; consuming collaboratively.[64] We have shared files, shared cars, shared pets, an updated version of the time-honored British standard of shared gardens, peer-to-peer renting, couch surfing, and we share knowledge in different ways than we have in the past.[65] Sharing of all kinds, as well as self-initiated downsizing, is certainly a reflection of a change in attitude toward the words *sharing* and *communal,* as much as it is about our current economic downturn.[66] Additionally, people are creating new systems for the way they live and work; building a social component that is desired. These "social innovations"[67] have the ability to support more sustainable ways of living.[68] In her edited book *Creative Communities, People Inventing Sustainable Ways of Living,*[69] architect and designer Anna Meroni offers over fifty case studies of social innovations. Inspired by Meroni's example of the "Living Room Restaurant"[70] the scene shown in Figure 66 points to where these social innovations challenge our notions of what is urban infrastructure—extending its

FIGURE 66   Collaborative consumption and social innovation: New scenarios for live/work sparking the need for change to existing zoning and regulations, as well as a need to support the success of these new strategies through design. Courtesy of Nadia Elrokhsy, digitally drawn by Eli Rosenbloom.

boundaries. Individuals come together, in various contexts, using their existing resources to develop new systems for living. Benefits and challenges are assessed under three categories—society, environmental, and economic—three areas commonly used to determine achievement in sustainable development. It is an excellent format for designers to use in assessing the potentials and pitfalls of various innovative scenarios for living.

Designers can play a role in furthering their success and help alleviate some of the challenges that arise with collaboration and sharing. The field of interior design should find these cases that rely on the design of place, objects, and human interactions over time interesting territory to study and engage with, especially since these are the services that their practice can provide.

ECONOMIC DRIVERS FOR CHANGE

Recent and various shocks to our systems have exposed what seems to be an increasingly destabilizing world. The ability to be resilient is challenged by these shocks to our network of systems. The Wall Street crisis, in September of 2008, has for many environmentalists and economists underscored the need for alternative and resilient frameworks for defining wealth and well-being.[71] Looking at the potentials in amplified bottom-up scenarios, similar to the initiatives of collaborative consumption and social innovations, economists such as David Korten[72] are favoring Main Street to Wall Street. In his book *Agenda for a New Economy: From Phantom Wealth to Real Wealth,* Korten[73] proposes creating a different system for measuring wealth other than money—quality of life over quantity of money. Korten[74] also states that any new framework, if it comes, will be "more diverse and decentralized and more supportive of local resilience and self organization." We are witnessing a paradigm shift away from individual ownership and self-reliance toward more resilient and flexible systems that are built on sharing and collaboration. Interior design can have a decisive impact on the social success of living more with less.

Service Design Thinking—In Service to the Service

Services now typically represent between sixty and seventy percent of the gross domestic product of developed nations and almost all new companies being founded and jobs created are in this so-called tertiary sector.[75]

The dominance of services in our global economy has resulted in particular attention to this sector, from economic scholars to governments, businesses, organizations, and designers. Hence, services emerged as a new design area of study in the early 1990s.[76] Because of the demand for improvements in public services, Europe is seen as the place where service design thinking first surfaced.[77] And in 2001, the first recognized service design consultancy, Live|Work,[78] opened in London, fostered by the British New Labour party politics of the 1990s, which imagined a cocreative engagement between the public and public service provider.[79]

A recurring aspect of the many and varied collaborations and social innovations is their reliance on the design and development of services. Services are an integral part of their success. The idea of sharing is achievable when the services supporting the shared events make the collaborative experience more rewarding than not sharing—focusing "on the services we need not the products we want."[80] In his LeNS (Learning Network on Sustainability) lecture, "Next—Design in the Age of Networks and Sustainability," Manzini[81] refers to this move in our worldwide economy as the "next economy," which is "not a utopia," but is "here" and is a potential for a "green, social and networked economy," affording great opportunities for designers. In this framework, design-led solutions move from a "product-centered dominant logic" to a "service-centered dominant logic."[82]

Designing services employs a range of tools and methods in the study of dynamic interactions of exchange that evolve over time. It begins with questioning what service needs to be offered and into what existing or newly desired system of operations it will be put. With user participation in a "cocreative" designing of the "customer journey," the users' experience is mapped and the interfaces or "touch points" (the sounds, script, smells, tastes, objects, spaces, visuals, etc. that are evidence that the service exists) are designed. With the goal of designing the conditions for more enjoyable experiences, the service designer assesses, with the user(s), the value and quality of the design touch points in the sequencing of the service offering (see Fig. 67).[83] It is important for interior designers to note that many of these touch points fall under their area of study and practice, and their design is significant, since touch points sustain the value of the service, making the nonmaterial characteristics of the service visible and therefore measurable and assessable.[84]

Interior designers are engaged in the design of interactions—humans with humans, humans with space, humans with objects, objects with space, objects with objects, and so on—to enable experience(s). Therefore, interior design can influence and foster interactions, behaviors, and experiences that encourage a more enjoyable life while consuming less stuff. Service design thinking methods and tools could provide further insight into how, opening the interior design process up to become even more integrative.

"How would you rate our service?"

FIGURE 67   Design for services and assessing the user(s) experience: The Wong-Baker Pain Assessment Scale was a tool developed to assist doctors in assessing the pain and discomfort levels experienced by their patients. Whether designing to improve an existing service or develop new service, it is essential that the design incorporate methods and tools to help assess the servicescape over time, especially for longterm and recurring services for our everyday needs and desires. *Source:* Wong-Baker FACES Pain Assessment Scale, http://www.wongbakerfaces.org/. Marc Stickdorn and Jakob Schneider, *This is Service Design Thinking. Basics, Tools, Cases* (Amsterdam: BIS Publishers, 2010). Courtesy of Nadia Elrokhsy, digitally drawn by Eli Rosenbloom.

AN INTEGRATIVE DESIGN PROCESS

As mentioned earlier, a wonderful collection of climatically responsive designs for comfort and delight are found in vernacular architecture; a testament to the value of the crafted creations of the preindustrial era.[85] The advent of the machine age and the mass-produced artifact alienated the local art- and craft-based process of producing objects with highly skilled laborers. The linear process of the assembly line was mirrored by an equally linear and efficient design process of defining the problem and solving the problem.[86] Designers envision what is possible but when faced with complex issues and "ill-defined problems"[87] the design process and thinking needs to be more engaging and integrative.[88]

Sustainability is a *wicked problem,* this being a term invented by theorists Horst Rittel and Melvin Webber.[89] Wicked problems are "a symptom or result of multiple, contingent, and conflicting issues."[90] They recognize change as a constant and a parameter for design and the design brief. They require a process that pushes disciplinary boundaries, while using knowledge and skills of the discipline(s) to analyze a problem by steadily reframing it. Therefore, broadening our design knowledge and skill sets—engaging with a wider range of methodologies and tools—and working in a more broadly integrative (beyond the related fields of the built environment) and reflective design process is essential to our understanding the role that interior design can play in addressing issues of sustainability.[91]

Best practice in environmental design and energy efficiency for the built environment is an interdisciplinary practice within related fields—architecture, interior design, product design, lighting, acoustics, engineering, and landscape. The interior designer is, primarily, associated with the role of interior/space planning and the selection of "finishes, furniture/fixtures, and equipment" (FFE). FFE product decisions have a significant influence on the reduction of our environmental impact, from healthy interiors to energy and water efficiencies. However, interior designers need to think and operate more strategically, redirecting unsustainable behaviors by questioning what needs to be designed. "Strategic design"[92] is about shifting the focus in innovating "from mainly product or mainly service design to an integrated product-service design strategy."[93] When designing within the framework of wicked problems, the role of the twenty-first-century interior designer needs to break free of the limitations of product-centered thinking and include service thinking. *The interior designer needs to reconnect with the role of envisioning what could be. How can we live differently? What conditions do we need to design that will support valuable alternative experiences and habits?* We need to insert ourselves in the questioning phase before a project has a clear position. This prepositioning work requires an exploration and questioning to develop the design brief, identifying new opportunities and assessing their environmental, social, and economic impacts before establishing the design proposal. Therefore, the interior designer will need to assert her or his role in the investigative "fuzzy front end"[94] (the other FFE) of an integrative design process, which goes beyond the inclusion of traditionally related fields. In the complexity of designing for sustainability, the interior design field is perfectly

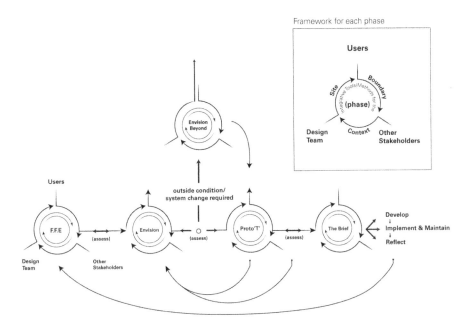

FIGURE 68   Prepositioning: a scalable process of co-creating alternatives ways of being. Designers, users, and related stakeholders for a given context/site (a defined but permeable boundary, leveraging the many assets that may lie outside of the boundary) seek and consider opportunities for more sustainable futures.

Prepositioning begins with the fuzzy front-end (FFE) phase of exploring and questioning what needs to be designed, both in the built environment and the related service systems. The team envisions what could be and, at times, envisions beyond the realm of current possibilities, requiring changes in codes, regulations, or infrastructures. Diverse sets of tools and methods (from service design, behavioral sciences, performance, etc.) are employed to understand the challenges and respond through protoTyping ("T" for integrating creative methods for testing), enacting, and visualizing ideas for feedback and reflection.

Each phase is marked by a moment of reflection to assess design decisions made socially, environmentally, and economically, both in terms of quantitative and qualitative assessments. All is applied to the development of the design proposal—the brief—from which other phases of a project are launched: programming, schematics, design development, implementation, maintenance, and reflection. Courtesy of Nadia Elrokhsy, digitally drawn by Eli Rosenbloom.

positioned to engage in a framework (see Fig. 68) that is significantly more inclusive in designing for efficiencies and beyond, with an eye toward more sustainable futures.

In a, brief, final project for a project-based seminar course on environmental design and sustainability[95], at Parsons the New School for Design, undergraduate interior design students modeled, the design process that is illustrated in Figure 68. The design challenge was to explore ways of "living more with less." The class did not have an external partner, so students were asked to develop characters from researched cases or connect with people they knew, using role-play and other exercises to practice empathy and understanding. In the fuzzy front end, students looked at current trends of shared and collaborative systems in urban life and presented personas that were created through observations, interviews, and research into specific urban stories. Working in groups, the students used and developed quantitative and qualitative assessment methods to establish design objectives—in well-being and happiness, as well as in environmental efficiencies and investigating frameworks for exchange. They were also introduced to exercises for assessing their own group dynamics. Based on the needs and desires identified in the fuzzy front-end (FFE) phase, the students envisioned new ways of living and prototyped aspects of these scenarios. This included modeling new service concepts while sketching, and performing, movement and layouts, as well as sampling other sensory considerations. They reflected and assessed the value of their proposal to the users and the strength of the idea socially, environmentally, and economically.

Outcomes addressed various topics of living our everyday. One group of students considered ways of addressing food-related concerns, from supply to waste. For example, students addressed the systems and elements that evidence homegrown foods, local farmers markets, and community supported agriculture services, designing to make them attractive and integrated into a building's system and services. One group studied how carefully designed social events (and the spaces where they occur) could, over time, encourage participation from the more reluctant persona to the motivated activist—looking at how and where foods can be grown, stored, exchanged, from roof to lobby and basement, as if they were the plumbing or electrical services of a building. Another group developed an idea for a green service business that would design for those who temporarily relocate, looking at ways of sourcing, repairing, and reselling or loaning interior elements—modeling the service script, as well as design options, for different types of space. At a more intimate scale, students envisioned ways of inserting density into a typical high-rise with purpose-built, communal living scenarios, designing conditions for more enjoyable experiences in sharing. Zooming in on ideas to support shared bathrooms, students considered how smart materials could be used to inform the bathers in conserving water and in consideration of others during potentially stressful, high-usage periods of the day. In one scene, a smart material would change color from multicolor swirls that move with your music, to orange then red, acting as a trigger and signal that the bather's time is coming to an end. In another scene, a thermochromic liquid crystal produces an image of a waiting person's hand on the bather's shower door; one iteration had the number of hands equal the number of people waiting. The shower door was the threshold where internal, behind the scenes, signals or interactive, front/backstage, signals would establish communication patterns to support desired cohousing behaviors. Students sought other opportunities to design for more successful experiences of sharing, while considering environmental design, water and energy efficiency. In a, stylistically eclectic design aesthetic, a student responded to the desire for personal toiletry space with an image of a highly decorative old, mailbox unit, a discarded artifact, that would be re-purposed as individually locked storage. These brief initial examples suggest how the interior designer would be of value in this prepositioning design phase and empowered to think broadly, imaging how we might live more sustainably and adapt to specific social, environmental, and/or economic pressures that call for a design for resilience.

A MISSION AND VISION FOR INTERIOR DESIGNERS

The evolution in collaborative ways of living, and bottom-up social innovations, along with the values they represent, all provide designers with an insight into cultural shifts. They identify opportunities to envision new sustainable ways of living that rely on design to succeed and grow. Designing for sustainability means designing the conditions—the sequence of events, the space(s), the tangible experiences of sight, sound, smell, taste, touch—that support new sustainable-everyday actions. Additionally, design could be used to amplify their benefits, and be furthered through policy and incentives.

In response to the challenge of designing for more sustainable ways of living, interior designers will have to be receptive to complexities—wicked problems—embrace collaboration, integrate knowledge more broadly, and become well-informed, quick to respond innovators. In a world where information is plentiful, designers can make sense of all the information by integrating diverse sets of data, mapping it and looking for emerging patterns of behavior, integrating stories that help us understand a larger landscape for design. There are many means to building this capacity, beginning with a design process that asks broader questions about how we live and work. Asking, What needs to be designed? What services, what experiences, what interfaces? to support more sustainable ways of being. It is heavy engagement with a prepositioning phase in the creation of the project design brief. Additionally, interior designers can use this prepositioning as a strategy for elevating the design potentials beyond the value of green finishes, furniture/fixtures, and equipment and engage in the fuzzy front end of designing for interactions that evolve more sustainable human behaviors.

In many areas of our society, people are pledging their commitment to an environmental or sustainable initiative of some kind—stewardship of our planet. Interior designers can join in those efforts by having a shared mission to reduce consumption—preserving and restoring essential planetary resources, while building resilience to the impacts of climate change through design—and a shared vision of welcoming the complexity of wicked problems, utilizing a design process that implements diverse methods for design research and practice, while integrating our depth in the knowledge and skills of the discipline—interior design. The process combines environmental design and energy efficiency with investigations in collaborative consumption and, cocreatively, designing the conditions for more enjoyable experiences through design. It considers sudden shocks to the system and can design for change or respond to the impact and rate of environmental change. This process for designing is executed as a means of supplying creative alternatives to the business-as-usual scenario of living. What is exciting for interior designers is that there is much research and work to be done in this area. In fact, it may be time to rethink what *discipline* means for interior designers in support of a greater understanding of the capability of design, "on its own terms."[96] Therefore, an interior designer who designs for sustainability would be defined as a designer who innovates collaboratively in the areas of services and the built environment to enhance experiences and overall quality of life, enacting a more sustainable way of living.

28

Interior Design, a Political Discipline

TERRY MEADE

INTRODUCTION

It is not unusual to observe that today, many of the certainties, both concrete and abstract, that we assume are the basis of our discipline are unsettled, displaced. Notions of progress, place, and meaning are all under assault. It is impossible now to retreat into the confines of any discipline or to engage in any form of practice without acknowledging the impact of the wider political realm on thinking, working, and teaching. As part of any conception of interiors, an outside is necessary for communication and connection to various networks and flows. This paper will attempt to tease out some of the challenges facing the discipline of interior design and examine the way it can redefine or reassert connections with the politics of particular situations in order to renew its position.

THE MOLE MAN OF HACKNEY

Writing in *The Guardian*[1] in August 2006, Paul Lewis described how a resident in Hackney, East London, had been digging a network of burrows underneath his house. According to the council, which used ultrasound scanners to ascertain the extent of the problem, almost half a century of nibbling away at the dirt with a shovel and home-made pulley had hollowed out a web of tunnels and caverns, some 26 ft. (8 m) deep, spreading up to 65 ft. (20 m) in every direction from his house. The council surveyors estimated that the resident, 75-year-old William Lyttle, known locally as the Mole Man, had scooped 3,530 cu ft. (100 cu m) of soil and debris from beneath the roads and houses that surrounded his twenty-room property. When his excavation work was uncovered in 2006, council officers found on his property four Renault cars, a boat, scrap metal, old baths, fridges, and dozens of TV sets.

"I often used to joke that I expect him to come tunneling up through the kitchen floor," said Marc Beishon, who lives a few yards from Mr. Lyttle's house.[2] His wife, Joy Beishon, understood the serious side of the issue, however. "We moved in six years ago and we've been complaining to the council ever since," she said. "Until six weeks ago they had the audacity to tell us the house was structurally sound. The whole of the opposite street lost power one day after he tapped into a 450-volt cable."[3] The council admitted that Lyttle has put the neighborhood at risk.

"I first tried to dig a wine cellar, and then the cellar doubled, and so on. But the idea that I dug tunnels under other people's houses is rubbish. I just have a big basement. It's gone down deep enough to hit the water table—that's the lowest you can go. I don't mind the title of inventor," said Lyttle. "Inventing things that don't work is a brilliant thing, you know. People are asking you what the big secret is. And you know what? There isn't one."[4]

This story is both funny and disturbing. On the one hand, it is a somewhat comical account of friction between neighbors, involving the violation of private property and planning laws. On the other hand, it is symptomatic of a certain state of society. The antics of the Mole Man testify to a solitary individual leading a fragmented life: isolated, self-justifying, bereft of social connectedness, unaware of the damage caused because of the lack of contact with neighbors. By digging to find out what lies beneath the surface, he undermined fixed structures and created a situation of precariousness and instability in the world above.

The story of the Mole Man raises issues of politics and space at both local and global scales. Locally, it immediately provokes questions of property, planning regulations, boundaries, and party walls, not to mention issues of order, stability, health, and safety. Private property is after all a concept essential and crucial to building and is so entrenched in every aspect of our culture. In a wider sense, it may also serve as a metaphor for a sense of alienation and anxiety, which appears to be haunting the collective unconscious of Western city dwellers in this twenty-first century. A profound insecurity fueled by the perception that the world is changing very fast and that our collective ability to shape that change is cripplingly weak. The Mole Man's excavations demonstrate the power of the interior to operate against the very architecture that hosts it. Different and even opposed spatial configurations succeed in forming and changing both the visible contours above and the underlying terrain below.

Creating space by excavating the ground indicates a search for substance, for evidence that something intangible can be given manageable, graspable shape. Redrawing boundaries in a space without any limits, disturbing foundations, and overturning the ground can also give rise to an illusion that something is there for the taking, that claims on territory can be settled through possession.

These issues, infused as they are with political content, are today unsettling spatial disciplines. The Mole Man raises questions about the causal relationships between functional space and informal, unanticipated, or nonprogrammable activities—about the coexistence of multiple and at times contradictory uses of space and about the psychological undercurrents and hidden assumptions lying behind alienation and deviant or mutant forms of occupation. His work engages with a politics of the continuous interior, a place with no outside—an interior continuously being created.

POPULATION

The United Nations recently reported that the world's population could more than double to reach fifteen billion by the end of this century, putting a potentially catastrophic strain on the planet's resources. This figure is far higher than many other current estimates. A previous UN calculation had expected the world to have more than ten billion people by 2100; currently, there are nearly seven billion. The new figure was in a landmark study by the UN Population Fund, "The State of World Population 2011." It was compiled to mark the expected moment in October 2011 when somewhere on Earth a birth would take the current population over the seven billion mark. The Earth has now doubled in population since the 1960s.[5]

Allied to this is the recent UN "State of the World's Cities 2010/2011" report, which pinpointed something unprecedented. For the first time in history, more people are living in cities than outside them. Megaregions are being formed by the spatial spread of geographically linked metropolitan areas and other urban configurations. As these gigantic urban areas push beyond their original boundaries, some are merging into new massive conurbations, urban corridors, and city regions. Such immense urbanization, covering vast areas, explodes the very notion of a bounded finite city. These conurbations will become the sites where the major challenges facing the world today—economic, environmental, security, sustainability, and dwelling—will be played out. It is clear that these changes are happening at a ferocious pace and with a scale and complexity that confronts traditional paradigms and renders many conventional tools and practices obsolete.

> Cities are becoming inhuman in both old and new ways—in the prodigious growth of slums, in the endlessness of megalopolitan sprawl, in the homogenizing routines of globalization, and in the alienating effects of disempowerment. But the scale has so shifted that the future of cities is now implicated with an inescapable immediacy in the fate of the earth itself.[6]

Familiar fears invariably attend discussions of population growth and the consequent migration (pollution, crime, terrorism). Fear is perhaps the most powerful of political emotions and also the most effective because it short-circuits and distorts political debate. As the global flow of people increases and as our cities and countries become more diverse, there is no shortage of clearly identifiable threats, which may be used to fantasize or manufacture anxiety. Such fears provoke a perhaps inevitable retreat. Separated territorial islands have proliferated in many of our cities in the form of settlements, gated communities, protected enclaves, urban villages, military zones, and pseudo country villages creating patchworks of discontinuous places set apart from each other. As a result, issues of exclusion and separation have become more pronounced than ever before. They spring from a desire or need for separated communities to completely remove the root causes of fear and disorder. Mike Davis, for instance, has written about the "greatest wave of wall building and border fortification in history."[7] These walls, between communities, between peoples, between nations, all have the intention of isolating, separating, and guarding against contact. As Stephen Graham writes, "Once again, nations are being (re)imagined as bounded, organized spaces with closely controlled and filtered relationships with the supposed terrors of the outside world."[8]

Walls are never inert. In spaces isolated and sealed by walls, the interior world can become intensified. Interiorization is a "progressive distancing of thought from the objects and events in the world."[9] It leads to a separation of thought from any here and now and may enhance notions of retreat and exclusion, acceptance and rejection. Definitions of insider and outsider now stretch beyond national borders. Certain groups, such as asylum seekers and refugees, have vastly increased in numbers and have now been assigned global identities. Exclusion is a major issue today, which promotes division and hierarchy (see for example the popular TV programs such as "Big Brother" or "The Weakest Link," which are all about exclusion).

AN AGE OF CONNECTING AND DISCONNECTION

What I fear for my grandchildren is a benign dystopia of ever present surveillance cameras watching us for our own good, a situation in which we will acquiesce, all too well aware of our attraction to danger.[10]

The impact of unresolved encounters and struggles between people threaten basic assumptions about inhabitation. Today, many categories with previously secure meanings are dissolving, together with the conceptual frameworks through which they have customarily been comprehended. Notions of place, dwelling, ties of family, class, religion, marriage, and other familiar settings of human life are all open to question. Emerging in their place are new ways of dwelling for a new age in history. Zygmunt Bauman has argued that people are more caught up in time than in space, embedded in a far more complex, interdependent, temporal world made up of ever-changing webs of human relationships and activity. "We engage in greater numbers of relationships, in a greater variety of forms, and with greater intensities than ever before. Descartes's dictum 'I think therefore I am' has been replaced by a new dictum: 'I am connected therefore I exist.' It's important to see this in the context of alienation today. We connect with large number of people through Facebook but we are alone when we do so."[11]

GATEKEEPERS

Along with the frantic quest for privacy and security, there is an equally frenzied hunger for connection. With the building of walls comes the question of access. The traditional city had gates where taxes and tolls had to be paid, where people such as gatekeepers, prostitutes, merchants, and hawkers congregated. The principle of selective passage regulated the exchanges between the inertia of place and transmigration. The old city edge has now given way to a new and different sense of boundary and different and more pervasive conditions of access.

> Everywhere we look today, access is becoming the measure of social relations. Our transportation, our neighborhood businesses, our personal health are being restructured to accommodate a new world defined by access relations. Access has slipped into the politics of society and nettled its way into virtually every nook and cranny of private and public life with little discussion.[12]

Power, therefore, resides with the gatekeepers who control access to properties, goods, popular culture, and geographic and cyberspace networks. Brian Massumi writes about gatekeeping as control mechanisms but not in the old sense of power over. He states, "It's control in Gilles Deleuze's sense, which is closer to 'check mechanism.' It's all about checkpoints."

> At the grocery store counter, the barcode on what you're buying checks the object out of the store. At the automatic bank teller, the PIN number on your card checks you into your account. The checks don't control you, they don't tell you where to go or what to be doing at any particular time. They don't lord it over you. They just lurk. They lie in wait for you at key points. You come to them, and they're activated by your arrival. You're free to move, but every few steps there is a checkpoint. They're everywhere, woven into the social landscape. To continue on your way you have to pass the checkpoint. What's being controlled is right of passage—access. It's about your enablement to go places and do things.[13]

Massumi maintains that society becomes an open field composed of thresholds or gateways—a continuous space of passage. We are no longer held by rigidly structured walled-in enclosures; "it's just that at key points along the way, at key thresholds, political power is tripped into action."[14] The exercise of this power places constraints on your movement but not so much on physical movement. It is, Massumi says, a constant play between constraint and room to maneuver, very convenient for surveillance or crime investigation but even more valuable for marketing. "In such a fluid economy, based so much on intangibles, the most valuable thing is information on people's patterns and tastes. The checkpoint system allows information to be gathered at every step you take. You're providing a continuous feed, which comes back to you in advertising and pushing new products."[15]

It is not that physical walls are no longer important; it is just that they no longer have the same role. They are no longer effective in physically holding on to a place. However tightly sealed and fortified they may be, walls are eminently permeable and can give no guarantee of security. They have other functions today. Walls have a psychological effect in the way they condition perception, blocking off some scenes from view while selectively allowing others through. Meanings attached to them or that resonate from them are translated as binary opposites to do with inside and outside. These further translate into public and private, restricted and open, order and chaos, us and them, included and excluded. Gated communities are prime examples of separated, walled enclaves, designed specifically to restrict access. Gatekeepers (security guards) are positioned at guardhouses at front entrances both to give the appearance of security and to make sure that only residents, their guests, and authorized visitors and vendors are allowed into the community.

POLITICS OF PLACE

Zygmunt Bauman has argued that politicians have abdicated any responsibility for moderating the impact of the inherent insecurity and instability associated with major economic, environmental, and social changes. So they attempt to compensate, through focusing on other types of insecurity, particularly protection and physical safety. This is concentrated in the increasing imposition of security and isolation in places of work, transport, and dwelling. We are therefore faced with a paradox. On the one hand, we are made aware of the loss of the defensive capacity of place, and, on the other, we are urgently engaged in a search for the security, certainty, and stability.[16]

> In the analysis of the migration and displacement of peoples, the normal reference is to the physical movement of bodies across boundaries. In a paradox that may well be a defining feature of our age, these boundaries have become at once increasingly mobile or porous (more and more people on the move as an effect of globalisation), and increasingly entrenched (more restrictions and policing of borders).[17]

Michael Kimmelman[18] maintains that "we tend to underestimate the political power of physical places. Politics troubles our consciences but places haunt our imaginations."
The sense of place is an important part of contemporary politics despite the fact that both our politics and economics have been steadily driving toward placelessness. People robustly defend their sense of belonging and commitment to place through a sense of belonging to communities and neighborhoods. Kimmelman maintains place is perhaps the most powerful mobilizing force and is still one of the most fundamental building blocks of politics. "It's a driver in human behaviour, particularly powerful in an age when we have become intoxicated by the technologies that shrink space. Now we are able to communicate immediately with almost anyone anywhere in the world, it has become all too easy to belittle or overlook the geographical identities that motivate us."[19] Where do you belong? Where are you from? Where is home? Such questions are deeply political and are inscribed in the passions that place provokes.

A POLITICAL DISCIPLINE?

These issues raise fundamental questions about the territory, practice, and boundaries of disciplines such as interior design. What may be understood or grasped about an interior in the twenty-first century, when a city becomes a formless global object and where, consequently, everything is inside? What happens when borders and boundaries are fragmented, turned inside out, and brought into private spaces? What do we understand of the politics of dwelling in the face of homelessness, increasing numbers of refugees, conflicting claims to territory, or the mobile nature of contemporary society? How is it possible to carve out meaningful spaces when confronted by a politics of separation, seclusion, and visual control requiring complex forms of access?

Too often in this profession, there is an avoidance of any significant debate about the ethics and values underlying interior design or design production. This situation has emerged perhaps because the profession has always considered itself free from political alignment. Indeed, the professional bodies that position themselves as gatekeepers for the discipline have preferred to become immersed in obsessions with restoration, historicism, and stylistic manipulation. Such disciplinary conservatism has prevented interior design from becoming a potentially broad and optimistic branch of learning. This ongoing, willed incapacity to think comprehensively about the realities and material transformations of the contemporary city now haunt the discipline. The result is that questions about the politics of spatial practice and about boundaries and contested territories that have influenced other disciplines (notably in cultural geography and critical art practices) have largely eluded interior design practice.

Lack of political content allows no external reference points through which to question or interrogate the framework of the discipline, even as the task grows in urgency and complexity. Disconnected from programs of use and alienated from significant theoretical debate, the discipline has largely remained as a vehicle for style, fashion, and arrangement, unable to make meaningful connections with the realities of cities. Designers must be aware of relationships between politics, place, and space. Such an understanding is indispensable for any sort of practice today and is in fact the source of much creative inspiration. It is thus important that interiors remain grounded in the complexities of everyday life, its politics, economics, and material conditions. Designers must be open to a range of alternative readings of territory and a range of spatial practices.

Expanding the scope of interior design to include the city's complex ecologies, its often-unpredictable human activities, its contending interests and actors, and its elusive and layered sites can lend intellectual authority to the discipline. Such a remit raises questions about the way new boundaries may be devised to make space apparent/present or about the way the conception of space might challenge the way we think of its inhabitation.

"Any concept of the interior asks questions of how, what and when is the interior."[20] It is a large and accumulative discipline in a very real and fruitful way. That it is fluid and mobile may be one of its great advantages and a reward for those who fully engage with it. The recent epidemic of books about the subject has occurred precisely because publishers understand the scope and the interest in its many aspects. Issues concerning interiors range from architecture at one end of a spectrum and stretch toward cultural geography at the other. Yet, although some of this terrain exerts considerable influence, none of it succeeds in fully gaining control over or defining the discipline. With such rich potential in terms of territory and community, a singular view is impossible. In the world of design, nothing remains constant or secure. Faced with a rapidly changing environment, it is impossible to predict the nature and scope of the field in ten or even five years time.

THE ACADEMY

Practicing or studying a discipline means working within the context of all its philosophical, cultural, and technological implications. This is important not only in the sense of giving a more broadly integrated view of the subject but also in assisting the design community in thinking through issues revealed through the new and often brutal processes that are now loosely defined as globalization. Any design education has its conditions in, and immediately takes its directions from, such issues. Disciplines cannot exist in isolation from each other or from global developments. This is a problem that relates back to specialized training and perhaps to a funding apparatus that is geared toward the fragmentation of knowledge. Such an approach suggests that there is no need to know the rest of the world. An awareness of overall society and where it is heading (whether this concerns the environment, the arts, or history) is diminished if a university does not communicate a broad academic mission. In such circumstances, a discipline is in danger of being reduced to little more than a technical training facility or corporate research institute.

THE MOLE MAN AND SPATIAL POLITICS

A counterpart to the frenetic and messy antics of the Mole Man exists in Walt Disney's planned community in Florida (Celebration). It is an example of a prepackaged lifestyle designed to produce a specific visual character linked to a fixed set of urban pleasures. The $2.5 billion community was built just outside Walt Disney World in Orlando. "The Celebration sales brochure emphasizes the way of life residents will experience rather than the features of the houses that were constructed, giving the clear impression that Celebration is more a celebration of lifestyle than living quarters."[21]

> There once was a place where neighbours greeted neighbours in the quiet of summer twilight. Where children chased fireflies. And porch swings provided easy refuge from the cares of the day. The movie house showed cartoons on Saturday. The grocery store delivered. And there was always that one teacher who always knew you had that special something. Remember that place? Perhaps from your childhood. Or maybe just from stories. It held a magic all of its own. The special magic of an, American home town.[22]

Celebration is the complete antithesis of the work of the Mole Man. However, the extraterritoriality described in both situations encapsulates many of the issues and problems facing interior design—the contrast between tamed domesticity and unruly formlessness. On one side is a partitioned, hierarchical, and disciplined way of living grounded in nostalgia and social cohesion. This is evident in the emphasis on the single-family house heavily protected against deviancy, its orderliness assured by strict covenants that conspire to produce both hygienic conformity and vaguely classical architectural forms. On the other side is a series of primitive, wild, mysterious, uncontrollable subterranean spaces that undermines the system of design by which spaces come into being. There is no design idea here or at least not one that is easily apparent. There appears to be no utilitarian basis for the work; no idea of use, distinction, or subdivision of functions; and no particular hierarchy or vantage point. In short, there is no sense of architectural organization or framework that might be driving a particular idea.

Both these situations interpret interior space as static confined and contained. What they both lack is any consideration about the way spatial boundaries are devised, about the social and temporal context that people move within, and about the presence of people as readers and projectors of ideas about interior space. The Mole Man, burrowing into the Earth reveals something of our world's damaged character. His sense of disconnection is manifested in the wider world through the deepening divisions that increasingly define our environment. The marking of subterranean space as a psycho-spatial terrain of those suppressed and exploited by the forces of so-called progress has long haunted Interior Design. Beneath the streets of many cities, a second city may often be found, where the vulnerable and the dispossessed congregate. Taking the ground from beneath our feet might rob us of what we take for granted, what we need to be sure of, in order for our sense of space to be certain. The common world pulled from underneath with no possibility for constructive response is the opposite of any generative act of communication.

The politics of interiors may be understood as a set of practices through which an order is created around human coexistence. Interior design proposes, performs, and embodies such an order and a position in life. Designers should maintain a point of view that encodes a political attitude on human life and its relationship with the wider environment. There is an obligation on designers not to repeat the past just as there is a responsibility for them to rebel against their inherited preferences. Issues of containment, separation, and occupation; struggles over the utilization of public places; disputes over real estate; and the formation of borders and boundaries are some of the vital political issues that interior designers will face in the twenty-first century.

The Blue Plaque Scheme in London was founded in 1868 and is now run by English Heritage. A blue plaque is placed on a building where a notable figure from the past lived and worked. It is a means of connecting such people with the places they inhabited. The Mole Man,

> Mr. Lyttle earned a mock "blue plaque" for his work, marking the dwellings of "English eccentrics." According to the *Londonist,* he claimed to be "digging to the local bank to rob it but when he arrived it had turned into a wine bar."[23]

REFERENCES

Bauman, Zygmunt. 2004. "Living (Occasionally Dying) Together in an Urban World." In *Cities, War, and Terrorism: Towards an Urban Geopolitics,* ed. Stephen Graham, 110–19. Oxford: Blackwell Publishing.

Ballard, J. G. 2004. *Quotes.* San Francisco: RE/Search Publications.

Davis, Mike. 2005 "The Great Wall of Capital." In *Against the Wall, Israel's Barrier to Peace,* ed. by Michael Sorkin, 88–99. London: New Press.

Graham, Stephen. 2004. *Cities, War, and Terrorism: Towards an Urban Geopolitics.* Oxford: Blackwell Publishing.

Harris, Paul. 2011. "Population of World 'could grow to 15bn by 2100'," *The Observer,* October 23, p. 1.

Hickman, Leo. 2011. "The Population Explosion," *The Guardian,* January 14, p. G2-4.

Judge, Brenda. 1985. *Thinking About Things, A Philosophical Study of Representation.* Edinburgh: Scottish Academic Press.

Kimmelman, Michael. 2011. "In Protest, the Power of Place," *The Observer/New York Times* supplement, October 23, p. 1

Massumi, Brian. 2002. "Navigating Movements, an Interview with Brian Massumi." Available at: http://www.brianmassumi.com/, accessed June 22, 2010.

Rifkind, Jeremy. 2001. *The Age of Access.* New York: Jeremy P. Tarcher/Putnam.

Rogers, Simon. 2011. "World Population by Country: UN Guesses the Shape of the World by 2100," *The Guardian,* October 26, http://www.guardian.co.uk/news/datablog/2011/may/06/world-population-country-un.

Rose, Jacqueline. 2007. *The Last Resistance.* London: Verso.

Sorkin, Michael. 2011. *All Over the Map, Writing on Buildings and Cities.* London: Verso.

29

Globalization: What Shapes a Global Interior?

ALISON B. SNYDER

INTRODUCTIONS: GLOBALIZATION AND THE AFFECTS ON DESIGN OF THE INTERIOR

If we search for the conditions of globalization and being global within the discipline and practice of interior design and interior architecture, we will find there is no cohesive or focused set of concepts, ideas, or theories. Maybe the lack of cohesion is appropriate as it calls attention to the dynamic aspect of being global today. In this chapter, this author proposes to define and make use of a new term, *global interior,* and poses questions concerned with how the design of the interior is theorized, taught, and practiced with regard to global issues. What are the key concepts and elements shaping the context of the interior as we move and work in the second decade of the twenty-first century? How can we speculate on and explore what the global interior looks and feels like?

If you ask practitioners, educators, and students in the United States and abroad, as this author has, What does a global interior mean today? or What might a global interior design be comprised of?, the responses pertain to a perceived knowledge of globalized or international issues concerning interior design. They include typical conditions such as working in foreign locales away from one's home base; suggesting this is another way of speaking about contemporary modern design; producing a general design all understand or could use; acknowledging that there is an increase in the need for multicultural expectations and how this affects our work as designers; suggesting this is about a global vernacular as compared to a local one; or assuming that global development relates to a modernization of traditional culture. The answers are put forth in a basic, cautious, or negative way with the notion of loss often associated. There is no reference to the body of global theory that might affect interior design.

Are we now so occupied by globalization, and accepting of the term, that we never take the time to analyze how this network, or the process of interrelated actions and conditions, has and is affecting the way we understand and approach the making of architecture and the design of interior space? In this chapter, the discussion concerning a global interior also focuses on a central paradox: does globalization actually shape us as designers and impact how we consider and create interior space, or does the interior design of space and place itself influence and shape people's views and their understanding of what is now considered global? Rooted within this paradox is the struggle to maintain a local or regional understanding of our relationship to place, culture, and client needs, as well as to be aware of a worldly view of design and all it might incorporate.

Presented here is a brief introduction into global theory and a small historical recap of how past interdisciplinary design movements relate to globalization concepts. Following is an analysis of how the terms *global* or *globalization* have entered the interior design discipline and practice so far, as evidenced by reviewing information accessed on the Internet and articles, book chapters, papers from conferences, and literature presented by professional companies and organizations. Later, the works of a few design strategists who, are furthering learning in many ways, are introduced. To begin to conclude the chapter, suggestions for a meaningful new pedagogy and professional method based on themes that express the processes and potentials associated with globalization and design of the interior are summarized.

UTILIZING GLOBAL THEORY AND STRESSING THE INTERDISCIPLINARY

The current status for what global and globalization means with regard to the discipline of interior design and interior architecture, and the academic pedagogy associated, is blurry and requires clarity. This author believes the acknowledgement of inter-, multi-, and transdisciplinary education and professional work is key to developing and focusing an open framework for considering design for the interior. The perspectives of sociologists, political scientists, economists, historians, philosophers, geographers, urban planners, and journalists can provide a means to convey the impact of globalization on the interior. The integration and use of new vocabulary and terminology allows for specifically placing and locating the global interior, and ideas about global space, in academia and the interior design work place. Developing the lexicon for the interior design field strengthens it and begins to align it with views associated with the humanities and social sciences as well as affects the interdisciplinary design dialogue among, for example, architecture, urban planning, and industrial or product design.

Global theory, or the study of globalism and its results, speaks of a dynamic state, and the vocabulary associated expresses open-ended potentials. Some of the provocative and conceptual words that describe this condition of globalization are *spread, movement, travel, flow, distribution, dissemination, diffusion, transformation, flexibility,* and *hybrid.*[1] These words can become terms that are useful for analyzing the incremental or grand-scale occurrences related to the process of globalization. This attitude relates to the work of planner Peter Marcuse and geographer Ronald van Kempen, who explain that globalization comprises many processes "such as the spatial integration of economic activities, movement of capital, migration of people, development of advanced technologies, and changing values and norms that spread among various parts of the world."[2] Related explanations of the effects of globalization are put forth by architect Patrik Schumacher, who follows geographer Edward Soja's stances, which are based on Henri Lefebvre's philosophy about economics and the production of space. Schumacher analyzed what he called post-Fordist globalization factors: "1. globalization, i.e. a new level of international integration of production 2. flexible specialization—made possible by the computer-revolution 3. the organizational revolution—i.e. the relative de-hierarchization and de-beaurocratization of work."[3]

To illustrate these ideas further, this author has written:

> Globalization is not "achieved." There are neither over-arching global goals nor specific global policies to implement; consequently, actual methods to assess change and its impact are elusive. World conditions seen, felt and described most often by journalists, economists and politicians, as well as historians and social science academicians suggest that globalization is a way to "re-read" or relate local, regional and national past and present histories in more universal or so-called global terms.[4]

The word global may be defined as an overarching idea that means full in form, whole, comprehensive, and worldwide; so by extension, globalization as a concept for design of the interior could mean and include many things. Global theory, then, reinforces concepts and questions concerning broad topics and processes such as change, permanence, and temporality. This theory directly involves how the individual and collective feel when they inhabit spaces, and contributes to how people from different disciplines and cultures work together, as well as what they gain from doing so (see Fig. 69 and Fig. 70).

Another context from which to consider how people engage in globalization relates to interdisciplinary collaboration. Looking into past arts movements and their schools shows there was a focus on training the individual while stressing different forms of working collaborations. These easily fit into the global dialogue about working together and producing alternative designs that reflect maintaining tradition and/or changing times.

There are several periods in history that relied on inter- or multidisciplinary knowledge. Ancient masters of construction and artisans were trained to work together to integrate a sophisticated knowledge about the use of space, light, and material detailing to compose large and small complexes globally. Probably the most prominent school still influencing Western pedagogy today is the seventeenth-century École des Beaux Arts in France, where students were schooled formally in classical and later historical precedent with a studio manner of work based in composing form by copying and rendering according to a master.

Rapid shifts in methods for design and production begin to occur during the nineteenth century Industrial Revolution and the machine age, which caused new wide spread

FIGURE 69   An intimate spatial volume for viewing and pondering with technology. Author's photograph and copyright with permission to publish by Zaha Hadid Architects.

modern development and communication possibilities, resulting in more competition, stratification, and class distinction. It is around this time that design, economics, social conditions, and politics intermix. The periods around the world wars influenced more art and design movements and schools. The constructivists in Russia, futurists in Italy, de Stijl in Holland, the Bauhaus in Germany, and later situationist international, brutalism

FIGURE 70 Smooth material detail provides for different auras. Author's photograph and copyright with permission to publish by Ateliers Jean Nouvel.

in the United Kingdom and beyond, or even Japan's *Butoh* embraced a notion of integrating many of the arts together such as color theory, architecture, music, industrial design, photography, dance, and set design. The work was experimental or became useful and was also a commentary on society since it engaged philosophical, political, secular, and spiritual approaches for social or revolutionary reform as seen through space and aesthetic. The members of the groups worked individually but were most remarkably collectives.

Globalization and its current ramifications for design thinking are perhaps most understandable when considering post-WWII technological production. The influence of radio along with the invention of television sped up and increased world communication. Materials development and innovation such as with plastics made huge changes for design impacting the environment. Marshall McLuhan, the 1960s media guru, prophesied our inability to live without global information pouring in and over us. Since the 1970s and especially now, everyone has become dependent on building technology and technology transfer. The use of the personal computer since the 1980s has increased the ability for individual production and mass trade all over the world. Now amidst the recall of ecological concerns and new call for sustainable practices, grassroots collectives and a DIY mentality are meshing with corporate structures.

SEARCHING THE INTERNET FOR GLOBAL REFERENCES RELATED TO THE INTERIOR AND DESIGN

The significance of attempting to define the global interior enables the ongoing development and deepening of design discourse. Using global theory aids analyzing different viewpoints in current interior design practice and pedagogy. Working to better understand globalization also strengthens how we might approach designing new interior spaces along with repurposing and readapting existing architecture and the sites it inhabits. This discourse deepens discussions based around interiority and use—such as behavioral sensitivity and working to achieve materiality that creates form and atmosphere.[5] And, while these interior-based topics obviously connect with the discipline of architecture, the methods for design and study of the global interior can be seen and understood separately. Each discipline informs the other.

Yet, when researching the terms global or globalization in association with design of the interior in published sources (including print and the Internet), the gap between awareness and specific knowledge and use of these ideas, is also very apparent. Using academic library or Web-browser databases to search under the terms listed below yields surprisingly few references or users of these as real terms.[6]

- *global interior*
- *global design*
- *global interior design*
- *global interior architecture*
- *globalization* and *interior*
- *globalization* and *interior design*
- *globalization* and *interior architecture*

The words are either separated inside of sentences or advertise a small group of companies that also use *global* to mean *world*, *international*, or *internationalization*. When surveying current published sources such as printed journals, newspapers, and books, the use of the suggested terms are also somewhat scarce and often separated.

On the Internet, the term *global design* yields some companies' advertising; they work with algorithms, mathematics, and computer programming as well as billboard advertising. For *global interior design,* a few companies publicize themselves as firms or contractors that work in several locales. A few construct and outfit transport vehicles such as airplanes and ships. Some firms that work on luxury commercial projects list multiple locations of European and mostly Asian or Middle Eastern locales. Yet, the most prominent use of global terminology is related to those people or companies that source, select, and apply materials; thus, global production and trade are linked. For these firms, some mention of sustainability as part of the design values is espoused, but there is no depth of description in this practice beyond an occasional reference to LEED or a similar international system.[7] When the word *globalization* plus *interior design* or *architecture,* instead of *global,* is used in the search, information or topics pertaining to geography and specific places for vernacular study are posted. It appears that people are publishing work that is concerned with globalization's positive and negative effects on traditional domestic space and nearby new development in what appear to be largely developing countries. Other kinds of professional design do not appear with these words or terms.

On the Internet, no one designer, researcher, agency, or professional firm was found that goes into any theory about what *global* or *globalization* means or how they can be understood (except when one reads the vernacular-based studies papers). Yet, it is interesting to realize that some of the key elements associated with interior design and practice such as material use and detailing, and the notion of transport or movement systems crossing local geographical boundaries, do exist. But, it appears that there is only a simple acknowledgement of using these words in relation to design.

A basic example of global theory and its terminology is found in simplified forms in the newspaper. Using the *New York Times* website as a database to search *design* plus *global* or *globalization* turns up articles related to computer software or cars as well as mass housing issues. And, most recently, some relation to the occupy Wall Street movement appears, the association being village-like design, politics, and economics coming together to form temporary grassroots habitats that sprang up in the summer, fall, and winter of 2011, mostly in the United States. Yet, when adding in to the search the words *global* plus *interior design,* little appears except for some references to real estate.

If the quickest technological portal to information on this subject yields so little, there is a missed opportunity regarding access to obvious relevant issues and concepts that pertain to global theory and design. For example, one can assume aspects of change occurring in this era of globalization relate to conditions urging flexibility and less homogeneity, economic responses to world markets, growing ecological values, seeing the need for workplace development because of generational changes, and recognizing that the many different innovative possibilities for integrating technology and smart manufacture are only a start.

ANALYZING CURRENT ACADEMIC AND PROFESSIONAL SOURCES FOR GLOBAL REFERENCES

Through reading academic and professional articles, papers, and policy, it is clear that design-based researchers, educators, and professional designers, their companies and organizations, and the interior design accrediting council do refer to global issues and trends. Mostly these are linked to broad aspects of defining global design as international and concerning culture, yet the notion of what *global* and *globalization* can mean as tantamount to the concepts driving the study and practice of designing the interior is just beginning to be presented and challenged. What follows are examples of what exists in the literature with some new comment on how other globalization issues fit into interior design study and practice.

Academic Papers

Interior design academics begin to call attention to the subject of globalization mostly through the term *international.* Professor Denise Guerin's important 1991 article "Issues Facing Interior Design Education in the Twenty-First Century" thoroughly covers concerns for the future of the profession. She highlights many meaningful issues that influence the profession and need to be part of design education, including "professional identity, liberal arts foundation, interdisciplinary elements, international concerns, technology integration, and scholarship activities."[8] She also questions what has to change pedagogically from what was then being done. Guerin identifies a consciousness of global commerce in the profession and also the ever-increasing global makeup of the United States. She states that we will have to be culturally responsive while being global, and the new internationalism should not result in a fragmented understanding of aesthetic. She also cites the importance of diverse design teams made of people from different locales and backgrounds and as an endpoint calls for study-abroad programs to be expanded.

One would expect that design conferences were the place that new ideas and issues would be experimented with and aired, yet only a few of the Interior Design Educators Council (IDEC) conferences and symposia over the last decade address international and global issues. The most comprehensive one relating to these topics was the regional conference in Oklahoma in 2006 called "Global Design Perspectives," which appeared to point designers toward teaching beyond their own culture and also brought up larger issues of economics and politics. Symposia papers focused on how globalization relates to Western and non-Western design history, how different cultures should be researched, and how to use technology to engage with people, and as well as many concepts surrounding the notion of modern compared to vernacular. In one paper, participant Abimbola Asojo's refers to a 1986 Alan Fairbrass and Ron Harris paper calling for "design educators to integrate international activities into their classrooms by exposing students to other cultures, their history, and life styles."[9] Another regional IDEC conference, in Pittsburgh in 2004 called "Taking the Lead," had a few papers with international and globalization issues as a focus. Donna Zimmerman and Kathe Stumpf's abstract focused on international study to give students broader inter- and multidisciplinary perspectives, and the previously mentioned Asojo paper focused on a project that gave students design problems related to low-cost slum redevelopment in Africa. This project mixed a global study with video conferencing to allow for students in all locales to collaborate, share, and compare their methods, aesthetics, and real needs. The 2010 joint symposium of IDEC, USA and Modern Interiors Research Center (MIRC), Kingston University, London, titled "Looking into the Modern Interior: History, Theory and Discipline in Education and Practice," might have linked the topic of globalization with modernity, though it was not their primary concern. Yet, Zamila Karimi does use some global theory vocabulary in relation to her research on new Muslim centers in the West. She writes that "this era of globalization when boundaries blur among communities of diverse backgrounds to create new narratives of identities in a wide range of settings."[10]

While these papers do bring up important issues, to explain how few are involved with these subjects, approximately 10 out of more than 100 papers and projects presented at the 2011 IDEC conference included the words *global* or *globalization,* with only about four that made attempts to suggest what this can mean for a student's growth or professional design work. Examples of topics are found in Hyung Chan Kim, Dong-Kwan Sheen and Yongrhip Kim's "Global Partner: International Design Exchange," which addresses the increase in professionals working on international design projects and developing knowledge of other cultures; and in Jun Zou and Phillip Tebbut's "Embracing Globalization in Junior Interior Design," which examines travel abroad, culture shock, and project collaboration resulting in more globalized perspectives. Mostly though, these authors refer to the Council for Interior Design Accreditation's (CIDA) standards and appear to be working their pedagogy toward them.[11] In both of these papers, designing with awareness of global issues more often refers to being out of the country and learning how to work in, or with cultures, other than formulating what design spaces and processes might entail.

Except for the aforementioned papers at recent IDEC conferences, it appears that there is a long academic gap before other scholars take on this subject matter. Professor Tiiu Poldma's 2008 article "Interior Design at a Crossroads: Embracing Specificity through Process, Research, and Knowledge" outlines the issues concerning the still-emergent interior discipline and solving design problems. Regarding what she calls the "evolution of societal paradigms," she echoes Guerin's observations that we are an increasingly changing global society.[12] She furthers the ideas and states that "our lives have become more insular and technology-oriented"[13] and that the way people work and live and relate to public space has changed dramatically, thus these spaces are multilayered, and the interior design practice and education must reflect this and the profession's specific abilities to deal with dynamic interplays and specific societal complexity. Her layered image and reference to global dynamics could lead to more specific, yet open, possibilities.

Books

A brief look at several books, in mostly chronological order, pertains to the subject of designing the interior and the possibility of how introducing global conditions yields different observations. John Kurtich and Garrett Eakin's book *Interior Architecture* (1993) looks at the profession and the nature of being global in a basic way. The book is not polemical, yet it is one of the early volumes identifying interior architectural space as worthy of separate study. It explains the interior within historical and cultural contexts from all over the world. The authors also recognized the concept of buildings changing and being reused and adapted over time, and they presented separate chapters on design components comprising the interior. Books such as John Pile's *Interior Design* from 1988/1995 and *The Fundamentals of Interior Architecture* (2007) by John Coles and Naomi House, are similar to Kurtich and Eakin's book in that they attempt to be all-encompassing books that express how history and precedent (primarily Western) in-fluence interior design, with chapters on many components, including professional of-fice practice. They do not reference the global phenomenon or what this might mean.

A few newer sources take us closer to laying out views about the global present and the future. Penny Sparke's and others' writings in Sparke's edited volume *Designing the Modern Interior, from the Victorian's to Today* (2009) addresses the relationship between modernism and modernity and a global view of design aesthetic from many viewpoints. Several authors mention the consumer and global economy, global communication media, the ecological footprint, and a general globalised context. Susan Winchip uti-lizes a case-study approach for her 2010 text, *Visual Culture in the Built Environment, a Global Perspective*. Globalism is explored historically and through global events as a means to "explain global styles and movements in the context of their development," and she hopes the approach "will stimulate perspectives regarding expectations for future in-terior environments and architecture."[14] She engages the reader in many case-study-like examples with many examples and exercises that are related to the notion of progress in a global world, thereby touching on some global theory in the subject matter. Lois Wein-thal's anthology *Toward a New Interior* (2011) presents a fresh and exciting approach to formulating and therefore comprehending that the disciplines of interior design and in-terior architecture do have particular design theories attached that are rooted in history but also to scale, place, psychology, and perception, all in relation to the body. Though inter-, multi-, and essentially transdisciplinary in approach, there is no real mention of globalization or how these ideas might relate to it. Finally, *Interior Architecture Now* (2007) by Jennifer Hudson, does not use the word global or reference globalization, but she makes a related point in her selection of "fifty-five of the most interesting people and practices designing interiors today—from the well known and long established to the young and experimental."[15] She presents the idea of using "common threads" such as adaptation, space over form, and a multidisciplinary approach to express design today and to begin to describe a body of interior work that references the dynamic flow and flexibility afforded by a global interior. There appears to be a visual style entering this discussion, but these are not the primary reasons for the examples selected. What is not presented is a clear sense of how scale and complexity of form or use of materials in single- or multi-roomed buildings should be understood (and there are only photographs, not plans), but the possibilities look and feel endless. Instead, a dogma needs to develop related to understanding time, behavior, emotion, culture, and space-making. Undoubtedly, new titles will continue to appear. Instead, a dogma needs to i develope related to understanding time, behavior, emotion, culture, and space-making.

Two Global Companies

Several professional companies have used their websites to go more deeply into some of the global issues and should or could be used as prototypical points of reference along with academic work. Interior design and architecture giant Gensler calls itself a "global architecture, design, planning and consulting firm."[16] The topics under "Viewpoint—Periodicals" include published titles called Annual Report, Dialogue and Design Update. Recently the subject matter of these publications have been provocatively titled "Redefining What's Possible," "Shift," and "Design Research" and "The Changing Nature of Work." These touch on the importance of integrated building and communication technology, respecting the client's cultural differences and arguing for an absolute awareness of producing rigorously researched sustainable design options. Surprisingly, though Gensler wins awards for its interior design, it does not specifically make reference to how it approaches the interior or what this means in the global spectrum. Another worldwide, product-oriented industry giant puts forth a related but different set of concerns. On Herman Miller's website under "Research," several conceptual papers deal with issues of diversity relating to both multicultural and generational stratification in the global workplace. Herman Miller researched specifically in the emergent BRIC countries—Brazil, Russia, India, and China—to locate how spatial behavior and use affect product development in the competitive global market. Though specific to office workplace furniture, the research calls for deep multicultural understanding. Herman Miller is also one of only a few global companies to reach toward 100 percent in sustainable ecological practices, signaling dynamic change in world industry.

Academic and Professional Organizations

Looking at IDEC's mission and vision statements, under "core values," the word *global* appears. IDEC states, "We believe the foundation of interior design education is grounded in ethics and encompasses environmental, cultural, social, global issues."[17] Following that is, "We believe in an open dialogue and collaboration among colleagues." And that is then followed by, "We believe a successful interior design education depends upon the participation of diverse groups of people." While IDEC's highlighting of global issues related to diversity and collaboration is important, the website does not have other permanent (or ephemeral) sections devoted to globalization, interior design pedagogy, or practice.[18]

Other global or international professional organizations such as International Interior Design Association (IIDA) and International Federation of Interior Architects/

Designers (IFI) and its partner the International Design Alliance (IDA) have different global approaches. In its vision and mission statement, IIDA states that it stands "for the future of design."[19] The organization specifically connects the professional world together by saying it is "committed to facilitating a global community for Members through the IIDA website" (linking to Twitter, Facebook, and the IIDA blogs). IFI "is the global voice and authority for professional Interior Architects/Designers. IFI is the sole international federating body for Interior Architecture/Design organizations, and acts as a global forum for the exchange and development of knowledge and experience."[20] IDA says its vision is to have the design community "working together for a world that is balanced, inclusive and sustainable."[21] In 2010, IFI held literal and virtual gatherings all over the world to discuss poetic and practical issues concerning interior design and the future of the profession. The new responses and trends, some of which relate to global issues, have been reported on but have not been formed into a useful or experimental pedagogy.[22]

CONCLUSIONS: CONSIDERING AND INTEGRATING A NEW INTERIOR THEORY AND MODEL

To address the movement and changes occurring within globalization, and in response to this author's research, offered here is a different beginning approach for the study and pursuit of designing the global interior. These ideas represent a possible shift and reorganization of how design is taught and how professional designers and clients refer to projects.

First, it is useful to look at the work of creative design strategists who identify and illustrate current paradoxes and paradigm shifts connected to global issues and the affects they have on many different professions and points of view. For example, William McDonough, who wrote with Michel Braungart *Cradle to Cradle: Re-Making the Way We Make Things* (2002); Bruce Mau, who wrote *Massive Change* (2004); and Daniel Pink, who wrote *A Whole New Mind* (2006), are a few of the most well-known names publishing and lecturing widely to audiences with mixed backgrounds. Their transdisciplinary ideas bring together people in all aspects of design and other fields such as those in science, business, environmental relations, sociology, and more. They believe and teach in different ways that design thinking and processes are key for advancement of many fields of study. Some of the things they advocate for related to globalization are working holistically with ecology so material use is considered deeply and is part of a sustainable process; urging collaboration through interdisciplinary and intercultural teams to illustrate how integrating processes can create new learning, products, and pedagogies; and learning to embrace and utilize technologically based communication methods including social media.[23] For example, on the subject of separate disciplinary work, Paddy Harrington, creative director in Mau's office, said in 2010 in a Radiolab discussion with another strategist, Jim Meredith,

> The complexity of global systems bring new challenges, demanding that disciplines that have traditionally worked quite separately now work together to find appropriately

complex solutions. The result is that the boundaries between disciplines seem to grow blurrier every day: architecture merges with graphic design merges with strategic consulting…Do we gain more by protecting the integrity of our practices from possible deterioration caused by outside forces, or are the possibilities generated in the friction caused by difference too great to ignore?[24]

People like McDonough, Mau, Pink, and others will aid the search for new pragmatic and creative methods that influence people about how to consider emerging conditions. This author recognizes that the processes and affects of globalization have the potential for wide-reaching spatial and social implications and that these realizations call for putting more attention on how to change and adapt the architectural disciplines.

A Model Proposed

Proposed here is a model for pedagogy resulting from and based on the global issues discussed. It is a proposition for instructional theory and method that challenges how a project is first labeled and affects how a project is planned for and subsequently designed. This proposition concentrates on the tangible human understanding of place and accesses intuitive behavior and sensing to link the conditions of globalization associated with concepts of interchangeability and timelessness as well as a beginning reinterpretation of cultural issues and values and the resulting use of technology and meaningful materiality. In addition to considering the paradox presented at the beginning of the chapter about whether globalization affects us and influences how we design or whether the design of space affects us and subsequently alters our view of global change, other specific questions include the following: in this global era of mixed-use facilities and the technological means of working almost anywhere, how else might interior designers refer to their work and modify their practice? What methods can integrate the movements of globalization and different individual and collective behavioral and cultural attitudes?

The new speculative pedagogy will begin to answer these questions and is therefore based on *themes* rather than typical types. Three sample themes are presented. The idea is to inspire a design process that is expressive of dynamic global terms such as *diffusion, flexibility,* and *hybrid* and also methods for interdisciplinary inclusion and/or mixed cultures and geographies. Often projects are categorized by project types named for the most obvious use. Designers and clients refer to, for example, residential, commercial, health care, hospitality, office, or institutional types such as a museum, library, or bank. The new pedagogy would invert the norm and make small groupings of types that fit under interrelated themes.

This approach is meant to provoke a dialogue and spark potential associations for configuring and planning global interiors today. It is not finite. David G. Shane's recent work on city morphology relates to processes of globalization, acceleration of communication networks, and consideration of new methods for design of the interior. "The process of recombination allows for change in actors and their responses to altered circumstances. Urban splicing analogously to genetic recombination, involves the sort layering, overlapping and combining of disparate elements to create new combinations."[25]

In planning and designing interiors, paying attention to themes could result in hybrids, combinations, and crossovers. New themes can also emerge or mutate.

Therefore, a project in a professional design office or a project given for school study would first be presented and discussed by a broad theme, thereby developing a different way to explain a new multifaceted type. Themes composed of verbs that describe and include interrelated subjects will embody today's needs and desires. The designer and client would consider which theme words work to describe the type of project desired and the planning needed. This will promote a multitude of methods for programmatic inclusion instead of assuming what is required. Global descriptors such as *interchangeability* will guide and influence design form and use. And the approach applies to all scales—from a space, a series of rooms, an entire adaptive reuse, or a large urban infill project (see Fig. 71 and Fig. 72, see Plate 30, Plate 31 and Plate 32).

Sample Themes with Crossovers

Theme 1: To View, to Exhibit, to Learn, to Entertain, to Meet, to Observe, to Nourish

Project types included in this group are institutions such as museums (gallery, installations), libraries, performing arts venues, tourist centers, schools, and restaurants, as well as hybrids of these.

FIGURE 71 A high tech integrated and encompassing monochromatic global interior within Jean Nouvel's 2009 Copenhagen Concert Hall. Author's photograph and copyright with permission to publish by Ateliers Jean Nouvel.

Explanation Example: In the global condition, this theme tries to look at the inherent qualities found in the included institutions such as museums/galleries, performance art venues, or schools. They could be described as an important purveyor of art and commodity and at the same time challenging craft or mass production or as spaces for teaching and collaborating. The scales of design as they relates to the interior identifies certain temporal notions of human interactivity and asks for new ideas pertaining to spatial flow of form and movement as well as a reliance on new smart technologies. Projects might endeavor to express and explain permanence and the opposite. Base needs require really establishing methods for seeing, viewing, and interacting. The act of exhibiting also asks for a careful set of intentions in many project types regarding local and global cultures and an adherence to the latest views on sustainability and material use by ecologically aware clients. All projects consider the location and context of site for adaptive reuse as key for interpretation.

Theme 2: To Live, to Work, to Age, to Learn

Project types included in this group are residences (including individual and shared domestic relationships and social housing prototypes), housing complexes, travel and hotel, aging developments, offices, and hybrids of these.

Explanation Example: In the global condition, this theme potentially defines and redefines individual domestic and group residential design and also office design to go beyond typical spatial problem solving. This theme depends on the mixture and careful incorporation of ages and behaviors of users and their cultures and vernacular or local knowledge of past and present. A combination of new programmed activities will depend on flexibility directly associated with the human scale, and, at the same time, the newest technologies that affect people and spatial design (e.g., smart sound and touch activated products and social interaction and networking abilities) must be investigated and reinterpreted.

Theme 3: To Contemplate, to Rest, to Revive, to Reevaluate, to Observe

Project types included in this group are sacred spaces, health venues/hospitals, spas, and also museums and libraries and hybrids of all of these.

Explanation Example: In the global condition, this theme potentially considers the attributes related to personal spiritual relationships supplied by sacred design or religious space anywhere while also suggesting that secular places can also embody aspects of monumentality and humble worldviews and ethics. While almost any project type could fit into this theme, the global considerations will depend on observing human perception and respecting behavioral differences. New designs will illicit emotions and responses through personal and cultural observation, or the study of signs and symbols, so meaningless decoration and pastiche will not occur.[26]

FIGURE 72 Respecting and adapting an industrial space in Istanbul by inserting the new in 2011. Author's photograph and copyright with permission to publish venue by Office of ryue nishizawa.

In summary, proposing a model and method for planning and designing a global interior project based on themes will rely on the following values and principles:

- Consider quality and aesthetic as meaningful.
- Respect the user and his or her health, welfare, and life safety.

- Provide chances for teamwork and collaboration inviting interdisciplinary sharing and learning.
- Utilize human diversity and/or cultural differences sensitively.
- Be cognizant of design ethics are influenced by politics and consumerism.
- Understand and respect historical precedence as a reference point but not a determinant for new design.
- Embody atmosphere and emotions through materials, use/touch, and lighting to allow designs to embrace and invite flexibility and transmutability.
- Depend on different technologies and communication systems.
- Be ecologically and sustainably conscious and progressive.
- Remain open and broad-minded towards changing and emerging themes.

The suggested concepts presented by focusing on interrelated themes instead of separate types alter how we understand space and form, and how we consider and create interior experience, and respond to existing conditions. As a result of globalization, interior designers and architects need to continually reinvestigate new methods and processes associated with the transformation occuring in local, regional, and global settings.

Representation and Fabrication

Introduction

Entitled "Representation and Fabrication," Part 3 explores how the interior can be the subject of a variety of mediated formats, each of which can create a particular interior condition. These various forms of representation create different understandings of the interior and can result in multiple readings of a space. As well, this medium of interior space can be utilized as a symbolic environment, a narrative instrument with which to describe human occupation. The second half of this part examines the atmospheric conditions of the interior, exploring how surfaces, light, color, and various technologies can impact upon the senses, as well as how esoteric dimensions such as trends and fashion can influence the interior and how it may look.

The ten chapters in this part are arranged in order to examine the various forms of representation and numerous ways in which atmosphere is produced in inside space.

SPECULATIVE FORMS OF PRODUCTION

Before an interior is actually built, it is subject to many forms of simulation. Drawing and model-making, often produced both by hand and also utilizing digital technologies, are representational tools that through various means suggest what a space might actually be like before it is built. Such visual material can demonstrate process in the form of sketch models and drawings, it can include factual information—such as production drawings or prototype models—and it will often include exhibition standard material such as presentation models and drawings. Drawing is one of the predominant forms of the representation of interior space, and in "The Art of Borrowing," the author Ro Spankie argues that there are a number of techniques of drawing that are particular to the design of interior space. The author argues that if adaptation and alteration are processes that are pertinent to interiors, then drawing processes such as collage and color experiments are particularly appropriate methods for depicting interior space. The process of designing space is represented in many forms of drawing, from sketch, to working drawing, layout, and presentation. In this chapter, Spankie examines Josef Albers's idea of the gap between the factual and the actual, the visually perceived and the physical reality of the image and the space. The central argument of the chapter is that drawing is central to the design process, a fact exemplified by its very name: *Designo,* or "drawing" in Italian also means "designer."

The three-dimensional qualities of space are often considered to be represented in the most convincing manner through the sculpting and modeling of their own forms. In the design process, this may take the form of analog modeling; that is, with a sharp knife and with card or foam board. It may also take the form of digital modeling with various sophisticated software packages such as Rhino or Vectorworks to name but two. It may involve prototyping through full-scale modeling of the intended finished pieces. Whichever method of representation, modeling attempts to convey the spatial and multidimensional qualities of interior space. In the chapter entitled "Model Behavior," author Nick Dunn explores both physical and digital model-making ideas and techniques, discussing their multifaceted aspects, which range from the abstraction of space to realization as a process or presentation tool. Using two key case studies and theories of modeling and scale, Dunn also examines emerging issues in modeling such as digital parametrics and full-size prototyping. He examines how they are incorporated in the design and representation of interior space.

Digital technology has impacted the processes of design in a number of ways: most notably, it has conflated the separation between idea, development, production, and fabrication. New methods of representation and fabrication are changing the processes of the design and construction of the interior by offering faster and more innovative solutions to the creation of space and its components. Evolving digital technologies are facilitating the development of alternative forms of space, exemplified by parametrically modeled and digitally enhanced structures and surfaces. In "Digital Representation and Fabrication," the author Igor Siddiqui examines how the transformable potentials of sophisticated digital technologies lie in their ability to produce integrated relationships between representation, fabrication, and construction by managing flows of complex information in the design process. This conflates the normally separate entities of design and making into one continuous flow of data, managed by mainframe technologies. Siddiqui introduces these new methods of technologies through the filters of continuity and pattern: two elements that he argues are integral features of the digital realm and two methods of surface and form-making that move away from traditional methods of construction. He argues that this is a situation that now characterizes contemporary interior space. The chapter shows a series of projects that highlight these new developments.

Conservative commentaries on developments in digital media and in particular the field of gaming often suggest that the underlying effect on the user is in relation to their isolation from society. In "The Interior: Television, Gaming, and New Media," Ed Hollis argues that the opposite is true and instead the eruption of the screen into our private spheres has reactivated and ultimately conflated distinctions between the private and the public. Hollis argues that the erosion of this threshold brings viewers and the public together in a variety of ways. The chapter is organized into six "scenes," starting in 1941 and culminating in the present day, with each one drawn from a significant event in the

Hollis family's history. The author suggests that, as Baudrillard has also stated, interior space and its occupants are given life through the screen and the reflected views of the lives of the actors playing them. Hollis argues that through representation, whether in the cinema, television, computer games, or on YouTube, the contemporary interior and its occupants have been deeply affected by this reflection, an image that has eradicated the threshold between private and public space. The screen has transformed the interior into the host of a series of data-streams and portals to many other worlds.

As well as being the subject of diverse forms of representation and fabrication, the interior is a space that can be utilized as a narrative instrument. As a backdrop to everyday life, the interior can be used as a device for structuring narrative in literature, films, games, and also on television. In books and novels, a specific scene or moment is often described within the setting of a particular space or room. These spaces exist only through the thoughts of the author and the imagination of the reader. Well-known literary spaces abound in famous books and novels. The material reconstruction of these scenes can provide a rich and detailed narrative on the use and role of the interior space in fiction and in film. In "Literary Narratives," the author Mark Taylor examines fictive and literary spaces, exploring their role as particular representations or reconstructions of relationships between occupants, rooms, and buildings. Taylor explores the novel, a literary device that is essentially domestic and one that can provide metaphorical connections of both the state of mind of the occupants as well as the character of the space. Taylor structures the chapter into three parts: he focuses on what he describes as the emotional and sensorial writings of the eighteenth century, the psychological and personal studies of the nineteenth century, and the social and spatial connections of the twentieth century.

ATMOSPHERIC CONDITIONS OF THE INTERIOR

The rendering of space through the creation of particular atmospheric conditions is one of the fundamental skills of the interior architect/designer/decorator. Through spatial and surface manipulation, the interior becomes a place of sensual occupation, an environment for the stimulation of less tangible effects such as light, color, and ambiance. The stimulation of atmosphere is created through sensual instruments such as color and light as well as technological developments. It is also promulgated through the placement of objects, the arrangement of ornaments, and the notion that these things are chosen because of their relationship with trends and fashion. Interior design has always had a close association to surface considerations and the application of applied embellishment, pattern, and the adornment of space. Modernism eschewed the allegedly superficial qualities of applied ornament and decoration. Instead, its agents advocated purity and the reduction of form and materials to their barest qualities, a strategy that ultimately resulted in the amalgamation of the room into the surface of the exterior. In "Ornament and Decoration," Jonathan Massey describes ornament as a relational device, one that differentiates things and people, frequently marking social status. Massey unpacks these associations and historically contextualizes the complicated debate of ornamentation and its relationship to the decoration of interior space. He posits a history of ornamentation and brings it right up to date by exploring contemporary obsessions with applied decoration. Massey focuses on the Western tradition of decoration as a mode of elaboration that performs a socializing function or ornament as an identifier of status.

Limiting the understanding of the interior to the assemblage of components such as light, color, furnishings, and materials overlooks the rich complexity of the development and understanding of atmosphere. The rendering of atmosphere through the selection of color and materials is an area of interior design that is often associated with decoration. The selection of color from swatches, color bands, charts, and samples is an important part of the development of space and, yet, at least in education, it is often overlooked. In "The Poetic Language of Interior Materials and Color," George Verghese and Dianne Smith draw on the work of Charles S. Pierce and Roman Jakobson in order to posit the notion that the interior is a holistic space that should be understood as a visual mode of communication. With appropriate semiotic analysis, the interior can be read as an environment where the language of each material, its color and texture along with their juxtaposition with each other, represents the poetry of interior space.

The close relationship between the interior and its human occupant has often led to its use as a prototype for the exploration and testing of new technological developments. Domestic space has often provided the test bed for experiments and innovation. In the early twentieth century, Le Corbusier described the home as a machine to live in. The integration of services, appliances, materials, and their fabrication was central to the modernist reformation project. The integration of new technologies into space and their impact upon the occupant is explored in "Technology and the Interior." In this chapter, Trevor Keeble examines the relationship of technology to the interior. He argues that technology is always described or perceived as rational, and mechanistic, yet this is not always so. Technology can also be a conditional instrument, open to different uses and even contingency. Keeble provides an overview of technological developments that are not exhaustive but instead explore how their development and incorporation into the interior has mediated the relationship between the occupant and the outside world. The chapter is structured in three parts; water, heat, and light; the technological interior; and the technological object.

In "Phenomenology and the Senses In Interiors," Christine Cantwell explores how phenomenology and the senses have the power to drive the fabrication and ultimately the identity of the interior. Cantwell describes how phenomenology is the discussion of structures of consciousness, and how through its senses the body reads its environment and understands ideas about the condition in which it is situated. The author suggests that the discipline of interior design intrinsically addresses the senses through the atmospheric and haptic conditions of lighting, sound, smell, and the touch of materials. Cantwell uses the color work of Josef Albers, Isamu Noguchi's sculpture gallery and garden in New York, and Peter Zumthor's Vals baths to describe the role of senses and atmosphere in interior space. She suggests that when developed together, the senses remain a subtle yet driving force in constructing an atmosphere for the interior.

The interior design profession is a tastemaking activity. Certain aspects of the discipline and the profession incorporate trend forecasting, an activity that is closely related to fashion. Tastemakers range from those who set trends in mainstream media, such as magazines and television, to those who act as trend forecasters, not only to interior designers but to product and fashion designers, determining colors, materials, and themes that will emerge as the next seasons trend, sometimes predicting styles or looks years in advance. In "Taste and Trends," Penny Sparke explores the big business of trend forecasting and looks into the alignment and implications of interiors with the fashion industry. Sparke suggests that one part of interiors is less related to other built environment disciplines, such as architecture, and instead is closely connected to fashion and socially defined concepts of taste. Sparke examines how trend forecasting is not new and was prevalent in the eighteenth century. She examines how fashion and dress are closely linked to the emergence of the role of women in the interior along with notions of trend and taste in the house. As a result, the interior is an ever-changing space, one that is intrinsically linked to new trends and fashionable styles. The influence of taste in the interior is ultimately affecting consumption and playing a role in the globalization of trends.

The chameleon-like quality of the interior allows it to be exemplified by many different mediated forms, a feature that promulgates the intrinsically indistinct characteristic of the interior and its reality as an edifice and as a set of ideas about communication. The chapters in this part have been compiled in order to establish the wide-ranging remit of the interior as a communicative device and how it can be used as a narrative instrument.

30

The Art of Borrowing

RO SPANKIE

INTRODUCTION

This chapter looks at representation, focusing in particular on the role of drawing in the production and the practice of interior design. At one level this feels like a contradiction as it could be argued that there is no such thing as *representational techniques specific to interior design* and that all the techniques used are borrowed from other disciplines. However, one could equally argue that if one understands interior design as a distinct practice, then it can be defined by what interior designers do, and drawing is integral to that process. In addition, if one accepts the definition of interior design as a discipline concerned with the re-reading and alteration of an existing context, then the borrowing of existing drawing techniques seems appropriate, as does their alteration.

What is meant by *borrowing* here? The term itself is "borrowed" from the fictional practice of borrowing described in Mary Norton's novel *The Borrowers* (1952). It does not refer to the everyday sense of borrowing where something is *borrowed* and *returned* (such as a stamp or a pencil), but rather to the borrowing of something to put it to another use and in doing so changing the object either conceptually or physically or both. In Norton's novel the borrowers are tiny people (compared to human beings), and thus scale becomes an instrument of change. The postage-sized stamp becomes a picture-sized portrait of the Queen when hung on their wall. I suggest the term *borrow* as a useful conceptual tool for interior designers that may give insight into interior practice, not just as an analogy with the reuse of existing buildings, but also as a means to foreground the creative potential of borrowing of ideas and techniques.

Why is Drawing Important?

Why is drawing important? Design is a drawing-based practice. Designers construct propositions on the page or screen, rather than the building itself, using drawing both as a tool to draw out and test an idea and as a language with which to communicate these ideas. Because interior design deals with buildings, it uses the same representational tools as architecture—orthographic projections such as plan, section, and elevation. These techniques are very adept at drawing form and make it possible to provide an accurate, measured description of a proposal. However, interior design is not just about form. It also deals with the effect a proposal induces in the user, and these more experiential and ephemeral qualities are not addressed by standard orthographic techniques by their nature of being unquantifiable, immaterial, and fluid.

While acknowledging the importance of conventional orthographic techniques, this chapter proposes to look at other drawing techniques relevant to interior design. Referring to the artist and educator Josef Albers's use of the terms *actual* and *factual* to describe the gap between space as it is visually perceived (*actual*) and the physical reality (*factual*), the chapter proposes to suggest ways one might begin to draw the "actual." What is interesting is that there are no set conventions in the way there are for orthographic techniques, and "actual" drawings refer to a variety of disciplines beyond architecture, such as fine art, animation, and advertising. These drawings are qualitative and subjective, rather than quantitative and measured, and respond to techniques of arrangement and association, rather than scale and proportion.

What is (a) Drawing?

The word *drawing* can be understood in two ways: as a verb meaning the practice "of drawing" and as a noun meaning "a drawing," as in the artifact. This dual nature is reflected in two styles of writing on drawing: first, the graphic manual that deals with the practice of drawing and explains *how* to draw; and, second, more theoretical writings that focus on the artifact and discuss *why* designers draw and *what* the drawing might represent. Such writings examine historical techniques, or extol new digital paradigms, and locate drawing in the wider field of representation, examining not just the act of drawing but also the expanded positions of the viewer and the viewed. Rarely do practice and theory combine.

In this chapter I propose to discuss the terms *why* and *what* in order to give an insight into *how*. Intriguingly the *why* and the *what* are answered relatively simply, while the seemingly more practical *how* is more complex, opening up questions about interior design as a discipline. I suggest this is because the *method* with which we choose to draw influences not only *what* we draw but also the way we *think* and therefore *design*. The proposition is that the question of how we draw should not be relegated to the graphics manual because in order to understand interior design as a practice we need to identify drawing techniques that, as we use them, allow us to *think through drawing* in an interior-specific way.

1: WHY DRAW?

I am my brain's publisher.

—Philippe Starck

I want to see things, that's why I draw.
Things show to me only when I draw them.

—Carlo Scarpa

There is no rule saying one *needs* to draw. Vernacular architecture and particularly domestic interiors have been created for centuries without the need for a lengthy and skilled drawing process. Many interiors simply evolve over time, in response to changes in use. For example, even a design classic such as Pierre Chareau's Maison de Verre in Paris (1931) was created with virtually no drawings. Once the steel work was in place, Chareau simply chose to discuss and modify on-site like a tailor altering the cut of a dress while the cloth is still pinned to the model.

So why *is* drawing important, and why do designers do it? There are a number of reasons. Historically, design has always been a drawing-based practice. In order to understand its significance, it may helpful to look back at how the role of drawing in the construction process has evolved.

Up until the fifteenth century the three visual arts—architecture, painting, and sculpture—were not seen as primarily intellectual activities, as they are today, but as mechanical skills confined to artisan guilds. Full-size templates were used to describe important features such as column capitals, but drawings in the sense that we understand them today were not such an important part of the building process. It was possible to build without representations of any kind because the designer and the maker were often one and the same person, and the desire for innovation was localized.

However, during the Renaissance a shift in this paradigm emerged, as designing and making became separate professions. Knowing how to draw began to distinguish the designer from the other occupations involved in building process. There are two reasons behind this shift. First, the rediscovery of perspective resulted in a change in the status of drawing. There was a growing understanding that the drawing could provide an accurate representation of the world around it and could therefore be a useful tool. Second, the term *designer* came into being. The word *design* is derived from the Italian word *disegno*, "meaning drawing, suggesting both the drawing of a line on paper and the drawing forth of an idea" from the mind.[1] Embodied in this concept was the assumption that the act of designing was a separate activity from the act of making. As design was constructed on the page, not the building site, the concern became not *how* to build but *what* to build and with that the justification *why*. This emphasis on the generating idea implied that intellectual labor was superior to manual labor.

No Watson, this was not done by accident but by design.

—Sherlock Holmes

So how does one draw forth an idea from the mind? If we understand the word *design* to be a kind of mapping out in the mind's eye, a proposition, a projection, an invention, a description, then the act of drawing (regardless of whether a pencil, pen, keyboard, or other medium is used) is a combination of the eye, the mind, the imagination, and the hand. It is an intellectual activity that links sensing, feeling, thinking, and doing. When ideas are at the embryonic stage there can be an almost subconscious dialogue between impulse, ideas, and marks, the brain receiving feedback from marks appearing on the page. Drawing becomes a mode of thinking. In the twenty-first century the concept of "disegno" has become so integral to the definition of design that we can say the ability to *think through drawing* has become the true mark of the professional designer.

2: WHAT SHOULD ONE DRAW?

To understand *what* to draw it may be useful to distinguish between how an artist draws and how a designer draws. An artist traditionally understands a drawing as a representation of something real or imagined. When artists put brush to canvas they set out to capture something of what they see, and the representation (the painting in this example) is the product. A designer works differently from an artist. Their drawing is a description of something that doesn't yet exist and has still to be made, a proposition rather than an observation. Designers' drawings are representations of an idea that originates in their imagination and are a means of communicating that idea to the wider world. The drawings are more like a set of instructions, done in order for the design to be realized, with the drawing preceding the design object as opposed to being the end product; it is a means to an end.

The "Existing" and the "Proposed"

This distinction is less clear, however, when it comes to the interior designer. The prevalent definition of interior design today is a discipline concerned with the re-reading, alteration, and/or reuse of an existing context, usually a building, regardless of scale or context (whether historical or contemporary). However, this definition implies a need to describe both the existing context *and* the design proposal, to observe or "read" the existing and to propose "alterations"—to draw, in other words, both as an artist and as a designer. The double role of the drawing (both observational and propositional) in the production of interiors can lead to confusion.

Form and Effect

But the artist, the architect, first senses the effect that he wishes to exert upon the spectator.... These effects are produced both by the material and the form of the space.

—*Adolf Loos, "The Principle of Cladding"*

There is a further complication. Because interior design conventionally practices at the scale of buildings, it naturally refers to architecture, borrowing its means of practice and

methods of representation and in particular the use of projective geometry to create orthographic and perspective projections. These techniques are very adept at drawing form
and make it possible to provide an accurate, measured description of a built proposal.
However, interior design is not just about form: it is also concerned with the effect a proposal induces in the user, and these more experiential qualities are not addressed by such
orthographic techniques. Anyone looking at a plan or section can see there is a huge gap
between the representation and the reality (see Fig. 73 and Plate 33). The abstraction
of the graphic conventions used refers to scale and measure, thickness and material,
but makes little attempt to "look like" the proposal. Techniques such as axonometric
projection provide a more realistic three-dimensional view, but because the underlying
geometry used to construct the image defines points in space drawn together by lines,
the interior space is defined only by its limits, its edges. On a very simplistic level the
difficulty arises because orthographic drawing describes the architecture or the form that
encloses the space, but the resulting space, the interior, is void (see Fig. 74).

   This is problematic as interior space is neither empty nor silent. The Austrian architect and theorist Adolf Loos, in the article "The Principle of Cladding" (1898), used the
terms *form* and *effect* to describe this dilemma.[2] Loos argued that the creation of interior
space should be driven primarily by the effect that the designer wishes to exert on the
spectator. What did Loos mean by "effect"? The effect is the experience, reading, or emotional response a space induces in the user. It is created by qualities such as texture, light,
and color, as well as association and memory. It can be an overwhelming experience or
just a gradual sense, but "effect" is the quality that allows us to use subjective terms such
as *cheerful* or *warm* in describing an interior. Rich in nuance but weak in character, the
power of effect should not be underestimated. The character of a space remains in the
head far longer than its more formal qualities, the mind often distorting the relationship
between actual form and perceived space.

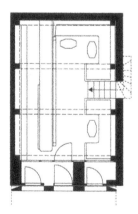

FIGURE 73   The Kärntner Bar (American Bar), Vienna, designed by Adolf Loos, 1908. "The sign of
a truly felt architectural work is that in plan it lacks effect" (A. Loos, "The Principle of Cladding," in
Spoken into the Void: Collected Essays 1897–1900 [Cambridge, MA: MIT Press, 1982], p. 66, originally
published in *Neue Freie Presse,* September 4, 1898). Note the effect of the mirrors, making the space
look larger than it actually is, and the reflection of the rectangular columns next to the mirror, giving the
illusion they are square. These are something the plan is unable to show. Courtesy of Graeme Brooker.

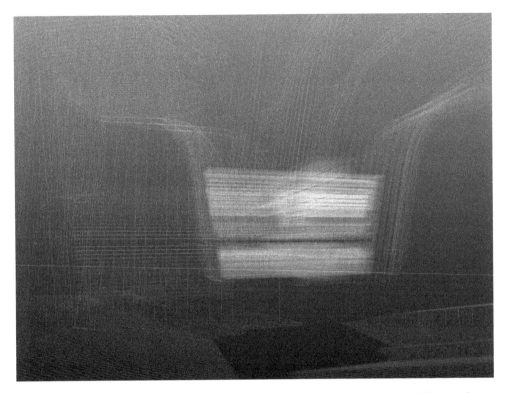

FIGURE 74 Victoria Watson: "Air Grid" is a method of describing the space created by an architectural form. Constructed as a digital model consisting of volumes of colored hatching in the air, air grid represents architectural space rather than the space of the interior. The interior designer is more concerned with occupation and effect. Courtesy of Victoria Watson.

The Beholder's Stare

The process of creating effect is not as straightforward as that of creating form, partly because in designing effect, form matters, but not so much the form itself as the ways in which the occupant reads the form. The occupant's visual perception is subject to what the art historian Ernst Gombrich has described as the "beholder's stare." According to Gombrich there is no such thing as an "innocent" look, as the viewer's perception is always influenced by his or her knowledge of the world and other images as much as by what he or she actually sees. "All art originates in the human mind, in our reactions to the world rather than in the visible world itself, and it is precisely because all art is 'conceptual' that all representations are recognisable by their style."[3] The viewer's experiences are therefore always implicated in this perceptual radar. The suggestion here is that just as Gombrich's artist cannot presume what the beholder will see, the interior designer cannot presume the effect of a space on the occupant. Each occupant will bring his or her own reading into the space, effectively becoming co-authors.[4]

Picking up on this concept, the writer Alain de Botton in a chapter entitled "Talking Buildings" suggests "our interest in buildings and objects is indeed determined as much by what they say to us as by how they perform their material function." He suggests this ability to read the spaces around us is fundamental to human nature and developed from our ability to read faces and body language, one of our key survival skills. "We can judge the personality of objects…because we first acquire this skill in relation to humans, whose characters we can impute from microscopic aspects of their skin tissue and muscle." "So refined is our skill at detecting parallels to human beings in forms, textures and colours that we can interpret a character from the humblest shape."[5]

The seeming aside into visual theory is important because it highlights the slippery nature of the effect. Interiors are both a material manifestation and a concept. (Confusingly, it implies that interior spaces themselves should be understood as representations, although this point is separate from the discussion of representational techniques.) Interiors, because of their scale, relationship to the occupant's body, and capacity to be altered, are subject to the beholder's stare to a far greater degree than the architectural host they inhabit. This throws up huge challenges in terms of representation because form can be accurately described and drawn out, but not the effect, even though it is precisely this quality that Loos argued should drive the design.

3: HOW SHOULD ONE DRAW?

The chapter opened by suggesting that the method we choose to draw, to draw out a design, influences not only what we draw but also the way we think and inevitably what we design.

The difficulty of borrowing techniques from other disciplines is that the technique, having been created for other purposes, may not describe the interior designer's concerns. An example of this could be the developed surface, a form of orthographic projection that provides a method of unfolding a room to see all the surfaces at once. It could be seen as an appropriate drawing technique for interior designers.

But as the architectural historian and theorist Robin Evans argues in his essay "The Developed Surface: An Enquiry into the Brief Life of an Eighteenth-Century Drawing Technique":

> Architectural drawing affects what might be called the architect's field of visibility. It makes it possible to see some things more clearly by suppressing other things; something gained, something lost. Its power to represent is always partial, always more or less abstract. It never gives, nor can it give, a total picture of a project, so in consequence it tends to provide a range of subject-matter that is made visible in the drawing, as opposed to all the other possible subject-matter that is left out of the drawing or is not so apparent from it.[6]

Describing the emergence and then decline of the technique, he points out that "the developed surface invites the draftsman to describe" primarily surface decoration such as "drapes, furnishings, fittings, wall coverings, plasterwork, floor and carpet"[7] but is unable to describe qualities such as the arrangement of the furniture in the room or a sequence of adjoining spaces. In other words, the technique both directs and limits the draftsman.

In an attempt to open up the designer's *field of visibility* I will describe two techniques that I suggest have potential to draw out form and also effect, offering a way of making and a way of thinking. With both techniques I will describe how they were originally used and then suggest ways they might be altered to become an interior design tool.

Factual and Actual

The first suggestion of *how* one might draw originates in art practice and concerns a method of *drawing out* color. The source is a book entitled *Interaction of Color,* by the artist and educator Josef Albers, originally published in 1963 (see Plate 34). The book is both a record and an analysis of experimental exercises that he conducted with his students for studying and teaching color. At that time, color was taught through the application of rules and theory, a method Albers found unsatisfactory. He explained the problem in the introduction:

> In visual perception a color is almost never seen as it really is
> —as it physically is.
> This fact makes color the most relative medium in art.
> In order to use color effectively it is necessary to recognize
> that color deceives continually.[8]

He continued, "Experience teaches that in visual perception there is a discrepancy between physical fact and psychic effect."[9]

Albers's solution was a teaching method that he termed "thinking in situations," where an understanding of color is gained, not through theory, but rather through practical exercises that introduced students to concepts such as "color relativity" and "vibrating and vanishing boundaries." In order to facilitate discussion, he suggested that "in dealing with color relativity or color illusion, it is practical to distinguish *factual* facts from *actual* facts."[10]

Albers introduced these terms in relation to color, but they are significant to this discussion because the gap between color and the perception of color is analogous to the gap between form and effect. "Factual facts" are physical facts that he defined as things that remain as they are, not undergoing change. For his students this was strips of colored paper; for the interior designer this would be the physical form of the building. "Actual facts," on the other hand, are the psychic effects on the viewer that he defines as things that change with time. For the interior designer this would be the effect.

Albers expands on the idea of *change* through an analogy relating the term *actual* to the noun *action* and to the verb *to act*. "Action is the noun for the verb 'to act.' Acting in visual presentation is to change by giving up, by losing identity. When we act, we change appearance and behavior, we act as someone else."[11] He cites the example of an actor appearing as Henry VIII. The audience both knows and temporarily forgets who he *factually* is, and (if the actor is good) he will have the same effect on the audience when he plays Henry IX or Henry X. Color acts in a similar way, with colors influencing and changing each other, continually interacting in our perception.

Looking at the examples of the studies shown (Figs. 75 and 76, Plate 34) one can see they are simple grids of color made of cut strips of colored paper rather than paint. Albers refers to them as "studies" or "experimental tryouts." As representations they are nonpictorial and are not meant to illustrate or to decorate. They are allographic rather than autographic, lacking the potential for self-expression. Because of this, as drawings they come under the "tool" category, providing the student with a technique that is able to produce a variety of desired effects that can then be compared and evaluated. Key to Albers's proposal is the idea of "praxis." The student gains an "eye" for color not through lectures but through repeated experiments with the exercises.

It is interesting to note that Albers's studies function in a manner not dissimilar to the mood boards or concept boards used by interior designers, techniques that use arrangement and association to describe effect. The mood board's weakness has always been a lack of precision. Albers's studies are more directed, offering a level of abstraction and a clear conceptual distinction between the role of the actual and the role of the factual. Rethought in this way mood boards could offer a far greater creative potential than the presentation format for which they are used today.

Collage and Montage

The second technique also originates in art practice and suggests an alternative to the strips of colored paper. Representation is traditionally about using one medium such as

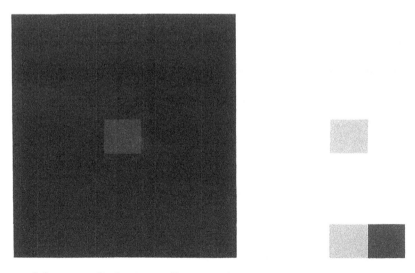

FIGURE 75   Subtraction of color: VII-7: illustration from *Interaction of Color* by Josef Albers. This study shows a very courageous solution to the problembecause it makes a very light grey and a dark, almost black-grey appear alike. Courtesy of Yale University Press.

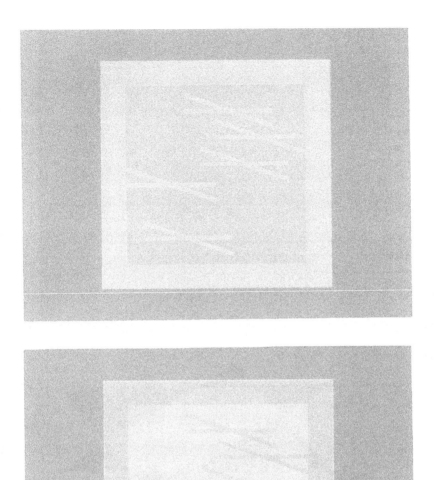

FIGURE 76   Vibrating boundaries: XXII-2 illustration from *Interaction of Color* by Josef Albers. 2 studies of precisely the same arrangement, but with reversed colors. That the vibrating boundaries look different on both sides is probably the result of the changing color quantities of figure and ground. Courtesy of Yale University Press. For color version, please see plate section.

paint to simulate something else. Collage, the application of real fragments like newspaper clippings onto the surface of paintings, was introduced just before World War I by the cubists Pablo Picasso and George Braque. Photomontage, the cutting and pasting of a number of photographs to make one image, came into being around the same time. The discovery was that the fragment, while still recognizable as, say, a newspaper clipping, could also be read as part of a new image, shifting, in Albers's terms, between factual and actual.

The word *collage* comes from the French *coller,* "to glue," while *montage* means "to put together," "to build," or "to organize." They can be further defined in many ways, but for the purpose of the interior drawing I would suggest collage is a fine art technique that works at the level of the drawing itself (and thus might be used to describe material qualities such as texture or form), while montage is a filmic technique using film or photographs that is affected by the context in which it operates and therefore refers to the wider culture beyond the drawing. Collage is perhaps more useful in the creation of more haptic or sensory effects, while montage refers to the "beholders' stare" and the associated readings or ideas created in one's head. In Gombrich's terms, collage relates to seeing, montage to knowing. My interest in both stems from their ability to translate from the painted canvas or photographic print into the abstract world of the orthographic projection. A fragment placed in plan or section becomes magically positioned in space, read at the scale of the drawing while still referring to its original context, responding, as it were, to both systems of measure.

Montage can also be understood in a more cinematic sense, as the juxtaposition and contrasting of images in cinematic sequence, a concept that implies time and space and opens intriguing questions between the construction of the image and its spatial application. The suggestion is that if the design is constructed using montage, the proposed space may function in a similar manner. The main difference between the drawing and an actual proposition would be that the effect could not be controlled in a proposed space in the way it can with a two-dimensional image. In montage the gaps between elements can be as important as the elements themselves (the gaps giving the image depth), yet in the proposed interior they will shift as the occupant moves through space, the montage endlessly made and remade by each user.

Traditionally, collage and montage were created with a scalpel and glue or editing tape. More recently, image-editing software means the whole process is often digitized, and the designer has the ability to manipulate both the fragment and the image as a whole. The scanner, the digital camera, and software that is able to import a variety of media have allowed designers to move with ease between techniques, and the hybrid drawing has emerged as the true medium of collage. In an example by Alessandro Ayuso, the collage drawing was created with a variety of techniques and could be said to exist both as a two-dimensional drawing and as a three-dimensional model (Plate 35). Because the animated figure moves around the three-dimensional model, the drawing can also be understood as a film still or moment in time.

The building was constructed in three dimensions in modeling software. A sectional cut through the staircase was selected and imported into Photoshop and colored in a beaux arts manner. The wire-frame "Putto" figure was created using animation software and let loose in the three-dimensional model. Stills were selected, some of which were rendered and imported into the section. The image was finally printed at a scale of 1:10, and Ayuso continued to work on the drawing by hand using colored pencils. His own figure can be seen faintly outlined in pencil at the bottom of the stair.

In fact, over-dependency on software is not an advantage, seducing designers into creating an almost-photographic likeness until it is not clear whether the image is a collage, a montage, or merely a photograph. In Albers's terms, such visualizations, as they are known, are simply deceits (as if the actor came on stage and claimed he was Henry VIII). The architect and academic Stan Allen illuminates this point, saying, "The ideology of visualization is both naïve and somewhat duplicitous. Its trajectory is not from image to reality, but from image to image."[12]

What these seamless images fail to utilize is the creative potential embedded in the techniques themselves. The ability to attract both the eye *and* the mind means collage and montage should not be understood merely as ways of constructing an image but also as ways of thinking about a proposition. They are physically and conceptually additive and as such are suggestive. Their creativity comes from surreal juxtapositions, the often-bizarre shift in scale between the fragment and the image, and the relationship of the gaps created in-between. The skill in constructing the image is based on the designer's selection, placement, and fixing of fragments, an intellectual activity requiring the placing of one fragment next to another in such a way that the net result is far greater than the sum of the parts. This ability to see the potential of the fragment in relation to the whole can be understood as an act of design and has a profound resonance with the interior practice of re-reading and altering an existing context through the placing of new elements. If we return to Albers's analogy of the actor, the interior designer becomes the director, directing "actors" on a stage.

The fragment doesn't have to be a physical object. The Smoking Room was the name of a lobbying room in the House of Commons; since the European Union ban on smoking, it is now known as the Strangers Bar. Members of Parliament and their guests come in the evening, to hear the gossip and have a drink. It is one of the few rooms where rumors are encouraged, and all political parties use the room as a space to allow leaks to be circulated to the press. Such a room has a clear function that is obviously not reliant on a particular architectural response, but more on the creation of an atmosphere or effect. In his collage "The Smoking Room," (Plate 36) Tom Holdom creates a visual analogy between the rumors and the smoke, using a technique in which he blew smoke onto a sticky film that he then stuck onto the drawing.

IN CONCLUSION

In conclusion to the questions of *why, what,* and *how* to draw, I would like to suggest the following: The traditional way to design buildings is reiterative; plan and section are drawn on tracing paper, overlaying sheets, tracing through some ideas, letting others submerge. More recently, there is an increasing trend to draw in a modeling software that allows one to construct a proposal in three dimensions, a process of building up not dissimilar to the construction process itself. The first technique gives an abstracted overview; the second is concerned with tectonics. Although much has been made of this shift from hand to digital, both techniques describe points in space through the use of geometry. They are essentially introverted activities allowing the design proposal to refer both to its own inner logic and to the language of architecture and design. This chapter suggests the interior designer's role is more extroverted, akin to the role of the director, in constant dialogue with the actor, understanding that the actors' performance is relative and will change in relation to the other actors, backdrops, and the audience.

The reason for this is that interior design is what the cultural critic and architectural theorist Mark Cousins would call a "weak discipline"[13] because it is both object based and also concerned with the effect of the object on a subject. As such (as I have already stated), interiors are both a material manifestation and a concept, answering both functional requirements while at the same time creating a dialogue with the occupant. The problem for the interior designer is that this dialogue is subjective and changes over time; the occupant's response is based as much on what something means to him or her as on what it "actually" is. The reason the practice of interior design is so difficult to define and therefore to draw is that it does not deal only with the stable geometry of the building but also with the less predictable effect, which relates to time, context, taste, and style.

Finally, it was suggested in the introduction that there are no drawing techniques specific to interior design; those that are used are borrowed from other disciplines. Traditionally, this would have negative connotations, as to borrow an idea is stealing or, as designers refer to it, copying. I have sought in this chapter to show how a more critical, creative reading of what it means to "borrow" might open up new representational possibilities for interior designers that may be used not just to *represent* a space or set of spaces but to *design* them as well. I hope to have shown that when a technique is borrowed and applied to a different context, such as the slip of colored paper or the collage fragment, it will be subject to change. This change will alter the original technique both as a way of making and as a way of thinking, and this process of reuse and alteration is analogous to the practice of interior design itself. And it is precisely because of the change embodied in the process that interior design remains creative, original, and relevant.

REFERENCES

Albers, J. 2006. *Interaction of Color.* New Haven, CT: Yale University Press.

Allen, S. 2000. *Practice: Architecture, Technique and Representation.* London: Routledge.

Cousins, M. 1998. "Building an Architect." In *Occupying Architecture: Between the Architect and the User,* ed. J. Hill, 13–21. London: Routledge.

de Botton, A. 2006. *The Architecture of Happiness: The Secret Art of Furnishing Your Life.* London: Penguin Books.

Evans, R. 1997. "The Developed Surface: An Enquiry into the Brief Life of an Eighteenth-Century Drawing Technique." In *Translations from Drawing to Building and Other Essays,* by R. Evans, 195–231. London: Architectural Association Publications.

Gombrich, E. H. 1960. *Art and Illusion: A Study in the Psychology of Pictorial Representation.* London: Phaidon.

Hill, J. 1998. "An Other Architect." In *Occupying Architecture: Between the Architect and the User,* ed. J. Hill, 135–159. London: Routledge.

Hill, J. 2006. *Immaterial Architecture.* London: Routledge.

Loos, A. 1898/1982. "The Principle of Cladding." *Neue Freie Presse,* September 4, 1898. Republished in *Spoken into the Void: Collected Essays 1897–1900.* Cambridge, MA: MIT Press.

Norton, M. 1952. *The Borrowers.* London: Puffin Books.

31

Model Behavior

NICK DUNN

The representation of creative ideas is of primary significance within any design discipline, and this is especially pertinent in interior design where we may not get to experience the final effects until the end of the design process.[1] Early ideas and concepts are developed through a design process that allows the designer to explore, edit, and further revise ideas, usually in increasing detail as time progresses, until such a stage that the project's design is appropriately consolidated and may be made. Models, both physical and digital, can be extraordinarily versatile tools within this process that allow designers to communicate thoughts and impulses in a creative manner. It is important to understand from the outset that modeling serves a dual function for designers, facilitating both the generation of ideas as well as their representation. Interior designers make models as a means to explore and communicate the conception and development of ideas in three dimensions. One of the key strengths of physical models is their immediacy as they are able to communicate ideas about form, material, shape, size, and color in a highly accessible manner. The size of such a model is often partially determined by the scale required at various stages of the design process, since models can illustrate a design project in relation to a wider context, as a remodeling or addition to an existing building; they can even be constructed as full-size versions, typically referred to as prototypes. More recently, the hybridization of digital and analog techniques has afforded designers even greater opportunity to explore their ideas.

Over the course of history, various types of models have been effectively used to explain gaps in knowledge. This is because models are able to provide easy understanding as a method of communication and interpretation. Our perception facilitates ready access to any part of a model and also to both specific as well as holistic views. Familiar features may be quickly understood, and this offers numerous ways for designers to draw attention to particular elements of a model. An important aspect of using models is that they are a potentially effective source of information about a design, giving three dimensions across which to communicate data and the capacity to include a spectrum of properties borrowed from the real world, such as size, shape, color, texture, and so on. Consequently, because the language of a model may be so rich, the encoding of each bit of information may be more compact with a resultant decrease in decoding time, thus facilitating our comprehension of it.

The final product of interior design may often require significant investment in relation to cost, materials, and time. Therefore, the opportunities that modeling affords the designer to rigorously describe, explore, predict, and evaluate various qualities of the design throughout the design process are considerable. This naturally leads us to the fundamental question of how best to represent the spatial experience of our interior design ideas. As professional creatives, interior designers are tasked or expected to be equipped with a highly developed set of design skills, not least of which is an innate capability to communicate their ideas across a variety of media. Similarly, for the interior design student, the issue of effectively expressing ideas so that the tutor may comprehend the design ideas is inherent to the practice of design education, as spatial ideas may become so complex that they have to be communicated in tangible form so that they may be discussed and developed further. On this latter use of modeling, it should be noted that the representation of design ideas is not solely for the tutor or reviewing audience in a formal review or crit. Modeling of interior design ideas has significant benefits for students as they seek to communicate their intentions, and these have to leap through space from the mind to be translated into two or three dimensions, enabling the initial concept to be defined. This process of transforming the mental image into a physical artifact, whether drawing or model, offers a springboard for further progression as well as a communication device for dialog with others. As such, this instigates a continuous flow between design ideas and methods of representation, a design discourse that advances until an appropriate level of definition is reached.

This raises an interesting point at this juncture since it is a reasonable assumption that an interior designer has enough experience and skills to be able to employ a range of design processes and techniques of communication as a response to the task in hand. However, in the scenario of a student developing design ideas as a response to project briefs, the use of a range of communication methods is a prerequisite for the thinking process required to deal with the complexity of interior design. In this educational environment, models and drawings are not necessarily viewed as end products through which to sell the solution to a client but rather as tools with which ideas may be developed and expressed. Furthermore, the use of various communication methods fosters greater generation and exploration of a student's ideas. There is a simple explanation for this as different representation methods and techniques stimulate different thought processes and provide greater insight during the design process. Rather than being an inert object, each model is much more usefully considered as having a particular purpose and user. Since it is not possible to include all possible design ideas within a single model, this typically results in a series of models exploring different aspects and elements of the design. Initially a model may simply act as a design tool, enabling the designer to investigate a specific idea or analyze successive developments. It may also be used to communicate design ideas to an audience, affording others to participate with the designer's vision. Therefore, far from being static things, models are actually dynamic and have, at the very least, a dual function depending on who is using them and why and when throughout the design process.[2]

This introduction has sought to explain the importance of models not only as dynamic tools in the decision-making process but also a means of generating, searching, and investigating creative impulses. Models enable designs to be explored and communicated in both a more experimental and more rigorous manner than two-dimensional media since various elements of the project may not appear to make much sense until visualized in three dimensions. Akiko Busch suggests that part of our attraction to models is because "the world in miniature grants us a sense of authority; it is more easily manoeuvred and manipulated, more easily observed and understood. Moreover, when we fabricate, touch, or simply observe the miniature, we have entered a private affair; the sense of closeness, of intimacy is implicit."[3] However, this really only addresses physical models, and the field of contemporary modeling is now much more expansive. The integration of digital technologies with more traditional modeling techniques has developed compelling and inspiring transformations in the way in which we engage with the process of designing interiors. The prevalence of computers in the design environment coupled with advanced modeling software have afforded professional interior designers and students alike the ability to create designs that would be very difficult to conceive using more traditional techniques, yet despite or perhaps even because of this, physical models appear to be experiencing something of a renaissance in both architecture and interior design. This return to analog models seems to be, as Peter Cook suggests, that "as we become cleverer at predicting colour, weight, performance or materiality, we are often in danger of slithering past the question of just what the composition of space may be" since "the tactile and visual nature of stuff may get you further into the understanding and composition" of it.[4] In addition, the implementation of CAD technologies as an integrated part of the making of physical models is increasingly growing via various CAD/CAM processes, including: CNC milling and routing, and rapid prototyping. Likewise, the translation of computer-generated data to physical object may be reversed with machines such as a three-dimensional scanner or digitizer that is able to trace the features of physical objects straight into the computer.

Computational modeling provides an additional set of tools and techniques for the interior designer in relation to traditional methods, in turn furthering the development of design innovation and the production of knowledge. For example, one of the key benefits of digital modeling is that it may facilitate the detailed scale of the temporal and animate interior to be investigated, further emphasizing the connections to the user(s) in a manner that conventional methods would find difficult to achieve. The tactile qualities of creating and using a physical model afford the designer connection with the real world, and so any overlap between different techniques and media, both digital and physical, may only serve to enhance the discourse within the discipline. These shifts are not the sole preserve of interior design and are occurring across a range of design disciplines, not least the highly interrelated one of architecture. For, as Karen Moon acknowledges, "even as architecture moves beyond the realm of the material, the physical model—contrary to expectation—may not lose its purpose. Models produced at the push of a button cannot offer the individuality and range of expression requisite for the task, nor can the imagination of architects be satisfied in this manner."[5] Thus the opportunities for computer technologies to run alongside or integral with manual techniques as part of the design process is a natural evolution that implies the time of physical models is far from over. At this standpoint, therefore, the future of interior design appears almost unquestionably to include physical models as vital tools that provide instrumentality for design generation and representation at the very core of both its practice and education. With this in mind, in the next section we will discuss a number of important aspects of modeling that are useful to consider before we engage with the process, since this affords us to be more effective in our design practice.

EFFECTIVE MODELING

The selection process for choosing appropriate materials with which to make a model is usually assisted if we consider three key factors: the speed of production, the stage of the design process, and what the purpose of the model is. However, by keeping an openminded attitude to materials, interior design ideas may emerge and be developed in unexpected ways. Core to this discovery is experimentation, particularly during the initial stages of the design process when ideas are perhaps more mutable and elastic. This not only stimulates creativity, as materials are handled and worked, but also facilitates different expressions of design ideas. This reiterates the notion stated earlier in this chapter— that is, that modeling might be as equally instrumental in the generation of ideas as in the representation of them. Clearly, it is valuable to consider the materials from which a model can be made as each different type of media has its own properties and implications that may also suggest how the embodied ideas are both explored and communicated. Many people new to modeling assume that a high level of realism is necessary, similar to a doll's house or toy train sets, but this may typically be very distracting to the eye and does not automatically convey the important aspects of the design. Therefore, in the first instance the modeler needs to think about the degree of abstraction.

All models by their very nature have a certain amount of abstraction, as there would not be value to a model if it merely described reality in every aspect. Perhaps more crucially, the degree of abstraction should be consistent, since it would be illogical to model a design's context with precision and then insert a very loosely defined and highly abstract model of the proposal in most situations. For the purpose of modeling, abstraction means removing any unnecessary components or detail that will not help the understanding of the design under exploration or being communicated. While there are no fixed guidelines for this process, novice designers should take some comfort from the knowledge that it is a skill that will develop accordingly through their experience of modeling. Despite this, a general rule of thumb typically indicates that the more precise and detailed a model is, the further the project is along the design process. This relates to all three factors outlined above since it would not make sense to waste valuable time and resources modeling accurate representations of early ideas that may be very susceptible to lots of changes later on. In relation to time, the primary constraint is what is technically possible within the time limits set aside to make the model. For example, if an element such as a staircase is too small to be made, it should be represented by simple angled pieces of material rather than laboriously making individual treads and risers.

The higher the degree of description and detail of materials, the more precise impression people viewing it will gain of the final intentions of the interior designer. As a consequence of this, the vast majority of presentation models made by both professionals and students are produced at a stage in the design process at which most of the design issues have been defined and addressed. This is because the more abstract a model is, the more it communicates conceptual ideas and facilitates the designer's imagination to flow and numerous interpretations of the design to be posited. This later aspect is especially useful in an educational environment but also during initial meetings with clients and public bodies. Professional model shops sell a considerable variety of components that may be included into models including figures, furniture, and fittings, and these may help overcome the scale difference between the model and reality. However, care should be taken not to unnecessarily detail a model as such information may distract from the qualities of the design and many interior designers frequently make their own versions of these elements, giving them more creative scope. The scale of the model typically offers clues as to the suitable degree of abstraction and is a useful starting point.

In the opening remarks of his essay for the catalog of the seminal *Idea as Model* exhibition, Christian Hubert states that "size and scale are not to be confused,"[6] and yet they so often are, so it is useful here to explain the difference. Size is directly connected to measurement and is therefore quantitative in nature, whereas by contrast, scale is relative—that is, a component is relationally smaller or bigger than another component and as a result is qualitative. However, this matter is further complicated since we need measurements so that we may set a scale up, and as a result the majority of models are made to a recognized conventional scale. So while an interior design model will frequently be produced at a different and smaller scale than the real thing, the various elements of the model all have the same scale relationship.

Why are interior design models typically made at smaller scales? The most immediate answers are related to cost, time, and effort. Models at a reduced scale are much quicker to produce and afford potential problems with installation sequences and materials to be forecast. The effort required in modeling enables the designer to assess creative ideas and refine the design accordingly. To this end, the type of model necessary at different progressive stages of the design process often outlines the amount of effort needed since a simple volumetric model will necessitate far less investment than a detailed sectional model of interior spaces. Obviously, the cost of even the most elaborate model is substantially less than that of making a real interior intervention or fit-out, and this allows the design to be examined further rather than made with any design flaws. However, beyond these reasons, there is another key factor to the role of models that is connected to the discipline itself. This is in connection to managing the design process, the fact that ideas are much easier to revise and edit when they are smaller and simpler than the real thing. The emergent quality of ideas within models provides dexterity for the benefit of the designer as models are dynamic tools of both exploration and communication at all stages of development.

As mentioned earlier, the choice of material to be used in modeling depends on the model's purpose, the stage of the design process, and how quickly it needs to be made. In order to assess which materials are suitable, it is useful to consider the degree of abstraction and the necessary scale. If a model is to be relatively abstract, it is logical to make it out of one material and focus on the formal qualities of the design. A single material may typically be manipulated and treated in numerous ways so this does not automatically constrain either the appearance or amount of detail. Monochromatic models are common in interior design; however, once the initial selection of material has been determined, a modeler then needs to decide whether additional materials will be used to develop a more representative model of the design. The integration of different surfaces, colors, and elements is a time-tested method of making interior design models, but consideration should be given to communicate the most significant qualities of the design and avoid extraneous information. A key issue here is in the handling of color since while colored elements may need to be incorporated into the model, care needs to be taken to get an appropriate balance; as Coles and House note, "Colour is not really a scalable entity, but somehow it has to be if it is not to appear overwhelming in miniature space."[7]

Combining materials to highlight their different qualities and make the most appropriate use of them needs significant experimentation, and modelers should be justifiably encouraged to explore the use of novel found materials as well as recycle packaging and other everyday objects in their quest for suitable materials. In a similar manner as to when laying out a drawing, the designer should give consideration to the composition of the model. Therefore, there are a few basic issues that are helpful to think about prior to modeling. First, what scale should be chosen, and how will this best relate to the level of detail required in the model? Second, is the proposed project to be centered within the overall model, or are there good reasons why this would not be the most suitable position—for example, specific relationship within an existing building? Third and finally, what are the desired interrelationships between elements in terms of color, proportion, and material that will communicate the design ideas in the most effective way?

Modeling in interior design is often perceived as a highly skilled craft concerned with precision, and while this may hold some truth in relation to presentation models it does not necessarily determine a good model. It is therefore important to state here that it is possible to make creative and provocative models without laborious and time-consuming techniques. After all, as Rolf Janke notes in his classic book on the subject of model-making, "The significance of a model lies not only in enabling (the designer) to depict in plastic terms the end-product of his deliberations, but in giving him the means—during the design process—of actually seeing and therefore controlling spatial problems."[8] However, when they are made with an appropriate degree of precision, it is possible to achieve superb effects with models as they may be carefully photographed, making it difficult for the viewer to easily distinguish between a modeled space and the real situation. It may also be useful to wall-mount interior design models, enabling the viewer to look into the contained space, rather than onto it. The obvious benefit of this technique is that it enhances our perception of the spaces, affording us to feel as if we are there. The two case studies that follow offer very different approaches to modeling for interior design. The first showcases a more traditional approach to modeling, making highly effective use of physical models, photography, and full-size prototyping to develop detailed design features and decisions. By contrast, the second demonstrates an innovative project that embraces the possibilities of digital technologies from concept, throughout the entire design process, and concluding in a final design made using digital fabrication techniques. Both case studies illustrate innovative ways in which modeling provides an essential part of the toolkit of any aspiring interior designer.

CASE STUDY 1: STEVEN HOLL—PHYSICAL MODELING AND FULL-SIZE PROTOTYPES

Interior design models are primarily made to explore and communicate the internal characteristics of space(s) and therefore may focus on a particular aspect of it rather than the overall design. Consequently, they may appear quite crudely finished externally since it is the interior elements and qualities that are of key interest. The designer's need to develop and understand a space in detail often leads to such models being produced at 1:20, 1:10, or 1:5 scales. This type of model frequently incorporates detailed components such as staircases, furniture, and miniature people, which need to be used cautiously as an integral part of the composition. Toward the end of the design process, interior design models seek to represent true spatial relationships, and so while a level of abstraction is acceptable due to their scale they afford the viewer to look inside the spaces and observe how they may actually appear in reality.

The architecture and interior design work of Steven Holl often celebrates a sophisticated interplay between light and shadow on his considered composition of forms. Writing about this quality, Holl opines, "Architecture transcends geometry. It is an organic link between concept and form . . . Forming a concept defines a field of inquiry— a territory of research for investigation that helps to form meaning. The idea is the force that drives the design. The field of inquiry sets the focus and the limit and, most importantly, the responsibility of work in rigor and depth."[9] This position and the quality of work developed through it has led to various commissions for gallery designs such as the Herning Center of the Arts, Denmark, 2009. Initiated as a fusion of landscape and architecture, the gallery spaces are orthogonal and simple with excellent proportions in relation to the art, while overhead the curved roof sections afford natural light to be brought into the spaces below. The nature of these gallery spaces was further explored using a sectional model (Fig. 77). By using photography to record the gallery spaces and the qualities of daylight within them, the sense of light and form achieved was enhanced by then using digital software to add people and thus afford the scale to be understood (Plates 37a and 37b). The careful positioning of the camera and setting up of each shot of the model is vital here since it adds to the illusion that we are entering real space. Clearly, a primary factor in nearly all gallery designs is the manipulation of daylight to ensure the exhibited artworks are not negatively affected by it. Therefore, in the final stage of this model series, the potential positions for paintings were subsequently added to communicate the practical qualities of the design in response to lighting criteria (Fig. 78). These accurately made but fairly simple interior design models are only part of the design process for this project.

Detailed spatial models are not the only types used in the field of interior design; sometimes structural or technical models, often known as details, are also required to contribute to the understanding of specific element. In theory, these models can be

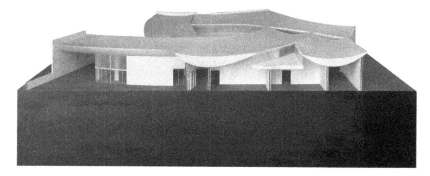

FIGURE 77   Herning Gallery, sectional model. Courtesy of Steven Holl Architects.

FIGURE 78   Herning Gallery space with added artworks. Courtesy of Steven Holl Architects.

made on a scale of up to 1:1, although at that stage they are more commonly referred to as prototypes. Thirty years ago, it was not unusual for architecture practices to make full-size prototypes of building components, interiors, and even entire floors of high-rise projects to explore the design implications involved. Of course this is an expensive process, and while it does still occur, especially in illustrious and high-profile projects, the use of CAD has afforded a considerable degree of a design's potential features and behavior over time to be predicted. However, this type of model is a useful tool for the designer who may have difficulty comprehending how complex combinations of elements connect in three dimensions. Full-size or 1:1 prototypes are typically constrained by the extent of their size in reality, and they therefore should function as tools to explore detailed components more rigorously, rather than merely replicate a portion of the design proposal. This is obviously not practical in situations where time and space are limited, but the advantages may be considerable. The appearance of materials may often be deceptive when shown on drawings and even the most sophisticated textured and colored computer renderings do not compensate for the loss of tactile data. This is one of the key reasons why interior designers may explore the possible materiality of a design's surfaces and components before their implementation within a design, especially where the materials have an unknown visual impact or other characteristics.

To return to Steven Holl's design for the galleries in Herning Center for the Arts, a 1:1 prototype was made (Fig. 79). This enabled the designers to fully comprehend the

FIGURE 79   Herning Gallery full-size prototype. Courtesy of Steven Holl Architects.

implications of connecting the various elements together to achieve the desired internal atmosphere. The curved roofs, a primary design feature, are a two-way truss system able to span in multiple directions, providing freedom between the roof structure and floor plan. The internal surfaces are lined with a white plaster, whose minimal appearance further emphasizes the geometry of the roof. The overall stability of the roof would be anchored by introducing thin rods within the clerestory glazing as tension elements intended to counterbalance any uneven forces over the gallery wall support, like a seesaw tied down on each side. By making a full-size prototype to address the possible difficulties on site, this method provided an effective tool through which the realities of the interior design and architecture could be tested.

CASE STUDY 2: MARK GOULTHORPE/DECOI—DIGITAL MODELING AND FABRICATION

The potential of emerging digital technologies in design, development, and fabrication processes for interior design is currently an area of inquiry and practice that is constantly evolving and providing new and exciting opportunities for the designer.[10] The widespread use of computers and advanced modeling software have enabled professional interior designers and students alike to develop designs that would be very difficult to conceive and make if traditional methods were used. More specifically, the emergence of new computational modeling software that enables parametric systems and complex biological organizations to be generated and explored in design terms has begun to offer avenues of holistic design production and detailed component manufacturing for the interior designer that had not previously existed. These huge transformations in design processes have implications in material culture far beyond the discipline of interior design as more and more research and developments are being conducted at cross-disciplinary levels around the globe. Furthermore, the use of CAD/CAM technologies as part of the production of physical models and prototypes is increasingly widespread through processes such as lazer cutting, CNC milling, and rapid prototyping. At the time of this writing, a number of these digital processes are sufficiently established, while retaining their high degree of innovation, to be discussed as a strand of closed-loop modeling— that is, where the complete design process uses digital technologies at every stage rather than as a hybrid process that integrates more traditional techniques.

Mark Goulthorpe is a leading figure in the field of digital design and fabrication and, through the various research and design projects his practice dECOi has produced to date, has demonstrated a breadth and depth of inquiry into the nature and opportunities of these digital processes. One of the most significant developments made possible through such technologies is the rise of bespoke, nonstandard production whereby one-off elements may be made at no additional cost due to the fabrication process. This important shift in the production of elements for architecture and interior design is often referred to as mass-customization where, as Branko Kolarevic has noted, "it is just as easy and cost-effective for a CNC milling machine to produce 1,000 unique objects as to produce 1,000 identical ones."[11] Describing the more recent output of dECOi, Goulthorpe explains that such projects "offer highly suggestive probes towards a radically revised design/build logic, where the nonstandard is thought through in methodological terms: the folding-back of disparate (industrial) element-ism into highly articulate singular processes, which allow differential attribute in material assemblies."[12]

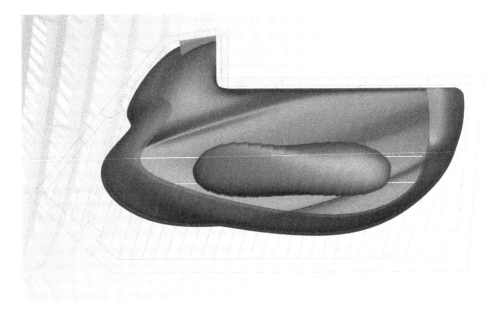

FIGURE 80   Initial 3D CAD model within plan of existing building. Courtesy of dECOi Architects.

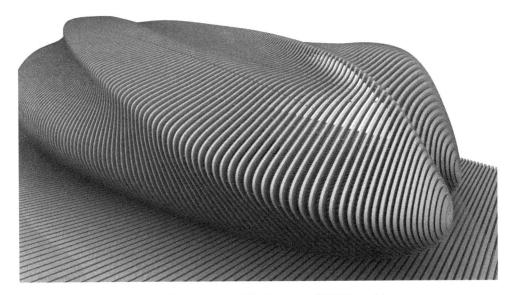

FIGURE 81   Later generation of 3D CAD model. Courtesy of dECOi Architects.

This approach is explicitly apparent in the design and fabrication of the project, Miran Galerie, Paris, 2003. This fashion showroom project utilizes Computer-Numerically Controlled (CNC) machining of plywood sheets to fabricate an interior form of a complex curved shell featuring a hanging display. The form is articulated as a highly sculptural, continuous surface through the composition of nonstandard planar elements. Despite using very different techniques to the previous case study, modeling was also at the very core of both the design development and realization of this project. The early stages of the design process used standard 3D software to develop a curvilinear surface that was then stretched out into the space of the existing building to maximize its impact and curvature in relation to its context (Fig. 80). This form was then further developed using computational scripting to drive parametric modeling software, enabling the designer to visualize the effects of changing different variables within the 3D digital model.[13] By using parametric modeling, the design was optimized in terms of geometry, structure, and material efficiency by allowing the designer to see where connections and so on were necessary (Plate 38). Once this stage of the design process had been completed, a revised 3D model of the design's final form could be produced in relation to its optimized state (Fig. 81). This model appears similar to the initial formal proposition, but there is a key difference since rather than being a continuous surface, the later version uses planar elements spaced apart to produce the effect of a homogenous form and thereby contains the vital information for the subsequent CAD/CAM process of CNC milling to make physical models.

The design was then further developed through a series of digitally fabricated models, affording the designer to revise and refine aesthetic considerations in relation to cost, thereby producing the most cost-effective means of translating the digital forms in material reality. Each component and connection was machined with the high degree of accuracy afforded by the CNC process, meaning that the models can be easily and quickly assembled (Plate 39). A subsequent computer script then divides the plywood rings into sections of appropriate dimensions for the CNC machine, automatically nesting these sections within the material sheet to minimize the amount of waste material. An interesting point to note here is that the modeling process used during design development stages and the final fabrication procedure are exactly the same, the only difference being one of scale. This is in direct contrast to traditional modeling techniques through which other materials almost always act as substitutes for those intended for the final design.

FUTURE MODELING

This chapter has described a number of key issues when using modeling as a means of generating design and communication tools. The two case studies discussed here have demonstrated just a few of the myriad possibilities that modeling may bring to the designer's ideas. Both examples illustrate a practice of sophisticated creativity that is pursued and articulated through the use of different types of models and modeling techniques. The use of models, therefore, as both a medium and tool through which the development of interior design ideas and innovation may be produced remains critical to the discipline and this seems unlikely to alter. However, what may be less certain is how this practice will change as a result of future developments and which aspects may evolve while others recede. From the current position, it appears that the role of models as generative and representative tools in interior design will continue to increase as the useful differences between various media and techniques continue to grow. Perhaps the most exciting field lies in the increasing overlaps between digital and traditional design processes and techniques. This ongoing development is characterized by the contemporary position offered by Bob Sheil:

> Never before have there been so many, or so varied, techniques and methods at our disposal, each the capacity to leap only previously imagined frontiers. Designing has become a liquid discipline pouring into domains that for centuries have been the sole possession of others, such as mathematicians, neurologists, geneticists, artists and manufacturers. Postdigital designers more often design by manipulation than by determinism, and what is designed has become more curious, intuitive, speculative and experimental.[14]

These huge shifts in design processes have implications far beyond the disciplines of interior design and architecture as more and more research and developments are being conducted at cross-disciplinary levels around the globe. The surge of interest in this field is perhaps typified by major international events exploring the design possibilities of important advances in technology and their application in the making of interior design and architecture.[15] In summary, the importance of modeling as both a medium for the development of interior design knowledge and as a dynamic tool that may catalyze and renegotiate relationships between concepts, techniques, and different modes of inquiry cannot be understated, and the realms of design opportunities await further exploration.

32

Digital Representation and Fabrication

IGOR SIDDIQUI

INTRODUCTION

In spatial design, digital technologies have prompted the development of a vast array of techniques for representing and fabricating the physical environment, from objects to landscapes. During the past twenty years, CAD/CAM software has afforded designers to conceive, visualize, develop, and construct their work in ways that were unimaginable only a few decades ago. While in some cases design professions have appropriated such technologies primarily to improve the efficiency of performing old tasks, innovative practitioners across multiple disciplines have engaged with computationally driven techniques in order to produce the kinds of material, formal, and spatial outcomes that would otherwise seem unlikely, if not impossible.[1] Digital technology continues to transform the procedures, sequences, feedback, workflow, and communication in the design process, and the designer's techniques[2]—the various specific ways of utilizing the given technology—profoundly impact the aesthetic, organizational, and performative character of contemporary environments, including building interiors.

A growing volume of contemporary interior spaces developed primarily through digital means from concept to realization—authored by designers, architects, decorators, and artists—suggests, as this chapter will explore, that the power of digital technology is neither in its sole capacity to represent spatial constructs in increasingly sophisticated ways nor is it only that it makes the fabrication of physical artifacts that are too complex or inefficient for analog production possible. Instead, the technology's transformative potential is in its ability to produce integrated relationships between representation and fabrication and to manage, through continuity, increasingly complex information that enters into and is generated by the design process. Framed in this way, representation[3] and fabrication—and by extension design and construction—are no longer understood as segregated pursuits but are rather interconnected entities that are a part of a continuous workflow. Although the interior projects that result from digital practices are undoubtedly diverse and greatly vary in spatial strategy and sensibility, two common tendencies—continuity and pattern—provide the means of organizing a range of exemplary works and the discourse that surrounds them. Continuous surfaces and aggregate patterns have been prioritized in contemporary design as facilitators of program, negotiators of site, givers of form, order, atmosphere, and decoration, and their at times relentless activity and seemingly ubiquitous presence both inside and out of building envelopes is technologically rooted, as will be discussed, in the digital realm. How the desire for surface continuity is linked to digital design techniques and why complex patterns have more recently proliferated across surfaces will be addressed by examining specific interior projects in relation to advances in digital technologies that informed their design and material manifestation. The discussion will conclude with a sampling of experimental works that hint at the potential future trajectories in digital interior design, in particular in relation to environments' responsiveness to human factors.

CONTINUITY

In their pioneering book *Digital Design Media* from 1991, written as a comprehensive introduction to digital processes for architects and allied design practitioners, William Mitchell and Malcolm McCullough state,

> All practical computation is based upon the idea of letting numbers represent things that interest us—counts, measures, characters, words, sounds, positions, shapes, gestures, and so on. These things may, in turn, represent other things, which may represent other things, in potentially endless chains of reference. We often use computers to process very complex, multilevel representations of this sort, but these representations all reduce to collections of numbers in the end.[4]

Although relatively straightforward and obvious from the standpoint of computer science, the authors' observations nonetheless touch upon at least two issues that are significant and central to architectural design. First is the notion of representation as a system based on numeric quantity rather than visual resemblance; second is the fact of computation as a platform that transforms diverse and at times otherwise incompatible informational inputs into common mathematical code. Both have a tremendous impact on the conceptual underpinnings of the digital design process as well as its pragmatic technical logic. In predigital design—that is, the design process based on manual and mechanical means of conceiving—when developing and disseminating information about a product or project at stake, or what we may at times refer to as analog design, representation is primarily understood as a visual matter, a set of two-dimensional notations and three-dimensional artifacts that describe a vast range of information about design intent, from depicting qualitative characteristics and describing precise geometries to diagramming instructions for both fabrication and occupation. While the same could be said about digital design—it is still after all the resultant drawings, renderings, and images of digital models that are produced for visual inspection, evaluation, and use—the difference is, as Mitchell and McCullough point out, that underlying such digitally processed artifacts is numerical data that can generate other types of output as well. For example, a line drawn on paper visually communicates its own geometry, direction, and dimension, but it requires additional acts of translation[5] such as measurement, scaling, or tracing before it can serve as a basis for material fabrication. A digitally drawn line, on the other hand, is essentially a set of numbers that can be directly processed in order to instruct digital fabrication machinery to produce the same line materially.[6] This is the core principle behind CNC—that is, the process of operating machinery not through manual or mechanical actions but rather through data, a continuous workflow that underlies all digital fabrication.[7] The power of digital representation is in large part in its ability to generate multiple modes of output, including the final product, without the additional interpretation or translation that is conventionally needed in analog production. Such a continuous process promises greater precision, increased efficiency, and a higher degree of customization and formal complexity; in other words, the technological links between representation and fabrication have presented designers with new opportunities for innovation.

Another kind of continuity is evident in contemporary digital design, one that addresses spatial, material, and formal connectivity through the articulation of smooth continuous surfaces. In the design of interiors specifically, this has resulted in the intensive questioning of the conventional distinctions between floors, walls, and ceilings, as well as the blurring of the boundaries between architectural elements and furnishings. Branko Kolarevic traces the discussion of the "fluid logic of connectivity" in architecture back to Greg Lynn's essay "Architectural Curvilinearity" from 1993 and acknowledges particular theoretical and philosophical influences on designers' intentions, but also identifies a much longer and broader trajectory of the development of such a formal language based on continuous, curvilinear surfaces. For him, the precedent for continuous form can be seen by not only looking backward toward baroque, *art nouveau,* and the 1960s plasticity but also outside of architecture in the world of industrially produced toothbrushes, toasters, computers, cars, and airplanes.[8] Volumetrically manipulated surface continuity appears as a spatial strategy in numerous interior projects of the past two decades, from Diller+Scofidio's Brasserie (1999) and Rem Koolhaas/OMA's Prada Epicenter New York (2001), to GRAFT's KU-64 Dental Clinic (2005) in Berlin, and Noé Duchaufour-Lawrance's Galerie BSL (2010) in Paris (Fig. 82), with each project's individual characteristics undoubtedly informed by various factors, from the designers' theoretical positions to the influence and referencing of aesthetic precedents. Though explorations of surface continuity clearly predate, and at times sidestep, the use of digital tools in design and fabrication, digital modeling has undoubtedly contributed to the exponential propagation and development of surface-driven spatial strategies. Digital modeling techniques are fundamentally surface-driven, whereby what is perceived visually as a solid volume, thickness, or mass is in fact a collection of two-dimensional surfaces seamed together to describe a three-dimensional form. The value of digital models is not only in their ability to visually and graphically convey spatial information but rather that their geometries also exist as numerical representations, thus making them readily editable, reproducible, and constructible. The computational logic and organization behind surface models varies depending on individual software packages as well as output formatting, but the most common types of digital surfaces are NURBS, polygon meshes, and subdivisions.[9] NURBS, the acronym for Non-Uniform Rational B-Splines, allow for what Kolarevic refers to as "rubber-sheet" geometries;[10] that is, the kinds of freeform surfaces that allow for a high degree of variation, while maintaining their overall continuity. While this has in many cases made NURBS surfaces desirable aesthetically—opening up a whole new set of formal possibilities in design—from the technical standpoint, what makes them valuable is the efficiency and accuracy with which they represent complex geometries, using a minimum amount of data and a relatively simple computational process.[11] Polygon meshes, on the other hand, approximate continuity of surface though tessellation (a point that will be addressed further in regard to surface patterning); that is, by constructing continuity not through smooth curvature but rather through the accumulation of flat polygonal tiles. Finally, subdivision models, too, are created using the logic of polygon modeling but have the added functionality of smoothing faceted curves and surfaces akin to NURBS construction. Whether spline-based or meshed, the digitally constructed surfaces have unleashed the technical ability of designers to generate and represent spaces whose geometries depart from the predigital Euclidian forms in Cartesian space.[12] Of particular importance for interior design,

FIGURE 82   Galerie BSL by NNoe Duchaufour Lawrance. Courtesy of Noe Duchaufour Lawrance/ Eric Laignel.

however, are those projects that synthesize the formal innovation achieved through the manipulation of continuous surfaces with the procedural continuity of the workflow between digital representation and fabrication.

One of the earliest and widely published interior architectural projects realized almost entirely through digital means from concept to construction is Ost/Kuttner Apartments by Kolatan/MacDonald (1997).[13] The project, sited on New York City's Upper West Side, deploys surface continuity as a connective tissue between and across a series of intended and potential microprograms. It occupies the footprint of two adjacent residencies in a 1933 building, and though it is designed to primarily serve as a single apartment, it can also be compartmentalized to function as two separate spaces that accommodate the occasional need for additional privacy between units. Within the prewar envelope of the existing building, a series of chromatically saturated volumes are inserted into the space—larger than single pieces of furniture but smaller than the size of a whole room—that merge the conventional distinctions between floor and wall surfaces, building and furnishing, object and paint but also blur the clear boundaries of use (Plate 40). In this way, a bright orange surface cascades down the wall to become the platform for a bed, only to spill out further and turn itself into an indented volume that serves as a bathtub before it completes its footprint as a floor finish. In another such volume—this one rendered in brushed metal—a sink is transformed into a vanity, which then swells up smoothly to form a full-height wardrobe (Plate 41). A plush upholstered windowsill morphs as it continues across the wall, past the window, and grows out to form the back of a built-in settee. Together, these interventions create an interior that has been stripped of most residential associations and yet highlights the sensual, informal, and voyeuristic aspects of contemporary domesticity.[14]

In the design process, Kolatan/MacDonald began with two-dimensional sections that index spatial occupation at the scale of the body as an initial input from which larger surfaces were digitally generated. Unlike conventional interior design practice in which standardized ergonomic proportion, shape, and scale are applied to the design of specific objects or spaces, the designers employed sampled sections from a variety of furnishings and household objects in order to embed them within surfaces that are typologically ambiguous yet rich in their potential to be occupied, engaged, and interacted with. In other words, while the presence of originally selected profiles alludes to certain conventionally understood uses, it is but a point of departure for the digital blending, lofting, extruding, and joining that produce a continuous terrain within which new relationships between the architectural form and the human body unfold. The designers state, "The ambivalence towards form and programme as relational constructs provides for the possibilities of appropriating, adapting and adopting those structures for the particular needs and desires of its inhabitants."[15] Kolatan/MacDonald took advantage of modeling software's ability to generate new data (the resultant surfaces) through the interpolation of information within a range of known limit conditions (the initial sectional curves). To physically construct the interior, the surface model is digitally contoured into serial sections that provide templates for the fabrication of the plywood ribs that structure the overall installation. In order to maintain the monolithic quality of the volumes, a thin skin of rigid fiberglass is draped over the structure, rendering the surfaces seamless, continuous, and with limited information about its tectonic properties. The space visually transmits many of the aesthetic qualities one is more likely to encounter within a virtual environment produced with software such as Maya than in a conventionally conceived architectural interior. While Kolatan/MacDonald regard fiberglass as a material without qualities[16]—perhaps not unlike NURBS surfaces themselves–Kolarevic explains that the effectiveness of such a material as a key ingredient in the physical construction of digital forms not because of the material's lack of qualities but rather because of its specific character. He writes, "The physical characteristics of fiberglass make it particularly suitable for the fabrication of complex forms. It is cast in liquid state, so it can conform to a mold of any shape and produce a surface of exceptional smoothness—a liquid, fluid materiality that produces liquid, fluid spatiality."[17] Implicit in such a discussion about the relationship between digital forms and material properties is the significant degree to which digital representations have shaped designers' desires and aesthetic sensibilities. In this particular project, choices of material, color, and finish work to reinforce the strategy of blurring distinctions across programs and uses, while at the same time fulfilling the visual desires generated by design software.

Whereas the surfaces of Ost/Kuttner Apartments seek to reterritorialize the activities that occur in the private realm, Restaurant Georges by Jakob + MacFarlene (2000) deploys surface continuity in order to inscribe a particular programmatic footprint within the larger institutional framework of a public museum (Plate 42). The restaurant occupies 15,000 sq.ft. (1,400 sq m) of the top floor at Centre Pompidou in Paris. The project's primary feature is a set of irregular, bulbous volumes clad in brushed aluminum, each of which strategically reveals an interior of a different color and contains a specific part of the restaurant's program. The largest volume contains the kitchen, while the smaller ones contain house coat-check and restrooms, a video bar, and a semiprivate dining area. Between, around, and extending out from these four defined forms is the matching aluminum floor surface that extends past the glass curtain wall onto the outdoor terrace, carrying most of the seating that accommodates the museum restaurant's diners. There is a clear contrast between not only the existing building's envelope—featuring exposed structural and mechanical systems designed by Renzo Piano and Richard Rogers and organized within a rigorous Cartesian grid—and the aluminum surfaces that define the restaurant but also between the luminous, yet achromatic, character of the aluminum and the richly saturated hues of rubber sheathing that lines the interiors of the volumes.

The material and formal continuity between the restaurant floor and the blobs that appear to emerge from it provides a conceptual framework for the design informed by the project's strict parameters. The primary site-based requirement that the designers had to address was the prohibition to intervene on or touch any of the building's interior surfaces but the floor. Their point of departure was a flat floor surface divided into a 31.5 in. (80 cm) grid—a dimension that echoes Centre Pompidou's architectural module—digitally deformed to create the three-dimensional interior volumes. By collaborating with a boat-building company from design to fabrication, Jakob + MacFarlane developed the project through a series of digital models that interpreted the continuous surfaces as a set of monocoque structures, constructed from intersecting ribs whose contours follow the deformed pattern of the initial grid. The models examined multiple technical properties of the system, from gravity and lateral loads to the contouring of the surface and fastening details, and served as a basis for templates from which structural ribs were digitally fabricated from 3/8 in. (10 mm) thick aluminum. Brendan MacFarlane refers to the ribs as the pure part of the construction because they were constructed entirely through digital means from modeling to fabrication. In contrast to the digital integration through which the structural ribs were developed and delivered, the process of constructing the aluminum skin ultimately required a strategic engagement with more traditional fabrication methods. The double-curved aluminum panels that make up the overall continuous skin were fabricated mechanically through a process borrowed from boat-building and their surfaces brushed on-site to produce the desired matte finish.[18] The strategy of deforming the floor surface, as if it were bubbling up from the pressure underneath, in and of itself produced an impenetrable volumetric condition that required another set of techniques for generating apertures with which to reveal and access the spaces within. The first technique was to truncate the form where necessary by slicing it across the surface with a flat cutting plane. The second was to cut an incision by following a curved path projected onto the continuous form, not unlike a knife that cuts through a material by moving perpendicularly to its surface, tracing the contours of the desired aperture.[19] Both follow a certain logic of surface editing inherent to digital modeling, resulting in formal effects that refer less to conventional doors and windows and are closer in resemblance to the arm and neck holes of a garment. In this way, the fluid geometry of the restaurant is experienced as a new layer between the surface of the body and the structure of the building, one that is seen as internal to the building, while at the same time containing, concealing, and framing its own interiority (Plate 43). The openings are crucial for other reasons, too: they impart a sense of scale and a depth of field by choreographing the occupants' movement and arranging the relationships between the foreground and the background. Furthermore, they provide evidence of the meeting between the project's digital and material means by revealing the profiles of the otherwise hidden structural ribs and exposing the material thicknesses of the aluminum and rubber surfaces, acknowledging the transpired transformation of the continuous NURBS surface into corporeal matter.

The two interior projects, produced at the turn of the century, capture the creative ambition as well as the technical limits that defined what might be considered the first wave of digitally produced architectural constructions. These designers and their peers sought to overcome–through digital fabrication–the limitations of formally extravagant but unbuildable digital architectural representations, while attempting to retain in their physical constructions both the quantifiable geometries and the aesthetic qualities produced in computer models, drawings, and renderings. While the computational continuity between representation and fabrication is central to the transformation of the image into material and space, the projects also reveal the amount of human judgment required along the way. Digital tools allow for the automation of processing and outputting information, but as the two discussed projects show, how the information is interpreted and deployed in architectural terms is still largely up to the designer. Both Ost/Kuttner Apartments and Restaurant Georges may be experienced as types of total immersive environments in which the surface acts as an omnifunctional entity capable of transforming itself in order to perform the work of any architectural component or piece of furnishing, yet they both also reveal the limits of a single homogenous system as the primary means of space-making. As it has been seen, the projects' encounters with materiality, structure, and use in the physical realm motivated the development of further design strategies to supplement the primary logic of the continuous digital surface. This is true of not only these two works but also can be understood as a broader trajectory in digital design, one that resonates in a wide range of realized interior projects from the first decade of the twenty-first century.

PATTERN

Parallel to and expanding the repertoire of continuous, curvilinear, and glossy digital environments first produced in the 1990s is the increased prevalence of patterns—graphic, material, structural, ornamental, and organizational geometries with varying degrees of repetition and difference within.[20] Such pattern-driven projects, in particular those for which the architectural surface is the primary carrier of repetitive geometries, intricate textures, and highly crafted reliefs, are as much a product of digital design techniques as are their smooth and blobby predecessors. The aesthetic qualities of these works have not only reinvigorated the once dormant discourse about ornament and decoration in architecture—a development particularly meaningful for the design of interiors—but also, to a large extent, reflect many of the pragmatic concerns related to the transformation of digital representations into viable material constructions.[21] As the previous case studies demonstrate, the continuous digital surfaces frequently require additional ordering devices or strategies before they can be fabricated and assembled at full scale. While for the projects preoccupied with surface continuity and seamlessness such strategies are secondary with their byproduct typically concealed by thin veneers of homogenous materials and layers of paint, the obsession with patterns yields works in which surface patterns that define material, structural, and scalar distribution of parts in fabrication are conceptually and technologically embedded into the design process from the onset of digital production. In this way, patterns provide a link between computation and construction and a means of continuous feedback between digital and material parameters in design.

Ongoing advances in software development, mainstream availability of once specialized digital tools, and the rapid distribution of digital scripts, plug-ins, and other means of generating, evaluating, and outputting digital designs have all contributed to the proliferation of pattern-based strategies both on computer screens and within buildings. Current digital tools expand the capacity of surfaces to address external demands that range from programmatic performance to material resolution, and through the use of patterns complex surfaces are able to be subdivided into smaller buildable elements on the one hand, or they can be generated through the multiplication and aggregation of predefined repeatable components on the other. Algorithmic scripts and parametric models allow for the dynamic exchange between digital data and form, with the resolution of design intent tested through an automated or live iterative process. That the embedded patterns have aesthetic consequences is undeniable; conceptually, however, it is also necessary to understand their role as highly organizational, as their geometries negotiate material limits (sizes of available materials and tooling tolerances based on their properties), labor distribution (how the components will be fabricated and assembled), human interaction (ways in which their geometries suggest use and occupation), and so on.

In the architecture of building interiors, digitally produced patterned surfaces take on the role of paneling, cladding, screens, suspended ceilings, and flooring systems, and their influence also permeates the realm of freestanding furnishings, decorative off-the-shelf products, even apparel. Their presence registers through various figure-ground relationships as well as in more nuanced topographic manipulations. Ranging from highly ordered matrices to intricate lace-like formations, and varying in depth from thin veneer to thick poché, the patterns are manifested as seams, reveals, gaps, edges, joints, apertures, perforations, protrusions, and reliefs across surfaces. Such conditions reflect not only the relationship between the cutting templates extracted from digital models and the cutting paths made by CNC tools but also the computer's capacity to generate and manage the levels of geometric complexity and variation unthinkable in the analog realm. Unlike the conventional patterns of assembly bound by the limits of standardized repetition on the one hand and laborious, resource-intensive customization on the other, digitally produced assemblies allow for high degrees of nonuniformity, while maintaining the production efficiencies otherwise associated with high degrees of repetition and standardization. This is commonly referred to as mass customization, a term originally coined to refer to competitively priced but highly customized goods and services tailored to their specific consumers' needs and desires in the information age,[22] but one that in architectural production primarily stands for the ability to serially fabricate uniquely differentiated material artifacts such as building components with the efficiency levels compatible to those of mass production.[23] The nonuniformity of patterns enables surfaces to respond to and accommodate a variety of conditions, while maintaining the overall continuity of the system. The variation of such patterns responds to programmatic requirements and site conditions, as well as environmental and performative criteria, and produces rich atmospheric effects through highly differentiated modulations of light, view, material, and texture.

In the past decade, the commercial availability and relative affordability of small-scale fabrication machinery such as laser cutters, CNC routers, and 3D printers, along with the earlier mentioned software developments, have allowed young architects to experiment with the design and delivery of digital projects from conceptualization to construction. Such experiments have resulted in gallery installations, temporary structures, and full-scale prototypes in which the use of pattern-based strategies is significant as the scalar limitations of fabrication machinery is negotiated vis-à-vis ambitions toward full-scale constructability. In other words, because the machinery produces artifacts of limited size, in order to construct an installation at the scale of a building, the overall digital form must be subdivided into much smaller components that can be individually fabricated and then reaggregated into the larger whole.[24] The puppet theater at the Carpenter Center for the Visual Arts at Harvard University (2004), a temporary pavilion tucked underneath the Le Corbusier–designed building, features a structural envelope defined by a tessellation of approximately 500 diamond-shaped components, each uniquely shaped in response to the distribution of forces across the overall surface. The tessellated pattern takes on the graphic form of seams between the components and contributes to various optical readings of the envelope depending on given lighting conditions. Brennan Buck's gallery installation *Technicolor Bloom* (2007) exploits surface subdivision as a technique for constructing a series of vibrant visual effects, distributing intricate voids across the plywood material so as to repress the material's original planar state (Plate 44). What is leftover appears like an elegant web of fragile edges, its thinness and layering amplified by strategic use of color. The spatial effects of the ornate latticework, not unlike those found in Andrew Kudless's cellular honeycomb experiments, are amplified by deliberate lighting. The intricate nature of Kudless's *C_Wall* (2006) is, for example, as evident in the physical construction of the paper cells of the porous Voronoi surface as it is in the cast shadows collected on the gallery floor. Although experimental in nature, such projects are nonetheless engaged in a productive exchange with commercial practice, undoubtedly expanding into and influencing more conventional modes of design, fabrication, and construction.

Japanese architect Kengo Kuma's interior design of a boutique for the fashion label Lucien Pellat-Finet (2009) deploys a three-dimensional honeycomb-like system as a primary spatial and tectonic element. Occupying 1,430 sq.ft. (133 sq m) divided into three stories of a compact building in the Shinsaibashi district of Osaka, the boutique also contains a café and a small library. From outside, the building appears as a thickened billboard, which visually blurs the distinction between the two-dimensional pattern imprinted onto the solid exterior surfaces of the building and a three-dimensional system within that is partially seen through two horizontal bands of frameless glass (Plate 45). In this project, the honeycomb pattern is based on irregular polygonal cells that include both pentagonal and quadrilateral shapes, a combination that suggests a degree of geometric order and repetition but also a level of flexibility and improvisation. Upon entering, visitors encounter the core of the boutique, a space where plywood honeycomb cells define most of the vertical wall surfaces as well as the ceiling. Along the walls the honeycomb has the depth of a typical storage shelf, acting both as a screen that filters views and a display system for merchandise. The vaulted ceiling appears as if it were designed by cutting a curvilinear incision into what would have been a solid mass of extruded honeycomb pattern, revealing as a result an array of irregular tessellated geometries (Plate 46). Upstairs, the program of the boutique continuous, as does a similar spatial strategy with the exception that along the exterior façade much of the pattern is removed to clear a direct panoramic view of the street framed by a band of glass. On the building's top floor, the pattern is further eroded, revealing more of the white background surfaces, with what is leftover of the pattern acting as strategically placed book displays for the informal library. In the basement, where the café is located, the pattern reappears again but is shallower and—with the exception of the fact that its depth is calibrated to house glassware at the bar area—appears tentative about accommodating program. Instead, the polygonal pattern is distributed as a decorative layer atop the neutrally painted background.[25]

Despite its high-end nature, the design achieves a richness of spatial experience with an economy of means. This is as evident in material and fabrication choices as it is clear from the deft deployment of pattern. The honeycomb pattern is entirely fabricated from ordinary plywood sheets and utilizes only three standard types of aluminum fasteners to address all the connections among the parts. The system's cells, with variant shapes and a range of depths, play multiple roles in the space, from defining overall wall and ceiling surfaces to acting as storage and display devices, see-through screens and surface-applied decorative wallpaper. In that sense, the nonuniform nature of the pattern is tailored according to variable site conditions, programmatic needs, and aesthetic desires and provides a sense of unity across the multiple levels of the building despite the embedded spatial differences and competing functional demands. Given its multifunctional nature, the system appears as efficient, but at its limits one also perceives its relentlessness and excess. This is most evident at the edges of the pattern where more ordinary, nearly ad hoc, devices are introduced to reinforce the utilities promised, but perhaps underdelivered, by the system. Conventional shelving and hanging rods introduce a tension between that which is programmatically essential and what is aesthetically and experientially desirable. The project nonetheless demonstrates the potential with which patterns that are ordinarily seen as graphic devices can be transformed into robust spatial constructs and does so by deliberately constructing a precise sequence of movement that leads one from the graphic exterior of the building to the immersive interior within.

In contrast to Kengo Kuma's boutique and all its exuberance, and with a remarkable restraint and rigor toward the integration of interior surfaces and patterns through digital means, is Marble Fairbanks's design for the Toni Stabile Student Center at Columbia University's School of Journalism in New York (2008). The project, completed in multiple phases, includes 9,000 sq. ft. (835 sq m) of renovated interior space spread over two floors and a new 1,000 sq. ft. (93 sq m) addition at the street level. In shaping the new interior spaces, the architects identified three particular surfaces and their individual roles in the project relative to programmatic and environmental requirements. The largest space within the project, the Social Hub, a multipurpose room for studying, meetings, and special events, contains two of the surfaces, a ceiling and a window wall. The ceiling is charged with the task of eliminating existing acoustic reverb and echo in the space, while the wall lends a new image to the space by graphically negotiating representational content (i.e., a photographic image embedded into its thickness) and abstract patterning. There is a third surface, another ceiling, that is a part of the new addition and acts as a rigid solar shade underneath a structural glass roof but is also a carrier of graphic content similar to that of the wall. Together, the three surfaces share common materiality, finish, and overall pattern geometry. All the paneling is fabricated from sixteen-gauge steel sheets, powder-coated white and perforated with an array of round apertures, ranging in size and shape from circles to ellipses.[26]

The central premise of the design for the Social Hub ceiling is that metal paneling conceals a layer of acoustic insulation and that it is perforated to expose the insulation wherever acoustically necessary. In addition, perforations for recessed lighting and a sprinkler system are integrated into the overall pattern. The overall form of the ceiling was manipulated through the introduction of strategically placed folds in order to maximize ceiling heights wherever possible. The design of the pattern was achieved digitally involving two related processes. First, a digital acoustic model was developed to evaluate sound conditions within the space. The model identified areas in the ceiling where the exposure of acoustic insulation aids the correction of existing reverb and echo issues in the space, thus requiring larger perforations in the metal surface. Second, through algorithmic scripting the exact distribution and size of perforations were determined along with the additional placement of lights and sprinklers. The script provided possible iterations based on preset rules: the overall pattern grid, the allowable range of perforation sizes and shapes, and various parameters for dealing with boundary conditions, such as the pattern's responsiveness as it encounters surface edges, creases, and preset fixture locations. The result is not just a highly differentiated gradient pattern but also the very patterns that are used, without the need for additional construction documents or shop drawings, for digital cutting and bending of the steel. The Social Hub wall, while similarly perforated, is different in its intent and process. Sited parallel to the tree-lined street outside, the intent was to transpose the view of the street, concealed by the solid walls of the building, as a virtual view on the inside but to do so with a level of abstraction that would allow the image to go in and out of focus, or rather, whose legibility would vary depending on the subject's distance from it. The process started with a digital image of the elevational view outside, which was then processed through another algorithmic script in order to transform tonal values of the image into apertures and convert that information into another set of cutting templates for fabrication.[27] The result is a cladding system whose pattern not only oscillates between abstraction and representation but also juxtaposes the virtual image of the street with the actual views framed by the existing windows inset into the paneled wall. The third surface, the café ceiling, is designed to eliminate 80 percent of the new addition's solar gain, while providing, not unlike the wall in the Social Hub, an aesthetic experience derived from graphic imagery. Through a combination of digital solar analysis models that quantify specific, maximum, and overall solar loads based on site information and, again, algorithmic scripting that automates pattern distribution according to preset criteria, the architects arrived at the final solution, which reduces solar gain but also produces a nuanced dappling of natural light as it is filtered through the ceiling and distributed to the space below. Together, the three surfaces deploy digital means not as methods for extravagant form-making but instead focus on the technology's ability to integrate, with high levels of precision, multiple sources of information, pragmatic demands, and aesthetic intentions in order to transform existing spatial conditions into preferred ones.

EXPANDED PERFORMANCE

As the case studies demonstrate, the significance of digital media in spatial design lies in its ability to connect generative, representational, and manufacturing tasks into continuous processes. Increasingly dynamic in nature, such projectsexceed the efficacy of static representations and artifacts in favor of dynamic relationships and reciprocal feedback. This means that the relationships between numerical inputs, digital geometries, and material outcomes are interdependent and adjustable, producing potentially infinite iterations and possibilities for fine-tuning and customization. The dynamic nature of digital processes has been exploited in ever-expanding facets of spatial design practices, from the mainstream integration of Building Information Modeling (BIM) in corporate architecture to the exploration of interactive technologies in more experimental contexts. What such digital projects have in common is the increased attention to performance in design; that is, how designed artifacts work in relation to their given tasks as well as ways in which digital technologies negotiate the responsiveness of those artifacts relative to the data that defines the performance criteria. As a result, contemporary digital models are dynamic in nature, only made static by their authors' judgment and will, and digitally fabricated material artifacts too frequently embody the kinetic properties of their virtual predecessors.

Marc Goulthorpe/dECOi's installation *Aegis Hyposurface* consists of tens of thousands of triangular panels connected by an elastic rubber membrane and a system of digitally controlled pistons that allow the overall surface to respond, through movement, deformation, and bulging, according to environmental stimuli such as light and sound.[28] The precedent-setting project, realized in 1999, is both continuous surface and pattern and its flexible, shifting form is a result of both physical and computational constraints. Exploiting the qualities of animate form is also evident in Ammar Eloueini's design for CoReFab chair.[29] Though static in its material state, Eloueini's chair is based on the fundamental premise that with digital fabrication, making a series of unique objects is as efficient as making reproductions of identical ones (Plate 47). As such, the chair is conceived as an animated lattice of interconnected members that is perpetually in motion, smoothly repatterning the chair as the animation unfolds in time until it is paused and 3D printed directly at full scale using a selective laser sintering machine.[30] Although the functional performance of the chair is not redefined—Eloueini intended CoReFab chairs to be used just like any other side chair—the design nevertheless seeks to redefine the status of uniqueness in product design relative to digital fabrication and addresses the value of one-off objects in the consumption of contemporary design. Also at the scale of furnishings is "Neri Oxman's Beast", an experimental prototype for a chaise lounge that synthesizes continuous surface and pattern in response to material and digital processes.[31] Designed as a monocoque surface, or a single structural skin, the chaise is modeled and patterned according to the structural requirements as a freestanding object as well as in response to the body's needs for comfort. The synthetic structure—also 3D printed and filled in with acrylic materials of varying levels of density, flexibility, stiffness, and translucency, depending on localized requirements—focuses on the issues of material performance at the scale of the body, zooming in, in order to address human factors at microscale.[32] The act of sitting, in a social context and aggregate form, is also addressed through digitally designed and fabricated furnishings in the Fleet Library at the Rhode Island School of Design, a project designed by Office dA and constructed in 2006. Faced with the programmatic requirement for multiple computer stations, the architects eschewed the standardized dimensions of workstations in favor of a parametric range that accommodates a diverse population of people of various sizes. In this way, the requirements for universal design are addressed not through rigid common denominators but rather through rule-based variation. Spatial and human performance is thus enhanced through customization, while maintaining and even increasing, as the architects acknowledge,[33] the economy of the project.

CONCLUSION

The notions of continuity and pattern have provided a useful framework for interrogating, relative to the design of interiors, the developments in digital representation and fabrication of the past two decades. It is hopefully clear, however, that despite the apparent aesthetic implications of these terms and the formal affinities among the discussed projects, the selection of the works is based primarily on the need to explain the crucial relationships between representation and fabrication in the digital realm in ways that are conceptually clear and visually explicit. Because the chapter focuses on these two areas of digital design as interrelated entities rather than separate areas of investigation and as such its ambition has been to examine the explicit continuum between specific techniques of visualizing and making, interior design has ultimately been treated primarily as a material practice. In the practice of interior design, whether as a specialization within architecture or within its own distinct disciplinary context, the use of digital tools is currently diverse and, in many cases, as compartmentalized as it is integrated in the discussed projects. The chosen examples deliberately demonstrate a degree of totalizing, allover design strategies that result in saturated, immersive environments, in part a reflection of the persistent dream in which a project is conceived in its entirety in the computer and then magically materialized with the touch of a button. While such visions of the future have undoubtedly shaped the ambitions that drive technological innovation, for interior design as a practice it may also be prudent to consider digital constructions as partial, incomplete, fragmented—in other words, not everything. The design of interiors after all requires a skilled synthesis of existing conditions, site-specific interventions, and off-the-shelf products as well as, inevitably, occupants' possessions.

In his essay "Relentless Patterns: the Immersive Interior," Mark Taylor discusses the work of Atelier Manferdini (Plate 48), known for its digitally crafted patterns embedded in everything from coffee cups and couture dresses to skyscraper curtain walls, and writes, "Operating at different scales, and cut into the material, this pattern is freed from the constraints of conventional ordering devices, and begins to take over, not to create an immersive environment but to immerse itself within the environment."[34] Contemporary interior designers, equipped with digital experience and with the drive to opportunistically co-opt technological advances unfolding around them, have the capacity to practice in ways that are at once expansive and focused. Equally fluent in site-specific interventions and industrial processes, and spanning multiple scales, markets, and media, the contemporary interior designer is positioned to influence material culture in ways that are perhaps, as of yet, unprecedented.

33

The Interior: Television, Gaming, and New Media

EDWARD HOLLIS

INTRODUCTION

This chapter is set in six scenes, some drawn from the authors own experience and others from wider research.

My grandmother watches *Gone with the Wind* in 1941. My father watches the coronation of Elizabeth II in 1952. I play Atari Pong in 1979. My work colleagues play Quake in 1997. A group of teenagers sit in the diary room at Madame Tussauds in 2008. Two hundred people dance to the sound of music in 2009. Each of these scenes represents a stage in a game: a negotiation or a battle, depending on your point of view between the two sides of a screen.

In *The Ecstasy of Communication* (1987), Jean Baudrillard described contemporary space as composed of

> great screens on which are reflected atoms, particles, molecules in motion. Not a Public space but gigantic spaces of circulation, ventilation and ephemeral connections.[1]

This chapter will follow Baudrillard's lead in investigating the interiors created by new media as, on the one hand, screen-like, and as, on the other, modulations of traditional conceptions of the public interior.

We use the word *screen* to denote the transparent film between ourselves and the digital, televised, or cinematic world, but the screen is also a veil. It is the site of trade—each side of the screen gives things to the other, and the interiors in which screens are watched and played with are just as fascinating as the interiors that appear, or seem to appear, inside them.

This chapter, which begins in a cinema and ends in a railway station, will examine the role of the screen in public as well private interiors. It will argue that the irruption of the screen into the contemporary interior has, rather than keeping us home alone as commonly supposed, revitalized the interiors we inhabit in the public and social sphere.

SCARLETT O'HARA MAKES A NEW DRESS

It is 1941, March. London is in blackout, and my grandmother, young, heavily pregnant, her husband away, is bored. She makes her way to the Palace Cinema in Harrow on the Hill and ensconces herself in its rich interior for an hour or two of celluloid escape.

Gone with the Wind is interminable, and my grandmother takes some time to warm to its infuriating heroine, Scarlett O'Hara. They have quite a bit in common: a youth spent in beautiful homes and a war that has deprived them of their former splendor.

There's a scene that really settles it for my grandmother: Scarlett walks in to her salon at Tara, now bedraggled and worn down by war. She has nothing to wear, and so, to the horror of her maid, Mamie, she tears down the green velvet curtains from the windows to make a dress, lest any gentleman call.

After the national anthem is played, my grandmother leaves the cinema determined to name her unborn child Scarlett. A few weeks later, she has saved up enough coupons to buy fabric—she opts for furnishing fabric, as it is cheaper than dress fabric, and she runs herself up a smart suit.

The world my grandmother set out to see on that March evening in 1941 was a fantasy. Tara is a set that, as Scarlett tears down her curtains, is turned into a prop. Like the steps of a Busby Berkely dancestravaganza, or the lurid color of Oz, the salon of Tara requires, despite its great elaboration, as much suspension of disbelief as the boards of the Shakespearean stage.

Tara was made of nothing but light projected onto a screen, and this screen formed but one wall of a room in Harrow on the Hill. My grandmother would have faced it sitting in a red velvet chair arranged in a row of many that raked down toward the screen. The four surfaces of the room that framed the screen were highly decorated, as was the frame of the screen itself, forming a proscenium arch.

The proscenium arch was a late arrival in the design of theaters. It is the invention of that prototype of the cinema, the masque, that saw the stage turned into a moving picture in the Renaissance. Like the stage, the cinema screen is an Albertian window, a picture that opens into another world. The rest of the room is just an elaborate three-dimensional frame for that picture. The cinema is a hybrid interior: a room that points outside itself to a world remote, imaginary, and ephemeral.

My grandmother knows that the curtains in the salon at Tara are hung from pasteboard flats in an industrial soundstage. The studio itself has already been dubbed the Dream Factory—by the manufacturers themselves. The whole machinery of that dream factory—the knowing artifice of the cinema and the film (and that other, implied invisible interior, the soundstage)—is designed to make her believe in it anyway. That is the magic of Hollywood.

It is a magic of strict hierarchy. At the end of the film, everyone in the cinema stands up for the national anthem. Passive spectators, who dutifully sit in the dark, they cannot intervene in the drama, which is made remote from them by the proscenium arch and the very immateriality of the interior that flickers inside it. Indeed, this interior has been sent to them as a gift from a remote and wonderful land, and once the film is over, it disappears.

THE CORONATION OF QUEEN ELIZABETH II

It is 1953, June. Everyone ought to be outside, but instead they are crowded into a gloomy cottage room, perched on the arms of chairs and on occasional tables, whose trinkets have been swept to the floor. There is no need for the fire to be lit, and although all the furniture in the room is oriented toward it, no one is looking that way. Instead they are staring intently at a tall cabinet in the corner. Toward the top of this cabinet, a tiny aperture flickers with light, and slots below it boom with indistinct sound.

The flickering becomes a head, surmounted by a magnificent crown, and it speaks, in a thin high voice. After it has finished speaking, the cabinet bursts into music: "Vivat Regina! Vivat! Vivat!" Then everyone in the room starts talking, and sherry is poured. Later on, everyone goes down to the Talbot Inn on New Street, where flags have been hung in the courtyard. They stand around the bar and drink a beer, and then they go to their own homes.

The coronation was the first televisual event in British national life. In order to watch *Gone with the Wind* in 1941, my grandmother had to go out in public. She watched the film in a grand public interior, and when it was over, she participated in a public ritual, standing for the national anthem and, perhaps, watching the Pathé news. In 1953, if you wanted to see the coronation the best place to stay was at home, in your living room.

FIGURE 83 A new hearth in the front room: watching television in 1958. Courtesy Evert F. Baumgardner.

Since the early nineteenth century, the furnishings of the British sitting room had been arranged of necessity around the fireplace. The arrangement and the growth of sofas in the nineteenth century or the inglenooks so beloved of the Arts and Crafts were, from a functional point of view, about huddling around the hearth for warmth, but the mantelpiece, surmounted by a mirror, invitations, clocks, candles, and ornaments, was a domestic ikonostasis: a shrine, the proscenium arch to other worlds.

As figure 83 illustrates, the television disrupted this arrangement. Its flickering screen was a rival to the fire, but it never occupied the privileged position on the axis of the room. Rather, the television was placed to one side, even when the fireplace was blocked up, or was omitted altogether. In many early instances, the screen itself was veiled when not in use, as if its blank and terrible eye could still survey what was happening in the room. The same fears surrounded the telephone—that other rude electronic incursion into the peace of the home. In Pierre Chareau's Maison de Verre (1927–1932), it is kept in a private box adjacent to the dining room. The proliferation of strange designs for that most curious (and now obsolete) piece of furniture, the telephone seat (usually placed in the liminal space of the hall), is testament to the anxieties that surrounded the introduction of what was essentially the public sphere into the home.

Like almost all early television, the coronation was broadcast live. It was not a dream but reality, and this meant that it needed to be staged specifically for the camera. The coronation had to look just as it always had, and that meant changing it completely. Richard Dimbleby, along with countless lights, and cameramen chosen for their diminutive stature were hidden in the triforium above the sanctuary of Westminster Abbey, from which they enjoyed a privileged view of the occasion denied to the peers of the realm who surrounded the young queen below. The Duke of Norfolk, whose role in the organization of the coronation ritual was as hereditary as his title, took some persuading to allow the event to be televised. Behind the concerns was a distaste for the idea of a crowd of lowborn journalists (let alone the viewing public) swarming around the monarch. Winston Churchill warned the queen that the lights would fatigue her and the broadcast damage her royal mystique, but the monarch was insistent.

The cameras followed the procession all the way to Westminster and showed scenes of public celebration along the way: floral arches, street parties, and all the rest of it. But they lingered in particular on one especially happy child who really expressed what the day was about. He was dressed in a cardboard box with a hole in it, and a coat hanger aerial was perched on his head. At the bottom of the box there was label: "1ˢᵗ television," it said. It is ironic, of course, that that child himself would have been unable to savor his moment of fame: running along the streets outside, he could not have been able to watch television.

PONG

It is Christmas morning, 1979, and my brother and I have been up for hours, watching television. It's only the test card—the girl with the alice band playing noughts and

FIGURE 84   A new toy for the bedroom: playing on the Amstrad in the 1980s. Courtesy Adrian
Pingstone.

crosses with her teddy—but it keeps us quiet, and for that reason, my parents allow us
to watch and buy themselves another hour or so in bed.

When it is time to open the presents, we are given a joint one. We unwrap the
paper and open the box and find within it a plastic box, dark brown on top and bright
orange everywhere else. The top is studded with knobs and dials, like the dashboard
of a spaceship.

We watch, jumping up and down, as my father—no technophile—swears and
sweats as he tries to work out which wire to insert into which plug at the back of the
television. There are countless false starts, but after an hour or so, he is able to switch
the bloody thing on.

The TV screen switches to black, bisected by a single vertical white line. At either
end of the screen, little white rectangles hang in the darkness, and almost immediately
a black square starts moving diagonally from one of these rectangles toward the other.
It hits it with a satisfying "ping" and floats back again.

My brother and I know exactly what to do. We have already played this game at
Jeremy's house—his father is in advertising, and he has everything. We are pried away
from the game several hours later for lunch, and our father has on his face an expression of sad amusement, puzzlement, and envy.

Pong wasn't meant to be a game at all. Developed in 1972 by Allan Alcorn, an engineer,
it was only meant to be a warm-up exercise, designed to introduce the unimaginative
scientist to the world of creative computing. To those who are used to the illusionism of
contemporary games, it doesn't really look like one either. Pong as the name suggest, is
a game of ping pong—at least, it represents a game of ping pong, in nothing more seductive than plan.

Pong was the descendant of one of the very first computer games, Tennis for Two, developed by William A Higginbotham in 1958, in which the screen of a cathode ray oscil-
loscope depicted a single pixel moving back and forth in elevation. Space Invaders (1978),
Tetris (1985), and Super Mario Bros. (1985) conjure worlds in section or elevation. Pac
Man wanders his labyrinth in a hybrid format: he, and the ghosts who want to eat him,
are drawn in elevation, their labyrinth in plan. In Asteroids (1979), abstracted vector nets
expand out from a central vanishing point, was an early attempt at perspective. Later, Sim
City and The Sims (2000) simulated worlds in axonometric and isometric.

Of course, that is all now ancient history, and the level of realism in current releases of
old classics such as Super Mario Bros. illustrates how far the graphics of computer games

have come. The screen has ceased to be a flat and has become, like the TV and the cinema screen before it, an aperture into other worlds. In games such as Prince of Persia(2003), motion capture, rendering, and the creation of virtual three-dimensional space have become so sophisticated that it is almost impossible to distinguish the live action spin-off movie (in itself, of course, heavily animated and rendered) from the original game.

The realism of Prince of Persia, Myst (1993), or Ico (2001) has a very specific purpose. In Prince of Persia or Ico, the point of the game is to escape from a palace—testing doorways, discovering tunnels, skittering over rooftops. This performance of parkour is complicated by the fact that the gamer must escort an ailing princess, who is unable to perform the gymnastic feats of the gamer. In Myst there is no explicit rule book at all, no apparent game, other than the interior itself, in which the gamer hunts for clues to events that might have taken place there, once upon a time. These magical interiors, glimpsed through screens of liquid crystal, are the game.

The first edition of Pong was installed not in a home but in Allan Alcorn's local bar in 1972. Alcorn had been to the local store to purchase a black-and-white TV, which he wired up and built into a wooden cabinet and placed by the pinball machine. It was only in 1976 that Atari released the home version of Pong onto the market, and even then, the video game was never really at home in the home. Rather it inhabited that other teenage haunt: the video arcade.

The video arcade started life as the pinball arcade, or the Vegas grind joint, its spatial syntax elucidated back in the 1970s by Robert Venturi:[2] the complete absence of natural light, the long, low spaces, glittering and twinkling away.

The video arcade has all too often been portrayed as an antisocial passive space, but in actual fact, it is crowded and social. Each video game holds a list of high scoring players, and players aim to enter their initials into that hall of fame with pride. The public side of video gaming has reached its apotheosis in the PC bangs of contemporary South Korea. Found on countless street corners, more popular than bars, they are spaces filled with PC monitors, filled with hundreds of players, and the sites of national leagues in video gaming.

The arcade is a space of physical activity, too. The mechanics of pinball machines require players to bump and grind the machine, jerking the ball into the desired holes, but even when such exertion is no longer required, arcade games suffer the same rough wooing. Gamers hunch into digital simulated rifles, punch fire buttons into breaking, and lean as their static car veers around virtual corners. In the arcade, the game is so real that it overflows the fixed frame of the screen and becomes one with the space in which it is situated.

But the real difference between the interior of Pong and those of Tara, or the coronation, is that I can affect it. The space of the computer game is one over which, through the dials and paddles of Atari, the joystick, the mouse, the Xbox, the Kinect, or the Wii players can exert control. These interfaces between one side of the screen and the other, now developed far beyond the primitive typewriter and telly format shown in figure 84, have transformed our understanding of the relationship between them.

On the real side of the screen, this has resulted in a detachment of the body from the screen. The earliest computer games were played by scientists in labs, feeding tape into computers so large that they were rooms. In early Dungeons and Dragons, gamers typed commands into the computer keyboard. The Atari console required players to sit (on the floor, significantly, rather than a chair) and manipulate dials through a console connected by wires to the television. The simple graphics enabled them to sit perhaps 6 ft. (2 m) away from the screen. The Xbox, lighter and more ergonomically designed, allowed them to move. In games such as Dance Dance Revolution, players manipulate the virtual interior by standing on a sheet on the floor.

> Players take advantage of this freedom in creative ways, incorporating spins, drop-ping to their knees, or even leaping over the safety bar for a grand entrance. Some players leave stage in the middle of the song to flirt or "take a phone call" for comic effect. On the website of DDRfreak.com one commentator recalls a player who left the arcade and ran all the way across the street in the middle of his performance, returning in time for the next step after a break in the music.[3]

The Wii removes any visible physical connection whatsoever, and the computer returns to being a room again. Some early users became so carried away that they started throw-ing the device around the room, smashing it, in a few instances, straight through the screen—revealing of course, only the empty space behind it.[4]

The interiors in which computer games are found are, like the cinema, portals to other worlds, but, unlike the cinema, they are active spaces in which players, rather than spectators, shout at the screen and thump the computer. In the video arcade, playing the game, both sides of the screen have started to become one.

QUAKE

> It is lunch hour, sometime in 1997, and I sit with my sandwich at the drawing board. I, having been the first to arrive in this architect's practice, before the computer, have never been given one. I leaf through *Building Design* as everyone else switches their machines from Autocad to Quake.
>
> Over partitions and from behind monitors, faces glow pale blue and crease up with laughter, curses, and whoops. The small office resounds with crashes, explosions, and the pings and pongs of lives lost and new levels attained, of boys playing games with toys.
>
> Each screen is set in motion at the end of a gun, whose sights navigate down cor-ridors in spaceships, through grimy concrete basements, over rooftops. Every sight chases elusive figures, who, if they pause too long, are blasted away.
>
> Each screen is different, but everyone is playing the same game in the same digitally imagined space—they are just seeing it from different points of view. Even Alan, our 3D modeling whizz, is playing, although he never gets out of bed before 4 p.m. He is on the Internet at home, playing from there.

Quake is what is known as a MUD, a multiuser dungeon. This means that Quake can be played by many people at the same time. It's not the first such game; Pong was designed for two players, for example, and in the space of the arcade, games had always been social. But the spaces inside Quake differ from their predecessors in important respects.

The first difference is in the representation of the space inside the game. Quake is a first-person shooter. Like Asteroids, it is visualized from the point of view of the player, in dynamic perspective. This is simple enough if there is one player in a game, but MUDs must deal with multiple perspectives: several players might be observing the same space at the same time from different points of view. In addition, MUDS must deal with dynamic and unpredictable spaces, since the movement of the players within the space will change them. Pong dealt with this problem by the use of a God's-eye view that allows different times and different places to be seen simultaneously. Quake, however, is the essence of interiority, since its labyrinths reveal themselves only through play and never in totality.

Second, the world of Quake is potentially unlimited. Played on countless machines at once, contained on a server belonging to the makers of the game rather than on the computers of the players, the spaces of the game may be added to or altered at will. It is possible for the player to switch off and return, only to find that the game has changed in the interim. Once upon a time, the illusion of a world beyond the screen was created by the horizontal scrolling of Super Mario, from left to right. Quake and other MUDS impose this condition of infinity in time as well as in space. Not only does the game continue beyond the edges of the screen, but it also continues to exist when the computer is off. Quake approaches the condition, more effectively than the original ever could, of a second life.

The world inhabited by the Quake screen is nothing like the privileged interiors of the cinema or arcade. Quake is played on a PC that could be used for anything and appropriates the mouse and the keyboard as lethal weapons. It shares something of the ad hoccery of the world of the television, which, shunted to one side of the fireplace, has always found it hard to find a home.

So has the computer. In the 1950s, computers were undomestic vast electronic interiors. By the 1970s, models like the Commodore had effected that unholy marriage between the typewriter and the television that formed the basis for the modern computer. By the late 1990s, these had become laptops. Jonathan Ive's work in reviving the Apple brand is design legend, but it was based around the observation that computers were pieces of home furniture.

The interior of the home, once sealed from the outside world, is now riddled with multiple apertures. Bill Gaver's work for the Equator project[5] created seemingly innocent home furnishings that were in fact ambient parasites, driven by data streams from the world beyond: from airplanes flying overhead or rates of data flow. It served to highlight the ways in which the contemporary domestic interior is alive, animated by and connected to the world outside.

Of a group of people playing Quake, it is possible that some of them are in the same room but that some others are, say, in the United States, and yet others are in Japan, and so on. Within the space of the game, they are indistinguishable from one another. Gilles Deleuze and Felix Guattari have dubbed this strange sort of space *rhizomic*. The rules and the spaces of the contemporary game operate as if Deleuze and Guattari had dug under the[forking] garden path of Borges (which, after all, was still a hierarchy of sorts) and had come up with an even more profound labyrinth…the potato root system has no beginning, no end, and grows outward and inward at the same time.[6]

Everything is connected to everything else, instantly. Like the endless corridors of Quake, rhizomic space goes on forever, without any discernible hierarchy. This is a radical answer to the architectural plan view of Pong or the neat perspectivity of Asteroids. The rhizomic space of Quake is the space of the contemporary interior, which is no longer an isolated space but connected to all other spaces by an infinite web of invisible connections, which may not be contemplated in plan, from afar, but only experienced in motion, from the inside.

THE DIARY ROOM

"This is Big Brother. You are live in Madame Tussauds; please do not swear." They don't. In fact, they really can't work out what to say or where to stand. They all try to pile on to the diary room chair, peering into the camera, and when they are seated, they wait, expectantly.

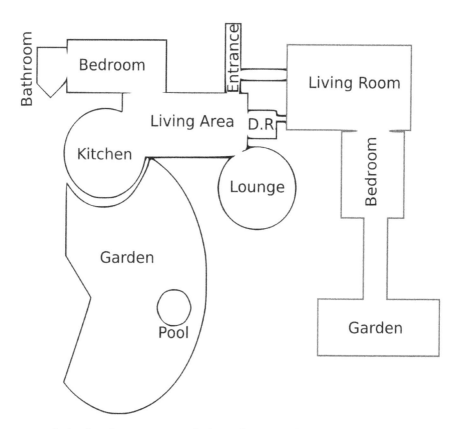

FIGURE 85   A plan for a house on screen: the house for *Big Brother*, season 7. Courtesy Alexj2002.

"This is Big Brother," says the room, and the teenagers burst in paroxysms of giggles and squeals. "How are you feeling today?" They just giggle: they are overwhelmed by the experience of sitting in the place of nasty Rex and sulky Nicole, screaming Samanda, and Nicky's tears and tantrums.

The diary room is the room to which the *Big Brother* housemates come to unburden themselves of private agonies, to confess their sins. They do so on a throne, to a camera that, they know, will broadcast their secrets to the entire nation. Only their housemates will remain ignorant of what is said.

For fifteen minutes, the kids in Madame Tussauds savor their fame and imagine that they have become as worthy of wax immortality as Davina herself, just outside. In the museum shop on the way out, they buy the video of their time in the diary room and upload it onto the Web to show their friends.

The irony of reality TV is that the classical relationship of active screen and passive spectator experienced by my grandmother in her cinema in 1941 has now been inverted: the home is on TV; and, with a plan as labyrinthine as quake (see fig. 85), and it has become a video game.

The world inside *Big Brother* is a real home, furnished in the latest taste every year. The decor is minutely described on the game's website, and designers compete to get their wares into the house for two months of unrivalled product placement. At the end of each game, the contents of the house are sold off to relic hunters. The house is stripped back to an empty frame, redesigned, and reassembled for the next game.

And the game is, apparently, not a game at all. All the housemates have to do is to live in the house, cut off from the world, as if they were holed up in some idealized Victorian domestic refuge. *Big Brother* turns the proscenium arch of the TV screen into a mirror, reflecting back into people's homes what is, apparently, already there. The home makeover show—from *Changing Rooms* to *60 Minute Makeover*—extended the format even further into reality. Ordinary homes were transformed in the televisual equivalent of Victorian advice literature.

But in 2005, *Big Brother* went evil: the spaces of the house were made as small as possible and then lined with mirrors, reflecting the housemates' every move. In 2003, the housemates woke up one morning to find that, in imitation of the Philadelphia experiment, the house had been divided by iron bars into a rich (captor) side and poor (captive) side, and the experiment was repeated in 2008. In 2005, a whole alternative house was constructed inside the house, into which inhabitants disappeared for weeks at a time. That trick appeared again for Aisleyne in 2006 and for Chantelle and Preston in celebrity big brother of the same year. By the time of the last series, in 2010, the house had revealed its true nature and was dressed as a circus sideshow.

The *Big Brother* house is no passive container but a toy box that springs open at will. Home makeover programs are, similarly, games: there is always the lack of time, the tight budget, and of course the dramatic reveal. It's the house, rather than its inhabitants, that is in charge.

Big Brother is the inversion of the coronation broadcast, in which television imposed a divinely appointed monarch on her subjects. Pressing the red dot on the remote reverses the flow, and we broadcast rather than receive. Uploading films of ourselves (like the teenagers in Madame Tussauds) on to YouTube does the same. Most extreme perhaps are phenomena such as Chat Roulette,[7] in which countless windows and people whirl past each other. It's Quake, played with real people.

OP ZOEK NAAR MARIA

It is March 2009, and the gaunt vaults of the hall of Antwerp-Centraal Station do little to dispel the commuter gloom. The tired voice of the announcer echoes formless through the heavy Sebaldian architecture, interrupted from time to time by the tuneless railway bell.

All of a sudden, the grey is pierced by alpine tones: "Let's start at the very beginning, a very good place to start. When you read you begin with A, B, C. When you sing you begin with Do Re Mi." People who would normally plod through raise their eyes quizzically, trying to discern the source of the song.

"Do re mi fa so la ti..." sings Julie. "Ah. Let's see if we can make it a little easier." And then an orchestra joins in: "Doe, a deer a female deer, ray..." A young man in a jacket, jeans, and a black scarf leaps in to dance and almost immediately he is joined by a Gretel-like little girl in a colored mac and a cute rucksack.

"Me, a name I call myself...," and as they do another man and another child do exactly the same. With every note, more and more passersby join in. Schoolchildren flood down the steps, and by the time we get to do re mi and so on the station hall has become a Von Trapp ball. All that's missing is the baroness.

Its all been organized by a wicked uncle Max of course—it's a promotion for a reality TV show, the Belgian version of "How Do You Solve a Problem Like Maria?"—but real people really do join in: they loved the movie; they've heard about this online; and they've been practicing in front of YouTube at home.

The first flashmob happened in Macy's, New York, in June 2003, when about 100 people all converged on an expensive rug on the home furnishings floor and tried to buy it at the same time. A few days later, 200 people burst into spontaneous applause in the lobby of the Hyatt Hotel, and then hundreds of people poured into a SoHo shoe store saying they'd been directed there by a tour guide.

In April 2006, about four thousand people in Victoria Station started dancing to whatever they had on their iPods. In March 22, 2008, pillow fights broke out in New York, Budapest, Copenhagen, Denver, Dublin, Hamburg, London, Los Angeles, Melbourne, Paris, Pécs, Roanoke, Stockholm, Sydney, Tel Aviv, Székesfehérvár, Szombathely, Vancouver, and other cities. A month later, several hundred people stood still for five minutes in Liverpool Street Station.

These outbreaks have all the absurdity of the situationists. They are gigantic games, and they bring to life the great public interiors of our cities: those ballroom-like station halls, the concourses of airports, metro stations, parks, shops. Such events represent quite as much a part of the revival of the old city centers as do coffee shops, independent boutiques, and renovated lofts.

They teeter only just on the right side of the law and then, not always. In 2006, the silent disco in Victoria Station had to be cleared by the police. The pillow fights of 2008 were a deliberate play on perceptions of safety and danger in a world threatened by shoe bombers and box cutters. The G20 protests, which have become as regular a fixture of the festival year as Christmas or Burning Man, are flashmobs of a sort. Protestors appear and move apparently at random, playing games of cat and mouse with the authorities reminiscent of nothing so much as an urban game of Quake.

Flashmobs aren't just games. They are computer games, and there is nothing random about them. The first flashmobs in 2003 were organized by Bill Wasik of *Harper's Magazine,* who wanted to poke fun at consumer society. He spread the word by e-mail. The first time, he got caught. The next time, he sent interested participants to several bars in the city, where they were given further instructions. Subsequent flashmobs have used Facebook, Twitter, and, of course, the mobile phone.[8] Flashmobs are organized through the computer, but this time, the computer controls the real, rather than the other way round.

This inversion has been explored through the medium of the computer game. In Can You See Me Now?, the world behind the screen is actually the city outside. It has been played in Sheffield, Rotterdam, Barcelona, and Tokyo. The world outside the screen is in fact inside the laboratory. In the lab, players run through a virtual model of the city. They are being chased by real people, through the real streets of the real city outside. Armed with portable computers, these runners can see where their victims are hiding, and they give chase to them. More innocently, there is the phenomenon of geocaching in which digital clues lead walkers across the countryside to hidden treasures. It's Myst played in some strange hybrid combination of real and virtual worlds.

Games like Can You See Me Now? are named ARGs (augmented reality games), and in them, as in the flashmob or Op zoek naar Maria, the screen has been released from its theatrical frame and has come out onto the streets, into the great public interiors of the city. It's a strange revival of public life—it's not as spontaneous or democratic as its seems: flashmobs, for example, are organized by mobile phone companies advertising the very spontaneity their products afford—once you are on a contract. These events are staged spectaculars on a scale of which the movie moguls could never have dreamed.

CONCLUSION

This account began in one public interior—an art deco cinema—and ended in another, a nineteenth-century railway station. It has often been argued that increasing use of new media represents a retreat from the social world and the formation of the interior as an increasingly private and hermetic cocoon.

But it is the argument of this chapter that the irruption of the screen into the interior over the last century has done anything but isolate us from one another. While passive isolation is indeed the implication of the classical space of the cinema, subsequent transformations of screen-space have transformed that model and have reactivated the sociality of both public and private interiors.

The television brought the screen—and the public world—into the domestic sphere, creating a virtual window from the living room into the nation, fomenting bonds with a wider community and also within the family, as it settled down to watch together.

The classical computer game contributed a new dimension to this social interaction, permitting people to influence what happens behind the screen. Transformed from passive spectators into active players, users, particularly teenagers, were able to inhabit a hybrid space, somewhere in between the Euclidean space of the arcade or bedroom and the virtual space of the world of the game.

But these virtual interior worlds, as they increase in sophistication and complexity, take on lives of their own. Like Quake, they become self-sufficient parallel universes with ties and connections of their own. They are interiors to which the interiors of the home, the video arcade, or the PC bag become mere portals, or nodal points, and parts of a system rather than self-sufficient enclosures.

Reality TV uses this self-sufficiency of the virtual world to posit it as equivalent to reality. The screen becomes a magic mirror, whose very cunning blurs and subverts the distinctions between the reality and the virtuality of the interior. The system and the interior (the nodal point) become one.

And last, mobile computing extinguishes the barrier formed by the screen altogether. The relationship between reality and the computer is in fact inverted, and the public interior becomes the game, the spectacle, manipulated ultimately from within the interiors of the private sphere.

My grandmother has stood up from her red chair. She has torn down the cinema curtains and has taken her place in the proscenium arch, where she stands draped in velvet. Scarlett O'Hara's face is projected onto her own and the two become one.

34

Literary Narratives

MARK TAYLOR

Unlike design critics, many novelists face the interesting challenge of trying to go beyond literal and material interpretations of the interior to convey other cultural, social, and psychological meanings. In their descriptions, spaces are often evoked as metaphors of the mind or realms for representing psychic and spiritual life. Across various texts, rooms and moments of transition such as ascending a stair can be a social, psychological, moral, or spiritual act. Although they focus primarily on persons, novelists, according to Karen Chase,[1] develop characters and story lines into which the charged system of spatial relations provides the imaginative condition of the novel.

The relationship between literature and architecture as outlined by Ellen Eve Frank is one in which "the particular subject, what may be thought of as the occasion, is the relationships between architecture and literature as announced in the writings of Walter Pater, Gerard Manley Hopkins, Marcel Proust, and Henry James; for each of these writers declares in one way or another that literature is like architecture."[2] For these and other authors, the house is often the focus—witness the number of novels with a house name in the title. Relative to this, Philippa Tristram suggests that "because the novel is invincibly domestic, it can tell us much about the space we live in; equally, designs for houses and their furnishings can reveal hidden aspects of the novelist's art. It is no accident that many of the terms used in critical discourse—*structure, aspect, outlook,* even *character*—are related to domestic architecture."[3] To some extent, we could argue as Kathy Mezei and Chiara Briganti have, that in a reciprocal relationship, people and characters create and shape their inhabitations, while both the spaces of domesticity and fiction shape the inhabitants.[4]

Many designers are drawn to literary narratives both for design inspiration and new interpretations of settings and environment, understanding that the novelists' space is an active contributor to the discourse of the interior. Unlike a real scene perceived by an individual, the literary narrative can offer a more detached or abstract view enabling the absorption of the scene as a whole. By taking in the scene in this manner, the visionary quality of the novelist can reveal a number of relations that normally go unnoticed when the individual is focused on particular aspects of the unfolding scene. In this short discussion, I will focus on emotional/sensorial writing of the eighteenth century, the psychological/personal studies that emerged in nineteenth century literary descriptions, and social/spatial connections that occur in twentieth century observations. This focus is not to declare these genres as characterizing all period writing but is representative of the way certain ideas are framed relative to characters and interiors. For example the eighteenth-century novels shamelessly promote pleasure and the intimacy of bodies, while their erotic imagining forges a connection between the body and interior space in the pursuit of aesthetic pleasure. The selection of nineteenth-century texts opens the discussion of personality and identification of rooms with the inhabitants' both physically and psychically. While one outcome is the drift toward decadence and ever more astonishing spatial tropes, another reflects the politically charged spaces of female subjectivity. This latter position also informs the early twentieth-century examples, whereas the final post-postmodern text is a more complex narrative in which the creation of rooms also constructs self.

EIGHTEENTH-CENTURY SEDUCTIVE SPACES

Among the variety of narrative texts produced during the eighteenth century, the libertine novel was a literary genre that blended eroticism and rationalism but is increasingly regarded as titillating or pornographic literature. As a genre, it offered explicit depictions of sexuality that often incorporated theatrical elements and provided a narrative that was both arousing and instructional. Authors who contributed to this literature include Jean-Baptiste de Boyer, the Marquis d'Argens (*Thérèse philosophe,* 1748), Denis Diderot (*Les Bijoux indiscrets,* 1748), Vivant Denon (*Point de lendemain,* 1777) Choderlos De Laclos (*Les Liaisons Dangereuses,* 1782), and the Marquis de Sade (*La Philosophie dans le boudoir,* 1795).

   One such text where the properly encoded interior advertises itself as a space for seduction is Jean-Francois de Bastide's *La Petite Maison* (1789), recently translated and published as *The Little House: An Architectural Seduction* (1996). This text, as Rodolphe el-Khoury argues, lies somewhere between literature and architectural theory, being the combination of two literary genres, the erotic libertine novella and the architectural treatise.[5] Informed by the writings and teachings of architectural educator Jacques-Francois Blondel, the text is located in the sensationalist theories developed by Etienne Bonnot de Condillac (1714–1780) in his *Treatise on Sensation* (1754)—a text that opened the body to new forms of spatial awareness. Individual aesthetic appreciation and a cultivation of the picturesque vision enabled architectural theorists such as Nicolas Le Camus de Mézières (1721–1789) to see architecture in a new way. His treatise *Le Génie de l'architecture* (1780), published one year after Bastide's novella, is primarily a detailed inventory of social and spatial rules for planning and organizing large-scale French residences,[6] which also advanced a new psychological reading of character proper to various rooms. By closely observing nature, Le Camus rationalized, in the manner of art theorist Charles Le Brun (1619–1690), that "every object possesses a character, proper to it alone"[7] and that the expression of character might be through a single line or plain contour. As a sensationalist text, character interpretation was made "solely through human sensations or responses: What emotions do we not feel in the contrast between deep shadow and limpid light, or between the delights of calm weather and the confusion of winds and tempests: Every nuance, every gradation, affects us."[8] Elsewhere[9] I have argued that both the interior and the garden were no longer regarded as a passive entity but were an active agent that engaged the emotional and sensorial aspects of inhabitation.

In *La Petite Maison,* Jean-Francois de Bastide narrates a plot of seduction between the Marquis de Trémicour and the young and virginal Mélite, who for some time had resisted his advances. The text begins with Mélite conceding to visit his *petite maison* not realizing it is tastefully arranged for love. During the visit, she is lead from one room to another, each more artfully arranged than the one before, but toward the middle of the narrative she is overcome by the many wonders and feels "weak, stifled even, and was forced to sit down 'I can take this no longer' she said 'This house is too beautiful. There is nothing comparable on earth…' Mélite's tone of voice betrayed a secret distress; Trémicour felt that she was nearly his."[10] Weak at the knees and betraying what Bastide calls a "secret distress," she was clearly aroused and overwhelmed by the architecture. To effect the seduction, Trémicour used both architecture (surfaces, artifacts, paintings, and sculpture) and special effects (fragrances, fireworks, and ethereal music).

In this novel, the architecture, as observed by Giuliana Bruno, has another role and reading since it also "stands for a lover's body and its traversal binds romantic touch to the taste for space."[11] Bruno further argues that in this processural narrative "where a woman is subject rather than object of (architectural) seduction," the story sensuously unfolds as every corner of the house and garden is explored.[12] The narrative plan attaches "eroticism to space" and engages the seduction of architecture, but as Mélite is lured into the architecture and seduced by the décor, Trémicour candidly reveals that "for the first time, the house meant less to him than the object he had brought to it."[13] Dianne Brown, a graduate of romance languages and literature, demonstrates how the narrative collusion between seduction in words and architectural detailing illustrated an inseparability that was also witnessed in *Le Sopha* (Paris, 1742) by Crébillon fils. To illustrate this, she quoted a moment when the narrator entered the cabinet, a place designed for seduction and where "everything radiated sensuality: the adornments, the furniture, the scent of the exquisite perfume that was always burning. Everything brought sensuality to the eye, everything transported it to the soul. This *cabinet* could have been taken for the temple of voluptuousness, for the indisputable seat of pleasure."[14]

Architectural historian and theorist Anthony Vidler has argued that space was crucial in establishing a "world apart," such as a world governed by an erotic narrative. He illustrated this by quoting from Vivant Denon's novel *Point de Lendemain* (1777), where he suggests the place of eroticism in architecture and architecture in eroticism is reversed "as when intrigued by a description of his lover's secret room, the narrator bluntly avows:

'I was very curious: it was no longer Madame de T— that I desired, but her *cabinet*,' thus reinstating architecture as the primary object of eroticism."[15] Dianne Brown pointed out that this account "exemplifies the lure of interior space, the erotic sensibilities it engenders, and the literary stakes in its exploration."[16] The narration in *Point de Lendemain* is primarily about a young man's one-night tryst with an older woman, one that Dianne Brown suggests traces a "migration from the public to the domestic sphere and, finally, to a secret, exotically appointed *cabinet*."[17] It is an erotic tale that centers on a hedonistic encounter between a young man who is "abducted" to the country estate of Madame de T— and embarks on a night of passion. Both interiors and landscape hold an important position in the novel, from the first moment in the carriage when leaning toward the same window, a jolt causes their faces to accidentally touch as they admire "the beauty of the landscape, the call of the night, the moving silence of nature."[18] Arriving at the house, the young man noted that its luxurious interior was filed with "images of sensual pleasure," and the young narrator could do little else but admire its magnificence. Following supper, Monsieur de T— retires early to bed, and Mme de T— and the young man took a stroll on the terrace. In the text, the narrator is drawn through a sequence of progressively more secluded spaces, which, Martin Calder observed, enabled the narrator to project a "libidinal specialization" into the garden, only to have the woman suggest they leave this "*dangerous séjour.*"[19]

While Bastide depicts an interior world that is open to the senses, in the way that one space unfolds into another, Dianne Brown indicates that architecture and erotic books shared "the isolated, private experience each could provide,"[20] particularly as they were designed to be read with one hand. In these texts and in real life, she argues, the eighteenth-century interior was fragmented into boudoirs, cabinets, alcoves, niches, and other small spaces partitioned by screens and curtains. These spaces offered a shift from outdoor pastoral encounters to the intimacy of the cabinet or boudoir, where, in a literary context, the opportunity for seclusion was matched by eavesdroppers and voyeurs. The seduction of Mélite is as much a seduction of architecture, implying as with other erotic libertine novels, seduction is spatial. Brown suggests that the moment that a room inflames arousal, when the cabinet supplants the body as the object of desire then, "the penetration of the inner sanctum is a figure for sexual penetration."[21] Moreover, her examination of the cabinet concludes that while it is both the site of seduction and observation, descriptions of curtains generate as much arousal as the outline of a naked body.

For the libertine novel and the erotic painting or illustration to achieve its characteristic frankness and directness of address, stories were set in specific itemized domestic interiors, notably boudoirs and cabinets, often containing a bed, bed linen, and swathes of curtains that frame or reveal the subject. Through the eighteenth century, the boudoir and the cabinet became a meeting point for a number of discourses around reading, viewing, and seduction. Thus sexualized, the space played a significant role in supporting and enhancing the mimetic identification of reader/audience with story/image.[22] Interiors were "pressed into the service of eroticism" and played a crucial role in housing sex, making it real for the reader, adding depth to characters, becoming an actor in the unfolding of story, and functioning as a critical stimulus to the sexual imagination.

Paul Young suggests the design of French libertine cabinets "commits itself unapologetically and wholly to pleasure...it is a self-conscious aesthetic chamber for sexual intimacy and discovery."[23] He adds, "The 'art' of the cabinet, in general, and painting, in particular, allow the libertine subjects to transpose the erotic into an aesthetic realm, in which these actors find their echoes in the works that surround them."[24] In Mathieu-François Pidanset de Mairobert's novel *Anecdotes sur Mme la Comtesse du Barry* (1775), Madame Gourdan initiated the young Mademoiselle Lançon (Comtesse du Barry) into her whorehouse by showing her through her apartments and, as she said, "my boudoirs fitted out for lovemaking where everything bespeaks pleasure and seduction...I urged her to examine the engravings that adorned the walls—nudes, suggestive positions, and all sorts of images for the arousal of sexual desire."[25] Here the descriptions of decorative furnishings are designed to reinforce the environment into which the hapless Comtesse has found herself, whereas other texts find occupants hidden in spaces that often do not feature in architectural treatises, particularly if they are behind movable or thin partitions. Similarly Diane Brown notes that in *Margot la Ravaudeuse* (1750) by Louis-Charles Fougeret de Monbron, Margot hides behind a screen that covers a niche. Here Margot is offered a layered spatial isolation for watching a sexual encounter, and confesses, "I slipped away in a niche in the *cabinet* that was closed by a simple screen with panels separated from each other by a good inch, sealed together with strips of paper. By means of a small opening that I made, it was easy to see all of their manoeuvres."[26] In a similar manner, the narrator, Thérèse—from the Marquis d'Argens's "pornographic" novel *Thérèse philosophe* (1748)—spies on the deceptive rape of her friend Eradice by the lecherous Jesuit, Father Dirrag.[27] Concealed in a cabinet, she is able to see Eradice assume an unorthodox prayer position, which she believed would allow Father Dirrag to purify her with "the cord of Saint Francis":

> I scurried into the closet...A hole in the closet door, as big as my hand and covered with an old, threadbare Bergamo tapestry, allowed me to see the entire room easily, without risk of being caught...I was positioned in such a manner as not to miss the slightest detail of the scene...the windows of the bedroom where this scene took place were directly across from the door of the *cabinet* where I was hidden.[28]

Many of these eighteenth-century "instructional" volumes were aimed at the sexual education of young women, and conversely the titillation of men, and included both physical and emotional interplay with architectural spaces/surfaces. Occasionally this was conveyed though the overwhelming effect that a decorated space had on the inhabitant as the story unfolded room by room (*enfilade*). Alongside this was the complicit role that concealment, as in being located in a hidden space within a room, and voyeurism play in watching and therefore educating the narrator in sexual acts. In most cases—whether "pornographic" novels or erotic literature—there are included descriptions of space, metaphors, and double entendres. What becomes apparent is that under this conception, an interior is not subservient to, or determined by, an existing built form but is generated from within, through pattern, ornamentation, and manipulation of surface, furnishing, and decorative effects.

NINETEENTH-CENTURY PSYCHOLOGICAL SPACE

In her analysis of Charlotte Brontë's novel *Jane Eyre* (1847), Karen Chase suggests that the text is spatially articulate and depicts several houses with multiple rooms, many of which are in continual upheaval as characters open and close doors and windows, ascend and descend staircases, and cross thresholds.[29] These houses preoccupy their inhabitants and rooms take on distinct personalities such that the protagonists' behavior is altered as their mental qualities come into play. The interior as a formal spatial (designed) arrangement is replaced by one that constructs new relationships through patterns of movement and inhabitation that occurs with each occupant's actions. Chase argues that in negotiating the five principal residences, Jane declares rooms to have personalities and constructs the houses relative to her mental state, as in one instance when Jane attempts to avoid other people in the house and "engages in architectural contortions in order to remain the unobtrusive governess."[30] The ability of the body to respond to spatial conditions and influence the narrative is further reinforced by Charlotte Brontë's lavish descriptions of rooms above those of the inhabitants and utilizing a number of devices to depict layers of containment, whether physical shells of enclosure or psychical descriptions of "dangerous" emotive energy. She portrays rooms within rooms, containers within containers, and the house as an outer shell for routes to intricate spaces.

The architectural interior holds other readings, as English literature academics Sandra Gilbert and Susan Gubar observe. Rooms are also used to contain passions and desires—particularly the confinement of female desire.[31] Their research on the interface of women and literature into the discourse on the interior links it to gender politics. In their work, literary techniques are used to discuss the interior through the topography of the occupant's innermost self, questioning the conflation between women, house, and inner being. In their examination of Charlotte Perkins Gilman short novel *The Yellow Wallpaper* (1892/1973),[32] they construct a feminist reading of a literary work in which a woman writer narrates her experiences of textual/architectural confinement. The importance of this study is that they demonstrate that women's writing is necessarily different from men's, and the gender (of the author's body) is inscribed in the text, and by implication, into the architectural surroundings under discussion.

Both *Jane Eyre* and *The Yellow Wallpaper* are stories of female confinement and escape. The latter volume, which Charlotte Perkins Gilman referred to as a description of a case of nervous breakdown, is, as Gilbert and Gubar argue "a first person account of a woman who is evidently suffering from a severe postpartum psychosis."[33] Confined in a large garret room in an "ancestral hall" the narrator is forbidden to write until she is well again. The room is lined with a sulfurous yellow paper, ripped and torn in a few areas and patterned with "lame uncertain curves" that "plunge off at outrageous angles" and "destroy themselves in unheard of contradictions." As the story unfolds the narrator confesses:

> I think there are a great many women both behind the paper and creeping in the garden, and sometimes only one, and she crawls around fast, and her crawling shakes [the paper] all over…And she is all the time trying to climb through. But nobody could climb through that pattern—it strangles so; I think that is why it has so many heads.[34]

By using the wallpaper in this manner, it soon becomes clear that the person creeping through and behind the wallpaper is both the narrator and the narrator's double. By the end of the story, moreover, the narrator has enabled this double to escape from her textual/architectural confinement: "I pulled and she shook, I shook and she pulled, and before morning we had peeled off yards of that paper."[35] Although there is a sense of horror much like in the earlier Edgar Allan Poe novel *The Fall of the House of Usher* (1840), the identification of gender and personality with the interior emerges in mid- to late-nineteenth-century novels and architecture. It is particularly evident in the conceptual shift from the home as repository for inherited artifacts to the home as an expression of the character and personality of the occupant. In a manner similar to the sensationalist approach of eighteenth-century French architectural theory, the nineteenth-century home as a collection of tastefully arranged furnishings was designed to arouse feelings and display imagination. To support this, a number of magazines and books provided advice on etiquette, taste, and how to negotiate the plethora of manufactured goods becoming available.

Paralleling this cultural change, a number of novels began to construct interiors that reflected the new discourse of the interior. Writing on French literature, Janelle Watson suggested that "many nineteenth-century novelists aspire to social analysis."[36] Linking descriptions of material objects with people, she argued that their interest in the densely decorated bourgeois interior is similar to that of the sociologist or social commentator. Watson noted that this was particularly evident in the ability to extract meaning from small but significant decorative objects. The importance of this connection for the discipline of interior design/architecture is that such novels become a source for rethinking both spatial and material culture. For example, connections are made through analogy, homology, and reciprocal influence, which Watson suggested occurs in the relationship of dweller and dwelling in Madame Vauquer's boarding house in *Le Père Goriot* (1835) by Honoré de Balzac. She observes that "the portrait of Madame Vaqueur is exemplary for the way it explicitly situates her in a mutually determining relationship to her environment, including her interior décor."[37]

While Balzac's novels were founded on social and zoological theories that enabled the inhabitants (such as Madame Vaqueur) to be determined by their environment[38] the nineteenth-century cultural phenomenon of the "artistic interior" gave rise to several new expressions of the collector's interior. These homes were not those of the antiquarian collectors of the past but were those of the new artistic or aesthetic collector who constructed a "close personal relationship between the 'artiste' and this objects...displayed gaily and warmly...providing a visual focal point."[39] One fictional aesthete that finds himself immersed in a delirious sensual environment is Duc Jean Floressas Des Esseintes, the principal character of Joris-Karl Huysmans's *A Rebours* (1884). In this text, Des Esseintes, an eccentric, reclusive aesthete and antihero, rejected his flamboyant Paris lifestyle for a new home at Fontenay, which he had colored and decorated as an artificially lit internal environment. A timber-clad dining room that resembled a ship's cabin, complete with bulkheads and pitch-pine floor, was built within the structure "like those Japanese boxes that fit one inside the other, this room was inserted within a larger one—the real dining room as designed by the architect."[40] This latter room had a specific interior décor, more akin to a decorous drawing room, inside the architecture proper and was provided with two windows:

> one of these was now invisible, being hidden by the bulkhead or partition wall, which could however be dropped by touching a spring, so that fresh air might be admitted to circulate freely around and within the pitch-pine enclosure; the other was visible, being situated right opposite the porthole contrived in the woodwork, but was masked in a peculiar way, a large aquarium filling in the whole space intervening between the porthole and the real window in the real house-wall.[41]

Des Esseintes also partitioned his salon into a series of niches, each designed with the character of the Latin and French books he liked. Each niche was differently hung and carpeted with a palate of colors that subtly linked them together. On the days he didn't want to play the eccentric, Des Esseintes would "settle himself down to read in which-ever of these recesses displayed in its scheme of decoration the closest correspondence with the intimate essence of the particular book his caprice of the moment led him to peruse."[42] At the same time, he covered the interior masonry architectural form and its original surface treatment, as if to erase the architectural limit and construct a psychic interior, an interior that turns inward and reflects his emotional states. Similarly, the semi-autobiographical *La Maison d'un Artiste* (1881) by Edmond de Goncourt (1822–1896) describes his own apartment in which the walls and ceilings are hidden under tapestries, china, watercolors, and books. The effect was to remove all physical markers of enclosure such that the mask erases the boundaries of architecture. Such observations recast the interior as a psychological retreat that defied regularity.

Huysmans's novel describes Des Esseintes's social engagements as being decadently eccentric, epitomized by the funereal feast to celebrate "the most unmentionable of personal calamities," which turned out to be a temporary loss of virility. For this occasion, "the dining room was hung with black and looked out on a strangely metamorphosed garden, the walks being strewn with charcoal, the little basin in the middle of the lawn bordered with a rim of black basalt and filled with ink."[43] Food such as "turtle soup, Russian black bread, ripe olives from Turkey…and sauces coloured to resemble liquorice water and boot-blacking" was served on black-bordered plates, and while guests were waited upon by "naked negresses wearing shoes and stockings of cloth of silver besprinkled with tears," funereal marches played in the background.[44]

TWENTIETH CENTURY AND BEYOND

Alongside her coauthored volume *The Decoration of Houses* (1898), the novelist Edith Wharton set many of her stories within complex social and spatial arrangements. Judith Fryer, in her analysis of Wharton's novel *The House of Mirth* (1905), proposes that the novel has a particular narrative that is "the downward path of the protagonist through a series of actual houses."[45] How we understand the houses is not so much through pictorial description but via the thoughts and feelings of the characters, in particular Lily

Bart. Gathered in our imagination, they exert a presence on the reader that is not fixed but is in flux, allowing us to individually build an understanding through the vividness of the narration. The character Lily Bart offers comments and criticizes rooms and spaces relative to her own value judgments of the occupants and is somewhat selective in her observations. On a number of occasions, Edith Wharton transposes architectural and character metaphors such that we often find room, occupant(s), and Lily Bart bound together. As the narrative revisits settings and rooms, Lily Bart offers a different slant conditioned by her reduced social and monetary circumstances. The faint sketches previously given are now replaced with new renderings. Similarly, the difference in how a room is perceived by two different intruders, such as Lawrence Seldon's and Lily Bart's separate visits to Gerty Farish's flat, confirm that architecture is more than the mere enclosing structure. Lawrence Seldon is able to compliment Gerty Farish on her apartment and both "fitted as snugly as bits in a puzzle,"[46] whereas Lily, after spending a restless night in the flat "looks about the poor slit of a room with renewal of physical distaste."[47] Literary academic John Clubbe comments on how the character Lawrence Seldon is able to respond sensitively and favorably to Gerty Farish's apartment, whereas Lily Bart finds disgust in being touched by ordinariness.[48]

In *The House of Mirth*, Lily Bart's social world remains static; the social order and the society she aspires to become constants. This is evidenced by her disappointment in returning to Lawrence Seldon's flat and finding it with "scene unchanged." Her world is found to be ordered, and it is through this that she descends. Lily Bart's journey passes through the most decorated of rooms, bringing her in contact with the fashionable "new moneyed" rich interiors of the Wellington Bry's and the now faded but once fashionable "old moneyed" dark interiors of her Aunt Peniston's home. It finishes via the less fashionable but more homely interior of Lawrence Seldon (the reader), the modest cozy apartment of Gerty Farish (the charitable), and the more spartan home of Nettie Struther (the mother). Throughout this room-by-room journey, Lily never manages to discern the relationship of room to occupier, always striving for some other vision. This series of rooms are criticized and rejected in a search for some "other" interior constructed in relation to herself.

Jacob's Room, To the Lighthouse, A Haunted House, A Room of One's Own, and *The Mark on the Wall* are titles of a number of Virginia Woolf's novels and essays, suggesting the key role that architectural and spatial concerns play in her work. Cities, buildings, spaces, elements perform a number of functions in her writing, serving as metaphors, structuring devices and facilitators of action or inaction.[49] Ruth Miller, in her investigation of "frames" in Woolf's texts, points out that rooms, windows, thresholds, and mirrors act as devices that structure her writing, as metaphors for consciousness and identity and as the medium for an awareness of the temporal.[50] Lyn Pykett explains that Woolf identifies the city with a freeing up of the imagination and a means for women to escape from the restricting interior spaces of the private domestic realm and to occupy "a different form of interiority in the public spaces of the streets."[51] The need to construct rooms as refuges against the perils of the outside world is a recurrent theme in Virginia Woolf's writing, just as the destruction or breaking of this enclosure signals fragility.

Virginia Woolf's novel *Orlando* (1928) is a mock biography in which the ageless Orlando lives for over 300 years and changes sex half-way through the narrative. In one section of the book, set in the mid-seventeenth century, the male Orlando was ensconced in his house, brooding and meditative. Focusing on the interior, Woolf depicted Orlando at night passing along the corridors, halls, and staircases and lingering in the crypts and tombs. This wandering through the interior of his house paralleled Orlando's retreat into his own internal world, where he thought and pondered deeply. Here, as in other texts by Woolf, rooms are seen as metaphors for the mind, such that the image of Orlando pacing through the galleries parallels the thought processes in his mind. Later, after the futility of all his thinking and writing, Orlando substitutes an architectural act of creativity for his failed literary one and redecorates his house. The redecoration becomes a material version of language, literally standing in for a conclusion, a "peroration," to an eloquent address he was making to his ancestors and his house. Writing and architecture are fused together, infecting one another. In this passage, Orlando's writing took on the qualities of decorating and decorating took on the qualities of inscription. Once Orlando's decorating frenzy was accomplished, right down to the last bowl of potpourri, he contemplates his handiwork and realized that it was not complete and that something more was needed. The furnishings and furniture were not enough, "people sitting in them, people lying in them improve them amazingly."[52] That is, by inhabiting the rooms and using the furniture, people became part of the overall decorative strategy.

Like many novels already discussed, Mark Z. Danielewski's *House of Leaves* (2000) contains numerous references to both fictitious and real events and sources, and contains many footnotes, some of which do not exist. Although Nele Bemong describes the home/book in terms of the "uncanny," trauma and Freud's concept of the death drive,[53] it is a difficult book to interpret and "many a critic has sighed that the book, since it incorporates almost all branches of critical discourse, explains, interprets, or reads itself, making the critic's work redundant."[54]

The opening autobiographical narrative is provided by the main protagonist, Johnny Truant, who works in a Los Angeles tattoo parlor. He moves into an apartment that once belonged to the blind and elderly Zampanò who is now deceased. In the apartment, he finds a manuscript, written by Zampanò, that is a careful study of a documentary film called *The Navidson Record*. This film, made by Will Navidson, records the strange events that occurred in the house he shared with his partner, Karen Green, and their children, Chad and Daisy. The plot is also complicated by other interjections from a number of interviews about the *Record* and some notes by unnamed "editors."

What is evident through the multiple texts of the anonymous editors, notes by Johnny Truant, the manuscript, and *The Navidson Record* is, as Nicoline Timmer observes, that the creation of "room" is connected to "constructing self." She notes that "structurally, thematically and even typographically, the novel is an exploration of personal space, of how to find room to become oneself—whereby the 'personal' turns out to be always and necessarily inter-personal and every 'space' already inhabited by traces of the other."[55]

Unlike the seductive, aesthetic, and gendered spaces already discussed, this novel or book creates an impossible spatial environment. The central character, Will Navidson, and his partner, Karen, move from New York to a suburban house in Virginia. On one occasion, they return from a visit to another town to find a dark room had appeared between the parents' and children's room. The children, Chad and Daisy, run through this space playing and giggling, whereas the *Navidson Record* shows Karen with hands to her mouth and Will almost amused by this change. Although not exactly threatening, like a robbery this spatial violation "still destroyed any sense of security or well-being."[56] This internal spatial change occurs while externally the house remained the same. That is, the house changes its dimensions and became spatially bigger on the inside, sprouting hallways, rooms, great halls and stairs, while still looking the same from the outside.

A maze-like hallway leading to an enormous room with a never-ending spiral staircase and endless corridors appears off the living room wall. Exploration #5 is Will Navidson's last hallway exploration, and he chooses not to head for the spiral staircase but ventures into one of the corridors. To record the adventure, he takes several cameras, a cassette recorder, and provisions for sleeping and eating while away. All of this is loaded onto a trailer attached to a mountain bike. After a couple of hours cycling, he has managed to go only 7 miles, but buy the evening 163 miles is covered—most freewheeling downhill. After camping overnight, he decides to return, a journey he estimates will take six to seven days, but after a few minutes cycling, he found the path was again going downhill; "confused he pulls into a large room and tries to gather his thoughts: it's as if I'm moving along a surface that always tilts downward no matter which direction I face."[57] The journey is not consistent as the corridor changes shape and size, and floors seem to rotate from horizontal to vertical without him noticing.

This series of never-ending passages reconceptualizes the home as a labyrinth, a disorientating space at the edge of our consciousness. The strange rooms and passages of this house are also metaphors of the mind and a reflection of the mental state of both main characters, the editors, and Jonny Truant; "the halls, and the rooms all become the self—collapsing, expanding, tilting, closing, but always in perfect relation to the mental state of the individual."[58] Nicoline Timmer observes that the notes left by Johnny Truant indicate that he loses his grip on the text after excessively exploring *The Navidson Record,* particularly as he "connects his own life story both to what is going on in the story (Navidson's story) and to intense reading and interpretation of the story."[59] In his notes, Truant uses similar spatial and emotional language to describe his own void as "profound darkness" and how "inside me, a long dark hallway . . . continued to grow,"[60] reflecting his own internal feelings.

Although these mental and physical spatial games might seem unreal, the vast space of the rooms and hallways has a close resemblance to secondary spaces in computer games, where a link opens a portal to another world or mission. In *House of Leaves,* the word *house* is printed in blue ink, referencing the blue highlighting of hyperlinks on Web pages and digital documents. This highlighting, as Mark Hansen notes, "transforms this keyword into something like a portal to information located elsewhere, both within and beyond the novel's frame."[61] Developing a discussion on the analog book's relationship to the digital, particularly the parametrically driven design techniques (where the range of virtual potentials is larger than the actualities), "what we encounter in this impossible house is a figure for a spatial dimension—a topological figure";[62] the house is a hypertext in which a small insertion opens another world. It is also a technique used in many computer games as spaces within spaces are explored. I suggest this because, while these texts are parallels between mental and physical space, this conception opens discussion on real and virtual spaces.

CONCLUSION

These novelists' observations are informed by changes in cultural, political, and social conditions and mirror, comment, or interpret these shifts through their text. Julie Park's comparison of Ian Watt's *Rise of the Novel* (1957) and Nancy Armstrong's *Desire and Domestic Fiction* (2000) is also pertinent to recall.[63] In her paper, she notes that Ian Watt finds equivalence between domestic life and the characters that inhabit these spaces, whereas Nancy Armstrong does not hold an architectural analogy between domestic space and the private self but conceptualizes the interior as "a politically charged setting for the containment of female subjectivity."[64] Her analysis also notes that Ian Watt, in equating the mind with room, finds coexistences between the pages of a novel and the domestic interior and the boundaries of the psyche. On the other hand, Armstrong, as Park observes, regards these as synonymous with "the domestication of female agency."[65] Many of the above examples adhere to this claim and provide a platform for women authors to represent their spaces as both a narrative and architectural endeavor, while engaging in the realities of architecture as a gendered practice and process.

For others, the narrative reveals the complicity between the imaginings of spatial encounters and architectural development. The cabinet as a site for voyeuristic activity shaped to reflect, imitate, and construct female subjectivity afforded a new sensationalist reading of space. Prior to this emotional engagement with surface and ornamentation through libidinal encounters, the architectural interior was filtered through rationalist, systematic thought that controlled its visibility. Reading the nineteenth-century narratives relative to Park's observations, the physical and psychical encounters between inhabitants, space, and the mind delimits the limit of the interior through effacement of physical form and character. In the twentieth century texts, the narrative revisits rooms, decorates obsessively, and endlessly explores mathematically impossible spaces, suggesting that subjectivity has slipped from person to room. Moreover, the lines between inside and outside are now blurred, enabling multiple spatialities that contribute to the discourse of interior architecture.

REFERENCES

Armstrong, N. 1987. *Desire and Domestic Fiction.* New York: Oxford University Press.
Bemong, N. 2003. "Exploration #6: The Uncanny in Mark Z. Danielewski's *House of Leaves.*" *Image and Narrative: Online Magazine of the Visual Narrative* 3 (2): 5. Available at: http://www.imageandnarrative.be/inarchive/uncanny/nelebemong.htm. Accessed September 23, 2011.

Brown, D. 2009. "The Female *Philosophe* in the Closet: The Cabinet and the Senses in French Erotic Novels, 1740–1800." *The Journal of Early Modern Cultural Studies* 9 (2): 96–123.

Bruno, G. 2007. *Atlas of Emotion: Journeys in Art, Architecture, and Film.* New York: Verso.

Calder, M. 2005. "The Experience of Space in the Eighteenth-Century French Garden: from Axis to Circuit to Closed Circuit." In *Space: New Dimensions in French Studies,* ed. Emma Gilby and Katja Haustein, 41–58. Bern: Peter Lang AG.

Chase, K. 1984. *Eros & Psyche: The Representation of Personality in Charlotte Brontë, Charles Dickens, and George Eliot.* London: Methuen.

Cleary, R. 1989. "Romancing the Tome; Or an Academician's Pursuit of a Popular Audience in 18th-CenturyFrance." *Journal of the Society of Architectural Historians* 48 (2): 139–49.

Clubbe, J. 1996. "Interiors and the Interior Life in Edith Wharton's *The House of Mirth.*" *Studies in the Novel* 28 (4): 543–64.

Danielewski, M. Z. 2000. *House of Leaves.* New York: Pantheon Books.

Darnton, R. 1995. *The Forbidden Best-Sellers of Pre-Revolutionary France.* New York: W. W. Norton.

de Bastide, J. F. 1996. *The Little House: An Architectural Seduction.* New York: Princeton Architectural Press.

de Crébillon, Claude-Prosper Jolyot. 1996. *Le Sopha.* Paris-Genève: Editions Slatkine.

Denon, V. 1997. "No Tomorrow." In *The Libertine Reader: Eroticism and Enlightenment in Eighteenth Century France,* ed. Michel Feher, trans. Lydia Davis, 732–47. New York: Zone Books.

Downey, G. and Taylor, M. 2010. "Curtains and Carnality: Processural Seductions in Eighteenth Century Text and Space." In *'Imagining': Proceedings from the 27th Annual Conference of the Society of Architectural Historians, Australia and New Zealand,* ed. Michael Chapman and Michael Ostwald, 121–26. Newcastle: University of Newcastle, Australia.

Frank, E. E. 1979. *Literary Architecture: Essays Toward a Tradition: Walter Pater, Gerard Manley Hopkins, Marcel Proust, Henry James.* Berkley: University of California Press.

Fryer, J. 1986. *Felicitous Space: the Imaginative Structures of Edith Wharton and Willa Cather.* Chapel Hill: University of North Carolina Press.

Gilbert, S. M. and S. Gubar. 1984. *The Madwoman in the Attic: The Woman Writer and the Nineteenth-Century Literary Imagination.* New Haven, CT: Yale University Press.

Gilman, C. P. 1973. *The Yellow Wallpaper.* London: Virago.

Hansen, M.B.N. 2004. "The Digital Topography of Mark Z. Danielewski's *House of Leaves.*" *Contemporary Literature* 45 (4): 597–636.

Huysmans, J. K. 1969. *Against the Grain (A Rebours).* New York: Dover Publications.

Le Camus de Mézières, N. 1992. *The Genius of Architecture; or, the Analogy of that Art with our Sensations.* Santa Monica: Getty Centre.

Mezei, K. and C. Briganti. 2002. "Reading the House: A Literary Perspective." *Signs* 27 (3): 837–47.

Miller, C. R. 1988. *Virginia Woolf: The Frames of Art and Life.* New York: St. Martin's Press.

Park, J. 2008. "Moving Parts: The Life of Eighteenth-Century Interiors." *Eighteenth-Century Fiction* 20 (3): v–ix.

Pykett, L. 1995. *Engendering Fictions.* New York: St. Martin's Press.

Sinclair, R. and M. Taylor. 2000. "Novel Architecture: The Settings of Virginia Woolf and Edith Wharton." In *Habitus 2000: A Sense of Place: Conference Proceedings* [CD-ROM], ed. J. R. Stephens. Perth: Curtin University.

Taylor, M. 2011. "Planting for Pleasure: The Eighteenth-Century Erotic Garden." *Interiors: Design, Architecture, Culture* 2 (3): 357–70.

Timmer, N. 2010. *Do You Feel It Too?: The Post-Postmodern Syndrome in American Fiction at the Turn of the Millenium.* Amsterdam: Editions Rodopi B.V.

Tristram, P. 1989. *Living Space in Fact and Fiction.* London: Routledge.

Watson, J. 2006. *Literature and Material Culture from Balzac to Proust: The Collection and Consumption of Curiosities.* Cambridge: Cambridge University Press.

Watt, I. 2000. *The Rise of the* Novel. London: Pimlico.

Wharton, E. 1987. *The House of Mirth.* New York: Macmillan.

Woolf, V. 1977. *Orlando.* [1928] St. Albans: Granada Publishing.

Young, P. J. 2008a. *Seducing the Eighteenth-Century French* Reader. Burlington: Ashgate.

Young, P. J. 2008b. "*Ce Lieu de delices:* Art and Imitation in the French Libertine Cabinet." *Eighteenth-Century Fiction* 20 (3): 335–56.

Wharton, E. and O. Codman. 1898. *The Decoration of Houses.* New York: Charles Scribner's Sons.

Atmospheric Conditions of the Interior

PLATE 33: The Kärntner Bar (American Bar) Vienna designed by Adolf Loos 1908. "The sign of a truly felt architectural work is that in plan it lacks effect."—Adolf Loos. Note the effect of the mirrors making the space look larger than it actually is and the reflection of the rectangular columns next to the mirror giving the illusion they are square. Photograph from RIBApix: Image number RIBA40277 by ORCH Orsenigo Chemollo.

PLATE 34: The relativity of color: IV–I: illustration from *Interaction of Color* by Josef Albers. A color has many faces, and one color can be made to appear as two different colors. In the original design for the study IV–I, horizontal dark blue and yellow stripes were on a flap that could be lifted to show that a vertical stripe of ochre is the same color at the top as at the bottom. Courtesy of Yale University Press.

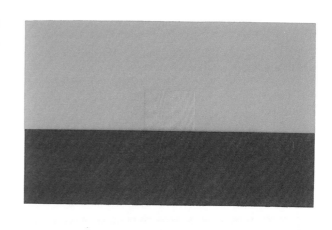

PLATE 35: Example of Hybrid Collage: Impromptu Bacchanalia on Stairwell: Alessandro Ayuso, 2011. The building was constructed in 3D in modeling software. A sectional cut through the staircase was selected and imported into Photoshop and colored in a Beaux-Arts manner. The wire frame putto figure was created using animation software and let loose in the 3D model. Stills were selected, some of which were rendered and imported into the section. The image was finally printed at scale 1:10 and Ayuso continued to work on the drawing by hand using colored pencils. His own figure can be seen faintly outlined in pencil at the bottom of the stair. Courtesy of Alessandro Ayuso.

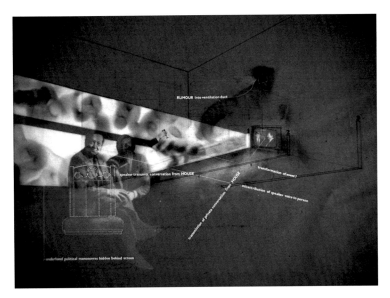

PLATE 36: Collage: The Smoking Room: Tom Holdom, 2009. The fragment doesn't have to be a physical object. The Smoking Room was the name of a lobbying room in the House of Commons, since the EU ban on smoking it is now known as the Strangers Bar. MPs and their guests come in the evening, to hear the gossip and have a drink. It is one of the few rooms where rumors are encouraged and all political parties use the room as a space to allow leaks to be circulated to the press. Such a room has a clear function that is obviously not reliant on a particular architectural response, more the creation of an atmosphere or effect. Holdom creates a visual analogy between the rumors and the smoke that is represented by literally smoking on film that is then stuck to the drawing. Courtesy of Tom Holdom.

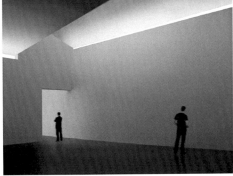

PLATE 37: (a) Herning Gallery, lobby; (b) Herning Gallery, space. Courtesy of Steven Holl Architects.

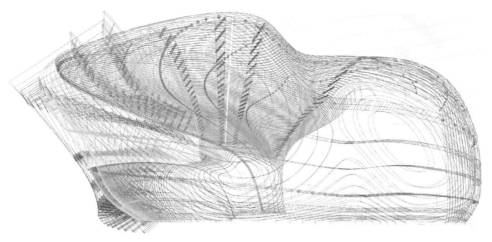

PLATE 38: Digital milling information generated by scripts operating on parametric sections. Courtesy of dECOi Architects.

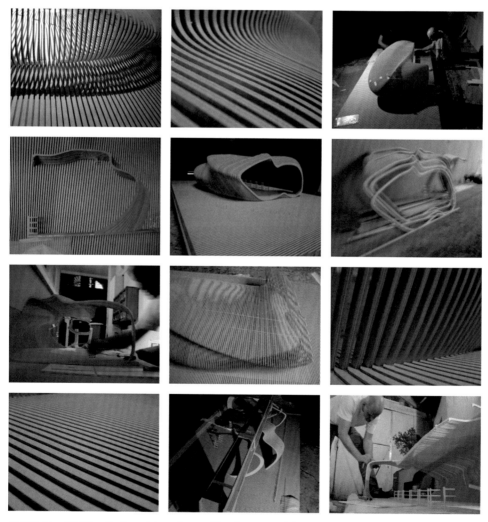

PLATE 39: CNC milled models and assembly. Courtesy of dECOi Architects.

PLATE 40: Ost Kuttner Apartment by Kol/Mac. Courtesy of Michael Moran/OTTO.

PLATE 41: Ost Kuttner Apartment by Kol/Mac. Courtesy of Michael Moran/OTTO.

PLATE 42:   Restaurant Georges. Copyright Jakob + MacFarlane - N. Borel photography.

PLATE 43:   Restaurant Georges. Copyright Jakob + MacFarlane - N. Borel photography.

PLATE 44:   Technicolor Bloom.
Courtesy of FreelandBuck.

PLATE 45:   Lucien Pellat-Finet Shinsaibashi by Kengo Kuma & Associates. Courtesy of Daici Ano.

PLATE 46: Lucien Pellat-Finet Shinsaibashi by Kengo Kuma & Associates. Courtesy of Daici Ano.

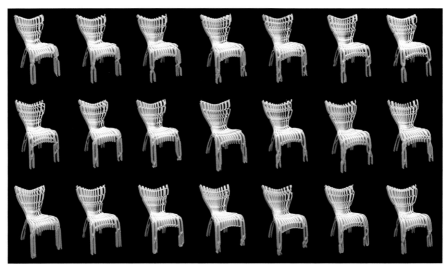

PLATE 47: CoReFab chair. Courtesy of Ammar Aloueini/AEDS.

PLATE 48: Cherry Blossom Collection, Spring/Summer 2007. Design by Atelier Manferdini Design Team: Elena Manferdini; Dorina Kastarti; Marisol Mejia; Photography: Robert Robert; Model: Lauren B @ FORD LA; Makeup: Samuel Paul; Hair: Tony Chavez (www.tonychavez.net) for Kerastase Paris Dear.

PLATE 49:   Curtains in a picture palace: the Piccadilly Cinema, Western Australia. Courtesy of Rob Chandler.

PLATE 50:   A new office window: online gaming in the 1990s. Courtesy of Love Krittaya.

PLATE 51: A city on screen: Antwerp Centraal Station. Courtesy of Ad Meskens.

PLATE 52: Owen Jones, *The Grammar of Ornament*, London, 1856.

PLATE 53: Frederick L. Trautmann, design exemplifying the system of projective ornament developed by Claude Bragdon, 1915. Claude Bragdon, *Projective Ornament*, Rochester, 1915: frontispiece.

PLATE 54: Miriam Schapiro and Sherry Brody, *Dollhouse*, wood and mixed media, 79 3/4 x 82 x 8 ½ inches, 1972. Smithsonian American Art Museum, museum purchase through the Gene Davis Memorial Fund.

The Poetic Language of Interior Materials and Colour   Photos by Imogen Moss , and George Verghese

The Poetic Language of Interior Materials and Colour   Photos by Imogen Moss , and George Verghese

PLATE 55: Visual Essay One. Courtesy of George Verghese and Imogen Moss.

PLATE 56: Visual Essay Two. Courtesy of George Verghese and Imogen Moss.

Visual Essay Three

The Poetic Language of Interior Materials and Colour   Photos by Imogen Moss, and George Verghese

PLATE 57: Visual Essay Three. Courtesy of George Verghese and Imogen Moss.

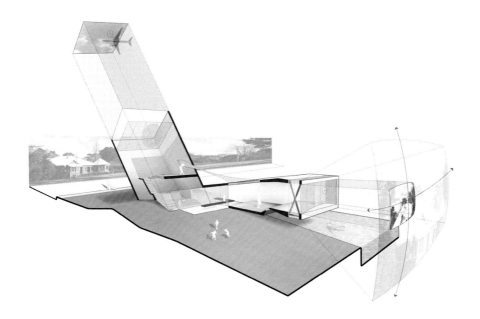

PLATE 58: Axonometric view of Mix House from the rear. Mix House was created by Joel Sanders Architect in collaboration with Karen Van Lengen/KVL and Ben Rubin/EAR Studio.

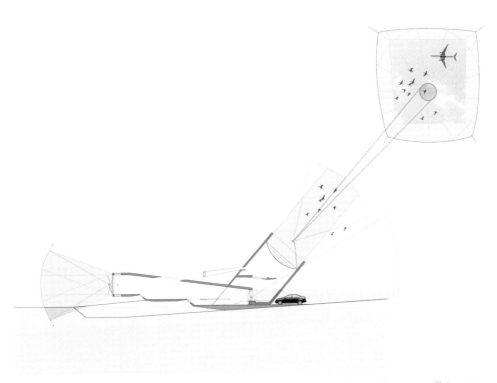

PLATE 59: Section of Mix House. Mix House was created by Joel Sanders Architect in collaboration with Karen Van Lengen/KVL and Ben Rubin/EAR Studio.

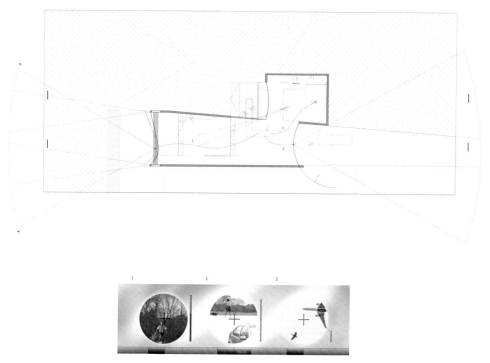

PLATE 60: Sectional plan and screen shot of Mix House demonstrating audio-targeting of environmental sounds. Mix House was created by Joel Sanders Architect in collaboration with Karen Van Lengen/KVL and Ben Rubin/EAR Studio.

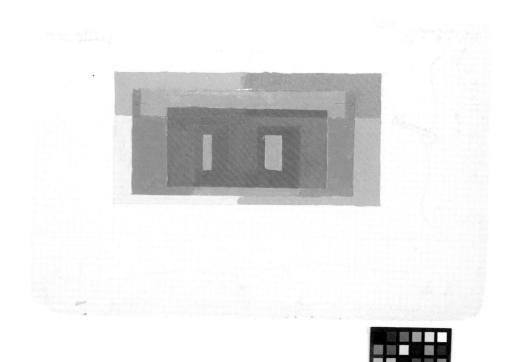

PLATE 61: Josef Albers, variant/adobe oil on blotting paper, c. 1947. The Josef and Anni Albers Foundation/ Artists Rights Society (ARS), New York.

PLATE 62:   Image from the film *Appalachian Spring*, produced by Nathan Kroll, 1958. Courtesy of The Criterion Collection.

PLATE 63:   Therme Vals spa exterior façade, architect Peter Zumthor, 1996. Courtesy of Jonathan Cantwell.

PLATE 64: Vibrating boundaries: XXII-2 illustration from *Interaction of Color* by Josef Albers. 2 studies of precisely the same arrangement, but with reversed colors. That the vibrating boundaries look different on both sides is probably the result of the changing color quantities of figure and ground. Courtesy of Yale University Press.

35

Ornament and Decoration

JONATHAN MASSEY

In the lobby of the Brooklyn Museum hangs a giant equestrian portrait in an elaborate gilt frame. Kehinde Wiley's *Napoleon Leading the Army over the Alps* (2005; Fig. 86) riffs on a celebrated painting by Jacques-Louis David that two centuries ago depicted General Bonaparte astride a rearing white steed on a rocky outcropping. In Wiley's canvas, the famous general has been replaced by a tattooed black man in camo jacket and cargo pants, Timberland boots, wristbands, and a bandana against a red background patterned with a gold floral motif. For the military uniform and decorations that marked Napoleon's high rank, Wiley substitutes the tattoos, street wear, and brand logos that serve as signs of distinction among the urban black men he most often paints. The background evokes damask or ornamental wallpaper (a specialty of eighteenth- and early nineteenth-century France, with roots in Renaissance wall-paintings), and in some places its motif occludes foreground figures, suggesting that the canvas itself is a kind of wallpaper decorating the walls of contemporary art collectors. The gilt frame, considered déclassé in today's art market, suggests a camp attitude toward forms of ornament that once conveyed importance through magnificence. Sperm wriggling across frame and canvas assert the masculinity of the portrait's subject, evoking the sexual braggadocio of gangster and hip-hop cultures even as they heighten the homoeroticism in this gay artist's paintings of working-class African American men.

By juxtaposing three ornamental codes—those of French high society circa 1800, contemporary urban black male culture, and today's institutionalized art world—Wiley's painting triggers our reflection on affinities, differences, and the disparities in status and power that accompany them. It reminds us that ornament makes things special. Ornament is a relational device that differentiates and associates things and people, frequently marking social status by signaling affiliations and distinctions. Ornament orders.

FIGURE 86   Kehinde Wiley, *Napoleon Leading the Army Over the Alps,* oil on canvas, 9 x 9 ft., 2005.
Copyright Kehinde Wiley. Used by permission.

We can recognize ornament in works from all times and places, but its nature and meanings change. Though frequently designed and conceptualized in ways specific to architecture and interior design, ornament is also used across boundaries of discipline and material—it is an arena in which these fields intersect with others such as the design of furniture, textiles, clothing, and jewelry. While *ornament* and *decoration* often have different meanings, with the former reserved for elements that clarify underlying form and the latter describing unrelated additions, or the former indicating socially meaningful elaboration and the latter designating less significant patterns, these distinctions are not stable or consistently observed. This chapter will focus on ornament in the Western tradition as a mode of elaboration that performs a socializing function.

Whether on clothing, furnishings, buildings, or even culinary dishes, ornament has often marked membership in particular grades and segments of society. It has distinguished sacred from profane, aristocrat from commoner, male from female, tribesman from stranger, high caste from low. In religious observance, and in buildings reserved for worship, ornament frequently indicates a believer's faith and denomination or sect. Concentrated on sites and instruments of particular liturgical significance, such as a church, synagogue, or mosque, or on an altar, ark, or mihrab, it can also mark degrees of closeness to divinity.

The differences marked by ornament are established not only stylistically but also through distinctions of material, finish, workmanship, size, scale, and position. A century ago, Columbia University professor A.D.F. Hamlin classified architectural ornament according to its way of covering space, the means of its production, the principles guiding its design, the object to which it is applied, and its relation to structure.[1] Each of these was further subdivided. Space-covering could be linear, allover, or radial, and each of these could in turn be continuous or discontinuous. Ornament could be produced by plastic or chromatic means. Its design principles could be conventional, naturalistic, or a hybrid, conventionalized-natural, which Hamlin further subdivided into the categories of regularization, abstraction, exaggeration, multiplication, and combination. Ornament could be applied to architecture or to objects of industrial production such as furnishings and clothing. Finally, it could be structural or applied, depending on whether it elaborated the structural and tectonic construction of an artifact or building or, conversely, was applied to the surface of its bearer independently of those factors. James Trilling recently outlined a classification system based on a series of dialectical concepts: movement versus stasis, grace versus strength, determinacy versus indeterminacy, comprehensibility versus complexity, stylization versus literalism, virtuosity versus truth to materials, application to versus integration with the object, convention versus innovation, the maker's versus the patron's imagination, and local tradition versus outside influence.[2]

Triglyph and metope, dentils and guttae; egg and dart, bead and reel, palmettes, anthemia, and rosettes—these and other elements of ancient Greek temple architecture claim pride of place in accounts of architectural ornament. The carved and painted entablatures and columns of antique temples constituted the orders of classical architecture (Fig. 87). Though conventionalized and significantly abstracted, these forms recalled the joints and construction details of the rustic wooden precursors built in sacred groves, as well as the sacrificial offerings hung on tree limbs and timber frames.[3] Doric, Ionic, and Corinthian, they expressed a temple's character and status through proportion and ornamental configuration. Vitruvius, the Roman author of the only architecture treatise surviving from antiquity, outlined the principles of decorum, whereby ornament—encompassing the order, the details of moldings, and figural motifs from mythology, history, or military observance—conveyed a building's purpose, status, and character.[4]

In Western societies from the Renaissance to the nineteenth century, ornament was largely based on reinterpreting the classical legacy of ancient Greece and Rome. Classicism constituted a lingua franca used across nearly every field of design, from the fine

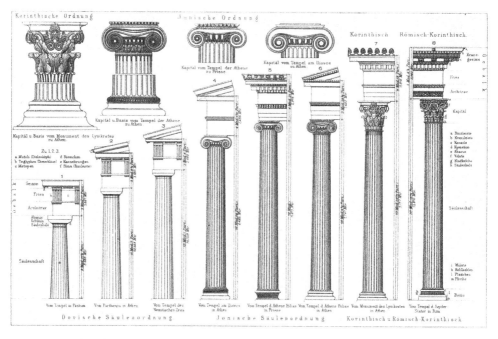

FIGURE 87 The classical orders as illustrated in Meyers kleines Konversations-Lexicon, Vienna, 1892–1893.

arts of painting and sculpture to architecture and printmaking to the crafting of furniture, dishware, and other housewares.[5] Prints and picture frames, vases and tables, building exteriors and interiors alike were ornamented with motifs such as the Roman candelabrum ornament, pilaster motifs, and moldings based on the architecture, art, and decoration of antiquity. In interior design, as in furniture and architecture, this classical system was valued in part for its modularity and formal systematicity, which made it a useful way to proportion and subdivide an object or surface, be it a piece of furniture, a baluster or mantelpiece, a wall, a room, a building, or an ensemble of buildings. Whether in stone, wood, plaster, metal, or paint, moldings based on those familiar from ancient temples disguised constructive joints, filled blank spaces, and established hierarchies of importance.

During this period, the economic surpluses generated by trade were often channeled into luxury goods. For these items, ornament of classical derivation served to mark status and signify elite taste. While fidelity to ancient models and their Renaissance emulation in northern Italy was an index of cosmopolitan sophistication—and can be used to reconstruct the routes along witch goods, ideas, and fashions traveled—these classical forms were always fused and transformed through the encounter with local styles, aesthetics, materials, and methods.[6]

In caste societies, ornament frequently marked hereditary rank or caste status, as when ancient Romans reserved the color purple for use by the emperor. Attitudes toward luxury found expression in sumptuary laws that at various times regulated what individuals could wear and eat, what kinds of furnishings they could possess, how they could conduct funerals and weddings, and what kinds of ornament they could use.[7] Ornament played a key role in the representation of power within early modern court societies, where it marked an individual's standing with a minutely graded prestige economy. Ornamental magnificence displayed the position of its bearer along a scale that ran from commoner to king. Architectural ornament was one among many facets of self-presentation that included laws and unwritten codes regulating the use of ornament in dress, dishware, coaches, and domestic furnishings such as cabinets and draperies.[8] In absolutist France, this representational system was codified through the architectural doctrine of *convenance*, usually translated as appropriateness and addressing concerns similar to those that Vitruvius treated when he discussed decorum. Treatise writers such as Philibert de l'Orme, Pierre Le Muet, and Michel de Frémin instructed architects on the proper use of the orders and other marks of architectural distinction to accurately represent the client's status, ensuring that the design of houses conformed to the ranked display of prestige that articulated power in court society.[9]

In parallel, however, some designers used ornament in a lighter mode characterized by worldliness, gallantry, and playfulness—values associated with a noble culture distinct from the bombastic and monumentalizing baroque décor favored by the royal court. In seventeenth-century grotesques and in eighteenth-century rococo compositions by Gilles-Marie Oppenord and Juste-Aurèle Meissonnier, for instance, ornament and interior decoration expressed a worldly noble sensibility marked by its aesthetic of wit, play, and pleasure (Fig. 88).[10]

In modernity, ornament began to take on new meanings as industrialization and political liberalization changed the nature of power, political authority, and taste. With the rise of large, imperial nation-states, mercantilist economists and social thinkers such as Adam Smith redefined luxury not as a necessary marker of status but as a category of expenditure with implications for individual economies and national prosperity. In both France and the United States, revolutionaries and republicans often rejected the sumptuous ornament of the old regimes, whether Bourbon or Georgian. And while richly ornamented architecture and interiors enjoyed a renewed life during the nineteenth century, eventually industrialization and the rise of the middle class led to the twentieth-century embrace of utility and restraint, with a concomitant decline in the taste for traditional luxury and the use of ornament. In the class societies that emerged from modernization, ornament often served as an instrument of what Thorstein Veblen called "invidious distinction," marking degrees of wealth rather than hereditary caste membership.[11]

As industrialization generated new wealth, artisanal workshops began to increase the scale and speed of their production, even before their own work integrated factory production. In mid-eighteenth century London the Adam Brothers established a system for expediting the creation of moldings and other wall and ceiling decorations. By creating a library of patterns and molds, their firm standardized detailing. This saved time and money in design, since draftsmen could specify motifs without having always to draw them out, as well as in construction, since these standard designs could be reproduced in

Cabinet de M.^r le Comte Bielénski Grand Marechal de la Couronne de Pologne executé en 1734
A Paris chés Huquier rue St Jacque au coin de celle des Mathurins CPR.

FIGURE 88 Juste-Aurèle Meissonnier, fireplace surround and wall treatment for Count Bielenski, Grand Marshal of Poland, 1734: engraving by Pierre Chenu, ca. 1745.

FIGURE 89   Robert Adam, drawing of door, fixture, and furnishing designs for the first floor of
Derby House, 26 Grosvenor Square, London, 1774.

plaster at the workshop for installation at the building site rather than being laboriously
carved or molded in situ by skilled craftsmen (Fig. 89).

By the mid-nineteenth century this kind of repetitive artisanal production had expanded into mass production of ornament and ornamented objects in the factory.

The casting, stamping, and tooling technologies of the new factory system turned out ornamental reproductions in cast iron, tin, plaster, and other materials (Fig. 90). Cornices, moldings, door and window frames, banisters, statuary, fountains, and other ornamental features were produced in quantity and sold in catalogues by the foot or the by the pound. Nailed up, like the pressed tin wall and ceiling panels in old restaurant and store interiors, or bolted together to create the iron fronts of mercantile districts, these mass-produced ornamental forms were often painted to emulate traditional materials such as limestone, marble, gold.

The extent to which industrial production had transformed the fabrication and social meaning of ornament became clear in the Great Exhibition of the Works of All Nations, the first of the major world's fairs, staged in London in 1851. Exhibitors showed manufactured goods of all description bearing ornament in many different styles. Owen Jones, the exhibition's superintendent of works, described and systematized this range of ornamental languages in *The Grammar of Ornament* (1856), an influential treatise that included Egyptian, Assyrian, Greek, and Roman ornament alongside less familiar pattern-languages such as the "Moresque," "Persian," "Indian," and "Hindoo" (Plate 52). This reflected not only the expansive geography of British colonialism but also the relativism introduced by archeological research and historicist thinking.

Beginning with the drawings of antique monuments published by Julien-David Le Roy in 1758 and by James Stuart and Nicholas Revett from 1762, the idea of classicism as a singular, ideal, and universal canon gave way to a recognition that classical designs had varied over time and space.[12] As archeologists documented not only the varieties of classicism but also an increasing number of the world's design traditions beyond Europe, they expanded the repertory of models available to contemporary artists, artisans, architects, and designers. Johann Gottfried Herder's philosophy of historicism, which presented art and architecture as facets of cultures rooted in particular times and places, fostered a growing attention to the historicity of particular styles and ornamental canons. Designers began to associate particular traditions with the values and characteristics attributed to the societies that had created them.

In the United Kingdom, architect and interior designer A.W.N. Pugin and critic John Ruskin successively promoted the revival of Gothic architecture, art, design, and handicraft as a way to reaffirm Christian values and preindustrial social order. Appalled by the Great Exhibition and its giant iron-and-glass Crystal Palace, Ruskin affirmed the value of handcrafted naturalistic ornament as an expression of integrated humanist creativity, Christian devotion to the beauty of God's creation, and the long time of tradition in the face of a rapidly accelerating modernity. Debates over the role ornament and the arts and crafts should play in an industrializing era gave rise to a design reform movement that made ornament an instrument of social and economic policy. Educational reformer and Great Exhibition commissioner Henry Cole introduced new design pedagogies through a series of societies and institutions, including the department of science and art at Britain's Board of Trade and the South Kensington (later Victoria and Albert) Museum. In the British and U.S. Arts and Crafts movements, the Vienna Secession, the German and Austrian Werkbunds, and

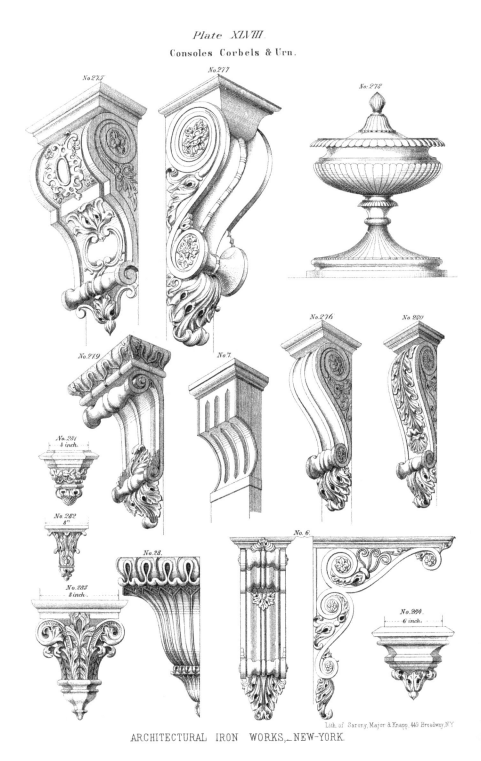

FIGURE 90 Mass-produced architectural ornaments illustrated in a plate from Daniel D. Badger, *Badger's Illustrated Catalogue of Cast-Iron Architecture*, New York, 1865

the Bauhaus, other "bureaucrats of beauty" likewise made ornament a lever for reforming the industrial system and modern society.[13]

Ornament and style also organized and articulated imperialism. British officers in India, for instance, synthesized Gothic and Mughal architectures in order to legitimize the hierarchies of imperial society. Colonial administrators developed a culture of ornamentalism that gave visual, tactile, and ceremonial expression to imperial hierarchy, order, and rank, while Cole's department of science and art restructured craft production of textiles and other goods, making South Asian ornament an instrument and figure of uneven development.[14] Early twentieth-century architects in South Africa, Australia, and other commonwealth colonies and dominions incorporated ornament based on regional flora and fauna—even sometimes on motifs from indigenous precolonial monuments—into classical and modernist buildings.[15]

This period from the mid-nineteenth century to World War I saw the intensive investigation of ornament as a topic of empirical, historical, and theoretical research, and a framework for experimental design production.[16] European designers employed exotic ornamental motifs and styles with increasing frequency as they developed a functional eclecticism rooted in the search for ways to communicate the growing array of modern institutions and programs. In Europe and the United States, the latter half of the nineteenth century was marked by a profusion of revivals sometimes romanticized as a battle of the styles.

European scholars, critics, architects, and designers studied the world's ornamental traditions for insight into how art functions and acquires meaning. Applying methods modeled on those of the natural sciences (especially biology) and linguistics, they sought in exotic and archaic ornamental motifs the basis for new theories of style and its development. French monument restorer Eugene-Emmanuel Viollet-le-Duc and German architect Gottfried Semper were among the theorists who analyzed ornament to derive comprehensive theories of architectural form that deeply informed architectural practice. The lessons that these artists, architects, designers, and art historians drew from ornament suggested strategies for resolving some of the new material, constructional, and pictorial problems of modernity.[17]

Ornament also became a medium for the cultivation of personal taste and aesthetic subjectivity on the part of designers and their clients. In redecorating the London dining room where one of his patrons kept a collection of Chinese blue-and-white porcelain, the painter James McNeill Whistler created a sumptuous interior that fused English medieval interior decoration with motifs from the art of China and Japan. Painted and gilt ornament complemented a society portrait and pictorial decoration to make Harmony in Blue and Gold: The Peacock Room (1876–1877; Fig. 91) a three-dimensional expression of Whistler's distinctive artistic persona. Others in the aesthetic movement projected subjectivity through ornament, as did the artists, architects, and designers of *l'art nouveau,* the transnational design movement that flourished from the 1890s to WWI. Whiplash lines and conventionalized nature motifs in the work of Hector Guimard, Victor Horta, Louis Comfort Tiffany, and others evoked vines, tendrils, and the vital energies coursing through living things (Fig. 92).

FIGURE 91   James McNeill Whistler, Harmony in Blue and Gold: The Peacock Room (1876–1877): north wall featuring *La Princesse du pays de la porcelaine,* photographed in Charles Lang Freer's Detroit home by George Swain, 1908. Charles Lang Freer Papers, Freer Gallery of Art and Arthur M. Sackler Gallery Archives, Smithsonian Institution, Washington DC. Gift of the Estate of Charles Lang Freer.

The artists of the affiliated Vienna Secession, including Josef Hoffmann and Joseph Maria Olbrich, revived baroque synthesis of the arts in compositions whose ornament integrated architecture with interior design, furnishing, and decorative art. In their work, characteristic ornament became a way to assert the generative capacity of individual subjectivity against industrial society's crystalline and geometric objectivity.[18] Seeing the architect as a poet-artist translating nature into architecture through the filter of a fecund imagination, their U.S. counterpart Louis Sullivan pursued similar goals. By animating the inert geometry of building masses with organic ornament, he aspired to master the inorganic and objective realities of industrial corporate society through the power of intense subjectivity. In some of his designs, Sullivan seems to have tested the capacity of ornament to serve as a site for working out formal ordering systems that could be scaled up to the urban or even territorial scale.[19]

A successor movement to *l'art nouveau* emerged from the Exposition Internationale des Arts Décoratifs et Industriels Modernes, held in Paris in 1925. A bid by France to sustain the leading role it had held in the eighteenth and nineteenth centuries as a maker of luxury goods that epitomized good taste, the exposition launched the *style moderne,*

FIGURE 92   Victor Horta, Hôtel Tassel, Brussels, 1893–1894: stair hall.

more often today characterized as Art Deco. Art Deco textiles, ceramics, furniture, jewelry, architecture, and interior design employed ornament extensively, combining figural sculpture with abstract geometric decoration and ornament based on conventionalized plants and flowers. Ornamented wallpapers, furnishings, and interiors such as those by French designer Émile-Jacques Ruhlmann represented opulent good taste from the mid-1920s through the Great Depression.

Modernists rejected the modes of ornamentation prevalent through the nineteenth century and found new ways for architecture and design to perform the relational work formerly done by ornament. Modernizers intent on promoting efficiency, productivity, and middle-class values associated ornament negatively with luxury, excess, and waste. Disparaged and disavowed, ornament came to be seen as a marker of time wasted, of times gone by, of being behind the times. As it regulated time, modernist discourse on ornament also policed social boundaries: of class, of race and ethnicity, of gender and sexuality. Ornament remained a site for working through the processes and implications of modernization and globalization.

By inaugurating an economy of imitation, mass production undermined the traditional role of ornament as a luxury item marking status and wealth. A rapid expansion in its use diluted its prestige power as ornament became devalued. Gilt finishes became shorthand for hollow pretension, inauthentic magnificence, kitsch. In *Style-Architecture and Building-Art* (1902), German architect and government minister Hermann Muthesius railed against the aristocratic pretensions of the middle class, which produced a sham culture manifest especially in the taste for rich ornament. Muthesius characterized the modern lack of decoration as a quintessentially middle-class trait to be celebrated for its rejection of aristocratic pomp and representation of status. In "Ornament and Crime" and other polemical essays, Vienna architect Adolf Loos campaigned to strip the ornament from language, from dress, and from dwelling.[20] "I have freed mankind from superfluous ornament," he bragged. "'Ornament' was once the synonym for 'beauty.' Today, thanks to my life's work, it is a synonym for 'inferior.'"[21] Espousing a middle-class ethos of functionalism, economic rationality, impersonality, and restraint, modernists redirected investment from luxury expenditures to factories, sanitary facilities, and municipal infrastructures. In place of individual expression they advocated standardized solutions, naked structures, white walls, and crisp geometric forms.

This shift in attitude drew in part from changes in theoretical conceptions of ornament.[22] With the rise of structural rationalism in France, ornament came to be seen as opposed not to poverty or low status (as in court society) but to structure.[23] The parallel redefinition of architecture as an art of space through empathy theory led architects to see ornament as superfluous and distracting.[24] For Marxist critics and cultural conservatives, ornament became a figure of mythical premodern wholeness that could only be ideological and mystifying in a disenchanted, rationalized modernity.[25] Weimar critic Siegfried Kracauer found in such quotidian pattern-making as rhythmic gymnastics a form of "mass ornament": an aesthetic reworking of industrial production logics that represented both regressive and progressive potentials in mass society.[26]

Modernist architects and designers sublimated ornament into industrial and aesthetic terms. Ornament's role of providing visual pleasure and making distinctions came to be fulfilled not by carved or gilt forms but by the grain of planed wood, the veining of stone veneer, the shine of chrome, the tint and reflectivity of glass, and the flatness and whiteness of paint.[27] This shift, evident already in the buildings of Loos, matured in the work of Ludwig Mies van der Rohe, whose Barcelona Pavilion (1928) employed smooth and polished industrial materials to satisfy the honorific requirements of a royal reception hall and model a new kind of sumptuousness.

When Le Corbusier proclaimed that "modern decorative art is not decorated," the seeming paradox manifested the rise of the aesthetic attitude, which privileged seemingly disinterested appreciation of formal and visual qualities.[28] But aesthetic disinterest, like the appreciation of magnificence in court society, served as a ruse for power, now recoded in liberal terms.[29] In a kind of culture war epitomized by Loos's essay "Ornament and Crime," many modernists stigmatized ornament by associating it with women, gay or effeminate men, the working class, and "savages" or colonized people.[30] The preoccupation with ornament in modernist discourse often reflected the exploitation of social differences to claim and assert authority on the part of a masculinist European elite.

Through the 1920s, the productivist ethos characteristic of European modernists had little impact on the ways architects and designers conceived and practiced modern architecture in the United States, where the modernization advocated by their European counterparts was already far advanced. U.S. architects committed to progressive social reform more often sought to invest ornament with new meanings so it could help their society negotiate the social tensions associated with immigration, industrialization, and increasing class stratification. Frank Lloyd Wright used conventionalization to abstract botanical forms into constituent geometries, which he made the basis for both planning and ornamentation in Prairie Style buildings and interiors. Wright's contemporary Claude Bragdon created "projective ornament," a system for generating geometric patterns and decorative motifs intended as a universal design language to replace the historical and national styles (Plate 53). While these U.S. progressives shared with European modernists the goal of changing modern society's patterns of consumption and representation, they reinvented ornament rather than eliminating or sublimating it.[31]

In the 1930s European modernism began to acquire momentum among U.S. elites, and attitudes toward ornament changed. When construction intensified following World War II international style modernism became the predominant language of authority and good taste in the United States as in Europe and many other parts of the world.

From the late 1960s into the 1980s, postmodernists revalorized ornament in terms shaped by modernist abstraction, pop art, and popular culture.[32] U.S. architects were particularly influential. Inspired by commercial signage and pop culture imagery, Robert Venturi and Denise Scott Brown developed an iconographic postmodernism in which ornament evoked historical precursors ranging from antique, Renaissance, and baroque classicism through nineteenth-century eclecticism to 1920s modernism. In the Piazza d'Italia (New Orleans, 1975–1977) and other commissions, Charles Moore used imaginative pop-inflected ornament to create scenographic compositions that celebrated poor taste and kitsch through exaggeration, stylization, and arch quotation. Michael Graves abstracted the classical language semi-ironically in buildings, interiors, furniture, and housewares, including the Portland Building (Portland, Oregon, 1982).

Although many critics decried postmodernism for its commercialism and nostalgia, postmodernist ornament also gave voice to sensibilities that had been marginal to canonical modernism, as when it conveyed a camp attitude associated with gay men or desublimated sexual identities that had been tacit in late modernism.[33] For U.S. artists in the pattern and decoration movement, ornament was a vehicle for aesthetic pleasures rooted in everyday crafts, techniques traditionally associated with women, such as weaving, and non-Western forms of art and culture. "It's a big world," observed the painter Robert Kushner, "look at your grandmother's quilt, look at the carpet you've been standing on, look at that ornament outside your building, look at what's happening in other countries... Enjoy it."[34] When Miriam Schapiro and Sherry Brody created the sculpture *Dollhouse* (1972; Plate 54), they used wallpaper, miniature furnishings, bits of lace and towel, and other decorative items to constitute a parlor, kitchen, boudoir, seraglio, nursery, and artist's studio that foregrounded the possibilities and limitations of agency for women in twentieth-century American modernity.

Postmodernism waned by the end of the 1980s, but beginning about a decade later neomodernist architects and designers gave ornament a new currency.[35] While a few experimented with retro-postmodernism, most explored the decorative dimension of pattern using the tools of parametric design and CAD-CAM milling.[36] Practitioners etched geometric patterns into facades, punched them through rain-screens, and tessellated them onto tiled walls. They modeled repetitive or self-similar patterns in 3D software, then output them using lasers, water-jets, CNC mills, and robotic assembly arms to give interior and exterior surfaces a range of new textures, visual qualities, and environmental capabilities. Reinterpreted in terms of contemporary techniques and aesthetics, ornament emerged as a tool for addressing varied audiences, augmenting building performance, and achieving novel structural and constructional effects.

In some of these projects, including department stores and retail establishments for luxury vendors such as Louis Vuitton and Christian Dior, ornament evoked brand identity in order to stimulate consumption. In others, designers collaborated with artists, graphic designers, and media specialists to create ornamented building surfaces that integrate architecture with visual and popular culture. Wallpaper made a comeback, with inexpensive on-demand printing enabling designers to create custom wall-coverings even for small jobs. Inspired by complexity theory and enabled by developments in digital technology, some architects and designers displaced the modernist opposition between structure and ornament. Innovative structural approaches and production techniques yielded intricate systems employing redundancy, pattern, and scalar homology to regulate the structural, constructional, and aesthetic performance of buildings. On the articulate surfaces of buildings by Herzog & de Meuron, Foreign Office Architects, and Atelier Hitoshi Abe, digital design, manufacturing, and engineering made ornament a territory of constructional innovation and interdisciplinary exchange.[37]

As in the past, much of this early twenty-first century ornament takes nature as its model. Drawing on complexity theory, crystallography, and bioinformatics, contemporary architects and designers update the long tradition of legitimating architecture by analogy with nature. In doing so, their designs frequently echo the art of previous eras. The artistic synthesis that marked the baroque and *l'art nouveau* recurs in projects by Reiser Umemoto and Ruy Klein, while Michael Hansmeyer's "Subdivided Columns" (2010; Fig. 93) reimagine the classical orders in biomorphic forms that evoke Borromini, Victorian finials or chess pieces, and science fiction fantasies. Contemporary theorists have drawn on the philosophies of Gilles Deleuze, Peter Sloterdijk, and others to describe ornament as a means of shaping perception, emotion, and subjectivity through affective rather than signifying means, but the social and cultural meanings of this work remain to be determined.[38]

In parallel with these shifts in practice, the conceptual apparatus shaping modernist and postmodernist attitudes toward ornament is challenged by new theories of history that dispute the premise of a radical break differentiating modernity from previous eras. Since at least the mid-nineteenth century, Western concepts and practices of ornament have been bound up in the modernist idea of time as a linear progression. When Ruskin celebrated hand-carved stone ornament for the slowness of its creation, its longevity, and the extended looking required for its appreciation, he mobilized ornament as a bulwark against the accelerating changes associated with modernization. When secessionists

FIGURE 93   Michael Hansmeyer, *Sixth Order,* installation at Gwangju Design Biennale, 2011, featuring selections from the series "Subdivided Columns," 2010: installation photograph by Kyungsub Shin. Courtesy of Michael Hansmeyer.

proclaimed "To the time its art, to art its freedom" as justification for original ornament, they made the case by appealing to the principle of historical progression. So too did Loos, their chief antagonist, in describing ornament as a sign of wasted time and a marker of evolutionary lag. When postmodernists revived traditional ornament, they often did so in the mode of nostalgia, reaffirming the association of ornament with bygone time.

But what might ornament mean if we set aside the premise that there is only one time and that it moves ineluctably forward? Drawing on anthropological theories of time, historian of science Bruno Latour has challenged the narratives of disenchantment and scientific revolution that describe Western modernity. If we have never been modern, then the modernist conceptions of time, history, and evolution that so powerfully shaped the discourse and practice of ornament are myths.[39] If we reject modernist temporality in favor of polytemporality or the coexistence of multiple times, then we must reconsider the historicist analytic through which ornament has been theorized and practiced in the West for 200 years. The outcome could be a range of amodern ways to understand and design ornament.

36

The Poetic Language of Interior Materials and Color

GEORGE VERGHESE AND DIANNE SMITH

INTRODUCTION

Among the essentials needed to turn mere survival into the art of living, perhaps none are more important than wisdom and knowledge. In a certain sense, these two human aptitudes are almost indistinguishable from each other; in another sense they are polar opposites. Wisdom is a putting together, knowledge is the taking apart. Wisdom synthesizes and integrates, knowledge analyzes and differentiates.[1]

A common misunderstanding of the role of an interior designer is that he or she is charged with the task of assembling the elements, materials, and colors to support and enhance the intent of the design and the functions to be undertaken within an interior space. As a result, those who have itemized such elements in an attempt to educate designers toward this goal have provided information but little understanding about the art of designing an interior. While information is essential, it is not the whole story. Awareness of the individual bits and pieces, such as light, color, materials, furniture, and/or furnishings, will not necessarily culminate in an understanding of an interior. Rather, the way that we experience an interior or place is through the immediacy of ourselves because we (or others) are located or immersed in a particular situation or setting (including the interior).

Reductionist approaches to investigating or constructing interior environments, which simply assemble or disassemble the components, are likely to be limited in capturing what it is to be in a particular place for the occupant in question. By adopting an approach that recognizes that multiple paradigms operate simultaneously—the sensorial experience, the cognitive or thoughtful, evaluative experience, and the immediate confrontation or immersive experience—a more holistic understanding is facilitated.

A holistic understanding of the role of an interior design also challenges the ways designers are educated and the way practitioners go about the design of places using materials and color. Any contained space consists of material matter of some form that encompasses volume—and in turn, is also a place that has inherent affordances. As James Gibson[2] defines: "The affordance of the environment is what it offers the animal, what it provides or furnishes"; that is, "if a terrestrial surface is nearly horizontal…and sufficiently extended…and if its substance is rigid…then the surface *affords support*…It is stand-on-able…walk-on-able and run-over-able" relative to humans, if it is of appropriate size and strength. Interestingly, Gibson also points out that affordance is both an objective and subjective property in that it is both "a fact of the environment and a fact of behavior."[3]

An interior can also be described as both shelter—the taken for granted attribute—and storyteller, indicative of its potency as a nonverbal communicator; the two spatial descriptions that follow will help to demonstrate this interrelationship between tangible (shelter) and intangible factors (narrative and meaning) within an interior. First, imagine entering an interior of a farmhouse. The timber floor, the narrow, full-height windows, the large spreading verandahs dappled in light through the vines and lattice set the scene. A gentle breeze stirs the gauze curtain, yet the echo of your footstep reflects the high ceilings and hard finishes. Memorabilia on the old, highly polished furniture tell of the children and past events on the property. The contrast between the dim interior and the glare of the daylight creates a sense of enclosure, mystery, coolness, and serenity within. Glimpses of garden and the paddocks are framed at the end of the corridor where gumboots stand and hats hang by the backdoor. The reflection on the floorboards, the patterns of the textiles strewn around, and the smell emanating from the kitchen beyond all reflect an interior that is lived in and appropriated through the demands of life.

Second, imagine a civic building in the capital city. As a reflection of the corporate world, it is located towering above the existing office blocks and associated laneways and social spaces. The foyer connects seamlessly with the outside as you wander through the glass entry across the polished granite foyer. Minimal chairs are artistically placed in clusters—spaces within spaces. Color is restrained and strategic to assist with navigation and to complement the symbolic value of glass, metal, water, and stone that dominate the entry and beyond. The users move into and past the entry toward their destinations. There is little time to dawdle so close to the final destination. The sound of the lifts as they ferry people vertically punctuates the otherwise neutral venue. There are no clues to who occupies the upper levels, but there is a sense of the power and potential of the organizations within.

For those who occupy either of these interiors, there is a sense of familiarity, and the environment over time becomes an extension of who they are in relation to these various aspects of their lives. For the visitor or passerby, the environments represent what the designer wishes to reveal to us about the organization or the occupant—the tangible stimulates the intangible aspects through the emotive responses and meaning-making. The exact story is tainted by our own experiences now and previously. The places have developed an identity, an atmosphere, and a meaning as a result. As designers, we select and specify the components that are the context of the attributes developed and held through these varied interpretations and experiences.

However, in addition, it is important that designers understand how the selections foster a sense of identity and what factors affect their selection. They must comprehend that meaning and atmosphere are the keys to promoting a sense of place that will offer various types of experiences beyond the mere sensory experience, for an interior place can also offer cognitive, thoughtful, and evaluative experiences and/or immediate confrontational or immersive experiences.

EXPERIENCE AND INTERPRETATION

The feelings aroused by different qualities of light are difficult to speak about clearly, much less define, for light has no intellectual meaning even though it touches the depths of our being in every way. We are subjected to the temperaments of light around us, we respond directly to their glow and color, but it is almost impossible to make any sense of the way they move us, which can only be felt as an indistinct murmur of the soul, moving the unconscious without our knowledge.[4]

Our experience may be a reaction to the interpretation concerning a place, or we may initially develop our interpretation from our immediate experiences. Either process involves the firsthand encounter with a place's potential instantaneously (as prethought). We order our environment by the parts and by subgrouping elements together to become the actual place, with particular attributes that we relate to (positively or negatively). In addition, we bring to the immediate experience our awareness of rituals, habits, or cultural/subcultural understandings. That is, we contextualize the present within both our knowledge of the past and our understanding of the future. These three aspects of the environmentalexperience are informed by C.S. Peirce's definitions of the three universes (outlined later) that we use when making meaning.

An aspect of experiencing an interior is the intangible dimension of color. It is well-documented that color is not inherent in the object. Instead, color is created by the integration of light source, path, or medium through which light passes, the object's surface properties, the pathway or medium between the object and the observer's eye, as well as the characteristics and experiences of the interpreter. The color, therefore, is an experience, although it may be described as an entity or attribute of something. Colors, when alone, do have spatial dimensions, and yet a particular color's ability to appear to move forward, to retreat, to expand, or to contract can be challenged or altered dramatically by adjacent colors, the extent of each color, the level of contrast, and/or the opacity or reflectance of the surfaces involved.

To claim that a design for an environment will potentiate a consistent appearance, or even experience, is naïve. For a person to see or experience color, light and surface are required. To experience materials, we need form, color, and light. However, as the quality of the light changes, so does the color and the perceived qualities of the material. We conceive both as though they are somewhat static, when in fact, the appearance, quality, and ambience change with the person (observer and interpreter) and with time and motion.

So how can we bring knowledge to the process of designing with materials and color if everything is in flux? First, we can understand how the nature of people, due to their characteristics and context, are most likely to understand a setting or place. Second, we can gather insights into how people go about interpreting their surroundings, using theories drawn from philosophers such as Roman Jakobson and C.S. Peirce. Both theorists unpack the way people create meaning. In order to do this, we will now explore relevant concepts, theoretical positions, and strategies in relation to color and materials. Finally, we can explore the impact of various settings by taking a multidimensional perspective, thereby developing a sense of how people may experience such environmental combinations or settings. A visual essay, which captures the interplay of color, light, and material (and their changes temporarily and spatially) will demonstrate the interdependency of these three aspects in the creation and experience of place. Identity and mood are captured through these examples, as is the fine-grain interplay of these three elements.

A SENSE OF PLACE

If place-making is the essence of interior design and the assemblage of materials elicits greater responses than those that arise from our reactions to the parts, how does an interior designer develop the ability to communicate the larger picture of a sense of place? Place needs to be experienced through all the senses in a four-dimensional manner. It should also be noted that the end result of an interior designed space that offers meaning and a sense of place cannot be easily portrayed in text and two-dimensional imagery. Many creative individuals, especially authors and poets, have eloquently described space through visuals and text. When we delve deeper into the realm of communication through text, we naturally arrive at the domain of the writer and particularly the poet, who have a limited pallet of devices to construct their visions. The words that they use are the elements—their materials—that they work within their craft. Regardless of whether it is the poet who combines words in a sequence to portray imagery or a filmmaker who manipulates scenes with the tools of motion, imagery, words, and sounds or the spatial designer who juxtaposes material, light, and color to create place, all are using the core structure of their particular language. The creator has fused together elements to give us a richness that we can recall and that may be triggered by any singular piece, such as a phrase or a scene. Sir Ernst Gombrich remarks that what we perceive is "the product of past experiences and future expectations."[5] "Places are spaces that you can remember, that you can care about and make a part of your life."[6] It is the person in combination with the material that constitutes the place, which in turn generates the experience and meaning. A space is made up of many vignettes involving the juxtaposition of materials, where any material could be substituted with another from a bank of known materials. However, a sense of place is developed through the connections established between materials and the understanding that arises in response to these vignettes and to the whole. Vignettes are contingent on space and time. The attainment and refinement of visual literacy develops understanding and a sense of place.

Personal responses to the environment are not only triggered by the material outcome of the designers' intentions but also by the viewers' own cultural and personal understandings. These are developed through personal, subcultural, and societal codes, whereby certain color, surfaces, material items, and collective settings come to have a common meaning for a group, individually or through association. If we unpack this idea of common meaning further, we enter the study of semiotics. The relationship between environmental design and semiotics has been established by researchers, including Umberto Eco and Charles Jencks,[7] Roland Barthes, Geoffrey Broadbent, Mark Gottdeiner, Susann Vihma, Bruce Dougherty, and Dianne Smith. However, when we look at key theorists of semiotics in the late nineteenth century and twentieth century, Charles Pierce and Roman Jakobson are the most noteworthy. Pierce was noted for describing a process of meaning-making and semiosis, and his acknowledgement of the real or material world made it applicable to the study of aesthetics and experience.[8] Jakobson explored the relationship between poetry and linguistics and the processes of selection and combination, which are also applicable to the built environment. If design deals with both the poetry of space and with the need for clarity of systems, then both Jakobson and Pierce are essential reading to ground our understanding of the relationship of color, materiality, and light with the poetics of space. Their theories will be discussed in a later section.

POETICS

Place-making is the poetry of the built environment: it is this poetic expression of space that many have written about or have demonstrated through their handling of material within a context. The development of poetic interiors is not a reductionist process of addressing each consideration in isolation. Instead, there is a constant dialogue between the separate elements to achieve the totality of the end result. Poetics is defined by Anthony Antoniades in *Poetics of Architecture: Theory of Design* as the Greek verb "to make ... making of space, making of poetry through words, making of art";[9] he describes this process in three ways: making through contemplative thought; making through tradition (mimesis); and, making through arbitrary means. In addition to the act is the impact. Gaston Bachelard[10] states, "[The creative act] through the poem, through its exuberance, awakened new depths in us." Terrance Hawkes writes, "According to Shklovsky, the essential function of poetic art is to counteract the process of habituation encouraged by routine everyday modes of perception ... the poet thus aims to disrupt 'stock responses,' and generate a heightened awareness: to restructure our ordinary perception of 'reality,' so that we end by *seeing* the world instead of numbly recognizing it."[11] Roman Jakobson extends the means to such awakenings further: "so what is important in any poem, is not the poet's or the reader's attitude to reality, but the poet's attitude towards *language* which, when successfully communicated, 'wakes up' the reader, and makes him see the structure of his language and so that of his 'world,' anew."[12]

Ways of working with materials and their context can achieve this end. Although sample boards show material juxtaposition, it is the history behind and meaning embedded in these juxtapositions that give an interior its meaning. In the past, all material and color texts concerning interior spatial design described separate materials to give you knowledge of each one's properties. Typically, it is here that knowledge of technical properties, economic factors, sustainable issues, aesthetics factors and usability, intention and functional aspects of use, and cultural concerns were discussed. Although important for understanding how they will react under various conditions, these resources did not explore how users react to them. This chapter highlights the importance of bringing together elements in combination rather than separating them. A sense of place results from the relationship of user and environment.

The creation of the built environment and the creation of the poetic involve the act of making through contemplative thought, traditions, imagination, and even the arbitrary. These acts can cause disruption, raise awareness, or facilitate seeing the situation differently. For example, on a recent trip to Japan (as a foreigner), the following experience was captured.

The afternoon sky was grey—fused together with the concrete and aluminum architecture of the prefecture near Kyushu University. As I stepped inside the space in the mid-afternoon my immediate impression was that I had stepped not into a coffee shop, but into a space familiar to me, but one that I had not seen before—a place. The slate floor at the entrance served as an extended threshold that allowed for a momentary pause before proceeding up one step into the small but endless seating area. Light poured into the space from the entrance and from the two small side windows. The soft sound of jazz filtered through the warm air as the smell of wood and coffee mingled together. The entire space, enclosed but open, was constructed of wood, unfinished and blemished, with rough plaster walls. The counter gently curved up in the middle to form a crown. The menu was hand-made paper with the fine calligraphy of Japanese Kenji characters describing the coffee options. The quite conversations of an elderly Japanese lady broke the ritualistic sound of the hand-blended coffee being made by the one worker.[13]

THE ACT OF DESIGNING WITH COLOR AND MATERIALS

It is important for spatial designers to make many decisions about various factors that will affect the final outcome. All these decisions sit within the realm of three areas of consideration—impetus, appropriate language, and desired meaning. Each consideration will now be discussed in detail.

Consideration of Impetus

Most design outcomes begin with a request to make a change in a particular condition. Spatial design usually begins with a site and an idea. The site may be real or hypothetical, and the idea may be initiated by the designer, the client, and/or by society as a whole. In terms of materials and color, this discussion of impetus will focus largely on the relationship with the site.

Although not always site specific, all interior spaces respond to a site in some manner. The understanding of the impact of the site plays a vital part in our approach to materiality and color. As designers, we need to fully comprehend the nature of our role, as we are charged with working with a client who desires that we make spatial modifications within a built environment. Light will occupy the site and the designated space to some degree and in doing so will illuminate the materials that constitute the forms that occupy that space. Together, the forms, materials, and light provide the user with a sense of place through the viewing of the space in different atmospheric conditions, notably natural, artificial, or a combination of light. It is the interplay of light with these elements that allows the user to experience color. Lois Swirnoff states, "It might be useful to state as a principle that color arises in the environment as a visual response to the stimulus of light."[14] Peter Zumthor clearly outlines the subtle elements that allow a piece of architecture to be able to provide an atmosphere or a sense of place. He understands the importance of light and materiality and makes a clear connection between the client, process, and materials when he talks about creating atmospheric architectural spaces:

> To do it I would need someone to be the owner, so we could get together and arrange things—first in our heads, and then in the real world. And we would look and see how things reacted together. And we all know there would be a reaction. Materials react with one another and have their radiance, so that the material composition gives rise to something unique.[15]

Zumthor's statement clearly communicates how material juxtapositions give rise to a series of reactions. Spatial design aims to examine and facilitate the relationship of these reactions.

Consideration of Appropriate Language

The second set of decisions rests with the appropriateness of the elements selected to respond to the consideration of impetus. When choices are made about a particular element to be used, they are made with reference to the alternative elements and involve the simultaneous interrelationship between many elements, particularly adjacent ones. When understanding the whole, the structure of the material language must be appreciated. It can be said that any assemblage of elements can create an interior space. However, it is not just the environment—the contained and the container—that is developed by the designer but, in addition, the potential for meaning. Meaning, as envisaged by the designer or creator, is manifested in the development of a place and involves both the original intention and the creation of an appropriate means to convey that message to the audience. Traditionally, designers present their ideas to their clients through the use of concept boards, mood boards, and/or sample boards. These boards are representations of colors and surfaces and as such indicate materiality. The owners or clients, for the most part, want to define a point of difference in the marketplace, so they will look to designers to provide that difference for them. Ultimately, designers respond to this professional request through the manipulation of materials in relation to color and light and their allocation within the spatial environment.

Consideration of Desired Meaning

Finally, the consideration of desired meaning establishes something that is more than the sum of the parts and may lead to a sense of place. This is in recognition of the role of chance, synchronicity, and those aspects not initially considered. Larger social factors may play a part in the manifestation of this consideration. Cultural understandings and practices influence both collective memory and personal memories, and as these are or become engrained within the user, a sense of place or connectedness is developed. As a result, the collective characteristics of situations or settings come to have meaning as a whole. The environmental attributes or the tangible materiality of color and the materials (surface or structural) act as cues or signs.

THEORETICAL FRAMEWORKS TO EXPLAIN THE IMPACT OF COLOR AND MATERIALS AS PART OF THE EXPERIENCE OF AN ENVIRONMENT

Having delved into place and poetics, as mentioned previously, the second means by which we can bring knowledge to the process of designing with materials and color when both the elements and meaning are in flux is to draw on theories from philosophers for insights into how people go about interpreting their surroundings. Roman Jakobson and C.S. Peirce are invaluable to this discussion. Both theorists unpack the way people create meaning. This knowledge provides insights into how various settings impact on the ways people may experience environmental combinations or settings.

Roman Jakobson on the Poetical Structure of Language

Jakobson was a formalist who viewed linguistics as the general field of which poetry formed one part. He focused on the text rather than the author as the symbolists and romanticists had done. If we consider that any visual means of expression can be considered as a text, then the visual can be read by different types of audiences, each with different levels of visual literacy. Looking at the idea of an interior place as a visual text leads us to Jakobson's understanding that the structure of any text is built on the interplay of two opposing considerations—substitution and combination. Bothprose and poetry are typically structured, sequential text; in contrast spatial reading is nonlinear and not sequential. Although users enter the space with a cultural identity and read the space through their particular bias and understandings, they end up comprehending the space and, in the case of the more visually literate, reading the space through a series of vignettes. These vignettes are composed of a juxtaposition of light interacting with the material surfaces and color.

Jakobson developed two key notions in regard to the poetic use of language: the notion of polarities and the notion of equivalence. Jakobson's most influential insight into the poetic function of language is that it is a process of "equivalence" in which both the selective and combinative dimensions are drawn upon to merge. Jakobson's theories applied to language and not just poetry, as he set out, in a formalist manner, the "poeticalness" of language. He said that the "poetic function is not the sole function of verbal art, but only its dominant, determining function, whereas in all other verbal activities it acts as a subsidiary, accessory constituent."[16]

Jakobson's detailed analysis of speech disorders defined a relationship to the rhetorical devices of metaphor and metonymy. These are figures of equivalence in that they present a secondary element that has the same status as the main subject. Building on Ferdinand de Saussure's ideas of messages being constructed from the inventory of available words selected to be placed in combination with other words in contiguity, sequentially ordered, Jakobson developed a model of binary opposites. It is this model of substitution (verticality) and juxtaposition (horizontality) that has a clear relationship to spatial design.

"Metaphor, to apply Saussure's concepts, is generally 'associative' in character and exploits languages 'vertical' relations, where metonymy is generally 'syntagmatic' in character, and exploits language's horizontal relations."[17] Jakobson noted that these were binary opposites that formed the key to the structure of linguistics and could be further described as a dual process of combination and selection. When linguistic signs are formed, "the given utterance (message) is a combination of constituent parts (sentences, words, phonemes, etc.) selected from the repository of all possible constituent parts (code)."[18]

The visual and sensual world of interior design is a world of enclosures constructed from materials to deliver a message. Jakobson's ideas of a selection merging with combinations can be viewed in a microcosm; within this world, the idea of selection of a material to be juxtaposed with another material gives the potential for poeticalness to be achieved. The diagram of binary opposites and the concept of poetic equivalence established by Jakobson can aid in establishing strategies toward designing and understanding an interior. The relationship of Jakobson's communication model to the interior allows us to understand the roles of an interior designer regarding the design outcome in a more comprehensive manner. The interior is captured as both the container and the contained. It also indicates many elements in the act of communicating. As Terence Hawkes[19] describes, Jakobson's approach to his model stressed that it is not only the message that allows for clear communication, it is also the context, code, and means of context that allows for total communication.

C.S. Peirce and the Material World

The material world offers opportunities for the users to interpret and to express meaning. It also allows people to understand what needs to be done and how to behave. Therefore, designers can facilitate the process of meaning-making. C.S. Peirce was a philosopher and scientist who theorized how people interpret and therefore experience the world. In doing so, he provides us with a means to understand the impact of the world we design.

Importantly, a designer, through his or her designs, including the selection of materials, color, and lighting, establishes the potential offered by an environment for people to create meaning. Meaning is not inherent in either the objects or places but is bestowed upon individual objects or aspects of them and the entire place by the observer through interpretative processes. The interior environment typically consists of furniture and furnishings and is molded by light and color. A designer, while creating, will undergo the same process of interpretation. As noted above, the final creation is in response to the design intention. Habits of practice noted by Peirce can be applied to the profession of interior design. Designers have common ways of doing things and this realization can be just as much a cautionary note as a benefit. Due to professional pressure and discipline expertise, a "habit of mind," as Peirce describes it, may result.[20] We must take care not to see material selection and outcomes of combinations as formulaic. Living by rules is a habit embedded in us.[21]

Peirce proposed that a person encounters the world and, therefore in this case, the interior in three different states, which he called universes, relating to modes of existence—firstness, secondness, and thirdness.[22] Firstness is the unanalyzed encounter that occurs before we reflect on a situation. It relates to the environment's potential to be a wide range of things. Secondness moves from potential to the reality; it occurs through the effect of the environment on a person as a result of the way he or she interprets it and how he or she perceives the constituent parts of the environment in relation to one another. Thirdness involves decision-making in regard to meaning. As a result, it influences how we understand what behaviors are expected of us.

A setting, therefore, has its own characteristics or qualities. For example, a restaurant setting is perceived as representing a situation and what it will be like to experience what is there. As a result, the setting is a vehicle by which images or ideas about the world we are in are conveyed into our thoughts. We interpret this filtered impression of what is perceived, and this is our understanding of the environment or place. These three components (the object, the referent, and the interpretant) constitute Peirce's sign: all three aspects of the triad are required for something—idea or tangible object or place—to act as a sign. To be a sign, something stands for something for somebody.

Important to note, an object such as a wallpaper panel or an entire restaurant is never seen in its totality but is always experienced as a sign, in that it is a culmination of the representation of both the original and the projection or proposition. It is the proposition that leads to subsequent interpretations. In keeping with Peirce's theory, Christensen[23] states that from the way an object may show itself qualitatively, we recognize its behaviors and how we need to adjust.[24]

Our interpretation can be emotional, energetic, or logical.[25] That is, the place acting as a text can arouse emotion, provoke action, and can result in new habits such as ideologies or fashions. Peirce believed that not only is there a conceptual reality but also in the existence of the material world. These real objects have effects that lead to or reinforce beliefs. Through reflected inquiry, a sense of reality is reached; yet with continuing experience of a particular venue or of similar places, the belief is reinforced, so that when the next example is encountered, assumptions about it or the genre will be based on the belief at a particular time.

Things come to have meaning through use, both in experience and projected future use. "Purposive bearing"[26] means that the outcome is more than action, as the person bestows meaning in terms of the predicted outcome of the action. On encountering an interior, we project how we may use it subsequently and the atmosphere it will have during use. Then, through use, how the interior was interpreted as a sign will be reinforced or challenged through use. The interior, as discussed earlier, is a text, a visual composition. The initial meaning we give to the situation is a proposition. Therefore, we translate the visual to a conceptual sign system.

The implications of Peirce's theories are many when it comes to selecting materials and colors that will be constructed as an interior. For example, although experienced as a whole, not all aspects of the interior will play a role in meaning-making at any one time or across time. However, those aspects that are selected—including the material surfaces, furnishings, furniture, light sources, and colors—establish the potential for an array of meanings, and depending on the social and cultural context of the users and the designers, this may also vary in nature and scope. Importantly, the visual language of the setting will become part of the interpretative process that integrates a triad involving the material world, the conceptual world, and the resultant interpretant or outcome. This is in contrast to Saussure's dyad of signifier: signified. As John Fiske[27] explains, for Saussure, "Gold is a symbol of wealth, power and status; whereas for Peirce, gold is an index of wealth and a symbol of power."[28]Indexically wealth and gold are related, whereas power is conceptually and collectively considered to be related to gold in certain societies. The user's interpretation or understanding will influence how the interior is perceived and used, and the experience of the interior will be influenced by the consistency between the belief and the reality. Interestingly, the meaning arising for the designer related to his or her design intention may differ significantly for the user and/or client once encountered and in use. The creation of meaning is a compositional process because we place things in relation to others.[29]

VISUAL ESSAY

The following images reflect an analysis of a range of interiors through the framework of the works of Jacobson and C.S. Peirce. The above theoretical summaries are thereby captured by a series of visual essays collected through numerous research fieldtrips and projects. Although these are descriptive in themselves, it is recognized that in keeping with the concepts raised, the reader will bring his or her own understandings to the task as part of his or her meaning-making strategies. Three essays are included and these represent, as well as facilitate, the three universes introduced by Peirce. The interior genre selected is public spaces, particularly restaurants. In conjunction, Jacobson's principles can be identified and applied to each.

Essay 1 (Plate 55)

Firstness captures the raw material of the interior or quality of feeling[30] as it presents to the viewer. Within this state of mind, the interior exists in its unfiltered potential. It exists without reference to anything else; it simply exists. As it is without reason or compulsion, it is defined as feeling.[31] For example, redness is a property that is not greenness and still exists whether brilliant or dull. Peirce states we have an immediate acquaintance with firstness in the qualities of feelings and sensations. Things in the material world have potential that we conceive as part of the material; although we do not observe it directly, we believe it is a continuing reality. For example, iron's property of attracting metal distinguishes it from brass.[32] It is in firstness that the full implication of the material juxtapositions impact on the viewers and form an initial impression upon them. Jacobson's theories of language structure assist in understanding this process. The viewer is treated to a sensory portrayal of the impetus of consideration. The outcome of this impetus is an interior that is witnessed by all through the impact of light on or through the material, giving rise to form and color. Appropriateness of the material language is witnessed but not assessed.

Essay 2 (Plate 56)

Secondness is the result of two things being brought into a relationship. It is the idea about things that arise as a reaction. This involves "a sense of acting and being acted upon."[33] It is how we engage in the brute reality of the world independent of rules or laws. It is at this point that we start to read—at a level dependent on our level of visual literacy—the various vignettes of material juxtapositions to form an understanding of the space. Jacobson's insights into combinations and selections can inform such considerations applicable to the design process and experience of design. When we experience space at this level, we experience not what the designer is saying but the understanding of previous material and spatial relationships enlisted to aid us in using the space. It is here that the relationships of juxtaposed materials are considered from a memory of previous combinations.

Essay 3 (Plate 57)

Thirdness is the thinking or decision-making that brings the elements together in such a way that they have meaning for the interpreter. It is the idea or representation of the original phenomenon and involves reason, rules, or habits that influence how to behave in this type of situation. Going beyond mere consideration of the appropriate material juxtapositions, it is at this point that the consideration of desired meaning is achieved through the interpretation of the viewer.

CONCLUSION

The consideration of how to work with materials and color in relation to one another presents challenges for the twenty-first century designer because of the constant advances in color pigmentation, dye chemistry, and material and fabrication technologies. These advances will exponentially increase in the future. Therefore, a focus on understanding the experience of the interior through the integration of materials and color seems more applicable than ever for current practitioners. This is not to undervalue the importance of technical knowledge, including installation, maintenance, life cycles, impact on the environment, and historical and cultural significance. Rather, a need to understand the impact of materials in combination and in association with the site context is highlighted. As a result, the probability of a distinction between designer's and users' interpretations becomes evident. Consequently, the reliance on styles and fashion is challenged as it is shown that the design of an interior is simply the basis on which users build their own meanings, which in turn construct and influence their experience.

In order to explore this process, it is proposed that designers need to envisage the physical environment of the interior as a visual mode of communication. This work builds on the work of Amos Rapport's seminal work on nonvisual communication by the built environment.[34] By merging the work of semiologist Roman Jakobson and pragmaticist C.S. Peirce with the particulars of interior design and interior architecture, this concept is extended. That is, the impact of surfaces, structure, furnishings, and finishes, as they are expressed through materials and color within the context of light, are married to theoretical frameworks originating in philosophy and language.

Edward Casey[35] discusses the dominance of logic and language in the twentieth century and states that the formalist ideas of Jakobson played a part in obscuring ideas of place. However, this chapter discusses how to use Jakobson's ideas of structure to demonstrate relationships and in doing so shifts the emphasis away from a highly definitive stance. What has arisen is an awareness of the importance of the nonreductionist approach to interior design. As long as individual items are selected in terms of their inherent character and technical properties, two key aspects are undervalued. The first is the impact of selections and combination of materials or colors, as well as those selections involving either colors or materials in relation to one another and/or with lighting. Obviously the relation of color and/or materials to form and space are implicated. The second is how propositions, which are built from the experience of the total environment, will influence how a person names, envisages, and reacts to a setting—and potentially how a sense of place is fostered.

Peirce identified that meaning involves translation from one sign system to another[36] and that this process is continual.[37] In relation to interiors, the ideas that are conceptualized are translated by the designer into a new system of potential signs—the physical elements and their relationships. In relation to these, the users in turn translate what they experience into their own expectations, beliefs, and experiences. As a result, the interior is defined through use.

The potential of the environment to raise awareness through emphasis on the poetic dimension is critical. At a time of homogenization and economic rationalism, attention to this responsibility is a mandate for a designer. Jakobson's analysis of poetic equivalence foregrounds the potential of language when it is structured as a merger of two binary opposites. Every text has the poetical embedded within it, but to emphasize the metaphorical allows the text to be poetic. Therefore, the consideration of the appropriate language sits within the domain of the designer and if he or she has the poetic intent then the potential of the space is realized. The aim is to make poetry through the built environment and in particular the interior. This can only occur through attending to the combination and the interdependency of the elements in creating the particular space, which through its use and interrelationship with people comes to have meaning— ideally a positive experience.

37

Technology and the Interior

TREVOR KEEBLE

INTRODUCTION

In his 1923 polemic *Towards a New Architecture,* Le Corbusier first proposed the notion that "the house is a machine for living in."[1] This proposition was to become one of the single most emblematic statements of the modernist project and remained fundamental to the ethos of its author and his many followers around the world.

Towards a New Architecture sought to equate architecture with machinery. The book proposed that architecture should, like machinery, be governed by system, purpose, and function. Expanding upon his thesis, Le Corbusier offered his reader "The Manual of the Dwelling."[2] This short list of principles instructs the modern dweller how to live in the modern age. In terms of economy, cleanliness, and efficiency, Le Corbusier presented the modern home as having "the most up-to-date fittings" such as shower-baths, ventilating panes, and gymnastic appliances. Stating that the mechanics of the "gramophone, pianola or wireless" could interpret first-rate music as well as any orchestra, Le Corbusier informed his reader that they should "demand concealed or diffused lighting...demand a vacuum cleaner."[3]

Placing the future of architecture and domesticity firmly within the terms of machinery and technology, Le Corbusier recognized the need for the dweller to comprehend the modernity of his or her existence, arguing that "every modern man has the mechanical sense."[4] Contrasting the modern dweller with his or her parents, Le Corbusier challenges his reader to "Bear in mind economy in your actions, your household management and in your thoughts."[5] In his essay, "The Sociology of Space" of 1903, the German writer Georg Simmel proposed that a social boundary "is not a spatial fact with sociological consequences but a sociological fact that forms itself spatially."[6] While his particular position might well be contested, Simmel's work voices the mutually dependent nature of society and the space in which it exists and echoes in Le Corbusier's instructional advice to the modern man or woman to learn how to live in the modern house. Perhaps more

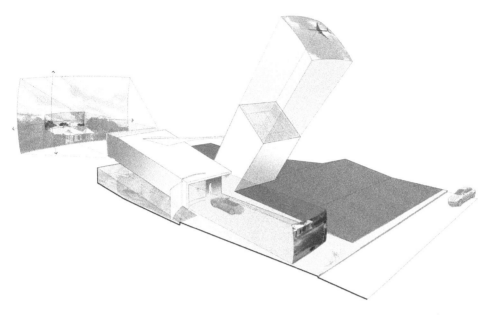

FIGURE 94   Axonometric view of Mix House seen from the front showing three sonic windows opening on to the garden, street, and sky. Mix House was created by Joel Sanders Architect in collaboration
with Karen Van Lengen/KVL and Ben Rubin/EAR Studio.

than any other of the modernist pioneers, Le Corbusier articulated his project as a physical, material, and visual manifestation and a conceptual, psychological, and behavioral
intervention. For Le Corbusier, his work was fundamentally about social and behavioral
change, and so it is not surprising therefore that technology as "the study or use of the
mechanical arts and applied sciences"[7] was so fundamental to his modernist project.

Throughout the history of humanity, technological change has been understood as
the key driver of social progress and the measure of human achievement. One might ask,
what form of creation is beyond the reach of technology? Whether it was the human
ability to harness the power of fire, fashion tools for himself or herself, or use the Earth's
resources to create things, technological innovation and change has always been the
register of progress. In his seminal essay *On Adam's House in Paradise,* Joseph Rykwert
stalked the mythological notion of the "primitive hut," which he argued had been fundamental to the critical discourse and understanding of architecture throughout history.[8] Initially drawing upon the writings of Le Corbusier, Frank Lloyd Wright, Mies
van der Rohe, and Adolf Loos, arguably the very authors of the modernist project, Rykwert proposed that in the builder of the primitive hut, these architects found an an-
cestor, "uncluttered by cultural baggage," for whom necessity and reason had been the
guiding lights.[9] Technology has always been characterized as rational, purposeful, and
functional, and in this sense what Rykwert's primitive hut offers is not just some mythical origin of the will to create architectural form but also a measure of just how far that
creative will has come. For Rykwert, the primitive hut offers a moment of purposeful
authenticity, which exists to fulfill some essential need.

Technology has long been implicated within the discussion of purpose and need, but as we well know from the consumerist perspective of the present century, needs are rarely essential or stable and can be created, satiated, and forgotten. This fact testifies to the role of humanity in the development, application, and design of technology and exposes the fact that all new technologies require willing consumers to use them. The flushable toilet, for example, is one form of technological innovation created long before it became commonly available. This was not due simply, however, to the constraints of availability but to a social and cultural willingness to accept such a device; the need for the moneyed people of the early nineteenth century to have a flushable toilet was simply not pressing while they had servants to remove their bodily waste in chamber pots.[10]

This chapter seeks to explore the relationship between technology, design, the interior, and its inhabitants in three sections. "Water, Heat, and Light" is concerned with the development of the interior as a technological infrastructure that mediates the relationship between the inhabitant and the outside world in pursuit of what are now thought of as basic human needs and comforts; "The Technological Interior" develops this discussion by considering the ways in which technological innovation through design creates both new types of interiors and new ways of experiencing and inhabiting them; and finally, "Technological Objects within the Interior" explores the ways technological objects and appliances have challenged and changed the design and experience of the interior. The chapter aims in no way to provide some exhaustive account of technological evolution but chooses instead to highlight some instances when technological innovation has changed both the interior and its inhabitants through design.

WATER, HEAT, AND LIGHT

Technological innovation has been the principal means by which physical comfort has been achieved throughout the history of architecture and interior design. This approach to comfort has historically been entirely dependent upon location and climate as the principal determinants of different types of need. In this sense, we might understand the essential needs of water, heat, and light to be some of the most fundamental design problems humanity has ever faced.

The harnessing and use of running water is a technology for which the Roman Empire has always been renowned, and the historical uses of water provide a very interesting case study through which to consider how technology fundamentally challenges and reinforces notions of public and private activity, the urban and the domestic space.

The location of Roman cities was often founded on the basis of geographic proximity to water, primarily freshwater rivers, and it is these rivers, along with captured rainwater, that provided water to the people. In time, however, the Roman's developed the technology to locate and draw from underground water sources and wells. This development was part of a much larger project to harness water in the service of agriculture and the construction of larger urban environments, a project that also developed the great brick aqueducts for which the Roman Empire is so famed.[11]

Initially the water was used in both civic and private buildings for its principal purposes of cooking, cleaning, and washing, and as the ruined city of Pompeii demonstrates, this clearly affected the layout and organization of buildings and interiors.[12] Most obviously, this meant that buildings were required to have purpose-built cisterns of varying size, but also it meant that a more systematic and constant supply of running water allowed the domestic spaces of the city to accommodate more easily some of those activities such as washing and bathing that until then had been done almost exclusively in public. This did not in any sense lessen the import of the public bath, which arguably served purposes far greater than those of washing, but it does offer an example of how technological development within interiors might alter the activities of those within them.

Perhaps the most innovative use of water by the Romans was, however, in the creation of a heating system known as the "hypocaust."[13] A forerunner of today's gas-fueled central heating system, the hypocaust was developed in the first century B.C. and used an underground furnace to heat water, which would be circulated in an entirely contained system that was networked throughout the building, thus providing the interiors with ambient heat. Hollow pillars and composite wall structures were redesigned to carry water throughout the building. This furnace would also heat the empty space of the hypocaust beneath the suspended floors of the structure, thus allowing warm air to seep through vents into rooms.

The effect of this system on interiors was both structural and experiential. The most striking innovation of the development was perhaps the way in which it removed the open furnace from the interior. Along with all other civilizations of its time, the Roman Empire continued to suffer the smoky side effects of open fires and hearths, but one of the key innovations of the hypocaust and its furnace was the way in which it used its hot but dirty by-product, smoke, as a means of clean radiant heat by expelling it through purpose-built cavities that ran the height of the interiors walls.[14]

In his study *The Invention of Comfort,* John E. Crowley has described some of the inherent problems posed by the open-hearth fires, which were typically used in buildings until the thirteenth century.[15] In rural dwellings throughout Europe, he argues, open fires were usually located in the center of large halls between facing doorways and windows from which they would draw air, and beneath shuttered smoke holes through which smoke would ideally be expelled. Offering an "unmediated relationship between heat and light," Crowley suggests this basic use of fire provided something of a baseline for the study of early modern comfort, demonstrating as it did the conflicting needs to keep the heat in while allowing the smoke out.[16] Needless to say, open hearth fires created a dim and smoky interior environment and, unguarded as they were, posed a very serious danger to anyone who got too close.

It was not until the thirteenth and fourteenth centuries that chimney fireplaces became common in Britain, and the spread and development of this mode of heating demonstrates very clearly the impact that technological change can have on interior spaces. Initially developed within the masonry architecture of castles, fireplaces with chimneys provided a concealed flue through which smoke escaped the interior. In so doing, the

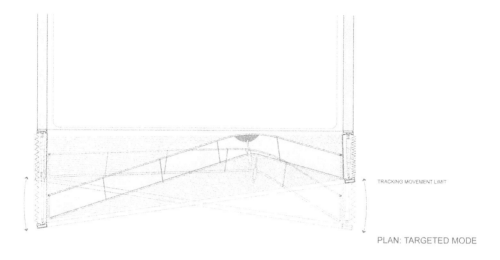

TRACKING MOVEMENT LIMIT

PLAN: TARGETED MODE

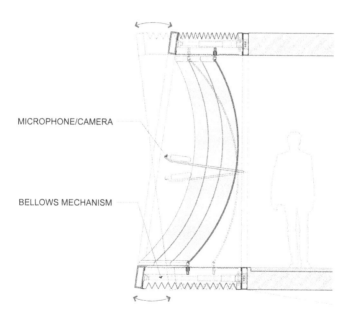

MICROPHONE/CAMERA

BELLOWS MECHANISM

FIGURE 95   Sonic window detail of Mix House. Mix House was created by Joel Sanders Architect in collaboration with Karen Van Lengen/KVL and Ben Rubin/EAR Studio.

fire was both physically removed from the center of the room to its wall and made considerably more controllable and regulated. This enabled the use of fireplaces beyond the great public rooms of a building and the proliferation of smaller closets and chambers.[17] There can be no doubt that this development served both to reorient and rearrange the space of the room and to offer a cleaner and more comfortable environment within it.

Technological innovation had the ability to quite fundamentally transform the experience of interior spaces of the past. One of the most common challenges to historic interiors was that posed by nightfall. As Witold Rybczynski has shown, although torches and crude oil lamps were used during the Middle Ages, until the eighteenth century candles provided the most common form of artificial light. These candles varied significantly in quality with the best beeswax being affordable by only the wealthiest in society. Most commonly used candles were made of tallow, hardened animal fat, which proved both smelly and irritating to the eyes when burnt.[18]

It was not until 1783 that a Swiss physicist named Ami Argand invented an oil-based lamp.[19] This lamp, essentially an oil bowl and meshed wick within a cylindrical glass shade, offered a more controlled and magnified flame. A fairly simple and easy article to produce, the Argand lamp proved extremely popular and was rapidly updated and imitated.[20] Kerosene lamps replaced these oil-based lamps during the late 1850s, although the most significant evolution in lighting technology at this time was an improved gaslight. Originally used in street lighting as early as the first decades of the nineteenth century, gas-fuelled lighting provided a variable quality of light accompanied by unpleasant and smelly fumes. Not surprisingly, its initial application within interiors was in public buildings, workshops, and factories, although it did become more commonly used in domestic interiors from the mid-nineteenth century, in spite of the fact it produced a considerable amount of soot, which blackened ceilings, furnishings, and textiles. Nevertheless, the desire for better artificial lighting evidently took priority over the demands of maintenance and cleaning.[21]

In Britain, the most significant and influential technological development in lighting came with the generation of electricity for sale during the 1880s. Used solely for artificial lighting, early commercial electricity supplies proved problematic due to the variability of demand. As Adrian Forty has demonstrated, the lulls and peaks in demand for artificial lighting according to the time of day meant its production proved very expensive.[22] This conundrum of uneven supply and demand is typical of technological innovation and change; new technological possibilities require further investment on the part of both producers and consumers before they become more widely viable. As a consequence, electricity suppliers sought to develop the demand for their product and focused upon its potential for heating and cooking. This led, in the first years of the twentieth century, to the rapid expansion of electric domestic appliances such as heaters, cookers, toasters, washing machines, and dishwashers.[23] Made in both Britain and America, these products became so pervasive that Forty has suggested that by 1914 almost every electrical appliance known today was available in some form.[24]

Of course in the twenty-first century, the provision of water, heat, and light within interiors has become one of the most pressing global concerns of our age. In the face of global warming, scientists, architects, designers, and householders have to find new ways to provide and use these utilities, and technology not surprisingly has been key to this. Yet, as the BedZED housing development in south London has shown, solutions can often be found in low-technology applications, reconsideration of materials use and application, and simple but strategic spatial arrangement. Comprising 100 homes, workspaces, and community facilities, BedZED was designed with the aim of reducing water consumption by 33 percent, power consumption by 60 percent, and space heating needs by 90 percent.[25] Just as the designers and builders of the Roman and medieval ages had to find ways to introduce water, heat, and light into their interiors, the designers of the twenty-first century have had to redesign the often wasteful and environmentally damaging technologies of the industrial and postindustrial centuries. By arranging buildings so that large triple-glazed, argon-filled windows facilitate passive solar gain and purpose-built sunspaces could be used to regulate the internal climate, BedZED demonstrates the importance that careful design plays in the use of technologies. Combined with a (300 mm/11.8 inches) layer of insulation applied to roofs, walls, and floors, this design meant that the ambient heat gained from human activity, lights, appliances, and hot water provided all necessary environmental heating.[26] By understanding the building and interior as a holistic entity of interrelated spaces, materials, and technologies, BedZed demonstrates the importance of strategic and technological application in the cause of environmental sustainability.

The long history of technological innovation within the infrastructure of the interior is largely a story of the interior becoming connected and eventually networked with the public realm of provision and supply. This is most obviously the case with those utilities that in the twenty-first century we understand as absolute necessities: electricity, gas, clean water, sewage disposal. The impact of these developments, among others, has been to fundamentally transform the expectations and understandings of both interior spaces and our physical, bodily interaction with them. Within the interior, the technological development of heating supply and appliances, of double-glazing and cavity wall insulation has without doubt changed the experience of what it is to feel hot or cold.

THE TECHNOLOGICAL INTERIOR

There can be no doubt that the technological innovation of materials and building processes has been a fundamental driver of progress within the design and construction of interiors, and while those material processes such as the manufacture of glazing developed progressively over many decades and centuries, it was during the industrial years of the nineteenth century that technology came to bear so fundamentally upon the creation of new types of interiors.

The most magnificent and new of these was undoubtedly the huge structure of the Great Exhibition of 1851, popularly known as the Crystal Palace. Located in London's Hyde Park, the vast exhibition structure was erected on site in less than eighteen months. This was due entirely to the standardized and prefabricated nature of its design and construction. Designed by Joseph Paxton, formerly in the service of the Duke of Devonshire, the skeletal iron-and-glass structure of the Crystal Palace manifested something of an outsized successor to the botanic glasshouses Paxton had designed for the Duke at Chatsworth.[27]

While Paxton's achievement was undoubtedly one of scale, his technological innovation was to design the building as standardized, interchangeable elements. By reducing the number of different elements of the building, whether these were the upright cast-iron mullions or the thousands of identical panes of glass, Paxton's design allowed rapid and systematic construction. Designing the building in what might best be understood today as kit-form allowed all of the pieces to be prefabricated to his specification off-site. Reducing the fabric of the building to just a cast-iron frame, sheets of glass, and wooden galleried flooring, this temporary structure achieved vast spans reminiscent of a medieval cathedral in its creation of interior space. Defined entirely by glazed walls, this interior offered its inhabitants unprecedented flexibility of creation and arrangement within.

The Crystal Palace was not, however, the first building to employ new cast-iron technologies in its construction. J. B. Bunning's City of London Coal Exchange (1847–1849) and Labrouste's Bibliotheque Sainte-Geneveieve in Paris (1843–1850) both used iron to great effect in their interiors. What is perhaps notable, however, in contrast to the Crystal Palace, is that these iron interiors where encased by neo-Renaissance stone facades and architectures.[28] This duality of interior and exterior testifies to the culturally ambiguous nature of industrial processes and materials that was current during the mid-nineteenth century and is most evident in the great brick-fronted iron

FIGURE 96   Interior view of Mix House showing the kitchen where the synchronized sights and sounds of the surrounding landscape are activated and arranged. Mix House was created by Joel Sanders Architect in collaboration with Karen Van Lengen/KVL and Ben Rubin/EAR Studio.

railway stations such as St Pancras and Paddington in London and the Venetian façade and iron structure of the National Museum and Art Gallery in Edinburgh.[29]

The notion of the standardized and interchangeable 'unit' has long preoccupied the ideas and intentions of architects and interior designers alike, and none more so than the continental modernists of the interwar years. Le Corbusier's aforementioned notion of the house as a machine for living in eventually evolved into the starkly incremental Domino House, a model arrangement designed for single or multiple productions. These ideals were made manifest by Walter Gropius and his colleagues when they designed and built the Dessau-Törten Estate between 1926 and 1928. This estate of 316 one-family dwelling units provided Gropius and his team with the opportunity to test out the mass production of architecture through the systematic construction of a largely standardized model dwelling, which it replicated.[30]

A significant aspect of this work was the way in which the component design of the housing units was integrated into the systematic process of their construction. The houses were designed not just for the purposes of dwelling but also for the purpose of their own manufacture. This interest in the systematic process of building and its impact upon design was fundamental to the discourses of the emergent modern movement and was made even more explicit in the Steel House also designed at the Bauhaus by George Muche and Richard Paulick in 1926. Prefabricated entirely from steel plate, the Steel House was designed as a flexible "type-house" that might be erected in days rather than weeks and that provided an organic flexibility for additions as and when inhabitants' needs changed.[31]

This polemical emphasis upon the role of new technologies in the fabrication and manufacture of new buildings, interiors, and furnishings was very heavily influenced by the rapidly developing manufacturing industries in the United States, where the early years of the twentieth century witnessed the development of scientific management. Pioneered by Frederick Winslow Taylor, who published *Principles of Scientific Management* in 1911, scientific management sought to apply the rational processes of scientific observation to the spatial arrangement and organization of the industrial workplace. Based on numerous observational time-and-motion studies, *Principles of Scientific Management* demonstrated the ways in which patterns of work and labor might be organized more efficiently, thus increasing productivity. So influential was this work that eventually it became known colloquially as Taylorism, and it played a prominent role in the rapid development of American manufacturing and mass production during the first half of the twentieth century, most notably in its influence upon Henry Ford's development of the moving production line, which from 1914 produced the Model T Ford motor car.[32]

Not surprisingly, Taylor's principles soon found application within the domestic interior through the writings and publications of Christina Frederick and Lillian Gilbreth among others.[33] These home Taylorists or household engineers concentrated upon the kitchen as the space in which most domestic production was undertaken and sought to demonstrate how a well-designed and well-arranged kitchen would improve efficiency while reducing labor in the home. With a focus entirely upon efficiency and utility, their plans for the modern scientific kitchen left little room for decoration and aesthetics and often invoked comparison with the laboratory.[34] The influence of this thinking was significant in the development of the fitted kitchen, which would subsequently become the overwhelmingly dominant model of kitchen design throughout the developed world. It is perhaps worth noting, however, that this particular application of scientific or technological principle came at a point of social change when the modern homes of the early years of the twentieth century were becoming increasingly without servants, and the inhabitants of the home were also its workers.

Whether in the workplace or the home, the emphasis of scientific management was upon the interaction of the human body and its environment, thus making it particularly important for interior design. Its methods and thinking proved highly influential to the design and manufacturing industries during the mid-twentieth century, and this encouraged further study into physical and environmental interaction. Known variously as human engineering, biotechnics, and, most commonly, ergonomics or anthropometrics, the human form was studied extensively so as to provide an overarching and rational explanation of its movement among spaces and things. As Jonathan Woodham has demonstrated, this work was taken up significantly by professional designers, and prescriptive books of analysis and models such as *Designing for People* by Henry Dreyfuss (1955) and *The Bathroom Book* by Alexander Kira (1966) became widely used and valued.[35]

The application of technological principal to the construction and arrangement of the interior has clearly influenced and shaped the physical experience of those spaces. However, technology has also been used to enhance and control the visual experience of interior space. The most famous and widely discussed early example of such an application of visual technology is the panopticon, a model prison designed by Jeremy Bentham in 1787. Designed on a circular plan, the panopticon placed the prisoner's cells on the periphery of the building and the guard's watchtower at its center. Through a number of devices such as venetian blinds, partitions, and strategically placed doors, the design maintained total vision by the guard while ensuring that he himself could never be seen. The French philosopher Michel Foucault has argued that this arrangement disassociated the relationship between seeing and being seen: "In the peripheric ring, one is totally seen, without ever seeing; in the central tower, one sees everything without ever being seen."[36]

The example of the panopticon is important because of the way it uses surveillance as a means to establish control, authority, and power within the interior. In the twenty-first century, this is achieved through extensive use of the closed-circuit television (CCTV). The widespread use of the CCTV has fundamentally challenged the concept of privacy within contemporary society, and the digital revolution has enabled and extended its use. Now, surveillance technologies proliferate in the name of security, but this development has arguably eroded social practices and conditions of trust, safety, and security; grainy images of missing children in shopping centers or hooded figures in tube stations intent on carnage almost serve to reinforce the need for such surveillance without actually changing the outcome of those unhappy surveyed events. This anxiety underpins the increasingly common practice of working parents being able to log on to CCTV to survey the spaces of their children's nurseries, and nursery workers.

FIGURE 97 Visual and audio activity as targeted from Mix House. Mix House was created by Joel Sanders Architect in collaboration with Karen Van Lengen/KVL and Ben Rubin/EAR Studio.

Few could have imagined the technological advances that have come as a consequence of the digital revolution, but the imagining of possibilities is arguably what designers of all kinds have in common, and the imagining of possible futures has informed the design of buildings and interiors since the days of Rykwert's primitive hut. The Mix House by Joel Sanders, Ben Rubin, and Karen van Lengen is a design project that sits on the cusp of innovation.[37]

The design explores the audiovisual experience of the domestic landscape. Arguing that the visual sense of the world has dominated human experience, the project's architects propose an environment where cutting-edge technology draws together the visual and audio so as to reengage these two principal human senses. Designed around two spatial volumes, each with a large, curved sonic window, the house presents a dynamic interior that engages the world beyond its walls (Figs. 94, 96, 98, and 99). Set into the windows are a small microphone and video camera, which are controlled on screens by the inhabitant so as to focus upon specific sounds such as planes or songbirds (Figs. 95 and 97). Set it as per style. The design also provides the opportunity not to control the technology and allow ambient sounds to come into the rooms in the way ambient images might be fleetingly glimpsed while passing a window. The design of the Mix House offers a perceptual challenge to both the inhabitant and designer of the interior. It suggests that technology may enable sound to inform interior design in the way that the visual has for so long.

TECHNOLOGICAL OBJECTS WITHIN THE INTERIOR

The use and deployment of technology within the interior has posed one of the most significant opportunities and challenges for the designer. One might even go so far as to say that it was precisely the need to integrate technology within our lives that brought about the profession of industrial product design.

As the industrial revolution continued to change and form the developing societies of the later nineteenth century, the manufacture and production of consumable things became the focus of industrial effort. Often attempting simply to mechanize existing processes and activities, this age of invention developed technology on a human and domestic scale. A number of writers have demonstrated how problematic the integration of technology within the domestic sphere was during the nineteenth century.[38] Given the widely held perception of the middle-class home as a private space, away from the worlds of work, industry, and commerce, mechanical objects and devices proved challenging to the domestic sensibilities of homeliness, comfort, and decoration.

One early object of mass production that proved particularly difficult within the domestic setting typifies the ways in which technology was required to be assimilated within the home. Sewing machines were available for domestic consumption from the beginning of the early 1850s. Manufactured in the United States and Britain by a number of firms including Wilcox & Gibbs, Wheeler & Wilson, and Singer, the sewing machine was essentially a mechanized tool created for the clothing industry. These manufacturers clearly understood the domestic potential for such machines, which were both affordable and easily useable within the home. At first, however, domestic consumers seemed reluctant to purchase these industrial mechanisms, and manufacturers realized the need to fundamentally differentiate those machines of the workplace from those made for the home. They did this by decorating and ornamenting the domestic machines so that they might blend more fully into the domestic setting. As Adrian Forty has shown, the domestic value of sewing machines became rapidly apparent to the householders, and the need to beautify them diminished as they became more readily accepted.[39] What this example demonstrates, however, is the need for domestic technologies to be designed and made consumable, perhaps especially when those technologies had no mechanized precedent within the home.

Of course not all domestic technologies and appliances were necessarily on show. The late nineteenth-century saw the rise of a number of large manufacturers associated with the new domestic technology of electricity. These included the General Electric Company (GEC) formed in 1892 and the Westinghouse Electric Company formed in 1886. GEC and Westinghouse realized that the opportunity for domestic electric technology lay primarily in creating objects to do domestic production and work such as cooking and the heating of water. These ambitions were, however, limited by problems with the networked supply of electricity to homes, mentioned already in this chapter.

By the second decade of the twentieth-century, consumer durable goods were being developed and manufactured extensively and were becoming increasingly available to affluent consumers in Europe and the United States. Design, however, was not much of a consideration in their creation. Much like the original sewing machines of the previous century, these devices and appliances were essentially pragmatic objects determined entirely by their purpose. They introduced to the home new materials such as plastic, itself a product of technological innovation, and this served only to heighten their disruptive sense of modernity and newness.

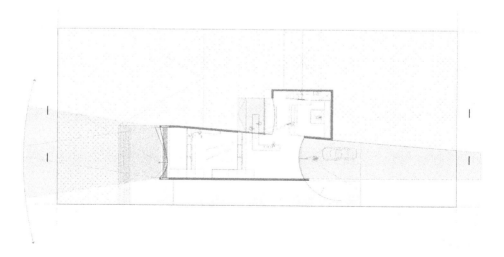

FIGURE 98 Visual and audio activity as targeted from Mix House Mix House was created by Joel Sanders Architect in collaboration with Karen Van Lengen/KVL and Ben Rubin/EAR Studio.

Increased competition between producers and a widening market for domestic goods eventually forced manufacturers to embrace design. A number of design historians have shown that in these early years of consumer capitalism, industrial or product design as it was subsequently to become known was not a defined area of specialization.[40] This being the case, manufacturers turned to people in the graphic and commercial arts who possessed the visual awareness and skills to characterize objects and to provide them with distinctive identity. The iconic pioneers of industrial design such as Raymond Loewy, Norman Bel Geddes, and Walter Dorwin Teague began their careers working in the commercial worlds of window design, fashion illustration, portrait painting, and advertising art. In turning their attentions to consumer objects, these designers not only advanced the role of technology within the interior but also provided it with a modern aesthetic.

The most celebrated examples of early designed products are perhaps the radio and the refrigerator. Having no real technological precedent other than perhaps musical boxes and gramophones, the radio presented a uniquely modern challenge, which a number of writers have explored.[41] Essentially just a collection of technical components such as wires and valves, the radio required an aesthetic character that both ameliorated the complexity of its technology and offered an appropriate visual contribution to the interior. As Adrian Forty has shown, initial designs took the form of radio cabinets, which were made of wooden veneers and took their inspiration from furniture. While these cabinets could to some extent express the modern styling of their day, they were essentially designed to blend in. In Britain it was not until the early 1930s that manufacturers began to commission modern designs that used modern materials such as Bakelite plastic, and the radio took on a distinctive character of its own, one that expressed the modernity of its technological innovation.

The refrigerator had a more solid precedent in the ice or cool box, which had been used in one form or another for several centuries. Defined by their function, these objects were transformed by the possibility of electricity and rapidly became an essential item, both in public and private spaces. The historical interest in the design of the refrigerator stems largely from the way in which it was designed into fashionability. During the 1930s, U.S. manufacturers such as Coldspot, Sunbeam, Maytag, and Hoover all presented iconic white refrigerators made of aluminum and chrome. These monolithic objects had more in common with streamlined automobiles than with other consumer durable goods, and like those automobiles they became objects of aspiration and status, and importantly they were subject to fashion change.

The refrigerator and the automobile may have shared an aesthetic styling and iconography during the 1930s, but they were objects aimed at very different consumers. Technology and the representation of technology have been fundamental to socially constructed notions of gender, and the car and refrigerator are perhaps emblematic of this. Commonly understood as a feature of rational, masculine thinking, technology has too often been understood in contrast to more feminine notions of artistry, decoration, and aesthetics. Paradoxically, the emergent role of technology within the domestic interior of the early twentieth century and the consumerist need for it to be styled and aestheticized served to both challenge and reaffirm this perception. In addition to this, the fact that the overwhelming majority of domestic labor-saving technologies were aimed specifically at the housewife has only added complexity to this understanding, even though it has been widely argued that the increased expectations and focus upon housework that these appliances created in fact increased her work.[42]

While designers and manufacturers addressed the perceived need for labor-saving technologies with vacuum cleaners, cooking appliances, and washing machines, the basic needs of housework were to some extent fixed. This is not to suggest, however, that the quest for better-performing technologies has not driven innovation and technological development, but by the mid-twentieth century all aspects of domestic labor had found some technological response. It is not surprising then that designers and manufacturers turned their attentions more fully toward technologies of leisure.

While the radio posed one of the first design challenges for domestic technology, it was the mass-consumption of television that had the most profound effect upon the space and inhabitation of the domestic interior. The rise of TV during the 1950s has commonly been understood to have reoriented the traditionally hearth-centered family away from one another and into a passive engagement with the rapidly expanding broadcast media. This perceived atomization of the family by technology was furthered in later decades due to the proliferation and personalization of entertainment technologies. No longer were televisions, videos, and music systems confined simply to the family living room. Instead, increased competition and affordability meant these consumer

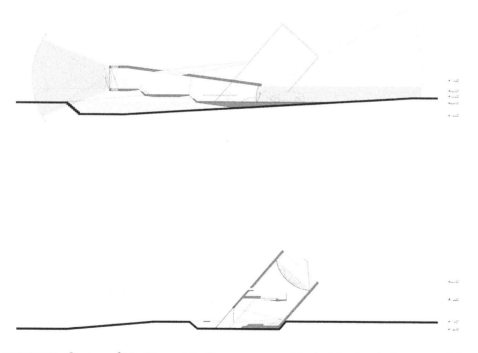

FIGURE 99   Sections of Mix House. Mix House was created by Joel Sanders Architect in collaboration with Karen Van Lengen/KVL and Ben Rubin/EAR Studio.

goods could be found throughout the house, and most primarily within children's bedrooms, thus further undermining familial collectivity.

Few could have predicted the extent to which the digital revolution would further personalize technologies. The development of the personal computer and home gaming console technologies, often associated with teenagers, have arguably hastened the retreat into the private space of the bedroom. At the heart of this development is a paradox: on the one hand, these technologies articulate the need for private spaces, but, on the other, they facilitate an engagement with the wider public world beyond the interior, an engagement that challenges all previous understandings of privacy. In an online world, where people can write messages to one another on their walls, we find the Facebook generation to have created fundamentally new ways in which to reinscribe and reengage physical spaces through technology.

CONCLUSION

At every stage of technological evolution, design has been required to mediate its innovation, novelty, and newness. Whether this mediation has taken the form of "The Manual of the Dwelling" or an aspirational future-gazing design for the *House of the Future*,[43] people have always required designers to show them the images, possibilities, and meanings of technology. These meanings, so often defined by notions of progress and evolution, have the power to show how life might be lived. Yet to many, such possibility comes as a challenge or a threat. Within the context of the interior, a space arguably defined by its physical proximity to the human body, technology has the ability to both comfort and disconcert its inhabitant. Whether through the relatively low technologies of heating, plumbing, and lighting and the purposeful and principled spatial arrangement of interiors or the more spectacular innovations of wireless connectivity and digital environments, the engagement of technology and humanity is possibly one of the most challenging and thrilling opportunities for the designer.

38

Phenomenology and the Senses in Interiors

CHRISTINE CANTWELL

These hours that with gentle work did frame
The lovely gaze where every eye doth dwell

—William Shakespeare, Sonnet V

THE HEURISTIC SKETCH MODEL AS A
LOCATION FOR SENSE AWARENESS

The notion of atmospheric conditions of the interior brings to mind vaporous attributes of air and water as much as the physical character of space. If water is symbolic of emotion, it makes sense to probe the emotional and poetic structure of the interior in its still plastic forms, when the designer is relating directly with the spatial qualities of an interior design proposal on paper or in three-dimensional sketches. The relational field between the structural and the ephemeral at play in interiors is engaged in the language of interior design—architectural drawing, three-dimensional scale model building, and images. All are informed by the visual arts and require the sensitivity and discipline of artists' visual-spatial sensibilities.

Materials, scale, desire, beauty, program, site are functions incorporated and modified in the synthesis of space by the manipulation of essential design elements. Essentials of interiors such as colors, acoustics, and light[1] carry qualitative and emotional weight in the perception and creation of interior space. Even in advance of conceptualizing a project, the designer knows that every decision made in the execution of a constructed work has a trajectory that eventually engages another person's subjective response to space. Ephemeral elements such as color or light acting on the body can be measured by scientific methods, but their antediluvian affect is measured more naturally with the precision that the senses gauge phenomena, and art. Literature as a case in point describes color, sound, and light as poetic, even mystical modalities that give expression to architecture and design because they are vehicles of the perception that buildings are light catchers, color is symbolic of nature, and materials vibrate with sound oscillation, memory, and life. Gaston Bachelard, whose phenomenological topics were wider ranging than the philosophy of science for which he was employed at the Sorbonne, wrote about the interior and things, amplifying the resonance that spaces and objects have with designer-as-artists' preoccupations. "The Poetics of Space," published in 1959, is a classic in the literature of interior design. The essay "The House from Cellar to Garret the Significance of the Hut" is a treatise on enclosure, intimacy, and complexity of the interior. A double meaning of interior—referring both to the room and the psychoanalytic reality within a person's psyche—is amplified. In Bachelard interior is rendered as a complex construction incorporating interior as space and as metaphor for the inner universe of the occupant of the space. Thus, the houses of dreams and memory are turned over like a stone and studied with the thoroughness of a naturalist and the mind of a literate. Bachelard created a repository of the concrete and ephemeral topologies of houses and rendered the topological conditions in language that enable the visualization of decorated, inhabited space with sensate qualities that reach below the surface. Bachelard attributes the house with being the primal site of dreaming and therefore of the emergence of image. Image is the language of the archetypal. Phenomenology literature observes intersections of the pragmatic logic of the senses with its wisdom of the body on the one hand and the logic of dream and its intuitive wisdom on the other. As they collide, a rich ground of the philosophical meeting the psychological is traversed. Phenomenology, the branch of philosophy that is pertinaciously interested in phenomena and structures of consciousness that pay attention to them, offers interiors the affirmation that each aspect of the interior can be regarded with intention to capture and clarify its detailed significance. Interior design handles the emergence of image and the particularity of its interest in detail (as it directly communicates with the body) in ways that are embedded in drawing and making such as three-dimensional scale-model sketching (also motivated by physical movement), instead of words.

Despite the high level of responsibility that interior designers have for the surfaces of things in projects, the work that designers do is not superficial. For the designer who understands architecture and engineering of structure and senses the body in space, practice is as much about intentionally constellating the reverse: engineering the environment that forms body-space by manipulating materials and light and having intuitive but reliable responses to the structural built environment. Perceiving and reflecting upon what is revealed by the making of the heuristic sketch model is a reflection upon an unreflected experience[2]—standing in for the future project. Here the interior design scale model provides the chance for a transcendental spark that leaps into the latent design idea. Existential phenomenology identifies the transcendental (by its nature a radical state) as an aspect of consciousness. In doing so, philosophy confers legitimacy on aspects of thought process repressed by rationality and embraced by practitioners engaged in synthesis and invention. Radical consciousness seeks the essential as much as it is a departure from common-sense patterns in everyday routines or an interruption in the rational methods of scientific thought pondering the structure of reality. The engaged architect of the interior relies on an ability to think abstractly and rigorously in three-dimensional sketch models—or in abstractions created by the application of high-performance computation that aids the visualization of space—in conjunction with a poetic, emotional contemplation of reality that depends on the senses to imagine the body in physical space. The creation of the built world depends on the integral interaction of these two disparate and oppositional thought forms—as design thinking in order to be materialized. In each new project that designers face, the intercourse of the rational (that knows the structure of reality at a constructed distance from self) and the physical (that knows the body in its intimate, self-motivated details and motions) is ratified.

EXISTENTIAL PHENOMENOLOGY

The essay "Cezanne's Doubt" by Maurice Merleau-Ponty lays out the significance of genius as it directly enters the unknown, not only the personal unknown but also the territory of unknown knowledge. Although artists have historically been ephemeralized and marginalized as possessing inborn talent, in fact the arts fields have acquired bodies of knowledge that have been gained or seized by practitioners who dedicate themselves to opening up ways of seeing. Seeing as insight and as collection of visual information is the basis for reorganizing thought forms that allow the arts and design to develop new aesthetic ideologies. For designers who read Merleau-Ponty's essay, there can be identification with the painter Cezanne as a genius who has provided the perceptual underpinnings of their own design work. He has articulated recognizable aspects of this to them and in so doing declared a reality and intelligence at work—in Cezanne's case, nurtured by compulsion and obsession[3]—but a logical reality nonetheless. A depiction of the *bardo* state—a term of Tibetan Buddhism that identifies a condition often thought of as the void between death and becoming that also exists in the construction of art—is articulated by the philosopher (but not named as such). Cezanne's perceptual breakthroughs were interspersed with voids, periods of not knowing or even madness as he discovered the behaviors of color in nature and portrayed the visible directly from the sensations of seeing and an intuitive mind of invention, not indirectly from thought. "We have to develop an optics," said Cezanne, "by which I mean a logical vision—that is, one with no element of the absurd."[4]

Cezanne's pursuit of looking at color and light directly in painting—even though color and light are habitually perceived with the peripheral vision associated with spontaneous perception—made possible the practice of optics that paved the way for the work of Josef Albers on the interaction of color and ultimately for other insights of modernism pertinent to interior design practice. Cezanne's discoveries about color at the edges of things was a small move, but painting as a condition of his insight took up his whole mind and life work and changed the world of knowledge about seeing. In the essay, Merleau-Ponty rendered Cezanne's purposefulness so that an appreciation of intentionality as critical to the understanding of abstract visual relationships and color as a structural element in painting was identified and broadened such that intentionality is also laid down and incorporated as a tenet of existential philosophy. His portrayal in effect rescued Cezanne's position in art history from the dismissal that his more conventional contemporaries inflicted upon him. Cezanne's doubt about what he was seeing and his pursuit of gazing into transitory, unreliable phenomena through insecure states of mind probing as-yet-unseen knowledge would later be described and studied by the Harvard cognitive psychologist Howard Gardner in his studies of multiple intelligence and genius.[5] If there was no legacy through direct knowledge of Cezanne by Josef Albers, it would not have mattered because in the narrative of perception, once something has been found to be true—like the activity of oscillating color relationships at the edge of form—it's emergence makes its way to the collective, not as digested, dry knowledge but as that theoretical basis from which optical experience can be discovered for one's self.

The primacy of perception[6] was already present in the formative Bauhaus preliminary course before Josef Albers directed it, and before Merleau-Ponty wrote about it. "Self-experience and self-knowledge"[7] were embedded in the course goals as a means of recognizing the necessity of allowing the creative abilities of the students. The Bauhaus school was grounded in a concept of apprenticeship "for the design experimentation or research on artistic and technical fundamentals."[8] Through mandatory construction of objects and spaces, perception belonged to the individual, and knowledge to the social collective. Notions of collaboration based on apprentice and workshop models from earlier forms of design production in Europe were integral to the discipline of the Bauhaus itself. Albers's progressive educational values emphasized the cultivation of engagement with social principles as discrete from but not less important than the artist's individual responsibility to develop, personally and aesthetically.[9] Through the rest of the twentieth century, for distinguished architects and designers this pedagogical concept and the brief existence of the Bauhaus in Weimar and Dessau was the center of gravity of modernism. It's rigor came from the very strong emphasis on doing. Invention was thought to kindle creative energies. Experimentation with materials and color was meant to awaken the optic and haptic senses with as much intensity as Cezanne mobilized in his painting. The perceptual foundation for what has evolved into contemporary forms of collaboration that utilize high-speed integrated design technologies and visualizing techniques—was in the last century, materials-based and touchable. Now, despite the distance introduced by nonphysical forms of communication and thinking, philosophically speaking the mandate for intellectual depth, imagination, and integral thinking that was concurrent with workshop activities of the Bauhaus remains operative and timely for interior design. Aesthetic education and the urge to design[10] things for use by others were primary then and are primary now, and they are tested in the studio and in the field by the parameters set by the body and senses at human scale. A designer's physicality and sensitivity are brought to bear on research, analysis, synthesis, and critique as sense memory that facilitates the designed inhabitation of space. At the Bauhaus, a sense of movement was nurtured by the performance of eurythmic exercises[11] to compliment learning. Photographs exist of Oskar Schlemmer's stage craft student groups conducting "equilibristics," exercises combining studies in choreographic and spatial relationships on the flat roof of the building in Dessau.[12] Movement was thought to be one of twelve senses of compositional phenomenology based on the Rudolf Steiner studies of the senses. A sense of life, sense of self-movement, and sense of balance were associated with touch. In the Steiner system, these are more fundamental than seeing. Art school is founded to serve a visual education, but the focus on it did not leave touch behind. Louis Kahn in a declaration with spiritual overtones also had sight be an aspect of primordial touch, with the eyes.

Without its former political and moral imperative, Albers's contribution to collaboration is profoundly resonant today when there is no interior design without working successfully as knowledgeable leaders with other designers and builders, but he is more well-known internationally by designers for the course developed during the time he was at Yale University: The Interaction of Color. The course consists of approximately twenty-three exercises related to principles present in arranging color on paper. Exercises give instructions that when followed cause the artist to discover certain effects of perception; the results demonstrate that surprising levels of control can be mastered through working nuanced differences in color in relationship to other colors. Albers taught this course at Black Mountain College and at Yale at the same time that he was producing the "Homage to the Square" paintings (see Plate 61). Also known as perceptual paintings, they utilized minimalist efficiency to attain discernable optic ends and perceptual and emotional affect.

The project was the product of work over the course of Albers's career. Perhaps rooted in the transparent stained-glass paintings that began before he was a student at the Bauhaus, he established a way for designers to initiate their own research on color and light. The course was carried out in many art schools in the United States in the 1960s and after by former student-artists who had dual careers as teachers, such as the painter Paul Rubin at Pratt Institute, who taught industrial designers, photographers, and future advertising executives in the foundation course on color. Albers also developed a language of terms that is used to describe color effects. Spoken mainly while simultaneously viewing the finished color plates that resulted from experimenting with pigmented color relationships, the menu of effects emphasized sensitivity and communicativeness through using color with attention. Phrases such as "reversed grounds," "subtraction of color," "after-image," "color mixture in paper," and "optical mixture"[13] were made concrete and spatial in the practice of working with color and then talking about the results while viewing them. Above all, for interior design and other fields, Albers's course introduced the significance of developing an individual practice through the senses to establish a relationship with matter and forms so that they are compelling. An excerpt from the introduction to the pocket edition of Albers's *The Interaction of Color* states,

> Practical exercises demonstrate through color deception (illusion) the relativity and instability of color. And experience teaches that in visual perception there is a discrepancy between physical fact and psychic effect. What counts here—first and last—is not so-called knowledge of so-called facts, but vision-seeing. Seeing here implies Schauen (as in Weltanschauung)[14] and is coupled with fantasy, with imagination.[15]

When artists and designers recognized aspects of color, physics, and psychology through the manipulation of Color-aid paper, scissors, rubber cement, magazine clippings, and Bristol board as in Albers's course, their insights gave substance to the aesthetic concerns of philosophy evoked in writing by the phenomenologists. Practice invokes the existential reality of an intentional transcendence that phenomenology names, and engages the mind in increasing its tolerance for ambiguity and its curiosity for what really happens with color on the surface of a page. Albers showed the way whereby the work in the studio, to develop understanding and depth and flexibility specifically about the use of color, is brought to bear in a wider context that includes the application of color in the built world where color has a cognitive and emotional impact on others. In this sense, understanding in an interiors project goes beyond how to manipulate the pigments, applications, and surfaces where color is to be used but also obtains the empathic force that communicates emotionally and physically. Color is a crucial means by which the interior designer reads three-dimensional space and through that reading delivers a rendering of the disposition of the architectural structure with an exactitude that produces an ideological result. This understanding is fundamental to modernism and to interior design.

THE SENSES FORM THE POWER TO DRIVE THE CONSTRUCTION OF AN ATMOSPHERE IN THE INTERIOR THROUGH CLOSE ATTENTION TO MATERIAL REALITY

Phenomenology speaks to perception as the experiential collection of data through the senses. A personal meaning about the sense of things is established through how objects look and feel, their contextual environment, and how they resonate in the interior experience of the viewer. By psychoanalytical and psychological projection—things that people make are imbued with sense memories and associations of the maker. This tremendously powerful inner directive can forcefully drive the construction of an architectural interior atmosphere with conscious or unconscious material. Gestalt psychology and anthroposophy, the background forebears of Maurice Merleau-Ponty's phenomenology, aimed to make the inner psychology transparent to its owner and to lighten unbearable loneliness and isolation of the subject. An artist through the work of art reaches out to touch another. Materially speaking, a signature that is an aggregate of optic, haptic, auditory, and other sense experiences recorded as smells or the taste of food is attached to this simple gesture. Theories of visual relationships such as those of Albers or Rowena Reed Kostellow that fostered the development of acuity in seeing and controlling design two- or three-dimensionally[16] only lead to the threshold that must be crossed when the mystery of the signature is synthesized.

Isamu Noguchi's oeuvre exemplifies an emotional connection with nature and his personal history as a Japanese American familiar with interstitial zones. He acknowledged in his writing that there was a relationship between loneliness and art. Seven years before his death, Noguchi created a foundation with the intention that a museum dedicated to the exhibition and study of his work would be developed in the warehouse adjacent to his Long Island City, New York, studio. The original name for the foundation, *Akari,* in Japanese means light. Noguchi's work perhaps more than that of any other twentieth-century artist could be said to exemplify the two meanings of the word *light,* one having to do with illumination and the other with weight.

Italo Calvino, a younger contemporary of Noguchi amplified the meaning of these double ambiances of the word when he wrote about literature. The essay called "Lightness" is the first of a collection of five lectures published as *Six Memos for the Next Millennium.*[17] The essays were written as lectures for delivery as the Charles Elliott Norton Lectures at Harvard University in 1985–1986. On the eve of his departure for Cambridge, Massachusetts, Calvino died without having spoken the words: "There remains one thread, the one I first started to unwind: that of literature as an existential function, the search for lightness as a reaction to the weight of living."[18]

Published posthumously, the collection is among the most illuminating of modern essays on qualities in art. A mature Noguchi could have reflected on his output by saying, as Calvino wrote, "My working method has more often than not involved the subtraction of weight...I have tried to remove weight from the structure of stories and language."[19] For Noguchi, it would have been about removing weight from the structure of space, so that the space could speak precisely. When the Noguchi Garden Museum opened in 1983 (and later to the public in 1985), these thoughts must have been on his mind.

Noguchi identified himself as a sculptor preoccupied with matter and space.[20] He saw them as conditions of modern sculpture—if it was to be relevant. In sculpture, conception and construction included the form and the space around it: the space that was formed by the presence of an ideational, abstract object was not conceptually and phenomenally separate. Gardens, interiors, lighting, and playgrounds were sculpture and environment, having aspects that made up the same whole and were dealt with as such. He had a keen sensitivity for seeing the negative space around things as positive, for creating placements that caused the invisible to become enlivened, as if visible—and for space to collect in it a positive feeling of being real (not empty). Relying on the movement of the eye of the viewer to follow the contours of sculptural form was one way this worked. He guided the eye over provocatively curved topologies of stone, thus creating a tension with the space it occupied. His way of working was as structural as it was visual, and his sculptural space spoke directly to a sense of mythical truth in the mind of the viewer. The structural integrity of individual stone sculptures took direction from the natural geometric structure that stones revealed when they were fractured. Noguchi mirrored the inner composition revealed in the fissures when he balanced the external forms. In his late work, the breaking of stone was referenced in the final pieces such as *Transfiguration of Nature* (1984) as a break in the piece, rearranged and placed so that it was read as a composition.[21] He preferred to invent the construction of a piece using gravitational forces as discovered by working stone, not mechanical fasteners. *Kouros* (1944–45, in the collection of the Metropolitan Museum of Art) was engineered so that the weight of the stones held it together.[22] Noguchi discovered that by presenting visual form that was figurative and of the scale and proportions of the body, he was driving its reception; the viewer's kinesthetic response was one that mimicked an experience of confronting another body in a room. In a written recollection of his collaboration with Martha Graham, he describes his stage sets as if they were parts of her anatomy (see Plate 62).[23] An interesting notion of their collaboration—one with no physical boundaries, as if they became one—is illuminated in his diary. Despite the sexual connotations of this image of set as co-figure as much as physical object supporting the dancer,[24] it calls to mind the submission and abandonment needed if an artist is to allow his or her physical body to inform and be the instrument of revealing qualities lying dormant in a work. The power of making brings forth kinesthetic and archetypal intelligence, as is possible when a dancer turns the body over to forces and expression that does not belong to the personal.

Creating the interior of the Noguchi Garden Museum was a culminating opus that spoke as an archive embodying the people, landscapes, and mythical narratives of Isamu Noguchi's life. The qualities at play in the original garden and interior were a mature and humble testament to space. The original Noguchi Museum held all of the delicate lightness and profundity of his late reflections. It had an atmosphere of imminence and impermanence revealed at first impression. The museum space visited on an unseasonably warm November Sunday more than twenty years ago had a dignified contained, pure presence. At that time, the museum closed in the fall until spring, much like a summerhouse, a place of lightweight construction not sturdy against the elements.[25] The steel framed windows were typical of light industrial structures of the 1950s. On Sundays, it was possible to take a bus ride from the Asia Society on Park Avenue in Manhattan across the Queensborough Bridge. Arrival, looking down on the museum door and garden gate from the height of a charter bus, aroused an anticipatory excitement invoked by scale: people scale for the door, sculpture scale for the grey painted garden gate. The Noguchi Museum was then an inward-looking museum that offered an intimate experience of the art and spaces and an imaginative evocation of the place as a working studio. As if it had the anthropomorphic capacity of being—with an open heart and open arms—a space receiving, it had an emotional mood established by the garden leaves and sky color in late fall warmth, the quiet sound of water overflowing along the surface of the basalt sculpture *The Well* (1982) from its carved bowl in a thin sheet. The entrance room was an area exposed to the outdoors through a triangular hole in the ceiling; beneath it young birch trees grew in an inner courtyard where monolithic stone sculptures were placed with perfection. North light was invited to enter indirectly as though mirroring its essential quality. This entrance space had an acoustical reverberation from a concrete floor being walked upon and concrete block wall forming an interior, private entrance. Memorializing stone sculptures—*Venus* (1980),[26] *Brilliance* (1982),[27] and *Deepening Knowledge* (1969)[28]—each of considerable weight that had been worked by Noguchi in Japan occupied the room in such a way as to effect the acoustical vibration. Open to the sky and to the garden, it was an interior and outdoor place (see Fig. 100). Traffic sounds, voices, distant sirens were modified as they entered through these apertures, but the adjacent urban sounds were invited to enter as in this personal recollection, "The first day of the return of standard time, darkness fell on Queens even as children and city softball leagues were playing in the disappearing afternoon light in Rainey Park, facing Roosevelt Island and Manhattan, and their delighted voices rose to the upper reaches of an atmosphere where they were to join more anonymous sounds of the city. The air was soft, enveloping."[29] Noguchi fully understood that placing the forms of sculpture in relation to one another with precision created an enlivened, imbued quality of space that defied it's actual emptiness. The place awakened eidetic capacities in the visitor; it was as if the space reflected and modeled the performance of the artist to a degree that seemed impossible in an old warehouse repurposed as a series of exhibition galleries. Noguchi sculptor and interior designer demonstrated that form and space are one three-dimensional reality. Interior design practice depends on them both in dynamic balance to communicate with architecture.

Memories of first viewing the early Noguchi Museum (and being profoundly moved) can be checked against images such as the ones made by John Berens when the museum opened (see Fig. 101). In them, the beauty of the light and shadows are revisited, and the images also report that the interior design really was not polished at the level of architectural detail. Brick exterior walls were covered with invasive ivy. The window paint color was in a hue close in tone to the brick, green oxide versus today's lighter tan color. Industrial steel windows let in cold air. There were no visually dominating wheelchair ramps. (I contend that Noguchi would have worked them out sculpturally to

FIGURE 100 The Noguchi Museum opening May 11, 1985. Interior view with stone sculpture: (l to r) *Deepening Knowledge,* 1969; *Brilliance,* 1982; *Venus,* 1983. Photo by Philip Galgiani. The Isamu Noguchi Foundation and Garden Museum, New York / Artists Rights Society (ARS), New York.

address ADA standards.) The suspended ceiling grids and industrial light fixtures with florescent lamps on the second floor were unacceptable by today's museum standards. These things went unnoticed in the integrated environment—until later when the museum was renovated for more visitors and more robust climate protection when various detailing entered as irritants disturbing to the purity of the early environment. With Noguchi's eye on the project, the earlier museum had a shimmeringly beautiful sense of unstudied proportion and fragility. It had an atmosphere that was authentic to the time when Noguchi worked in it and across the street on the corner of 10th Street. Two objects placed in a room that was swept clean constitute an interior design full of character that evokes a visceral sense memory that can be felt twenty years later, as if in a dream. The sculpture forms of the Noguchi Museum are not furniture forms that contemporary interior designers place in buildings, but for industrial and interior designers who have experienced this space, the placement and distribution of human scale elements in their rooms and the visual structure of countless furniture purchases and placements in interiors has been informed by Noguchi's space, as a precedent that has analytical and emotional value (see Fig. 102).

FIGURE 101 The Noguchi Museum Garden showing *The Well,* 1982 (foreground), *Basin and Range,* 1984 (center), and *Unmei,* 1970 (background). Photo by John Berens. The Isamu Noguchi Foundation and Garden Museum, New York/Artists Rights Society (ARS), New York.

FIGURE 102   The Noguchi Museum. Area 4. showing *This Place,* 1968 (foreground), and *Origin,* 1968. Photo by Reiter Dulberg. The Isamu Noguchi Foundation and Garden Museum, New York/ Artists Rights Society (ARS), New York.

The urban garden of the museum was then as now entered through the interior by crossing the threshold of a wide opening on the south of the entrance area. It is open to the sky and literally to the interior. Noguchi saw the garden area as part of the whole first level, a concept that returns to an internalized understanding in Noguchi of the traditional places of Kyoto that moved him. The garden and room spaces were two kinds of interiors, rather than the more familiar dialogue about the dialectic between inside and outside.[30] The garden proper was a place to view sculpture with focus on the fourth dimension—time—because of the weathering of materials and the presence of moving water. In it, Noguchi dealt more casually but no less seriously with placement, scale, and time than in his enclosed plaza landscape projects such as the Chase Manhattan Plaza or the narrative interior garden *California Scenario* in Costa Mesa,[31] but he allowed time to take its place as if the senses that pick out time's passage, hearing, smell, seeing were privileged. Concrete pathways directed the visitor on a walk through the garden that was less choreographed and smaller scale than the UN garden in Paris where perspective, elevation, and size are organized to contribute to the pleasure of the views. The *Well, Variation on a Tsukubai* (1982) was the dominant force of the museum garden. People who entered the space responded to its multisensory stimuli. Even today after the renovation reopening in 2004, some visitors overtly go to it fascinated to see how it works; some sit nearby and listen, while others look at other pieces and indirectly let *The Well* evoke strong sense reciprocities in them, working on their emotions through a more introverted engagement.

INTERIORS, PHENOMENOLOGY, AND CRITIQUE

The world of perception, or in other words the world which is revealed to us by our senses and in everyday life, seems at first sight to be the one we know best of all. For we need neither to measure nor to calculate in order to gain access to this world and it would seem that we can fathom it simply by opening our eyes and getting on with our lives. Yet this is a delusion. In these lectures, I hope to show that the world of perception is, to a great extent, unknown territory as long as we remain in the practical or utilitarian attitude. I shall suggest that much time and effort, as well as culture, have been needed in order to lay this world bare and that one of the great achievements of modern art and philosophy (that is, the art and philosophy of the last fifty to seventy years) has been to allow us to rediscover the world in which we live, yet which we are always prone to forget.[32]

Peter Zumthor's Therme Vals is a contemporary interior that is the numenistic equivalent of an interior room in a Bachelard essay, an interior that possesses philosophical and psychoanalytic atmospheric conditions and translates rational sources such as geology and landscape into its poetic reality. In that sense, the project has a kinship with the materiality and mythos of the Noguchi Museum and the pragmatic poesis in the painting and furniture made by Albers. Zumthor's design practice, like Noguchi's, is an art practice that is more favorable toward optical reality, synthesis, and manifestation than to the philosophical reveries on objects within the purview of philosophy. The interests of phenomenology in the writings of Merleau-Ponty and Bachelard seem integrally related to the sense awareness required for interior design practice. Their existential phenomenology purports a primacy of perception that drives the intention to directly experience and appreciate the life of things. Yet in Zumthor's work—as in that of Juhanni Pallasmaa, Noguchi, and Albers—the primacy of perception that comes from an experience of making is deeper than the theoretical narratives of phenomenology. The primordial state of mind and existential struggle made up of associations, insights, memory, poetry, and direct physical experience that are the base material of the designer's art are directly related to the profundity of results in an architectural interior built project. Therme Vals is an elemental, spatially rich ground where the human desire to float, submerge, and be warmed is activated. Perhaps because interior architects are performing operations on design in the studio in the present moment, an ambiguity arises for them when philosophy as adopted by architecture assumes that the main value of the perceptual categories such as sight, hearing, touch, and other sets of concepts about the logic of the senses is to serve as a theoretical antidote to the rational suppositions of architecture, as a means of humanizing it. The function and praxis of interiors is not to humanize architecture (although it often achieves that) but to seek its own spatial relationship with the elements of design given to affecting the body. The function of interiors is to meet the architecture (or engineering) and critically work out the interstitial edge they share.

While the Bauhaus may have thought of the practice of deepening perception in the process of making as in the realm of personal development (based on the German roots of phenomenology in Goethe) and collective well-being (based on the social needs magnified by postwar conditions), postmodern era criticism identified with phenomenology focused on a more self-conscious social critique of a set of concerns about alienation and sense repression resulting from the domination of technology and divided representation.[33] K. Michael Hays pointed out in his introduction to Alberto Perez-Gomez's 1983 essay "Introduction to Architecture and the Crisis of Modern Science"[34] that the search for order within the philosophical realm of phenomenology as a basis for criticism is generally made unreliable by the certainty of an interpretive position that is burdened with reactive, predigested value judgments (i.e., humanism is good; science is bad.). This relegated its use in design theory to strategies of resistance to technology, more suited to warning or prediction than to hypothesis. An interpretive position that seeks a more fluid transposition of the rational and subjective may be well suited to inform the production of contemporary interior design. High technology that interior designers deal with also may require a high level of sense imagination since the media of technologies is physically an out-of-body experience. Using them to develop interiors does not diminish the requisite that the results of thinking must create architecture that meets the needs of the body at the scale of the body.

Teachers such as Pallasmaa and Zumthor (who has an education in form based industrial design) have encouraged a materials emphasis based on the sense of touch and spatial memory to enhance the architect's and user's relationship with architecture. Using a sailing analogy, the Australian Glenn Murcutt raises the physics and causal nature of designing structures: how the wind flows over a building, how air pressure works when it meets resistance,[35] and, by projection, how that feels in the hand of the drawing architect, in the architect's corporeal imagination. Pallasmaa, Murcutt, and Zumthor's influence on designers has been broad but not received unconditionally because of their unusual confidence in the dominant need of the body as it meets the forces of nature as the generator of architecture.[36] Zumthor and Pallasmaa in particular have become known for architectural practices associated with phenomenology. For Zumthor, phenomenology takes the form of addressing the essential ideas of architecture, place, and purpose as much as it is about the use of materials. The core symbols that create the image of his projects are informed by an intimate relationship with and feel for elemental materials and geologic site.

The Therme Vals (opened 1996) in the Grabunden area of Switzerland is an intensely affective interior space. It exists largely as an underground stone structure that is approached by a tunnel extending from the preexisting hotel on site. There are no exterior doors. The building has one exterior façade, more because it is situated on a mountainside than due to the ambition of the architecture to represent itself as a building (see Plate 63). The roof is camouflaged with grass and Alpine plants. Natural springs emerge from the Earth at warm temperatures determined by the Earth and fill multiple bathing pools. (The temperatures of some of the pools are heated and cooled to provide restorative water therapies.) The mineral content of the water, valued for its health benefits, is related to the minerals found in the stone of the mountain, and the stone from the local mountains is the building material of the pools and structure. Valser quartzite cut in slabs is used structurally as a building block construction material (in an unprecedented relationship with concrete). A description of the qualities of the native quartzite make it possible to think of its embedded translucent crystals as captured light that has once again been released. "Fine grained, massive, slated, micaceous quartzite with rough banding of green, light bluish, micaceous layers, some eyed, alternating with light grey to white quartz layers."[37] In describing the architectonic language that appears at Therme Vals, Zumthor gives an account of a searching design process that itself could be an answer to looking for a phenomenologically active basis for inventing a surprising and atmospheric interior:

> The lengthy projection process culminating in the finished artefact [sic] of the spa was initially a process of playful discovery, of a patient and enjoyable quest far beyond the architectonic ideals. The fascination for the mystic qualities of a world of stone within the mountain, for darkness and light, for light reflections on the water or in the steam saturated air, pleasure in the unique acoustics of bubbling water in a world of stone, a feeling for warm stones and naked skin, the ritual of bathing—these notions guided us.[38]

A personal, intimate response is not only hoped for in the user, it is in the design process, correspondently delivered by the architect of the interior (where the anticipated experience is profoundly internal). The embodied response to being in the Vals baths is sensate, as if the body listens to the interior spaces, in part, because partaking in the baths results in relaxation that awakens sensation including that of the experience of place itself. In drinking the bottled mountain water of Vals, visitors are taking in the same minerals that are embedded in the architecture. One woman related, "I had a profound experience being in that space and it is all still very immediate three or four years later. The darkness of the stone, the dim and then selective strategic lighting, the smells…all very visceral and moving."[39] Therme Vals was a memorable interior space for another visitor. It evoked in him a strong response of being within, held, bathed, and cleansed. It was a surprise to have a strong embodied reaction to an architectural interior for this person. While the project by its built presence critiques an alienating rationality, it also almost lovingly embraces science and engineering and proposes a theoretical basis for invention of structured experience. Much of the writing about Therme Vals and critics' responses to it could be concerning ancient structures, yet the Vals baths is thoroughly contemporary architecture. The lines are clean; the sections indicate carved, minimalist spaces. The stone slab material creates a horizontal emphasis. Insulated glass is used abundantly. Long slits of light enter through high-tech, lens-like expansion joints in the roof. Despite the presence of steam and ice (surrounding the exterior pool) the environmental controls were invented with well-ordered acoustical, thermal, moisture, and electrical systems. Pools joined by water corridors presented unusual coating and joinery technical challenges. The stone was cut, ground, and layered with very fine exactitude. The interior volumes have geometric traits that make water seem lighter than it is. The relationship of interior and the scenic view of mountains is unmitigated. Strategic thinking about lighting and color is not seen as a disingenuous manipulation or decoration.

For Pallasmaa, being a phenomenologist is related to his identity as a Finnish architect. As writers, both men are concerned with qualities of things in direct relationship with the individual subject. They generate observations that shed light on the character of buildings and on the personal experience of architecture as place, and the place of beauty in life. In the annals of phenomenology, theirs is the message of the practitioner as corrective force against a rationalist takeover of architecture, and yet they are not as practitioners or teachers limited by their held views on phenomenology; the principles seem to inspire *Areté:* excellence and knowledge. Zumthor's enduring decision to focus on percepts as touchstones of reality linked to construction is more contemporary than it seems. Through the lenses of perception and phenomenology, the same design elements that are submitted to science and technology, such as compound masonry, *verbundmauerwerk,*[40] and mechanical and acoustical resonance, are indemnified with theoretical and poetic inquiry and substance. Once belonging to the humanities in opposition to science, phenomenology in Zumthor's architectural interiors now stands closer to science—that is, physics, biology, and neuroscience—in its examination of praxis and theory. Although interior design is determined to make life practicable at the scale of the body, it is the additive and subtractive phenomena of color, sound, physical sensation, and light that are carriers of interiors' atmospheric character and authenticity. The occupant consciously or subconsciously listens to architecture with his or her skin and senses. The state of the finished and lived-in interior that offers transcendence like the baths at Vals or the original Noguchi studio museum also offers consciousness that is a product of thinking that integrates many sources and sensations by grounding them in the sensorial-based empirical—the world as lived.

39

Taste and Trends

PENNY SPARKE

In the early twenty-first century anyone, from an amateur home decorator to a professional interior designer, in search of new trends in interior decor can search the Internet and discover multiple sites that claim to predict the future. From www.cosmoworlds. com to www.lenzing.com/fasern/de/trends to www.interiordesigntrends.co.uk to www.trendir.com (and many more besides), the Web provides a wealth of information and advice about next year's colors, patterns, and general interior trends. "Staying in is the new going out," one contemporary website tells us, adding that, as we will all be wanting to retreat from the economic crisis and seek comfort in our interiors, we need to think, "Chesterfield wingback chairs, cosy textiles, shag-pile carpets; all creating a serene and comforting living environment."[1] Others predict what they describe as "main trends," such as "Folk Style; Big Blooms; Natural Materials; Retro/Vintage and Country House Glamour";[2] others stick to color predictions: "We'll find unexpected-looking colours created from historical natural dye developments such as 'baby indigo' and 'madder red,'" for instance;[3] while yet others focus on new developments in textiles and patterns.

Such predictions can also be accessed at trade shows and in the pages of home and lifestyle magazines—from Condé Nast's *House & Garden* to the BBC's *Good Homes.* While they all emphasize the aesthetic and stylistic characteristics of the highly desirable interior spaces that they are anticipating, more importantly, perhaps, they are rooted in a psychological reading of the zeitgeist. The anxieties of an era inevitably lead, it is implied, to a particular way of thinking about our interior spaces. In turn, those spaces can play a role in alleviating them. In an age that has no anxieties, our interiors, presumably, would be able to express that fact equally well.

Clearly forecasting what our home interiors (and, inasmuch as they depend on the appearance of our domestic interiors to a considerable extent, our inside public spaces as well) are going to look like is clearly big business in the early twenty-first century. The phenomenon has enormous implications for the paint, wallpaper, textiles and furniture industries, and interior decorating and design businesses, which can either thrive or fail on the basis of a sentence uttered on a website. This is not a new phenomenon, however; nor did it emerge in isolation. Rather, the concept of interior design forecasting flowed directly from the world of fashion predictions that preceded it. Interiors share much with fashion items and are determined by similar, if not identical, socioeconomic and psychological forces.

This chapter sets out to explore when, why, how, and by whom interior design came to be aligned with the world of fashion and some of the implications of that alignment. Through the twentieth century and up to the present, one face of interior design depended less on its relationship with architecture and more upon its rapport with the fashion-dependent and socially defined concept of taste. Indeed, that concept lies at the heart of the historical and contemporary definition of interior design. The fact, also, that interior design has historically been identified with feminine taste has led to its cultural marginalization, especially by architects.[4] Indeed, the gap that developed through the late nineteenth century and early twentieth century between the fashion- and style-oriented modern interior and the model that was developed by modernist architects has, today, become almost unbridgeable.

A study of the modern interior through the lens of its relationship with fashion and taste also allows us to focus on the experience and the aesthetic of what has been called "feminine modernity."[5] Importantly, one contemporary website claims that, while the forecasting of trends in interior design are linked to that of fashion items, it lags one year behind it. That would suggest that fashion sensitivity is at its strongest in our choice of clothing items, which are located nearest to our bodies and, only after that, in the spaces of the interior that encompass the (usually) clothed body. The cultural historian Regina Lee Blaszczyk has provided an account of the development of color standards for manufacturers, which facilitated the matching of color across fashion items and accessories, including components of the interior.[6] "Color forecasting," she tells us, "is a profession with a long history, going back to the late 1800s when French textile mills first issued colour cards. These foldout books, made from paper and ribbon samples, showed what colors were popular among French dressmakers and milliners in the current season."[7] The practice was subsequently emulated across the Atlantic in the United States where "French color cards became valuable tools for textile mills, tanneries, straw makers, and feather importers—the industries that supplied the ready-to-wear business, hat-makers and shoe factories."[8] Following the outbreak of the WWI, the American equivalent of the French fashion industry, which could no longer import French color cards at that time, took guidance from its newly formed Textile Color Card Association, which took responsibility for color standards in that country. In the 1920s, a certain Margaret Hayden Rorke became, in Blaszczyk's words, "America's first color forecaster" and the head of the association for nearly four decades.[9] Given America's commercial preeminence in those years, that development proved to be hugely significant for fashion and subsequently for interior design forecasting in general, and by helping to inform manufacturers about women's tastes and preferences, it provided the basis of an industry that was to exert a huge influence on the commercial practices of all the fashion-related industries (including interior design) across the globe. In particular, it served to prioritize color as a key means of evoking desire in consumers and of encouraging them to purchase the material goods that formed the backcloth to their everyday lives and through which they formed their modern identities. Blaszczyk also tells us that, in the mid-1920s, "Macy's promoted color in the kitchen to sell blue brooms and mottled mops," showing that, once standards had been established, colors used for fashionable dress could be matched to those used for the components of the domestic interior.[10]

Color standardizing and forecasting provided, therefore, one means through which the interior became aligned with the world of fashionable dress and accessories in the early twentieth century. It also confirmed the importance of feminine consumption to both areas and the link to feminine culture in general. That link between fashion, the interior, and the female body was discussed by the American cultural historian Beverley Gordon in her 1996 essay "Women's Domestic Body: The Conceptual Conflation of Women and interiors in the Industrial Age," in which she argued that women's bodies (and by extension their dress) and the domestic interior were, in the late nineteenth and early twentieth centuries, symbolically linked.[11] Furthermore, she contended, dress was frequently associated, through its fabrics and its colors, with specific locations within the domestic interior. Light airy cottons, for example, she claimed, were worn in the breakfast room.[12] The linking factor, Gordon explains,[13] is women's notions of self, or identity, which is formed and reinforced by the fashionable dress and interiors they simultaneously wear and inhabit.

The convergence between feminine culture, fashion, taste, and the interior had been in place long before the twentieth century, however. As far back as the eighteenth century, the idea of being fashionable had been a prerequisite for women who were part of the French court or of noble society. Madame de Pompadour, for example, was frequently painted in fashionable dress framed by a fashionable, neoclassical interior. Both constituted important markers of her social status, which is turn was confirmed by her personal taste. In his little book *Bricobracomania: the bourgeois and the biblelot,* Remy G. Saisselin addressed this issue, explaining that the nobility was expected to possess art as it defined, and was inseparable from, rank and social function.[14] Indeed, at that time the possession of art was, he explained, synonymous with the ideas of landed wealth and lineage. He also suggested that it was the ownership of art by the nobility that conferred status upon artworks, not the other way round.

By the mid-nineteenth century, the Industrial Revolution had brought about a democratization of fashion and taste through increased wealth and the enhanced availability of luxury goods. The expanding social mobility of that era meant that the possession of fashionable taste became a requirement for all people with social ambition, and it revealed itself, largely, through the acquisition of fashion items and the decoration and furnishing of the domestic interior. In that context, the alignment between fashionable dress and the interior grew strong, facilitated by the expanding numbers of mechanisms of dissemination—magazines and exhibitions among them.

At that time, the idea of the modern interior, and the possibility for ever larger numbers of people of embellishing it in the fashionable taste of the day, came into being. In France, the publication of Charles Percier and Antoine Fontaine's *Receuils de decorations interieures,* which was published as articles in 1801 and in book form in 1812, was closely followed by the Englishman Thomas Hope's 1807 *Household Furniture and Interior Decoration.* Those publications marked the emergence of a modern concept of interior decoration that was accessible to people from an extended range of social backgrounds. The early decades of the nineteenth century also saw the idea of fashion expand its influence. According to several writers—from Charles Baudelaire to George Simmel to Walter Benjamin—fashion was a defining component of modernity, embodying what Baudelaire described in 1863 as the "ephemeral, the fugitive, the contingent."[15] That abstract definition of fashion as something that could be expressed through dress, but which was, essentially, a socioeconomic, cultural symptom of the modern condition, was easily transferred from dress to a range of other goods and environments. Goods and environments, in turn, responded to, and defined themselves through, the media. Fashion was, as we have seen, most easily and naturally extended to objects and spaces that enjoyed a close relationship with the female body, including fashion accessories and the domestic and commercial interiors that contained fashionably dressed female bodies.

In Britain and America, the 1870s and 1880s witnessed the development of an even closer relationship among taste, fashion, the interior, and feminine culture. By that time, the aesthetic movement, which embraced the idea that good taste, the capacity, that is, not to be vulgar, had replaced salvation as *the* mark of social status or distinction—it had moved down-market. That was made possible by the expanding desire of the lower-middle classes, stimulated by exhibitions, magazines, journals, and trade catalogues, to express their social status and aspirations through their interior furnishings, and, with the growth of mechanized mass-production and mass retailing, the increasing availability of artistic furnishings in the marketplace.

While the mechanisms for the widespread production, dissemination, and consumption of the aesthetic interior were fully in place by the 1870s, the understanding and the visual skills needed to produce it were frequently absent. A means was needed, therefore, through which uneducated consumers could acquire the knowledge and discrimination required to make what were considered to be the right aesthetic decisions. Not only did that involve, as it had for the nobility of the previous century, choosing the right chairs, tables, upholstery fabrics, wallpapers, tiles, and decorative artifacts for the home but also, more importantly, having the ability to combine them in particular ways into beautiful and effective ensembles. That involved the exercising of taste, which, inextricably linked as it was to the workings of the fashion system, had become, rather than wealth per se, a marker of social status in its own right.

An especially close alliance existed between the aesthetic interior, as defined by the élite group of artistic individuals who created it, and the ideas expressed in the early decorating and furnishing advice literature that targeted the uneducated housewife/homemaker. These artistic individuals emerged simultaneously, arguably as part of the same impetus to highlight the home and its self-consciously acquired and arranged furnishings and decoration, as a social and cultural priority and the main means through which people (especially women) were able to negotiate their modern identities. The 1870s and 1880s saw middle-class women taking more responsibility for the decoration of the home, aided by the new advice books. Indeed, a significant number were written by women.[16] As manifested in the paintings of James McNeil Whistler, the writings of Oscar Wilde, and the architecture and design of Richard Norman Shaw and William Nesfield, Edward William Godwin and Thomas Jeckyll and others, the aesthetic movement only involved women in a passive sense, as symbols, that is, of the beauty that those painters, for instance, desired in their immediate environments, which in turn acted as mirrors for their narcissism. As the movement moved down the social ladder, however, woman became the active agents of its entrance into the middle-class home, albeit implemented with more conservative values and intentions than their progressive male counterparts. In an attempt to resolve the apparent contradiction, the art historian Michael Hatt has claimed that, so risqué were the lifestyles of the aesthetes that middle-class respectability was required to rescue the aesthetic movement from being seen as deviant and decadent.[17] Interestingly, given that gendered divide, and the social transformations that it underwent, the language of the aesthetic interior remained remarkably consistent across the spectrum from artistic innovation to domestic conservatism. Dependent as it was upon a specific set of recognizable colors, symbols, decorating devices, and furniture types, it was easily emulated.

Mrs. Haweis's advice books were all aimed at upper-middle-class female home decorators. In both *The Art of Beauty* and *The Art of Decoration*, which covered a lot of the same ground, the author was critical about the slavishness to fashionable style that she had observed in the adoption, by a large sector of society, of the key features of the aesthetic interior—be those the use of certain colors, such as olive green, "the inescapable blue china,"[18] or Japanese parasols. Going against the grain of the design reformers of the era—John Ruskin, William Morris, and others—who sought a democratic solution to the problem of taste, she encouraged people to discover and implement their individual tastes. That did not mean that she was averse to offering her readers a set of abstract principles to guide them in the decoration of their homes, such as decorating with "feeling, devotion and knowledge."[19] She was also remarkably liberal is her definition of taste, explaining that "good taste has a wider margin than some would allow."[20]

By the end of the nineteenth century, fashionable dress and interior decoration had been raised to the level of modern art forms. As Lisa Tiersten has explained, "Late-nineteenth-century taste media proclaimed fashion and home decorating to be not simply art forms, but art forms inscribed in modernity."[21] Being elevated to the status of art compensated for the increasingly overt, and much derided, commercialism of both practices. The emphasis on taste in the negotiations that took place between artistic practitioners and clients in both areas concealed, for instance, the large amounts of money that passed hands and the fact that both class and modernity could now be bought in the marketplace. The close proximity between fashion and the interior was manifested in increasingly numerous ways and within several different areas. When fashion designers engaged with the interior, they tended to approach it with the same attitude as they did dress, that is as an extension of women's relationship with modernity, as a setting within which fashionable dress could express, and indeed extend, its values, and as part of women's discoveries of their own identities. That in turn came to define an important face of the modern interior.

In the years between the mid-nineteenth century and WWI, numerous professional links were established between the creators of fashionable dress and the decorated interior. Above all, helping to reinforce the synergies between them, common values defined both areas. These were originally formed and developed in the private sphere, in the context of private subjectivity, but were subsequently transferred into the public sphere through the commercial infrastructure provided by the theater, the department store, the world exhibition, and the mass circulation woman's fashion magazine. Department stores, in particular, emphasized the important relationship between them. In the 1850s and 1860s, a number of such stores were established, including the Bon Marché, the Louvre store, and Au Printemps in Paris, and Macys and Lord and Taylor, among others, in New York. At the time of the opening of its new store in Paris, in 1869, the Bon Marché department store, for instance, focused on a range of cheap goods—*nouveautés*—aimed to appeal to women, from clothing to fabrics to sewing goods to interior furnishings. Beds were available from the 1850s, and rugs from the 1860s, while the following decade saw the introduction of tables, chairs, and upholstery. Some displayed deluxe cabinetwork and others country furniture. House and kitchen wares could be purchased in the store by 1900. A decade later, complete modern room sets were also available.

The stores presented those goods as extensions of traditional decorative items, thereby providing bourgeois women with complete material environments. From a dress to a furnishing fabric to a lamp to a cupboard, consumers could purchase a range of goods with which they could self-fashion themselves. A strong link between dress and the interior was thus reinforced through the process of shopping for them in a single store. As Michael Miller has explained, "The Bon Marché showed people how they should dress, how they should furnish their homes."[22]

The United States provided the upper-class French couture trade with a mass market so the couturiers were keen to show their work on live mannequins across the Atlantic. The department stores gave them the opportunity to do so. In the 1890s, Lord & Taylor imported designs by Jacques Doucet, while Paul Poiret, a French couturier who understood the links between fashion and the interior, undertook a tour of American department stores in 1913, orchestrating fashion shows for eager customers. A handful of couturiers also established their own individual outlets across the Atlantic. Madame Paquin, for example, opened a shop for furs in New York in 1913. At around the same time as American stores became sites for fashion shows, they also began to establish departments dedicated to goods for the decorated interior. The journalist-turned-decorator Ruby Ross Wood, for example, directed the Wanamaker store's first atelier, named Au Quatrième, which opened in 1913, just a year after the fashionable French store Au Printemps had established its Atelier Primavera. Other French stores followed in the early 1920s: Galeries Lafayettes with La Maîtrise, the Louvre department store with its Studium Louvre, and Bon Marché with its Atelier Pomone.

World exhibitions provided yet another important shop window for the public's en-counter with fashionable dress and interiors. Worth exhibited designs at the French universal exhibitions of 1855 and 1889, while at the Paris 1900 exhibit the department stores Bon Marché, the Grands Magasins du Louvre, and Au Printemps all created indi-vidual pavilions in which they exhibited a wide range of their wares. They did so again at the 1925 Exposition des Arts Decoratifs in Paris, where the emphasis was on complete interiors created by the leading decorators of the day.

Women's mass-circulation fashion magazine provided yet another important me-dium for taste dissemination, embracing both dress and the interior. When Condé Nast first launched *Vogue* magazine in the United States in 1909, for example, he was deeply committed to showing interior decoration alongside couture fashion. At the level of the market at which he was directing his publication, the assumption was that *Vogue* readers would be able both to purchase couture clothes and hire an interior decorator. Architec-tural and decorative arts magazines of the period, the *Studio* among them, also included interiors within them, although, in that architectural context, their fashionable face was less in evidence.

The group of professional female interior decorators who had begun to practice at the turn of the century in the United States, led by the actress-turned-decorator Elsie de Wolfe, saw themselves as operating within the same fashion system as Worth and his followers, and they emulated, as a consequence, a number of their commercial strate-gies. De Wolfe was among the first of her generation to understand the workings of the fashion system and its relevance to the interior. That was largely due to the fact that she had moved into interior decoration as an amateur from an earlier career in the theater. She had done so in the 1890s, a time when, being the years before the English couturier Lucile had pioneered the fashion parade, the theatrical stage was the only place where couturiers could display their wares on live models.

In search of wealthy clients, like Parisian couturiers before her, de Wolfe mixed with America's aristocracy and new rich; she opened a furniture and furnishings showroom; she socialized with artists so that their image would rub off on to her; and she presented herself (also like couturiers before her) as a brand. That last commercial strategy was es-pecially apparent in the pages of her highly successful advice book, *The House in Good Taste*. On the first page, she included an elegant portrait of herself below which she had added her signature. Just as, by adding his personal artistic genius to an item of clothing, Worth had been able to dictate the course of fashionable dress in France through the sec-ond half of the nineteenth century, so, in the United States, de Wolfe and her followers set out to persuade wealthy clients that the association of their names with interiors had the effect of making the people who commissioned them highly fashionable and seen as having good taste. Also, de Wolfe understood the importance of dress and the interior to modern women's search for self-identity in a world in which flux was the only constant.

The model of the fashionable signature-decorator that de Wolfe established was emulated and built upon by several other female decorators in the first half of the twentieth century, among them Ruby Ross Wood, Frances Elkins, Rose Cummings, Dorothy Draper, and Syrie Maugham. Like their dress-oriented counterparts, those twentieth-century interior decorators presented themselves, first and foremost, as fashionable beings. By extension, their work was seen as fashionable and their clients as fashion-conscious, modern, and discerning.

By the 1920s, as we have seen, color standardization and fashion forecasting had been firmly established and interiors forecasting was following close behind. This was accompanied and supported by an elaborate fashion/taste-forming system that comprised exhibitions, magazines, books, the branding and marketing of the interior decorators and designers, and, eventually, by film, which also (Hollywood film in particular) recognized the double appeal of fashionable clothing and interiors being depicted together on the silver screen. Following WWII, the expansion of the mass media to include television and the Internet served to render the network of influencing forces around taste and fashion even more complex and sophisticated. Also in the years after 1945, the growth in the accessibility of fashionable dress and household goods and furnishings, combined with the huge expansion of the DIY movement in Britain and the United States transformed the picture once again. That was especially visible in the new suburban areas where social mobility and aspiration were at their most extreme at that time.

While color and visual style remained key fashion indicators, together with the use of certain materials and forms, the discussion about fashion and taste that took place in the media was, from the 1960s onward, taken to another level. The concept of lifestyle emerged as a mass phenomenon at that time through the pages of color newspaper supplements and the efforts of the pioneers of lifestyle retailing, Terence Conran and his Habitat store among them. The idea of lifestyle, of, that is, a sense that fashionable artifacts and spaces both facilitate and represent the full range of activities that constitute people's lives—from domestic family rituals to sports activities and traveling and eating outside the home—became increasingly democratized as consumption increased; necessities became luxuries, and people's possessions took on new meanings. Magazines mixed articles about fashionable dress with others about interiors. The dress designer Mary Quant, for example, designed her own kitchen, which found its way on to the pages of a color newspaper supplement. Both her dresses and her kitchen showed the influence of op art, especially the work of the artist Victor Vasarely, which was in vogue at the time. When the pop revolution in art and design took hold in the second half of the 1960s and the two-dimensional image took precedence over the three-dimensional object or space, the symbiotic relationship between fashion and the interior grew even stronger, and motifs—union jacks, stripes, and targets among them—embellished the surfaces of dresses, walls, and pine dressers alike, pulling them together into a single fashionable statement and eroding the distinctions among them.

The "Challenge of Pop," as an article in *Design* magazine called it, served to consolidate the consumer-led definition of the interior that had been both developing and becoming increasingly democratized over the two preceding centuries.[23] In that process of development and democratization, the worlds of fashion and the interior had become inextricably linked as the consumer gaze became the most dominant defining force behind the popular understanding of mass-produced visual, material, and spatial culture. So strong was the pull of this popular understanding that even the revived modernist interior came to be seen as a fashion rather than the timeless architecturally related concept that it had been originally conceived as.

By the end of the twentieth century, the holistic idea of lifestyle had taken over from discrete design media—fashion items, furniture pieces, or domestic ceramic or glass objects. It was the ensemble, rather, that mattered. A plethora of lifestyle television programs focused on people's fashion choices, interiors, house purchases, holidays, and eating habits, and, as these lifestyle choices came within the reach of the majority of the population, a pluralistic set of tastes, rather than a single taste, came to the fore. Fashion possibilities became plural and fragmented and interior choices also became multiple and varied.

By the early twenty-first century, the multiple choices on offer on interior forecasting websites had come to demonstrate the plurality of possibilities. Distinct trends were still discernible, but they were lifestyle rather than, or as well as, stylistic choices. The Independent: House and Home/Life & Style website tells us, for example, that Pantone's color of the year is turquoise, explaining that this is not just because it is appealing to the eye but because it "inspires thoughts of soothing, tropical waters and a comforting escape from the everyday troubles of the world."[24] It is the evocative, symbolic, lifestyle implications that really matter, we are told. The same website tells us that IMM Cologne's recent annual trend book focused on the themes of "Trickery, Rehab and Discipline," adding yet another level of abstraction and showing how far interior trends, following yet again on the world of fashion proper, have come from the visual styles of a few decades earlier. It also suggested that another trend was emerging, however, that turned that historical pattern completely on its head. Whereas, for at least two centuries, interior design trends had been dependent on fashionable dress to lead the way, that site proposed, instead, that fashion was finding its inspiration in "artwork, nature, mathematics and interior design."[25] The time lag between fashion and interior design seemed to have closed, and, for the first time, the latter was leading the way, showing fashionable dress where to go.

Over two centuries, therefore, fashionable dress, with the fashionable interior following fast on its heels, has functioned in a sociocultural context that has enabled it to become the visual symbol of social mobility, identity formation, and cultural transformation. Arguably, with the fashion cycle moving so rapidly that it has become virtually impossible to see it happening, and it appears that multiple influences are in operation at the same time, cross fertilizing each other and making it impossible to detect where innovation is actually occurring, the slower cycle of fashion change in the interior has bestowed greater visibility on that cultural form than on dress. Thus, in the early twenty-first century, the ever-increasing number of television programs and the plethora of magazines and journals dedicated to the interior are markers of its contemporary preeminence as a key social symbol.

At the same time the design profession is embracing cocreation and participatory design such that the ideas that one group of people can control the taste of another and that it is possible to forecast tastes and trends are rapidly becoming outmoded. Arguably, this significant shift suggests that the interior is entering a period in its history in which anything might be possible.

NOTES

1 MODERN HISTORY AND INTERIOR DESIGN

1. Emma Ferry, "Introduction," in *Designing the Modern Interior: From the Victorians to Today,* ed. Penny Sparke, Anne Massey, Trevor Keeble, and Brenda Martin (Oxford: Berg, 2009), pp. 13–29.

2. Friedrich Engels, *Die Lage der arbeitenden Klasse in England,* 2nd ed. (Leipzig, Germany: Otto Wigand, 1848), pp. 36–37, quoted in Walter Benjamin, *The Arcades Project,* trans. Howard Eiland and Kevin McLaughlin (London: Belknap Press of Harvard University Press, 1999), pp. 427–28.

3. Charles Eastlake, *Hints on Household Taste,* 4th ed. (Mineola, NY: Dover, 1986; originally published by London: Longmans, Green, 1878), pp. vi, v.

4. Ibid., pp. 162–63.

5. Juliet Kinchin, "Interiors: Nineteenth Century Essays on the 'Masculine' and the 'Feminine' Room," in *The Gendered Object,* ed. Pat Kirkham (Manchester: Manchester University Press, 1996), p. 12.

6. Benjamin, *Arcades Project,* pp. 8–9.

7. Engels, *Die Lage der arbeitenden Klasse,* pp. 36–37.

8. Jean Baudrillard, "Structures of Interior Design," in *The Everyday Life Reader,* ed. Ben Highmore (London: Routledge, 2002), p. 309.

9. Lucy Orrinsmith, *The Drawing Room,* Macmillan's Art at Home Series (London: Macmillan, 1877), p. 6, quoted in Emma Ferry, "The Later Nineteenth Century Interior, 1870–1900," in Sparke, Massey, Keeble, and Martin, *Designing the Modern Interior,* p. 14.

10. See Beatriz Colomina, *Privacy and Publicity: Architecture and Mass Media* (Cambridge, MA: MIT Press, 1994).

11. See Penny Sparke, *The Modern Interior* (London: Reaktion, 2008).

12. Le Corbusier, *Towards a New Architecture,* trans. Frederick Etchells (1931; repr. enlarg., London: Architectural Press, 1987), p. 227.

13. See Hilde Heynan and Gulsum Baydar, eds., *Negotiating Domesticity: Spatial Productions of Gender in Modern Architecture* (London: Routledge, 2005); and Christopher Reed, *Not at Home: The Suppression of Domesticity in Modern Art and Architecture* (London: Thames & Hudson, 1996).

14. Gay McDonald, "Selling the American Dream: MoMA, Industrial Design and Post-War France," *Journal of Design History* 17, no. 4 (2004): 397–412; see also Mary Anne Staniszewski, *The Power of Display: A History of Exhibition Installations at the Museum of Modern Art* (Cambridge, MA: MIT Press, 1998).

15. Quoted in Anne Massey, *Interior Design since 1900,* 3rd ed. (London: Thames & Hudson, 2008), p. 161.

16. See Penny Sparke, *Elsie de Wolfe: The Birth of Modern Interior Decoration* (New York: Acanthus, 2005).

17. See Anne Massey, *The Independent Group: Modernism and Mass Culture in Britain, 1945–1959* (Manchester: Manchester University Press, 1995).

18. See John Stonard, "Pop in the Age of Boom: Richard Hamilton's *Just What Is It That Makes Today's Homes So Different, So Appealing?*" *The Burlington Magazine,* September 2007, 607–620.

19. Reyner Banham, "Vehicles of Desire," *Art,* September 1955, p. 3.

20. For a full set of photographs and plans, see Dirk van den Heuvel and Max Risselda, eds., *Alison and Peter Smithson—from the House of the Future to a House of Today* (Rotterdam, the Netherlands: 010 Publishers, 2004), pp. 80–95.

21. John McHale, "Technology and the Home," *ARK,* no. 19 (March 1957): p. 25.

22. For an expansive overview of postmodern design, see Glenn Adamson and Jane Pavitt, eds., *Postmodernism: Style and Subversion, 1970–1990* (London: V & A Publications, 2011).

23. See Daniel Miller, *The Comfort of Things* (Cambridge, UK: Polity Press, 2008).

2 RETHINKING HISTORIES, CANONS, AND PARADIGMS

1. Alun Munslow, *Deconstructing History* (New York: Routledge, 2006), p. 15.

2. Keith Jenkins, *On "What Is History?"* (London: Routledge, 1995), p. 15.

3. See Robin George Collingwood, *The Idea of History* (Oxford: Clarendon, 1946); and Edward Hallett Carr, *What Is History?* (New York: Vintage, 1961).

4. Joyce Appleby, Lynn Hunt, and Margaret Jacob, *Telling the Truth about History* (New York: W. W. Norton, 1994).

5. Mary Anne Beecher, "Toward a Critical Approach to the History of Interiors," *Journal of Interior Design* 24, no. 2 (1998): pp. 4–11.

6. Benjamin Bloom, *The Taxonomy of Education Objectives: The Classification of Educational Goals* (New York: Longmans, Green, 1956).

7. Albert Jacquemart, *A History of Furniture,* ed. Bury Palliser (London: Reeves and Turner, 1878), p. 1.

8. Thorstein Veblen, *The Theory of the Leisure Class* (New York: Macmillan, 1899).

9. Amy Sue Bix, "Equipped for Life: Gendered Technical Training and Consumerism in Home Economics, 1920–1980," *Technology and Culture* 43, no. 4 (2002): pp. 728–54.

10. John Summerson, *Georgian London* (London: Pleiades Books, 1945).

11. Mark Girouard, *Life in the English Country House* (New Haven, CT: Yale University Press, 1978), p. v.

12. Charles Jencks, *The Language of Post-Modern Architecture* (New York: Rizzoli, 1977), p. 9.

13. See John Turpin, "The History of Women in Interior Design: A Review of Literature," *Journal of Interior Design* 33, no. 1 (2007): pp. 1–16; and John Turpin, "Omitted, Devalued, Ignored: Re-Evaluating the Historical Interpretation of Women in the History of the Interior Design Profession," *Journal of Interior Design* 27, no. 1 (2001): pp. 1–11.

14. Linda Nochlin, "Why Have There Been No Great Women Artists?" *Art News* 69, no. 9 (January 1971): pp. 22–39; reprinted in Linda Nochlin, *Women, Art and Power and Other Essays* (New York: Harper & Row, 1988).

15. Dolores Hayden, *The Grand Domestic Revolution* (Cambridge, MA: MIT Press, 1981).

16. Isabelle Anscombe, *A Woman's Touch: Women in Design from 1860 to the Present Day* (London: Virago, 1984), p. 11.

17. See Penelope Corfield, *Language, History and Class* (Oxford: Cambridge University Press, 1991); and Joan Wallach Scott, *Gender and the Politics of History* (New York: Columbia University Press, 1988).

18. Jeremy Aynsley and Charlotte Grant, eds., *Imagined Interiors: Representing the Domestic Interior since the Renaissance* (London: V&A Publications, 2006).

19. Mihaly Csikszentmihalyi and Eugene Rochberg-Halton, *The Meaning of Things: Domestic Symbols and the Self* (London: Cambridge University Press, 1981).

20. Appleby, Hunt, and Jacob, *Telling the Truth*, p. 10.

3 INHABITED SPACE

1. Gaston Bachelard, *The Poetics of Space,* trans. Maria Jolas (Boston: Beacon, 1994), p. 47.

2. Gwendolyn Wright, *Building the Dream: A Social History of Housing in America* (Cambridge, MA: MIT Press, 1983), p. 13; Mark Taylor and Julieanna Preston, eds., *Intimus: Interior Design Theory Reader* (Chichester, UK: Academy Press, 2006) and Lois Weinthal, ed., *Toward a New Interior* (New York: Princeton Architectural Press, 2011).

3. Anthropologist Mary Douglas, quoted in Diana Fuss, *The Sense of an Interior: Four Writers and the Rooms That Shaped Them* (London: Routledge, 2004), p. 66.

4. Lynne Walker, "Home Making: An Architectural Perspective," *Signs* 27, no. 3 (2002): p. 823.

5. See, for example, Joan DeJean, *The Age of Comfort: When Paris Discovered Casual—and the Modern Home Began* (repr., New York: Bloomsbury USA, 2010).

6. Walter Benjamin, *The Arcades Project*, trans. Howard Eiland and Kevin McLoughlin, (Cambridge, MA: Belknap Press of Harvard University Press, 2002)

7. Fuss, *Sense of an Interior*, p. 182; and Joris-Karl Huysmans, *Against Nature: A Rebours,* ed. Nicholas White and Margaret Mauldon (repr., Oxford: Oxford University Press, 2009).

8. Benjamin, *The Arcades Project*, p. 879.

9. Ibid., p. 216.

10. Catherine Murphy, "Transitional (Object) Space" (master's thesis, School of Constructed Environments, Parsons the New School for Design, 2011).

11. Sigmund Freud, "Introductory Lectures on Psychoanalysis. Lecture XIX: Resistance and Repression," in *The Standard Edition* 16 (New York: W. W. Norton, 1976 London: The Hogarth Press, 1953–74), pp. 295–96, quoted in Fuss, *Sense of an Interior*, p. 6.

12. Fuss, *Sense of an Interior,* p. 100.

13. Fyodor Dostoevsky, *Crime and Punishment,* trans. Richard Pevear and Larissa Volokhonsky (New York: Vintage, 1993), p. 417.

14. Georges Perec, *Species of Spaces and Other Pieces,* trans. John Sturrock (London: Penguin Classics, 2008), p. 37.

15. Benjamin, *Arcades Project,* p. 221; and Adolf Behne, quoted in Karina Van Herck, "Only Where Comfort Ends, Does Humanity Begin: On the 'Coldness' of Avant-Garde Architecture in the Weimar Period," in *Negotiating Domesticity: On the Spatial Productions of Gender in Modern Architecture,* ed. Hilde Heynen and Gülsüm Baydar (London: Routledge, 2005), p. 123.

16. Charles Rice, *The Emergence of the Interior: Architecture, Modernity, Domesticity* (London: Routledge, 2005), p. 34.

17. Sarah Wigglesworth, "A Fitting Fetish: The Interiors of the Maison de Verre," in, *Intersections: Architectural Histories and Critical Theories,* 1st ed., ed. Iain Borden and Jane Rendell (London: Routledge, 2000), p. 101.

18. Jean Baudrillard, *The System of Objects,* trans. James Benedict (London: Verso, 2005), p. 43.

19. Sylvia Lavin, "Open the Box: Richard Neutra and the Psychology of the Domestic Environment," *Assemblage,* no. 40 (December 1999): p. 11; and Margaret Maile Petty, "Scopophobia/Scopophilia: Electric Light and the Anxiety of the Gaze in Postwar American Architecture," in *Atomic Dwelling: Anxiety, Domesticity and Postwar Architecture,* ed. Robin Schuldenfrei (London: Routledge, 2012), pp. 45–66.

20. Benjamin, *Arcades Project,* p. 220.

21. Frank Trentmann, "Materiality in the Future of History: Things, Practices, and Politics," *Journal of British Studies* 48, no. 2 (2009): p. 283.

22. Bill Brown, quoted in Victoria Rosner, *Modernism and the Architecture of Private Life* (New York: Columbia University Press, 2008), p. 128. On this conflation of people and things, Brown elsewhere cites the French philosopher Bruno Latour, who wrote on this same issue that "things do not exist without being full of people" Quoted in Brown, "Thing Theory," *Critical Inquiry* 28, no. 1 (2001): p. 12.

23. Lytton Strachey, quoted in Rosner, *Modernism and the Architecture of Private Life,* p. 76.

24. Trentmann, "Materiality in the Future of History," p. 297.

25. Daniel Roche, *A History of Everyday Things: The Birth of Consumption in France, 1600–1800,* trans. Brian Pearce (Cambridge: Cambridge University Press, 2000), p. 174.

26. Baudrillard, *System of Objects,* pp. 13–14.

27. Ibid., p. 97.

28. Benjamin, *Arcades Project,* p. 9.

29. Ibid.

30. Roche, *History of Everyday Things,* p. 168.

31. Walker, "Home Making," p. 826.

32. Ibid., p. 831.

33. Henri Lefebvre, *The Production of Space,* trans. Donald Nicholson-Smith (Maiden, MA and Oxford, UK: Blackwell Publishing, 1991) pp. 1–68.

34. Baudrillard, *System of Objects,* pp. 27–28.

35. Rosner, *Modernism and the Architecture of Private Life,* p. 128.

36. Bachelard, *Poetics of Space,* p. 17.

37. Ibid., p. 47.

38. Ibid., p. 81.

39. Henry Urbach, "Closets, Clothes, disClosure," in *Gender Space Architecture: An Interdisciplinary Introduction,* ed. Jane Rendell, Barbara Penner, and Iain Borden (London: Routledge, 2000), pp. 342–52.

40. Jasmine Rault, "Designing Sapphic Modernity," *Interiors: Design, Architecture, Culture* 1 (July 2010): p. 35.

41. George Wagner, "Lair of the Bachelor," in Taylor and Preston, *Intimus*, pp. 375–79, previously published in Debra Coleman, Elizabeth Anne Danze, and Carol Jane Henderson, eds., *Architecture and Feminism* (New York: Princeton Architectural Press, 1996), pp. 183–220.

42. Ibid., p. 376.

43. Lucinda Havenhand, "A View from the Margin: Interior Design," *Design Issues* 20 (Autumn 2004): pp. 32–42.

4 METHODS OF RESEARCH AND CRITICALITY

1. Gianni Ottolini, "Ricerca scientifica e progetto di interni nell'esistente," in *Gli interni nel progetto sull'esistente,* ed. Adriano Cornoldi, Giampiero Bosoni, Imma Forino, Paolo Giardiello, and Gennaro Postiglione (Padua, Italy: Il Poligrafo, 2007), p. 20.

2. Over time the discipline of architecture has been defined in different ways. Such definitions may be divided into three main families (Eberhardt Richtin and Mark W. Maier, *The Art of Systems Architecting* [New York: CRC Press, 1996]): architecture as a principle of organization of objects and complex systems (29-30 B.C., Marcus Vitruvius Pollio, *On Architecture*, ed. Richard Schofield (London: Penguins Books, 2009) 1923, Le Corbusier, *Towards a new architecture* (New York: Dover Publications, 1986) John Fleming, Hugh Honour, Nikolaus Pevsner, *Dictionary of Architecture* (London: Penguins Books, 1991) 1799, Étienne-Louis Boullée, *Treatise on Architecture*, ed. Helen Rosenau (London: Alec Tiranti, Ltd. 1953)); architecture as art and practice, with the architect as its actor (1799, Étienne-Louis Boullée, *Treatise on Architecture*, ed. Helen Rosenau (London: Alec Tiranti, Ltd. 1953); Christian Norberg-Schultz, *Intentions in Architecture* [Cambridge, MA: MIT Press, 1968]; Gianni Ottolini, *Forme e Significato in architettura* [Bari-Roma: La Terza, 1996]); and architecture as science and theory, or an objective domain of knowledge of works and practices (Aldo Rossi, *The Architecture of the City*, Cambridge MA: MIT Press, 1982, Saverio Muratori, *Studi per una operante storia urbana di Venezia*, in "Palladio", no. 3-4, 1959, pp. 46-63, Giorgio Grassi, *La costruzione logica dell'architettura* (Padova: Marsilio, 1967)).

3. Stéphane Hanrot, *A la recherche de l'architecture: essai d'épistémologie de la discipline et de la recherche architecturales* (Paris: L'Harmattan, 2002), pp. 47–74.

4. Philipe Boudon, *Architecture et architecturologie* (Paris: Atelier de recherche et d'études d'aménagement, 1975); and Alexander Tzonis, *Towards a Non-Oppressive Environment* (Cambridge, MA: MIT Press, 1972).

5. In epistemology, *doctrine* is the group of rules developed to address a problem. Theories are analytical tools for understanding, explaining, and making predictions in and about a field of knowledge (Hanrot, *A la recherche de l'architecture,* pp. 83–91).

6. Christopher Frayling, "Research in Art and Design," *Royal College of Art Research Papers* 1, no. 1 (1993): pp. 1–5.

7. "Research into (or about) design is the oldest and most widespread form of research, where design itself is the thematic object of analysis" (Uta Brandes, "Research," in *Design Dictionary,* ed. Michael Erlhoff and Tim Marshall [Basel: Birkhäuser, 2008, pp. 316–317.]); "research for design empirically supports the design process and its concretisation in artefacts" (Eleonora Lupo, "For a Practice-Led PhD Design Research in Action: Make a Work

That Is Viewed from the Inside," in *Notes on Doctoral Research in Design,* ed. Luca Guerrini [Milan: FrancoAngeli, 2010], p. 67).

8. James C. Snyder, ed., *Architectural Research* (New York: Van Nostrand Reinhold, 1984); and Marieke Van Ouwerkerk, ed., *Research by Design,* Proceedings A&B International Conference (Delft: TU-Delft University Press, 2001).

9. Lunenfeld (2007); Simon Grand, "Theory," in *Design Dictionary: Perspectives on Design Terminology,* ed. Michael Erlhoff and Tim Marshall (Basel: Birkhäuser, 2008), pp. 379–380; and Angelus Eisinger, "Stop Making Sense," in *Explorations in Architecture: Teaching Design Research,* ed. Reto Geiser (Basel: Birkhäuser, 2008).

10. Gennaro Postiglione, "The Paradox of Construction," in *Otras Vias 2: Homage to Lewerentz* (Avila, Spain: Colegio Oficial de Arquitectos de Castilla y Leon, 2006), pp. 35–47.

11. The analysis of the rules of making and building underlies the construction of a work that denies the very process that brought it to light. Free from the obligation to interpret a canon, and working exclusively with building materials, in Klippan the Swedish master overcame the definition of architecture given by Friedrich Von Schelling in his *Philosophie der Kunst* (1802; *The Philosophy of Art,* [Minneapolis: Minnesota University Press, 1989]), where he states, "Architecture is a representation of itself as construction fulfilling a purpose," proposing, with this work, an entirely new definition: architecture as paradox of construction.

12. Snyder, *Architectural Research,* p. 2.

13. Linda Groat and David Wang, *Architectural Research Methods* (New York: John Wiley & Sons, 2002); Ranjit Kumar, *Research Methodology* (London: Sage, 2005); and Snyder, *Architectural Research.*

14. Groat and Wang, *Architectural Research Methods;* Kumar, *Research Methodology;* and Snyder, *Architectural Research.*

15. Groat and Wang, *Architectural Research Methods;* Kumar, *Research Methodology;* and Snyder, *Architectural Research.* Particularly emblematic instances of pure research in the interiors field are, for example, the studies developed by Stanley Abercrombie (*A Philosophy of Interior Design* [New York: Harper & Row, 1990]), Imma Forino (*L'interno nell'interno. Una fenomenologia dell'arredamento* [Firenze: Alinea, 2001]), Gianni Ottolini (*Forme e Significato in architettura*), and Charles Rice (*The Emergence of the Interior: Architecture, Modernity, Domesticity* [London and New York: Routledge, 2007]).

16. Groat and Wang, *Architectural Research Methods;* Kumar, *Research Methodology;* and Snyder, *Architectural Research.*

17. The book deals with the domestic interior and its historical emergence as a condition of modernity related to privacy and comfort on the one hand and to consumption and self-representation on the other. Utilizing the thinking and writings of Walter Benjamin and Sigmund Freud as a point of departure, the research reexamines the emergence of the interior from its bourgeois origin into its modernist architectural manifestations by means of case studies. Consequently, the book argues that the interior emerged as an inherently dual spatial and image-based concept, an interpretation Rice proposes as a point of departure for future architectural orientations of domesticity (Marie Frier in Gennaro Postiglione's "*Mapping Interiors Research and Methods,*" research study in progress).

18. Abercrombie defines what he calls "the primacy of concept," through which he locates the task of "thinking" philosophically about the interior as the point of departure for its practice. Due to its dual content, the study can be considered as both pure and applied research (Frier in Postiglione's Mapping Interiors Research and Methods, research study in progress).

19. Michela Bassanelli in Postiglione's "Mapping Interiors Research and Methods," research study in progress.

20. The study surveys the connections linking form and life in private space by retracing them in archetypal places, in the emblematic interpretations of those places given by modern architecture, and in their stimulating contaminations offered by the current main practitioners of domestic design. The book presents a lively portrait of the ideal house in the past, the four main models of the house in the Western world, and, finally, sketches of the features of houses and domestic design in the near future (Bassanelli in Postiglione's *Mapping Interiors Research and Methods,* research study in progress).

21. Groat and Wang, *Architectural Research Methods;* Kumar, *Research Methodology;* and Snyder, *Architectural Research.* In developing a study one often returns to inquiry modes, as happens, for example, with the historical-critical research developed by Renato De Fusco (*Storia dell'arredamento. Dal '400 al '900* [Milano: FrancoAngeli, 2004]), Roderick J. Lawrence (*Housing, Dwellings and Homes: Design Theory, Research and Practice* [Chichester: John Wiley & Sons, 1987]), Anne Massey (*Interior Design of 20th Century* [New York: Thames & Hudson, 1990]), Mario Praz (*An Illustrated History of Interior Decoration: From Pompeii to Art Nouveau* [London: Thames & Hudson, 1964]), or Peter Thornton (*Authentic Decor: The Domestic Interior, 1620–1920* [London: George Weindenfeld & Nicholson, 1984]). In these studies, descriptive research is based on the scientific collection of documents (mainly secondary sources) that are often also of a quantitative kind.

22. Ottolini's and De Prizio's research—which relies on the case study method—rethinks the domestic interior as an architectural discipline by analyzing the connections between built-in furniture and architecture. The book's original contribution is its mapping of equipment organized into typologies (Bassanelli in Postiglione's *Mapping Interiors Research and Methods,* research study in progress).

23. Primary sources are original documents from the time period involved in the study, and not filtered through interpretation or evaluation. Secondary sources are almost always the result of elaborations and previous research aimed at understanding the work. Reneesh, "Primary Data," *Scridb* (August 4, 2007), http://www.scribd.com/doc/222326/Primary-Data, accessed May 18, 2012.

24. In general terms, critical practice work refers to an approach to cultural studies that, in the act of research, focuses on the semantic and cognitive value of language, such as writing and reading; the social and cultural dimension of ideologies; the value of the body and gender in the production and understanding of works and phenomena; the role of psychoanalysis in pursuing new forms of knowledge; and the cross-disciplinary nature of knowledge (Catherine Belsey, *Critical Practice* [London: Methuen, 1980]).

25. The "interior in the interior" is a definition that implies a spatial device comprising a void (the space it is possible to live in) and an envelope (the boundaries defining the space of gesture and life) in turn contained in a room. Forino surveys architectural interiors looking for meaningful case studies where this phenomenon is clearly evident.

26. De Giorgi's text comprises two parts. The first is a "cinematic" interpretation of Carlo Mollino's work with particular focus on his ideas of interior design as an interpenetration of spaces, due to his passion for photography, surrealism, and furniture design as catalyzing aspects. The second part proposes a monographic description of three designs—two houses, Minola and Devalle, and a ballroom, Lutrario, as emblematic cases of Mollino's theory of

design (Bassanelli in Postiglione's *Mapping Interiors Research and Methods,* research study in progress).

27. Sara Marinelli, "Per una topografia carnale," *Atlas,* 10, no. 23 (June 2007), pp. 6–7.

28. Operative research should not be confused with the wider and more general approach related to critical practices (Belsey, *Critical Practice*). Hence, in the domain of interiors research, critical practices should be conceived as a specific way of conducting studies that belongs, as a method, to logical argumentation and, in its objectives, to interpretative research. Clear examples are a number of studies, including Iñaki Abalos' *The Good Life: A Guided Visit to the Houses of Modernity* (Barcelona: Gustavo Gili, 2001), Gaston Bachelard's *The Poetics of Space* (New York: Orion Press, 1964), and Anthony Vidler's *The Architectural Uncanny. Essays in the Modern Unhomely* (Cambridge, MA: MIT Press, 1992).

29. Grand, "Theory," p. 335.

30. Ibid.

31. The essay "Il progetto storico" was published as a whole for the first time in Manfredo Tafuri, *La sfera e il labirinto: avanguardie e architettura da Piranesi agli anni '70* (Turin, Italy: Einaudi, 1980).

32. Colin Rowe, *The Mathematics of the Ideal Villa and Other Essays* (Cambridge, MA: MIT Press, 1976); and Tafuri, *La sfera e il labirinto.*

33. Michel Foucault, "Les intellectuals et le pouvoir, a conversation with Gilles Deleuze," *L'Arc,* no. 49 (1972), pp. 3–10.

34. Ignasi De Sola Morales, "Pratiche teoriche, pratiche storiche, pratiche architettoniche," in *Decifrare l'architettura* (Turin, Italy: Allemandi, 2001), pp. 145–57, first published in *Zodiac,* no. 21 (December 1999).

35. "*La Casa all'italiana* [the Italian-style home] is not a crammed and closed refuge against the harshness of the climate…: the Italian house is a place we choose to enjoy the beauty that our land and our sky bestow upon us during the long seasons. In the Italian house there is no clear architectural distinction between inside and outside: elsewhere there is even separation of forms and materials: here outer architecture penetrates inside and even uses stone, plasterwork and fresco…. Its design is not the mere result of the material necessities of living, it is not a mere *machine à habiter.* So-called *comfort* in the Italian-style home does not refer just to how things respond to necessity, requirements, comforts of our life and to the organization of services. Such comfort is somewhat superior, it occurs when we give architecture a measure for our own thoughts,… and in this consists the full meaning of this beautiful Italian word, *conforto.*" Gio Ponti, "*La casa all'italiana* [The Italian-style Home]," *Domus* 1, no. 1 (1928): p. 3.

36. Fulvio Irace, *Giò Ponti* (Milan, Italy: Electa, 1988).

37. Ed. Jane Rendell, Jonathan Hill, Murray Frazer, and Mark Dorrain, *Critical Architecture* (London & New York: Routledge, 2007); and Michael Osman, Adam Ruedig, Matthew Seidel, and Lisa Tilney, "Mining Authonomy," special issue, *Perspecta* no. 33, (Cambridge, MA: MIT Press, 2002).

38. "Koolhaas shows how modernity opposes integrity with fragmentation, contemplation with dynamic consumption, structural sincerity with separation between inside and outside. In other words, modernity generates what we might call a polytheist aesthetics, a sum of beliefs with no unifying ideal binding them together." Luigi Prestinenza Puglisi, "Rem Koolhaas: una morale amoralità," *Prestinenza,* http://www.prestinenza.it/scrittibrevi/articoliDomus/, accessed May 18, 2012.

39. Bernhard E. Burdek, *Design: History, Theory and Practice of Product Design* (Basel: Birkhäuser, 2005), p. 133.

40. Andrea Branzi, *No-Stop City* (Orléans, France: Editions HYX, 2006). As its authors defined it, *No-Stop City* is "a theoretical design for a widespread metropolitan system" (back cover): it is a hugely enlarged building, so big its boundaries actually become invisible. Inside it is a hollow, wired, air-conditioned, and protected space that may both accommodate activities and offer a place where the residents may rest from their nomadic wandering. "They erase all difference between architecture and urban planning thus showing that, in a society made of fluxes and relations, there is just one problem: managing a space that is only made of communication; they contrast the principles of *existenz minimum* made of walls and boundaries enclosing cramped and tayloristically organized environments with those of free bodies and objects in a limitless space; by focusing on what is immaterial, ephemeral, changing, they denounce the end of traditional architecture conceived as a composition of objects, forms, styles." Luigi Prestinenza Puglisi, "Burkhardt—Branzi," *Prestinenza,* http://www.prestinenza.it/articolo.aspx?id=95, accessed May 18, 2012.

41. Andrea Branzi, *Modernità debole e diffusa* (Milan, Italy: Skira, 2006), p. 14; translation by Ilaria Parini.

42. The main function of a research study is to explain how answers will be found to research questions, defining the logic of the inquiry. It could be understood as a *strategy,* a plan of actions designed to achieve the particular goal the research wishes to reach.

43. It is worth noting that since the 1920s Italian schools of architecture have had architects who, being both practitioners and professors, taught furniture design and interior decoration (a tradition inaugurated, for example, at the Politecnico di Milano by Giò Ponti and followed first by Franco Albini and Carlo De Carli, and later by Vittoriano Viganò and others).

44. Vera De Prizio and Gianni Ottolini, *La casa attrezzata* (Naples, Italy: Liguori, 2005); and ed. Roberto Rizzi, *Culture of Living* (Milan, Italy: Lybra, 2003).

45. Ed. Adriano Cornoldi, *L'architettura della casa* (Rome: Officina edizioni, 1988); and ed. Adriano Cornoldi, *Architettura dei luoghi domestici: Il progetto del comfort* (Milan, Italy: Jaca Book, 1994).

46. Alison's work focuses on a particular history-related investigative research method that by using surveys, redrawing, and modeling, as well as the critical and historical analysis of the subject and its author, sometimes results in prototypes and even in products. In the different phases of its development, this operation pursues an immediate primary goal: propagating universally shared cultural values by offering "reconstructed" furniture designs for current use. Filippo Alison, *Le sedie di Charles Rennie Mackintosh,* ed. Grafiche Milani (Milan, Italy: Documenti di Casabella, 1973); Filippo Alison, *E.G. Asplund. Mobili ed oggetti* (Milan, Italy: Electa, 1985); and Filippo Alison, *Frank Lloyd Wright, Designer of Furniture* (Naples, Italy: Fratelli Fiorentino, 1997).

47. Groat and Wang, *Architectural Research Methods;* Kumar, *Research Methodology;* and Snyder, *Architectural Research.* This is the typical case of historical studies like Stefan Muthesius's *The Poetic Home: Designing the 19th-Century Domestic Interior* (London: Thames & Hudson, 2009), John Pile's *A History of Interior Design* (London: Laurence King, 2005), Witold Rybczynski, *Home: A Short History of an Idea* (New York: Viking Penguin, 1986), and Peter Thornton, *Authentic Decor: The Domestic Interior, 1620–1920* (London: George Weindenfeld & Nicholson, 1984).

48. The leading idea of Rybczynski's work is that in each age humankind has a different relation with domestic space due to the different home-living cultures that alternate over time. The narration is developed across ten chapters, each identified by a name that summarizes the main value of the historical age in question. Each chapter is introduced by an emblematic work that is analyzed in terms of its technical development of furniture and tools and, most of all, the modifications brought by social and cultural changes that affected the individuals' perception of themselves and their surroundings and that inevitably reflect on the organization of living spaces (Bassanelli in Postiglione's "Mapping Interiors Research and Methods," research study in progress).

49. These are studies that use approaches typical of cultural studies and critical practices.

50. Hanrot, *A la recherche de l'architecture.* Examples of such an approach are, besides others already mentioned, John Baudrillard's *The System of Objects* (Brooklyn, NY: Verso, 1996), Carlo De Carli's *Architettura: spazio primario* (Milan: Hoepli, 1982), and Norberg-Schultz's *Intentions in Architecture.*

51. Robert K. Yin, *Case Study Research: Design and Methods* (Thousand Oaks, CA: Sage, 2009).

52. Research in interiors that uses large work catalogs include Cornoldi, *Architettura dei luoghi domestici;* and De Prizio and Ottolini, *La casa attrezzata.*

53. *Critical cases* are case studies chosen because they do not contain what the research is looking for even though they should. *Extreme cases* are cases that present extremely strong and defined individual elements that the research intends to understand (describing and/or explaining and/or interpreting). *Emblematic cases* are special case studies chosen because they contain what the research is looking for, as already known findings: through the analysis of accurately selected case studies, the research verifies the principles hypothetically assumed and/or develops comparative studies to identify their commonalities and differences.

54. Yin, *Case Study Research.*

55. Morales proceeds by using two narrative devices: on the one hand, he describes the designs and their related cultural movements; on the other hand, he interrelates them in a comparative manner, thus highlighting their shared features and differences. The collection of case studies starts in the 1930s, the age of art avant-garde, and continues through the contemporary age of "dissolution of the room" when technology has overridden space (Bassanelli in Postiglione's *Mapping Interiors Research and Methods,* research study in progress).

56. Peter Reason and Hilary Bradbury, eds., *Handbook of Action Research* (London: Sage, 2001); and Kurt Lewin, "Action Research and Minority Problems," *Journal of Social Issues* 2, no. 4 (1946): pp. 34–46.

57. Stephen Kemmis and Robin McTaggart, *The Action Research Planner* (Victoria, Australia: Deakin University Press, 1982).

58. This is how most of the already above-mentioned historical studies have been developed.

59. Ed. Philippe Ariès and Georges Duby, *Histoire de la vie privèe* (Paris: Editions du Seuil, 1987); and Susan Kent, *Domestic Architecture and the Use of Space: An Interdisciplinary Cross-Cultural Study* (New York: Cambridge University Press, 1990).

60. In this special issue of *Domus,* "Domus d'Autore" (no. 1, 2006), OMA and Rem Koolhaas as guest editors develop an analysis of some of their own works aimed at verifying the conditions of their interiors and users' satisfaction rate with architectural space just a few years after the buildings were occupied.

61. One could refer to the multiple calls for papers connected to international conferences, such as the biannual Interiors Forum World promoted by the Politecnico di Milano, the

Interiors Forum Scotland meetings, and the annual meeting launched by the Modern Interiors Research Centre at Kingston University, as well as the related "call for contributions" for *Interiors: Design, Architecture, Culture,* a peer-reviewed journal of interior studies established in 2010. Similarly, other initiatives are promoted by the Interior Design/Interior Architecture Educators Association in Australia and New Zealand, including calls for papers in connection with both international conferences and the publication of the peer-reviewed journal *IDEA.*

5 PROTECTED TITLE IN BRITAIN

1. Recommended reading is Megan Aldrich, ed., *The Craces, Royal Decorators 1768–1899* (Brighton, UK: John Murray, The Royal Pavilion, Art Gallery and Museums, 1990).
2. De Montfort University, Leicester, and its preceding iterations in art and design.
3. BIID Interior Design Yearbook, article Michael Leese Giles, Godfrey Giles, Master Worshipful Company Painters Stainers, PP British Institute of Interior Design (1899–1988 then merged Chartered Society of Designers).
4. John Dibblee Crace.
5. Paul Binski, "Prince, Gilbert (d. 1396)," in *Oxford Dictionary of National Biography* (Oxford: Oxford University Press, 2004), http://www.oxforddnb.com/view/article/55379, accessed June 8, 2011.
6. Peer Monamy was later known for his marine paintings of shipping, but in September 1696 the Painter–Stainers' Company records Monamy as being indentured for seven years to William Clarke, a leading house painter and former master of the company. Pieter van der Merwe, "Monamy, Peter (bap. 1681, d. 1749)," in *Oxford Dictionary of National Biography,* http://www.oxforddnb.com/view/article/18935, accessed April 12, 2011.
7. http://www.paintershall.co.uk/history/.
8. A *plafond* is a flat surface, normally a ceiling that is "art-painted."
9. William Sandby, *The History of the Royal Academy of Arts* (1862), vol. 2, p. 13.
10. Alan Borg, *The History of the Worshipful Company of Painters, Otherwise Painter Stainers* (UK: Jeremy Mills, 2005).
11. The Incorporated Institute of British Decorators was formed by the Worshipful Company of Painters and Stainers principally as an educational institute for the development and promotion of decoration.
12. "Crace and Sons—His Royal Highness the Prince of Wales Quitted the Pavilion on Friday, for London, but Is Expected," *Hampshire Telegraph and Sussex Chronicle* (Portsmouth, UK), April 16, 1804.
13. Robin Stummer, "High-Level Schism Opens Up at Royal Academy," *The Guardian,* March 15, 2004.
14. M. H. Port, "Founders of the Royal Institute of British Architects (act. 1834–1835)," in *Oxford Dictionary of National Biography,* online ed. (Oxford : Oxford University Press, May 2009), http://www.oxforddnb.com/view/theme/97265, accessed June 29, 2011.
15. http://www.architecture.com/TheRIBA/AboutUs/Ourhistory.aspx. The first compulsory examinations for the RIBA were held in 1882.
16. Nash and Fredrick Crace collaborated on the Royal Pavilion in Brighton, http://openlearn.open.ac.uk/file.php/2339/!via/oucontent/course/597/plates1–11.pdf.

17. Pugin and J. G. Crace worked together on Pugin's House, Ramsgate, and the Palace of Westminster. E. W. Pugin, "Who Was the Architect of the Parliament Houses," *The Times,* September 7, 1867, p. 11.

18. James Green, *Building News,* 1867, p. 257, quoted in Helen Smith, *Decorative Painting in the Domestic Interior in England and Wales, c. 1850–1890* (New York: Garland, 1984), p. 224.

19. Select Committee (1849), p. 531, clauses 2093.

20. Records from the Victoria and Albert Museum, Summary.

21. *Report from the Select Committee on the School of Design together with the Proceedings of the Committee, Minutes of Evidence, Appendix and Index, Ordered by the House of Commons to be printed July 27, 1849,* available at http://books.google.co.uk/books?id=BI0SAAAAYAAJ&pg=PA476&dq=crace+schools+of+design &hl=en&sa=X&ei=zbX-TrOCNoTR8gOAlKGtCA&ved=0CEUQ6AEwAA#v.

22. Ibid., p. xxix.

23. Ibid.

24. "Royal College of Art," *Survey of London* 38: *South Kensington Museums Area* (1975): pp. 260–61, http://www.british-history.ac.uk/report.aspx?compid=47535, accessed August 31, 2011.

25. *Report from the Select Committee on the School of Design.*

26. "Proposed Leicester School of Design," *The Leicester Chronicle or, Commercial and Agricultural Advertiser,* January 13, 1849.

27. Gale Document Number: R3213102377.

28. Gale Document Number: R3213102377.

29. *The Leicester Chronicle or, Commercial and Agricultural Advertiser,* March 1, 1862, p. 1.

30. James Astbury Hammersley on Government Schools of Art, *Nottinghamshire Guardian,* March 18, 1862, p. 7.

31. "Leicester School of Art," *Leicester Chronicle and the Leicestershire Mercury,* February 26, 1870, p. 8, available from *19th Century British Library Newspapers: Part II Online,* http://gale.cengage.co.uk/.

32. *Leicester Chronicle and the Leicestershire Mercury,* April 16, 1870.

33. Recommended reading: Ro Spankie.

34. Howard W. Binns, "History of British Decorators Association" pamphlet (British Decorators Association, 1994).

35. "Art Training," *The Sydney Morning Herald* (New South Wales), July 10, 1871, p. 3.

36. Crace reputedly sold the business after a series of pay demands and strikes by artisan workmen. Cowtan Cowtan or Cowtan and Sons, Decorators and Upholsterers, Records 1881–1959, deposited in the London Metropolitan Archives, City of London, GB 0074 B/CWT.

37. Spencer replaced Walter Crane as head of the Royal College of Art (previously known as the South Kensington School or National School for Art).

38. Pamphlets and records held by the author in trust. Incomplete set of pamphlets of lectures held by IIBD. Some copies in the RIBA library.

39. "1933–34 Prospectus, House Painting, Decorating and Sign Writing, Cont'd." (Leicester: Leicester College of Art and Technology, 1934), p. 34.

40. "Prospectus Faculty of Three-Dimensional Design" (Leicester: Leicester College of Art, 1966), p. 7. Leicester College of Art was part of Leicestershire College of Art and Technology

and was part of Leicestershire Education Department of Leicestershire County Council, the local authority.

41. Ibid., p. 8.

42. Brian Aylward, "The Oxford 'A' Level Examination in Design: An Interim Appraisal of an Experimental Approach," *Studies in Design Education Craft & Technology* 4, no. 1 (1971). Aylward was the Leicestershire County Council advisor on crafts and design for primary and secondary schools. A. W. Hodge was head of the Faculty of Design at Leicester College of Art, and Ken Baynes at Hornsey College of Art constructed the curriculum for this experimental project.

43. http://vads.ac.uk/diad/article.php?year=1971&title=273&article=d.273.27.

44. The Gateway Grammar School in Leicester was a technical grammar school formed in 1922.

45. The author of this chapter attended this school, being the last cohort to pass the selection process as a 13+ candidate . To the detriment of his formal academic achievement he made full use of this approach, which formed the spark that ignited his design career.

46. http://www.nationalarchives.gov.uk/catalogue/displaycataloguedetails.asp?CATID=73&CATLN=1&accessmethod=5&j=1.

47. Appendix 1, Memorandum and Articles of British Institute of Interior Design.

48. http://www.facultyofdecoration.org/.

49. UCAS information.

6 REGULATIONS AND CONVENTIONS

The author wishes to thank the following contributors to the survey: Naning Adiwoso, Indonesia; Constance Ann, Singapore; Joan Aragones, Spain; Carlo Beltramelli, Italy; Vanessa Brady, United Kingdom; Yao Cheng Chung, Taiwan; Cindy Coleman, United States; Kerstin Geppert, Germany; Ellen Klingenberg, Norway; Madeline Lester, Australia; Thomas Ness, Norway; Davina Preca, Malta; Per Reinholtz, Sweden; Andrew Schuncke, Australia; Thomas Wachter, Switzerland; Benedict Weiss, Switzerland.

1. Leadership in Energy and Environmental Design, a green building certification system developed by the U.S. Green Building Council (http://www.usgbc.org).

2. "North American Industry Classification System," U.S. Census Bureau, http://www.census.gov/eos/www/naics/, accessed March 10, 2013.

3. "Detailed Structure and Explanatory Notes: ISIC Rev.4 Code 7410," United Nations Statistics Division, http://unstats.un.org/unsd/cr/registry/regcs.asp?Cl=27&Lg=1&Co=7410, accessed March 3, 2013.

4. *Klassifikation der Wirtschaftszweige, Ausgabe 2008* (Herausgeber: Statistisches Bundesamt, Wiesbaden).

5. Directive 2005/36/EC of the European Parliament and of the Councilon the Recognition of Professional Qualifications. EU member states must implement this directive in their national legislation. "Free Movement of Professionals," European Commission, last updated November 26, 2012, http://ec.europa.eu/internal_market/qualifications/future_en.htm, accessed March 10, 2013.

6. Conseil Français des Architectes d'Intérieur, http://www.cfai.fr.

7. California Council for Interior Design Certification, http://www.ccidc.org.

8. "Codex Alimentarius: Food Hygiene: Basic Texts, Second Edition," Secretariat of the Joint FAO/WHO Food Standards Programme, http://www.fao.org/docrep/005/Y1579E/Y1579E00.htm, accessed March 10, 2013.

9. European Council of Interior Architects, http://www.ecia.net.

10. *Locke versus Shore,* U.S. District Court for the Northern District of Florida, Case No. 4:09-cv-00193-RH-WCS,February 4, 2010, Florida Department of Business and Professional Legislation, http://www.myfloridalicense.com/dbpr/pro/arch/documents/id_opinion.pdf, accessed March 10, 2013.

11. American Society of Interior Designers, http://www.asid.org.

12. "ASID Legislative Policy," American Society of Interior Designers, http://www.asid.org/custom/ASID2013/documents/LegislativePolicy_1207.pdf, March 10, 2013.

13. Conseil Français des Architectes d'Intérieur, http://www.cfai.fr.

14. National Council for Interior Design Qualification, http://www.ncidq.org.

15. Sveriges Arkitekter, http://www.arkitekt.se.

16. Design Institute of Australia, http://www.dia.org.au.

17. Institute of Designers in Ireland, http://www.idi-design.ie.

18. European Council of Interior Architects, http://www.ecia.net.

19. Asian Pacific Space Designers Association, http://www.apsda.net.

20. Consejo Iberoamericano de Diseñadores de Interiores, http://www.cidi-iberomericano.blogspot.com.

21. American Society of Interior Designers, http://www.asid.org.

22. International Interior Design Association, http://www.iida.org.

23. Interior Designers of Canada, http://www.idcanada.org.

24. International Federation of Interior Architects and Designers, http://www.ifiworld.org.

25. Council for Interior Design Accreditation, http://www.accredit-id.org.

26. Akkreditierungsverbund für Studiengänge der Architektur und Planung, http://www.asap-akkreditierung.de.

27. "ECIA Educational Recognition Program," ECIA, http://www.ecia.net/ home/blogs/ecia-recognition-and-educational-membership.

28. Interior Design Educators Council, http://www.idec.org.

29. Interior Educators, http://www.interioreducators.co.uk.

30. Interior Design Educators Association, http://www.idea-edu.com.

31. Interiors Forum Scotland, http://www.interiorsforumscotland.com.

32. Interiors Forum World, http://www.interiorsforumworld.net.

33. Among others: Special Publication 1032 of the National Institute of Standards and Technology in the United States, http://fire.nist.gov/CDPUBS/NISTSP_1032/Data.htm.

7 THE PROFESSION THAT DARE NOT SPEAK ITS NAME

1. International Federation of Interior Architects/Designers, *http://www.ifiworld.org.*

2. Philip M. Parker, *Report on Interior Design Services: World Market Segmentation by City* (San Diego, CA: ICON Group International, 2009).

8 INTERIORIZT

1. John Gigli, Frazer Hay, Edward Hollis, Alex Milton, Andy Milligan, and Drew Plunkett, eds., *Thinking inside the Box: A Reader in Interiors for the 21st Century* (London: Middlesex University Press, 2007), p. xi.

2. John Pile, *A History of Interior Design*, 3rd ed. (London: Laurence King, 2009), p. 11.

3. Shashi Caan, "IFI President's Update," International Federation of Interior Architects/ Designers, September 22, 2010, http://ifiworld.org/presidents_update/?p=20#Homepage. See also Shashi Caan, *Rethinking Design and Interiors: Human Beings in the Built Environment* (London: Laurence King, 2011).

4. Michel Foucault and Gilles Deleuze, "Intellectuals and Power: A Conversation between Michel Foucault and Gilles Deleuze," in *Language, Counter-Memory, Practice: Selected Essays and Interviews,* by Michel Foucault, ed. Donald Bouchard (Ithaca, NY: Cornell University Press, 1977), p. 208.

5. Walter Benjamin, *The Arcades Project* (Cambridge, MA: Harvard University Press, 2002), p. 19.

6. Ibid., p. 206.

7. Ibid., pp. 8–9.

8. Ibid., p. 20.

9. Ibid., p. 211.

10. Ibid., p. 216.

11. Charles Rice, "The Geography of the Diagram: The Rose Seidler House," in *Designing the Modern Interior: From the Victorians to Today,* ed. Penny Sparke, Anne Massey, Trevor Keeble, and Brenda Martin (Oxford and New York: Berg, 2009), p. 132.

12. Charles Rice, *The Emergence of the Interior: Architecture, Modernity, Domesticity* (London: Routledge, 2007), p. 9.

13. Graeme Brooker and Sally Stone, *What Is Interior Design?* (Mies, Switzerland: RotoVision SA, 2010), p. 8.

14. Graeme Brooker and Sally Stone, *Re-Readings: Interior Architecture and the Design Principles of Remodelling Existing Buildings* (London: Royal Institute of British Architects Enterprises, 2004), p. 19.

15. Ibid.

16. Michael Benedikt, "Environmental Stoicism and Place Machismo," *Harvard Design Magazine* 16 (2002), pp. 1–8, 4.

17. Ibid.

18. Ibid., p. 2.

19. Ibid., p. 4.

20. Andrea Branzi, "Retailing in the Globalisation Era," in *Places and Themes of Interiors: Contemporary Research Worldwide,* ed. Luca Basso Peressut Imma Forino, Gennaro Postiglione, and Francesco Scullica (Milan, Italy: FrancoAngeli, 2008), p. 94.

21. Andrea Branzi, "Provocation: Ten Modest Suggestions for a New Athens Charter," *IDEA Journal* (2010): p. 12.

22. Branzi, "Retailing in the Globalisation Era," p. 96.

23. Suzie Attiwill, "Introduction: Composing Forces," special issue, *IDEA Journal: INSIDE-OUT* (2005): pp. 1–6, http://www.idea-edu.com/Journal/2005/2005-IDEA-Journal, accessed June 24, 2010.

24. Elizabeth Grosz, *Chaos, Territory, Art: Deleuze and the Framing of the Earth* (New York: Columbia University Press, 2008), p. 12, originally published in *IDEA Journal: INSIDEOUT* (2005), http://www.idea-edu.com/Journal/2005/Chaos-Territory-Art.-Deleuze-and-the-Framing-of-the-Earth, accessed June 24, 2010.

25. Gilles Deleuze, *Foucault* (Minneapolis: University of Minnesota Press, 1988).

26. Gilles Deleuze, "Ethology: Spinoza and Us," in *Incorporations,* ed. Jonathan Crary and Sanford Kwinter (New York: Zone Books, 1992), pp. 626 and 628.

27. Erin Manning, "Creative Propositions for Thought in Motion," special issue, *INFLEX-ion: A Journal for Research Creation: How Is Research-Creation?* (2008): p. 20, http://www.inflexions.org, accessed March 7, 2010.

28. Anna Kajumulo Tibaijuka, "Inaugural Address UN Pavilion Lecture Series," Shanghai World Expo 2010, May 1, 2010, http://www.unhabitat.org/content.asp?cid=8273&catid=560&typeid=8&subMenuId=0, accessed April 24, 2011.

29. Vittoria di Palma, Diana Periton, and Marina Lathouri, eds., "Introduction," in *Intimate Metropolis: Urban Subjects in the Modern City* (London: Routledge, 2009), pp. 1–8.

30. Felix Guattari, *The Three Ecologies* (London: Continuum, 2008).

31. Adolf Loos, "The Poor Little Rich Man," in *Spoken into the Void: Collected Essays 1897–1900* (Cambridge, MA: MIT Press, 1982), pp. 125–27, originally published in *Neues Wiener Tagblatt,* April 26, 1900.

32. Michael Meredith, "Whatever Happened to 'Whatever Happened to Total Design?' The Momentary Utopian Jouissance of the Bouroullec Brothers," *Harvard Design Magazine* 29 (Fall/Winter 2008): p. 109.

9 SURFACE DEMONSTRATIONS, NEUTRAL, NOT SO

1. Diana Young, "The Material Value of Colour: The Estate Agent's Tale," *Home Cultures* 1, no. 1 (2004): p. 9.

2. Francis Ching and Cassandra Adams, *Building Construction Illustrated,* 3rd ed. (New York: John Wiley & Sons, 2001), p. 10.10.

3. Mark Burry and Julieanna Preston, *Construction Primer* (Wellington, Australia: Victoria University Wellington Press, 2000), p. 154.

4. Edward Allen and Joseph Iano, *Fundamentals of Building Construction Materials and Methods,* 4th ed. (Chichester: John Wiley & Sons, 2004), p. 775.

5. George Sher, *Beyond Neutrality: Perfection and Politics* (Cambridge: Cambridge University Press, 1997), p. 1.

6. Philip C. Jessup and Francis Deák, *Neutrality: Its History, Economics and Law,* vol. 1, *The Origins* (New York: Octagon Books, 1976), p. 249.

7. Department of Building and Housing (Te Tari Kaupapa Whare in Maori), *Residential Tenancy Agreement* (Wellington: New Zealand Government, 2005), p. 4, http://www.dhb.govt.nz, accessed June 23, 2010.

8. *GIB Site Code for Residential and Commercial Installations: CBI 5113* (New Zealand: Winstone Wallboards, May 2006), p. 92, http://www.gib.co.nz/assets/Uploads/Gib-Site-Guide-2003.pdf, accessed June 24, 2010.

9. Robin Kinross, "The Rhetoric of Neutrality," *Design Issues* 2, no. 2 (1985): p. 27.

10. Ibid., p. 25.

11. Nils Brunsson and Bengt Jacobson, *A World of Standards* (New York: Oxford University Press, 2000), pp. 138–50.

12. Allen and Iano, *Fundamentals of Building Construction Materials,* p. 761.
13. Luce Irigaray, *To Speak Is Never Neutral,* trans. Gail Swab (London: Continuum, 2002), p. 137.
14. Ibid., p. 138.
15. Ibid., p. 140.
16. Lorraine Daston and Peter Galison, *Objectivity* (New York: Zone Books, 2007), p. 17.
17. Gui Bonsiepe, "Visual/Verbal Rhetoric," *Ulm* 14–16 (1965): p. 30.
18. Kinross, "Rhetoric of Neutrality," pp. 29–30.
19. Jacques Rancière, *The Politics of Aesthetics: The Distribution of the Sensible,* trans. Gabriel Rockhill (London: Continuum, 2004), p. 16.
20. Kinross, "Rhetoric of Neutrality," pp. 20–21.
21. Young, "Material Value of Colour," p. 9.
22. Ibid., p. 13.
23. Ibid., p. 15.
24. Lesley Naa Norle Lokko, *White Papers, Black Marks: Architecture, Race, Culture* (London: Athlone, 2000), p. 18.
25. Craig L. Wilkins, *The Aesthetics of Equity: Notes on Race, Space, Architecture and Music* (Minneapolis: University of Minnesota Press, 2007), p. 10.
26. Mark Wigley, *White Walls, Designer Dresses* (London: MIT Press, 1995), p. 362.
27. Ibid., p. 361.
28. Naa Norle Lokko, *White Papers, Black Marks,* p. 27.

10 A SHORT HISTORY OF THE ROOM

1. Robin Middleton, "Soane's Spaces and the Matter of Fragmentation," in *John Soane, Architect: Master of Space and Light,* ed. Margaret Richardson and Mary Anne Stevens (London: Royal Academy of Arts, 1999 p. 32).
2. Ibid.
3. Jean-Nicolas-Louis Durand (b. Paris, September 18, 1760, d. Thiais, December 31, 1834).
4. Augustus Welby Pugin, *Contrasts* (1836; repr., Leicester: Leicester University Press, 1969). An excellent description of the arguments accompanying the development of a modern Gothic in the nineteenth century is included in George L. Hershey, *High Victorian Gothic, a Study in Associationism* (Baltimore: John Hopkins University Press, 1972).
5. Le Corbusier, *Vers une Architecture* (*Towards a New Architecture*) (Paris: G. Cres et Cie, 1924).
6. Ibid., 82.
7. The phenomenon of the triumph of the pure surface over the articulated classical surface at the beginning of the twentieth century probably deserves a book of its own. Perhaps a contribution to understanding the classical order can be found in *The Art of Memory* by Frances Yates (Chicago: University of Chicago Press, 1966), which investigates in part the use of classical architecture as a device for lodging specific facts at specific places as part of a spatial matrix of memory, in the mind and in the world. It can be understood that this is an ability of the classical facade that would be found missing in the plain, undifferentiated modernist facade. One is tempted to say that the nonreferential nature of undecorated modernism is the clearest sign of its progressive nature, and so to forget the past.

8. "Ornament and Crime," first published in German in 1929 by the *Frankfurter Zeitung,* despite it already having appeared in *l'Esprit Nouveau* and elsewhere

9. Theo Van Doesburg, *Towards a Plastic Architecture* (1924), sixteen points of the principles of a new architecture, (quoted in T. M. Brown Gerrit Rietveld, p.68) "*Point 8. PLAN.* The new architecture has broken through the wall and in so doing has completely eliminated the divorce of inside and out. The walls are no longer loadbearing; they are reduced to points of support. And as a result there is generated a new, open plan, totally different from the classic because inside and outside spaces interpenetrate." First published in Cahiers D'aujourd'hui, Paris May 1913.

10. Gerrit Rietveld, "View of Life as a Background for My Work," in *The Work of G. Rietveld, Architect,* by Theodore Brown (Utrecht, the Netherlands: A. W. Bruna and Zoon, 1958), p. 162. This quote and the later Van Doesburg quote are cited from an as yet unpublished dissertation by William Fisher, "Life without Walls, Modernist Approaches to the Domestic Free Plan."

11. The increase in privacy and the decline of conviviality in the history of the house was a constant theme of the work of Diploma 4 at the Architectural Association in the 1970s, devoted to the architecture of the house, which was taught by Robin Evans and me. The best published descriptions of the thinking underlying the Unit's work are contained in the articles by Robin Evans, "Figures, Doors and Passages," *Architectural Design* 4 (1978), and Fred Scott, "Pictorial and Sensual Space," *AAQ* 8, no. 4 (1976).

12. Life in the modern home as proposed in *Space in the Home,* metric ed. (London: HMSO, 1968) is made up of a sequence of sedentary situations, mainly sitting and sleeping. The proposition quietly censures the other more rambunctious social occasions, parties, for instance, and dancing. William Fisher Life Without Walls School of Architecture, London Metropolitan University, March 2009 p.9.

13. Fred Scott, *On Altering Architecture* (New York: Routledge, 2008), p. 148.

11 NEW OCCUPANCY

1. Christian Norberg-Schulz, *Genius Loci: Towards a Phenomenology of Architecture* (London: Rizzoli International Publications, 1979), p. 7.

2. Christian Norberg-Schulz, *Existence, Space & Architecture* (Praeger Publishers, 1974). William Fisher Life Without Walls School of Architecture, London Metropolitan University, March 2009 p.9.

3. Norberg-Schulz, *Genius Loci,* p. 6.

4. Ibid., p. 23.

12 PROGRAM, FUNCTION, AND FABRICATION

1. Terence Riley, "The Architect's Room," in *Fabricaciones/Fabrications,* ed. Terence Riley (Barcelona: Museu d'Art Contemporani de Barcelona and ACTAR, 1998), pp. 87–95. The *Oxford English Dictionary* definition of *fabrication* is 1. (n) The action or process of fabricating (fabricate v.1a); construction, fashioning, manufacture; also, a particular branch of manufacture. Now *rare.* 2. The action of fabricating or "making up"; the invention (of a statement); the forging (of a document). Also *concr.* An invention; a false statement; a

forgery. OED online, http://www.oed.com/view/Entry/67399?redirectedFrom=FABRIC ATION#eid, accessed 21 May 2013.

2. "Internet of Things: What Is It," *Council: The Internet of Things,* http://www. theinternetofthings.eu/internet-of-things-what-is-it%3F, accessed October 5, 2011.

3. *Mouseions* were often described as temples of the muses; see Richard W. Budd and Brent D. Ruben, *Beyond Media: New Approaches to Mass Communication,* 2nd rev. ed. (Piscataway, NJ: Transaction, 1988).

4. Pierre Von Meiss, *Elements of Architecture, from Form to Place* (New York: E&F Spon, 1990), p. 101. See also Leland Roth, *Understanding Architecture: Its Elements, History, and Meaning,* Icon Editions Series, 2nd ed. (New York: Westview, 2006), pp. 90–103.

5. Floating Lab Collective, http://floatinglabcollective.com/?page_id=133, accessed June 10, 2012.

6. Juhani Pallasmaa, "Hapticity and Time: Notes on Fragile Architecture," *Architectural Review* 207, no.1239 (May 2000): pp. 78–84, 82.

7. Pierre Von Meiss, in *Elements of Architecture, from Form to Place (New York: E&F Spon, 1990), in chapter two Phenomena of Perception,* pp. 16–20.

8. Von Meiss, *Elements of Architecture,* pp. 15–20.

9. Matiu Carr, *Barcelona Pavilion: Projection, Interpretation and Reflection,* quoting Gill Matthewson, "Standing in the Shadows," Paper presented at the ACCESSORY/architecture Conference 1995 held by the School of Architecture at the University of Auckland, has suggested that the authorship of the Barcelona Pavilion may at least in part be attributed to Lilly Reich, an accomplished designer who worked with Mies van der Rohe for a large part of his early career; Projection, Interpretation and Reflection, http://archpropplan.auckland.ac.nz/ virtualtour/barcelona/bptxt.htm, accessed July 12, 2011.

10. Charles Rice, "For a Concept of the Domestic Interior: Some Historical and Theoretical Challenges," in *Thinking inside the Box: A Reader in Interiors for the 21st Century,* ed. Edward Hollis, Andrew Milligan, John Gigli, Drew Plunkett, Frazer Hay, and Alex Milton (London: Middlesex University Press, 2007), p. 180.

11. Gaston Bachelard, *The Poetics of Space,* new ed. (Boston: Beacon, 1992), p. 36.

12. Rice, "For a Concept of the Domestic Interior," pp. 177–85.

13. "Glasgow Riverside Museum of Transport," Zaha Hadid Architects, http://www.zaha-hadid. com/architecture/glasgow-riverside-museum-of-transport/, August 2, 2012.

14. Pamela Robertson, *The Mackintosh House* (Glasgow, UK: Hunterian Art Gallery, University of Glasgow, 2008), p. 24, http://www.gla.ac.uk/hunterian/collections/permanentdisplays/ themackintoshhouse/#d.en.199546, accessed March 5, 2012.

15. Ibid.

16. W. H. Auden, "Writing," in *The English Auden* (London: Faber and Faber, [1932] 1978), p. 303

17. Philip Ursprung, "Anachronism and Entropy," in *Almost Everything* (Barcelona: Ediciones Poligrafa, 2008), p. 167.

18. Ibid.

19. "History," *Sir John Soane's Museum,* http://www.soane.org/history, accessed March 29, 2013.

20. Rice, "Concept of the Domestic Interior."

21. Carole Dingle, *Memorable Quotations: French Writers of the Past* (Bloomington, IN: iUniverse, 2000)

22. *MoLI, the Museum of Lost Interactions,* University of Dundee, Department of Digital Interaction Design, http://imd.dundee.ac.uk/moli/, accessed December 3, 2011.

23. Graham Pullin, "Statement of Practice: Curating and Creating Design Collections, from 'Social Mobiles' to the 'Museum of Lost Interactions' and 'Six Speaking Chairs,'" *Journal of Design and Culture* 2, no. 3 (2010): pp. 309–28.

24. H. Glenn Penny, *Objects of Culture: Ethnology and Ethnographic Museums in Imperial Germany,* (Chapel Hill: University of North Carolina Press, 2002), p. 296.

25. Sverre Fehn, quoted in Per Olaf Fjeld, *The Pattern of Thoughts* (New York: Monacelli, 2009), p. 127.

26. See Kerstin Leder et al., "Tagging is Connecting: Shared Object Memories as Channels for Sociocultural Cohesion," *M/C Journal* 13, no. 1 (2010), http://journal.media-culture.org. au/index.php/mcjournal/article/viewArticle/209, accessed February 9, 2011. TOTeM is a £1.39 million ($2.1 million) research project exploring social memory in the emerging culture of the *Internet of Things.* This term is used to describe the increasingly popular use of tagging technologies to track physical objects in the real world. TOTeM focuses instead on existing artifacts that hold significant personal resonance, not because they are particularly expensive or useful, but because they contain or "evoke" memories of people, places, times, events, or ideas. Objects across a mantelpiece can become conduits between events that happened in the past and people who will occupy the future.

27. "Technology Strategy Board to invest £5m into the 'Internet of Things'," Technology Strategy Board, May 11, 2011, http://www.innovateuk.org/content/news/technology-strategy-board-to-invest-5m-into-the-in.ashx, accessed June 9, 2011.

28. Nigel Rix, "'Internet of Things' Convergence Competition," Technology Strategy Board, September 26, 2011, https://connect.innovateuk.org/web/connected-world/articles/-/blogs/internet-of-things-convergence-competition, accessed December 21, 2011.

29. Russell M. Davies, "The Next Technological Revolution," *Four Thought,* prod. Giles Edwards, BBC Radio 4, September 22, 2011, http://www.bbc.co.uk/programmes/b014qndl#synopsis, accessed January 1, 2012.

30. Bill Moggeridge, "Multisensory and Multimedia," in *Designing Interactions,* 1st ed. (Cambridge, MA: MIT Press, 2007), chap. 8.

31. Wendy Vogel, "Interview: Josef Helfenstein," *By Any Means Necessary* 157 (November 12, 2010), http://www.fluentcollab.org/mbg/index.php/interview/index/157/85, accessed November 23, 2011.

32. "MERZbau reconstruction," YouTube, July 29, 2011, http://www.youtube.com/watch?v= 4cF2Qb4bNm0, accessed March 29, 2013.

33. Gwendolyn in Webster's essay entitled 'Kurt Schwitter's Merzbau' *Color and Collage,* ed. Isabel Schulz (New Haven, CT: Yale University Press, 2010), p. 130 in Webster's essay entitled 'Kurt Schwitter's Merzbau'.

34. *Kurt Schwitters: Color and Collage,* exhibit at Princeton University Art Museum, March 26 to June 26, 2011, originating at the Menil Collection; see "Kurt Schwitters: Color and Collage," Princeton University Art Museum, press release, http://artmuseum.princeton.edu/about/press-room/announcement/kurt-schwitters-color-and-collage, accessed March 29, 2013.

35. *Simulacrum* (plural: *simulacra*) comes from the Latin *simulare,* "to make like, to put on an appearance of," originally meaning a material object representing something (such as a cult image representing a deity, or a painted still-life of a bowl of fruit). By the 1800s it developed a sense of a "mere" image, an empty form devoid of spirit, and descended to connote a specious or fallow representation; "Simulacrum," *Psychology Wiki,* March 23, 2006, http://psychology.wikia.com/wiki/Simulacrum, accessed April 23, 2011.

36. Mark Robbins, "Construir/Edification," in *Fabricaciones/Fabrications,* pp. 99–100.

37. The "Daguerre Diorama" was a popular entertainment that originated in Paris in 1822. An alternative to the also popular "panorama" (panoramic painting), the diorama was a theatrical experience viewed by an audience in a highly specialized theater.

38. Riley, "The Architect's Room," p. 88.

39. Charles Rice, *The Emergence of the Interior: Architecture, Modernity, Domesticity* (Routledge, New York, 2006), p. 2.

40. Aaron Betsky, "Bodybuildings: Towards a Hybrid Order of Architecture," in *Fabricaciones/Fabrications,* p. 119.

41. Robbins, "Construir/Edification," p. 98.

42. Debra Wilbur and Christopher Scoates, *Custom Built: A Twenty Year Survey of Work by Allan Wexler,* at Atlanta College of Art and City Art Gallery at Chastain (New York: Distributed Art Publishers, 1999), p. 6.

43. Aaron Betsky, "Furnishing the Primitive Hut: Allan Wexler's Experiments beyond Building," in *Custom Built,* p. 19.

44. Frederic Schwartz, Billie Tsien, Allan Wexler, and Tod Williams, *Home Rooms,* exhibit at the Fine Arts Center at University Museum of Contemporary Art, the University of Massachusetts Amherst, September 7 to December 15, 1991; See http://www.umass.edu/fac/calendar/universitygallery/events/HomeRooms.html, accessed September 20, 2012.

45. Allan Wexler, quoted in Bernd Shulz, *Allan Wexler* (Barcelona: Gustavo Gili, 1998), p. 52.

46. Betsky, "Furnishing the Primitive Hut," p. 11.

47. Eric L. Santner, *On Creaturely Life: Rilke, Benjamin, Sebald* (Chicago: University of Chicago Press, 2006), p. 50.

48. John Tusa, "Transcript of the John Tusa Interview with Rachel Whiteread," *The John Tusa Interviews,* BBC Radio 3, January 4, 2004, http://www.bbc.co.uk/radio3/johntusainterview/whiteread_transcript.shtml, accessed May 21st 2013.

49. Adrian Searle, "Rachel Doesn't Live Here Anymore," *Freize* 14 (January/February 1994), http://www.frieze.com/issue/article/rachel_doesnt_live_here_anymore/, accessed April 7, 2011.

50. Rachel Whiteread describes her work as creating fossils that are excavated through a process of casting that exposes traces of lives lived and highlighting combined layer, edges, volumes,and boundaries of domestic occupation. In "*Ghost,* her breakthrough piece from 1990,[we see]...a plaster cast of a living room, modeled on a typical Victorian terraced house in north London, similar to the one in which the artist grew up. In its melancholic beauty, Ghost is a resonant monument both to the individuals who once occupied this room, and to our collective memories of home"; "Rachel Whiteread: Biography," Tate, http://www.tate.org.uk/whats-on/tate-modern/exhibition/unilever-series-rachel-whiteread-embankment/rachel-whiteread-0, accessed August 8, 2011.

51. Robbins, "Construir/Edification."

52. Rachel Carley, "Domestic Afterlives," in "Interior Atmospheres," ed. Julieanna Preston, special issue, *Architectural Design* 78, no. 3 (2008): p. 27.

13 LIVES IN LARGE INTERIORS

The author wishes to acknowledge the assistance of photographer Justin Zhuang, who has patiently captured a slice of interior lives within Changi Airport and the underground subway stations in Singapore.

1. Michael Bednar, *Interior Pedestrian Places* (New York: Whitney Library of Design, 1989).

2. Trevor Brody, "Underground and Overhead: Building the Analogous City," in *Variations on a Theme Park: The New American City and the End of Public Space,* ed. Michael Sorkin (New York: Hill and Wang, 1992), pp. 123–53.

3. Ibid., p. 153.

4. Margaret Crawford, "The World in a Shopping Mall," in Sorkin, *Variations on a Theme Park,* pp. 4–30.

5. Walter Benjamin, *The Arcades Project,* trans. Howard Eiland and Kevin McLaughlin (Cambridge, MA: Harvard University Press, 2002).

6. Rem Koolhaas, "Bigness or the Problem of Large," in *Small, Medium, Large, Extra-Large,* by Rem Koolhaas and Bruce Mau (Rotterdam, the Netherlands: 010 Publishers, 1995), p. 515.

7. Kristine F. Miller, *Designs on the Public: The Private Lives of New York's Public Spaces* (Minneapolis: University of Minnesota Press, 2007).

8. I first came across this term in an essay, "Architecture as a Continuation of the City by Other Means," by Andreas Ruby, published in *Daidalos* 72 (1999). Ruby highlighted the works of architect Wilfried Hackenbroich, which exemplified the spatial and programmatic folding of the city's activities into the building interior. However, it was Rem Koolhaas's OMA proposal for the Library of Jussieu in Paris in 1993 that Ruby identified as the "paradigmatic model" of an architecture of interior urbanism.

9. The notion of the "Asian century" is itself a contentious issue among intellectuals from the West and East. See Christopher Lingle, "The Propaganda Way," *Foreign Affairs,* May/June 1995, http://www.foreignaffairs.com/articles/50983/christopher-lingle/the-propaganda-way; and Kishore Mahbubani, "The Case against the West," *Foreign Affairs,* May/June 2008, http://www.foreignaffairs.com/articles/63402/kishore-mahbubani/the-case-against-the-west.

10. Peter Gordon, "Deciding the Fate of Times Square," *The Standard,* last modified April 9, 2008, http://www.thestandard.com.hk/news_detail.asp?pp_cat=15&art_id=64124&sid=18407014&con_type=3.

11. "Provision of Public Facilities in Private Developments," Buildings Department, Government of Hong Kong Special Administrative Region, last modified July 28, 2011, http://www.bd.gov.hk/english/dedicated_areas.html.

12. "World Airports Award," Skytrax, 2010, http://www.worldairportawards.com/Awards_2010/Airport2010.htm.

13. "Be a Changi Millionaire," Changi Airport Singapore, 2010, http://www.changiairport.com/at-changi/events-and-promotions/millionaire/how-to-win, accessed December 7, 2010.

14. Timothy Chui, "MTR Walks into Fire from Disabled over Fares," *The Standard,* last modified April 20, 2009, http://www.changiairport.com/at-changi/events-and-promotions/millionaire/how-to-win.

15. "Singapore Parliamentary Debates," Parliament of Singapore, 2006, http://www.comp.nus.edu.sg/~ipng/pol/parl_2006/20060306.pdf, accessed December 20, 2006.

16. A vivid memory of the Golden Mile Complex that I could still recall was seeing an old lady selling vegetables inside the mall. She laid a plastic sheet on the ground and placed a variety of leafy vegetables on it. I was initially shocked to find this practice inside an air-conditioned mall in Singapore but also could not help but feel a sense of joy at discovering this spatial subversion by an ordinary resident.

17. "Statistics and Charts, Housing and Development Board Annual Report 2007/2008," Singapore Government, 2010, http://www.hdb.gov.sg/fi10/.../STATISTICS%20 AND%20CHARTS.pdf, accessed December 7, 2010.

18. Vicky Cheng, "Understanding Density and High Density," in *Designing High Density Cities: For Social and Environmental Sustainability,* ed. Edward Ng (London: Earthscan, 2010), p. 3.

19. Louis Wirth, "Urbanism as a Way of Life," *American Journal of Sociology* 44, no. 1 (1938): pp. 2–24.

20. Sze Lai Shan, "Karen and Peter Fung, Cherish Their Innocence," in *Our Life in West Kowloon,* ed. Iman Fok (Hong Kong: Society for Community Organization, 2007), pp. 74–77.

21. Wing Lun Luk, "Privately Owned Public Space in Hong Kong and New York," in *The Urban and Spatial Influence of the Policy* (2009), http://newurbanquestion.ifou.org/ proceedings/.../d056_luk_winglun_Revised.pdf.

22. Richard Sennett, *The Uses of Disorder* (New York: Alfred A. Knopf, 1970).

23. Leslie Lu, "The Asian Arcades Project: Progressive Porosity," *Perspecta 36: Juxtapositions, The Yale Architectural Journal* (2005): pp. 86–91.

24. "Civic and Community Institution Space," National Council of Social Services, 2010, http://www.ncss.org.sg/VWOcorner/cci.asp, accessed December 7, 2010.

25. Jonathan D. Solomon, "Learning from Louis Vuitton," *Journal of Architectural Education* 63, no. 2 (2010): pp. 67–70.

26. Brian Caplan, "Hong Kong: The Envy of Lee Kuan Yew," Library of Economics and Liberty, last modified April 5, 2009, http://econlog.econlib.org/archives/2009/04/hong_kong_ the_e.html.

27. Carol Lim, "Cash In on More: Underground Pedestrian Links," Skyline, Singapore: Urban Development of Singapore, 2004: p. 14, http://www.ura.gov.sg/skyline/skyline04/skyline04-02/ text/p14.html.

14 SWISS CHEESE AND BEANBAGS

1. Notions of the public and the private have long been identified as mutable and socially relative; it is the distinction between the terms that is pervasive and persistent. On the shifting sense of the private and the public see, for example, Antoine Prost, Gerard Vincent, Philippe Aries, Georges Duby, Arthur Goldhammer, Roger Chartier, Michelle Perrot, Patricia M. Ranum, and Paul Veyne, *A History of Private Life,* 5 vols. (Cambridge, MA: Harvard University Press, 1987–1991); and Norbert Elias, *The Civilizing Process,* 2 vols. (1939; repr., New York: Pantheon, 1982). The close connection between the intimate and the social is discussed by Hannah Arendt in *The Human Condition* (Chicago: University of Chicago Press, 1958) and is also developed by Richard Sennett in *The Fall of Public Man* (1974; repr., London: Penguin, 2003). The way such notions construct one another while discursively shifting and sliding in use is taken up in relation to architecture and the interior within Vittoria Di Palma, Diana Periton, and Marina Lathouri, eds., *Intimate Metropolis: Urban Subjects in the Modern City* (New York: Routledge, 2009).

2. On airport cities, see "What is an Airport City," World Conference and Exhibition on Airport Cities, http://www.globalairportcities.com/what-is-an-airport-city.html, accessed July 14, 2010.

3. Office for Metropolitan Architecture (OMA), Rem Koolhaas, and Bruce Mau, *Small, Medium, Large, Extra-Large* (New York: The Monacelli Press, 1995), p. 515. This book is popularly known as *S, M, L, XL*.

4. Mark Pimlott subtly evokes this atmosphere of a spreading, pervasive, supremely interior condition in his writing on the tactics of surveying and controlling space in the United States: Mark Pimlott, *Without and Within: Essays on Territory and the Interior* (Rotterdam, the Netherlands: Episode, 2007).

5. Charles Rice, "The Atmosphere of Interior Urbanism: OMA at IIT," *Architectural Design* 78 (2008): pp. 88–91, 90.

6. Chuihua Judy Chung, Jeffrey Inaba, Rem Koolhaas, and Sze Tsung Leong, eds., *The Harvard Design School Guide to Shopping* (New York: Taschen, 2002).

7. To draw out just two examples that contribute to recent discussion of this connection: Setha M. Low and Neil Smith, eds., *The Politics of Public Space* (London: Routledge, 2006); and Bruce Robbins, *The Phantom Public Sphere* (Minneapolis: University of Minnesota Press, 1993).

8. For instance, it is claimed that as spaces become more controlled, filtered, and exclusive this leads to the occlusion and exacerbation of social inequalities. See, for instance, Margaret Kohn, *Brave New Neighborhoods: The Privatization of Public Space* (New York: Routledge, 2004); Don Mitchell, *The Right to the City: Social Justice and the Fight for Public Space* (New York: Guilford, 2003); and Richard Sennett, *The Uses of Disorder: Personal Identity and City Life* (1970; repr., New Haven, CT: Yale University Press, 2008).

9. On these distinctions between, and overlapping qualities of, public space, public realm, and public sphere and their implications for urban design, see, for example, Matthew Carmona, Tim Heath, Taner Oc, and Steve Tiesdell, *Public Places—Urban Spaces* (Oxford: Architectural Press, 2003); Marcel Henaff and Tracy B. Strong, *Public Space and Democracy* (Minneapolis: University of Minnesota Press, 2001); and Ali Madanipour, *Public and Private Spaces of the City* (London: Routledge, 2003).

10. FAT stands for Fashion Architecture Taste.

11. Paul ONeal, "Fat Fantasy," *On Office Magazine*, March 14, 2007, http://www.onofficemagazine.com/projects/item/226-fat-fantasy, accessed October 27, 2010.

12. "Ørestad College," *3XN*, http://www.3xn.dk/, accessed October 27, 2010.

13. "One Shelley Street," *Clive Wilkinson Architects*, http://www.clivewilkinson.com/work/macquarie_sydney_desc.html, accessed July 14, 2010.

14. It is also interesting to note that typically private, domestic objects and spaces are introduced within the project alongside the "urban" or "public" (e.g., the tree house, the playroom). Their elevation within the new workplace sees an equivalency of spatial categories afforded by the interior territory, which accommodates conjugated programs and smoothes their distinctions.

15. Two key examples are found in the work of Jürgen Habermas and, more recently, Ray Oldenburg. For Habermas the new social venue of the English coffee house was a key site for the establishment of the public sphere; see Habermas, *The Structural Transformation of the Public Sphere* (1989; repr., Cambridge, MA: MIT Press, 1991). For Oldenburg coffee houses are an example of third places, or "great good places": public places on neutral ground that promote social equality by leveling the status of guests; see Oldenburg, *The Great Good Place: Cafés, Coffee Shops, Community Centers, Beauty Parlors, General Stores, Bars, Hangouts, and How They Get You through the Day* (New York: Marlowe, 1997).

16. Regarding urban activity in this way is not new; an obvious example is Hannah Arendt's conception of the citizen-actor and the importance of his or her visible deeds in the public realm. Arendt borrows the ancient theatrical concept of persona—the mask that actors wore during plays—to explain the difference between a private individual and a citizen. Arendt opposes persona to "natural man," who is outside the range of law and the body politic of citizens; see Arendt, *The Human Condition*, 2nd ed. (1958; Chicago: University of Chicago Press, 1988). We also find a concern with performance in Henri Lefebvre's work, where place is characterized by the mobilities that course through it; see particularly Lefebvre, *Rhythmanalysis: Space, Time, and Everyday Life* (London: Continuum, 2004). Jane Jacobs also provides a well-known example in her comparison of the successful city street to a dance: "an intricate ballet"; see Jacobs, *The Death and Life of Great American Cities* (1961; New York: Vintage Books, 1992).

17. Charles Moore, "You Have to Pay for the Public Life," *Perspecta* 9–10 (1965): p. 59.

18. Ibid., p. 65.

19. Ibid, pp. 57–65, 68–106

20. Louis Marin, *Utopics: The Semiological Play of Textual Spaces*, trans. Robert A. Vollrath (Atlantic Highlands, NJ: Humanities Press International, 1990).

21. Ibid.

22. Ibid.

23. "What We Do," *Jerde*, http://www.jerde.com/Jerde-Philosophy.html, accessed March 14, 2013.

24. Jon Adams Jerde, "Visceral Reality," in *The Jerde Partnership International* (Milan, Italy: L'Arca Edizioni, 1998).

25. An understanding of the enclave as critical to the spatiality of the postmodern city is found in Steve Graham and Simon Marvin, *Splintering Urbanism: Networked Infrastructures, Technological Mobilities and the Urban Condition* (New York: Routledge, 2001); Setha Low, *Behind the Gates: Life, Security, and the Pursuit of Happiness in Fortress America* (New York: Routledge, 2003); Mike Davis, *City of Quartz: Excavating the Future in Los Angeles* (London: Verso, 1990); Reinhold Martin, *Utopia's Ghost: Architecture and Postmodernism, Again* (Minneapolis: University of Minnesota Press, 2010); and Lieven de Cauter, *The Capsular Civilization: On the City in the Age of Fear* (Rotterdam, the Netherlands: NAi Publishers, 2004). Peter Sloterdijk's "theory of spheres" has received recent attention, its emphasis on co-isolation, co-fragility, and processuality providing a useful counterpoint to the rigid, stable, and largely physical divisions discussed elsewhere. See Peter Sloterdijk, "Foam City," *Log* 10 (Winter/Spring 2007): pp. 63–76; and Peter Sloterdijk, "Cell, Block, Egospheres, Self-Container," *Log* 9 (Summer/Fall 2007): pp. 89–109.

26. Jean Baudrillard, "The Ecstasy of Communication," in *The Anti-Aesthetic: Essays on Postmodern Culture*, ed. Hal Foster (Port Townsend, WA: Bay Press, 1983), pp. 129–30.

27. Michael Sorkin, ed., "Introduction: Variations on a Theme Park," in *Variations on a Theme Park: The New American City and the End of Public Space* (New York: Noonday Press, 1992), p. xv.

28. Mike Davis, *City of Quartz: Excavating the Future in Los Angeles* (London; New York: Verso, 1990); Sharon Zukin, *Landscapes of Power: From Detroit to Disney World* (Berkeley: University of California Press, 1991); Richard Sennett, *Flesh and Stone: The Body and the City in Western Civilization* (New York: W. W. Norton, 1994); and Neil Smith, *The New Urban Frontier: Gentrification and the Revanchist City* (New York: Routledge, 1996). Not all of these books

provided lapsarian narratives; there was also recognition that older urban forms should not be idealized in relation to the accessibility and equity of their public spaces. However, what tended to be consistent was an understanding of public space as the material space of appearance, that is, an emphasis on individuals and groups being *seen* in public in order to be part of a/the public. Kurt Iveson provides a very useful critique of this "topographical" fetish in *Publics and the City* (London: Blackwell, 2007), chap. 1: "The Problem with Public Space."

29. Sorkin, "Introduction," p. xiii.

30. Trevor Boddy, "Underground and Overhead: Building the Analogous City," in Sorkin, *Variations on a Theme Park,* pp. 135–36.

31. M. Christine Boyer, "Cities for Sale: Merchandising History at South Street Seaport," in Sorkin, *Variations on a Theme Park,* p. 184.

32. Jacobs, *Death and Life,* p. 57.

33. Boddy, "Underground and Overhead," p. 152.

34. For a representative example of such an investigation, see "Diagram Work: Data Mechanics for a Topological Age," special issue, *ANY,* no. 23 (June 1998). In a previous essay I have specifically examined historical shifts in the conception and structuring of bodily flows and encounter within architecture, and their materialization in specific buildings; see Lee Stickells, "Conceiving an Architecture of Movement," *arq: Architectural Research Quarterly* 14, no. 1 (2010): pp. 41–51.

35. OMA, Koolhaas, and Mau, *S, M, L, XL,* pp. 1310–26.

36. Brendan McGetrick and Rem Koolhaas, eds., *Content* (Cologne, Germany: Taschen, 2004), p. 73.

37. For an overview of Tiravanija's work, see Rirkrit Tiravanija, Frank Hyde-Antwi, and Rein Wolfs, *Supermarket: Migros Museum für Gegenwartskunst, Zurich, Wexner Center for the Arts, the Ohio State University, Columbus, De Appel, Amsterdam, le Consortium, Centre d'art contemporain, Dijon* (Zurich: Migros Museum fur Gegenwartskunst, 1998).

38. "Rirkrit Tiravanija interview by Hans Ulrich Obrist," *Art Text Translation Archive,* December 1993 and July 2002, http://www.atta-project.net/en/node/220, accessed June 3, 2011.

39. Nicolas Bourriaud, *Relational Aesthetics* (1998; Dijon, France: Les Presses du réel, 2002), p. 112.

40. Ibid., p. 28.

41. Nicolas Bourriaud, "Berlin Letter about Relational Aesthetics," in *Contemporary Art: From Studio to Situation,* ed. Claire Doherty (London: Black Dog, 2004), p. 44.

42. Bourriaud sees this as a key distinction between the generation of artists he focuses on (emerging in the 1990s) and earlier ones. He suggests that the constitution of convivial relations has been a historical constant within art since the 1960s. However, he argues that where a key earlier concern was the broadening of art's boundaries, a more pressing recent motivation has been to experience art's "capacities of resistance within the overall social arena"; Bourriaud, *Relational Aesthetics,* pp. 30–31. In this regard, as well as Tiravanija, he cites the work of artists such as Angela Bulloch, Philippe Parreno, and Liam Gillick. However, that concern for a "micro-utopics" can also be seen in much recent urban intervention that intertwines architecture, art, and activism: for example, projects such as EXYZT and Sara Muzio's Southwark Lido, the ECObox project of Atelier d'Architecture Autogérée, and projects by San Fransicsco's Re:Bar collective.

43. Multiple media, the web, and transnational associations and economies have produced a global space of flows that is argued to have a far greater role in the production of public

spheres. New media and communication practices especially stretch conceptions of public spaces—which are now often seen as diffused through radio, television, and the Internet; see, for example, Mimi Sheller and John Urry, "Mobile Transformations of 'Public' and 'Private' Life," *Theory, Culture & Society* 20, no. 3 (2003): pp. 107–25; and Ash Amin, "Collective Culture and Urban Public Space," *City* 12, no. 1 (2008): pp. 5–24.

44. Vito Acconci, "Public Space in a Private Time," *Critical Inquiry* 16 (1990): p. 917.

45. Creativity (materialized in "creative cities" and a "creative class") is now a central concept for government policy makers, planners, and others attempting to stimulate economic and cultural life in twenty-first-century cities; see Richard Florida, *The Rise of the Creative Class: And How It's Transforming Work, Leisure, Community and Everyday Life* (New York: Perseus Books, 2002). On historical shifts in management concepts and the recent fostering of creativity and flexibility, see, for example, Howard Davis and Richard Scase, *Managing Creativity: The Dynamics of Work and Organization* (Buckingham, UK: Open University Press, 2000). A recent example of the promotion of "proactive" rather than "reactive" employees can be found in Michael Frese and Doris Fay, "Personal Initiative: An Active Performance Concept for Work in the 21st Century," *Research in Organizational Behavior* 23 (2001): pp. 133–87. On the entrepreneurialism of the contemporary university, see Michael Gibbons, "Globalization, Innovation and Socially Robust Knowledge," in *The University in the Global Age,* ed. Roger King (Basingstoke, UK: Palgrave Macmillan, 2004), pp. 96–115. For an example of the contemporary emphasis on innovation and creativity for schoolchildren, see Partnership for 21st Century Skills, *Framework for 21st Century Learning,* 2007, http://www.21stcenturyskills.org/index.php?optio=com_content&task=view&id=254&Itemid=120, accessed September 20, 2011.

46. The schools included Madison Middle School in Seattle, Washington; St. Philip Catholic High School in Battle Creek, Michigan; and Western Heights College, Victoria, Australia. See Frank M. Locker, "Swiss Cheese Schools," SchoolFacilities.com, June 18, 2007, http://www.schoolfacilities.com/_coreModules/content/contentDisplay.aspx?contentID=2891, accessed July 7, 2010.

47. Locker, "Swiss Cheese Schools."

48. Ibid. (my italics).

49. Ibid.

50. Prakash Nair and Annalise Gehling, "Life between Classrooms: Applying Public Space Theory to Learning Environments," in *Reshaping Our Learning Landscape: A Collection of Provocation Papers* (British Council for School Environments, 2010), p. 29.

51. Mimi Sheller, "Mobility," *Sociopedia.isa,* 2011, p. 1; http://www.sagepub.net/isa/resources/pdf/Mobility.pdf, accessed September 20, 2011.

52. Ibid., p. 2. Sheller offers an excellent overview of "mobilities research," stressing its critique of generalizing conceptions of societies of "flow": "For mobilities researchers today it is not a question of privileging flows, speed, or a cosmopolitan or nomadic subjectivity, but rather of tracking the power of discourses, practices and infrastructures of mobility in creating the effects of both movement and stasis." For a selection of mobility-related research with particular resonance for spatial design, see Tim Cresswell, *On the Move: Mobility in the Modern Western World* (London: Routledge, 2006); Stephen Graham and Simon Marvin, *Splintering Urbanism: Networked Infrastructures, Technological Mobilities and the Urban Condition* (London: Routledge, 2001); Arjun Appadurai, *Modernity at Large: Cultural Dimensions of Globalization* (Minneapolis: University of Minnesota Press, 1996); Marc Augé,

Non-Places: An Introduction to the Anthropology of Supermodernity (London: Verso, 1995); and John Urry, *Sociology beyond Societies: Mobilities for the Twenty-First Century* (London: Routledge, 2000).

53. Sennett, *Flesh and Stone,* pp. 255–56.

54. "Rolex Learning Center / Lausanne / Switzerland / SANAA," *archiCentral,* January 14, 2009, http://www.archicentral.com/rolex-learning-center-lausanne-sanaa-3752/, accessed October 27, 2010.

55. "EPFL—Ecole Polytechnique Federale de Lausanne Rolex Learning Center Press Information," Ecole Polytechnique Fédérale de Lausanne, revised June 7, 2010, http://www.rolexlearningcenter.ch/documents/english_kit_revised.pdf, accessed October 27, 2010.

56. On recent innovative school design, see, for example, Mark Dudek, *Architecture of Schools: The New Learning Environments* (Boston: Architectural Press, Butterworth-Heinemann, 2000); and Rotraut Walden, *Schools for the Future: Design Proposals from Architectural Psychology* (Cambridge, MA: Hogrefe, 2009).

57. Ross Collin and Michael W. Apple, "Schooling, Literacies and Biopolitics in the Global Age," *Discourse: Studies in the Cultural Politics of Education* 28, no. 4 (2007): pp. 433–54.

58. Majia Nadesan, "The MYD Panopticon: Neo-Liberalism, Governmentality and Education," *Radical Pedagogy* 8, no. 1 (2006). Accessed via *Radical Pedagogy* online archives, http://www.radicalpedagogy.org/Radical_Pedagogy/Volume_8__Issue_1.html, accessed September 20, 2011.

59. Locker, "Swiss Cheese Schools."

60. One of the learning expectations at the Australian Science and Mathematics School is that students will "be autonomous, self-directing and self-perpetuating learners and accept the associated responsibilities to self and others." "Curriculum," *Australian Science and Mathematics School,* http://www.asms.sa.edu.au/curric/learning/Pages/LearningExpectations.aspx, accessed September 20, 2011.

61. Nair and Gehling, "Life between Classrooms."

62. It is interesting to note the similarities in the ambience of new school spaces such as 3XN's "storey lounges" (beanbags, WiFi connections, and sprawling students) with those produced by relational artist Angela Bulloch's "Bean-Bag Works." For *Flexible* (1997) at the Art Club Berlin she provided large, brightly colored beanbags, a CD player, and headphones so that visitors could chill out on the beanbags listening to music.

63. See Low and Smith, *Politics of Public Space.*

15 THE PUBLIC PRIVATE INTERIOR

1. Adolf Loos, "Heimat Kunst," in *Adolf Loos: Trotzdem 1900–1930* (1931; Vienna: Georg Prachner, 1982).

2. Susan Sidlauskas, *Body, Place and Self in Nineteenth-Century Painting* (Cambridge: Cambridge University Press, 2000), p. 20.

3. Charles Rice, *The Emergence of the Interior: Architecture, Modernity, Domesticity* (London: Routledge, 2007), p. 2.

4. Diana Fuss, *The Sense of an Interior: Four Writers and the Rooms That Shaped Them* (New York: Routledge, 2004), p. 10.

5. Walter Benjamin, *The Arcades Project,* trans. Howard Eiland and Kevin McLaughlin (Cambridge, MA: Belknap Press of Harvard University Press, 1999), p. 220.

6. Ibid., p. 216.

7. Gulsum Baydar Nalbantonglu, "Thresholds of Privacy and the Ideal(ized) Home," *Singapore Architect,* special issue on housing, no. 189 (1995): p. 27.

8. For a history of the separation of home and workspaces see, for example, Dona Birdwell-Pheasant and Denise Lawrence Zuniga, eds., *HouseLife. Space, Place and Family in Europe* (Oxford: Berg, 1999); and Hilde Heynen, "Modernity and Domesticity: Tensions and Contradictions," in *Negotiating Domesticity: Spatial Productions of Gender in Modern Architecture,* ed. Hilde Heynen and Gulsum Baydar, 1–29 (London: Routledge, 2005).

9. Robbie Goh, "Things to a Void," in *Theorizing the Southeast Asian City as Text: Urban Landscapes, Cultural Documents, and Interpretive Experiences,* ed. Robbie Goh and Brenda Yeoh (Singapore: World Scientific, 2003), p. 64.

10. The single most comprehensive academic paper written on the HDB interior so far is by Jane Jacobs and Stephen Cairns, on the decoration of households as traced through the HDB newsletter *Our Home.* From conversation with the authors, it is apparent that there is a dearth of public information on how the interior is lived. See Jane M. Jacobs and Stephen Cairns, "The Modern Touch: Interior Design and Modernization of Post-independence Singapore," *Environment and Planning A* 40 (2008): pp. 572–95.

11. Giuliana Bruno, *Atlas of Emotion: Journeys in Art, Architecture, and Film* (New York: Verso, 2002), p. 6.

12. Cyril Wong, "First House," in *Unmarked Treasure* (Singapore: Firstfruits, 2004), p. 11.

13. Jane Pek, "Memory," in *No Other City: The Ethos of Urban Poetry,* ed. Alvin Pang and Aaron Lee (Singapore: Ethos Books, 2000), p. 172.

14. Ibid., pp. 172–73.

15. Ibid.

16. For a comprehensive history of the early years of the HDB, its objectives and output, see *First Decade in Public Housing, 1960–1969* (Singapore: Housing and Development Board, 1970); A. K. Wong and S.H.K. Yeh, eds., *Housing a Nation: Twenty-five Years of Public Housing in Singapore* (Singapore: Housing and Development Board, 1985), and Beng Huat Chua, "Not Depoliticized but Ideologically Successful: The Public Housing Programme in Singapore," in *Understanding Singapore Society,* ed. Ong Jin Hui, Tong Chee Kiong, and Tan Ern Ser, 307–27 (Singapore: Times Academic Press, 1997).

17. *Report on New Life in New Homes* (Singapore: Persatuan Wanita Singapura, 1965), p. 18.

18. In 1961, 2,642 families were made homeless because of six fires; in 1962, 81 families suffered a similar fate as nine fires destroyed the slum areas. See *Annual Report of the Housing and Development Board* (Singapore, 1961), p. 53; and *Annual Report of the Housing and Development Board* (Singapore, 1962), p. 51.

19. "Our History: Development," http://app.www.sg/who/40/Development.aspx, accessed June 20, 2011.

20. Chua, "Not Depoliticized but Ideologically Successful," p. 315.

21. Sishir Chang, "A High-Rise Vernacular in Singapore's Housing Development Board Housing," *Berkeley Planning Journal* 14 (2000): pp. 97–116.

22. C. J. Wan-Ling Wee, *The Asian Modern: Culture, Capitalist Development, Singapore* (Singapore: National University of Singapore Press, 2007), p. 22.

23. Ibid., p. 84.

24. Ibid., p. 85, 86. The People's Action Party has been in power and almost unopposed since Singapore's independence.

25. Alfian Sa'at, "Corridor," in *Corridor: 12 Short Stories* (Singapore: Raffles, 1999), p. 41.

26. Ibid., p. 52.

27. Martin Perry, Lily Kong, and Brenda Yeoh, *Singapore: A Developmental City State* (Chichester, UK: John Wiley & Sons, 1997), p. 11. The other two elements of control are a network of "parapolitical" community-based, grassroots institutions linked to the state and a series of public campaigns and programs designed to alter behavior such as productivity, public hygiene, courtesy, family planning, energy use, moral values, and use of Mandarin. From 1968 to 1982, sixty-six campaigns were launched.

28. Ibid., p. 6.

29. Ching Ling Tai, *Housing Policy and High-Rise Living: A Study of Singapore's Public Housing* (Singapore: Chopmen, 1988), p. 114.

30. Perry, Kong, and Yeoh, *Singapore,* p. 115.

31. As early as 1959, the People's Action Party government recognized unchecked population growth as an obstacle to economic development and the potential cause of serious social, political, and economic problems.

32. Peter S. J. Chen and James T. Fawcett, *Public Policy and Population Change in Singapore* (New York: Population Council, 1979). During the period 1957–1970, the proportion of one-family-nucleus households increased from around 64 to 72 percent, whereas the combined no-family-nucleus and single-person households dropped from 26 to 17 percent. The estimated proportion of nuclear-family households increased from 51 percent in 1957 to 57 percent in 1970.

33. *Report on New Life,* p. 42.

34. *Berita Singapura: Housing Week,* videocassette, Singapore National Archive, accession number 2004001774 (Singapore: Ministry of Culture, Broadcasting Division, 1967).

35. Baydar Nalbantonglu, *Singapore Architect,* p. 28.

36. Mark Wigley, "Untitled: The Housing of Gender," in *Sexuality and Space,* ed. Beatriz Colomina (New York: Princeton Architectural Press, 1992), pp. 336 and 339.

37. Ibid., p. 331.

38. See model of one-room unit furnished with low-cost furniture in *Annual Report of the Housing and Development Board 1960* (Singapore: Housing Development Board, 1960), p. 45; and "The Winning Set of Furniture at the Housing and Development Board Exhibition of Low-Cost Furniture at Macpherson Road on August 12–20, 1961, submitted by S.P.A.S.," *Dimension Annual: Journal of the Singapore Polytechnic Architectural Society 1* (1962): pp. 32–34.

39. "Winning Set of Furniture," p. 33.

40. Ibid.

41. *Annual Report* (1960), p. 44.

42. The circulation of this magazine was 161,000 in 1973, and this number grew to 440,000 by 1989.

43. Jacobs and Cairns, "The Modern Touch," p. 592.

44. Ibid.

45. "Wallpaper of New Design to Give an Illusion of Depth and Calm Beauty," *The Straits Times* August 30, 1967, p. 10.

46. Jacobs and Cairns, "Modern Touch," p. 592.

47. Abidin Kusno, *Beyond the Postcolonial: Architecture, Urban Space and Political Cultures in Indonesia* (London: Routledge, 2000), p. 204.

48. Excerpt from *12 Storeys,* dir. Eric Khoo (Singapore: Zhao Wei Films, 1997).

49. Jacobs and Cairns, "Modern Touch," p. 591.

16 THE EVOLUTION OF WORKSPACE DESIGN

1. In March 2008 BBC News selected the Google Zurich office as an exemplar of new ways of working. See Jane Wakefield, "Sliding into Work at Google HQ," *BBC News,* prod. Fiona Graham, March 13, 2008, http://news.bbc.co.uk/1/hi/technology/7292600.stm, accessed August 2010.

2. Architect Frank Duffy vividly describes the "paper factory" layout of the Larkin Building in "Office Futures That Work," *Design* (April 1983): p. 53, published by the Design Council.

3. James Woudhuysen in "Tayloring People for Production," *Design* (August 1984): pp. 34–37, presents a critique of Frederick Taylor in which he describes his influence on modern office design as greater than that of the Bauhaus.

4. See Judith Merkle, *Management and Ideology* (Berkeley: University of California Press, 1980).

5. Le Corbusier, *Towards A New Architecture* (New York: Brewer, Warren and Putnam, 1946), p. 87.

6. Tom Wolfe, *From Bauhaus to Our House* (London: Jonathan Cape, 1981), p. 47. Wolfe satirically branded Mies van der Rohe as "White God No. 2," after "White God No. 1" Le Corbusier.

7. Charles Handy, *The Age of Unreason* (London: Arrow Books, 1990), p. 146. Here Handy provides an excellent critique of mechanistic management practices.

8. This point is expanded in Gavin Turner and Jeremy Myerson's discussion of management barriers to change in *New Workspace New Culture* (Aldershot: Gower, 1998).

9. See Thomas Davenport, Robert J. Thomas, and Susan Cantrell, "The Mysterious Art and Science of Knowledge Worker Performance," *MIT Sloan Management Review* 44, no. 1 (2002): pp. 23–30. It is one of the few academic papers to shed new light on office design for knowledge workers.

10. Peter Drucker made this claim in "The Next Society: A Survey of the Near Future," supplement to *The Economist* (November 3, 2001). See also Peter Drucker, "Knowledge Worker Productivity: The Biggest Challenge," *California Management Review* 41 (1999): pp. 79–94.

11. Frank Duffy first outlined the three waves of workplace change in detail at the Workplace Trends: Global Arena Conference, Tate Britain, London, 2006.

12. See Adrian Forty, *Objects of Desire: Design and Society 1750–1980* (London: Thames & Hudson, 1986). In this book Forty also explains how modern work interiors like the Larkin Building deprived office clerks of their status as masters of their own domain by removing the high backs on chairs that afforded a degree of privacy and introducing more rigid, machine-like fittings, such as fixed, pivoting seats.

13. Lance Knobel, *Office Furniture* (London: Unwin Hyman, 1987), p. 65.

14. The idea of the network—social, technical, organizational, economic, and so on—is an important recurring theme in the development of workplace design. This chapter builds on ideas expressed in a keynote paper given by the author at the Networks of Design Annual International Design History Conference, University College Falmouth, United Kingdom, 2008.

15. See Jeremy Myerson, *International Interiors 5* (London: Laurence King, 1995), pp. 12–17.

16. See Jane Jacobs, *The Death and Life of Great American Cities* (New York: Random House, 1961). In her famous book, Jacobs castigated Le Corbusier's "Radiant City" as among the models deeply unhelpful to urban planning because they present a barrier to dynamic social community.

17. See Jeremy Myerson and Phillip Ross, *The 21st Century Office* (London: Laurence King, 2003).

18. See Frank Duffy, "Does the Big Corporate Office Still Have a Future in the UK?" *Building Design: Office,* December 23, 2008.

19. There is an extensive review of narrative-based office design in Myerson and Ross, *21st Century Office.*

20. Pringle Brandon Consulting/UCL, "Occupier Density Study" (London: British Council of Offices, 2008), http://www.bco.org.uk/Research/Publications/OccupierD2582.aspx, accessed March 31, 2013.

21. Charles Armstrong, interviewed by author, March 2, 2011. Armstrong was a keynote speaker at the Intersections: Redesigning the Future of Business Conference, March 2010, Eden Project, Cornwall, United Kingdom.

22. Ibid.

23. See Jeremy Myerson, Jo-Anne Bichard, and Alma Erlich, *New Demographics, New Workspace: Office Design for the Changing Workforce* (Aldershot: Gower, 2010), pp. 54–85 for an in-depth description of the Welcoming Workplace study.

17 INSTALLATION AND PERFORMANCE

1. Aldert Vrij, Sharon Leal, Par Anders Granhag, Samantha Mann, Ronald Fisher, Jackie Hillman, and Kathryn Sperry, "Outsmarting the Liars: The Benefit of Asking Unanticipated Questions," *Law and Human Behavior* 33 (2009): pp. 159–66.

2. Maurice Merleau-Ponty, *The World of Perception* (London: Routledge, 2008), p. 43.

3. Ibid., pp. 53–54.

4. John Berger, *Ways of Seeing* (London: Penguin, 1972), pp. 8–9.

5. This film is available on YouTube, posted July 8, 2010, http://www.youtube.com/watch?v=OnUEr_gNzwk, accessed December 2, 2011.

6. Jens Hoffmann and Adriano Pedrosa, eds., *Companion to the Istanbul Bienali 2011* (Istanbul: Istanbul Foundation for Culture and Arts, 2011), p. 220.

7. Ibid., p. 223.

8. Richard Wollheim, *Art and Its Objects* (London: Penguin, 1978), p. 102.

9. Quoted in John Willett, *Brecht on Theatre* (London: Eyre Methuen, 1977), p. 187.

10. This program of work is being undertaken by David Littlefield of the University of the West of England, Ken Wilder of Chelsea College of Art and Design (University of the Arts London), and Mathew Emmett of the University of Plymouth. Grouped under the title Estranged Space, the project seeks to find aesthetic value in spaces that lie beyond the architectural or social norm.

11. Anthony Vidler, *The Architectural Uncanny: Essays in the Modern Unhomely* (Cambridge, MA: MIT Press, 1994), p. 6.

12. Notions of heritage and authenticity, and their definitions, have been the subject of much discussion and debate since the end of the nineteenth century. The international heritage body UNESCO (the United Nations Educational, Scientific, and Cultural Organization)

has invested considerable time and energy in attempting to reach consensus on these issues, notably with its 1994 meeting in Nara, Japan, which led to the publication of the "Nara Document on Authenticity" (available at http://whc.unesco.org/uploads/events/documents/event-833-3.pdf, March 8, 2013). See also the UNESCO documents that emerged from the San Antonio and Great Zimbabwe International meetings.

13. This work at the Roman baths in Bath has been presented by the author at the following conferences: Narrative Space, University of Leicester and University of Nottingham (March 2010); Mapping Spectral Spaces, University of Ireland, Maynooth (May 2011); and Peripheries, Queens University Belfast (October 2011), for the Architectural Humanities Research Association.

14. Christopher Tilley, Sue Hamilton, and Barbara Bender, "Art and the Re-Presentation of the Past," *Journal of the Royal Anthropological Institute* 6, no. 1 (March 2000): p. 60.

15. Ibid., p. 52.

16. Ibid., p. 60.

18 EXHIBITION DESIGN

1. Nicholas Serota, *Experience or Interpretation: The Dilemma of Museums of Modern Art* (London: Thames & Hudson, 1996), p. 42.

2. Ibid., p. 55. Other key works include Mary Anne Staniszewski's *The Power of Display: A History of Exhibition Installations at the Museum of Modern Art* (Cambridge, MA: MIT Press, 1998); and Reesa Greenberg, Bruce W. Ferguson, and Sandy Nairne, eds., *Thinking about Exhibitions* (London: Routledge, 1996).

3. It is useful to reflect that apart from formal exhibitions, there are all kinds of exhibition design going on. Exhibition making is an innate activity: everyone's home is an exhibit in some way, and people display objects to inform themselves, and others, about their lives and needs. People are also instinctively adept at public display: arrangements of personal possessions, clothes, and gestures constantly declare a set of values, attitudes, and aspirations. Markets, street stalls, and window dressings are casual exhibitions that happen as part of the textures of every day life. Sometimes surprising, but always effective, informal display plays an important role in how we express ourselves.

4. B. Joseph Pine II and James H. Gilmore, *The Experience Economy: Work Is Theatre and Every Business Is a Stage* (Boston: Harvard Business School Press, 1999).

5. George Cochrane, "Creating Tate Modern 1996–2000," in *Beyond the Museum Art Institutions,* People Museum of Modern Art Papers 4, ed. Ian Cole and Nick Stanley (Oxford: Museum of Modern Art, 2000).

6. The image of a *museum without walls* is taken from André Malraux's book of the same title, *Le Musée Imaginaire* (Paris: Gallimard, 1965), which discusses questions of the autonomy of art. My analogy here is about connectedness, a museum whose boundaries are as much about opening up relationships as controlling a rarified interior. For a discussion of this text, see the work by Rosalind E. Kraus, "Postmodernism's Museum without Walls," in *Thinking about Exhibitions,* pp. 341–48.

7. "Cottonopolis" denotes a metropolis of cotton and cotton mills, inspired by Manchester and its status as the international center of the cotton and textile-processing industries during the nineteenth century.

8. There is a useful survey in Vikki Bell, ed., *Performativity and Belonging* (London: Sage, 1999).

19 REDESIGNING FOR THE BODY

1. Le Corbusier, *Precisions on the Present State of Architecture and City Planning,* trans. Edith Schreiber Aujame (Cambridge, MA: MIT Press, 1930), p. 108.

2. A note on the book's publication history: the report was first published by Cornell University in 1966 and was then published in paperback by Bantam Books in 1967. Because the latter version is in much wider circulation than the former, I have referenced it throughout. Alexander Kira, *The Bathroom: Criteria for Design* (Ithaca, NY: Cornell University Center for Housing and Environmental Studies, 1966); and Alexander Kira, *The Bathroom: Criteria for Design* (New York: Bantam Books, 1967).

3. Stephen Pheasant, *Bodyspace: Anthropometry, Ergonomics and the Design of Work,* 2nd rev. ed. (London: Taylor & Francis, 1996), p. 109.

4. Walter Arensberg, quoted in William A. Camfield, *Marcel Duchamp: Fountain* (Houston: Menil Collection/Houston Fine Art Press, 1989), p. 25.

5. Nancy Newhall, ed., *The Daybooks of Edward Weston 1: Mexico* (Rochester, NY: George Eastman House, 1973), p. 132.

6. Siegfried Giedion, *Mechanization Takes Command: A Contribution to Anonymous History* (New York: Oxford University Press, 1948), pp. 691–92.

7. R. Buckminster Fuller, "Influences on My Work," in *The Buckminster Fuller Reader,* ed. James Meller (London: Jonathan Cape, 1970), p. 64.

8. For an excellent discussion of these issues, see David Serlin, "Pissing Without Pity: Disability, Gender, and the Public Toilet," in *Toilet: Public Restrooms and the Politics of Sharing,* ed. Harvey Molotch and Laura Norén (New York: New York University Press, 2010), pp. 167–85.

9. Kira, *The Bathroom,* pp. vi–vii.

10. A summary of this survey, however, is provided in an Appendix. Kira, *The Bathroom,* pp. 209–19. Full results are published in Marilyn Langford, *Personal Hygiene Attitudes and Practices in* 1000 *Middle-Class Households* (Ithaca, NY: Cornell University, Agricultural Experiment Station, New York State College of Home Economics, 1965).

11. Kira, *The Bathroom,* p. vi.

12. Ibid., pp. 174–77.

13. Ibid., pp. 187–90.

14. See Serlin, "Pissing Without Pity," pp. 167–69. Also highly relevant is Lance Hosey, "Hidden Lines: Gender, Race, and the Body in 'Graphic Standards,'" *Journal of Architectural Education* 55, no. 2 (2001): pp. 101–12.

15. Kira, *The Bathroom,* pp. 98–106.

16. Ibid., p. 106.

17. Ibid., p. vii.

18. Alexander Kira, *The Bathroom, New and Expanded* (New York: Viking Press, 1976), p. vii. For more on the impact of the sexual revolution, see also pp. 170–76.

19. Ariel Levy, "Doing It: A New Edition of *The Joy of Sex,*" *The New Yorker,* January 5, 2009, p. 67.

20. All quotes from Kira, *The Bathroom, New and Expanded,* pp. 143–44. Note, however, that Kira stopped short of filming his model urinating while holding her labial folds apart; for these findings, he was content to simply reference pioneering sexologist Havelock Ellis's 1902 article, "The Bladder as a Dynamometer." Kira, *The Bathroom, New and Expanded,* fn. 3, p. 262.

21. For an expanded discussion, see Barbara Penner, "(Re)Designing the 'Unmentionable': Female Toilets in the Twentieth Century," in *Ladies and Gents: Public Toilets and Gender,* ed. Olga Gershenson and Barbara Penner (Philadelphia: Temple University Press, 2009), pp. 141–50.

22. Kira, *The Bathroom, New and Expanded,* p. 143.

23. For his proposals, see Kira, *The Bathroom, New and Expanded,* pp. 232–37.

24. Rebecca Solnit, *River of Shadows: Eadweard Muybridge and the Technological Wild West* (London: Penguin Books, 2003), p. 225.

25. Lillian Gilbreth, Orpha Mae Thomas, and Eleanor Clymer, *Management in the Home: Happier Living through Saving Time and Energy,* rev. ed. (New York: Dodd, Mead & Company, 1964), pp. 59–73.

26. Lillian Gilbreth interview (1926), quoted in Laurel D. Graham, "Domesticating Efficiency: Lillian Gilbreth's Scientific Management of Homemakers, 1924–1930," *Signs* 24, no. 3 (1999): p. 652. Extended descriptions of micromotion studies can also be found in Lillian M. Gilbreth, *The Home-Maker and Her Job* (New York: D. Appleton-Century Company, 1938), pp. 95–97; and Gilbreth, Thomas, and Clymer, *Management in the Home,* pp. 89–99. Gilbreth had initially developed these techniques in partnership with her husband, Frank Gilbreth, in an industrial setting. The Gilbreths began as disciples of Frederick W. Taylor but grew disillusioned with what they saw as his crude use of time as a measure of efficiency and his disregard for worker satisfaction. Rather, Lillian held that eliminating waste through motion, skill, and fatigue studies and creating positive benefits for workers was key to the successful adoption of scientific management methods (see Graham, "Domesticating Efficiency," pp. 633–75). Lillian remained active in the field of household engineering, into the 1960s, and enthusiastically embraced the idea that families might do micromotion studies using home-movie cameras. Gilbreth, Thomas, and Clymer, *Management in the Home,* p. 97.

27. Glenn H. Beyer, ed., *The Cornell Kitchen: Product Design through Research* (Ithaca: New York State College of Home Economics, in association with the Cornell University Housing Research Center, 1952).

28. Kira, *The Bathroom,* p. ix.

29. These tests were overseen by associate professor of household management Mary Koll Heiner, who knew Gilbreth's techniques well. See Mary Koll Heiner and N. Maude Vedder, "Studies in Dishwashing Methods: An Attempt to Apply Methods of Job Analysis to a Household Process," *Journal of Home Economics* 22, no. 5 (1930): p. 396. For more on the product design and laboratory criteria, see Beyer, *Cornell Kitchen,* pp. 56–73, 74–80.

30. Gardner Soule, "New Kitchen Built to Fit *Your* Wife," *Popular Science,* September 1953, p. 172.

31. For Kira's use of anthropometric data and the way he defines his design population, see Appendix A in Kira, *The Bathroom,* pp. 197–201.

32. Ibid., p. 45.

33. On cleaning the bathroom, see Kira, *The Bathroom,* pp. 42–43, 72–73, 89–90, 136–37, 162–64.

34. See Annmarie Adams, *Architecture in the Family Way: Doctors, Houses, and Women, 1870–1900* (Montreal and Kingston: McGill-Queen's University Press, 1996), pp. 73–102.

35. Kira, *The Bathroom,* pp. 10–11, 174.

36. Ibid., pp. 18–20.

37. American Standard eventually put one of Kira's designs into production, a posture-mold seat (for a photo, see Kira, *The Bathroom, New and Expanded*, p. 132), and he consulted on other products for the company, notably the prefabricated Spectra 70 bath and enclosure, which included most of his design criteria from multiple shower heads to a lumbar support to a fold-out tray. Rita Reif, "The Bathtub Gradually Takes on a 20th Century Look," *New York Times,* January 13, 1969, p. 24.

38. Kira, *The Bathroom,* p. 175.

39. This appeared to be the consensus among those professionals who gave any serious consideration to bathrooms. See also Julius Panero and Martin Zelnik, *Human Dimension & Interior Space* (New York: Whitney Library of Design, an imprint of Watson-Guptill Publications, 1979), pp. 163–68, 275–78.

40. Denise Scott Brown, "Planning the Powder Room," *AIA Journal* (April 1967): pp. 81–83.

41. Kira quotes Scott Brown on signage and location instead. Kira, *The Bathroom, New and Expanded,* p. 205.

42. Ibid., p. viii. See, for instance, the bathroom-related pages in Charles G. Ramsey and Harold R. Sleeper, *Architectural Graphic Standards,* 4th ed. (New York: John Wiley & Sons, 1951), pp. 341–50; or "Bathrooms," in Ernst Neufert, *Architect's Data,* ed. Vincent Jones, 2nd ed. (London: Granada, 1980), pp. 61–64.

43. This account of *Graphic Standards* is primarily drawn from Paul Emmons, "Diagrammatic Practices: The Office of Frederick L. Ackerman and *Architectural Graphic Standards,*" *The Journal of the Society of Architectural Historians* 64, no. 1 (2005): pp. 4–21. See also George Barnett Johnston, *Drafting Culture: A Social History of Architectural Graphic Standards* (Cambridge, MA: MIT Press, 2008).

44. Kira, *The Bathroom, New and Expanded,* p. 176.

45. For graffiti, see ibid., p. 210; for a sample a dirty joke, see ibid., p. 18.

46. Ibid., p. viii.

47. Ibid., p. vii.

48. See Kira, *The Bathroom,* p. 76.

49. Ralph Nader, *Unsafe at Any Speed: The Designed-In Dangers of the American Automobile* (New York: Grossman, 1965).

50. "Examining the Unmentionables," *Time,* May 20, 1966; and "Bathrooms for Living," *Time,* December 22, 1975.

51. An important exception is planner Clara Greed's *Inclusive Urban Design: Public Toilets* (Oxford: Architectural Press, 2003).

52. The German company Röhm (described as one of Kira's "greatest fans" in one trade journal) designed a modular bathroom system and a low-level lavatory based on his ideas. Louis Wilkins, "Fitting Out," *Building Design,* November 19, 1976, pp. 18–19. See also Philippe Daverio, Enrico Finzi, Anna Lombardi, and Vitaliano Pesante, *Hic Licet: Bathrooms and Wellness. The Story of Pozzi-Ginori* (Spilimbergo: Pozzi-Ginori, 2004), pp. 108–9.

53. Judith Davidsen, "Talking: Alexander Kira," *Interior Design,* September 1, 1989, http://www.highbeam.com/doc/1G1-7978569.html, March 6, 2010.

54. Kira, *The Bathroom, New and Expanded,* p. 49; and Nader, *Unsafe at Any Speed,* p. vii.

55. Kira, *The Bathroom, New and Expanded,* p. 212.

56. Kira, *The Bathroom,* p. 12.

57. Ibid., p. 13.

58. This is adapted from a remark by Beyer in *The Cornell Kitchen*, p. 14: "A reciprocity also exists between this area of space [i.e., the kitchen] and the homemakers, in that any alterations which she may make in the 'space relations' to suit her own preferences in turn operate to change, in some way, those preferences."

59. See Clara Greed, "The Role of the Public Toilet in Civic Life," in *Ladies and Gents: Public Toilets and Gender* (Philadelphia: Temple University Press, 2009), pp. 35–47.

60. A recent article, for instance, positively considers "modern-day squat evangelists" in the West who encourage a return to squat toilets for health reasons. Not surprisingly, Kira is prominently cited. Daniel Lametti, "Don't Just Sit There!" *Slate*, August 26, 2010, http://www.slate.com/id/2264657/, December 12, 2010.

61. Molotch writes an illuminating behind-the-scenes account of trying and failing to redesign the bathroom in his department at New York University. Harvey Molotch, "On Not Making History: What NYU Did with the Toilet and What it Means for the World," in *Toilet: Public Restrooms and the Politics of Sharing*, ed. Harvey Molotch and Laura Norén (New York: New York University Press, 2010), pp. 255–72.

62. Molotch, "On Not Making History," p. 256.

63. Tim Ostler, "Four Vases Do Not Make a Bathroom: An Interview with Alexander Kira," *World Architecture* 51 (1996): p. 132.

64. Ibid.

65. For a helpful introduction to these representational issues and techniques, see Ro Spankie, *Drawing Out the Interior* (Lausanne: AVA Publishing, 2009).

20 AN ENVIRONMENTAL PSYCHOLOGY APPROACH

1. David M. Buss, "Selection, Evocation, and Manipulation," *Journal of Personality and Social Psychology* 53 (1987): pp. 1214–21; and William B. Swann, "Identity Negotiation: Where Two Roads Meet," *Journal of Personality and Social Psychology* 53 (1987): pp. 1038–51.

2. Buss, "Selection, Evocation, and Manipulation," pp. 1214–21.

3. Samuel D. Gosling, Sei Jin Ko, Thomas Mannarelli, and Margaret Morris, "A Room with a Cue: Judgments of Personality Based on Offices and Bedrooms," *Journal of Personality and Social Psychology* 82 (2002): pp. 379–98.

4. Roy F. Baumeister, "A Self-Presentational View of Social Phenomena," *Psychological Bulletin* 91 (1982): pp. 3–26; Swann, "Identity Negotiation," pp. 1038–51; and William B. Swann, Peter J. Rentrow, and Jennifer S. Guinn, "Self-Verification: The Search for Coherence," in *Handbook of Self and Identity*, ed. Mark R. Leary and June Price Tangney (New York: Guilford, 2003), pp. 367–83.

5. Lindsay T. Graham, Carson J. Sandy, and Samuel D. Gosling, "Manifestations of Individual Differences in Physical and Virtual Environments," in *Handbook of Individual Differences*, ed., Tomas Chamorro-Premuzic, Adrian Furnham, and Sophie von Stumm (Oxford: Wiley-Blackwell, 2011), pp. 773–800.

6. Edward O. Laumann and James S. House, "Living Room Styles and Social Attributes: The Patterning of Material Artifacts in a Modern Urban Community," *Sociology and Social Research* 54 (1970): pp. 321–42.

7. Samuel D. Gosling, Kenneth H. Craik, Nicholas R. Martin, and Michelle R. Pryor, "Material Attributes of Personal Living Spaces," *Home Cultures* 2 (2005): pp. 51–88.

8. Joyce V. Kasmar, "The Development of a Useable Lexicon of Environmental Descriptors," *Environment and Behavior* 2 (1970): pp. 153–69.

9. Gosling et al., "A Room with a Cue," pp. 379–98; and Samuel D. Gosling, Kenneth H. Craik, Nicholas R. Martin, and Michelle R. Pryor, "The Personal Living Space Cue Inventory: An Analysis and Evaluation," *Environment and Behavior* 37 (2005): pp. 683–705.

10. Gosling et al., "The Personal Living Space Cue Inventory," pp. 683–705.

11. Gosling et al., "A Room with a Cue," pp. 379–98; Gosling et al., "The Personal Living Space Cue Inventory," pp. 683–705; and Gosling et al., "Material Attributes of Personal Living Spaces," pp. 51–88.

12. Harriet L. Rheingold and Kaye V. Cook, "The Content of Boys' and Girls' Rooms as an Index of Parents' Behaviors," *Child Development* 46 (1975): pp. 459–63.

13. Dana R. Carney, John T. Jost, Samuel D. Gosling, and Jeff Potter, "The Secret Lives of Liberals and Conservatives: Personality Profiles, Interaction Styles, and the Things They Leave Behind," *Political Psychology* 29 (2008): pp. 807–40.

14. Graham et al., "Manifestations of Individual Differences."

15. Oliver P. John, Laura P. Naumann, and Christopher J. Soto, "Paradigm Shift to the Integrative Big-Five Trait Taxonomy: History, Measurement, and Conceptual Issues," in *Handbook of Personality: Theory and Research,* ed. Oliver P. John, Richard W. Robins, and Lawrence A. Pervin (New York: Guilford, 2008), pp. 114–58.

16. Gosling et al., "A Room with a Cue," pp. 379–98.

17. James C. McElroy, Paula C. Morrow, and Ronald J. Ackerman, "Personality and Interior Office Design: Exploring the Accuracy of Visitor Attributions," *Journal of Applied Psychology* 68 (1983): pp. 541–44.

18. William B. Hansen and Irwin Altman, "Decorating Personal Places: A Descriptive Analysis," *Environment and Behavior* 8 (1976): pp. 491–504.

19. Anne Vinsel, Barbara Brown, Irwin Altman, and Carolyn Foss, "Privacy Regulation, Territorial Displays and Effectiveness of Individual Functioning," *Journal of Personality and Social Psychology* 39 (1980): pp. 1104–15.

20. Meredith M. Wells and Luke Thelen, "What Does Your Workspace Say About You? The Influence of Personality, Status, and Workspace on Personalization," *Environment and Behavior* 34 (2002): pp. 300–21.

21. Meredith M. Wells, "Office Clutter or Meaningful Personal Displays: The Role of Office Personalization in Employee and Organizational Well-Being," *Journal of Environmental Psychology* 20 (2000): pp. 239–55; and Meredith M. Wells, Luke Thelen, and Jennifer Ruark, "Workspace Personalization and Organizational Culture: Does Your Workspace Reflect You or Your Company?" *Environmental and Behavior* 39 (2007): pp. 616–34.

22. Rheingold and Cook, "The Content of Boys' and Girls' Rooms," pp. 459–63.

23. Randall M. Jones, Denise E. Taylor, Andrew J. Dick, Archana Singh, and Jerry L. Cook, "Bedroom Design and Decoration: Gender Difference in Preference and Activity," *Adolescence* 42 (2007): pp. 539–53.

24. Gosling et al., "Material Attributes of Personal Living Spaces," pp. 51–88; Hansen and Altman, "Decorating Personal Places," pp. 491–504; and Vinsel et al., "Privacy Regulation, Territorial Displays and Effectiveness of Individual Functioning," pp. 1104–15.

25. Sommer, R. *Social Design: Creating Buildings with People in Mind* (Englewood Cliffs, NJ: Prentice-Hall 1983).

26. Egon Brunswik, *Perception and the Representative Design of Psychological Experiments* (Berkeley: University of California Press, 1956).

27. Andrew Baum and G. E. Davis, *Journal of Personality and Social Psychology* 53 (1976): pp. 1214–21.

28. James Jerome Gibson, *The Senses Considered as Perceptual Systems* (Boston: Houghton Mifflin, 1966); and James Jerome Gibson, *The Ecological Approach to Visual Perception* (Boston: Houghton Mifflin, 1979).

29. James Jerome Gibson, "The Theory of Affordances and the Design of the Environment," Paper presented at the annual meetings of the American Society for Aesthetics, Toronto, 1976.

30. Daniel E. Berlyne, *Aesthetics and Psychobiology* (New York: Appleton-Century Crofts, 1971); and Daniel E. Berlyne, ed., *Studies in the New Experimental Aesthetics: Steps Toward an Objective Psychology of Aesthetic Appreciation* (New York: Halsted Press, 1974).

31. Amos Rapoport and Robert E. Kantor, "Complexity and Ambiguity in Environmental Design," *Journal of the American Institute of Planners* 33 (1967): pp. 210–21; and Robert Venturi, *Complexity and Contradiction in Architecture* (New York: Museum of Modern Art, 1966).

32. Joachim F. Wohlwill, "Environmental Aesthetics: The Environment as a Source of Affect," in *Human Behavior and Environment*, vol. 1, ed. Irwin Altman and Joachim F. Wohlwill (New York: Plenum, 1976), pp. 37–86.

33. Gary W. Evans, Elsye Kantrowitz, and Paul Eshelman, "Housing Quality and Psychological Well-Being Among the Elderly Population," *Journals of Gerontology: Series B: Psychological Sciences and Social Sciences* 57 B (2002): pp. 381–83.

34. Robert Gifford and Cécile Lacombe, "Children's Socioemotional Health and Housing Quality," *Journal of Housing and the Built Environment* 21 (2006): pp. 177–89.

35. William M. Michelson, *Environmental Choice, Human Behavior and Residential Satisfaction* (New York: Oxford University Press, 1977).

36. Paramjeet K. Dhillon and Minni Bhalla, "The Impact of Built-Living Environment on Human Behavior: An Empirical Study," *Journal of the Indian Academy of Applied Psychology* 14 (1988): pp. 16–25; Omer R. Galle and Walter R. Gove, "Crowding and Behavior in Chicago, 1940–1970," in *Residential Crowding and Design*, ed. John R. Aiello and Andrew Baum (New York: Plenum, 1979), pp. 23–39; Robert Gifford, "The Consequences of Living in High-Rise Buildings," *Architectural Science Review* 50, no. 1 (2007): pp. 2–17; and Willem van Vliet, "Families in Apartment Buildings: Sad Storeys for Children?" *Environment and Behavior* 15 (1983): pp. 211–31.

37. Janet Frey Talbot and Rachel Kaplan, "The Benefits of Nearby Nature for Elderly Apartment Residents," *The International Journal of Aging & Human Development* 33 (1991): pp. 119–30.

38. Andrea Faber Taylor, Frances E. Kuo, and William C. Sullivan, "Views of Nature and Self-Discipline: Evidence from Inner City Children," *Journal of Environmental Psychology* 22 (2002): pp. 49–63.

39. John C. Baird, Barbara Cassidy, and Jennifer Kurr, "Room Preference as a Function of Architectural Features and User Activities," *Journal of Applied Psychology* 63 (1978): pp. 719–27.

40. Michael R. Cunningham, "Notes on the Psychological Basis of Environmental Design: The Right-Left Dimension in Apartment Floor Plans," *Environment and Behavior* 9 (1977): pp. 125–35.

41. David L. Weisenthal and Joseph H. Tubiana, "Apartment Design Choices: A Study of Israeli and Non-Israeli University Students," *Environment and Behavior* 13 (1981): pp. 677–84.

42. Frank H. Mahnke and Rudolf H. Mahnke, *Color and Light in Man-Made Environments* (New York: Van Nostrand Reinhold, 1987).

43. Anya C. Hurlbert and Yazhu Ling, "Biological Components of Sex Differences in Color Preference," *Current Biology* 17 (2007): pp. 623–25.

44. Stephen E. Palmer and Karen B. Schloss, "An Ecological Valence Theory of Color Preferences," *Proceedings of the National Academy of Sciences* 107, no. 19 (2010): pp. 8877–82.

45. Michiko Kunishima and Takuko Yanase, "Visual Effects of Wall Colors in Living Rooms," *Ergonomics* 28 (1985): pp. 869–82.

46. Robert Gifford, *Environmental Psychology: Principles and Practice,* 4th ed. (Colville, WA: Optimal Books, 2007).

47. Robert Gifford, "Performance and Related Outcomes of Inadequate Offices: An Annotated Bibliography" (Report to the British Columbia Buildings Corporation, Victoria, British Columbia, 1992).

48. For extensive reviews, see Gifford, *Environmental Psychology;* David J. Oborne and Michael M. Gruneberg, eds., *The Physical Environment at Work* (New York: John Wiley & Sons, 1983); and Eric Sundstrom, *Work Places: The Psychology of the Physical Environment in Offices and Factories* (Cambridge: Cambridge University Press, 1986).

49. Jennifer A. Veitch, Donald W. Hine, and Robert Gifford, "End-Users' Knowledge, Beliefs, and Preferences for Lighting," *Journal of Interior Design* 19, no. 2 (1993): pp. 15–26.

50. J. F. Barnaby, "Lighting for Productivity Gains," *Lighting Design and Application,* February 1980, pp. 20–28; and Robert Gifford, Donald W. Hine, and Jennifer A. Veitch, "Meta-Analysis for Environment-Behavior Research, Illuminated with a Study of Lighting Level Effects on Office Task Performance," in *Advances in Environment, Behavior, and Design* 4: *The Integration of Theory, Research, and Utilization,* ed. Gary T. Moore and Robert W. Marans (New York: Plenum, 1997), pp. 223–53.

51. Peter Robert Boyce, *Human Factors in Lighting* (London: Applied Science Publishers, 1981).

52. Jean D. Wineman, "The Office Environment as a Source of Stress," in *Environmental Stress,* ed. Gary W. Evans (Cambridge: Cambridge University Press, 1982), pp. 256–85.

53. Phil Leather, Michael Pygras, Di Beale, and Claire Lawrence, "Windows in the Workplace: Sunlight, View, and Occupational Stress," *Environment and Behavior* 30 (1998): pp. 739–62.

54. Toni Farrenkopf and Vicki Roth, "The University Faculty Office as an Environment," *Environment and Behavior* 12 (1980): pp. 467–77; and Leather et al., "Windows in the Workplace," p. 30.

55. Mohamed Boubekri, Robert B. Hull, and Lester L. Boyer, "Impact of Window Size and Sunlight Penetration on Office Workers' Mood and Satisfaction: A Novel Way of Assessing Sunlight," *Environment and Behavior* 23 (1991): pp. 474–93.

56. Nancy J. Stone and Joanne M. Irvine, "Direct or Indirect Window Access, Task Type, and Performance," *Journal of Environmental Psychology* 14 (1994): pp. 57–63.

57. Mary C. Finnegan and Linda Z. Solomon, "Work Attitudes in Windowed vs. Windowless Environments," *Journal of Social Psychology* 115 (1981): pp. 291–92.

58. S. P. Banbury and D. C. Berry, "Office Noise and Employee Concentration: Identifying Causes of Disruption and Potential Improvements," *Ergonomics* 48 (2005): pp. 25–37.

59. Sheldon Cohen, Gary Evans, Daniel Stokols, and David Krantz, *Behavior, Health and Environmental Stress* (New York: Plenum, 1991); David Glass and Jerome Singer, *Urban Stress: Experiments on Noise and Social Stressors* (Chichester, UK: Academic Press, 1972); and Andrew Smith, "A Review of the Effects of Noise on Human Performance," *Scandinavian Journal of Psychology* 30 (1989): pp. 185–209.

60. Edward Donnerstein and David W. Wilson, "Effects of Noise and Perceived Control on On-going and Subsequent Aggressive Behavior," *Journal of Personality and Social Psychology* 34 (1976): pp. 774–81.

61. Greg Oldham, Anne Cummings, Leann Mischel, James Schmidtke, and Jin Zhou, "Listen While You Work? Quasi-Experimental Relations Between Personal-Stereo Headset Use and Employee Work Responses," *Journal of Applied Psychology* 80 (1995): pp. 547–64.

62. John G. Fox, "Industrial Music," in *The Physical Environment at Work,* ed. David J. Oborne and Michael M. Grunberg (New York: John Wiley & Sons, 1983).

63. Ibid.

64. J. Richard Jennings, Robert Nebes, and Kay Brock, "Memory Retrieval in Noise and Psychophysiological Response in the Young and Old," *Psychophysiology* 25 (1998): pp. 633–44; and Kari Lahtela, Pekka Niemi, Vesa Kuusela, and Kimmo Hypen, "Noise and Visual Choice-Reaction Time: A Large-Scale Population Survey," *Scandinavian Journal of Psychology* 27 (1986): pp. 52–57.

65. Cheuk Fan Ng, "Office Worker Performance and Satisfaction: The Effects of Office Noise and Individual Characteristics," *Dissertation Abstracts International* 50, no. 5 B (1989): pp. 2190–91; and Lionel Standing, Danny Lynn, and Katherine Moxness, "Effects of Noise Upon Introverts and Extroverts," *Bulletin of the Psychonomic Society* 28 (1990): pp. 138–40.

66. Glenn A. Toplyn, "The Differential Effect of Noise on Creative Task Performance," *Dissertation Abstracts International* 48 (1988): p. 3718.

67. Bruce L. Welch, "Extra-Auditory Health Effects of Industrial Noise: Survey of Foreign Literature," Aerospace Medical Research Laboratory, Aerospace Medical Division, Airforce Systems Command, Wright-Patterson AFB, June 1979.

68. Gary W. Evans and Dana Johnson, "Stress and Open-Office Noise," *Journal of Applied Psychology* 85 (2000): pp. 779–83.

21 GUILTY BY DESIGN/GUILTY BY DESIRE

1. Shame is a fundamental component of homosexual identity and life. More recently, some ground-breaking scholarship addressing this issue has been published, and in the limited space here, it is too difficult to attend to. See David M. Halperin and Valerie Traub, eds., *Gay Shame* (Chicago and London: University of Chicago Press, 2009); and Eve Kososky Sedgwick, *Tendencies* (Durham, NC: Duke University Press, 1993).

2. Aaron Betsky, *Queer Space: Architecture and Same-Sex Desire* (New York: William Morrow and Co., 1997), p. 5.

3. See, for example, Neil Bartlett, *Who Was that Man? A Present for Mr. Oscar Wilde* (London: Serpent's Tail, 1988); Matt Cook, *London and the Culture of Homosexuality, 1885–1914* (Cambridge: Cambridge University Press, 2003); John Potvin, "Vapour and Steam: The Victorian Bath, Homosocial Health and Male Bodies on Display," *Journal of Design History* 18, no. 4 (2005): pp. 319–33; and Andrew Stephenson, "Precarious Poses: The Problem of Artistic Visibility and its Homosocial Performances in Late Nineteenth-Century London," *Visual Culture in Britain* 8, no. 1 (2007): pp. 73–104.

4. See Jon Binnie, *The Globalization of Sexuality* (London: Sage, 2004); Marianne Blidon, "Jalons pour une géographie des homosexualités," *Espace géographique* 2, no. 37 (2008):

pp. 175–89; Michael Brown, *Closet Space: Geographies of Metaphor from the Body to the Globe* (London: Routledge, 2000); Lynda Johnston and Robyn Longhurst, *Space, Place and Sex: Geographies of Sexualities* (Lanham, MA: Rowman and Littlefield, 2010); Rob Kitchin, "Sexing the City: The Sexual Production of Non-Heterosexual Space in Belfast, Manchester and San Francisco," *City* 6, no. 2 (2002): pp. 205–18; and Natalie Oswin, "Critical Geographies and the Uses of Sexuality: Deconstructing Queer Space," *Progress in Human Geography* 32, no. 1 (2008): pp. 89–103.

5. I am not suggesting that there are not excellent studies on sexuality and the interior. Rather, I simply and importantly want to highlight the current imbalance, which privileges the public domain over the domestic realm. The study of the home and its interiority in many disciplines has only come into its own in the past two or so decades.

6. Walter Benjamin, *The Arcades Project,* ed. Rolf Tiedemann (Cambridge, MA: Harvard University Press, 1999), p. 19.

7. John Ruskin, *Sesame and Lilies* (New Haven, CT: Yale University Press, 2002), p. 122.

8. David Sox, *Bachelors of Art: Edward Perry Warren and the Lewes House Brotherhood* (London: Fourth Estate, 1991), pp. 44–45.

9. Ibid., p. 44.

10. Osbert Burdett and E. H. Goddard, *Edward Perry Warren: The Biography of a Connoisseur* (London: Christopher's, 1941), p. 131.

11. See John Potvin, "Askesis as Aesthetic Home: Edward Perry Warren, Lewis House and the Ideal of Greek Love," *Home Cultures: The Journal of Architecture, Design and Domestic Space* 8, no. 1 (2011): pp. 71–90.

12. William G. Holzberger and Herman J. Saatkamp, eds., *Persons and Places: Fragments of an Autobiography* (Cambridge, MA: MIT Press, 1986), p. 81.

13. William Rothenstein, *Men and Memories: Recollections of William Rothenstein,* 1900–1922 (London: Faber & Faber, 1932), p. 343.

14. John Tosh, *A Man's Place: Masculinity and the Middle-Class Home in Victorian England* (New Haven, CT: Yale University Press, 1999), p. 173.

15. Katherine V. Snyder, *Bachelors, Manhood, and the Novel, 1850–1925* (Cambridge: Cambridge University Press, 1999), p. 21.

16. Ibid., p. 7.

17. Burdett and Goddard, *Edward Perry Warren,* p. 144.

18. Rothenstein, *Men and Memories,* p. 167.

19. Benjamin, *Arcades Project,* p. 19.

20. Ricketts Letter to Michael Fields, February, 26 1899; Paul J. G. Delaney, ed., *Some Letters from Charles Ricketts and Charles Shannon to "Michael Field" (1894–1902)* (Edinburgh: The Tragara Press, 1979), n.p.

21. Jean Paul Raymond and Charles R. Ricketts, *Oscar Wilde: Recollections* (London: Nonesuch Press, Bloomsbury, 1932), p. 40.

22. Rothenstein, *Men and Memories,* p. 174.

23. *News of the World,* May 26, 1895.

24. *Star,* April 26, 1895.

25. *Evening News,* April 26, 1895.

26. Ed Cohen, *Talk on the Wilde Side: Toward a Genealogy of a Discourse on Male Sexualities* (London: Routledge, 1993), p. 180.

27. Italics emphasized by author from Jeffrey Weeks, *Coming Out: Homosexual Politics in Britain from the Nineteenth Century to the Present* (London: Quartet Books, 1977), p. 14.

28. Erik Näslund, *Rolf de Maré: Art Collector, Ballet Director, Museum Creator,* (Stockholm: Dance Books, 2009), pp. 74–75.

29. Russel W. Belk and Melanie Wallendorf, "Of Mice and Men: Gender Identity in Collecting," in *Interpreting Objects and Collections,* ed. Susan M. Pearce (London: Routledge, 1994), pp. 240–53.

30. Max Nordau, *Degeneration,* 2nd ed. (London: Heineman, 1895), p. 2.

31. Näslund, *Rolf de Maré,* p. 90.

32. In addition to a number of periodicals, de Maré was the founder of *Monsieur,* the first men's fashion magazine in the West. For more on the magazine, see John Potvin, "The Vaseline Mafia: Rolf de Maré and a Certain Monsieur," in "Queer Fashion," special issue, *Lambda Nordica: Journal for LGBT Studies* 14, no. 3/4 (2009): pp. 160–90.

33. Betsky, *Queer Space,* p. 20.

34. Michel Foucault, *History of Sexuality,* vol. 1 (New York: Vintage Books, 1990).

22 TOWARD SENTIENCE

1. Charles Leadbetter and Jake Garber, *Dying for Change* (London: Demos, 2010).

2. Atul Gwande, "Letting Go: What Should Medicine Do When It Can't Save Your Life?" *The New Yorker,* August, 2, 2010, http://www.newyorker.com/reporting/2010/08/02/100802fa_fact_gawande, accessed April 13, 2011.

3. King's College London Exhibits and Galleries, Ruth Richardson, "Florence Nightingale and Hospital Design," November 2010, http://www.kingscollections.org/exhibitions/specialcollections/nightingale-and-hospital-design/florence-nightingale-and-hospitaldesign, accessed April 13, 2011.

4. Roger S. Ulrich, "View Through a Window May Influence Recovery From Surgery," *Science* 224 (1984): pp. 42–421.

5. Gwande, "Letting Go."

6. Leadbetter and Garber, *Dying for Change,* p. 59.

7. Fukushima nuclear disaster at the Fukushima I Nuclear Power Plant, Japan that followed the 9.0 magnitude earthquake and tsunami on March 11, 2011. It is considered to be the second largest nuclear accident after the Chernobyl disaster.

8. Richard Smith, "Medicine's Need for the Humanities," December 30, 2010, http://blogs.bmj.com/bmj/2010/12/30/richard-smith-medicines-need-for-the-humanities, accessed March 1, 2011.

9. Ibid.

10. "Definition of Hippocratic Oath," MedicineNet.com, http://www.medterms.com/script/main/art.asp?articlekey=20909, accessed March 4, 2011.

11. Jonah Lehrer, *Proust Was a Neuroscientist* (Boston: Houghton Mifflin, 2007).

12. Marcel Proust, *A la Recherche du Temps Perdu* (France: Grasset and Gallimard, 1913–1927).

13. James Auger, Royal College of Art Website, http://www.di.research.rca.ac.uk/content/projects/39/Smell%2B#, accessed February 28, 2011.

14. Ibid.

15. Lehrer, *Proust Was a Neuroscientist,* p. 190.

16. Charles Percy Snow, *The Two Cultures,* 2nd ed. (Cambridge: Cambridge University Press, 1993), p. 181.

17. Welcome Trust, http://www.wellcome.ac.uk.

18. Arts for Health, http://www.artsforhealth.org.

19. "Enhancing the Healing Environment," The Kings Fund, April 2009, http://www.kingsfund.org.uk/current_projects/enhancing_the_healing_environment/, accessed March 4, 2011.

20. Ulrich, "View Through a Window."

21. Roger S. Ulrich, "Effects of Health Facility Interior Design on Wellness: Theory and Recent Scientific Research," *Journal of Health Care Design* 3 (1991): pp. 97–109.

22. Ibid.

23. *Soylent Green* (1973) is an American science fiction film directed by Richard Fleischer and staring Charlton Heston. Set in a dystopian New York in 2022, the film dramatizes a world plagued with overpopulation, pollution, and food shortages. As a consequence, the population lives off rations made by the Soylent Corporation, including a rare new product called "soylent green." The film's plot revolves around the police investigation of the murder of the head of the Soylent Corporation and the subsequent uncovering of the secret behind soylent green itself.

24. *Hay Wain* is an oil painting by John Constable. It was finished in 1821 and shows a hay wain near Flatford Mill on the River Stour in Suffolk. *Hay Wain* is revered today as one of the greatest British paintings, but in a health setting it runs the risk of being seen as a saccharine chocolate box image.

25. *My Bed* (1998) is an art installation piece by Tracey Emin first displayed at the Tate Gallery in 1999. It depicts an unmade bed, with various objects littered on the floor. The work shortlisted for the Turner Prize in the same year. It became a cause celebre in the media through its uncompromising use of real objects including, among other things, stained bed-sheets, condoms, and dirtied underwear. Emin defended the content of the work by stating that the room was an actual representation of the room where she spent several days suffering from suicidal depression in the wake of a relationship breakdown.

26. MoMA, http://www.moma.org/meetme.

27. Michael Craig-Martin, *KIDS* (2011), see http://www.michaelcraigmartin.co.uk, and also http://news.bbc.co.uk/1/hi/uk_politics/8650553.stm.

28. Rosalia Staricoff, Jane P. Duncan, and Melissa Wright, "A Study of the Effects of Visual and Performing Arts in Health Care" (London: Chelsea and Westminster Hospital, 2004).

29. D. Kirk Hamilton, "The Four Levels of Evidence-Based Practice," *Healthcare Design* 3 (2003): pp. 18–26.

30. Tony Blair, cited in "Enhancing the Healing Environment" (Kings Fund Report, September 2005).

31. Mary G. Lankford, Teresa R. Zembower, William E. Trick, Donna M. Hacek, Gary A. Noskin, and Lance R. Peterson, "Influence of Role Models and Hospital Design on the Hand Hygiene of Health-Care Workers," *Emerging Infectious Diseases* 9, no. 2 (2003), http://wwwnc.cdc.gov/eid/article/9/2/02-0249_article.htm.

32. Bromley by Bow Centre, http://www.bbbc.org.uk/pages/about-us.html.

33. See http://www.maggiescentres.org/about/whowasmaggie.html.

34. Richard Dawkins, Daniel Dennett, Sam Harris, and Christopher Hitchens, "Four Horsemen Discussion," YouTube, posted May 6, 2012, http://www.youtube.com/watch?v=rRLYL1Q9x9g, accessed July 28, 2012.

35. Research undertaken as part of the Invest to Save: Arts in Health Project, http://www.miriad.mmu.ac.uk/investtosave/.

36. Kate Kellaway in an article for *The Observer,* "Maggie's Centres: How One Woman's Vision is Changing Cancer Treatment," February 20, 2011, http://www.guardian.co.uk/society/2011/feb/20/maggie-keswickjencks-centres-cancer-design, accessed February 21, 2011.

37. Charles Jencks, "The Maggie Centres Movement, Eight Years In," *Fourth Door Review, Architexts 1, Design with Care* (2005), http://sust.org/pdf/The%20Maggie%20Centres%20Movement%20eight%20years%20in.....pdf, accessed July 20, 2011.

38. Maggie's Centres, "Maggie's Centre Architectural Brief," http://www.maggiescentres.org/about/our_publications.html, accessed May 20, 2012.

39. Jencks, "The Maggie Centres Movement."

40. Maggie Keswick Jencks, *A View From the Front Line* (London: Maggie Keswick and Charles Jencks, 1995), p. 21, http://www.maggiescentres.org/newspublications/publications.html.

41. Dome of Discovery, http://en.wikipedia.org/wiki/Dome_of_Discovery.

42. Darren Browett, http://darrenbrowett.wordpress.com/.

43. Anne Basting, http://forgetmemory.org.

44. Gene Cohen, "Research on Creativity and Aging: The Positive Impact of the Arts on Health and Illness," *(The American Society on Aging) Generations* 30, no. 1 (2006): pp. 7–15.

45. Anne Basting, *Forget Memory: Creating Better Lives for People with Dementia* (Baltimore: Johns Hopkins University Press, 2009).

46. Cohen, "Research on Creativity and Aging," pp. 7–15.

47. Department of Health, "National Dementia Strategy," 2010, http://www.dh.gov.uk/en/SocialCare/NationalDementiaStrategy/index.htm, accessed March 18, 2011.

48. Constantin Boym, http://www.boym.com.

49. Darren L. Browett, http://darrenbrowett.wordpress.com/.

50. Darren L. Browett, "Fortuitous Novelties: Creative Engagement in Dementia Care" (thesis submitted in partial fulfillment of the Requirements of The Manchester Institute of Research and Innovation in Art and Design at Manchester Metropolitan University for the Degree of Master of Arts, 2010).

51. Donald F. Duclow, "'Ars Moriendi: Conversation, Guidance and Rituals' to Support Someone to Have a 'Good Death,'" *Encyclopedia of Death and Dying,* http://www.deathreference.com/A-Bi/Ars-Moriendi.html, accessed March 12, 2012.

52. Recorded interview with staff as part of Browett, "Fortuitous Novelties," May 2010

53. Browett, "Fortuitous Novelties."

54. Iona Heath, "Combating Disease Mongering: Daunting but Nonetheless Essential," *PLoS Medicine* 3, no. 4 (2006): p. e146, doi:10.1371/journal.pmed.0030146 11:04:06.

55. Lehrer, *Proust Was a Neuroscientist,* p. 191.

56. Ibid., p. 197.

57. Iona Heath, "What Do We Want To Die From?" *British Medical Journal* 341, 21 July 2010. BMJ2010;341:c3883, http://dx.doi.org/10.1136/bmj.c3883.

58. Ibid.

59. Ibid.

60. Iona Heath, What do we want to die from in British Medical Journal, 21 July 2010 BMJ2010;341:c3883 http://dx.doi.org/10.1136/bmj.c3883.

61. Kath Weston, *Render Me, Gender Me* (New York: Columbia University Press, 1996).

62. Paul Bate and Glenn Robert, "Experience-Based Design: From Redesigning the System Around the Patient to Co-Designing Services with the Patient," *Quality and Safety in Health Care* 15 (2006): pp. 307–10, doi:10:1136/qshc.2005.016527.

63. Lauren Tan and Deborah Szebeko, "Co-Designing for Dementia: The Alzheimer 100 Project," *Australasian Medical Journal* 1, no. 12 (2009): pp. 185–98, doi:10.4066/AMJ.2009.97.

64. Cohen, "Research on Creativity and Aging," p. 14.

65. Smith, "Medicine's Need for the Humanities."

66. As used by clinicians in Sweden a "breakpoint discussion" is a systematic series of conversations that enable patients to move from fighting a disease to actively focusing on their priorities and quality of life.

23 DESIGN FOR AGEING-IN-PLACE FOR HIGH-DENSITY LIVING IN ASIA

1. "Report on Aging Population," Singapore Committee on Aging Issues, Singapore: CAI (2006).
2. Toru Suzuki, "The Latest Development in the Population of Japan: The 2008 Revision," *The Japanese Journal of Population* 8 (2010), http://www.ipss.go.jp/webj-ad/WebJournal.files/population/2010_Vol.8/Web%20Journal_Vol.8_04.pdf, accessed September 25, 2011.
3. Government of Hong Kong, "Statistics Table," Census and Statistic Department, http://www.censtatd.gov.hk/hong_kong_statistics/statistical_tables/index.jsp?charsetID=1&subjectID=1&tableID=160#1, accessed November 2010.
4. United Nations, "Population Report" (2005), Table II.5, p. 36.
5. "Report on Aging Population," Singapore Committee on Aging Issues.
6. Ibid.
7. "Ageing-in-place" is defined as the ability for elderly people to live in their own home, comfortably and without much third-party assistance.
8. The basic idea behind assisted living is to provide professional but limited health care to vulnerable and frail people within a residential rather than institutional environment; Victor A. Regnier, *Assisted Living Housing for the Elderly: Design Innovations from The United States and Europe* (New York: Van Nostrand Reinhold, 1994).
9. Andreas Huber, "New Housing Model in Practice," in *New Approaches to Housing for Second Half of Life,* ed. Andreas Huber (Basel: Birkhäuser, 2008), pp. 77–83.
10. Universal design broadly refers to the design ideas that will create environments, products, or buildings that can be easily used by the able-bodied or those with physical disabilities. Now, this concept has often been employed for designing barrier-free environments used by three generations.
11. Regnier, *Assisted Living Housing for the Elderly.*
12. *Overcare* is defined as "the provision of inappropriate long-term care"; from Kathryn Lawler, *Aging-in-Place* (Cambridge, MA: Harvard University, 2001). It will occur when the aged individual is presented with too few options, either due to issues of costs or lack of available options.
13. *Undercare* is defined as the inadequate provision of healthcare services within the housing environment with regards to the individual's level of need; from Lawler, *Aging-in-Place.* It will occur when the aged individual is living in a house that is too big to be maintained without assistance or larger than necessary.
14. Regnier, *Assisted Living Housing for the Elderly.*
15. Ibid.
16. A. Huber, M. Hugentobler, and R. Walthert-Galli, "New Housing Models in Practice," in *New Approaches to Housing for the Second Half of Life,* ed. A. Huber (Basel: ETH, Birkhäuser, 2008), pp. 77–169.
17. Government of Hong Kong, "Statistics Table."
18. The Hong Kong Housing Authority (HKHA) is a statutory body established in 1973 responsible for implementing the majority of Hong Kong's public housing programs.
19. The Hong Kong Housing Society (HKHS) is an independent statutory organization established in 1948 for providing specific categories of subsidized housing to help meet the housing needs of the community.
20. Government of Hong Kong, "Statistics Table."

21. Ibid.
22. This program helps to provide 100 percent lift accessibility for all flats wherever feasible.
23. The Main Upgrading Programme (MUP) was launched by the government in 1990 to enhance the overall living environment of Housing and Development Board estates. It is part of the government's continual efforts to enhance the quality of life of Singaporeans through its public housing program. Established community ties are also preserved, as residents are able to enjoy a better living environment without the need to move out from their familiar surroundings. See Housing Development Board statistics (2010).
24. Raj Basu, "Improving Home Care," *The Straits Times,* December 20, 2010, pp. A16, 11.
25. Hong Kong Housing Society, Hong Kong Special Administrative Region Government, *Universal Design Guidebook for Residential Development in Hong Kong,* http://www.hkhs.com/eng/info/udg.asp, accessed November 2010.
26. Lions Befrienders Service Association is a Voluntary Welfare Organization that was founded in 1995 by the Lions Clubs of Singapore and a Lions District Project. Its core mission is to aid in the social, psycho-emotional, and physical well-being of lonely seniors through community participation while upholding the belief that every older person is a valued member of society and deserves to age with grace and dignity.
27. CHEER stands for Community and HDB Engaging Elderly Residents. Under Project CHEER, the Housing and Development Board facilitates corporations and companies that volunteer their time and funds in reaching out to senior citizens living in rental blocks.
28. SPHERE stands for Students, Singapore Pools and HDB Enriching and Reaching out to the Elderly. Under Project SPHERE, students from the participating schools adopt a Housing and Development Board rental block or studio apartment. They work toward enriching the lives of the elderly who live in these adopted blocks by organizing community activities for them.

24 DEMOGRAPHICS AND IDENTITY

1. Michiel Horn, *Becoming Canadian: Memoirs of an Invisible Immigrant* (Toronto: University of Toronto Press, 1997).
2. Jane Hamlett, "Managing and Making the Home: Domestic Advice Books," in *Imagined Interior: Representing the Domestic Interior Since the Renaissance,* ed. Jeremy Aynsley and Charlotte Grant (London: V&A Publications, 2007), pp. 184–85.
3. Martin Hall, "Virtual Colonization," *Journal of Material Culture* 4, no. 1 (1999): pp. 39–55.
4. Stuart Hall, "Who Needs Identity?" in *Questions of Cultural Identity,* ed. Stuart Hall and Paul De Gay (London: Sage, 1996), pp. 1–14.
5. "Do Bidets Save Forest and Water Resources?" *Scientific American,* December 16, 2009, http://www.scientificamerican.com/article.cfm?id=earth-talks-bidets, accessed 20 October 2010.
6. Kathleen L. Endres and Therese Lueck, *Women's Periodicals in the United States: Consumer Magazines* (Westport: Greenwood Publishing Group, 1995).
7. Betty Friedan, *Feminine Mystique* (New York: W. W. Norton, 1963).
8. Diana Rowntree, *Interior Design* (London: Penguin Classics, 1964).

9. Alison. J. Clarke, "The Aesthetics of Social Aspiration," in *Home Possessions: Material Culture Behind Closed Doors,* ed. Daniel Miller (Oxford: Berg, 2001), pp. 23–46.

10. Pierre Bourdieu, *The Field of Cultural Production* (New York: Columbia University Press, 1993).

11. Hall, "Who Needs Identity?"

12. Stephen Calloway and Stephen Jones, *Style Traditions. Recreating Period Interiors* (New York: Rizzoli, 1990).

13. Steven Parissien, *Interiors: The Home Since* 1700 (London: Laurence King, 2009), p. 284.

14. Economic Dispatch, *The Guardian,* June 8, 2004, http://www.guardian.co.uk/business/2004/jun/08/usnews.economicdispatch, accessed November 28, 2010.

15. Bourdieu, *The Field of Cultural Production.*

16. Brian James Barr, "Now Brewing, Starbucks Gets a Makeover," *The New York Times,* January 11, 2010, http://tmagazine.blogs.nytimes.com/2010/01/11/now-brewing-starbucks-gets-a-makeover/.

17. Bryant Simon, *Everything But the Coffee: Learning About America from Starbucks* (Berkeley: University of California Press, 2009).

18. Antanas Sileika, *Buying on Time* (Erin, Ontario: Porcupine's Quill, 1997).

19. Harriet McKay, "Designing Lifestyles: Retail Catalogues," in *Imagined Interior: Representing the Domestic Interior Since the Renaissance,* ed. Jeremy Aynsley and Charlotte Grant (London: V&A Publications, 2007), pp. 242–43.

20. Richard Jenkins, *Social Identity* (London: Routledge, 2008).

21. Neil Bissoondath, *Selling Illusions: The Cult of Multiculturalism in Canada* (Toronto: Penguin Canada, 2002).

22. Mark Gottdiener, *Postmodern Semiotics: Material Culture and the Forms of Postmodern Life* (Oxford: Blackwell, 1995).

23. For a discussion about a discernible shift away from aspiration, see Neil Davenport, "The Strange Death of Social Aspiration," *Spiked Essays,* August 11, 2004, http://www.spiked-online.com/articles/0000000CA663.htm, accessed October 20, 2010.

25 THE THIN EDGE OF THE WEDGE

1. For instance, five essays on ethics can be found in one recently published overview of the interior design profession. See Judith Fosshage, "The Ethical Imperative: Relevancy of the Interior Design Profession"; Allan Guinan, "Commoditization of Interior Design"; Cindy Coleman, "Ideals + Ideas + Infringements"; Susan E. Farley, "When Is and Imitation an Illegal Knockoff"; and H. Ladon (Don) Baltimore, "What is the Effect of Regulation on Liability," in *The State of the Interior Design Profession,* ed. Caren Martin and Denise A. Guerin, (New York: Fairchild Books, 2010), pp. 219–25, 226–31, 232–37, 238–42, 243–47, respectively. The underrepresentation of philosophical approaches to ethics in design practice is discussed in Michael P. Levine, Kristine Miller, and William Taylor, "Introduction: Ethics and Architecture," *The Philosophical Forum* 32, no. 2 (2004): p. 106.

2. Merriam Webster Online Dictionary, "Ethics," http://www.merriam-webster.com/dictionary/ethics, accessed January 15, 2011.

3. Francis T. Ventre, "Regulation: A Realization of Social Ethics," *VIA: Ethics and Architecture* 10 (1990): p. 51.

4. Clive Edwards, *Interior Design: An Introduction* (Oxford: Berg, 2011), pp. 15–16.

5. Lois Weinthal, "Towards a New Interior," in *Thinking Inside the Box: A Reader in Interiors for the 21st Century,* ed. Edward Hollis, Andrew Milligan, Drew Plunkett, John Gigli, and Frazer Hay (London: Middlesex University Press, 2007), pp. 113–21.

6. Judith Fosshage, "The Ethical Imperative: Relevancy of the Interior Design Profession," in *The State of the Interior Design Profession,* ed. Caren Martin and Denise A. Guerin (New York: Fairchild Books, 2010), p. 224 (italics are mine).

7. Arian Campo-Flores, "In Florida, Interior Decorators Have Designs on Deregulation," *Wall Street Journal,* April 15, 2011, http://online.wsj.com/article/SB10001424052748703 5513045762607422093153376.html?mod=WSJ_WSJ_US_News_10_1, accessed on April 16, 2011.

8. Christopher Day, *Places of the Soul: Architecture and Environmental Design as a Healing Art* (London: The Aquarian Press, 1990), p. 187.

9. Mark Taylor and Julieanna Preston, "Proximities" in *Intimus: Interior Design Theory Reader,* ed. Mark Taylor and Julieanna Preston (Chichester: Wiley-Academy, 2006), p. 11.

10. Weinthal, "Towards a New Interior," pp. 113–21.

11. *A Report on Waste Management for the Construction Industry,* The Canadian Construction Association, August 1992, p. 13; "LEED," Canadian Green Building Council, http://www.coolearth.ca/LEED%20description.html, accessed February 19, 2011; and "Construction Waste Management," *Whole Building Design Guide,* http://www.wbdg.org/resources/cwmgmt.php, accessed February 19, 2011. Also, the building industry is estimated to contribute 35 percent of waste in landfills in the UK; "Reducing and Managing Waste," http://www.sustainablebuild.co.uk/ReducingManagingWaste.html, accessed February 19, 2011.

12. While no single date can be used to establish the date on which interior designers began to address issues of sustainability en masse, the topic appears with some regularity in popular and scholarly design literature after 1990 and increases dramatically in publications dating to 2000 and beyond.

13. Mihyun Kang and Denise Guerin, "The Characteristics of Interior Designers Who Practice Environmentally Sustainable Interior Design," *Environment and Behavior* 41, no. 2 (2009): p. 180.

14. "Editorial," *Interiors,* February 1945, p. 8.

15. Kang and Guerin, "Characteristics of Interior Designers," p. 180.

16. Karrie Jacob, "Too Virtuous," *Metropolis,* July/August 2010, p. 42.

17. Jacob, "Too Virtuous," p. 45.

18. Craig Delancey, "Architecture Can Save the World: Building and Environmental Ethics," *The Philosophical Forum* 35, no. 2 (2004): pp. 151–52.

19. Elissa Auther, "The Decorative, Abstraction, and the Hierarchy of Art and Craft in the Art Criticism of Clement Greeberg," *The Oxford Art Journal* 27, no. 3 (2004): p. 342.

20. Walter Benjamin, "The Work of Art in the Age of Mechanical Reproduction," in *Illuminations,* ed. Hannah Arendt (New York: Schocken Books, 1978), p. 236.

21. Leslie C. Smith, "Social Media Consciousness," *Canadian Interiors,* January/February 2011, pp. 8–9.

22. Author's notes from keynote lecture, September 24, 2010.

23. Saul Fisher, "How to Think about Architectural Ethics," in *Ethics and the Built Environment*, ed. Warwick Fox (New York: Routledge, 2000), p. 179.
24. Gerry Beegan and Paul Atkinson, "Professionalism, Amateurism, and the Boundaries of Design," *Journal of Design History* 21, no. 4 (2008): p. 8.

26 DESIGNING DESIRE

1. In May 2007 with Gregory Krum, director of retail, The Shop at Cooper-Hewitt, National Design Museum.
2. *The Wrong Gallery*, New York (2002), installation by Maurizio Cattelan, Massimiliano Gioni, and Ali Subotnick; moved into the Tate Modern collection in 2005.
3. Including unique pieces, such as headgear by Dutch industrial designer Hella Jongerius, a perfume concocted by Swiss architects Herzog & de Meuron, and a wireless Jawbone headset from San Francisco–based designer Yves Béhar.
4. Of course, in utter private contradiction of itself—consumption will not be denied—the shop was available for purchase, wholesale, by a single collector.
5. Rem Koolhaas, *The Harvard Design School Guide to Shopping* (New York: Monacelli, 2000).
6. *Bazaar* means "place of prices" in Middle Persian.
7. From the British, a dealer in cloth or clothing and dry goods.
8. Bainbridge opened in 1838 in Newcastle-upon-Tyne, England, and reorganized itself by department in 1849.
9. An Austrian immigrant to the United States, Victor Gruen is credited for the design of the mall as we know it today.
10. The Future Laboratory (retail newsletter, November 2010, London).
11. "H&M Goes Augmented," VR-News, November 17, 2010, http://www.vr-news.com/2010/11/17/hm-goes-augmented/.
12. The Future Laboratory, "Beyond Retail" (report, April 2010, London).
13. Interview with author.
14. Ibid.
15. October–November 2010. The content of this series of six one-week public events, collaborations between architects and fashion designers, was determined through competitions and sponsored by Boffo, a nonprofit arts and culture organization based in New York City with the mission "to educate and inform the public through innovative exhibitions and events while providing exposure for artists and designers."
16. Shonquis Moreno, "Foam Alone," *Frame* magazine 79 (March/April 2011): pp. 44–45.
17. Ibid.
18. Rebecca Velt, "Prada's Subversive Style," MetropolisMag.com, September 28, 2007, http://www.metropolismag.com/story/20070928/pradas-subversive-style, accessed April 2, 2013.
19. Interview with author, November 2010.
20. As of 2011, Agneessens also directs an eponymously named New York studio that focuses on design, whereas Formavision seeks out and creates art and design mash-ups.
21. Shonquis Moreno, "Acid Flashback," *Frame* magazine 67 (March/April 2009): pp. 153–59.
22. Interview with author, August 2011.
23. Shonquis Moreno, *MiND* magazine 6 (January 2011).
24. Impractical for the customer trying to make a worthwhile purchase; practical, of course, for a brand trying to conceal poor quality.

25. Shonquis Moreno, *MiND* magazine 6 (January 2011).

26. Lolë, September 2010, http://www.lolewomen.com/blog/.

27. Shonquis Moreno, *Frame* 70 (September/October 2009): pp. 48–49.

27 DESIGNING FOR SUSTAINABILITY

1. Birgit Mager, "Service Design," in *Design Dictionary, Perspectives on Design Terminology*, ed. Michael Erlhoff and Tim Marshall (Basel: Birkhäuser, 2008), p. 355.

2. Buckminster Fuller, in *The World of Buckminster Fuller*, film, directed by Robert Snyder (New York: Mystic Fire Video, 1971).

3. The report is frequently referred to as the Brundtland Report. Gro Harlem Brundtland, then prime minister of Norway, was asked to chair the UN's World Commission on Environment and Development (also referred to as the Brundtland Commission). The committee was charged with investigating the social, economic, and environmental problems associated with growth and development and put forward recommendations for a more sustainable future; see "Biography of Dr Gro Harlem Brundtland," http://www.un.org/News/dh/hlpanel/brundtland-bio.htm, accessed September 2012.

4. United Nations World Commission on Environment and Development, "Report of United Nations World Commission on Environment and Development: Our Common Future" (1987), Part I, Chapter. 2, p.41, http://www.un-documents.net/our-common-future.pdf, accessed September 2012.

5. Bill McKibben, *Deep Economy, the Wealth of Communities and the Durable Future* (New York: Henry Holt, 2007).

6. Ibid., p 41.

7. Ibid., p 42.

8. The term *ecological footprint analysis* originates from the research of William Rees and Mathis Wackernagel of the University of British Columbia, School of Community and Regional Planning. Rees describes ecological footprint analysis as a method that "enables us to estimate the resource consumption and waste assimilation requirements of a defined human population or economy in terms of a corresponding productive land area"; Mathis Wackernagel and William E. Rees, *Our Ecological Footprint, Reducing Human Impact on the Earth* (Gabriola Island: New Society Publishers, 1996), p. 3. Furthermore there is growing concern for water and water scarcity—alternative energy systems exist, but there are no alternative sources for freshwater—therefore Water Footprint calculators have been developed. An example can be found at the website of the Water Footprint Network, created by scientists Arjen Y. Hoekstra and Ashok K. Chapagain (http://www.waterfootprint.org/index.php?page=files/home).

9. William E. Rees, "Ecological Footprints and Biocapacity: Essential Elements in Sustainability Assessment," in *Renewables-Based Technology, Sustainability Assessment*, ed. Jo Dewulf and Hermen Van Langenhove (New York: John Wiley & Sons, 2006), pp. 144, 145, 150.

10. Global Footprint Network, Advancing the Science of Sustainability, "Living Planet Report 2010: Biodiversity, Biocapacity and Development," 2010, http://www.footprintnetwork.org/en/index.php/GFN/page/Living_Planet_Report_2010_dv/, accessed January 2011.

11. Rees, "Ecological Footprints and Biocapacity," p. 152.

12. Al Gore, *An Inconvenient Truth, The Planetary Emergency of Global Warming and What We Can Do About It* (New York: Rodale, 2008); Richard Heinberg, "The Post Carbon Reader

Series: Foundation Concepts, Beyond the Limits to Growth," in *Post Carbon Reader, Managing the 21st Century's Sustainability Crises,* ed. Richard Heinberg and Daniel Lerch (Berkeley: University of California, 2010), no. 1;Sandra Postel,"Water: Adapting to a New Normal," in *Post Carbon Reader, Managing the 21st Century's Sustainability Crises,* ed. Richard Heinberg and Daniel Lerch (Berkeley: University of California, 2010), no. 7.

13. Michael Erlhoff and Tim Marshall, eds., *Design Dictionary, Perspectives on Design Terminology* (Basel: Birkhäuser, 2008).

14. Cameron Tonkinwise, "Sustainability," in *Design Dictionary, Perspectives on Design Terminology,* ed. Michael Erlhoff and Tim Marshall (Basel: Birkhäuser, 2008), pp. 380–86.

15. Tonkinwise, "Sustainability," p. 380.

16. C. S. Holling, "Resilience and Stability of Ecological Systems," *Annual Review of Ecology and Systematics* 4 (1973): pp. 1–23, doi:10.1146/annurev.es.04.110173.000245.

17. Carl Folke, "How Much Disturbance Can a System Withstand? With Roots in Ecology and Complexity Science, Resilience Theory Can Turn Crises into Catalysts for Innovation," *SEED Magazine,* December 13, 2010, http://seedmagazine.com/content/article/on_resilience, accessed February 2011.

18. Abiotic interactions have importance in understanding environmental impacts related to the built environment, as well as the biotic because they, too, are natural resources; Joshua Farley, "Ecological Economics," in Richard Heinberg, "The Post Carbon Reader Series: Foundation Concepts, Beyond the Limits to Growth," in *Post Carbon Reader, Managing the 21st Century's Sustainability Crises,* ed. Richard Heinberg and Daniel Lerch (Berkeley: University of California, 2010), Part 9, Economy, no. 20. The definition of *abiotic* refers to that which is not a living organism but is physical, such as light. "Abiotic," Oxford Dictionary Online, http://oxforddictionaries.com/definition/english/abiotic?q=abiotic, accessed November 6, 2010.

19. Fritjof Capra, *The Hidden Connections, A Science for Sustainable Living* (London: Flamingo, 2003).

20. Ibid., p. 201.

21. Rachel Carson, *Silent Spring,* 40th ed. (Boston: Houghton Mifflin, 2002).

22. *An Inconvenient Truth,* directed by Davis Guggenheim (Hollywood: Paramount Classics, 2006), film.

23. Tonkinwise, "Sustainability," p. 382.

24. Ezio Manzini and François Jégou, *Collaborative Services, Social Innovation and Design for Sustainability* (Milan: Edizioni Poli Design, 2008).

25. Anna Meroni, ed., *Creative Communities, People Inventing Sustainable Ways of Living* (Milan: Edizioni Poli Design, 2007), p.14.

26. The term is used here as it suggests—to amplify—but it also references The New School's DESIS Lab research project, Amplyfying Creative Communities, funded in part by the Rockefeller Foundation's 2009 NYC Cultural Innovation Fund. The project extends the international research of the DESIS Network to the United States and New York City (led through Parsons DESIS Lab). It explores emerging and established, sustainable, and innovative ways of living that often circumvent existing systemic roadblocks and assist efforts in making the experiences easier and more enjoyable while mapping ways of replicating these innovations through service design (see http://amplifyingcreativecommunities.net/#p8 and http://desis.parsons.edu); DESIS (Design for Social Innovation and Sustainability), "What We Do,"

2010, http://desis.parsons.edu/, http://desis.parsons.edu/2010/07/amplify-creative-sustain-able-lifestyles-in-the-lower-east-side/, accessed January 2011; and Sustainable Everyday Project, http://www.sustainable-everyday.net/SEPhome/home.html, accessed July 2010.

27. *Greenhouse effect*—the term, widely, used to correlate the effect that the atmosphere plays in warming planet Earth's surface with the effect that a glass-enclosed space—a greenhouse—plays in warming that space for plants. The correlation is helpful when visualizing how our atmosphere and its composition of gasses warm Earth, but, scientifically, the correlation is not strong. Atmospheric gasses, also widely referred to as greenhouse gasses, include carbon dioxide and methane, which are two main gases causing scientific concern for climate change, as well as oxygen and other gases that play an important role in the habitability of planet earth; Frederick K. Lutgens and Edward J. Tarbuck, *The Atmosphere, An Introduction to Meteorology,* 9th ed. (Upper Saddle River: Pearson, Prentice-Hall, 2004), p. 52.

28. Spencer R. Weart, *The Discovery of Global Warming,* New Histories of Science, Technology, and Medicine (Cambridge, MA: Harvard University Press, 2003), pp. 1–19.

29. Ibid., p. 74.

30. Charles David Keeling, "The Concentration and Isotopic Abundances of Carbon Dioxide in the Atmosphere," *Tellus* 12 (1960): 200–203, http://scrippsco2.ucsd.edu/publications/scientific_literature.html, accessed August 8, 2010; See National Oceanic and Atmospheric Administration (NOAA): www.esrl.noaa.gov.

31. International Panel on Climate Change (IPCC), IPCC Fourth Assessment Report: Climate Change (2007), "Contribution of Working Groups I, II and III to the Fourth Assessment Report of the Intergovernmental Panel on Climate Change," in *AR4 Synthesis Report* (Geneva: IPCC, 2007), http://www.ipcc.ch/publications_and_data/ar4/syr/en/contents.html and http://www.ipcc.ch/publications_and_data/ar4/syr/en/spm.html, accessed July 2009.

32. Ibid., "Summary for Policymakers: The Long-term Perspective," no. 5.

33. Gore, *An Inconvenient Truth,* pp. 214–55; William N. Ryerson, "Population: The Multiplier of Everything Else," in *Post Carbon Reader, Managing the 21st Century's Sustainability Crises,* ed. Richard Heinberg and Daniel Lerch (Berkeley: University of California, 2010), Part 6, no. 12.

34. Paul Oliver, ed., *Encyclopedia of Vernacular Architecture of the World* (Cambridge: Cambridge University Press, 1998). An interior example of providing comfort relative to temperature can be found in the use of the wingback chair, which protects the occupant from rear drafts and provides a place to rest the head while receiving radiant heat from an adjacent fireplace. Other modest examples include the use of textiles: enclosing space within a space, reducing a room's volume with a thermally resistant material (e.g., a canopy bed with heavy draperies), and hanging tapestries and curtains, which protected occupants from drafts and cold wall surfaces, as well as being decorative works. A description of thermal comfort can be found in The THERMIE Programme of the European Commission DGXVII, (EC THERMIE, EUR18944), Architect's Council of Europe (ACE), Eoin O Cofaigh; Energy Research Group (ERG), Eileen Fitzgerald, Ann McNicholl, Robert Alcock, J. Owens Lewis; Suomen Arkkitehtiliitto (SAFA), Vesa Peltonen; Softech, Antonella Marucco, *A Green Vitruvious, Principles and Practice of Sustainable Architectural Design* (London: James & James, 1999).

35. Thomas Randall, ed., Environmental Design, An Introduction for Architects and Engineers, 2nd ed. (London: E & F Spoon, 1999), pp. 3–5; Louise Jones, ed., *Environmentally Responsible Design: Green and Sustainable Design for Interior Designers* (New York: John Wiley &

Sons, 2008); Grazyna Pilatowicz, *Eco-Interiors: A Guide to Environmentally Conscious Interior Design* (New York: John Wiley & Sons, 1995).

36. International Energy Agency (IEA), *IEA Statistics, CO2 Emissions from Fossil Fuel Combustion, Highlights* (2010), p. 9, http://www.transport2012.org/bridging/ressources/files/1/868,CO2highlights.pdf, accessed January 7, 2011.

37. Victor Papanek, *The Green Imperative: Ecology and Ethics in Design and Architecture* (London: Thames & Hudson, 1995), pp. 76–78, 99–103; Building Research Establishment Environmental Assessment (BREEAM), "About," 2010, http://www.breeam.org/page.jsp?id=66, accessed October 2010

38. BREEAM, "About."

39. U.S. Green Building Council (USGBC), "LEED," and "About," n.d., http://www.usgbc.org/, accessed October 2010.

40. Jones, ed., *Environmentally Responsible Design,* pp. 251–288

41. Randall, *Environmental Design,* pp. 29, 68–70; Susan M. Winchip, *Sustainable Design for Interior Environments* (New York: Fairchild Publications, 2007), p 234.

42. William McDonough and Michael Braungart, *Cradle to Cradle: Remaking the Way We Make Things* (New York: Strauss and Giroux, 2002), p. 27.

43. Papanek, *The Green Imperative,* pp. 159–82.

44. According to the National Oceanic and Atmospheric Administration's National Ocean Service website, the "garbage patch" is marine debris that "can easily be ingested by marine species causing choking, starvation, and other impairments." It is also not limited to a patch area in the North Pacific Ocean alone but is also in various other areas and typically consists of small pieces of plastic debris that are not easily visible to the naked eye; NOAA National Ocean Service, Marine Debris Program, http://marinedebris.noaa.gov, accessed November 3, 2011.

45. In his book, *The Green Imperative: Ecology and Ethics in Design and Architecture* (Singapore: Thames and Hudson, 1995), Victor Papanek presents "Ten Questions Before Buying" (p. 187), which leads readers to consider the alternative solution to addressing a need—"sharing not buying" (pp. 183–202).

46. McDonough and Braungart, *Cradle to Cradle.*

47. Victor Papanek, *Design for the Real World: Human Ecology and Social Change* (London: Thames & Hudson, 2000),. pp. 250, 251; Carlo Vezzoli and Ezio Manzini, *Design for Environmental Sustainability* (London: Springer-Verlag, 2008), pp. 215–43.

48. International Standards Organization, "ISO Standards for Life Cycle Assessment to Promote Sustainable Development, Ref. 1019," July 7, 2006, http://www.iso.org/iso/pressrelease.htm?refid=Ref1019, accessed November 6, 2011.

49. Helen Lewis and John Gertsakis, with Tim Grant, Nicola Morelli, and Andrew Sweatman, *Design and Environment: A Global Guide to Designing Greener Goods* (Sheffield, UK: Greenleaf Publishing, 2001); Vezzoli and Manzini, *Design for Environmental Sustainability,* pp. 51–197, 243–50.

50. Sarah Darby, *The Effectiveness of Feedback on Energy Consumption, A Review for DERFA of the Literature on Metering Billing and Direct Displays* (Oxford: University of Oxford, 2006), http://www.eci.ox.ac.uk/research/energy/electric-metering.php, accessed March 11, 2011; Dean C. Mountain, *Real-Time Feedback and Residential Electricity Consumption: British Columbia and Newfoundland and Labrador Pilots* (Ontario: Mountain Economic Consulting, 2007), power.com/…/residential_energy_use_behavior_change_pilot.pdf, accessed February 9, 2011.

51. Tonkinwise, "Sustainability," p. 382.

52. Paul Hawken, Amory Lovins, and L. Hunter Lovins, *Natural Capitalism, Creating the Next Industrial Revolution* (New York: Little Brown and Co. 1999); McKibben, *Deep Economy.*

53. Elinor Ostrom, "A Multi-Scale Approach to Coping with Climate Change and Other Collective Action Problems," *Solutions* 1, no. 2 (2010): pp. 27–36, http://www.thesolutions-journal.com/node/565, accessed October 2010. See also Meroni, *Creative Communities;* and Papanek, *The Green Imperative,* pp. 183–202.

54. Dolores Hayden, *The Grand Domestic Revolution: A History of Feminist Designs for American Homes, Neighborhoods, and Cities* (Cambridge, MA: MIT Press, 1981).

55. Dolores Hayden, *Seven American Utopias, The Architecture of Communitarian Socialism, 1790–1975* (Cambridge, MA: MIT Press, 1976).

56. Chris Colin, "To Your Left, a Better Way of Life?," *New York Times,* June 11, 2009, http://www.nytimes.com/2009/06/11/garden/11cohousing.html, accessed February 13, 2010. Daniel Browne, Mark Woltman, Laurel Tumarkin, Sabine Dyer, and Kristina Mazzocchi, "Sharing Old Age: Alternative Senior Housing Options," Office of Public Advocate for the City of New York, Betsy Gotbaum, Public Advocate for the City of New York, 2008, pp. 19–26, www.pubadvocate.nyc.gov; publicadvocategotbaum.com/policy/ . . . / SeniorHousingReport_web_.pdf, accessed February 2011; Homeshare International, "About Us" n.d., http://homeshare.org/aboutus.aspx, accessed March 2011; Meroni, *Creative Communities.*

57. The Cohousing Association of the United States; Linda Collins, "After 3+ Years, Brooklyn Cohousing Abandons Efforts," October 4, 2010, http://www.brooklyneagle.com/categories/ category.php?category_id=5&id=38523, accessed October 2010; Vivian S. Toy, "Abandoning a Bid to Create an Urban Village," *New York Times,* October 5, 2010, http://cityroom. blogs.nytimes.com/2010/10/05/abandoning-an-attempt-to-create-an-urban-village/, accessed January 2011.

58. Dan Fost, "They're Working on Their Own; Just Side by Side," *New York Times,* February 20, 2008, http://www.nytimes.com/2008/02/20/business/businessspecial2/20cowork.html, accessed July 2010.

59. This references the social networking portal Meetup, cofounded by Scott Heiferman. Meetup is an online place for community organizing, of any kind, that then takes place offline.

60. Laura Forlano, "Work and the Open Source City," *TTI Vanguard. Urban Omnibus,* June 3, 2009, http://urbanomnibus.net/2009/06/work-and-the-open-source-city, accessed March 2010.

61. Sindya N. Bhanoo, "At Shared Offices, How Green Is My Work Space," *New York Times,* February 15, 2010, http://www.nytimes.com/2010/02/15/nyregion/15green.html, accessed July 10, 2010; Fost, "They're Working on Their Own."

62. Architecture 2030, "The Economy—Current Situation: The Imminent Commercial Real Estate Meltdown," 2011, http://architecture2030.org/the_problem/problem_economy, accessed February 2011.

63. Jade Chang, "Behind the Glass Curtain," *Metropolis Magazine,* June 19, 2006, http://www. metropolismag.com/story/20060619/behind-the-glass-curtain, accessed November 12, 2011; Jane Wakefield, "Google Your Way To A Wacky Office," *BBC News,* March 13, 2008, http://news.bbc.co.uk/2/hi/7290322.stm, accessed January 2011.

64. Rachel Botsman and Roo Rogers, *What's Mine Is Yours, The Rise of Collaborative Consumption* (New York: Harper Collins, 2010), pp. XV, 71, 95–119; Vezzoli and Manzini, *Design for Environmental Sustainability,* pp. 26, 204–6.

65. Botsman and Rogers, *What's Mine Is Yours,* pp. XV, 71, 95–119; FlexPetz, "About Us," n.d., http://www.flexpetz.com/, accessed April 2010. Penelope Green, "Living Together, A Modern Answer to the Commune," *New York Times,* September 30, 2009, http://www.nytimes.com/2009/10/01/garden/01collective.html?pagewanted=all, accessed February 2010.

66. Matthew Danzico, "Cult of Less: Living Out of a Hard Drive," *BBC News,* August 16, 2010, http://www.bbc.co.uk/news/world-us-canada-10928032, accessed March 13, 2010.

67. Vezzoli and Manzini, *Design for Environmental Sustainability,* p. 261.

68. Meroni, *Creative Communities;* Manzini and Jégou, *Collaborative Services, Social Innovation*

69. Meron, *Creative Communities.*

70. Ibid., p. 62.

71. Adbusters Media Foundation, Adbusters Culture Jammer Head, "#OccupyWallStreet." July 13, 2011, http://www.adbusters.org/blogs/adbusters-blog/occupywallstreet.html, accessed October 17, 2011; Heinberg, "The Post Carbon Reader Series"; David Korten, *Agenda for a New Economy: From Phantom Wealth to Real Wealth,* 2nd ed. (San Francisco: Berrett-Koehler Publishers, 2010).

72. Korten, *Agenda for a New Economy,* pp. 43–45.

73. Ibid.

74. Ibid., p. 7.

75. Mager, "Service Design," p. 354.

76. Mager, "Service Design"; Stephen L. Vargo and Robert F. Lusch, (2004), "Evolving to a New Dominant Logic for Marketing," *Journal of Marketing* 68 (January 2004): pp. 1–17. Available at: *courses.ischool.berkeley.edu/i210/f07/readings/VargoLusch.pdf,* accessed January 2011.

77. Lara Penin, in Laura Forlano, "What is Service Design?" *TTI Vanguard. Urban Omnibus,* October 27, 2010, http://urbanomnibus.net/2010/10/what-is-service-design, accessed November 2010.

78. Live|work, "Home: A Brief Introduction to Service Design," n.d., http://www.livework.co.uk, accessed March 2010.

79. Mark Bevir and David O'Brien, "New Labour and the Public Sector in Britain." *Public Administration Review* 61 (2001): pp. 535–47, http://escholarship.org/uc/item/3383t35k, accessed October 2010.

80. Cameron Tonkinwise, in Laura Forlano, "What is Service Design?" *TTI Vanguard. Urban Omnibus,* October 27, 2010, http://urbanomnibus.net/2010/10/what-is-service-design, accessed November 2010.

81. Ezio Manzini, "NEXT Design in the Age of Networks and Sustainability," Lens Lecture, Milano, May 20, 2010, http://www.slideshare.net/vezzoliDSS/next-design-manzini-4176911, October 2010.

82. Vargo and Lusch, "Evolving to a New Dominant Logic for Marketing"; Manzini and Jégou, *Collaborative Services, Social Innovation;* Stephen L. Vargo and Robert F. Lusch, "Why 'Service'?" *Journal of the Academy of Marketing Science* 36, no. 2 (2008): pp. 5–38, doi:10.1007/s11747-007-0068-7.

83. Marc Stickdorn and Jakob Schneider, *This is Service Design Thinking. Basics, Tools, Cases* (Amsterdam: BIS Publishers, 2010), pp. 38, 39, 198–201.

84. Stickdorn and Schneider, *This is Service Design Thinking;* Vargo and Lusch, "Why 'Service'?".

85. Oliver, *Encyclopedia of Vernacular Architecture of the World;* Bernard Rudofsky, *Architecture Without Architects: A Short Introduction to Non-Pedigreed Architecture* (New York: MoMA, 1964).

86. Richard Buchanan, "Wicked Problems in Design Thinking," in *The Idea of Design: A Design Issues Reader,* ed. Victor Margolin and Richard Buchanan (Cambridge, MA: MIT Press, 1998), pp. 3–20; Papanek, *The Green Imperative,* pp. 103, 104, 113–38, 211–22; Rittel and Webber, "Dilemmas in a General Theory of Planning."; Steven Parissien, *Interiors: The Home Since 1700* (London: Laurence King, 2009), pp. 11, 133–77.

87. Horst W. Rittel and Melvin M. Webber, "Dilemmas in a General Theory of Planning," *Policy Sciences* 4 (1973): pp. 160, http://www.jstor.org/stable/4531523, accessed January 22, 2009.

88. Papanek, *Design for the Real World,* pp. 285–321; Vezzoli and Manzini, *Design for Environmental Sustainability,* pp. 46–50; Rittel and Webber, "Dilemmas in a General Theory of Planning."

89. Rittel and Webber, "Dilemmas in a General Theory of Planning."

90. Tim Marshall, "Wicked Problems," in *Design Dictionary, Perspectives on Design Terminology,* ed. M. Erlhoff and T. Marshall (Basel: Birkhäuser, 2008), pp. 447.

91. Tim Marshall, "Designing Design Education," *Form Magazine* 224 (2009), http://www.icograda.org/education/education/articles1397.htm, accessed January 2011; Papanek, *The Green Imperative,* pp. 203–5; Peter G. Rowe, *Design Thinking* (Cambridge, MA: MIT Press, 1987); Donald Schön, *The Reflective Practitioner, How Professionals Think In Action* (New York: Basic Books, 1983).

92. Anna Meroni, "Strategic Design: Where Are We Now? Reflection Around the Foundations of a Recent Discipline," *Strategic Design Research Journal* 1, no. 1 (2008): pp. 31–38, www.unisinos.br/_diversos/revistas/design/pdf/57.pdf, accessed July 2011; Vezzoli and Manzini, *Design for Environmental Sustainability,* pp. 48, 49, 212, 261.

93. Meroni, "Strategic Design: Where Are We Now?" p. 37.

94. A conventional Product Development and Management Association (PDMA) term that describes the actions in the early stages of product development, which are "chaotic, unpredictable and unstructured" and allow for exploration, creativity, and innovation; Product Development and Management Association (PDMA),"Get Knowledge: The New Product Development Glossary," www.pdma.org, accessed May 14, 2011.

95. A required course that introduces the topic of sustainability and environmental design within the AAS (Associate in Applied Science) interior design program at Parsons the New School for Design. This specific class, taught by the author in the academic spring of 2011 and the fall of 2011, was an opportunity to apply her research, specifically in the role that interior design can play in reducing material consumption through shared and collaborative systems thinking and design. Material and exercises applied in the curriculum development for the Parsons BFA in Integrated Design program, which included sustainability and a new area of study, service design (established and coordinated by Lara Penin, assistant professor of transdisciplinary design at Parsons), were integrated into the study of designing for sustainability in interior design.

96. Nigel Cross, "Designerly Ways of Knowing," *Design Studies* 3, no.4 (1982): pp. 221–27, design.open.ac.uk/cross/documents/DesignerlyWaysofKnowing.pdf, accessed June 15, 2010; Nigel Cross, "Designerly Ways of Knowing: Design Discipline Versus Design Science," *Design Issues* 17, no.3 (2001): 49–55, http://design.open.ac.uk/cross/publications. htm, accessed January 2011

28 INTERIOR DESIGN, A POLITICAL DISCIPLINE

1. Paul Lewis, "The Mole Man of Hackney," *The Guardian,* August, 8, 2006, http://www.guardian.co.uk/society/2006/aug/08/communities.uknews, accessed March 7, 2013

2. Ibid.

3. Ibid.

4. Ibid.

5. Leo Hickman, "The Population Explosion," *The Guardian,* January 14, 2011, p. G2-4; Paul Harris, "Population of World 'could grow to 15bn by 2100'," *The Observer,* October 23, 2011, p. 1; Simon Rogers, "World Population by Country: UN Guesses the Shape of the World by 2100," *The Guardian,* October 26, 2011, http://www.guardian.co.uk/news/datablog/2011/may/06/world-population-country-un.

6. Michael Sorkin, *All Over the Map Writing on Buildings and Cities* (London: Verso, 2011), p. 308.

7. Mike Davis, "The Great Wall of Capital," in *Against The Wall, Israel's Barrier to Peace,* ed. Mickael Sorkin (London: New Press, 2005), p. 88.

8. Stephen Graham, *Cities, War, and Terrorism: Towards an Urban Geopolitics* (Oxford: Blackwell Publishing, 2004), p. 10.

9. Brenda Judge, *Thinking About Things A Philosophical Study of Representation* (Edinburgh: Scottish Academic Press, 1985).

10. J. G. Ballard, *Quotes* (Re/Search Publications, 2004), p. 203.

11. Madeleine Bunting, "Passion and Pessimism," *The Guardian,* April 5, 2003, in "Reviews," p. 20.

12. Jeremy Rifkind, *The Age of Access* (New York: Jeremy P Tarcher/Putnam, 2001), p. 115.

13. Brain Massumi, "Navigating Movements, an interview with Brian Massumi," 2002, http://www.brianmassumi.com/, accessed June 22, 2010.

14. Ibid.

15. Ibid.

16. Zygmunt Bauman, "Living (Occasionally Dying) Together," in *Urban World in Cities, War, and Terrorism: Towards an Urban Geopolitics,* ed. Stephen Graham (Oxford: Blackwell Publishing, 2004), pp. 110–19.

17. Jacqueline Rose, *The Last Resistance* (London: Verso, 2007), p. 41.

18. Michael Kimmelman, "In Protest, the Power of Place," *The Observer/New York Times* supplement, October 23, 2011, p. 1.

19. Madeleine Bunting, "As Strong as Faith and Race, It Is Place that Defines Our Sense of Identity," *The Guardian,* September 19, 2011, p. 27

20. From a discussion led by Michael Ostwald at Interior Spaces in Other Places Conference, Brisbane, February 3–5, 2010.

21. Rifkind, "The Age of Access," p. 117.

22. Ibid.

23. Kevin Rawlinson, "Mole Man William Lyttle's house: For £500,000, the perfect place for the downwardly mobile," *The Independent,* October 4, 2011, http://www.independent.co.uk/news/uk/this-britain/mole-man-william-lyttles-house-for-500000-the-perfect-place-for-the-downwardly-mobile-2365169.html#, accessed March 7, 2013.

29 GLOBALIZATION

1. In addition to consulting the fourth edition of the *American Heritage Dictionary,* these defining vocabulary words (and later writings in this chapter) associated with globalization come

from this author's research through independent fieldwork and from urbanists/architects/ theorists, such as Hans Ibelings, Nezar Al-Sayyad, and Herbert Marcuse. The selection of only one book by each of these authors listed in the bibliography is meant to signify only a small portion of their important contribution to the subject.

2. Peter Marcuse and Ronald van Kempen, eds., *Globalizing Cities: A New Spatial Order* (New York: Blackwell Publishers, 2000), p. 6.

3. Patrik Schumacher, "Soja's 'Postmodern Geographies'—A Political Reading", Architectural Association, London, 1996), http://www.patrikschumacher.com/Texts/soja.htm, p.4, accessed march 4, 2012.

4. Alison B. Snyder, "Flexibility and Hybridity: Learning from the Contemporary Village in Anatolian Turkey," in *On Global Grounds: Urban Change and Globalization,* ed. Julia Nevarez and Gabriel Moser (New York: Nova Science Publishers, 2008), pp. 1–26.

5. Phenomenology, a form of philosophy concerned with conscious experience, relates to design and how people are affected by feeling, emotion, and atmosphere in the built environment. Well-known works by authors such as Gaston Bachelard, *The Poetics of Space* (Boston: Beacon Press, 1964); Martin Heidegger, *Basic Writings: From Being and Time (1927) to The Task of Thinking (1964)* (New York: Harper Collins, 1993); and Christian Norberg-Schulz, *Genius Loci: Towards a Phenomenology of Architecture* (New York: Rizzoli Publications, 1980), are some of the key works known to have begun this spatial conversation.

6. The period of Internet research for putting these words together ends in late 2011.

7. The names of companies listed on the Internet are only described, rather than citing commercial entities.

8. Denise Guerin, "Issues Facing Interior Design Education in the Twenty-First Century," *Journal of Interior Design Education and Research* 17, no. 2 D (1992): pp. 9–16.

9. Abimbola Asojo, "Community, Technology and Environment: Cross Cultural Design Collaborations via Distance Learning," presented in SW Regional Conference in Oklahoma, Global Design Perspectives, IDEC (2006), p. 19.

10. Zamila Karimi, "Tradition is the Tending of the Fire, Not the Worship of the Ashes," in Joint Symposium of IDEC, USA and Modern Interiors Research Center (MIRC), Looking into the Modern Interior: History, Theory and Discipline in Education and Practice, IDEC (2010), p. 12.

11. CIDA's recently changed requirements implemented in 2009 are concerned with the terms *global* and *globalization.* CIDA states, "Adaptation to change requires that graduates draw on history and on the experience of many cultures," and CIDA most clearly list global understanding under what the organization calls "Global Context for Design." CIDA requires "entry-level interior designers have a global view and weigh design decisions within the parameters of ecological, socio-economic, and cultural contexts." The organization asks for student performance criteria that shows an understanding of "globalization and the implications of conducting the practice of design within a world market." CIDA also focuses on "how design needs may vary for different socio-economic populations." Thus, CIDA acknowledges some of the mainstream global particulars, yet the organization does not refer to global theory per se. Caren Martin and Michael Kroelinger's article "2009 Accreditation Requirements: Comparison of CIDA and NAAB" (*JID* 35, no. 2 [2010]: pp. ix–xxxii) was written before the full adoption of the accreditation standards.

12. Tiiu Poldma, "Interior Design at a Crossroads: Embracing Specificity Through Process, Research, and Knowledge," *Journal of Interior Design* 33, no. 3 (2008): p. ix.

13. Ibid., p. x.

14. Susan Winchip, *Visual Culture in the Built Environment: A Global Perspective* (New York: Fairchild, 2010), pp. xvi–xvii.

15. Jennifer Hudson, *Interior Architecture Now* (London: Laurence King, 2007), p. 6.

16. "Viewpoint," Gensler, http://www.gensler.com/#viewpoint.

17. "Mission," IDEC, http://www.idec.org/who/mission.php.

18. IDEC. These statements represent 2012 research.

19. "Vision and Mission," International Interior Design Association, http://www.iida.org/content.cfm/vision-mission.

20. "About Us," International Federation of Interior Architects/Designers, http://www.ifiworld.org/#About_IFI.

21. "IDA," International Council of Societies of Industrial Design, http://www.icsid.org/about/IDA.htm.

22. The author participated in an all-day roundtable in September 2010 in Portland, Oregon, that brought candid conversations from directors of Oregon, Washington, and Vancouver interior design programs together with students.

23. The expertise and publications from the three strategists listed represent only a portion of their larger works.

24. For the full transcript from the November 10, 2010, airing, see http://glasshouse conversations.org/in-your-opinion-is-there-still-a-benefit-to-boundaries-between-disciplines-why-or-why-not/.

25. David G. Shane, *Recombinant Urbanism: Conceptual Modeling in Architecture, Urban Design and City Theory* (New York: John Wiley & Sons, 2005), p. 6.

26. A beginning list of contemporary and emerging designers, architects, and artists who may be working to rethink how a global interior may be designed are how a global interior may be designed are: OMA (Office for Metropolitan Architecture), Petra Blaise, Elizabeth Diller and Ricardo Scofidio, Jo Noero, Han Tumertekin, Tadoa Ando, Jacques Herzog and Pierre de Meuron, Alvaro Siza, B.I.G.–Bjarke Ingels, Teddy Cruz, Sanaa—Kazuyo Sejima + Ryue Nishizawa, Steven Holl, Peter Zumthor, and many others. A beginning list of artists to learn from may include those who specialize in light and material and form and sound such as James Turrell, Bill Viola, Richard Serra, Rachel Whiteread, Michael Heizer, Maya Lin, Eindhoven Group, and James Carpenter, to name only a few. The hope is that we will learn from a transdisciplinary approach from people in different countries that depends upon a variety of methods and discussions.

30 THE ART OF BORROWING

1. Jonathan Hill, *Immaterial Architecture* (London: Routledge, 2006), p. 33.

2. Adolf Loos, "The Principle of Cladding," *Neue Freie Presse,* September 4, 1898, re-published in *Spoken into the Void: Collected Essays 1897–1900* (Cambridge, MA: MIT Press, 1982).

3. Ernst H. Gombrich, *Art and Illusion: A Study in the Psychology of Pictorial Representation* (London: Phaidon, 1960), p. 89.

4. Jonathan Hill, "An Other Architect," in *Occupying Architecture: Between the Architect and the User,* ed. J. Hill (London: Routledge, 1998), pp. 135–159.

5. Alain De Botton, *The Architecture of Happiness: The Secret Art of Furnishing Your Life* (London: Penguin Books, 2006), pp. 78, 87, 89.

6. Robin Evans, "The Developed Surface: An Enquiry into the Brief Life of an Eighteenth-Century Drawing Technique," in *Translations from Drawing to Building and Other Essays* (London: Architectural Association Publications, 1997), p. 199.

7. Ibid., p. 209.

8. Josef Albers, *Interaction of Color* (New Haven, CT: Yale University Press, 2006), p. 1.

9. Ibid., p. 2.

10. Ibid., p. 71.

11. Ibid., p. 72.

12. Stan Allen, *Practice: Architecture, Technique and Representation* (London: Routledge, 2000), p. 149.

13. Mark Cousins, "Building an Architect," in *Occupying Architecture: Between the Architect and the User,* ed. J. Hill (London: Routledge, 1998), pp. 16–17.

31 MODEL BEHAVIOR

1. For a general overview on various approaches and techniques, see, for example, Maureen Mitton, *Interior Design Visual Presentation: A Guide to Graphics, Models, and Presentation Techniques,* 3rd ed. (New York: John Wiley & Sons, 2008).

2. This notion of the implementation of models at different stages of the design process and a detailed explanation of the various reasons for this is given extensive coverage, especially in the third section, "Application" in Nick Dunn, *Architectural Modelmaking* (London: Laurence King, 2010), pp. 150–79.

3. Akiko Busch, *The Art of the Architectural Model* (New York: Design Press, 1991), p. 11.

4. Peter Cook, "View," *The Architectural Review* CCXXIII, no. 1333 (2008): p. 38.

5. Karen Moon, *Modeling Messages: the Architect and the Model* (New York: Monacelli, 2005), p. 211.

6. Richard Pommer and Christian Hubert, *Idea as Model. Institute for Architecture and Urban Studies, Catalogue 3* (New York: Rizzoli, 1980), p. 17.

7. John Coles and Naomi House, *The Fundamentals of Interior Architecture* (Lausanne: AVA Publishing SA, 2007), p. 163.

8. Rolf Janke, *Architectural Models* (London: Thames & Hudson, 1968), p. 15.

9. Steven Holl, *Intertwining* (New York: Princeton Architectural Press, 1996), p. 15.

10. For an overview of different approaches using these technologies and further examples, as three books following are recommended: Lisa Iwamoto, *Digital Fabrications: Architectural and Material Techniques* (New York: Princeton Architectural Press, 2009); and Jacobo Krauel, *Contemporary Digital Architecture: Design & Techniques* (Barcelona: Links International, 2010); or Nick Dunn, *Digital Fabrication in Architecture* (London: Laurence King, 2012).

11. Branko Kolarevic, ed., *Architecture in the Digital Age: Design and Manufacturing* (New York: Spon Press, 2003), p. 52.

12. Mark Goulthorpe, *The Possibility of (an) Architecture: Collected Essays by Mark Goulthorpe, DECOi Architects* (Oxon: Routledge, 2008), p. 255.

13. Computational scripting and algorithmic design are extensive areas in their own right, and it would be futile to attempt to give a concise description in such a limited context here, so for

further explanation I direct the reader to Kostas Terzidis, *Algorithmic Architecture* (Oxford: Architectural Press, 2006).

14. Bob Sheil, ed., *Protoarchitecture: Analogue and Digital Hybrids* (New York: John Wiley & Sons, 2008), p. 7.

15. For example, the groundbreaking *Design and the Elastic Mind* exhibition held at the MOMA, New York, 2008, and the seminal Fabricate conference, London 2011.

32 DIGITAL REPRESENTATION AND FABRICATION

1. Greg Lynn, "Constellations in Practice," *Praxis: New Technologies:///New Architectures* 6 (2004): pp. 8–17.

2. For a further discussion about the relationships between technologies and techniques, see Ali Rahim, "Techniques and Technology," in *Catalytic Formations: Architecture and Digital Design* (New York: Taylor & Francis, 2006), pp. 10–21.

3. Here and elsewhere in this article, I am referring to representation not as broader set of cultural, social, and political constructs but rather as a series of commonly used and understood notational conventions specific to architectural and by extension, interior design. Graphic drawings, physical models, digital imagery, and data are all modes of representation through which design intent is communicated prior to physical fabrication and construction.

4. William Mitchell and Malcolm McCullough, *Digital Design Media* (New York: Van Reinhold, 1991), p. 25.

5. For theoretical discussions about translations from drawing to building in architecture, see Robin Evans, "Translation from Drawing to Building," *AA Files* 12 (1986): pp. 3–18.

6. The same could be said of pixels that convey information about color. Rather than simply approximating the appearance of a color, a pixel contains data that can be precisely matched in digital printing. A CMYK-formatted image, for example, is the data that controls the distribution of ink as it is output from the cartridge of a printer onto a material surface.

7. For a further discussion about the evolution of computer numerical control, see Kiel Moe, "Automation Takes Command: the Nonstandard, Unautomatic History of Standardization and Automation in Architecture," in *Fabricating Architecture: Selected Readings in Digital Design and Manufacturing,* ed. Robert Corser (New York: Princeton Architectural Press, 2010), pp. 152–67.

8. Branko Kolarevic, *Architecture in the Digital Age: Design and Manufacturing* (New York: Spon Press, 2003), pp. 4–6.

9. For a thorough conceptual and technical discussion regarding NURBS surfaces, meshes, and subdivisions, see Helmut Pottman, Andreas Asperl, Michael Hofer, and Axel Kilian, *Architectural Geometry* (Exton, PA: Bentley Institute Press, 2007), pp. 377–409.

10. Kolarevic, *Architecture in the Digital Age,* p. 15.

11. Ibid.

12. In the earlier stages of digital production in spatial design, at a moment when the commercial availability of fabrication technology lagged behind visualization software, design practices like Asymptote produced innovative virtual environments that allowed users to experience such spatiality through digital interactive walk-throughs and animations. In particular, see

Asymptote's Guggenheim and New York Stock Exchange projects for reference, Lise Anne Couture and Hani Rashid, *Asymptote: Flux* (New York: Phaidon, 2002).

13. The project has been extensively published and exhibited in both professional and popular venues. For the project authors' discussion about the design process, see Sulan Kolatan, "More than One / Less Than Two_RESIDENCE(S)," in *Digital Real, Blobmeister: First Built Projects,* ed. Peter Cachola Schmal (Basil: Birkauser, 2001), pp. 70–80; and also, Sulan Kolatan and William MacDonald, "Lumping," in *Architectural Design: Contemporary Techniques in Architecture,* ed. Ali Rahim(London: Academy Editions, 2002).

14. The project's contribution to the discussion about the transformations in the domestic design realm and the innovation with which notions of privacy and publicity are addressed is evident by its inclusion in the exhibition *The Un-Private House* at the Museum of Modern Art in New York, July 5 to October 1, 1999. For the catalog of the exhibition, see Terrence Riley, ed., *The Un-Private House* (New York: Museum of Modern Art, 2002).

15. Kolatan and MacDonald, "Lumping," p. 79.

16. Ibid., p. 83.

17. Kolarevic, *Architecture in the Digital Age,* p. 50.

18. Brendan MacFarlane, "Making Ideas," in *Architecture in the Digital Age: Design and Manufacturing,* ed. Branko Kolarevic (New York: Spon Press, 2003), pp. 181–97.

19. Ibid., p. 191.

20. Mark Garcia, "Introduction: Prologue for a History, Theory and Future of Patterns of Architecture and Spatial Design," in *Architectural Design: Patterns of Architecture,* ed. Mark Garcia(New York: John Wiley & Sons, 2010), pp. 6–17.

21. Branko Kolarevic and Kevin Klinger, *Manufacturing Material Effects: Rethinking Design and Manufacturing in Architecture* (London: Routledge, 2008), p. 13.

22. The term *mass customization* in Stan Davis's 1987 book *Future Perfect,* but one of the first authors that defined the term as it has been appropriated by design discourse is Joseph Pine in the book that bears the coined term as its title: Joseph Pine, *Mass Customization: The New Frontier in Business Competition* (Boston: Harvard Business School Press, 1993).

23. Stephen Kieran and James Timberlake, *Refabricating Architecture* (New York: McGraw Hill, 2004), p. xiii.

24. For a comprehensive overview of numerous digitally designed and fabricated installations that primarily take on experimental, research-driven agendas, see Lisa Iwamoto, *Digital Fabrications: Architectural and Material Techniques* (New York: Princeton Architectural Press, 2009).

25. For photographic documentation of the project, as well as its statistics, see "Lucien Pellat-Finet, Shinsaibashi," interior by Kengo Kuma and Associates, http://kkaa.co.jp/works/lucien-pellat-finet-shinsaibashi/, accessed May 28, 2011.

26. The architects maintained an extensive online journal of the project's process and progress, including comprehensive technical information and insight: Marble Fairbanks, "Project Journal: Toni Stabile Student Center," http://marblefairbanks.com/?p=785, accessed May 28, 2011.

27. Similar techniques of producing patterns through image transformation have, admittedly, become ubiquitous. The façade of Herzog & de Meuron's deYoung Museum in San Francisco was one of the first projects to deploy a comparable strategy, but because it predated many of the digital tools that have since become available, it required a high level

of innovation throughout the research and development part of the project. For a thorough discussion about the process, see Alayna Fraser, "Translations: de Young Museum and the Walker Art Center by Herzog and de Meuron," *Praxis: Expanding Surface* 9 (2007): pp. 68–85.

28. Kolarevic, *Architecture in the Digital Age,* p. 51.

29. Paola Antonelli, ed., *Design and the Elastic Mind* (New York: Museum of Modern Art, 2008), p. 75.

30. While most of the digital fabrication techniques that have been discussed so far are subtractive in nature—that is, the process of shaping material into a desired geometry involves removing material by, for example, cutting into it or drilling through it—other methods of digital fabrication, such as selective laser sintering, stereolithography, and 3D printing, are additive in nature; that is, only the material that is needed to describe a three-dimensional form is composited, usually in layers, to produce the larger whole. Such additive methods are commonly referred to as rapid prototyping and, when utilized toward the production of a final product, rapid manufacturing. Although significant advances have been made in the field of rapid manufacturing, available technologies presently still place a limit on the scale and quality of finished products. As such, at the architectural scale of building interiors, use of additive rapid manufacturing has been limited and selective. For an overview of the present discussion surrounding rapid manufacturing, specifically as defined in the field of engineering, see Neil Hopkinson, Richard Hague, and Philip Dickents, eds., *Rapid Manufacturing: An Industrial Revolution for the Digital Age* (New York: John Wiley & Sons, 2006).

31. Neri Oxman, "Beast," http://web.media.mit.edu/~neri/site/projects/beast/beast.html, accessed May 28, 2011.

32. Also, see Neri Oxman's wearable wrist splint "Carpal Skin," http://web.media.mit.edu/~neri/site/projects/carpalskin/carpalskin.html, accessed May 28, 2011.

33. Vernon Mays, "Office dA: The Boston Firm Combines Intellectual Rigor with Sensitivity to Site, Material, and Process in Three New Projects," *Architect* (June 2007), http://www.architectmagazine.com/architects/office-da.aspx, accessed May 20, 2011.

34. Mark Taylor, "Relentless Patterns: the Immersive Interior," in *Architectural Design: Patterns of Architecture,* ed. Mark Garcia(New York: John Wiley & Sons, 2010), p. 47.

33 THE INTERIOR

The author would like to thank Andrew Milligan of Duncan of Jordanstone College of Art, University of Dundee, for his assistance in the *Big Brother* section of this paper.

1. Cited in Grace Lees-Maffei and Rebecca Houze, *The Design History Reader* (Oxford: Berg, 2010), p. 183.

2. Robert Venturi and Joseph Rykwert, *Learning from Las Vegas: the Forgotten Symbolism of Architectural Form* (Cambridge, MA: MIT Press, 1977).

3. Gillian Andrews, "Dance Dance Revolution: Taking Back Arcade Space," in *Space Time Play Computer Games, Architecture and Urbanism: the Next Level,* ed. Friedrich von Borries, Steffen Walz, and Matthia Boettger (Basel: Birkhauser, 2007), p. 21.

4. See http://www.youtube.com/watch?v=gDiqQgZkw3E&feature=related.

5. See www.equator.ac.uk.

6. Janet Murray, "Inventing the Medium," in *The New Media Reader,* ed. Noah Wardrip Fruin and Nick Montfort (Cambridge, MA: MIT Press, 2003), p. 9.

7. See http://www.chatroulette.com.
8. Judith Nicolson, "Flash! Mobs in the Age of Mobile Connectivity," *The Fibreculture Journal* 6 (2005), http://journal.fibreculture.org/issue6/issue6_nicholson.html.

34 LITERARY NARRATIVES

1. Karen Chase, *Eros & Psyche: The Representation of Personality in Charlotte Brontë, Charles Dickens, and George Eliot* (London: Methuen, 1984), p. 65.
2. Ellen Eve Frank, *Literary Architecture: Essays Toward a Tradition: Walter Pater, Gerard Manley Hopkins, Marcel Proust, Henry James* (Berkley: University of California Press, 1979), p. 3.
3. Philippa Tristram, *Living Space in Fact and Fiction* (London: Routledge, 1989), p. 2.
4. Kathy Mezei and Chiara Briganti, "Reading the House: A Literary Perspective," *Signs* 27, no. 3 (2002): 837–47.
5. Jean-Francois de Bastide, *The Little House: An Architectural Seduction,* trans. Rodolphe el-Khoury (New York: Princeton Architectural Press, 1996).
6. Nicolas Le Camus de Mézières, *The Genius of Architecture; or, the Analogy of that Art with Our Sensations* (Santa Monica: Getty Centre, 1992).
7. Ibid., p. 70.
8. Ibid., p. 71.
9. Georgina Downey and Mark Taylor, "Curtains and Carnality: Processural Seductions in Eighteenth Century Text and Space," in *Imagining: Proceedings from the 27th Annual Conference of the Society of Architectural Historians, Australia and New Zealand,* ed. Michael Chapman and Michael Ostwald (Newcastle, Australia: University of Newcastle, 2010), pp. 121–26; and Mark Taylor, "Planting for Pleasure: the Eighteenth-Century Erotic Garden," *Interiors: Design, Architecture, Culture* 2, no. 3 (2011): pp. 357–70.
10. Bastide, *The Little House,* p. 83.
11. Giuliana Bruno, *Atlas of Emotion: Journeys in Art, Architecture, and Film* (New York: Verso, 2007), p. 234.
12. Ibid.
13. Bastide, *The Little House,* p. 59.
14. Diane Brown, "The Female *Philosophe* in the Closet: The Cabinet and the Senses in French Erotic Novels, 1740–1800," *The Journal of Early Modern Cultural Studies* 9, no. 2 (2009): p. 102.
15. Bastide, *The Little House,* p. 12.
16. Brown, "The Female *Philosophe* in the Closet," p. 97.
17. Ibid.
18. Vivant Denon, "No Tomorrow," in *The Libertine Reader: Eroticism and Enlightenment in Eighteenth Century France,* ed. Michel Feher, trans. Lydia Davis (New York: Zone Books, 1997), p. 733.
19. Martin Calder, "Experience of Space in the Eighteenth-Century French Garden: from Axis to Circuit to Closed Circuit," in *Space: New Dimensions in French Studies,* ed. Emma Gilby and Katja Haustein (Bern: Peter Lang AG, 2005), p. 55.
20. Brown, "The Female *Philosophe* in the Closet," p. 97.
21. Ibid., p. 98.
22. Paul J. Young, *Seducing the Eighteenth-Century French Reader* (Burlington: Ashgate, 2008).

23. Paul J. Young, "*Ce Lieu de delices:* Art and Imitation in the French Libertine Cabinet," *Eighteenth-Century Fiction* 20, no. 3 (2008): p. 353.

24. Ibid.

25. Robert Darnton, *The Forbidden Best-Sellers of Pre-Revolutionary France* (New York: W. W. Norton, 1995), p. 345.

26. Brown, "The Female *Philosophe* in the Closet," p. 103.

27. Robert Darnton suggests this book is as close as possible to "pure" pornography and argues that the term *pornographe* hardly existed in eighteenth-century France, although some books celebrated reading as a "stimulus of sexual pleasure and sometimes recommended works that provided it" (Darnton, *Forbidden Best-Sellers of Pre-Revolutionary France,* p. 89).

28. Darnton, *Forbidden Best-Sellers of Pre-Revolutionary France,* p. 235.

29. Chase, *Eros & Psyche,* pp. 47–65.

30. Ibid., p. 59.

31. Sandra M. Gilbert and Susan Gubar, *The Madwoman in the Attic: The Woman Writer and the Nineteenth-Century Literary Imagination* (New Haven, CT: Yale University Press, 1984).

32. Charlotte Perkins Gilman, *The Yellow Wallpaper* (London: Virago, 1973).

33. Gilbert and Gubar, *The Madwoman in the Attic,* p. 16.

34. Gilman, *The Yellow Wallpaper,* p. 30.

35. Ibid., p. 32.

36. Janell Watson, *Literature and Material Culture From Balzac to Proust: The Collection and Consumption of Curiosities* (Cambridge: Cambridge University Press, 2006), p. 145.

37. Ibid.

38. Ibid., p. 147.

39. Ibid., p. 64.

40. Joris-Karl Huysmans, *Against the Grain (A Rebours)* (New York: Dover Publications, 1969), p. 16.

41. Ibid., pp. 18–19.

42. Ibid., p. 10.

43. Ibid., p. 11.

44. Ibid.

45. Judith Fryer, *Felicitous Space: the Imaginative Structures of Edith Wharton and Willa Cather* (Chapel Hill: University of North Carolina Press, 1986), p. 75.

46. Edith Wharton, *The House of Mirth* (New York: Macmillan, 1987), p. 206.

47. Ibid., p. 223.

48. John Clubbe, "Interiors and the Interior Life in Edith Wharton's *The House of Mirth,*" *Studies in the Novel* 28, no. 4 (1996): pp. 543–64.

49. Rebecca Sinclair and Mark Taylor, "Novel Architecture: The Settings of Virginia Woolf and Edith Wharton," in *Habitus 2000: A Sense of Place: Conference Proceedings,* ed. John R. Stephens (Perth: Curtin University, 2000), CD-ROM.

50. C. Ruth Miller, *Virginia Woolf: The Frames of Art and Life* (New York: St. Martin's Press, 1988).

51. Lyn Pykett, *Engendering Fictions* (New York: St. Martin's Press, 1995), p. 104.

52. Virginia Woolf, *Orlando* (St. Albans: Granada Publishing, 1977), p. 70.

53. Nele Bemong, "Exploration #6: The Uncanny in Mark Z. Danielewski's *House of Leaves,*" *Image and Narrative: Online Magazine of the Visual Narrative* 3, no. 2 (2003): p. 5, http://www.imageandnarrative.be/inarchive/uncanny/nelebemong.htm, accessed September 23, 2011.

54. Nicoline Timmer, *Do You Feel It Too?: The Post-Postmodern Syndrome in American Fiction at the Turn of the Millenium* (Amsterdam: Editions Rodopi B.V., 2010), p. 264.

55. Ibid., p. 244.
56. Mark Z. Danielewski, *House of Leaves, by Zampanò, With Introduction and Notes by Johnny Truant* (New York: Pantheon Books, 2000), p. 28.
57. Ibid., p. 425.
58. Ibid., p. 165.
59. Timmer, *Do You Feel It Too?*, p. 256.
60. Danielewski, *House of Leaves*, p. 425.
61. Mark B. N. Hansen, "The Digital Topography of Mark Z. Danielewski's *House of Leaves*," *Contemporary Literature* 45, no. 4 (2004): p. 598.
62. Ibid., p. 608.
63. Julie Park, "Moving Parts: The Life of Eighteenth-Century Interiors," *Eighteenth-Century Fiction* 20, no. 3 (2008): pp. v–ix.
64. Park, "Moving Parts," p. vi.
65. Ibid.

35 ORNAMENT AND DECORATION

1. Alfred Dwight Foster Hamlin, *A History of Ornament: Ancient and Medieval* (New York: Century Company, 1916).
2. James Trilling, *The Language of Ornament* (London: Thames & Hudson, 2001).
3. George Hersey, *The Lost Meaning of Classical Architecture: Speculations on Ornament from Vitruvius to Venturi* (Cambridge, MA: MIT Press, 1988).
4. Vitruvius, *The Ten Books on Architecture*, trans. Morris Hicky Morgan (Cambridge MA: Harvard University Press, 2006), http://www.gutenberg.org/ebooks/20239, accessed April 25, 2012.
5. Michael Snodin and Maurice Howard, *Ornament: A Social History Since 1450* (New Haven, CT: Yale University Press, 1996).
6. Peter Thornton, *Form and Decoration: Innovation in the Decorative Arts 1470–1870* (London: Weidenfield and Nicolson, 1998).
7. Alan Hunt, *Governance of the Consuming Passions: A History of Sumptuary Law* (New York: St. Martin's Press, 1996).
8. Norbert Elias, *The Court Society*, trans. Edmund Jephcott (New York: Pantheon, 1983).
9. Marc Grignon and Juliana Maxim, "*Convenance, Caractère*, and the Public Sphere," *Journal of Architectural Education* 49, no. 1 (1995): pp. 29–37.
10. Jean-François Bédard, *Decorative Games: Ornament, Rhetoric, and Noble Culture in the Work of Gilles-Marie Oppenord (1672–1742)* (Newark: University of Delaware Press, 2011).
11. Thorstein Veblen, *The Theory of the Leisure Class: An Economic Study in the Evolution of Institutions* (New York: Macmillan, 1899).
12. Julien-David Le Roy, *Les Ruines des plus beaux monuments de la Grèce* (Paris, 1758); and James Stuart and Nicholas Revett, *The Antiquities of Athens* (London, 1762ff).
13. Arindam Dutta, *The Bureaucracy of Beauty: Design in the Age of Its Global Reproducibility* (London: Routledge, 2007).
14. David Cannadine, *Ornamentalism: How the British Saw Their Empire* (New York: Oxford University Press, 2001); Dutta, *The Bureaucracy of Beauty*.
15. Federico Freschi, "'Unity in Diversity': The Representation of White Nationalisms in the Decorative Programmes of Public Buildings, 1930–1940," in *The Visual Century 1*, ed. Jillian Carman (Johannesburg: Wits University Press, 2011), pp. 156–73.

16. Isabelle Frank, ed., *The Theory of Decorative Art: An Anthology of European and American Writings, 1750–1940* (New Haven, CT: Yale University Press, 2000).

17. Debra Schafter, *The Order of Ornament, the Structure of Style: Theoretical Foundations of Modern Art and Architecture* (Cambridge: Cambridge University Press, 2003).

18. Massimo Cacciari, *Architecture and Nihilism: On the Philosophy of Modern Architecture,* trans. Stephen Sartarelli (New Haven, CT: Yale University Press, 1993).

19. Louis H. Sullivan, *A System of Architectural Ornament According with a Philosophy of Man's Powers* (New York: Press of the American Institute of Architects, 1924); and David Van Zanten, *Sullivan's City: The Meaning of Ornament for Louis Sullivan* (New York: W. W. Norton, 2000).

20. Adolf Loos, "Ornament and Crime," in *Programs and Manifestoes on 20th Century Architecture,* rev. ed., ed., Ulrich Conrads, trans. Michael Bullock (Cambridge, MA: MIT Press, 1970), pp. 19–24.

21. Adolf Loos, "Foreword," in *Trotzdem* (Innsbruck: Brenner-Verlag, 1931), p. 5; author's translation.

22. Frank, *The Theory of Decorative Art.*

23. Annemarie Sankevitch, "Structure/Ornament and the Modern Figuration of Architecture," *Art Bulletin* 80, no. 4 (1998): pp. 687–717.

24. Jonathan Massey, *Crystal and Arabesque: Claude Bragdon, Ornament, and Modern Architecture* (Pittsburgh: University of Pittsburgh Press, 2009).

25. Cacciari, *Architecture and Nihilism;* and Karsten Harries, *The Ethical Function of Architecture* (Cambridge, MA: MIT Press, 1997).

26. Siegfried Kracauer, *The Mass Ornament: Weimar Essays,* trans. and ed. Thomas Y. Levin (Cambridge, MA: Harvard University Press, 1995).

27. Mark Wigley, *White Walls, Designer Dresses: The Fashioning of Modern Architecture* (Cambridge, MA: MIT Press, 1995).

28. Le Corbusier, *The Decorative Art of Today,* trans. James I. Dunnett (Cambridge, MA: MIT Press, 1987).

29. Jonathan Massey, "New Necessities: Modernist Aesthetic Discipline," *Perspecta* 35 (2004): pp. 112–33.

30. Jacques Soulillou, *Le décoratif* (Paris: Klincksieck, 1990); and Jacques Soulillou, "Ornament and Order," in *Crime and Ornament: The Arts and Popular Culture in the Shadow of Adolf Loos,* ed. Bernie Miller and Melony Ward (Toronto: YYZ Books, 2002).

31. Massey, *Crystal and Arabesque.*

32. Glenn Adamson and Jane Pavitt, eds., *Postmodernism: Style and Subversion, 1970–1990* (London: V&A Publishing, 2011).

33. Timothy M. Rohan, "Rendering the Surface: Paul Rudolph's Art and Architecture Building at Yale," *Grey Room* 1 (2000): pp. 84–107.

34. Anne Swartz, ed., *Pattern and Decoration: An Ideal Vision in American Art, 1975–1985* (Yonkers, NY: Hudson River Museum, 2007), p. 14.

35. Emily Abruzzo and Jonathan D. Solomon, eds., *Decoration 10* (New York: 306090 Books, 2006).

36. Paul Andersen and David Salomon, *The Architecture of Patterns* (New York: W. W. Norton, 2010).

37. Ben Pell, *The Articulate Surface: Ornament and Technology in Contemporary Architecture* (Basel: Birkhäuser, 2010).

38. Farshid Moussavi and Michael Kubo, eds., *The Function of Ornament* (Barcelona: Actar, 2006); and Alejandro Zaera Polo, "The Politics of the Envelope: A Political Critique of Materialism," *Volume* 17 (2008): pp. 76–105.

39. Bruno Latour, *We Have Never Been Modern,* trans. Catherine Porter (Cambridge, MA: Harvard University Press, 1991).

36 THE POETIC LANGUAGE OF INTERIOR MATERIALS AND COLOR

1. György Doczi, *The Power of Limits: Proportional Harmonies in Nature, Art, and Architecture* (Boulder: Shambhala Publications, 1981), p. 127.

2. James J. Gibson, *The Ecological Approach to Visual Perception* (New Jersey: Lawrence Erlbaum, 1986), p. 127.

3. Ibid., p. 129.

4. Henry Plummer, *Light in Japanese Architecture* (Tokyo: A+U Publications, 1995), pp. 15–16.

5. Cited in Cathy Treadaway (p. 233) in Ernst Hans Gombrich, *The Image and the Eye: Further Studies in the Psychology of Pictorial Representation* (London: Phaidon, 1994), p. 28; and cited in Cathy Treadaway, "Materiality, Memory and Imagination: Using Empathy to Research Creativity," *Leonardo* 42, no. 3 (2009): pp. 231–37, http://muse.jhu.edu/, accessed August 17, 2010.

6. Donlyn Lyndon and Charles W. Moore, *Chambers for a Memory Palace* (Cambridge, MA: MIT Press, 1994), p. xii.

7. Joy Monice Malnar and Frank Vodvarka, *The Interior Dimension: A Theoretical Approach to Enclosed Space* (New York: Van Nostrand Reinhold, 1992), p. 284.

8. Bruce Travis Dougherty, *Architecture as Communication: An Application of Semeiotic* (master's thesis, Texas Tech University, Lubbock, 1990); John Fiske, "Introduction to Communication Studies," in *Communication, Meanings, and Signs,* 2nd ed., ed. John Fiske, (London: Routledge, 1990), pp. 39–63.

9. Anthony Antoniades, *Poetics of Architecture: Theory of Design* (New York: Van Nostrand Reinhold, 1992), p. 3.

10. Gaston Bachelard, *The Poetics of Space,* trans. Maria Jolas (Boston: Beacon Press, 1994), p. xxiii.

11. Terence Hawkes, *Structuralism & Semiotics* (London: Methuen, 1977), p. 62.

12. Ibid., p. 70.

13. George Verghese (research field notes, unpublished, 2010).

14. Lois Swirnoff, "The Visual Environment: Consider the Surface," *The Environmentalist* 2 (1982): p. 218.

15. Peter Zumthor, *Atmospheres: Architectural Environments, Surrounding Objects* (Basel: Birkhäuser, 2006), pp. 22–24.

16. Roman Jakobson, "Closing Statement: Linguistics and Poetics," cited in Thomas Albert Sebeok, *Style in Language* (Cambridge, MA: MIT Press, 1966), p. 356.

17. Hawkes, *Structuralism & Semiotics*, p. 77.

18. Roman Jakobson and Morris Halle, *Fundamentals of Language* (Berlin: Mouton de Gruyter, 2002), p. 75.

19. Closing statement by Roman Jakobson, cited in Hawkes, *Structuralism & Semiotics*, p. 83.

20. John Dewey, "The Pragmatism of Peirce," in *Chance, Love, and Logic: Philosophical Essays,* ed. Charles Sanders Peirce and Morris R. Cohen (Lincoln: University of Nebraska Press, 1998), p. 301.

21. Ibid., p. 307.

22. Charles S. Peirce, "What Is a Sign?" in *The Essential Peirce: Selected Philosophical Writings 2 (1893–1913),* rev. ed. (Indianapolis: Indiana University Press, 1998), pp. 4–10; Charles S. Peirce "What Pragmatism Is?" in *The Essential Peirce: Selected Philosophical Writings 2 (1893–1913),* rev. ed. (Indianapolis: Indiana University Press, 1998), pp. 331–45; and Winfried Nöth, *Handbook of Semiotics* (Indianapolis: Indiana University Press, 1990), pp. 39–47.

23. Carleton B. Christensen, "Peirce's Transformation of Kant," *The Review of Metaphysics* 48, no. 1 (1994): pp. 91–121.

24. Charles S. Peirce, "Pragmatism", in *The Essential Peirce: Selected Philosophical Writings* 2 *(1893–1913),* rev. ed. (Indianapolis: Indiana University Press, 1998), p. 409; Dianne Smith, *Architecture: A Composition of Viewpoints* (PhD thesis, Queensland University of Technology, Brisbane, Australia, 2000) p. 109.

25. Based on Smith, *Architecture: A Composition of Viewpoints.*

26. Nöth, *Handbook of Semiotics.*

27. Dewey, "The Pragmatism of Peirce," p. 303.

28. Fiske, "Introduction to Communication Studies."

29. Smith, *Architecture: A Composition of Viewpoints,* p. 252.

30. Joseph Ransdell, "Some Leading Ideas of Peirce's Semiotic," version 2.0 (1997), http://www.door.net/arisbe/menu/library/aboutcsp/ransdell/leading.htm, accessed March 2, 1999.

31. Charles S. Peirce, "The Categories Defined," in *The Essential Peirce: Selected Philosophical Writings 2 (1893–1913),* rev. ed. (Indianapolis: Indiana University Press, 1998), p. 160.

32. Peirce, "What Is a Sign?" p. 5.

33. Peirce, "The Categories Defined," p. 269.

34. Peirce, "What Is a Sign?" p. 4.

35. Amos Rapaport, *The Meaning of the Built Environment: A Non-Verbal Communication Approach,* rev. ed. (Tucson: University of Arizona Press, 1990).

36. Edward S. Casey, *The Fate of Place: A Philosophical History* (Berkeley: University of California Press, 1997), p. xii.

37. Nöth, *Handbook of Semiotics,* pp. 39–47.

38. Charles S. Peirce, "Immortality in the Light of Continuity," in *The Essential Peirce: Selected Philosophical Writings 2 (1893–1913),* rev. ed. (Indianapolis: Indiana University Press, 1998), pp. 160–78.

37 TECHNOLOGY AND THE INTERIOR

1. Le Corbusier, *Towards a New Architecture,* rev. ed. (London: Butterworth Architecture, 1989), p. 4.

2. Ibid., pp. 122–23.

3. Ibid., p. 123.

4. Ibid.

5. Ibid.

6. Georg Simmel, "The Sociology of Space" in *Simmel on Culture,* ed. David Frisby and Mike Featherstone (London: Sage, 1997), p. 143.

7. Della Thompson, ed., *Oxford English Dictionary,* 9th ed. (New York: Oxford University Press, 1995).

8. Joseph Rykwert, *On Adam's House in Paradise* (New York: Museum of Modern Art, 1972).

9. Ibid., pp. 190–91.

10. May N. Stone, "The Plumbing Paradox: American Attitudes Toward Late Nineteenth-Century Domestic Sanitary Arrangements," *Winterthur Portfolio* 14, no. 3 (1979): pp. 284–85.

11. Jean-Pierre Adams, *Roman Buildings: Materials and Techniques,* trans. Anthony Matthews (London: Routledge, 2005), p. 235.

12. Ibid., p. 264.

13. Ibid., pp. 266–67.

14. Ibid., pp. 268–69.

15. John E. Crowley, *The Invention of Comfort: Sensibilities and Design in Early Modern Britain and Early America* (Baltimore: John Hopkins University Press, 2001), pp. 3–44.

16. Ibid., p. 8.

17. Ibid., pp. 32–36.

18. Witold Rybczynski, *Home: A Short History of An Idea* (London: Heinemann, 1988), p. 138.

19. Ibid.

20. Ibid., p. 139.

21. Ibid., p. 141.

22. Adrian Forty, *Objects of Desire: Design and Society Since* 1750 (London: Thames & Hudson, 1986), pp. 183–85.

23. Ibid., p. 187.

24. Ibid.

25. Anne Chick, "Living the Sustainable Life: A Case Study of the Beddington Zero Energy Development (BedZED) Sustainable Interior," in *Designing the Modern Interior: From the Victorians to Today,* ed. Penny Sparke, Anne Massey, Trevor Keeble, and Brenda Martin (Oxford: Berg, 2009), p. 278.

26. Ibid., p. 278.

27. John McKean, *Crystal Palace* (London: Phaidon, 1994).

28. David Watkin, *A History of Western Architecture* (London: Barrie & Jenkins, 1986).

29. Penny Sparke, *The Modern Interior* (London: Reaktion, 2008), pp. 119–20.

30. Gillian Naylor, *The Bauhaus Reassessed: Sources and Design Theory* (London: Herbert Press, 1985), pp. 138–42.

31. Ibid., pp. 141–42.

32. David A. Hounshell, *From the American System to Mass Production, 1800–1932* (Baltimore: John Hopkins University Press, 1985).

33. Sarah A. Leavitt, *From Catherine Beecher to Martha Stewart: A Cultural History of Domestic Advice* (Chapel Hill: University of North Carolina Press, 2002), pp. 41–72.

34. Penny Sparke, *As Long As It's Pink: The Sexual Politics of Taste* (London: Pandora, 1995), pp. 85–87.

35. Jonathan M. Woodham, *Twentieth-Century Design* (New York: Oxford University Press, 1997), p. 181.

36. Michel Foucault, *Discipline and Punish: The Birth of the Prison* (London: Allen Lane, 1977).

37. Karen Van Lengen and Joel Sanders, "Re-Envisioning Audio Techno Culture: Synthesis of Design and Technology in Support of Communicative Architectures," in *The International Journal of Technology, Knowledge and Society* 6, no. 6 (2010): pp. 15–28.

38. Hounshell, *From the American System to Mass Production;* Forty, *Objects of Desire;* and Sparke, *As Long As It's Pink.*

39. Forty, *Objects of Desire,* p. 99.

40. Penny Sparke, *An Introduction to Design and Culture* (London: Routledge, 2004); and Woodham, *Twentieth-Century Design.*

41. Forty, *Objects of Desire;* and Woodham, *Twentieth-Century Design.*

42. Ruth Schwartz Cowan, *More Work for Mother: The Ironies of Household Technology from the Open Hearth to the Microwave* (New York: Basic Books, 1983); and Sparke, *As Long As It's Pink,* p. 168.

43. The *House of the Future* was a much publicized and discussed exhibit designed by Alison and Peter Smithson for the Daily Mail Ideal Home Exhibition in March 1956; see Anne Massey, *The Independent Group: Modernism and Mass Culture in Britain, 1945–1959* (Manchester: Manchester University Press, 1995), pp. 103–4.

38 PHENOMENOLOGY AND THE SENSES IN INTERIORS

1. Or in cases such as when a window opens onto a garden or food preparation in a kitchen is meant to enhance the experience of occupancy, smell is an essential of interiors.

2. Maurice Merleau-Ponty, "The Phenomenal Field," in *The Phenomenology of Perception,* rev. ed., trans. Colin Smith (London: Routledge, 1994), p. 63.

3. Possibly brought on by diabetes.

4. Maurice Merleau-Ponty, "Cezanne's Doubt," in *Sense and Nonsense,* trans. Hubert L. Dreyfus and Patricia Allen Dreyfus (Evanston, IL: Northwestern University Press, 1964), p. 237.

5. Howard Gardner, *Creating Minds: An Anatomy of Creativity as Seen Through the Lives of Freud, Einstein, Picasso, Stravinsky, Eliot, Graham, and Gandhi* (New York: Basic Books, 1993).

6. This term is used here colloquially, but it owes its use to the title of the dissertation of Merleau-Ponty that established his philosophical work for the rest of his life.

7. Rainer K. Wick, *Teaching at the Bauhaus* (Ostfildern, Germany: Hatje Cantz, 2000), p. 60.

8. Ibid., p. 58.

9. Ibid., p. 173.

10. Ibid., p. 185.

11. Introduced by Itten.

12. Hans M. Wingler, *The Bauhaus: Weimar, Dessau, Berlin, Chicago,* trans. Wolfgang Jabs and Basil Gilbert (Cambridge, MA: MIT Press, 1969), pp. 468–70.

13. Josef Albers, *The Interaction of Color,* rev. ed. (New Haven: Yale University Press, 1975), pp. 77–81.

14. German for worldview; often used to identify a comprehensive worldview based on perception.

15. Albers, *Interaction of Color,* p. 2.

16. Gail Greet Hannah, *Elements of Design: Rowena Reed Kostellow and the Structure of Visual Relationships* (New York: Princeton Architectural Press, 2002), pp. 16–18.

17. A sixth lecture was planned but not written.

18. Italo Calvino, *Six Memos for the Next Millennium* (New York: Vintage Books, 1993), p. 26.

19. Ibid, p. 3.

20. Diane Apostolos-Cappadona and Bruce Altshuler, eds., "What's the Matter with Sculpture," in *Isamu Noguchi, Essays and Conversations* (New York: Harry N. Abrams, 1994), p. 18.

21. Dore Ashton, *Noguchi East and West* (Berkeley: University of California Press, 1993).

22. Diane Apostolos-Cappadona and Bruce Altshuler, eds., "An Interview with Isamu Noguchi by Katherine Kuh (1962)," in *Essays and Conversations* (New York: Harry N. Abrams, 1994), p. 133.

23. Ibid., p. 121.

24. Perhaps drawn from their relationship as lovers.

25. Modernist seasonal cottages built on outer Cape Cod (Massachusetts), 1945–1960, by architects and industrial designers, many of whom were friends, were lightweight constructions and experimental in nature. Surviving structures, now mainly within the boundaries of the Cape Cod National Seashore National Park, are a rare collection of assemblages that embody fragile qualities characteristic of the pleasures of living close to nature in summer. The spatial qualities embedded in them, although different, are moving in the idealistic, playful promise attributed to space and time as alive elements in design and building.

26. Basalt.

27. Manazuru stone.

28. Basalt.

29. Christine Cantwell, from an unpublished journal entry, ca. 1992

30. The dialectic between opposites has become a contemporary way of discussing architectural elements in the studio but also as a means of introducing a category of analysis of precedent with architecture and landscape architecture or architecture and site.

31. Ana Maria Torres, "Gardens, Plazas, and Parks," in *Isamu Noguchi: A Study of Space* (New York: Monacelli, 2000), pp. 50–244.

32. Maurice Merleau-Ponty, *The World of Perception*, trans. Oliver Davis (London: Routledge, 2009), pp. 31–32.

33. See Dalibor Vesely, *Architecture in the Age of Divided Representation: The Question of Creativity in the Shadow of Production* (Cambridge, MA: MIT Press, 2004).

34. Vesely and the notion of phenomenology as a "therapeutic corrective" to the overly "anti-humanist machinations" of architectural theory is referenced by K. Michael Hays in his introduction to the essay "Introduction to Architecture and the Crisis of Modern Science" by Alberto Perez-Gomez, which was excerpted as a 1983 essay in K. Michael Hays, ed., *Architecture Theory Since* 1968 (Cambridge, MA: MIT Press, 1998), pp. 462–63.

35. Glen Murcutt, recorded conversation with Juhani Pallasmaa, Architalx Architectural Lecture Series, September 9, 2001.

36. I would purport that this would not be a problem in interiors or industrial design.

37. Peter Zumthor, "Therme Vals," ca. 2000, http://www.therme-vals.ch, accessed February 2011.

38. Ibid.

39. Elizabeth Dranitzke, e-mail correspondence with the author. February 2011.

40. Sigrid Hauser, *Peter Zumthor Therme Vals,* trans. Kimi Lum and Catherine Scheibert (Zürich: Scheidegger & Spiess, 2007), p. 168.

39 TASTE AND TRENDS

1. http://www.independent.co.uk/life-style/house-and-home/2010-interior-design-trends-02/11/2010.

2. http://www.channel14.com/4homes/design-style/trend-watch/decorating-design-interior 02/11/2010.

3. http://www.lwnzing.com/fasern/de/trends/6558.jsp 01/11/2020, accessed August 31, 2011.

4. See Penny Sparke, *As Long As It's Pink: The Sexual Politics of Taste* (London: Pandora, 1995).

5. See Alison Light, *Forever England: Femininity, Literature and Conservatism Between the Wars* (London, New York: Routledge, 1991).

6. Regina Lee Blaszczyk, "The Color of Fashion," *Humanities* 29, no. 2 (2008): pp. 1–5, http://www.neh.gov/news/humanities/2008–03/Color_of_Fashion.html 03/11/10, accessed August 31, 2011.

7. Ibid., p. 2.

8. Ibid.

9. Ibid., p. 3.

10. Ibid.

11. Beverly Gordon, "Woman's Domestic Body: The Conceptual Conflation of Women and Interiors in the Industrial Age," *Wintherthur Portfolio: A Journal of American Culture* 31, no. 4 (1996): pp. 281–90.

12. Ibid., p. 282.

13. Ibid., p. 283.

14. See Rémy G. Saisselin, *Bricobracomania: The Bourgeois and the Bibelot* (London: Thames & Hudson, 1985).

15. For further ideas about the relationship between fashion and modernity see Ulrich Lehmann, *Tigersprung: Fashion in Modernity* (Cambridge, MA: MIT Press, 2000); Elizabeth Wilson, *Adorned in Dreams: Fashion and Modernity* (London: Virago, 1985); and Christopher Breward and Caroline Evans, eds., *Fashion and Modernity* (Oxford, New York: Berg, 2005). The Baudelaire quote is from Charles Baudelaire, "The Painter of Modern Life," in *The Painter of Modern Life and Other Essays,* trans. Jonathan Mayne (London: Phaidon Press, 1964), p. 12.

16. Advice books in the "Art at Home" series written by women included Agnes Garrett and Rhoda Garrett, *House Decoration* (London: Macmillan, 1877); Martha Jane Loftie, *The Dining Room* (London: Macmillan, 1888); and Lucy Orrinsmith, *The Drawing Room* (London: Macmillan, 1889).

17. See Michael Hatt, "Space, Surface, Self: Homosexuality and the Aesthetic Interior," *Visual Culture in Britain* 8, no. 1 (2007): pp. 105–12.

18. Mary Eliza Haweis, *The Art of Decoration* (London: Chatto and Windus, 1889), p. 52.

19. Mary Eliza Haweis, *Beautiful Houses* (New York: Scribner and Welford, 1882), p. iii.

20. See Haweis, *Beautiful Houses,* pp. xviii, 225.

21. Lisa Tiersten, *Marianne in the Market: Envisioning Consumer Society in Fin-de-Siecle France* (Berkeley: University of California Press, 2001), p. 125.

22. See Michael Miller, *The Bon Marché: Bourgeois Culture and the Department Store*, 1869–1920 (Princeton: Princeton University Press, 1994).
23. Paul Reilly, "The Challenge of Pop," *Architectural Review*, October 1967, pp. 255–57.
24. http://www.google.co.uk/search?sourceid=navclient&ie=UTF-8&rlz=1T4SKPT_enGB4 01GB436&q=Independent%3a+House+and+home%2ftaste+and+style, accessed August 31, 2011.
25. Ibid.

CONTRIBUTORS

Suzie Attiwill is associate professor of interior design and deputy dean of learning and teaching in the School of Architecture and Design, RMIT University, Melbourne, Australia. Since 1991, Attiwill has had an independent practice that includes exhibition design, curatorial work, writing, and a range of interdisciplinary projects in Australia and overseas. She holds a PhD as well as master's and bachelor's degrees in art history and interior design. She was the inaugural artistic director of Craft Victoria from 1996 to 1999, and chair of IDEA (Interior Design/Interior Architecture Educators Association; www.idea-edu.com) from 2006 to 2012. Attiwill is a founding member of the Urban Interior research group (www.urbaninterior.net) and a professional member of the Design Institute of Australia.

Mary Anne Beecher, PhD, is an associate professor and head of the Interior Design Department at the University of Manitoba in Winnipeg, Canada. Beecher has a master's degree in interior design from Iowa State University and a PhD in American studies from the University of Iowa. She is the current chair of the Alliance of Canadian Educators in Interior Design and is an active member of the Interior Design Educators' Council and the Vernacular Architecture Forum. Beecher's research areas include vernacular modern American interiors and the history of the interior design profession in North America.

Christine Cantwell is the principal and owner of Industrial Design Studio, an award-winning design consultancy based in Portland, Maine, United States. She has been a faculty member in industrial design, interiors, and architecture at Harvard University, the University of Texas at Austin School of Architecture, and Rhode Island School of Design, as well as a visiting design critic at the Southern California Institute of Architecture, Parsons the New School for Design, and Bauhaus—Universität Weimar, among others. Cantwell received a bachelor of industrial design from Pratt Institute and a master's in design studies in history, theory, and criticism from Harvard University Graduate School of Design.

Lilian Chee obtained her doctorate from the Bartlett, University College London, in 2006 and is assistant professor at the National University of Singapore. Her publications include "An Architecture of Twenty Words," in *Negotiating Domesticity* (2005); "A Web in the Garden," in *Haecceity Papers* (2007); "Living with Freud," in *Interior Atmospheres* (AD, 2008); "Performing Domesticity: Ma Qingyun's Father's House," in *Haecceity Papers* (2009); "Under the Billiard Table," in the *Singapore Journal of Tropical Geography* (2011); "Materializing the Tiger in the Archive," in *Feminist Practices* (2011); and "The Domestic Residue," in *Gender Place Culture* (2012). She is co-editor of *Asian Cinema and the Use of Space: Interdisciplinary Perspectives* (Routledge, forthcoming 2014). Her current research on domesticity in the Singapore context is captured in the film *Three Flats* (13 Little Pictures and National University of Singapore, 2013 forthcoming). She also serves as regional editor for the *Journal of Architecture.*

David Dernie, RIBA, is professor of architecture and dean, faculty of architecture and built environment, at the University of Westminster, UK. His research focuses on representation and the use of materials in architecture. Having left Cambridge University with a starred distinction in 1988 he went on to become Rome Scholar in Architecture (1991–1993). He was elected a fellow at Fitzwilliam College, Cambridge (1999). His published books include *Architectural Drawing* (2010), *Exhibition Design* (2006), *Material Imagination* (2005), *New Stone Architecture* (2003), *Villa d'Este at Tivoli* (1996), and *Victor Horta* (1995).

Nick Dunn is professor of urban design at the Lancaster Institute for the Contemporary Arts, University of Lancaster. His primary research interests are in the fields of visualization, modeling, mapping, representation in architecture, infrastructure, postindustrial landscapes, and urbanism. His work responds to the contemporary city as a series of systems, flows, and processes, explored through experimentation and discourse addressing the nature of urban space: its perception, demarcation, and appropriation. His recent publications include *Digital Fabrication in Architecture* (Laurence King, 2012) and the coauthored *Urban Maps: Instruments of Narrative and Interpretation in the City* (Ashgate, 2011).

Nadia Elrokhsy is assistant professor of sustainable interior design and associate member of the Parsons DESIS Lab, School of Design Strategies, Parsons the New School for Design. She is a licensed architect, LEED-accredited professional, and principal of a creative practice firm that specializes in environmental design. Her built works include full and partial structures, as well as a diverse range of project interiors. An original trainee in Al Gore's Climate Project, Elrokhsy gives presentations that continue to raise awareness about climate change. Her academic research goes beyond environmental design, uncovering connections between the social, economic, and environmental, and leverages broadly integrative tools and methods in the design for more sustainable ways of being.

Lorraine Farrelly is professor of architecture and design at the University of Portsmouth. She has interests and experience associated with areas in architecture and interior and urban design. Her research interests include a multidisciplinary approach to architecture at various scales, through understanding ideas of interior detail to urban concepts. This scale shift from the object in the interior to the building in a cityscape informs her teaching and professional work. As an architect Farrelly's own completed projects range from the interior fitting-out of bars and restaurants and retail design through to individual house designs and designs for public spaces. Previous publications include *Materials and the Interior, Drawing for Urban Design, Fundamentals of Architecture, Representational Techniques,* and *Construction and Materiality*

Robert Gifford is professor of psychology and environmental studies at the University of Victoria and a fellow of the American Psychological Association, the Canadian Psychological Association, and the Association for Psychological Science. The author of over 100 refereed publications and book chapters plus four editions of *Environmental Psychology: Principles and Practice,* Gifford is also the editor of the *Journal of Environmental Psychology* and served as president of the American Psychological Association's Population and Environment Division and the environmental psychology division of the International Association of Applied Psychology. He is the founding director of the University of Victoria's Human Dimensions of Climate Change program.

Samuel Gosling is a professor of psychology at the University of Texas, Austin. He did his doctoral work at the University of California at Berkeley, where his dissertation focused on personality in spotted hyenas. He has published broadly on the topics of Internet-based methods of data collection, personality in nonhuman animals, and ways in which human personality is manifested in everyday contexts like bedrooms, offices, web pages, music preferences, and social media; this latter work is described in his book, *Snoop: What Your Stuff Says about You.* Gosling is the recipient of the American Psychological Association's Distinguished Scientific Award for Early Career Contribution.

Edward Hollis is reader in design, and head of interior design, at Edinburgh College of Art. He originally trained and practiced as an architect, and his research writing concerns the historiography of the built environment, in particular its relationship to entropic processes of ruination. His first book, *The Secret Lives of Buildings,* was published in 2009, and his second, *The Memory Palace, a Book of Lost Interiors,* will appear in August 2013. He is also secretary of the Interiors Forum Scotland, which has edited two readers in interior theory: *Thinking inside the Box* (2007) and *Interior Tools, Interior Tactics* (2012).

Ong Swee Hong has been lecturer (2008 to 2010) and section head (2010 to 2011) in the School of Design at Temasek Polytechnic; he is now the director of ONG&ONG Lighting. Swee Hong graduated with a bachelor of arts (architecture) from the School of Architecture, National University of Singapore, in 2003. In 2005 she was awarded the National University of Singapore Research Scholarship for her postgraduate thesis, "Design Basis for Quality Urban Lighting Masterplanning." Besides practicing, she has written on topics such as participatory urban design, and during her teaching at the Temasek Design School, she focused on topic of aging and design. Since 2006, she has contributed to various publications locally and internationally and has been invited to give lectures on lighting design at major international lighting design conferences.

Trevor Keeble is Director of Research & Enterprise at the University for the Creative Arts (UCA). He has recently coedited the collection of essays *Performance, Fashion and the Modern Interior* (Berg, 2011).

Thomas Kong is an associate professor at the School of the Art Institute of Chicago and a licensed architect in Singapore. His research and creative practice are focused on works of architecture as anthropological objects and the cultural geographies of Asian cities. He has written and lectured at international conferences on themes relating to the changing role of public spaces and architectural education, and has received national and international recognition for his work. In 2009 Kong was the third Jaap Bakema Fellow, an international fellowship administered by the Netherlands Architecture Institute, and a co-recipient of the Motorola Foundation grant for his community-based studio in Beppu, Japan. He was awarded the David Marshall Distinguished Fellowship by the School of the Arts, Singapore, in 2012 in recognition of his contribution to the integration of the arts in architectural design education.

David Littlefield is a senior lecturer in the School of Architecture at the University of the West of England, Bristol, United Kingdom. Littlefield has authored, or made major contributions to, more than ten books on architecture, including *Architectural Voices: Listening to Old Buildings* and *London (Re)generation* (a special edition of the journal *Architectural Design*). He also curated the exhibition *Unseen Hands: 100 Years of Structural Engineering,* which ran at the Victoria & Albert Museum, London, in 2008. He has worked as an artist in residence at the Roman baths in Bath, England, and is a member of the PLaCE and Mapping Spectral Traces academic networks.

Anne Massey is professor of design at Middlesex University. Her writing on interior design includes *Interior Design since 1900* (Thames & Hudson, 3rd edition, 2008), *Designing Liners: Interior Design Afloat* (Routledge, 2006), and *Chair* (Reaktion, 2011). She is the founding editor of the academic journal *Interiors: Design, Architecture, Culture,* published by Berg since 2010. She has researched and lectured widely on the subject of the Independent Group, including *The Independent Group: Modernism and Mass Culture, 1945–59* (Manchester University Press, 1995) and *Out of the Ivory Tower: The Independent Group and Popular Culture* (Manchester University Press, 2012).

Jonathan Massey, an architect and historian, is Meredith Professor of Teaching Excellence at Syracuse University, where he has chaired the bachelor of architecture program and the University Senate. His research shows how architecture mediates power by giving form to civil society, shaping social relations, and regulating consumption.

A cofounder of the Transdisciplinary Media Studio and the Aggregate Architectural History Collaborative, Massey is the author of *Crystal and Arabesque: Claude Bragdon, Ornament, and Modern Architecture* (2009). He has also published in many journals and essay collections, including *Governing by Design: Architecture, Economy, and Politics in the Twentieth Century* (2012).

Lindsay McCunn is a PhD student in environmental psychology at the University of Victoria, Canada. Her research has been presented at conferences such as the Environmental Design Research Association, the International Association for People-Environment Studies, and the International Congress of Psychology. She also consults for a British Columbia–based planning firm.

Terry Meade is a principal lecturer and academic program leader of the Interior Architecture and Urban Studies Programme at the University of Brighton. He has a background in architecture, fine art, and engineering and is currently undertaking a PhD. His recent publications include "Violence and Domestic Space," in the *Journal of Architecture* (2011), and "Camps," published in *Interior Wor(l)ds* (2010). More recently he has been working in Palestine, helping to build houses with an Israeli peace group. This has led to the exploration of the way issues of security (walls, borders, and barriers) have contributed to a particular shaping of domestic space.

Andy Milligan is course director of interiors at Duncan of Jordanstone College of Art and Design, University of Dundee and cofounder of Interiors Forum Scotland. He is a fellow of the Higher Education Academy and a member of GIDE, the Group for International Design Education network. Recently funded AHRC and EPSRC research explores, urban green spaces, flexible dwelling for older generations, and pro-environmental behavior change in the workplace. He is a member of TRIGGER ArtWorks Scotland: Artist Peer to Peer Learning Networks. Publications include Domestechtopias at Interior Futures (2011), co-editor of *Interior Tools Interior Tactics* (2011), *Thinking inside the Box* (2007), and Crossing Design Boundaries, of *CoDesign Journal: special issue* (2006).

Shonquis Moreno is a freelance journalist and design consultant living and working between Brooklyn and Istanbul who contributes to publications such as *Wallpaper, Case da Abitare, T, the New York Times Style Magazine,* and *Whitewall.* In the past, she has served as the design editor for *Surface, Dwell,* and *Frame* magazines. She is also the author of a number of books by Gestalten, Birkhauser, and Frame Publishers on topics ranging from window display and product design to architecture, interiors, furniture, and packaging. Her website is http://shonquismoreno.com.

Jeremy Myerson is director of the Helen Hamlyn Centre for Design at the Royal College of Art, which he cofounded in 1999. An internationally recognized author, academic, and activist in design and innovation, he is also chair of the InnovationRCA network for business and the first Helen Hamlyn Professor of Design. Workplace design has been a long-term research interest, and his many books on this subject include *The*

21st Century Office, Space to Work, The Creative Office, and, most recently, *New Demographics, New Workspace.*

Helen O'Connor is a senior lecturer and the undergraduate course director in architecture at the University of Dundee, Scotland, where she runs design research and masters thesis units under the theme of 'rooms and cities'. She is a registered architect and takes an active interest in architectural pedagogy, acting as an external examiner and as a lead examiner for the Architects Registration Board. Her recent publications include "LaTourette" (*Architects Journal,* 2007). She is a regular contributor to Higher Education Academy (HEA) subject center conferences on architectural design studios.

Clive Parkinson is the director of Arts for Health at Manchester Metropolitan University—the longest-established unit of its kind. He has worked variously within the National Health Service and the voluntary sector. He began his career as an artist working in a hospital for people with learning difficulties: a position that enabled him to see the potential of the arts to impact on individual well-being and broader society. His current research is focused around dementia and issues around end-of-life care. Parkinson's most recent paper, "Fur Coat and No Knickers," explores the sometimes superficial place of art in the public realm (available at http://www.publicartonline.org.uk/whatsnew/news/article.php/FcNK). He is a regular speaker at international conferences and blogs at http://artsforhealthmmu.blogspot.com.

Barbara Penner is senior lecturer in architectural history at the Bartlett School of Architecture, University College London. She is author of *Newlyweds on Tour: Honeymooning in Nineteenth-Century America* (University Press of New England, 2009) and coeditor of *Ladies and Gents: Public Toilets and Gender* (Temple University Press, 2009) and *Gender Space Architecture* (Routledge, 2000). She has most recently contributed essays to *Toilet: The Politics of Sharing* (New York University Press, 2010) and *Globalization in Practice* (Oxford University Press, forthcoming) and is completing *Bathroom* (Reaktion, 2013).

Drew Plunkett graduated from the Royal College of Art in 1981 and for twenty-five years, until 2010, was head of interior design at Glasgow School of Art. Throughout that time he continued to practice, working on projects, primarily restaurants and exhibitions, in Glasgow, London, Dubai, and Beijing. He now writes on interior design; his recent published work includes "Drawing for Interior Design" and "Construction and Detailing for Interior Design." He has contributed to *Blueprint, Designers Journal,* and *Architects Journal.* He was elected a fellow of the Royal Society of Arts in 1996 and was the first fellow of Interior Educators in 2010.

Gennaro Postiglione is associate professor in Architecture of Interiors and member of the PhD Board in Interiors at the Politecnico di Milano (http://www.lablog.org.uk). His research activity focuses mainly on domestic interiors, on museography, and on the preservation and diffusion of collective memory and cultural identity (connecting the museographic issues with the domestic ambit). Since 2004 he has been the promoter of "Public Architecture at POLIMI", an interdisciplinary research and operative group that puts the resources of architecture in the service of the public interest. His main publications include *The Atlantikwall as Military Archaeological Landscape* (coedited with M. Bassanelli, Siracusa: LetteraVentidue, 2011), *Norwegian Talks* (coedited with N. Flora, Macerata, 2010), and *Interior Wor[l]ds* (coedited with L. Basso Peressut and I. Forino, Torino: F. lli Allemandi, 2010).

John Potvin is associate professor at Concordia University in Montreal. He is the author of *Material and Visual Cultures beyond Male Bonding, 1880–1914* (2008), *Giorgio Armani: Empire of the Senses* (2013), and *Bachelors of a Different Sort: Queer Aesthetics, Material Culture and the Modern Interior* (2014). He is also editor of *The Places and Spaces of Fashion* (2009) and coeditor of both *Material Cultures, 1740–1920: The Meanings and Pleasures of Collecting* (2009) and *Fashion, Interior Design and the Contours of Modern Identity* (2010). Potvin also serves as book review editor for *Interiors: Design, Architecture, Culture.*

Julieanna Preston is a transdisciplinary spatial designer and artist practicing through sculptural objects, performative installations, interior interventions, speculative furniture designs, and site-writing essays. Her recent projects include *BALE* (Snowhite Gallery, 2011), *No Fixed Seating* (Whirlwinds, London, 2010), and *Interior Weather Watch* (Wellington LUX, New Zealand, 2011). These creative works are contextualized and expanded in her recent books and book chapters: *Interior Atmospheres* (AD, 2008), *Intimus: Interior Design Theory Reader* (coedited with Mark Taylor, Wiley, 2006), "Blazing Inter-Alia: Tropes of a Feminist Interior Practice" (published in *Feminist Practices,* edited by Lori Brown, 2011), "Fossicking for Interior Design Pedagogies" (published in *After Taste,* edited by Klein, Merwood-Salisbury, and Weinthal, 2011), and a forthcoming issue of *IDEA* journal entitled "Interior Economies" (2012). Preston is an associate professor and director of research and postgraduate studies within the College of Creative Arts, Massey University, Wellington, New Zealand.

Fred Scott, Des. RCA, graduated in 1961 from the School of Industrial Design. He was part-time tutor in industrial design at Hornsey College of Art in 1967–1968; part-time or full-time and unit master at the Architectural Association from 1966 to 1981; tutor at the School of Environmental Design, Royal College of Art, in 1975–1976; tutor and course leader in interior design at Kingston University from 1985 to 2004; and visiting professor in interior architecture at Rhode Island School of Design and in industrial design at La Sapîenza, University of Rome. He has published articles and book reviews in various magazines, including *Architectural Design, Building Design,* and *Architecture Today;* in addition, he is author of *On Altering Architecture* (Routledge, 2008) and has carried out various design commissions including a library for U2 in Eze sur Mer, near Nice, and an exhibition in association with Kerr Noble at the Architectural Foundation. Images of his own apartment were published in *Abitare* 7/8 in 1981.

Igor Siddiqui is an assistant professor at the University of Texas at Austin School of Architecture. He is also the principal and cofounder of the New York City–based

ISSSStudio, an emerging practice whose work has been published, exhibited, and critically assessed internationally. Siddiqui's current scholarship and teaching consider the contemporary interior as a framework for examining encounters between architectural spaces and fabricated products. Among his recent publications are essays "Surface Fatigue," in Sophia Vyzoviti's book *Soft Shells: Porous and Deployable Architectural Screens* (2011)*,* and "Tessellated Floorscape (2010–): Interior Acts of Production, Siting and Participation," in *IDEA Journal* (2010).

Dianne Smith is Associate Professor and Head of Interior Architecture at Curtin University, Western Australia. Her research focuses on the person-environment relationship—with particular reference to discriminatory design, interpretation and meaning, and the impact of colour and light on the experience of place. She currently leads a research team investigating design in relation to occupation, health and wellbeing. Dianne co-edited Life from the Inside: Perspectives on Social Sustainability and Interior Architecture and is currently co-editing another book on trans-disciplinary community engagement methods and practices. She has participated in key professional and academic bodies including the national boards of Design Institute of Australia (DIA) and IDEA (Interior Design/Interior Architecture Educators Association).

Alison B. Snyder is an associate professor and architect. She focuses her work on revealing how places, buildings, and interiors transform over time. She often conducts fieldwork in Turkey, and her investigations consider both local and global conditions in sacred and secular contexts. Snyder has published chapters in *A Historical Archaeology of the Ottoman Empire* and *On Global Grounds: Urban Change and Globalization,* and articles in several international art and architecture journals such as *2A,* the *METU Journal Faculty of Architecture,* and *Dosya.* Snyder directs the Interior Architecture Program at the University of Oregon, where she has taught since 1997, teaching courses and studios involving research, culture, and design theory.

Kees Spanjers is a registered interior architect and architect who lives and works in Amsterdam and New York. He is the director of Zaanen Spanjers Architects in Amsterdam, specializing in cultural buildings and public interiors. He is the recipient of numerous awards, including the Architectural Record Interiors Award. Spanjers was the president of the European Council of Interior Architects and served as a co-opted board member of the International Federation of Interior Architects/Designers. He is a past president and now honorable member of Beroepsvereniging Nederlandse Interieurarchitecten (BNI), the Dutch Association of Interior Architects. Spanjers has written many professional articles and has been active on many international panels and juries.

Ro Spankie is course leader for the bachelor with honors in interior architecture at the University of Westminster. Following a master in computing and design she developed a fascination with the role of the drawing in the design process that combines with research into the interior. She is currently enrolled in the PhD in architectural design at the Bartlett School of Architecture, University College London, supervised by Professor Philip Steadman. Her thesis, "Thinking through Drawing," is focused on drawing out interior-specific practice. She has exhibited and published work both in the United Kingdom and abroad, including *Drawing Out the Interior* (2009), *Modelling the Domestic: Revisiting the Doll's House* (2011), and *An Anecdotal Guide to Sigmund Freud's Desk* (2013).

Penny Sparke is professor of design history, director of the Modern Interiors Research Centre, and the pro vice-chancellor for research at Kingston University, London. She has lectured, published, and broadcast widely on the subject of design history, with an emphasis, over the last decade, on the history and meaning of the modern interior.

Lee Stickells is a senior lecturer in architecture and urban design at the University of Sydney, where he directs the master of architecture program. His research is characterized by an interest in relationships between architecture and the city, with a focus on the construction of encounter. He was coeditor of *The Right to the City* (2011) and has contributed to anthologies, including *Beyond Utopia* (2012), *Trash Culture* (2010), and *Heterotopia and the City* (2009). His essays have appeared in journals such as *ARQ: Architectural Research Quarterly* and *Transition*. He is currently coeditor of the journal *Architectural Theory Review*.

Graham Stretton is a senior lecturer in interior design at Leicester School of Design, De Montfort University. Until recently program leader, Stretton has returned to interests in research and publication activities; immersive interiors, blending real and augmented realities using scale models and 1:1 installations. As a practicing designer for more than forty years, he has designed across most areas of interior design in practice, working on major interdisciplinary projects around the world. He was a fellow of both and VP BIID and liaison officer/negotiator with the CSD at the time of the merger (1988) and was awarded the BIID medal for services to design. Stretton's interests lie in the history of and relationship between interiors education and the professions. He is chair of the membership panel of Interior Educators.

Mark Taylor is professor of architecture at the University of Newcastle, Australia. His research on the interior has been widely published in journals and books, and he has taught both theory and design studio courses. He is a visiting professor at Universiti Teknologi Mara, Malaysia, a research fellow at the Spatial Information Architecture Laboratory and currently holds an Australian Research Council Discovery Grant. He coedited (with Julieanna Preston) *Intimus: Interior Design Theory Reader* (Wiley, 2006) and edited *Interior Design and Architecture: Critical and Primary Sources* (Bloomsbury, 2013). He has also published chapters in *Diagrams of Architecture* (Wiley, 2010), *Performance Fashion and the Modern Interior* (Berg, 2011), and *Domestic Interiors: Representing Homes from the Victorians to the Moderns* (Bloomsbury, 2013).

John C. Turpin, PhD, FIDEC, is dean of the School of Art and Design at High Point University. His research focuses on the development of the interior design profession in North America with emphasis on the intersection of social values, material culture, and gender constructs. He is currently the coeditor of the scholarly journal *Interiors: Design,*

Architecture, Culture. His most recent work includes chapters for *Intimus: Interior Design Theory Reader, The State of the Interior Design Profession, Gender and Women's Leadership: A Reference Handbook,* and *Domestic Interiors: Representing Homes from the Victorians to the Moderns.*

George Verghese is currently the executive director for the Institute of Material Innovation at Kwantlen Polytechnic University in Canada. Prior to this position, he was dean of the Faculty of Design at Kwantlen. With thirty-two years of experience he has previously held positions as director of postgraduate design, course director in interior design, and associate head of school at University of Technology Sydney in Australia, and he was also chair of the School in Interior Design at Ryerson University in Canada and a visiting professor at King Mongkut's University of Technology Thonburi in Thailand. His doctorate research is in grounded theory and innovative materiality within interior practice. He has published widely on topics of new materials in design. He is now currently involved with technical textile research and the impact of materials in birthing centers.

Stephanie White is the editor of *On Site* review, a journal that discusses architecture and urbanism in various ways—socially, culturally, geologically, and infrastructurally. She studied architecture, practiced it, and taught it for many years. She has a doctorate in urban geography and lives in Calgary, Alberta.

Alexa Griffith Winton is an independent design historian in New York City. Her work investigates the history and theory of the domestic interior, with a particular emphasis on the mid-twentieth century. Her work has been published in the *Journal of Modern Craft,* the *Journal of Design History,* and the *Archives of American Art Journal.* She is on the faculty of Parsons the New School for Design, where she teaches in the master of fine arts programs in lighting and interior design.

INDEX